The Classic 1000 Chicken Recipes

The Classic 1000 Chicken Recipes

foulsham

LONDON • NEW YORK • TORONTO • SYDNEY

foulsham
The Publishing House, Bennetts Close,
Cippenham, Berkshire SL1 5AP, England

ISBN 0-572-02646-3

Printed in Great Britain by St Edmundsbury Press, Bury St Edmunds, Suffolk

Contents

Introduction	6
Here's to a Healthy Diet	7
Notes on the Recipes	11
Choosing, Preparing and Carving Your Birds	12
Starters	19
Soups	42
Light Bites	64
Pan-fried Specials	87
Grills and Barbecues	122
Roasts and Oven Bakes	143
Pastry Dishes	183
Casseroles	202
Pasta and Rice Meals	239
Curries	286
Salads	303
Sauces	333
Those Little Extras	347
Index	358

Introduction

Chicken, turkey, duck, goose and all the more exotic game birds make mouth-watering eating. Whether you're having a family meal or serving up something special for a dinner party, poultry is always the perfect choice. Naturally lower in fat than red meat, almost always guaranteed to be more tender, more succulent and more versatile, it can be cooked with confidence to create sensational dishes.

This book has been written to give you all your favourite recipes – and some you've never heard of before – from every corner of the world.

You won't find just main courses either. There are soups to savour, starters such as Chicken and Bacon Terrine with Pistachio Nuts and Quails' Egg Tartlets, light snacks and every sauce and accompaniment you will ever need to complement your birds. Whether you enjoy eating a hot and fiery Chicken Vindaloo, crispy Peking Duck, a splendid roast turkey with all the trimmings, or a bold, impressive game pie, they are all here and much, much more. So cook, eat and enjoy!

Here's to a Healthy Diet

I'm not going to go on about eating the right amounts of carbohydrates, protein and other foods in this book. We all know that a good, balanced diet is essential. I just want to say the word 'bacteria'. There are many forms of micro-organisms, called bacteria, living in us. There are 'friendly' bacteria that help us fight off illness, digest our food and fulfil many other useful functions. We also use some types of bacteria in food in a 'good' way – for instance to make cheese and yoghurt. But there are other strains of bacteria, called pathogenic micro-organisms, which cause food poisoning. They are naturally present in all living things, but if they infect us we can become seriously ill; they can even be fatal. It is therefore vital to practise good hygiene in the kitchen and to store and cook foods properly to kill any bacteria that may be present and to avoid infection. Poultry, in particular, can cause food poisoning so it is vital that it is handled correctly.

BUYING YOUR BIRDS

It's up to you whether you choose frozen or fresh birds, free-range or intensively farmed. The flavour and texture is undoubtedly better from fresh, free-range birds and, especially for those with a conscience, it is worth paying the extra for them. However, it is true that once masked in a highly flavoured sauce, an inexpensive frozen chicken, for instance, will taste perfectly succulent and delicious. Look out, too, for special offers for your freezer, such as the fresh birds that have been reduced because they are only one day before their sell-by date. Provided you buy, take home and freeze immediately or cook first, then freeze, they will be perfect for use up to three months later.

There are some simple shopping rules you should follow:

- Always buy your birds (and other perishables for that matter) from a reputable source.
- Buy from a shop with a quick turnover, and where the chiller cabinets are clean and working efficiently.
- Buying from over-stocked refrigerated cabinets should be avoided as the temperature may not be cold enough.
- If buying frozen birds, make sure the freezers are not over-full. There is a load line on the cabinet. If food is stacked above this line, it will not be stored at the correct temperature. Make sure too that the bag wrapping the chicken is not torn and that there are no signs of freezer burn (pale dried-up patches on the skin) which would mean that the wrapping has been damaged and the flavour will be impaired.
- Preferably have an insulated cool bag with you at the store for carrying home chilled or frozen food.
- Always wrap frozen birds in a separate bag so no cross-contamination can occur. NEVER put raw meats next to cooked meats. The plastic wrappers they are in may well be perished and contamination can occur.
- Always take chilled and frozen foods straight home and store in the appropriate place immediately. Never leave them lying around in a warm car, office or kitchen or any bacteria will multiply.

SENSIBLE STORAGE

The Fridge

- Your fridge should be running at a temperature of between 0°C and 4°C. It is worth investing in a fridge thermometer to check this regularly. Any warmer than this and bacteria can multiply even as food sits there in so-called cool conditions.
- Never leave the door open longer than absolutely necessary. If you do, warm air circulates and raises the temperature considerably.
- Don't overload the fridge. If you do, air can't circulate and the temperature will rise.
- Never put warm or hot foods in the fridge. They should always be thoroughly covered and left in the kitchen to cool completely. As soon as they are cold, they should be transferred to the fridge. If you put in hot foods they will, obviously, raise the temperature of the whole fridge.
- Always store cooked meats at the top of the fridge and raw ones at the bottom, ideally in covered, sealed containers. That way, no drips will fall from the raw meat to the cooked. NEVER store raw and cooked meat on the same shelf. It is far too easy for the raw to contaminate the cooked.
- Wipe up any spills or drips as soon as you spot them. Always use disposable cloths and use a solution of bicarbonate of soda (baking soda) to wash the surfaces. Wash the cloth thoroughly, preferably in an anti-bacterial solution or a mild bleach. Never wipe up blood spills, then wipe another surface; you will simply spread the germs.
- If your fridge is not self-defrosting, make sure you defrost it regularly.
- Use chilled foods by their best-before date – preferably before.

The Freezer

- Your freezer should be running between –18°C and –23°C. If you notice it is icing up quickly, constantly running or, worst of all, that your food is not thoroughly frozen, you have a problem and should call an engineer immediately. If the temperature is constantly much above these recommended temperatures, bacteria can grow. Freezing doesn't kill bacteria, it just stops its growth so, as the food warms, the bacteria can multiply.
- Your freezer should have a **** rating to freeze fresh foods. Those with *** or ** markings are suitable only for storing commercially frozen produce.
- Unless self-defrosting, defrost your freezer regularly. Do not allow a massive build up of ice or the freezer will not work efficiently. When you do defrost it, make sure you wrap any foods in cool boxes or insulate them in several layers of blankets to prevent thawing taking place. Any food that does thaw should be cooked and either used straight away or cooled quickly before re-freezing.
- NEVER re-freeze thawed foods without cooking first. It is perfectly safe to re-freeze poultry or game once it has been thoroughly cooked after thawing, as long as it is cooled quickly and frozen immediately it is cold.
- NEVER store frozen poultry or game for more than three months.
- Always freeze foods on the day of purchase.

THAWING BIRDS

- Always thaw poultry and game thoroughly before cooking, preferably slowly in the fridge.
- Always put it on a plate or shallow dish to catch any drips.
- Leave it in its original wrapper until thawed.
- Cook as soon as possible after thawing.
- If you forget to take it out of the freezer in time to thaw slowly, you can speed up thawing by placing the wrapped bird in cold water. Change the water often and never use hot water or bacteria will grow.
- Defrosting can be done in your microwave using the manufacturer's instructions. Whole birds are best started in the microwave then left to thaw naturally. If you microwave too much, even on a low setting, you will start to cook the thin parts of the bird and this can cause bacteria to grow. Also it is more likely you will end up with a 'cold' spot in the centre of the bird. This may then not reach a high enough temperature on cooking and so become a breeding ground for germs.
- Always check there are no ice crystals left in the body cavity. Rinse the inside in cold water if in any doubt to help finish the thawing.
- Never use a cloth to wipe a bird, then use it for other cleaning jobs. Kitchen paper (paper towels) that will be instantly thrown away is much more hygienic.

COOKING AND REHEATING POULTRY AND GAME

- Don't cook poultry from frozen unless a commercially prepared dish specifically tells you to. All birds in any form should be thawed before cooking.
- Only stuff the neck end of the bird. The body cavity does not reach a high enough temperature to ensure that germs will not breed.
- Always follow any cooking instructions given on wrappers.
- To test if a bird is cooked through, pierce the thickest part of the thigh with a skewer and the juices should run clear. If they are at all pink, cook for a little longer.
- It is advisable to roast larger birds upside-down for the first half of cooking to ensure the thick parts of the legs and thighs cook through. This also helps ensure the breast stays succulent.
- If reheating cooked poultry (or any other dish), make sure it is piping hot throughout before serving. To test a made-up dish, insert a knife down through the centre for 5 seconds, then remove the knife. If the blade feels very hot, the dish is hot through: if not, heat for a little longer.
- Once cooked, cover any leftovers and cool quickly, then wrap thoroughly and store in the fridge for up to three days. If you have a very large bird (like the Christmas turkey), take all the leftover meat off the bones, make the carcass into stock (pages 43, 57, 61, 63) and store the meat in a sealed container in the fridge. If you are not going to eat it within three days, freeze the meat in suitably sized portions for use at a later date.

KITCHEN CLEANLINESS

- It should be automatic to keep everything in the kitchen scrupulously clean. Keep work surfaces clean and tidy and wipe up spills straight away.
- Always wash your hands in hot, soapy water before preparing any food at all, after going to the loo, handling your pets, gardening or tending the indoor plants or flowers, or taking out the rubbish. Don't think that because you are wearing rubber gloves, it doesn't matter. Your hands might be clean, but your gloves could be festering!
- Don't use the same utensils for preparing raw and cooked foods without washing them thoroughly in between. Ideally use separate utensils.
- Ideally use non-porous chopping boards. If you do use wood, scrub it thoroughly after use and preferably use an anti-bacterial agent as well. Use separate boards for smelly foods like garlic and onion, raw poultry, fruit and vegetables, and bread.
- Keep pets out of the kitchen and always wash pet food bowls and other equipment separately from the human ones and using different cleaning utensils.
- Never wipe a chopping board you have been cutting raw poultry on with a cloth, then use it to wipe the work surface. You will simply spread the germs from one place to another.
- Use disposable cloths and kitchen paper (paper towels) instead of re-usable cloths. They are far more hygienic.
- Don't lick your fingers and never taste raw poultry or partially cooked dishes.
- If you have a tummy upset, avoid handling food. Also, cover any wounds – even the tiniest cut – with a clean waterproof dressing or antiseptic plastic 'skin'.
- Keep rubbish bins covered, out of the immediate food preparation area and always use disposable bin liners (or leakproof carrier bags).

Notes on the Recipes

- All ingredients are given in metric, imperial and American measures. Follow one set only in a recipe.
- American terms are given in brackets.
- All spoon measurements are level: 1 tsp = 5 ml; 1 tbsp = 15 ml.
- Eggs are medium unless otherwise stated.
- Always wash, peel, core and seed, if necessary, fresh produce before use.
- Seasoning and the use of strongly flavoured ingredients such as garlic or chillies are very much a matter of personal taste. Adjust seasonings to suite your own palate.
- Always use fresh herbs unless dried are specifically called for. If you wish to substitute dried for fresh, use only half the quantity or less as they are very pungent. Chopped, frozen varieties have a better flavour than dried.
- All can sizes are approximate as they vary from brand to brand. For example, if I call for a 400 g/ 14 oz/1 large can of tomatoes and yours is a 397 g can – that's fine.
- I have given the choice of butter or margarine in the recipes. Use a different spread if you prefer but check that it is suitable for general cooking, not just for spreading.
- Cooking times are approximate and should be used as a guide only. Always check that poultry is thoroughly cooked through before serving.
- Where stock is called for, use home-made (pages 43, 57, 61, 63) or stock cube and water.
- I have used medium-fat soft cheese in these recipes. Use a low-fat variety if you prefer.

Choosing, Preparing and Carving Your Birds

POULTRY

Chicken

This is the generic term for the barnyard fowl of every shape and size, from the baby poussin (Cornish hen) to the large, plump capon. You have a choice between fresh or frozen, battery-reared, barn-reared (where they are, at least, not caged even if they have very little room to move) and free-range (where they can scratch around outside in a controlled environment). You may have come across corn-fed birds, too, which are fed a special diet to give their flesh a particular yellow colour and distinctive flavour. A fresh chicken should have a plump, firm breast, smooth, pliable legs and a pliable breastbone.

Poussin (Cornish hen): a very young bird, 4–6 weeks old and weighing up to 450 g/1 lb. Allow 1 per person.

Double Poussin: a 6–10 week-old bird, weighing around 900 g/2 lb. Serves 2.

Roasting Chicken: 1.25–2.75 kg/ 2½–6 lb, 4–9 months old. The very small roasters are also known as spring chickens. If carved, the smaller birds will serve 4 people, the larger 6–8 or even 10. But if you cut it into portions, you will still have only four quarters, however large the bird! These are also available as joints, portions or breast fillets.

Boiling Fowl: these used to be very easy to come by but not any more. They are usually hens at the end of their laying time, about 1 year old, weighing about 2.75 kg/6 lb. They are inexpensive and ideal for stocks, soups and casseroles. They require longer, slower cooking than other birds to make them tender but their flavour is very good.

Capon: young, sometimes castrated, cockerels bred to give a large proportion of flesh to bone with an excellent flavour. 10–12 weeks old, they weigh 2.75–3.5 kg/6–8 lb and will serve 8–10 people.

Turkey

Now on sale all year round, the turkey is still considered by many to be *the* festive bird. But you can now enjoy breast steaks, breast and dark meat joints, wings, thighs and leg roasts as well as the whole bird.

The bird can range from about 2.75 to 15.5 kg/6 to 35 lb in weight. An average one will weigh around 4.5–6.4 kg/10–15 lb. The best ones are hens, about 6–8 months old. The legs should look dark, the breast very plump and the flesh pale white with a bluish tinge. Allow about 350 g/ 12 oz per person when deciding what weight to buy but remember that you may want some left over to serve cold or to make into other dishes.

Duck

Aylesbury ducks are the best known breed in the UK. In France, they favour Nantais and the larger Rouen varieties and in the USA, the Long Island duckling. The French Barbary duck is widely available in the UK but is not highly prized by gourmets. A duck usually weighs 1.75–2.75 kg/4–6 lb and will serve up to 4 people. Ducks have a large amount of bone to flesh and are fatty. For this reason it is a good idea to prick the skin all over to allow the fat to drip out during cooking. This also helps to crisp the skin. Available all year fresh or frozen, but fresh are best between August and December. Choose one with a plump breast and creamy-coloured skin.

Duckling

A young duck for roasting weighing 1.6–1.75 kg/3½–4 lb. Fresh ones are best between April and July. Serves 2.

Goose

Thought by many people to be the best of all poultry, goose is rich, well flavoured and succulent. However, in my opinion, it needs careful cooking to become tender. Fresh birds are best between October and February. A goose usually weighs 2.75–5.4 kg/ 6–12 lb. Allow at least 350 g/12 oz per person. Choose one with a plump breast and creamy-coloured skin with a pale pinky-orange tinge. Avoid any with blue or brown tinges.

Guinea Fowl

These used to be game birds but are now farmed so have lost that status. They should be hung for several days to improve their flavour and tenderise the flesh. They weigh up to 1.6 kg/3½ lb and should have firm, creamy-white flesh. Small ones are sold as squab (weighing up to 550 g/ 1¼ lb) and guinea chicks (up to 1 kg/ 2¼ lb).

GAME

This is the term applied to birds (and furry animals) that are hunted for food. In Britain there is a closed season for most game when it is forbidden to shoot them. Only pigeons and quails (and rabbits) are not in this category; however it is illegal to shoot wild quail in the UK. Game birds are hung unplucked and undrawn by their beaks (wild ducks and geese by their feet) for several days to give them their 'gamey' flavour and to help tenderise the meat. If you are given an unplucked bird, I recommend removing the skin with the feathers; it is a lot less messy. To draw a bird, you simply cut off the neck then pull out the entrails and wash the bird thoroughly. Use the heart, liver, gizzard and neck for giblets and discard the remaining entrails. Make sure you bard the breast before cooking (that is, cover it thoroughly with fat bacon) to keep the breast moist.

When choosing all-feathered game, choose birds that have a firm, plump breast and tight skin.

Capercaillie

Also known as wood grouse, this is the largest of the grouse family with a strong pine flavour. For this reason, gourmands tend to leave the legs, which have the strongest flavour. If you want to reduce this taste, soak the bird in milk with a little vinegar added for 24 hours before cooking. A capercaillie will serve 4 people. The season runs from 1 August to 31 January.

Grouse

Red or Scottish grouse are the most common birds. Others are the black grouse and hazel grouse (or hazel hen). Hang for three days. Young birds will serve 1 person and should be roasted: older ones, serving 2–3 people, are probably better casseroled. The season runs from 12 August to 10 December.

Mallard

This is the largest of the wild ducks. It has dark, dry flesh but a good flavour. Hang for a day. Serve roasted, allowing 1 bird for 2–3 people. The season runs from 1 September to 28 February.

Ortolan

The smallest of the long-beaked birds. They are good grilled (broiled) or wrapped in vine leaves and roasted quickly. They can be prepared like snipe, if you wish. The season runs from 1 September to 28 February.

Partridge

The English or grey partridge is considered the superior bird: the other, larger one is the French red-leg. Hang for three days. Roast, grill (broil) or braise. The season runs from 1 October to 31 January.

Pheasant

Pheasant are often sold as a brace – one cock bird and one hen bird – but they can also be bought separately. The hen bird is smaller and usually the more tender of the pair. It will serve 2–3 people. A large cock will serve 4 people. Hang for 3–10 days depending on the weather (and how high you like your game). The season runs from 1 October to 31 January in England and 1 October to 10 December in Scotland.

Pigeon

Pigeon is in season all year round, but best from August to October. Choose young birds with pink legs; older birds have much darker flesh. They can be roasted but are best braised, casseroled or cooked in a pie as the flesh can be dry. Do not overcook.

Ptarmigan

This is also known as white grouse and is prepared and cooked like grouse. The season runs from 20 August to 10 December.

Quail

Wild quail are rare; the birds are now farmed and also imported from Europe. They are best eaten fresh, not hung first. Roast, grill (broil) or casserole. There is no season but they are at their best from June to September.

Snipe

Small birds, not often seen in the shops. Some gourmets say you shouldn't draw them before cooking but should tuck the head underneath, using the long beak to skewer the wings and legs. The head is split open after cooking so the brains (a delicacy) can be eaten! Personally, I prefer to prepare them in the usual way with a good knob of butter inside and a simple trussing of string. A good bird will have a round, plump breast and pliable legs. Hang for 3–4 days. Serve 1 per person. The season runs from 12 August to 21 January.

Teal

This is the smallest of the wild ducks. Do not hang. Serve 1 per person. The season runs from 1 September to 20 February.

Widgeon

The most highly prized of the wild ducks, widgeon is plump and rich in flavour. Hang for 1 day only. One bird will serve 2 people. The season runs from 1 September to 20 February.

Woodcock

Choose a bird with a plump, well-rounded breast and pliable legs. Prepare as for snipe, if you wish. Roast or braise. Serve 1 per person. The season runs from 1 October to 31 January.

JOINTING A BIRD INTO PORTIONS

❶ Gently pull the leg away from the body and cut through the skin and flesh down to the joint.

❷ Break the leg joint, then cut through the remaining flesh and remove the leg portion. Repeat with the other side. For eight portions, separate the leg and thigh by cutting through the joint.

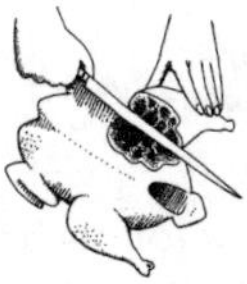

❸ Cut down one side of the breastbone, easing the breast meat away from the carcass.

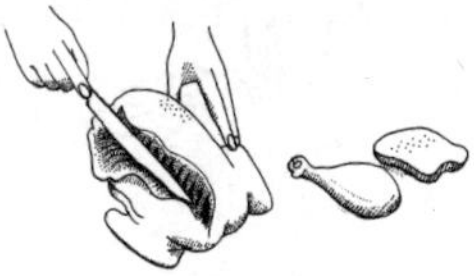

❹ Find the wing joint and cut through, then cut away the remaining skin and remove the breast portion. Repeat with the other side. For eight portions, separate into the breast and wing by cutting through the wing where it joins the breast.

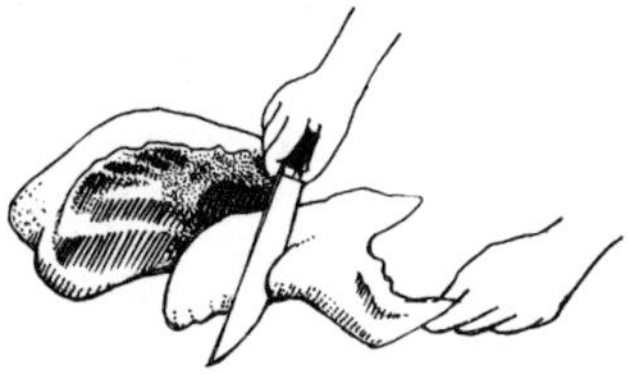

BONING A BIRD

❶ Cut off the wing pinions.

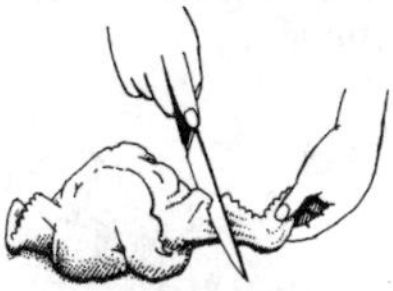

❷ With the bird upside-down, make a cut along the backbone, starting at the neck end and carefully cut the flesh away from the rib cage on each side, down towards the wing joints.

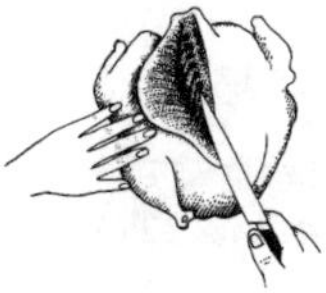

❸ Cut through the sinews at the wing joint and scrape away the flesh from along the wing bone down towards the body. Repeat with the other wing.

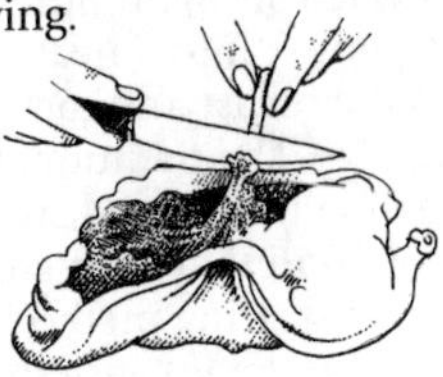

❹ Cut through the sinews at the leg joint, turn the leg inside-out and scrape the flesh away from the bone down towards the body. Repeat with the other leg.

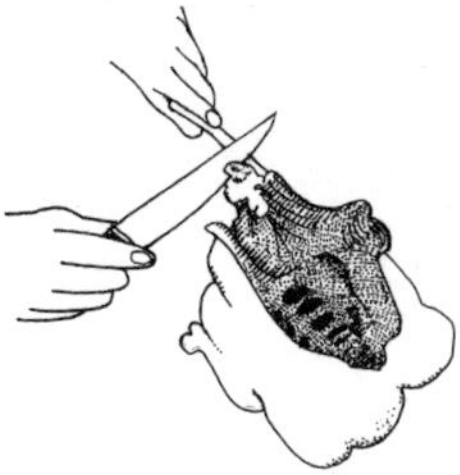

5 Gently continue cutting and scraping down either side of the breastbone, being careful not to puncture the skin.

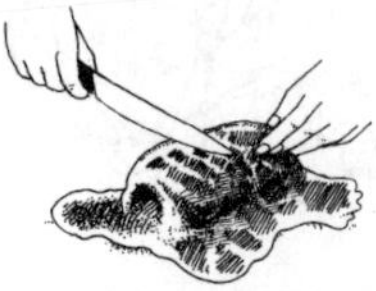

6 Lastly, cut the flesh away from the top of the breastbone, not cutting through the skin and lift away the carcass.

TRUSSING A BIRD

Many birds come already trussed with elasticated string. If not, you will need to tie it into a neat shape to plump up the breast and tuck in the wings and legs. The traditional way is with a trussing needle and string but most people find that a bit arduous. The skewer and string method is still very effective and a lot easier!

1 Place the bird breast-side down on a board. Fold any loose neck skin over the back, closing the neck opening (over stuffing if there is any). Fold the wing tips over the body to hold the skin in place and to keep them neatly tucked underneath when the bird is upright. Also, for a large turkey, poke the parson's nose up through a slit in the skin above the body cavity.

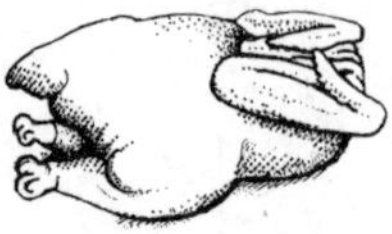

2 Push the legs up towards the neck and insert a metal skewer through the bird just below the thigh bones.

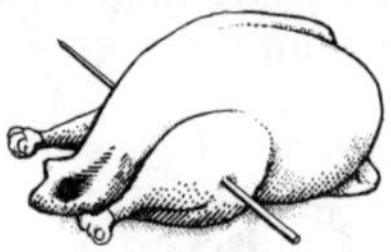

3 Turn the bird on its breast again and tie string round the wing tips leaving two long ends, then round the ends of the skewer and cross the string over its back.

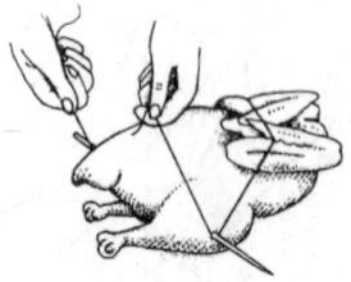

4 Turn the bird over, loop the string round the drumsticks and parson's nose and tie securely.

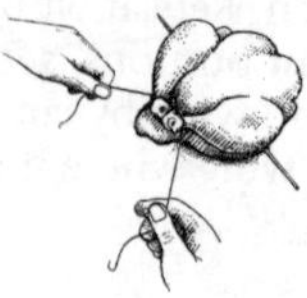

CARVING LARGE BIRDS

In all cases, remove the trussing string and any skewers before carving. For large turkeys, you may wish to carve the leg meat off the bones, in downward slices from the bone end.

1. Cut off the drumsticks.

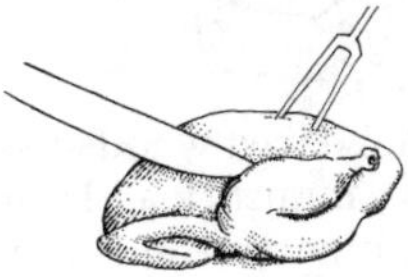

2. Cut off the thighs at the thigh joint next to the body. Alternatively, cut the leg and thigh joint off in one portion.

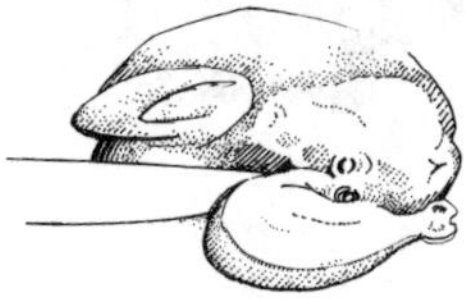

3. Cut off a little breast with the wing joints each side of the body.

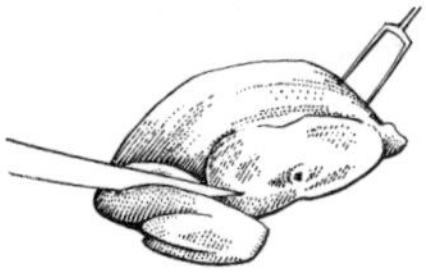

4. If the bird has been stuffed, carve the stuffing in thick slices across the bird.

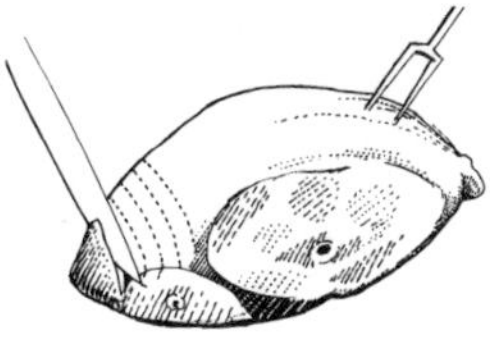

5. Carve the breast in thin, downward slices for turkey or chicken, thicker ones for duck or goose.

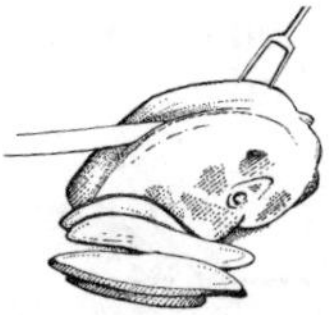

HALVING OR QUARTERING SMALLER BIRDS

1. Use poultry shears or a sharp carving knife. Start at the centre of the neck end and cut through the centre of the breastbone to the body cavity.

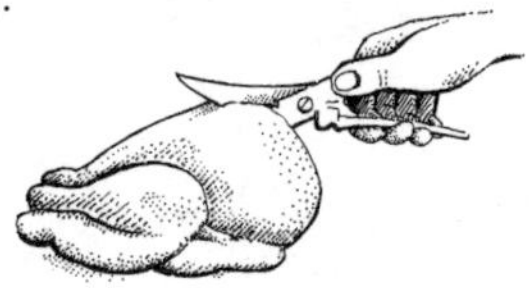

2. Pull the two parts of the bird in half, then cut through the centre of the backbone to divide completely.

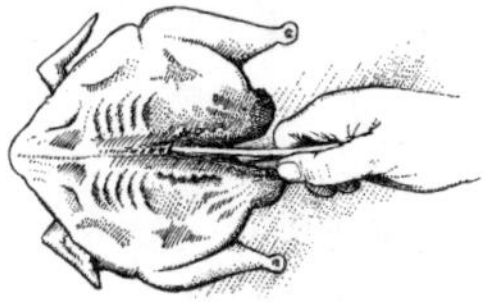

3. To quarter, lay the halves on a board and cut directly in half behind the leg. Alternatively, cut through the natural division between the leg portion and the breast portion and divide the bird at the thigh joint.

TO SPATCHCOCK POUSSINS (CORNISH HENS) OR LARGER BIRDS

❶ Cut through both sides of the backbone from the parson's nose to the neck with poultry shears or a sharp kitchen knife.

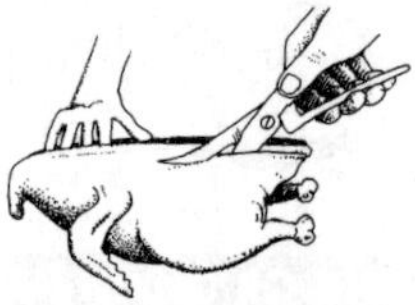

❷ Remove the backbone.

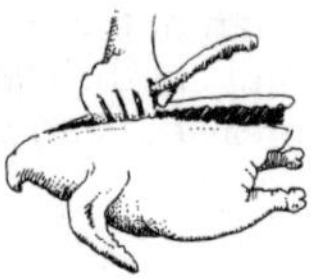

❸ Turn the bird over, flatten out by pressing the breastbone down and fold the drumsticks towards the centre.

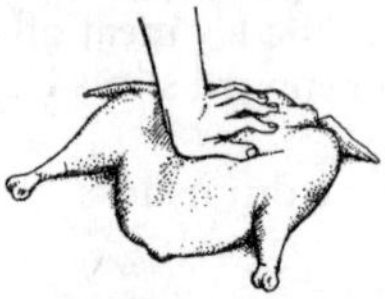

❹ Push one soaked wooden skewer through one drumstick and out through the other one and a second one through the wings, the same way. This will hold the birds flat.

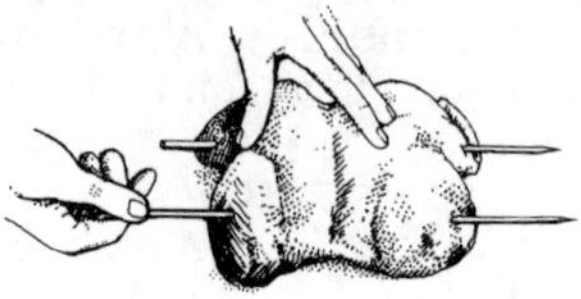

Starters

All kinds of poultry and game make delicious starters. Tiny morsels of succulent meat or the livers, served in so many ways – every one designed to whet the appetite, not satiate it! You will also find many of these recipes make ideal light lunches, perhaps served with a side salad and some crusty bread.

CHICKEN

Chicken Baked Custard

SERVES 4

100 g/4 oz frozen mixed vegetables
175 g/6 oz/1½ cups cooked chicken, chopped
2 eggs
300 ml/½ pt/1¼ cups milk
2.5 ml/½ tsp dried mixed herbs
Salt and freshly ground black pepper
Parsley sprigs

Cook the mixed vegetables in plenty of boiling salted water for 5 minutes. Drain. Mix with the chicken and divide between four individual ovenproof dishes. Beat together the eggs and milk with the herbs and some salt and pepper. Pour over the chicken and vegetables. Stand the dishes in a roasting tin containing 2.5 cm/1 in hot water. Bake at 190°C/375°F/gas mark 5 for about 30 minutes until set. Serve hot, garnished with parsley sprigs.

Huevos à la Cubana

SERVES 4

175 g/6 oz/¾ cup long-grain rice
1 onion, finely chopped
1 small garlic clove, crushed
60 ml/4 tbsp olive oil
100 g/4 oz/1 cup cooked chicken, chopped
2 bananas, cut into thick chunks
4 eggs

Cook the rice in plenty of boiling, salted water for 10 minutes or until tender. Drain. Meanwhile, fry (sauté) the onion and garlic in 15 ml/1 tbsp of the oil until soft and brown. Add the chicken and fry for a further 2 minutes. Remove from the pan with a draining spoon and keep warm. Add a further 15 ml/1 tbsp of the oil to the pan and fry the bananas until just cooked but still holding their shape. Add to the chicken mixture. In a clean frying pan (skillet), heat the remaining oil and fry the eggs until set. Pile the rice on to four warm plates. Slide an egg on top of each and garnish with the chicken mixture.

Chicken, Ham and Pineapple Cocktail

SERVES 6

75 g/3 oz/⅓ cup long-grain rice
50 g/2 oz frozen peas
30 ml/2 tbsp olive oil
10 ml/2 tsp lemon juice
5 ml/1 tsp soy sauce
2 spring onions (scallions), finely chopped
100 g/4 oz/1 cup cooked chicken, diced
100 g/4 oz/1 cup cooked ham, diced
225 g/8 oz/1 small can of pineapple chunks in natural juice, drained, reserving the juice
30 ml/2 tbsp mayonnaise
12 stoned (pitted) black olives

Cook the rice in plenty of boiling salted water for 10 minutes until just tender. Add the peas half-way through cooking. Drain, rinse with cold water and drain again. Mix together the oil, lemon juice, soy sauce and spring onions. Add to the rice, toss well and divide between six small serving plates. Mix together the chicken, ham and pineapple with the mayonnaise. Slice 6 of the olives and fold in. Thin the mixture with a little of the pineapple juice if necessary. Pile on to the rice and garnish each with an olive.

Chicken and Mushroom Cocktail

SERVES 4

½ small iceberg lettuce, shredded
100 g/4 oz small button mushrooms
100 g/4 oz/1 cup cooked chicken, diced
75 ml/5 tbsp mayonnaise
75 ml/5 tbsp plain yoghurt
30 ml/2 tbsp tomato ketchup (catsup)
15 ml/1 tbsp lemon juice
Salt and freshly ground black pepper
4 lemon and 4 cucumber slices, to garnish
Brown bread and butter, to serve

Put the lettuce in four large wine goblets. Put the mushrooms in a bowl, cover with boiling water and leave to stand for 2 minutes. Drain, rinse with cold water and drain again. Pat dry on kitchen paper (paper towels). Mix with the chicken and spoon into the goblets. Blend together the remaining ingredients and spoon over, seasoning to taste with salt and pepper. Make a small slit from the centre to the edge of each slice of lemon and cucumber and hang one of each on the side of each glass. Serve with brown bread and butter.

Chicken and Prawn Cocktail

SERVES 4

Prepare as for Chicken and Mushroom Cocktail, but omit the mushrooms and add 100 g/4 oz cooked, peeled prawns (shrimp), well drained on kitchen paper (paper towels). Add 5 ml/1 tsp Worcestershire sauce to the mayonnaise mixture and hang a cooked, unpeeled prawn on the side of each goblet with the lemon and cucumber slices.

Chicken, Ham and Olive Cocktail

SERVES 4

Prepare as for Chicken and Mushroom Cocktail, but omit the mushrooms and use cooked diced ham instead. Add 50 g/2 oz sliced stuffed olives to the mixture, reserving 4 slices to put on top of the sauce in the goblets.

Chicken and Avocado Cocktail

SERVES 4

Prepare as for Chicken and Mushroom Cocktail, but omit the mushrooms and add a diced ripe avocado, tossed in 5 ml/1 tsp lemon juice, with the chicken. Spike the sauce with 5 ml/1 tsp Worcestershire sauce.

Chicken and Prawn Wontons with Sweet and Sour Sauce

SERVES 4

100 g/4 oz/1 cup cooked chicken, finely chopped
25 g/1 oz cooked, peeled prawns (shrimp), finely chopped
10 ml/2 tsp caster (superfine) sugar
1 small garlic clove, crushed
2.5 cm/1 in piece of cucumber, finely chopped
15 ml/1 tbsp soy sauce
A pinch of Chinese five spice powder
A pinch of salt
20 wonton wrappers
Oil, for deep-frying
Sweet and Sour Dipping Sauce (page 337), to serve

Mix together the chicken, prawns, sugar, garlic and cucumber with the soy sauce, five-spice powder and salt. Dampen the wonton wrappers. Divide the filling between the wrappers. Dampen the edges again and draw the corners together twisting to form little pouches. Heat the oil in a wok or frying pan (skillet) and fry (sauté) the wontons for about 2 minutes until golden. Drain on kitchen paper (paper towels) and serve hot with the hot Sweet and Sour Dipping Sauce in small bowls.

Chinese Meatballs with Ginger

SERVES 6

450 g/1 lb minced (ground) chicken
2 spring onions (scallions), finely chopped
1 small garlic clove, crushed
225 g/8 oz/1 small can of water chestnuts, drained and finely chopped
15 ml/1 tbsp oyster sauce
25 g/1 oz/½ cup fresh breadcrumbs
1 egg, beaten
Oil, for shallow-frying
120 ml/4 fl oz/½ cup pineapple juice
120 ml/4 fl oz/½ cup chicken stock
10 ml/2 tsp grated fresh root ginger
10 ml/2 tsp soy sauce
15 ml/1 tbsp clear honey
30 ml/2 tbsp cider vinegar
30 ml/2 tbsp cornflour (cornstarch)

Mix the chicken with the spring onions, garlic, water chestnuts, oyster sauce and breadcrumbs. Mix with the egg to bind. Shape into 48 small balls. Heat a little oil in a wok or frying pan (skillet) until a cube of day-old bread browns in 30 seconds. Fry (sauté) the balls about 12 at a time for about 4 minutes until golden brown all over and cooked through. Drain on kitchen paper (paper towels). Put the pineapple juice, stock, ginger and soy sauce in a saucepan with the honey. Stir well. Blend the cornflour with the vinegar and stir in. Bring to the boil and cook, stirring for 2 minutes. Place the meatballs in the sauce, turning gently until coated and simmer gently for about 5 minutes. Serve the meatballs on cocktail sticks (toothpicks).

Chinese Spring Rolls

SERVES 4

100 g/4 oz/1 cup cooked chicken, chopped
1 spring onion (scallion), chopped
50 g/2 oz button mushrooms, finely chopped
50 g/2 oz/1 cup beansprouts
15 ml/1 tbsp cooked, peeled prawns (shrimp)
15 ml/1 tbsp soy sauce
A pinch of ground ginger
10 ml/2 tsp caster (superfine) sugar
7.5 ml/1½ tsp cornflour (cornstarch)
8 small or 4 large filo pastry (paste) sheets
Oil, for deep-frying

Mix together the chicken, onion, mushrooms, beansprouts and prawns with the soy sauce, ginger, sugar and cornflour. If using large filo sheets, cut each in half. Lay the pastry sheets on the work surface and fold in halves. Divide the mixture between the pastry squares in the centre of one edge. Brush all round the edges with water. Fold in the sides, then roll up firmly. Deep-fry in hot oil for about 5 minutes until golden brown. Drain on kitchen paper (paper towels) and serve hot.

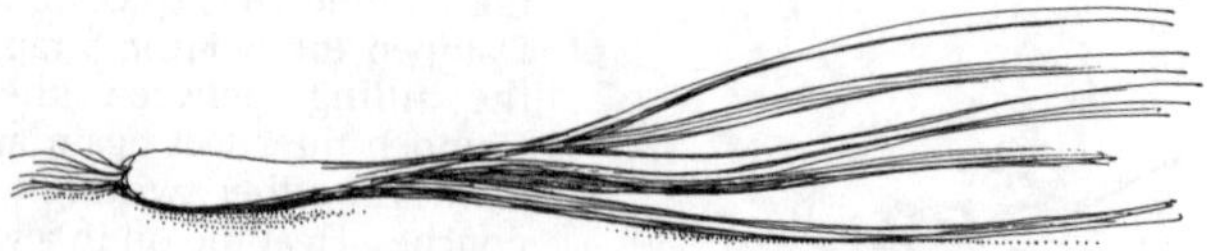

Marbled Tea Eggs with Sesame Chicken

SERVES 4

4 eggs
300 ml/½ pt/1¼ cups cold water
A pinch of salt
2 star anise
100 ml/3½ fl oz/scant 1 cup soy sauce
15 ml/1 tbsp Chinese five spice powder
2 tea bags
10 ml/2 tsp clear honey
15 ml/1 tbsp sesame oil
175 g/6 oz/1½ cups cooked chicken, cut into neat pieces
2 spring onions (scallions), chopped
15 ml/1 tbsp toasted sesame seeds
Round lettuce leaves

Put the eggs in the water. Bring to the boil and simmer for 10 minutes. Lift the eggs out of the pan and plunge into cold water to cool. Add the salt, star anise, 75 ml/5 tbsp of the soy sauce, the five spice powder, tea bags and honey to the pan with the boiling water. Tap the eggs gently with a teaspoon all over to crack the shells and return to the pan. Bring back to the boil and simmer for 30 minutes. Remove from the heat and leave to stand for several hours or overnight.

One hour before serving, mix the remaining soy sauce with the sesame oil and add the chicken and spring onions. Arrange lettuce leaves on four small serving plates. Put a pile of the chicken mixture in the centre and sprinkle with the sesame seeds. Remove the shells from the eggs. There should be a beautiful marbled pattern on them. Cut in halves and place rounded-sides up on top of the chicken. Serve cold.

Simple Dolmas

SERVES 6

6 large outer cabbage leaves
100 g/4 oz frozen diced mixed vegetables
100 g/4 oz/1 cup cooked chicken, chopped, all skin removed
2.5 ml/½ tsp dried thyme
Salt and freshly ground black pepper
1 egg, beaten
250 ml/8 fl oz/1 cup passata (sieved tomatoes)
60 ml/4 tbsp grated Cheddar cheese

Cut out any thick central stalk from the leaves. Blanch the leaves in boiling water for 5 minutes. Drain and rinse with cold water. Meanwhile, cook the vegetables according to the packet directions. Drain and mix with the chicken, thyme, a little salt and pepper and the egg. Lay the cabbage leaves on a board and divide the chicken and vegetable mixture between the leaves. Fold in the two sides and roll up to form parcels. Place rolled-sides down in a single layer in an ovenproof dish. Spoon the passata over, sprinkle with the cheese and bake in a preheated oven at 190°C/375°F/gas mark 5 for 15–20 minutes until tender and the cheese has melted and is turning golden brown. Serve on warm plates.

Avocado à l'Indienne

SERVES 4

2 ripe avocados, halved and stoned (pitted)
Lemon juice
100 g/4 oz/½ cup cottage cheese with (bell) peppers
100 g/4 oz/1 cup cooked chicken, diced
1 small green chilli, seeded and chopped
30 ml/2 tbsp mayonnaise
2.5 ml/½ tsp curry paste
10 ml/2 tsp curried fruit chutney
15 ml/1 tbsp chopped coriander (cilantro)
4 coriander leaves and lemon wedges, to garnish
Mini popadoms, to serve

Place the avocados in four avocado dishes or other suitable small dishes. Brush with lemon juice to prevent browning. Mix the cottage cheese with the chicken and chilli and spoon into the cavities. Blend the mayonnaise with the curry paste, chutney and coriander and add a dash of lemon juice to taste. Spoon a little over each avocado and garnish with a coriander leaf. Put a lemon wedge to the side of each and serve with mini popadoms.

Chinese Chicken Fries

SERVES 4

1 skinless chicken breast
1 spring onion (scallion)
½ small green chilli, seeded
Salt and freshly ground black pepper
5 ml/1 tsp lemon juice
2.5 ml/½ tsp garlic purée (paste)
8 slices of white bread from a large sliced loaf
40 g/1½ oz/⅓ cup sesame seeds
Oil, for deep-frying
90 ml/6 tbsp soy sauce
30 ml/2 tbsp medium-dry sherry

Mince (grind) the chicken, spring onion and chilli in a mincer (grinder) or food processor. Season with a little salt and pepper and stir in the lemon juice and garlic purée. Cut the crusts off the bread and spread on one side with the chicken mixture. Sprinkle with the sesame seeds and cut each slice into four triangles. Heat the oil until a cube of day-old bread browns in 30 seconds. Deep-fry the triangles until golden brown. Drain on kitchen paper (paper towels). Mix together the soy sauce and sherry in a small bowl and serve the triangles warm with the sauce to dip into.

Chicken, Olive and Avocado Mousse

SERVES 6

1 chicken stock cube
300 ml/½ pt/1¼ cups boiling water
15 ml/1 tbsp powdered gelatine
2 ripe avocados
15 ml/1 tbsp lemon juice
2.5 ml/½ tsp grated onion
50 g/2 oz stuffed green olives, sliced
175 g/6 oz/1½ cups cooked chicken, finely chopped, all skin removed
A few drops of Tabasco sauce
A few drops of Worcestershire sauce
2 egg whites
150 ml/¼ pt/⅔ cup whipping cream
A few extra sliced olives, to garnish
Warm pitta bread fingers, to serve

Dissolve the stock cube in the boiling water. Sprinkle the gelatine over and stir until completely dissolved. Halve the avocados, remove the stones (pits) and scoop the flesh into a bowl. Mash thoroughly with the lemon juice until smooth. Stir in the dissolved gelatine mixture, the onion, olives and chicken and flavour to taste with Tabasco and Worcestershire sauces. Whisk the egg whites, then the cream until peaking. Fold the cream, then the egg whites into the avocado mixture. Turn into one large or six small serving dishes and chill until set. Garnish with the extra olives and serve with warm pitta bread fingers.

Potted Chicken with Sherry and Herbs

SERVES 8

1.5 kg/3 lb oven-ready chicken
60 ml/4 tbsp medium-dry sherry
15 ml/1 tbsp chopped parsley
15 ml/1 tbsp chopped tarragon
100 g/4 oz/½ cup unsalted (sweet) butter
1 onion, quartered
1 carrot, roughly chopped
1 celery stick, roughly chopped
600 ml/1 pt/2½ cups water
Salt and freshly ground black pepper
A pinch of ground mace
A sprig of parsley, to garnish
Crusty bread, to serve

Remove any fat from just inside the body cavity of the chicken and remove any giblets. Take these out of the bag and place alongside the chicken in a large, flameproof casserole (Dutch oven). Add the sherry, herbs, half the butter, the onion, carrot and celery. Cover and cook in a preheated oven at 180°C/350°F/gas mark 4 for 1½ hours. Remove from the oven. When cool enough to handle, remove all the meat from the chicken, discarding the skin. Return the carcass to the casserole and add the water. Bring to the boil on top of the stove and boil rapidly until the liquid has reduced by half. Meanwhile, finely chop the chicken in a food processor or pass through a mincer (grinder). Strain the reduced stock and stir in. Season to taste with salt, pepper and the mace. Turn into an attractive serving bowl and leave until cold. Melt the remaining butter and pour over the surface. Chill until firm. Garnish with a sprig of parsley and serve with crusty bread.

Smoked Chicken with Scrambled Egg

SERVES 4

15 g/½ oz/1 tbsp butter, plus extra for spreading
4 eggs, beaten
150 ml/¼ pt/⅔ cup single (light) cream
100 g/4 oz smoked chicken, cut into thin strips
Freshly ground black pepper
Salt
4 slices of granary bread
2 tomatoes, cut into small wedges, and parsley sprigs, to garnish

Melt the butter in a saucepan. Add the eggs and cream and whisk together lightly. Cook over a gentle heat, stirring all the time, until just beginning to scramble. Add the chicken and season with pepper. Continue cooking until the egg is scrambled but creamy and the chicken is piping hot. Do not allow to boil. Taste and add a little salt if necessary. Meanwhile, toast the bread, cut off the crusts and spread with a little butter. Cut into triangles. Spoon the egg mixture on to warm plates. Arrange the toast triangles around and garnish with tomato wedges and parsley sprigs on the side.

Cajun Chicken Wings

SERVES 8

20 ml/4 tsp paprika
5 ml/1 tsp ground cumin
10 ml/2 tsp ground coriander (cilantro)
2.5 ml/½ tsp chilli powder
5 ml/1 tsp celery salt
2.5 ml/½ tsp onion salt
45 ml/3 tbsp sunflower oil
30 ml/2 tbsp red wine vinegar
1 garlic clove, crushed
16 chicken wings, wing tips removed
Lettuce leaves

Mix the spices with the celery and onion salt and 15 ml/1 tbsp of the sunflower oil, the vinegar and garlic. Rub this mixture all over the wings. Place in a roasting tin (pan) and chill for at least 1 hour. Drizzle the remaining oil over and roast in a preheated oven at 200°C/400°F/gas mark 6 for 15–20 minutes, basting with the juices several times until well coloured and cooked through. Serve hot on a bed of lettuce.

Piquant Spinach and Chicken Rolls

SERVES 6

For the rolls:
12 spinach leaves
200 g/7 oz/scant 1 cup medium-fat soft cheese
15 ml/1 tbsp chopped parsley
15 ml/1 tbsp chopped dill (dill weed)
Finely grated rind of 1 lemon
10 ml/2 tsp chopped capers
Freshly ground black pepper
15 ml/1 tbsp milk
6 thin slices of cooked chicken breast
For the dressing:
45 ml/3 tbsp olive oil
15 ml/1 tbsp lemon juice
5 ml/1 tsp balsamic vinegar
2.5 ml/½ tsp caster (superfine) sugar
15 ml/1 tbsp chopped dill
Salt
A few mixed salad leaves, to garnish

To make the rolls, trim the stalks from the spinach and plunge the leaves into boiling water for 1 minute. Drain, rinse with cold water and drain again. Pat dry on kitchen paper (paper towels). Mash the cheese with the herbs, lemon rind and capers. Season to taste with pepper. Stir in the milk to thin slightly. Cut the chicken in halves lengthways. Spread each piece gently with the cheese mixture and carefully roll up. Lay each on a spinach leaf, fold in the sides, then roll up tightly. Chill.

To make the dressing, place all the ingredients in a screw-topped jar with a good grinding of pepper and a pinch of salt. Shake well. To serve, place two rolls on each of six serving plates. Cut into attractive slices and garnish with salad leaves. Shake the dressing and spoon a little over the slices before serving.

Baked Avocados with Chicken

SERVES 4

2 ripe avocados
5 ml/1 tsp lemon juice
2 spring onions (scallions), finely chopped
75 g/3 oz/⅓ cup soft cheese with garlic and herbs
100 g/4 oz/1 cup cooked chicken, chopped, all skin removed
Salt and freshly ground black pepper
A few drops of Tabasco sauce
15 g/½ oz/1 tbsp butter or margarine
25 g/1 oz/½ cup white breadcrumbs
15 ml/1 tbsp grated Parmesan cheese

Halve the avocados, remove the stones (pits) and scoop the flesh into a bowl, reserving the skins. Mash well with the lemon juice. Stir in the spring onions, soft cheese and chicken. Season to taste with salt, pepper and Tabasco sauce. Spoon this mixture back into the shells. Melt the butter or margarine and stir in the breadcrumbs and Parmesan cheese. Spoon over the filling. Place in a shallow baking dish and bake in a preheated oven at 200°C/400°F/gas mark 6 for about 10–15 minutes until the top is golden brown and the filling is piping hot. Serve straight away.

Stuffed Peaches

SERVES 4

175 g/6 oz/¾ cup cottage cheese
2 celery sticks, finely chopped
15 ml/1 tbsp chopped walnuts
100 g/4 oz/1 cup cooked chicken, diced, all skin removed
30 ml/2 tbsp mayonnaise
15 ml/1 tbsp tomato relish
Salt and freshly ground black pepper
8 canned peach halves
Lettuce leaves
4 walnut halves, to garnish

Mix the cheese with the celery, chopped walnuts and chicken. Blend the mayonnaise with the tomato relish and fold in. Season to taste. Pile into the peach halves and place on lettuce leaves. Garnish with the walnut halves and chill before serving.

Cottage Cheese, Chicken and Prawn Cups

SERVES 4

350 g/12 oz/1½ cups cottage cheese with chives
100 g/4 oz/1 cup cooked chicken, finely chopped
150 ml/¼ pt/⅔ cup plain yoghurt
15 ml/1 tbsp tomato purée (paste)
5 ml/1 tsp lemon juice
Salt and freshly ground black pepper
100 g/4 oz cooked, peeled prawns (shrimp)
4 small parsley sprigs, to garnish

Mix together all the ingredients except the prawns and spoon into four ramekins (custard cups). Press down firmly. Top each with the prawns and a small sprig of parsley and chill for at least 1 hour before serving.

Stuffed Cucumber Boats

SERVES 6

2 cucumbers, halved lengthways
1 red eating (dessert) apple, diced
10 ml/2 tsp lemon juice
30 ml/2 tbsp sultanas (golden raisins)
100 g/4 oz/1 cup cooked chicken, chopped, all skin removed
50 g/2 oz button mushrooms, finely chopped
1 spring onion (scallion), finely chopped
60 ml/4 tbsp mayonnaise
5 ml/1 tsp Dijon mustard
Salt and freshly ground black pepper
Lettuce leaves, to serve
Paprika, for dusting

Scoop the seeds out of the cucumbers with a small spoon. Cut each half into three pieces. Blanch in boiling water for 2 minutes. Drain, rinse with cold water and drain again. Mix together the remaining ingredients. Spoon into the cucumber. Arrange the lettuce leaves on six individual plates. Place two cucumber boats on each plate, dust with paprika and serve.

Pompeii Eggs

SERVES 4

45 ml/3 tbsp chopped parsley
10 ml/2 tsp chopped basil
1 garlic clove, crushed
12 stoned (pitted) green olives
1 small onion, quartered
1 sun-dried tomato in oil
15 ml/1 tbsp oil from the jar
100 ml/3½ fl oz/scant ½ cup olive oil
6 hard-boiled (hard-cooked) eggs, sliced
4 tomatoes, sliced
Lettuce leaves

Put the parsley, basil, garlic, 8 of the olives, the onion, sun-dried tomato and the sun-dried tomato oil in a blender or food processor and blend until smooth. With the machine running, gradually add the oil in a trickle until a smooth glossy sauce is formed. Arrange the egg and tomato slices on a bed of lettuce on plates. Spoon the sauce over and garnish with the remaining olives, sliced.

Grilled Chicken Bites

SERVES 6

350 g/12 oz skinless chicken breasts, cut into bite-sized pieces
1 egg, beaten
90 g/3½ oz/1 small packet of parsley and thyme stuffing mix
Sunflower oil, for brushing
Shredded lettuce and lemon wedges, to garnish

Toss the chicken in the egg, then in the stuffing mix to coat completely. Chill for at least 30 minutes. Place on foil on the grill (broiler) rack, brush all over with oil and grill (broil) for about 8 minutes, turning frequently, until crisp and cooked through. Serve on a bed of shredded lettuce and garnish with lemon wedges.

Spicy Grilled Chicken Bites

SERVES 6

Prepare as for Grilled Chicken Bites but add 1.5 ml/¼ tsp hot chilli sauce to the beaten egg before dipping and substitute sage and onion stuffing mix for parsley and thyme.

Oriental Chicken and Prawn Salad

SERVES 6

175 g/6 oz/3 cups beansprouts
1 small red (bell) pepper, chopped
100 g/4 oz cooked, peeled prawns (shrimp)
100 g/4 oz/1 cup cooked chicken, diced, all skin removed
10 ml/2 tsp soy sauce
10 ml/2 tsp cider vinegar
5 ml/1 tsp caster (superfine) sugar
15 ml/1 tbsp sesame oil
15 ml/1 tbsp sunflower oil
Salt and freshly ground black pepper
Lettuce leaves
2 spring onions (scallions), chopped

Wash the beansprouts and place in a bowl with the chopped pepper, prawns and chicken. Whisk together the soy sauce, vinegar, sugar, oils and seasoning and pour over. Toss gently. Arrange the lettuce leaves on a serving plate and pile the chicken and prawn mixture over. Sprinkle with the chopped spring onion.

Prune and Chicken-stuffed Tomatoes

SERVES 4

4 beefsteak tomatoes
Salt and freshly ground black pepper
100 g/4 oz/½ cup soft cheese with chives
8 ready-to-eat prunes, chopped
1 spring onion (scallion), finely chopped
100 g/4 oz/1 cup cooked chicken, skinned and finely chopped
Lettuce leaves

Cut the rounded ends off the tomatoes and scoop out the seeds. Season inside with salt and pepper and tip upside down on kitchen paper (paper towels) to drain. Beat together the cheese, prunes, spring onion and chicken and season with salt and pepper. Spoon into the tomatoes and replace the lids. Chill until ready to serve on a bed of lettuce.

Chicken Samosas

MAKES 16

150 g/5 oz/1¼ cups plain (all-purpose) flour
5 ml/1 tsp salt
2.5 ml/½ tsp baking powder
25 g/1 oz/2 tbsp butter or margarine
90 ml/6 tbsp water
225 g/8 oz minced (ground) chicken
2.5 ml/½ tsp turmeric
5 ml/1 tsp ground cumin
5 ml/1 tsp ground coriander (cilantro)
2.5 ml/½ tsp chilli powder
5 ml/1 tsp caster (superfine) sugar
10 ml/2 tsp cornflour (cornstarch)
Oil, for deep-frying
Shredded lettuce and lemon wedges, to garnish
Lime pickle, to serve

Sift the flour, half the salt and the baking powder into a bowl. Rub in the butter or margarine. Mix with the water to form a soft but not sticky dough. Knead gently until smooth, then wrap in clingfilm (plastic wrap) and chill. Put the remaining ingredients except the cornflour in a saucepan and cook, stirring, until the chicken is no longer pink and all the grains are separate. Stir in the cornflour. Leave to cool.

Divide the dough into eight pieces. Roll out each piece to a very thin round. Cut each in half. Hold a semi-circle of dough in your hand and brush the cut edge with water. Fold in half and press the cut edges together to form a cone. Gently spoon a little of the meat mixture into the cone, brush the edges with water and press together to seal. Repeat with the remaining ingredients. Heat the oil until a cube of day-old bread browns in 30 seconds. Deep-fry the samosas for about 6 minutes or until crisp and golden. Drain on kitchen paper (paper towels). Serve hot, garnished with shredded lettuce and lemon wedges, with lime pickle.

Savoury Stuffed Mushrooms

SERVES 4

8 large open mushrooms
225 g/8 oz chicken livers, trimmed
2 rindless streaky bacon rashers (slices), cut into pieces
1 small onion, quartered
50 g/2 oz/¼ cup butter or margarine
1.5 ml/¼ tsp dried oregano
75 g/3 oz/1½ cups white breadcrumbs
Salt and freshly ground black pepper
30 ml/2 tbsp water
Parsley sprigs, to garnish
French bread, to serve

Peel the mushrooms and trim off the stalks. Mince (grind) or process the mushroom stalks, livers, bacon and onion in a food processor. Melt nearly all the butter or margarine in a saucepan. Add the liver mixture and cook gently, stirring, for 2 minutes. Stir in the oregano and breadcrumbs and a little seasoning. Spoon into the mushroom caps. Grease a shallow roasting tin (pan) with the remaining butter. Place the mushrooms in the pan and add the water. Cover with foil and bake in a preheated oven at 180 °C/350 °F/gas mark 4 for 30 minutes until the mushrooms are cooked through. Transfer to warm plates and garnish with parsley sprigs. Serve hot with French bread.

Chicken and Bacon Terrine with Pistachio Nuts

SERVES 8

450 g/1 lb chicken stir-fry meat
225 g/8 oz chicken livers, trimmed
100 g/4 oz bacon pieces, all rind and bone removed
1 large onion, quartered
1 large garlic clove, crushed
30 ml/2 tbsp chopped parsley
5 ml/1 tsp dried thyme
30 ml/2 tbsp medium-dry sherry
Salt and freshly ground black pepper
1 egg, beaten
8–10 rindless streaky bacon rashers (slices)
50 g/2 oz/½ cup shelled pistachio nuts
1 chicken breast, thickly sliced
Hot toast, to serve

Put the chicken stir-fry meat, the chicken livers, bacon pieces and onion through a coarse mincer (or drop into a food processor with the machine running until coarsely chopped). Stir in the garlic, herbs and sherry and season well with salt and pepper. Mix with the egg to bind. Scrape the rashers with the back of a knife to stretch slightly. Use to line a 1.2 litre/2 pt/5 cup terrine or loaf tin (pan). Spoon a quarter of the minced mixture into the tin and top with half the pistachio nuts. Add a further quarter of the minced mixture and lay the chicken breast pieces on top. Add half the remaining meat mixture, then the remaining pistachios, then the remaining meat mixture. Cover with foil. Place in a roasting tin (pan) containing 2.5 cm/1 in boiling water. Bake in a preheated oven at 160°C/325°F/gas mark 3 for 2 hours or until cooked through and firm to the touch.

Remove the terrine from the roasting tin and pour off any juices. Cover with clean foil and weigh down with heavy weights. Leave until cold then chill, preferably overnight. Gently loosen the edge all round with a knife and turn out on to a serving dish. Serve sliced with hot toast.

Oriental Chicken Livers with Spinach and Toasted Sesame Seeds

SERVES 4

10 ml/2 tsp sesame seeds
15 ml/1 tbsp sunflower oil
15 ml/1 tbsp sesame oil
350 g/12 oz fresh leaf spinach, well washed and shredded
4 spring onions (scallions), finely chopped
225 g/8 oz chicken livers, trimmed and cut into bite-sized pieces, if necessary
30 ml/2 tbsp medium-dry sherry
30 ml/2 tbsp soy sauce
30 ml/2 tbsp apple juice
Prawn crackers, to serve

Toast the sesame seeds in a dry frying pan (skillet) or wok, stirring until golden. Immediately tip out of the pan on to a cold plate and reserve. Heat about half of each oil in the frying pan or wok. Add the spinach and spring onions and stir-fry for 3–4 minutes until tender. Remove from the pan and keep warm. Add the remaining oil to the pan. Add the chicken livers and stir-fry for 3–4 minutes until tender but still soft. Stir in the remaining ingredients except the sesame seeds. Heat through. Divide the spinach mixture between four small warm bowls. Spoon the chicken livers on top and sprinkle with the sesame seeds before serving with prawn crackers.

Velvety Chicken Liver Pâté

SERVES 6

1 small onion, finely chopped
1 small garlic clove, crushed (optional)
200 g/7 oz chicken livers, trimmed and roughly chopped
30 ml/2 tbsp water
15 ml/1 tbsp brandy
2.5 ml/½ tsp dried mixed herbs
200 g/7 oz/scant 1 cup medium-fat soft cheese
Salt and freshly ground black pepper
Lemon wedges and parsley sprigs, to garnish
6 slices of toasted wholemeal bread, to serve

Put the onion and garlic in a saucepan with the chicken livers, water, brandy and herbs. Cook, stirring, for 5 minutes or until the chicken livers are just cooked and the onion is softened. Cool slightly, then purée in a blender or food processor. Add the cheese and run the machine again until well blended. Season with salt and pepper. Turn into a small container, cover and chill. When ready to serve, divide the pâté between six serving plates, garnish with lemon wedges and parsley sprigs and serve with triangles of hot toast.

Pâté Nests

SERVES 6

6 slices of white bread, crusts removed
Butter or margarine
175 g/6 oz smooth chicken liver pâté
30 ml/2 tbsp mayonnaise
2 hard-boiled (hard-cooked) eggs, finely chopped
10 cocktail gherkins (cornichons)
Freshly ground black pepper
6 small parsley sprigs

Spread the bread on both sides with butter or margarine. Press into the sections of a tartlet tin (pan). Bake in a preheated oven at 190°C/375°F/gas mark 5 for about 25 minutes until golden brown and crisp. Leave to cool. Mash together the pâté, mayonnaise and eggs. Chop 4 of the gherkins and add to the mixture. Season with pepper. Spoon into the cases. Make fans out of the remaining gherkins by making a series of cuts from the point not quite through the stalk end, then opening out gently to form a fan. Lay one on top of each nest and add a sprig of parsley to each. Serve within 1 hour.

Warm Chicken Livers with Blueberries

SERVES 4

450 g/1 lb chicken livers
25 g/1 oz/2 tbsp butter or margarine
Salt and freshly ground black pepper
175 g/6 oz blueberries
15 ml/1 tbsp port
175 g/6 oz mixed salad leaves
30 ml/2 tbsp raspberry vinegar
15 ml/1 tbsp olive oil
5 ml/1 tsp wholegrain mustard

Trim the chicken livers. Heat the butter or margarine in a non-stick frying pan (skillet). Add the chicken livers and a little seasoning and toss quickly for 4–5 minutes until just cooked but still soft. Remove from the pan and keep warm. Add the blueberries and port, cover and cook gently for 1 minute. Meanwhile, arrange the salad leaves on four serving plates. Whisk together the vinegar, oil and mustard, season with salt and pepper and spoon over the salad. Top with the chicken livers and spoon over the blueberries and their juices. Serve warm.

Grilled Aubergine Slices with Chicken Livers and Peanut Sauce

SERVES 6

1 large aubergine (eggplant), sliced
Sunflower oil
Salt and freshly ground black pepper
225 g/8 oz chicken livers, trimmed and cut into bite-sized pieces, if necessary
5 ml/1 tsp grated fresh root ginger
15 ml/1 tbsp medium-dry sherry
30 ml/2 tbsp snipped chives
Peanut Sauce (page 336)

Lay the aubergine slices on a piece of foil on the grill (broiler) rack. Brush with oil and sprinkle with salt and pepper. Grill (broil) until golden, then turn over the slices, brush with oil and season again and cook until golden and tender. Meanwhile, heat 15 ml/1 tbsp oil in a small saucepan. Add the chicken livers and ginger and season lightly. Toss over a moderate heat until the chicken livers are pink, just cooked but still soft. Stir in the sherry and half the chives. Arrange the aubergine slices and livers on warm serving plates, sprinkle with the remaining chives and serve with the warm Peanut Sauce.

Pâté and Horseradish Dip

SERVES 4

100 g/4 oz/½ cup medium-fat soft cheese
60 ml/4 tbsp single (light) cream
15 ml/1 tbsp creamed horseradish
100 g/4 oz smooth chicken liver pâté
Milk
Salt and freshly ground black pepper
3 stuffed olives, sliced, to garnish
Carrot, cucumber and red (bell) pepper sticks, to serve

Beat the cheese with the cream, horseradish and pâté until smooth. Thin with milk to a soft dropping consistency. Season to taste. Turn into four small bowls. Garnish with a few olive slices and serve with a pile of carrot, cucumber and red pepper sticks to dip in.

Chicken Liver and Mushroom Pâté with Celery

SERVES 4–6

25 g/1 oz/2 tbsp butter or margarine
1 small onion, chopped
200 g/7 oz chicken livers, trimmed and finely chopped
225 g/8 oz button mushrooms, chopped
15 ml/1 tbsp lemon juice
200 g/7 oz/scant 1 cup medium-fat soft cheese
30 ml/2 tbsp chopped parsley
Celery sticks, to serve

Melt the butter or margarine in a saucepan. Add the onion and fry (sauté) for 3 minutes until lightly golden. Add the chicken livers and mushrooms and cook, stirring, until no liquid remains. Purée in a blender or food processor. Leave to cool for 5 minutes, then beat in the lemon juice, cheese and parsley. Turn into small pots, cover and chill. To serve, place each pot of pâté on a small serving plate with plenty of celery sticks. To eat, either use as a dip or spread the pâté in the celery.

Sherried Pâté Pears

SERVES 4

100 g/4 oz smooth chicken liver pâté
15 ml/1 tbsp medium-dry sherry
4 eating (dessert) pears, peeled, halved and cored
Lettuce leaves
175 g/6 oz/¾ cup medium-fat soft cheese
45 ml/3 tbsp mayonnaise
15 ml/1 tbsp milk
Salt and white pepper
75 g/3 oz seedless black grapes, halved
75 g/3 oz seedless green grapes, halved
Hot wholemeal rolls, to serve

Mash the pâté with the sherry until smooth. Spoon into the cavities of the pears and place rounded-sides up on lettuce leaves on four plates. Beat the cheese with the mayonnaise and milk and season to taste. Spoon over the pears and garnish with the black and green grapes. Serve with hot wholemeal rolls.

TURKEY

Jalopeño Hoppin' John

SERVES 6

15 g/½ oz/1 tbsp butter or margarine
4 turkey rashers (slices), diced
1 onion, finely chopped
100 g/4 oz/½ cup long-grain rice
Boiling water
425 g/15 oz/1 large can of black-eyed peas, drained
Salt and freshly ground black pepper
1 jalopeño pepper, seeded and chopped
Corn chips
Orange and Mango Salsa (page 336), to serve

Melt the butter or margarine in a large frying pan (skillet). Add the meat and onion and fry (sauté) for 3–4 minutes. Add the rice and cook for 1 minute. Just cover with boiling water, bring to the boil, reduce the heat and simmer for 10–15 minutes until the rice is tender, topping up with boiling water if necessary. Stir in the peas, a good seasoning of salt and pepper and the jalopeño pepper. Toss gently. Spoon on to plates and serve with corn chips and the Orange and Mango Salsa.

Cypriot Stuffed Aubergine

SERVES 6

3 aubergines (eggplants)
40 g/1½ oz/3 tbsp long-grain rice
175 g/6 oz minced (ground) turkey
1 onion, finely chopped
1 garlic clove, crushed
30 ml/2 tbsp tomato purée (paste)
5 ml/1 tsp ground cinnamon
90 ml/6 tbsp water
2.5 ml/½ tsp dried oregano
Salt and freshly ground black pepper
40 g/1½ oz/⅓ cup Cheddar cheese, grated

Halve the aubergines lengthways. Boil in a large flameproof casserole (Dutch oven) in lightly salted water until just tender. Drain, rinse with cold water and drain again. Using a spoon, carefully scoop out the flesh, leaving a shell about 5 mm/¼ in thick. Chop the scooped-out flesh. Cook the rice in boiling salted water until tender. Drain. Dry-fry the turkey in a saucepan with the onion, stirring, for 3–4 minutes until all the grains of meat are separate and no longer pink and the onion is soft. Add the chopped aubergine, rice and all the remaining ingredients except the cheese, seasoning to taste with salt and pepper. Return the aubergine shells to the casserole dish in a single layer. Spoon the filling into the shells and sprinkle the cheese on top. Add enough boiling water to come half-way up the aubergine shells. Cover and simmer gently for 15 minutes. Transfer to warm plates and serve.

Turkey and Pink Grapefruit Pâté

SERVES 4–6

225 g/8 oz/2 cups cooked turkey
1 small onion
2 slices of white bread, cut into pieces
1 pink grapefruit
5 ml/1 tsp dried oregano
30 ml/2 tbsp chopped parsley
Salt and freshly ground black pepper
1 egg, beaten
Butter or margarine, for greasing
Parsley sprigs, to garnish
Toast triangles, to serve

Finely mince (grind) the turkey, onion and bread or process finely in a food processor. Thinly pare half the grapefruit rind and reserve. Finely grate the remainder and squeeze the juice. Mix the finely grated rind and the juice into the turkey mixture with the oregano, parsley and some salt and pepper. Mix in the egg to bind. Turn into a greased 450 g/1 lb loaf tin (pan). Bake in a preheated oven at 180°C/350°F/gas mark 4 for about 40 minutes or until firm to the touch and beginning to shrink from the sides of the tin. Leave to cool in the tin, then turn out and chill.

Cut the reserved grapefruit rind into thin strips and boil in water for 3 minutes. Drain, rinse with cold water and drain again. Slice the pâté and garnish with parsley sprigs and the shredded grapefruit rind and serve with toast triangles.

Quick Turkey and Liver Pâté

SERVES 4

100 g/4 oz continental liver sausage
1 small garlic clove, crushed
50 g/2 oz/¼ cup butter, softened
50 g/2 oz/¼ cup medium-fat soft cheese
15 ml/1 tbsp milk
5 ml/1 tsp lemon juice
100 g/4 oz/1 cup cooked turkey, finely chopped, all skin removed
Salt and freshly ground black pepper
A pinch of grated nutmeg
A sprig of parsley, to garnish
Hot toast, to serve

Mash the liver sausage with the garlic, butter, cheese, milk and lemon juice. Stir in the turkey. Season with salt and pepper and the nutmeg. Pack into a small pot, garnish with a sprig of parsley and serve with hot toast.

Turkey and Spring Onion Wontons with Chilli Dipping Sauce

SERVES 4

Prepare as for Chicken and Prawn Wontons (page 21), but substitute finely chopped turkey for the chicken and 2 finely chopped spring onions (scallions) for the prawns. Omit the garlic. Serve with Chinese Chilli Dipping Sauce (page 337) instead of Sweet and Sour Sauce.

Egg and Turkey Rashers in Green Sauce

SERVES 4

450 g/1 lb frozen peas
5 ml/1 tsp dried mint
25 g/1 oz/2 tbsp butter or margarine
30 ml/2 tbsp double (heavy) cream
Salt and freshly ground black pepper
4 eggs
4 turkey rashers (slices)
Chopped parsley, to garnish
Crusty bread, to serve

Boil the peas with the mint for 5 minutes. Drain. Purée in a blender or food processor with the butter or margarine, cream and some salt and pepper. Meanwhile, boil the eggs in water for 4 minutes. Drain, rinse with cold water and drain again. Carefully remove the shells and place in four ramekins (custard cups). Grill (broil) the turkey rashers and cut into small pieces. Scatter over the eggs. Spoon over the sauce and place under a hot grill (broiler) until glazed on top. Sprinkle with chopped parsley and serve with crusty bread.

Smoked Turkey and Cheese Balls

SERVES 6–8

225 g/8 oz/1 cup medium-fat soft cheese
50 g/2 oz/¼ cup butter or margarine, softened
225 g/8 oz smoked turkey, finely chopped
75 g/3 oz/¾ cup smoked Bavarian cheese, grated
30 ml/2 tbsp chopped parsley
Tomato and cucumber slices, to garnish
Oatcakes, to serve

Beat together the soft cheese and butter or margarine until smooth. Beat in the turkey, smoked cheese and parsley. Roll into small balls and chill for 1 hour. Arrange on serving plates, garnish with tomato and cucumber spices and serve with oatcakes.

Turkey, Prawn and Cucumber Boats

SERVES 6

Prepare as for Stuffed Cucumber Boats (page 27), but substitute turkey for the chicken and 50 g/2 oz chopped, cooked peeled prawns (shrimp) for the mushrooms. Add a dash of lemon juice to the mixture and garnish with a few whole peeled prawns.

Devilled Turkey-stuffed Eggs

SERVES 6

6 hard-boiled (hard-cooked) eggs
100 g/4 oz/½ cup medium-fat soft cheese
5 ml/1 tsp anchovy essence (extract)
100 g/4 oz/1 cup cooked turkey, finely chopped, all skin removed
15 ml/1 tbsp snipped chives
2.5 ml/½ tsp chilli powder
Milk
Salt and freshly ground black pepper
Lettuce leaves
45 ml/3 tbsp Worcestershire sauce
45 ml/3 tbsp tomato ketchup (catsup)
15 ml/1 tbsp lemon juice
30 ml/2 tbsp chilli relish
5 ml/1 tsp made English mustard
A few drops of Tabasco sauce

Shell the eggs, halve lengthways and scoop the yolks out into a bowl. Mash with a fork. Work in the cheese, anchovy essence, turkey, chives and chilli powder. Moisten with a little milk and season with salt and pepper. Pile this mixture back in the egg whites and arrange on small plates on a bed of lettuce. Mix together the remaining ingredients and spoon a little over each egg. Serve cold.

Hot Leerdammer and Turkey Bites

MAKES 20

5 slices of white bread, crusts removed
50 g/2 oz/¼ cup butter or margarine
30 ml/2 tbsp sunflower oil
100 g/4 oz/1 cup cooked turkey, finely chopped, all skin removed
15 ml/1 tbsp sweet pickle
15 ml/1 tbsp mayonnaise
5 slices of Leerdammer cheese
50 g/2 oz/1 small can of anchovies, drained and halved widthways

Cut the bread into quarters and fry (sauté) in the butter or margarine and oil until golden on both sides. Drain on kitchen paper (paper towels). Mix the turkey with the pickle and mayonnaise. Put the bread squares on the grill (broiler) rack and pile the turkey mixture on top. Cut the cheese slices into quarters and put one on top of each. If you do not have 20 halved anchovy fillets, cut some in halves lengthways. Roll up and place one roll on top of each cheese square. Cook under a moderate grill (broiler) until the cheese has melted and the bites are piping hot. Serve hot.

Savoury Jellied Egg Ramekins

SERVES 4

300 ml/½ pt/1¼ cups chicken stock
10 ml/2 tsp powdered gelatine
15 ml/1 tbsp medium-dry sherry
4 eggs
4 turkey rashers (slices)
Chopped parsley, to garnish
Crusty bread, to serve

Put 30 ml/2 tbsp of the stock in a small bowl. Sprinkle the gelatine over and leave to soften for 5 minutes. Place the bowl in a pan of hot water or heat in the microwave briefly to dissolve completely. Stir well. Stir in the remaining stock and the sherry and leave until cold and on the point of setting. Meanwhile, put the eggs in a saucepan of cold water. Bring to the boil, cover and cook for 4 minutes. Drain immediately and cover with cold water. When cold, peel off the shells and place an egg in each of four ramekins (custard cups). Meanwhile, grill (broil) the turkey rashers. When well cooked, cut into small pieces and scatter over the eggs. Spoon the stock over the eggs and chill until set. Sprinkle with chopped parsley and serve with crusty bread.

Mushroom, Sausage and Egg Cups

SERVES 4

225 g/8 oz turkey sausages, cut into small pieces
100 g/4 oz button mushrooms, sliced
1 garlic clove, crushed
150 ml/¼ pt/⅔ cup chicken stock
4 eggs
15 ml/1 tbsp chopped parsley
Freshly ground black pepper
20 ml/4 tsp double (heavy) cream
Parsley sprigs, to garnish
Crusty bread, to serve

Dry-fry the sausages in a non-stick frying pan (skillet), stirring, for about 4 minutes until lightly golden all over. Add the mushrooms, garlic and stock. Bring to the boil, cover with a lid or foil and simmer for 10 minutes. Spoon the mixture into four ramekins (custard cups). Break an egg into each and sprinkle with the parsley and some pepper. Pour 5 ml/1 tsp cream over each. Bake in a preheated oven at 180°C/350°F/gas mark 4 for 10 minutes or until the eggs are just set. Cook a little longer if you like your eggs well done. Add a sprig of parsley to each and serve hot with crusty bread.

Polish Stuffed Cabbage Leaves

SERVE 4 OR 8

8 large green cabbage leaves
8 rindless streaky bacon rashers (slices), chopped
1 onion, chopped
15 ml/1 tbsp sunflower oil
175 g/6 oz minced (ground) turkey
50 g/2 oz/¼ cup long-grain rice
15 ml/1 tbsp chopped parsley
30 ml/2 tbsp tomato ketchup (catsup)
Salt and freshly ground black pepper
Chicken stock
45 ml/3 tbsp tomato purée (paste)
A pinch of caster (superfine) sugar

Cut out the thick part of the central cabbage leaf stalk. Blanch the leaves in boiling water for 3 minutes. Drain, rinse with cold water, drain again and dry on kitchen paper (paper towels). Cook the bacon and onion in the oil for 2 minutes. Mix with the turkey, rice, parsley, ketchup and some salt and pepper. Divide this between the cabbage leaves. Fold in the sides, then roll up. Pack in a single layer in a flameproof casserole (Dutch oven). Pour just enough stock over to cover. Bring to the boil, reduce the heat, cover and simmer gently for 1½ hours. Lift out the rolls and keep warm. Stir the tomato purée and sugar into the stock. Bring to the boil and boil rapidly until reduced to about 450 ml/¾ pt/2 cups and the sauce has thickened slightly. Taste and re-season, if necessary. Transfer the cabbage rolls to warm serving plates. Spoon a little sauce over each and serve.

Potted Turkey Livers

SERVES 6

225 g/8 oz turkey livers, trimmed and cut into small pieces
50 g/2 oz rindless streaky bacon rashers (slices), diced
1 garlic clove, crushed
1.5 ml/¼ tsp dried thyme
75 g/3 oz/⅓ cup butter
Salt and freshly ground black pepper
15 ml/1 tbsp brandy
Lemon wedges and toast, to serve

Fry (sauté) the livers, bacon, garlic and thyme in 50 g/2 oz/¼ cup of the butter for about 6 minutes or until the livers are tender and cooked but not hardening. Transfer to a blender or food processor and add a little salt and pepper and the brandy. Blend until smooth. Turn into a small pot and leave to cool. Melt the remaining butter and pour over. Chill. Serve with lemon wedges and toast.

Velvety Turkey Liver Pâté with Port

SERVES 6

Prepare as for Velvety Chicken Liver Pâté (page 31) but substitute turkey livers for the chicken livers and port for the brandy. If available, garnish the pâté with small sprigs of redcurrants on the side.

Brandied Turkey Liver and Walnut Pâté

SERVES 4

275 g/10 oz/1¼ cups unsalted (sweet) butter
550 g/1¼ lb turkey livers, trimmed
1 bunch of spring onions (scallions), roughly chopped
5 ml/1 tsp dried oregano
1 large garlic clove, crushed
30 ml/2 tbsp brandy
30 ml/2 tbsp double (heavy) cream
Salt and freshly ground black pepper
100 g/4 oz/1 cup walnut halves
Lemon wedges and parsley sprigs, to garnish
Rye bread, to serve

Melt 100 g/4 oz/½ cup of the butter in a saucepan. Add the turkey livers and spring onions and cook, stirring, for 3–4 minutes until the livers are pink and cooked but still soft. Stir in a further 100 g/4 oz/½ cup of the butter, the oregano, garlic, brandy and cream and season to taste. Purée in a blender or food processor until smooth. Reserve two or three walnut halves for garnish, roughly chop the remainder and stir into the pâté. Taste and re-season if necessary. Turn into an attractive serving dish and leave until cold. Melt the remaining butter and pour over. Arrange the remaining walnut halves on top to garnish, then chill until set. Garnish with lemon wedges and parsley sprigs and serve with rye bread.

Highland Pâté

SERVES 6

75 g/3 oz/⅓ cup butter
225 g/8 oz turkey livers, trimmed and chopped
50 g/2 oz raw smoked ham, diced
1 garlic clove, crushed
2.5 ml/½ tsp dried thyme
Salt and freshly ground black pepper
20 ml/4 tsp Scotch whisky
A sprig of parsley and lemon slices, to garnish
Oatcakes, to serve

Melt 50 g/2 oz/¼ cup of the butter in a saucepan. Add the turkey livers, ham, garlic and thyme. Stir well, cover and cook gently, stirring occasionally, for 6 minutes until the livers are cooked but not hardening. Season to taste and stir in the whisky. Purée in a blender or food processor and turn into a small pot. Leave until cold. Melt the remaining butter and pour over. Chill until firm. Garnish with a sprig of parsley and lemon slices and serve with oatcakes.

Highland Pâté with Pickled Walnuts

SERVES 6

Prepare as for Highland Pâté but add 2 chopped pickled walnuts after the mixture is puréed before turning into the pot. Garnish the top with a sliver of pickled walnut and a sprig of parsley and omit the lemon.

DUCK

Duck with Orange Terrine

SERVES 10

1.75 kg/4 lb oven-ready duck
350 g/12 oz diced stewing pork
100 g/4 oz chicken livers, trimmed
1 small leek, roughly chopped
2 oranges
1 garlic clove, crushed
5 ml/1 tsp salt
Freshly ground black pepper
2.5 ml/½ tsp dried sage
15 ml/1 tbsp chopped parsley
25 g/1 oz/½ cup fresh breadcrumbs
45 ml/3 tbsp brandy
Oil, for greasing
1 chicken stock cube
15 ml/1 tbsp powdered gelatine
300 ml/½ pt/1¼ cups boiling water
Parsley sprigs, to garnish
Hot French bread, to serve

Remove all the skin and fat from the duck. Cut off the breast fillets and reserve. Remove all the remaining meat from the bones, scraping it away with a knife where necessary. Place the duck flesh (not the fillets) in a food processor. Run the machine and drop in the pork, chicken livers and leek until finely chopped. Alternatively, pass through a fine mincer (grinder). Finely grate the rind from one of the oranges. Remove all the pith, then cut the flesh into segments. Finely chop. Add the rind and chopped fruit to the meat with the garlic, salt and lots of pepper, the sage, parsley, breadcrumbs and 30 ml/2 tbsp of the brandy. Mix well. Spoon half the meat mixture into a lightly oiled 1.2 litre/2 pt/5 cup terrine or other attractive ovenproof serving dish.

Place the duck breasts in a plastic bag and beat lightly with a rolling pin to flatten slightly. Lay over the meat mixture, then top with the remaining meat mixture. Cover with foil and place in a roasting tin (pan) containing 2.5 cm/1 in boiling water. Bake in a preheated oven at 160°C/325°F/gas mark 3 for 2½–3 hours or until cooked through and firm to the touch. Remove from the baking tin, weigh down with heavy weights or cans of food and leave until cold, then chill overnight.

Next day, dissolve the stock cube and gelatine in the boiling water. Stir in the remaining brandy. Leave until cold and the consistency of egg white. Remove the weights and foil from the terrine and discard any fat. Slice the remaining orange and arrange over the top of the terrine. Spoon the jellied stock over and chill again until firmly set. Garnish with parsley sprigs and serve sliced with hot French bread.

Potted Duck with Port and Sage

SERVES 8–10

Prepare as for Potted Chicken with Sherry and Herbs (page 25) but substitute a 1.75 kg/4 lb oven-ready duck for the chicken, port for the sherry and sage for the tarragon. Cook for 2 hours, instead of 1½ hours and omit the mace.

Potted Duck with Stilton and Redcurrants

SERVES 4

1 duck portion
50 g/2 oz/½ cup white Stilton, crumbled
50 g/2 oz/¼ cup unsalted (sweet) butter
15 ml/1 tbsp creamed horseradish
Salt and freshly ground black pepper
4 small redcurrant sprigs
Oatcakes, to serve

Place the duck portion under the grill (broiler) and grill (broil) for about 25 minutes, until cooked through and the skin is well browned and crisp. Remove the skin, shred and reserve. Cut all the meat off the bones and place in a food processor with the cheese, butter and horseradish. Run the machine until the mixture forms a paste, stopping the machine and scraping down the sides if necessary. Season to taste, spoon into a small dish and chill. To serve, spoon on to four small plates. Top with the skin. Lay a sprig of redcurrants to the side of each and serve with oatcakes.

Oriental Sesame Bites

SERVES 4–6

225 g/8 oz duck meat, minced (ground)
Soy sauce
Salt and freshly ground black pepper
1 spring onion (scallion), finely chopped
1 garlic clove, crushed
30 ml/2 tbsp sunflower oil, plus extra for shallow-frying
45 ml/3 tbsp plain (all-purpose) flour
2 eggs, beaten
90 ml/6 tbsp sesame seeds
Chilli sauce, to serve

Mix the duck with 45 ml/3 tbsp soy sauce, a good pinch of salt and lots of black pepper. Stir in the onion, garlic and oil. Shape the mixture into small, flat cakes about 2.5 cm/1 in diameter. Dip in the flour, then the egg, then the sesame seeds to coat completely. Chill for 30 minutes. Shallow-fry in hot oil for about 4 minutes or until golden brown on both sides and cooked through. Drain on kitchen paper (paper towels). Serve with bowls of soy sauce and chilli sauce for dipping.

GAME

Quails' Egg Tartlets

SERVES 6

150 ml/¼ pt/⅔ cup boiling water
1 chicken stock cube
10 ml/2 tsp powdered gelatine
150 g/5 oz/1¼ cups plain (all-purpose) wholemeal flour
A pinch of salt
65 g/2½ oz/⅓ cup butter, cut into pieces
Cold water to mix
For the filling:
6 quails' eggs
75 g/3 oz smooth chicken liver pâté
75 g/3 oz/⅓ cup medium-fat soft cheese
15 ml/1 tbsp brandy
1 egg white
Salt and freshly ground black pepper
12 stoned (pitted) black olives
12 stoned green olives
6 small parsley sprigs

Pour the boiling water on to the stock cube in a measuring jug. Stir until dissolved. Sprinkle on the gelatine and stir until completely dissolved. Leave to cool until the consistency of egg white. Meanwhile, mix the flour and salt in a bowl. Add the butter and rub in with the fingertips. Mix with enough cold water to form a firm dough. Knead gently on a lightly floured surface. Use to line six individual flan rings set on a baking (cookie) sheet. Prick the bases with a fork and line with crumpled foil. Bake in a preheated oven at 200 °C/400 °F/gas mark 6 for 10 minutes, then remove the foil and return to the oven for 5 minutes to dry out. Remove from the oven and leave to cool.

To make the filling, place the quails' eggs in a pan and cover with cold water. Bring to the boil, cook for 3 minutes, then drain and cover with cold water. When cold, carefully remove the shells. Beat the pâté with the cheese and brandy until smooth. Whisk the egg white until stiff and fold into the mixture with a metal spoon. Season to taste. Spoon the pâté mousse into the pastry cases (pie shells). Place a quail's egg gently on top in the centre of each. Arrange the olives attractively around. Spoon the almost-jellied stock over, garnish each with a tiny sprig of parsley and chill until set.

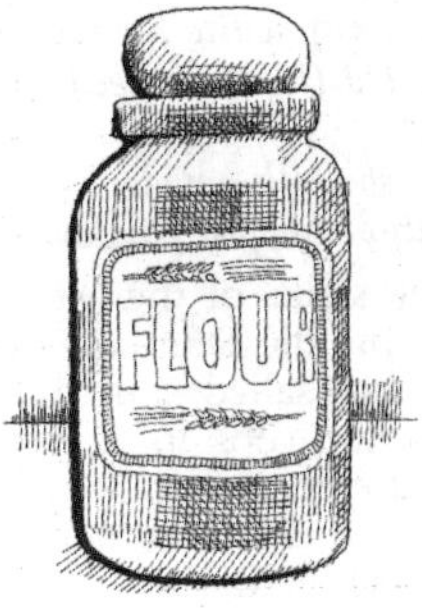

Asparagus, Strawberry and Quails' Egg Salad

SERVES 6

12 quails' eggs
350 g/12 oz/1 medium can of asparagus spears, drained
225 g/8 oz strawberries, sliced
50 g/2 oz/½ cup pecan halves
½ cucumber, sliced
75 ml/5 tbsp fromage frais
75 ml/5 tbsp mayonnaise
10 ml/2 tsp creamed horseradish
Salt and freshly ground black pepper
Paprika, for dusting

Place the quails' eggs in cold water, bring to the boil and cook for 3 minutes. Drain, rinse with cold water and drain again. Shell and halve. Arrange the asparagus, strawberries, pecans and cucumber slices attractively on small plates with the halved quails' eggs. Mix together the fromage frais, mayonnaise and horseradish with a little salt and pepper and spoon to one side. Dust with paprika and chill before serving.

Gamekeeper's Asparagus

SERVES 4

450 g/1 lb baby asparagus spears
75 g/3 oz/⅓ cup unsalted (sweet) butter
100 g/4 oz/1 cup cooked pheasant meat, finely chopped
50 g/2 oz/1 cup white breadcrumbs
2 hard-boiled (hard-cooked) eggs, chopped
2.5 ml/½ tsp chilli powder
15 ml/1 tbsp chopped parsley

Trim the stalks of the asparagus and tie in a bundle. Stand the bundle in a pan of boiling salted water. Cover with a lid or foil and cook for 8 minutes. Lift out of the pan, drain and untie. Meanwhile, melt the butter in a frying pan (skillet). Add the pheasant meat and breadcrumbs and toss until the bread is golden. Stir in the eggs, chilli and parsley. Lay the asparagus spears on warm plates, scatter the pheasant mixture over and serve hot.

Potted Game

SERVES 4

350 g/12 oz/3 cups cooked game bird meat, such as pheasant or grouse
100 g/4 oz/1 cup cooked ham
1.5 ml/¼ tsp ground mace
1.5 ml/¼ tsp dried oregano
15 ml/1 tbsp medium-dry sherry
Salt and freshly ground black pepper
75 g/3 oz/⅓ cup unsalted (sweet) butter
A small bay leaf, to garnish
Hot toast, to serve

Mince (grind) the game and ham finely. Place in a saucepan with the mace, oregano, sherry, a little salt and pepper and 50 g/2 oz/¼ cup of the butter. Cook gently, stirring, for 5 minutes. Turn into a small pot and press down well. Leave until cold. Melt the remaining butter and pour over. Garnish with a small bay leaf and chill until ready to serve with hot toast.

Fresh Potted Pheasant

SERVES 6

1 large oven-ready pheasant
Salt and freshly ground black pepper
350 g/12 oz/1½ cups unsalted (sweet) butter
30 ml/2 tbsp medium-dry sherry
1.5 ml/¼ tsp ground cumin
Hot crusty bread, to serve

Wipe the pheasant inside and out and season inside and out. Melt 50 g/2 oz/¼ cup of the butter in a flameproof casserole (Dutch oven). Place the pheasant in the casserole. Pour over the sherry and sprinkle with the cumin. Cover with the lid and cook gently for 1½ hours, turning occasionally until the bird is really tender. Remove from the oven. When cool enough to handle, remove all the meat, discarding the skin and bones. Mince (grind) finely or process in a food processor. Add 100 g/4 oz/½ cup of the remaining butter and the cooking juices and beat in thoroughly. Taste and re-season, if necessary. Pack into small pots. Melt the remaining butter and pour over to seal completely. Leave until completely cold, then chill. Store for up to one month in the fridge. Once the butter seal is broken (i.e. if you eat half a pot) use the remainder within two days.

Sweet and Sour Pheasant with Beans

SERVES 6

750 g/1¾ lb runner beans, diagonally sliced
1 orange
30 ml/2 tbsp olive oil
1 small onion, finely chopped
100 g/4 oz button mushrooms, sliced
100 g/4 oz/1 cup cooked pheasant, cut into small pieces, all skin removed
30 ml/2 tbsp Worcestershire sauce
15 ml/1 tbsp soy sauce
30 ml/2 tbsp light brown sugar
30 ml/2 tbsp white wine vinegar

Cook the beans in lightly salted boiling water for 5 minutes or until just tender. Drain and return to the pan. Meanwhile, thinly pare the rind from the orange, place in a colander or steamer over the pan of beans and cook for 3 minutes. Remove from the pan. Squeeze the juice from the orange. Heat the oil in a frying pan (skillet), add the onion and mushrooms and fry (sauté) for 2 minutes, stirring. Stir in the pheasant and toss for 2 minutes. Add the orange juice, Worcestershire sauce, soy sauce, sugar and vinegar. Cook, stirring, for 1 minute. Tip into the beans and toss over a gentle heat for 2 minutes. Pile on to warm plates, scatter the orange rind over and serve straight away.

Potted Pheasant with Two Cheeses

This is also good served with water biscuits (crackers) instead of a cheese course.

SERVES 4–6

100 g/4 oz/1 cup Cheddar cheese, finely grated
100 g/4 oz/1 cup Stilton cheese, crumbled
100 g/4 oz/½ cup unsalted (sweet) butter, softened
100 g/4 oz/1 cup cooked pheasant, finely chopped
60 ml/4 tbsp port
A good pinch of ground mace
Hot French bread, to serve

Mash the cheeses with the butter until fairly smooth. Work in the pheasant and port. Season with the mace. Pack into a small pot. Cover with clingfilm (plastic wrap) and chill, preferably overnight. Serve with hot French bread.

Soups

Soups make wonderful lunches or suppers, when served with crusty bread. They are also perfect as a starter before a fairly light main course at a special meal. All the birds are so versatile that you can make soup out of every bit of them – even the giblets!

CHICKEN

White Chicken Stock

If you can't get a boiling fowl use the cheapest small chicken you can find and thaw it well, if frozen, before cooking. After boiling, pick off all the meat and use it for any recipe calling for cooked chicken.

MAKES 1 LITRE/1¾ PTS/4¼ CUPS

1 boiling fowl
2 litres/3½ pts/8½ cups water
1 celery stick, chopped
1 onion, quartered
1 leek, white part only, chopped
1 bouquet garni sachet
Salt and freshly ground black pepper

Put the boiling fowl in a saucepan and cover with the water. Add the remaining ingredients. Bring to the boil, skim the surface, reduce the heat and simmer gently for 2–2½ hours. Remove the scum from the surface several times during cooking. Strain the stock through a sieve (strainer) into a bowl and leave until no more dripping occurs. Taste the stock and re-season if necessary. Leave until cold, then chill. Skim off any fat and use the stock as required.

Chicken Carcass Stock

MAKES 900 ML/1½ PTS/3¾ CUPS

1 chicken carcass
1 onion
1 bay leaf
1 carrot, cut into chunks
Salt and freshly ground black pepper

Break up the carcass and put in a saucepan with the onion, bay leaf and carrot. Add a little salt and pepper. Cover with water. Bring to the boil, cover, reduce the heat and simmer very gently for 2 hours. Strain the stock. Leave until cold, then chill or freeze in two or three portions for use as required.

Chinese Chicken Stock

MAKES 1.5 LITRES/2½ PTS/6 CUPS

1 chicken carcass
1.75 litres/3 pts/7½ cups water
2.5 cm/1 in piece of fresh root ginger, chopped
1 leek, chopped
3 garlic cloves, halved
Salt and freshly ground black pepper

Break up the carcass and place in a saucepan with the remaining ingredients. Bring to the boil. Skim the surface, cover, reduce the heat and simmer gently for 1½ hours. Strain and leave to cool. Skim off any fat and use the stock as required.

Oriental Chicken, Spinach and Egg Noodle Soup

SERVES 6

1.5 litres/2½ pts/6 cups chicken stock
225 g/8 oz Chinese egg noodles
225 g/8 oz/2 cups cooked chicken, diced
Soy sauce
Freshly ground black pepper
30 ml/2 tbsp sunflower oil
225 g/8 oz frozen leaf spinach, thawed
50 g/2 oz button mushrooms, sliced

Heat the stock in a large saucepan. Add the noodles and simmer gently for 4–10 minutes, depending on the make, until cooked. Add the chicken and soy sauce and pepper to taste. Heat the oil in a frying pan (skillet). Add the spinach and toss over a high heat for 2 minutes. Stir into the soup, add the mushrooms and simmer for 5 minutes. Serve hot.

Chilli Winter Warmer

SERVES 4

100 g/4 oz minced (ground) chicken
2 onions, finely chopped
2 carrots, finely chopped
2.5 ml/½ tsp chilli powder
15 ml/1 tbsp tomato purée (paste)
900 ml/1½ pts/3¾ cups chicken stock
5 ml/1 tsp yeast extract
100 g/4 oz/1 cup soup pasta shapes
15 ml/1 tbsp cornflour (cornstarch)
30 ml/2 tbsp water
Chopped parsley

Put the chicken, onions and carrots in a large saucepan and cook, stirring, until the grains of meat are brown and separate. Stir in the chilli powder, tomato purée, stock and yeast extract. Bring to the boil, reduce the heat and simmer for 20 minutes, stirring occasionally. Add the pasta and cook for a further 10 minutes. Blend the cornflour with the water. Stir into the soup and cook, stirring, for 1 minute. Serve hot garnished with chopped parsley.

Wontons in Garlic Soup

SERVES 6

50 g/2 oz peeled prawns (shrimp), chopped
50 g/2 oz minced (ground) pork
50 g/2 oz/½ cup cooked chicken, chopped
5 ml/1 tsp soy sauce
1 bunch of spring onions (scallions), chopped
½ garlic bulb, separated into cloves and crushed
Salt
100 g/4 oz/1 cup plain (all-purpose) flour, sifted
2 eggs, beaten
15 ml/1 tbsp sunflower oil
1 onion, finely chopped
1.75 litres/3 pts/7½ cups chicken stock

Mix the prawns with the pork, chicken, soy sauce, half the spring onions, 1 of the garlic cloves and a pinch of salt. Put the flour in a separate bowl. Add the eggs and work into a dough with the fingers. Add a little water, if necessary, to form a soft but not sticky dough. Knead gently on a lightly floured surface and roll out thinly. Cut into 7.5 cm/3 in triangles. Divide half the prawn and meat mixture between the triangles. Dampen the edges. Fold in the two side points and roll up. Heat the oil in a large saucepan or wok. Fry (sauté) the remaining garlic and the chopped onion until lightly golden. Add the remaining filling and fry, stirring, for 3 minutes. Add the chicken stock and season to taste with salt. Bring to the boil, drop in the dumplings, cover and simmer for about 15 minutes. Sprinkle the remaining spring onions into the pot just before serving ladled into warm soup bowls.

Caribbean Chicken with Coconut Soup

SERVES 4

4 spring onions (scallions), chopped
1 garlic clove, crushed
30 ml/2 tbsp sunflower oil
5 ml/1 tsp turmeric
300 ml/½ pt/1¼ cups canned coconut milk
900 ml/1½ pts/3¾ cups chicken stock
50 g/2 oz spaghetti, broken into small pieces
1 lemon slice
100 g/4 oz/1 cup cooked chicken, diced
Salt and freshly ground black pepper
4 coriander (cilantro) leaves

Fry (sauté) the spring onions and garlic in the oil for 2 minutes, stirring, until softened but not browned. Add the turmeric, coconut milk, stock, spaghetti and lemon slice. Bring to the boil, reduce the heat, cover and simmer gently for 10 minutes. Discard the lemon, stir in the chicken and season with salt and pepper. Heat through for 2 minutes. Ladle into warm bowls and garnish each with a coriander leaf.

Eastern Saffron Soup

SERVES 6

2 onions, thinly sliced
15 g/½ oz/1 tbsp butter or margarine
2 potatoes, thinly sliced
600 ml/1 pt/2½ cups chicken stock
45 ml/3 tbsp dried milk powder (non-fat dry milk)
Salt and freshly ground white pepper
2.5 ml/½ tsp powdered saffron
A pinch of turmeric
225 g/8 oz/2 cups cooked chicken, cut into small strips
50 g/2 oz/½ cup cooked basmati or fragrant Thai rice
300 ml/½ pt/1¼ cups crème fraîche
6 thin lemon slices
Chopped parsley

Fry (sauté) the onions in the butter or margarine gently for 2 minutes, stirring, until softened but not browned. Add the potatoes and stock. Bring to the boil, cover and simmer for about 5 minutes until tender. Purée in a blender or food processor, then return to the rinsed-out pan. Stir in the milk powder and season with salt, pepper, the saffron and turmeric. Stir well. Add the chicken and rice and heat through for 2–3 minutes. Stir in the crème fraîche and heat through again. Taste and re-season if necessary. Ladle into warm bowls and garnish each with a slice of lemon and a little chopped parsley.

Almond Cream of Chicken Soup

SERVES 6

100 g/4 oz/1 cup ground almonds
1.2 litres/2 pts/5 cups hot chicken stock
Salt and freshly ground white pepper
100 g/4 oz/1 cup cooked chicken, finely chopped
50 g/2 oz/¼ cup long-grain rice
150 ml/¼ pt/⅔ cup double (heavy) cream
2 egg yolks

Put the almonds in a saucepan. Add about 300 ml/½ pt/1¼ cups of the hot stock, whisking all the time until the mixture is smooth. Blend in the remaining stock and a little salt and pepper. Bring to the boil, reduce the heat and simmer for 20 minutes. Add the chicken and rice and continue cooking for 10 minutes. Whisk the cream and egg yolks together. Whisk in a ladleful of the hot soup. Return this mixture to the saucepan and heat through, stirring, but do not allow to boil. Serve straight away, ungarnished.

Meatballs in Greek Broth

SERVES 4

175 g/6 oz minced (ground) chicken
100 g/4 oz/½ cup long-grain rice
1 small egg, beaten
10 ml/2 tsp chopped mint
Salt and freshly ground black pepper
A little plain (all-purpose) flour
1.2 litres/2 pts/5 cups chicken stock
2 eggs
Juice of 1 large lemon

Mix the chicken with the rice, egg, mint and a little salt and pepper. Shape into small balls and roll in flour. Bring the stock to the boil, drop in the meatballs and simmer gently for 15 minutes. Beat together the eggs and lemon in a large soup tureen. Gradually strain the chicken stock into the egg, whisking all the time. Add the meatballs and serve straight away.

White Chicken Soup

SERVES 6

Prepare the White Chicken Stock (page 43). When the stock has finished dripping, remove all the meat from the carcass and chop. Return to the stock, then season and heat through. Sprinkle with chopped parsley before serving.

Chicken, Mushroom and Noodle Soup

SERVES 6

900 ml/1½ pts/3¾ cups chicken stock
1 bay leaf
1 leek, thinly sliced
1 small skinless chicken breast
100 g/4 oz button mushrooms, sliced
50 g/2 oz vermicelli, broken into small pieces
150 ml/¼ pt/⅔ cup dry white wine
Salt and freshly ground black pepper
15 ml/1 tbsp chopped parsley

Place the stock in a saucepan with the bay leaf, leek and chicken breast. Bring to the boil, reduce the heat, part-cover and simmer gently for 10 minutes until the chicken is really tender. Lift out of the pan with a draining spoon and cut into small pieces. Add the mushrooms and pasta to the pan with the wine. Bring to the boil and simmer for 6 minutes until the pasta is tender. Return the chicken to the pan. Discard the bay leaf and season to taste with salt and pepper. Ladle into warm soup bowls and sprinkle with the parsley before serving.

Japanese Chicken and Shiitake Mushroom Clear Soup

SERVES 6

15 ml/1 tbsp soya or sunflower oil
1 small onion, chopped
250 g/9 oz minced (ground) chicken
4 spring onions (scallions), finely chopped
1 carrot, finely chopped
1 garlic clove, crushed
1 star anise or 1 clove
1 bouquet garni sachet
25 g/1 oz dried shiitake mushrooms
1 stalk of lemon grass, lightly crushed
6 black peppercorns
1 egg white
1.5 litres/2½ pts/6 cups chicken stock, cooled
Salt
Snipped chives, to garnish

Heat the oil in a large saucepan. Add the chopped onion and fry (sauté) for 4–5 minutes until golden brown. Leave to cool. Add the chicken, spring onions, carrot, garlic, star anise or clove, bouquet garni, mushrooms, lemon grass and peppercorns. Whisk the egg white until stiff and stir into the mixture. Stir in the cold stock. Bring just to the boil, stirring frequently, until the egg white sets. Reduce the heat immediately, then simmer gently for 45 minutes. Do not let the mixture boil again.

Lay a piece of muslin (cheesecloth) or a new disposable kitchen cloth in a sieve (strainer) and pour the soup through this into a clean pan. Add salt to taste. Reheat and skim the surface again, if necessary. Pour into warm soup bowls and sprinkle with snipped chives before serving.

Chinese Hot and Sour Soup

SERVES 4

30 ml/2 tbsp sunflower oil
8 dried shiitake mushrooms, soaked and sliced
30 ml/2 tbsp pure orange juice
30 ml/2 tbsp soy sauce
15 ml/1 tbsp clear honey
30 ml/2 tbsp red wine vinegar
100 g/4 oz/1 cup cooked chicken, chopped
1.2 litres/2 pts/5 cups chicken stock
2 spring onions (scallions), finely chopped

Heat the oil in a saucepan. Add the mushrooms and stir-fry for 1 minute. Add the remaining ingredients except the spring onions. Bring to the boil and simmer for 3 minutes. Add the spring onions, cook for a further minute and serve.

Chinese Chicken and Spring Onion Soup

SERVES 4

15 ml/1 tbsp sunflower oil
1 garlic clove, crushed
5 cm/2 in piece of fresh root ginger, grated
2 chicken leg portions, skinned and cut into two pieces
15 ml/1 tbsp oyster sauce
1.5 litres/2½ pts/6 cups water
Salt and freshly ground black pepper
50 g/2 oz button mushrooms, sliced
1 bunch of spring onions (scallions), cut into long, thin shreds
1 green (bell) pepper, thinly sliced
60 ml/4 tbsp dry sherry

Heat the oil in a saucepan and stir-fry the garlic and ginger for 30 seconds. Add the chicken, oyster sauce and water. Add a little salt and pepper and bring to the boil. Reduce the heat, part-cover and simmer for 30 minutes or until the chicken is tender. Lift the chicken out of the pan with a draining spoon. Cut all the meat off the bones, cut into neat pieces and return to the pan. Add the mushrooms, spring onions, green pepper and sherry. Simmer for about 6 minutes until tender. Taste and re-season if necessary. Ladle into warm bowls and serve piping hot.

Chicken and Saffron Soup

SERVES 6

1 skinless chicken breast, cut into very thin strips
1 large onion, sliced
1 large potato, sliced
600 ml/1 pt/2½ cups milk
1 chicken stock cube
Salt and white pepper
5 ml/1 tsp powdered saffron
450 ml/¾ pt/2 cups crème fraîche
Chopped parsley and croûtons, to garnish

Poach the chicken in just enough lightly salted water to cover for a few minutes until tender. Drain and reserve. Put the onion, potato and milk in a saucepan with the stock cube. Bring to the boil, reduce the heat and simmer gently until tender. Tip into a blender or food processor and run the machine until smooth. Return to the saucepan. Add some salt and pepper, the saffron and 300 ml/½ pt/1¼ cups of the crème fraîche. Heat gently, stirring, until the mixture boils, reduce the heat and simmer for 5 minutes. Add the chicken, taste and re-season. Heat through for a few minutes, then ladle into bowls. Garnish with spoonfuls of the remaining crème fraîche, the croûtons and parsley and serve hot.

Peasant Pottage

SERVES 6

2 onions, finely chopped
2 carrots, finely chopped
1 small red (bell) pepper, finely chopped
25 g/1 oz/2 tbsp butter or margarine
1 chicken portion, all skin removed
100 g/4 oz French (green) beans, cut into quarters
2 tomatoes, skinned and chopped
¼ green cabbage, finely shredded
400 g/14 oz/1 large can of chick peas (garbanzos), drained
1 litre/1¾ pts/4¼ cups vegetable stock, made with 2 stock cubes
Salt and freshly ground black pepper
1 bay leaf
45 ml/3 tbsp grated Parmesan cheese

Fry (sauté) the onions, carrots and pepper in the butter or margarine for 2 minutes, stirring. Add the remaining ingredients except the cheese, bring to the boil, reduce the heat, part-cover and simmer gently for 30 minutes. Lift out the chicken and remove the bay leaf. Cut all the meat of the chicken portion, chop and return to the pan. Taste and re-season if necessary. Ladle into warm bowls and sprinkle a little of the Parmesan over each serving.

Chicken and Prawn Bouillabaisse

SERVES 4

1.5 kg/3 lb oven-ready chicken
Thinly pared rind of ½ orange
30 ml/2 tbsp plain (all-purpose) flour
15 ml/1 tbsp paprika
Salt and freshly ground black pepper
60 ml/4 tbsp olive oil
1 large onion, finely chopped
1 large garlic clove, crushed
1 fennel bulb, chopped, reserving the feathery fronds for garnish
1 large carrot, finely diced
5 ml/1 tsp dried thyme
1 bay leaf
400 g/14 oz/1 large can of chopped tomatoes
900 ml/1½ pts/3¾ cups water
2 chicken stock cubes
2 large potatoes, diced
150 ml/¼ pt/⅔ cup dry white wine
175 g/6 oz raw, peeled tiger prawns (jumbo shrimp)
30 ml/2 tbsp chopped parsley
Rouille (page 339), to serve

Cut the chicken into 8 pieces (page 15), discarding the skin. Mix the orange rind with the flour, paprika and some salt and pepper. Toss the chicken in this mixture. Heat the oil in a large saucepan. Add the chicken and brown quickly. Remove from the pan. Add the onion, garlic, fennel and carrot and fry (sauté), stirring, for 2 minutes. Return the chicken to the pan and add the thyme, bay leaf, tomatoes, water and stock cubes. Bring to the boil, reduce the heat, part-cover and simmer gently for 45 minutes. Add the potatoes and wine and simmer for a further 15 minutes. Add the prawns and cook for 5 minutes until pink and cooked through. Remove the bay leaf. Taste and re-season if necessary. Ladle into warm soup bowls, garnish with parsley and serve with Rouille.

Quick Scottish Chicken Soup

SERVES 4–6

2 × 295 g/2 × 10½ oz/2 medium cans of condensed cream of chicken soup
Milk
45 ml/3 tbsp Scotch whisky
60 ml/4 tbsp single (light) cream
15 ml/1 tbsp chopped parsley

Empty the soup into a pan and add milk according to the instructions. Whisk in the whisky. Heat through until piping hot. Ladle into warm bowls. Add a swirl of cream to each and sprinkle with chopped parsley before serving.

Iced Chicken and Mango Mulligatawny

SERVES 6

1 small, ripe mango
25 g/1 oz/2 tbsp butter or margarine
1 onion, finely chopped
1 carrot, finely chopped
30 ml/2 tbsp plain (all-purpose) flour
15 ml/1 tbsp Madras curry powder
1.2 litres/2 pts/5 cups chicken stock
100 g/4 oz/1 cup chicken, finely chopped, all skin removed
6 coriander (cilantro) leaves, to garnish

Peel the mango and cut all the flesh off the stone (pit). Heat the butter or margarine in a saucepan and cook the onion and carrot for 5 minutes until soft and lightly golden. Stir in the flour and curry powder and cook for 3 minutes, stirring, until a rich brown colour. Remove from the heat and gradually blend in the stock. Bring to the boil, stirring until thickened. Add the mango flesh. Reduce the heat, part-cover and simmer gently for 20 minutes. Purée in a blender or food processor, then pour into a container and leave to cool. Stir in the chopped chicken, cover and chill until ready to serve. Ladle into chilled soup bowls and garnish each bowl with a coriander leaf.

Chicken and Potato Chowder

SERVES 4–6

4 large potatoes, diced
1 onion, finely chopped
3 rindless streaky bacon rashers (slices), chopped
25 g/1 oz/2 tbsp butter or margarine
1 small bay leaf
300 ml/½ pt/1¼ cups chicken stock
15 ml/1 tbsp plain (all-purpose) flour
300 ml/½ pt/1¼ cups milk
100 g/4 oz/1 cup cooked chicken, chopped, all skin removed
30 ml/2 tbsp chopped parsley
Salt and freshly ground black pepper

Fry (sauté) the potatoes, onion and bacon in the butter or margarine in a saucepan for 3 minutes, stirring. Add the bay leaf and stock. Bring to the boil, reduce the heat, part-cover and simmer for 20 minutes. Blend the flour with a little of the milk, then stir in the remaining milk, then stir into the soup with the chicken. Bring to the boil, stirring, and simmer for 5 minutes, stirring occasionally. Stir in the parsley and season to taste. Serve in warm bowls.

Cock-a-leekie Soup

SERVES 6

2 large leeks, thinly sliced
2 chicken portions, skin removed
75 g/3 oz/scant ½ cup pearl barley
1 bouquet garni sachet
1.75 litres/3 pts/7½ cups chicken stock
A pinch of salt
Freshly ground black pepper
8 prunes, quartered and stoned (pitted)
30 ml/2 tbsp chopped parsley

Put all the ingredients except the prunes and parsley in a large saucepan. Bring to the boil, reduce the heat, part-cover and simmer gently for 1 hour. Add the prunes and cook for a further 30 minutes until the chicken and barley are tender. Lift the chicken out of the soup. Take the meat off the bones and cut into small pieces. Return to the pan and simmer for a further 5 minutes. Taste and re-season, if necessary. Discard the bouquet garni and stir in the parsley.

Chicken and Rice Soup

SERVES 4

Prepare as for Turkey, Onion and Rice Soup (page 60), but use a chicken carcass instead of turkey, use only one onion and substitute sherry for the vermouth.

Chicken and Corn Chowder

SERVES 4

1 chicken portion, all skin removed
450 ml/¾ pt/2 cups water
1 bunch of spring onions (scallions), chopped
2 potatoes, finely diced
Salt and freshly ground black pepper
350 g/12 oz/1 large can of sweetcorn (corn)
300 ml/½ pt/1¼ cups milk
30 ml/2 tbsp dried milk powder (non-fat dry milk)
30 ml/2 tbsp chopped parsley

Put the chicken portion in a pan with the water. Bring to the boil, reduce the heat, part-cover and simmer gently for 45 minutes. Carefully lift out the chicken, remove all meat from the bones, chop and reserve. Add the spring onions, potatoes and some salt and pepper to the chicken stock and simmer for 10 minutes. Add the chicken and corn. Blend a little of the milk with the milk powder and stir until smooth. Stir into the pan with the remaining milk. Bring to the boil and cook for 2 minutes, stirring all the time. Stir in the parsley and re-season, if liked. Ladle into bowls and serve hot.

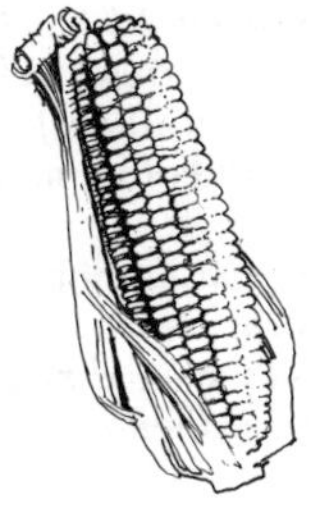

Creamed Chicken and Tarragon Soup

SERVES 6

1 chicken carcass
1 large carrot, roughly chopped
1 large onion, roughly chopped
1.5 litres/2½ pts/6 cups water
Salt and white pepper
15 ml/1 tbsp chopped tarragon
40 g/1½ oz/⅓ cup plain (all-purpose) flour
150 ml/¼ pt/⅔ cup milk
150 ml/¼ pt/⅔ cup single (light) cream
6 tarragon sprigs, to garnish

Break up the chicken carcass and place in a large saucepan with the carrot, onion and water. Season fairly well and add the tarragon. Bring to the boil, skim the surface, reduce the heat, part-cover and simmer gently for about 1½ hours. Strain the stock and return to the rinsed-out saucepan. Bring to the boil and boil rapidly until reduced to about 900 ml/1½ pts/3¾ cups. Pick any chicken meat off the carcass. Chop and reserve. Blend the flour with the milk. Whisk into the simmering stock and cook, stirring, until thickened and smooth. Cook for a further 2 minutes. Stir in the chicken meat and cream. Reheat but do not boil again. Taste and re-season, if necessary. Ladle into warm bowls and garnish each with a tiny sprig of tarragon before serving.

Sherried Chicken and Pasta Soup

SERVES 4

1 small skinless chicken breast, cut into thin strips about 2.5 cm/1 in long
900 ml/1½ pts/3¾ cups chicken stock
4 spring onions (scallions), chopped
100 g/4 oz small button mushrooms, sliced
50 g/2 oz soup pasta shapes
1 bouquet garni sachet
Salt and freshly ground black pepper
60 ml/4 tbsp medium-dry sherry

Put all the ingredients except the sherry in a saucepan. Bring to the boil, reduce the heat and simmer for 10 minutes. Stir in the sherry, taste and re-season if necessary. Ladle into warm bowls and serve hot.

Oriental Chicken and Sweetcorn Soup

SERVES 6

900 ml/1½ pts/3¾ cups chicken stock
2 thin slices of fresh root ginger
1 garlic clove, halved
350 g/12 oz/1 medium can of sweetcorn (corn)
100 g/4 oz/1 cup cooked chicken, finely chopped and all skin removed
30 ml/2 tbsp dry sherry
15 ml/1 tbsp soy sauce
1 spring onion (scallion), very finely chopped
15 ml/1 tbsp cornflour (cornstarch)
30 ml/2 tbsp water
Salt and white pepper

Put the stock in a saucepan with the ginger and garlic. Bring to the boil, cover, reduce the heat and simmer for 5 minutes. Remove the ginger and garlic with a draining spoon and discard. Add the remaining ingredients except the cornflour, water and seasoning. Bring to the boil, reduce the heat and simmer gently for 3 minutes. Blend the cornflour with the water and stir into the soup. Simmer for a further 2 minutes, stirring. Season to taste with salt and pepper and add little extra soy sauce, if liked. Ladle into warm bowls and serve.

Chinese Chicken and Vegetable Soup

SERVES 4

1 small skinless chicken breast
5 ml/1 tsp cornflour (cornstarch)
15 ml/1 tbsp soy sauce
2 carrots, coarsely grated
5 cm/2 in piece of cucumber, coarsely grated
1.2 litres/2 pts/5 cups chicken stock
15 ml/1 tbsp medium-dry sherry
Salt

Cut the chicken into thin slices, then the slices into thin strips. Place in a bowl. Toss in the cornflour, then add the soy sauce and toss again. Leave to stand for 10 minutes. Put in a saucepan and stir in the remaining ingredients. Bring to the boil, reduce the heat and simmer for 8 minutes until the chicken is really tender. Taste and add a little more soy sauce, if liked. Ladle into soup bowls and serve.

Oriental Chicken and Soy Soup

SERVES 4

15 ml/1 tbsp sesame oil
30 ml/2 tbsp soy sauce
10 ml/2 tsp cornflour (cornstarch)
1 skinless chicken breast, very thinly sliced widthways
1 carrot, very thinly sliced
1.2 litres/2 pts/5 cups chicken stock

Mix together the oil, soy sauce and cornflour in a shallow dish until smooth. Add the chicken and toss to coat completely. Leave to marinate for at least 15 minutes. Meanwhile, put the carrot and stock in a saucepan. Bring to the boil and simmer gently for 5 minutes. Add the chicken mixture to the pan, stir well and simmer gently for 8 minutes. Taste and add more soy sauce, if liked. Ladle into warm bowls and serve hot.

Rich Chicken and Mushroom Soup

SERVES 6

1 small onion, very finely chopped
350 g/12 oz button mushrooms, very finely chopped
15 g/½ oz/1 tbsp butter or margarine
150 ml/¼ pt/⅔ cup chicken stock, made with ½ stock cube
100 g/4 oz/1 cup cooked chicken, very finely chopped, all skin removed
30 ml/2 tbsp plain (all-purpose) flour
450 ml/¾ pt/2 cups milk
A pinch of salt
Freshly ground black pepper
30 ml/2 tbsp finely chopped parsley
30 ml/2 tbsp fromage frais

Cook the onion and mushrooms in the butter or margarine gently for 3 minutes, stirring until soft but not brown. Add the stock and chicken, stir, cover, reduce the heat to low and simmer gently for 10 minutes, stirring occasionally, until tender. Blend the flour with a little of the milk. Stir into the mushrooms with the remaining milk. Bring to the boil and cook for 2 minutes, stirring. Season with the salt and some pepper, then stir in the parsley and fromage frais. Reheat but do not boil. Ladle into warm bowls and serve.

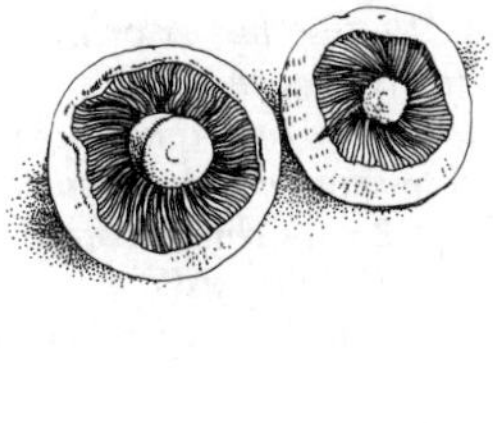

Chicken, Mushroom and Pasta Chowder

SERVES 4

1 onion, finely chopped
2 rindless, streaky bacon rashers (slices), finely diced
1 garlic clove, crushed
30 ml/2 tbsp olive oil
15 ml/1 tbsp plain (all-purpose) flour
600 ml/1 pt/2½ cups chicken stock
300 ml/½ pt/1¼ cups milk
1 bay leaf
50 g/2 oz soup pasta shapes
100 g/4 oz button mushrooms, sliced
100 g/4 oz/1 cup cooked chicken, chopped, all skin removed
Salt and freshly ground black pepper
15 ml/1 tbsp chopped parsley

Fry (sauté) the onion, bacon and garlic in the oil for 2 minutes, stirring. Add the flour and stir for 1 minute. Remove from the heat and gradually blend in the stock. Stir in the milk and add the bay leaf. Bring to the boil, stirring. Add the pasta and mushrooms and simmer gently for 15 minutes. Stir in the chicken and season to taste. Cook for a further 5 minutes. Discard the bay leaf. Ladle into warm bowls and sprinkle with parsley before serving.

Chicken, Corn and Peanut Chowder

SERVES 6

20 g/¾ oz /1½ tbsp butter or margarine
1 onion, finely chopped
50 g/2 oz/¼ cup light brown sugar
60 ml/4 tbsp smooth peanut butter
450 ml/¾ pt/2 cups chicken stock
300 ml/½ pt/1¼ cups milk
200 g/7 oz/1 small can of sweetcorn (corn)
100 g/4 oz/1 cup cooked chicken, finely chopped, all skin removed
Salt and freshly ground black pepper
15 ml/1 tbsp chopped parsley
175 g/6 oz/1½ cups Cheddar cheese, grated, to serve

Melt the butter or margarine in a saucepan. Add the onion and fry (sauté) for 4 minutes until browned. Stir in the sugar and cook for a further 2 minutes. Stir in the peanut butter. Remove from the heat and gradually blend in the stock and milk. Return to the heat, bring to the boil, reduce the heat and simmer for 10 minutes. Add the corn and chicken and season to taste. Simmer for a further 10 minutes. Stir in the parsley. Taste and re-season, if necessary. Ladle into warm bowls and serve with grated Cheddar cheese.

Chinese Egg Flower Soup

SERVES 4

900 ml/1½ pts/3¾ cups chicken stock
15 ml/1 tbsp soy sauce
30 ml/2 tbsp dry sherry
A pinch of ground ginger
25 g/1 oz frozen peas
½ red (bell) pepper, cut into tiny diamond shapes
1 egg, beaten

Put all the ingredients except the egg in a saucepan and bring to the boil. Simmer for 5 minutes until the peas and pepper pieces are tender. Remove from the heat and pour the egg in a thin stream through the prongs of fork so it solidifies in 'flowers'. Let the soup stand for 20 seconds to allow the egg to set, then ladle into warm soup bowls.

Straciatella

SERVES 4

2 eggs
25 g/1 oz/¼ cup Parmesan cheese, grated
15 ml/1 tbsp chopped parsley
15 ml/1 tbsp chopped basil
A pinch of grated nutmeg
Salt and freshly ground black pepper
1.2 litres/2 pts/5 cups chicken stock

Whisk together the eggs, cheese, herbs and nutmeg with a little salt and pepper. Bring the stock to the boil. Whisk a ladleful of the stock into the egg mixture. Pour into the remaining stock. Whisk and serve straight away.

Sopa di Agio

SERVES 4

45 ml/3 tbsp olive oil
1 large garlic clove, crushed
100 g/4 oz/2 cups white breadcrumbs
750 ml/1¼ pts/3 cups chicken stock
Paprika
Salt
4 eggs

Heat the oil in a saucepan. Add the garlic and fry (sauté), stirring, for 2 minutes. Stir in the breadcrumbs and stock. Season to taste with the paprika and salt. Bring to the boil. Ladle into four ovenproof bowls. Break an egg into each. Bake in a preheated oven at 180°C/350°F/gas mark 4 for about 10 minutes until the eggs are just set and a crust has formed on the top. Serve straight away ungarnished.

Garlic and Chicken Soup

SERVES 4

Prepare as for Sopa di Agio but reduce the quantity of breadcrumbs to 75 g/3 oz/1½ cups and add 100 g/4 oz/ 1 cup finely chopped cooked chicken.

Woodland Chicken Soup

SERVES 6

100 g/4 oz/1 cup hazelnuts (filberts)
15 g/½ oz/1 tbsp unsalted (sweet) butter
1 onion, finely chopped
1 large chicken breast fillet, cut into small pieces
100 g/4 oz chestnut mushrooms, chopped
900 ml/1½ pts/3¾ cups chicken stock
30 ml/2 tbsp chopped parsley
1 egg yolk
150 ml/¼ pt/⅔ cup double (heavy) cream
Salt and freshly ground black pepper

Dry-fry the hazelnuts in a frying pan (skillet), tossing until golden brown. Remove from the pan and grind in a food processor until coarsely ground. Heat the butter in a saucepan. Add the onion and fry (sauté) gently for 3 minutes until softened but not browned. Add the chicken, mushrooms, stock and half the parsley. Stir in the hazelnuts. Bring to the boil, reduce the heat and simmer for 7 minutes. Blend the egg yolk with the cream and stir into the soup. Re-heat but do not boil. Season to taste. Ladle into warm bowls and sprinkle with the remaining parsley before serving.

Kosher-style Chicken Soup

Serve the cooked chicken and vegetables with plain boiled potatoes and mustard on the day the soup is made or use it for any recipes calling for cooked chicken in this book.

SERVES 6

1 large boiling fowl
10 ml/2 tsp salt
10 black peppercorns
1 turnip, cut into chunks
1 small swede (rutabaga), cut into chunks
1 large onion, cut into chunks
2 celery sticks, chopped
2 large carrots, cut into chunks

Wash the chicken inside and out and place in a large saucepan. Add the salt, peppercorns and prepared vegetables. Cover with cold water. Bring to the boil and skim the surface. Cover the pan, reduce the heat and simmer very gently for at least 2 hours, ideally 3–4 hours. Carefully lift out the chicken and vegetables and use as required. Pour the soup into a cold container and leave to cool, then cover and chill, preferably overnight. Skim off any fat, reheat and serve.

Kosher-style Chicken Soup with Noodles

SERVES 6

Prepare as for Kosher-style Chicken Soup. Cook 100 g/4 oz vermicelli, broken into short lengths, in boiling water until just tender. Drain and return to the pan. Add the chilled chicken soup and bring to the boil, stirring. Taste and re-season if necessary. Serve very hot.

Chicken Soup with Matzo Meal Dumplings

SERVES 6

Kosher-style Chicken Soup (page 53)
225 g/8 oz/2 cups matzo meal
A pinch of salt
A pinch of white pepper
30 ml/2 tbsp chopped parsley
30 ml/2 tbsp sunflower oil
1 egg, beaten
250 ml/8 fl oz/1 cup boiling water

Put the chilled chicken soup in a large saucepan and bring to the boil, then reduce the heat to moderate. Meanwhile, put the matzo meal, salt and pepper in a bowl and stir in the parsley. Make a well in the centre and add the oil and the egg. Beat in the water to form a soft dough. Drop 12 small spoonfuls of the dough into the simmering soup. Cover and simmer for about 10 minutes until fluffy. Ladle into warm bowls and serve straight away.

Chicken Soup with Lemon Dumplings

SERVES 6

50 g/2 oz/1 cup white breadcrumbs
2.5 ml/½ tsp finely grated lemon rind
A pinch of grated nutmeg
15 ml/1 tbsp chopped parsley
1.5 ml/¼ tsp dried thyme
25 g/1 oz/2 tbsp butter, softened
1 egg yolk
Salt and freshly ground black pepper
Kosher-style Chicken Soup (page 53)
6 thin lemon slices

Mix together the breadcrumbs, lemon rind, nutmeg, herbs and butter, then work in the egg yolk and a little salt and pepper. Shape into 24 tiny balls. Heat the soup until boiling, reduce the heat, drop in the dumplings, cover and poach gently for 15 minutes. Serve ladled into warm bowls and garnish each with a thin slice of lemon.

Cream of Chicken and Walnut Soup

SERVES 6

1 cooked chicken carcass
1 large onion
1 large carrot
1.2 litres/2 pts/5 cups chicken stock
2 cloves
8 black peppercorns
50 g/2 oz/½ cup walnut pieces, chopped
50 g/2 oz/½ cup plain (all-purpose) flour
150 ml/¼ pt/⅔ cup milk
150 ml/¼ pt/⅔ cup single (light) cream
Salt
15 ml/1 tbsp chopped parsley

Break up the carcass and place in a large saucepan with the onion and carrot. Add the stock, cloves and peppercorns. Bring to the boil, cover, reduce the heat and simmer for 1 hour. Strain the stock and return to the saucepan. Remove any meat from the carcass. Chop and return to the pan. Add the walnuts. Blend the flour with the milk until smooth and stir into the saucepan. Bring to the boil and cook for 2 minutes, stirring all the time. Stir in the cream and season to taste with salt. Stir in the parsley. Ladle into warm bowls and serve hot.

Quick Greek-style Chicken and Vegetable Soup

SERVES 4

100 g/4 oz frozen mixed vegetables
450 ml/¾ pt/2 cups chicken stock
100 g/4 oz/1 cup cooked chicken, finely chopped, all skin removed
1 egg yolk
300 ml/½ pt/1¼ cups Greek-style plain yoghurt
Salt and freshly ground black pepper
Finely grated rind and juice of 1 small lemon
15 ml/1 tbsp chopped mint

Simmer the vegetables in the stock for 5 minutes. Add the chicken and simmer for a further 3 minutes. Whisk together the egg yolk and yoghurt in a bowl. Whisk in four ladles of the hot stock and whisk well. Stir this back into the hot soup. Heat through but do not boil. Add lemon juice to taste. Ladle into warm bowls and sprinkle with the grated lemon rind and mint before serving.

Curried Chicken and Apple Warmer

SERVES 4

1 onion, roughly chopped
2 green eating (dessert) apples, peeled, cored and chopped
25 g/1 oz/2 tbsp butter or margarine
5 ml/1 tsp curry powder
450 ml/¾ pt/2 cups chicken stock
Salt and freshly ground black pepper
150 ml/¼ pt/⅔ cup crème fraîche
50 g/2 oz/½ cup cooked chicken, finely chopped, all skin removed
30 ml/2 tbsp flaked (slivered) almonds

Fry (sauté) the onion and apples in half the butter or margarine for 3 minutes, stirring. Add the curry powder and stir for 1 minute. Pour in the stock and add a little salt and pepper. Bring to the boil, reduce the heat and simmer for 5 minutes. Purée in a blender or food processor. Return to the pan and stir in the crème fraîche. Heat through. Taste and re-season, if necessary. Meanwhile, melt the remaining butter or margarine in a frying pan (skillet), add the chicken and nuts and toss quickly until the nuts are golden. Drain on kitchen paper (paper towels). Ladle the soup into warm bowls and top with the chicken and almond mixture.

Avocado and Chicken Soup

SERVES 6

1 large onion, finely chopped
1 garlic clove, crushed
25 g/1 oz/2 tbsp butter or margarine
25 g/1 oz/¼ cup plain (all-purpose) flour
2 large ripe avocados
Finely grated rind and juice of ½ small lemon
2.5 ml/½ tsp ground coriander (cilantro)
900 ml/1½ pts/3¾ cups chicken stock
100 g/4 oz/1 cup cooked chicken, finely chopped
Salt and white pepper
150 ml/¼ pt/⅔ cup crème fraîche
A little milk
30 ml/2 tbsp chopped parsley

Fry (sauté) the onion and garlic gently in the butter or margarine for 4 minutes until softened but not browned. Add the flour and cook for 1 minute, stirring. Remove from the heat. Halve the avocados, remove the stones (pits) and scoop out the flesh into a bowl. Make sure you scrape all the flesh near the skin, to give the soup a rich, green colour. Mash thoroughly with the lemon rind and juice until smooth. Stir into the flour mixture with the coriander. Blend in the stock. Bring to the boil, reduce the heat and simmer gently for 2 minutes. Stir in the chicken and heat through. Season to taste. Stir in half the crème fraîche and thin with a little milk, if necessary. Heat through again but do not boil. Ladle into warm soup bowls. Top each with a little of the remaining crème fraîche and sprinkle each with a little chopped parsley before serving.

Tuscan Chicken Liver Soup

SERVES 6

200 g/7 oz chicken livers, trimmed and chopped
15 g/½ oz/1 tbsp unsalted (sweet) butter
1.75 litres/3 pts/7½ cups chicken stock
100 g/4 oz/½ cup risotto rice
Salt and freshly ground black pepper
30 ml/2 tbsp chopped parsley
Freshly grated Parmesan cheese

Fry (sauté) the chicken livers in the butter for about 2–3 minutes until pink and almost firm. Put the stock in a large saucepan and bring to the boil. Add the rice, reduce the heat and simmer for 12 minutes. Add the chicken livers and their juice and continue to cook for 4 minutes. Season to taste and stir in the parsley. Ladle into soup bowls and sprinkle with freshly grated Parmesan.

Chicken Giblet Soup

SERVES 4

50 g/2 oz/¼ cup butter or margarine
1 small onion, finely chopped
15 ml/1 tbsp plain (all-purpose) flour
1.2 litres/2 pts/5 cups water
Giblets and neck from a chicken, rinsed in cold water
1 bay leaf
1 large sprig of parsley
1 sprig of thyme
Salt and freshly ground black pepper
30 ml/2 tbsp sherry (optional)
30 ml/2 tbsp chopped parsley, to garnish

Melt the butter or margarine and fry (sauté) the onion for 2 minutes, stirring. Stir in the flour and cook for 2 minutes. Blend in the water and bring to the boil. Add the giblets and neck and herbs and simmer gently for 1 hour or until the giblets are really tender. Remove the giblets from the pan. Take off all the meat from the neck and discard any hard bits of gizzard. Discard the bay leaf and parsley from the soup, then purée the giblets and the soup in a blender or food processor. Return to the pan. Season to taste, then flavour with the sherry, if liked. Serve garnished with chopped parsley.

Chicken Soup with Chopped Liver Dumplings

SERVES 6

225 g/8 oz/2 cups plain (all-purpose) flour
Salt and freshly ground black pepper
3 eggs
15 ml/1 tbsp water
1 small onion, finely chopped
15 ml/1 tbsp sunflower oil
225 g/8 oz chicken livers, trimmed and finely chopped
30 ml/2 tbsp chopped parsley
Kosher-style Chicken Soup (page 53)

Sift the flour and a pinch of salt into a bowl. Beat 2 of the eggs and stir in with the water. Mix to form a soft but not sticky dough. Knead gently on a lightly floured surface, then wrap in clingfilm (plastic wrap) and chill for 30 minutes.

Meanwhile, fry (sauté) the onion in the oil for 2 minutes, stirring. Add the livers and fry, stirring, for 2 minutes or until the livers are just cooked but still pink and soft. Remove from the heat. Stir in the parsley and season to taste with salt and pepper.

Roll out the dough thinly and cut into 18 5 cm/2 in squares. Divide the filling between the squares. Brush the edges with water, then fold the dough over the filling to form little triangles. Press the edges well together to seal. Bring a large pan of water to the boil and add a good pinch of salt. Drop in the dumplings and simmer for about 15 minutes or until cooked and they float on the surface. Remove from the pan with a draining spoon and drain on kitchen paper (paper towels). Bring the chicken soup to the boil, add the dumplings and simmer for 10 minutes, then serve piping hot.

Chicken Liver and Pea Pottage

SERVES 6

1 onion, finely chopped
1 garlic clove, crushed
25 g/1 oz/2 tbsp butter or margarine
100 g/4 oz chicken livers, trimmed and finely chopped
350 g/12 oz frozen peas
1 potato, finely diced
1.2 litres/2 pts/5 cups chicken stock
5 ml/1 tsp dried mint
Salt and freshly ground black pepper

Fry (sauté) the onion and garlic in the butter or margarine for 2 minutes, stirring. Add the chicken livers and fry for 1 minute. Add the peas, potato, stock and mint. Bring to the boil, part-cover and simmer gently for 10 minutes. Lift out about 15 ml/1 tbsp of the peas to reserve for garnish, then purée the soup in a blender or food processor and return to the pan. Season to taste. Reheat, ladle into bowls and top each with the reserved peas.

TURKEY

Turkey Carcass Stock

MAKES 1.2 LITRES/2 PTS/5 CUPS

Prepare as for Chicken Carcass Stock (page 43), but use a cooked turkey carcass and a bouquet garni sachet instead of the bay leaf.

Turkey Broth

SERVES 4–6

Turkey Carcass Stock, chilled
Salt and freshly ground black pepper
15 ml/1 tbsp chopped parsley
30 ml/2 tbsp medium-dry sherry (optional)

Skim off any fat from the stock. Reheat, season to taste, stir in the parsley and flavour with the sherry, if liked.

Curried Turkey and Lentil Soup

SERVES 4

100 g/4 oz/⅔ cup brown or green lentils, soaked for several hours or overnight
1 onion, finely chopped
15 ml/1 tbsp sunflower oil
15 ml/1 tbsp Madras curry powder
1 litre/1¾ pts/4¼ cups chicken stock (or half stock, half turkey gravy)
225 g/8 oz/2 cups cooked turkey, diced, all skin removed
30 ml/2 tbsp raisins
Salt and freshly ground black pepper
Plain yoghurt and chopped mint, to garnish

Drain the lentils. Cook the onion in the oil in a large saucepan for 2 minutes, stirring. Add the curry powder and stir for a further minute. Blend in the stock and lentils. Bring to the boil, reduce the heat, part-cover and simmer for 40 minutes or until the lentils are tender. Add the turkey and raisins and season to taste. Simmer for a further 10 minutes. Ladle into warm bowls, add a spoonful of yoghurt to each and sprinkle with chopped mint before serving.

Turkey Sausage Soup

SERVES 4

4 turkey sausages
25 g/1 oz/2 tbsp butter or margarine
2 onions, thinly sliced
900 ml/1½ pts/3¾ cups chicken stock
5 ml/1 tsp Dijon mustard
Gravy block or browning
1.5 ml/¼ tsp dried sage
Salt and freshly ground black pepper
100 g/4 oz/1 cup Cheddar cheese, grated
Crusty bread, to serve

Brown the turkey sausages in the butter or margarine in a large saucepan. Remove from the pan and drain on kitchen paper (paper towels). Cut into small chunks. Fry (sauté) the onions in the pan for 3–4 minutes until softened and golden. Add the stock, mustard and gravy block or browning to taste. Add the sage, bring to the boil, reduce the heat and simmer for 20 minutes. Add the sausage chunks, season to taste and simmer for a further 10 minutes. Stir in the cheese until melted and serve piping hot with crusty bread.

Baked Main Meal Turkey, Ham and Vegetable Soup

SERVES 6

30 ml/2 tbsp olive oil
3 celery sticks, chopped
2 carrots, coarsley grated
1 large onion, coarsely grated
½ small white cabbage, shredded
1 red (bell) pepper, sliced
1 garlic clove, crushed
1.2 litres/2 pts/5 cups chicken stock
30 ml/2 tbsp snipped chives
Salt and freshly ground black pepper
1 small baguette, cut into chunks
100 g/4 oz/1 cup cooked turkey, cut into small pieces, all skin removed
2 slices of ham, diced
100 g/4 oz/1 cup Gruyère (Swiss) cheese, grated

Heat the oil in a large saucepan. Add the prepared vegetables, stir well, cover and cook gently for 5 minutes, stirring once or twice. Add the stock and chives and seasoning to taste. Bring to the boil, reduce the heat, part-cover and simmer gently for 30 minutes. Meanwhile, spread out the bread on a baking (cookie) sheet. Bake in a preheated oven at 220°C/425°F/gas mark 7 for about 8 minutes until crisp and golden. Put a layer of half the bread in a large casserole dish (Dutch oven). Stir the turkey and ham into the soup, taste and re-season. Spoon half the soup into the casserole. Sprinkle with half the cheese. Repeat the layers of bread, soup and cheese. Return to the oven for 10 minutes until the cheese is golden and bubbling. Ladle into large warm bowls and serve.

Cream of Turkey and Pecan Soup

SERVES 6

Prepare as for Cream of Chicken and Walnut Soup (page 54) but use a small turkey carcass instead of the chicken carcass, pecan nuts instead of the walnuts and substitute snipped chives for the parsley before serving.

Turkey Minestrone

SERVES 8

1 turkey leg
1.5 litres/2½ pts/6 cups water
1 chicken stock cube
2 onions, sliced
2 carrots, diced
2 celery sticks, chopped
1 bay leaf
½ small, green cabbage, shredded
50 g/2 oz frozen peas
400 g/14 oz/1 large can of chopped tomatoes
50 g/2 oz quick-cook macaroni
Salt and freshly ground black pepper
Grated Parmesan cheese, to serve

Put the turkey leg in a large saucepan with the water and stock cube, onions, carrots, celery and bay leaf. Bring to the boil, skim the surface, reduce the heat, part-cover and simmer gently for 1½ hours. Lift the turkey out of the pan. Discard the skin. Cut all the meat off the bone, cut into small pieces and reserve. Add the cabbage, peas, tomatoes and macaroni to the pan and season to taste. Cover and simmer for 10 minutes or until the pasta and cabbage are tender. Return the turkey to the pan and heat through. Taste and re-season. Discard the bay leaf. Ladle into warm bowls and serve sprinkled with grated Parmesan cheese.

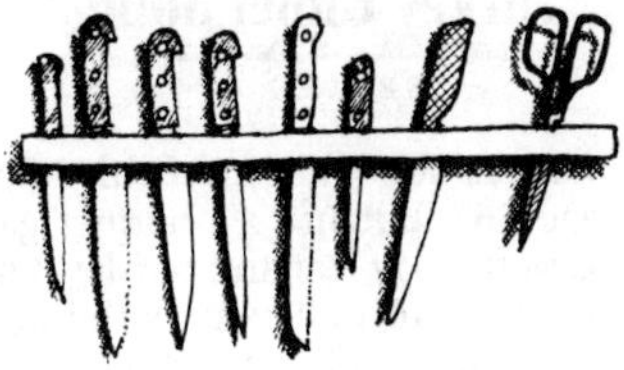

Brown Turkey Potage

SERVES 6–8

1 turkey carcass
1 large onion
1 clove
1 small bay leaf
15 g/½ oz/1 tbsp butter or margarine
1 onion, finely chopped
15 ml/1 tbsp light brown sugar
1 large potato, finely diced
1 large carrot, finely diced
Salt and freshly ground black pepper
30 ml/2 tbsp cornflour (cornstarch)
30 ml/2 tbsp cold water
Chopped parsley, to garnish

Break up the carcass and place in a large saucepan. Stud the large onion with the clove and add to the pan with the bay leaf. Just cover with water. Bring to the boil, reduce the heat, part-cover and simmer gently for 2 hours. Strain into a bowl. When the bones are cool enough to handle, pick off any meat from the bones and add to the stock. Discard the bones. Heat the butter or margarine in the rinsed-out saucepan. Add the chopped onion and fry (sauté) for 3 minutes. Add the sugar and continue to cook, stirring, until a rich brown. Add the potato and carrot and pour on the stock. Stir well. Bring to the boil, reduce the heat and simmer for 20 minutes until the potato and carrot are really tender. Season to taste. Blend the cornflour with the water and stir into the soup. Bring to the boil and simmer for 1 minute until slightly thickened. Ladle into warm bowls and garnish with chopped parsley before serving.

Sherried Turkey Pottage

SERVES 6–8

Prepare as for Brown Turkey Potage, but use a bouquet garni sachet instead of a bay leaf for flavouring and substitute sherry for the water to blend the cornflour (cornstarch).

Turkey Bean Chowder

SERVES 6

2 leeks, thinly sliced
2 carrots, finley chopped
1 onion, finely chopped
25 g/1 oz/2 tbsp butter or margarine
600 ml/1 pt/2½ cups turkey or chicken stock
400 g/14 oz/1 large can of chopped tomatoes
400 g/14 oz/1 large can of baked beans
100 g/4 oz/1 cup cooked turkey, chopped, all skin removed
5 ml/1 tsp dried oregano
Salt and freshly ground black pepper
Grated cheese, to serve

Fry (sauté) the leeks, carrots and onion in the butter or margarine in a saucepan for 4 minutes, stirring, until softened. Add the stock, bring to the boil, reduce the heat and simmer gently for 15 minutes. Add the remaining ingredients, bring back to the boil and simmer for a further 10 minutes. Taste and re-season if necessary. Ladle into warm bowls and serve with grated cheese to sprinkle over.

Turkey, Onion and Rice Soup

SERVES 4

1 turkey carcass
1.75 litres/3 pts/7½ cups water
1 bouquet garni sachet
2 large onions, finely chopped, reserving the skins
Salt and freshly ground black pepper
50 g/2 oz/¼ cup long-grain rice
15 ml/1 tbsp cornflour (cornstarch)
30 ml/2 tbsp dry vermouth
Chopped parsley, to garnish

Pick any meat off the carcass and chop. Break up the bones and place in a large saucepan with the water, bouquet garni and the onion skins. Add some salt and pepper. Bring to the boil, skim the surface, cover, reduce the heat and simmer for 2 hours. Strain and return the stock to the rinsed-out saucepan. Add the onions, rice and chopped turkey meat to the stock, bring to the boil and simmer for 20 minutes. Blend the cornflour with the vermouth and stir in. Bring back to the boil and cook for 1 minute, stirring. Taste and re-season if necessary. Ladle into warm bowls, garnish with chopped parsley and serve hot.

Swiss Turkey Soup

SERVES 4–6

1 large onion, finely chopped
1 celery stick, finely chopped
25 g/1 oz/2 tbsp butter or margarine
5 ml/1 tsp light brown sugar
750 ml/1¼ pts/3 cups turkey or chicken stock
100 g/4 oz stuffed green olives, sliced
100 g/4 oz/1 cup cooked turkey, chopped, all skin removed
1 small bay leaf
Salt and freshly ground black pepper
4–6 slices of French bread, toasted
75 g/3 oz/¾ cup Gruyère or Emmental (Swiss) cheese, grated

Fry (sauté) the onion and celery in the butter or margarine for 3 minutes to soften. Stir in the sugar and cook for a further 2 minutes. Add the stock, olives, turkey and bay leaf. Bring to the boil, reduce the heat and simmer for 15 minutes. Discard the bay leaf and season to taste. Ladle into flameproof bowls. Float the toasted French bread on top and sprinkle with the cheese. Place under a hot grill (broiler) until the cheese melts. Serve straight away.

Turkey Giblet Soup

SERVES 4

Prepare as for Chicken Giblet Soup (page 56), but use a bouquet garni instead of the bay leaf and parsley. Once cooked and puréed, flavour with brandy instead of sherry, if liked, before serving.

DUCK

Duck Carcass Stock

MAKES 900 ML/1½ PTS/3¾ CUPS

Prepare as for Chicken Carcass Stock (page 43), but add 2 fresh sage sprigs and omit the bay leaf.

Plain Duck Broth

SERVES 4–6

Duck Carcass Stock, chilled
Salt and freshly ground black pepper
15 ml/1 tbsp snipped chives
30 ml/2 tbsp Madeira or sherry (optional)

Skim off all the fat from the stock. Reheat and season to taste. Stir in the chives and flavour with Madeira or sherry, if liked.

Duck and Barley Broth

SERVES 4

1 duck carcass
1 large sprig of sage
1.75 litres/3 pts/7½ cups water
50 g/2 oz/scant ⅓ cup pearl barley
2 onions, finely chopped
2 carrots, coarsely grated
1 turnip, grated
Salt and freshly ground black pepper
15 ml/1 tbsp chopped parsley

Break up the carcass and place in a saucepan with the sage and water. Bring to the boil, skim the surface, cover and simmer gently for 1½ hours. Strain the stock, reserving the bones, and return to the rinsed-out pan. Add the barley and simmer for 30 minutes. Add the prepared vegetables and simmer gently for a further 30 minutes. Meanwhile, pick any meat off the duck carcass. Taste the soup and season well. Add the duck meat and heat through. Serve piping hot, sprinkled with the chopped parsley.

Creamy Duck and Spinach Soup

SERVES 6

1 duck portion
450 ml/¾ pt/2 cups water
1 onion, finely chopped
25 g/1 oz/2 tbsp butter or margarine
25 g/1 oz/¼ cup plain (all-purpose) flour
175 g/6 oz frozen chopped spinach, just thawed
600 ml/1 pt/2½ cups milk
Soy sauce
Freshly ground black pepper
Grated nutmeg
60 ml/4 tbsp double (heavy) cream, to garnish

Put the duck portion and water in a saucepan. Bring to the boil, reduce the heat, cover and simmer gently for 1 hour. Strain the stock. Remove all the meat from the duck, discarding the skin. Chop.

Brown the onion in the butter or margarine in the rinsed-out saucepan for 3 minutes. Add the flour and cook for 1 minute, stirring. Remove from the heat. Spoon off as much fat as possible from the top of the stock. Blend the stock into the flour mixture, stirring all the time. Add the spinach and stir in the milk. Return to the heat and bring to the boil, stirring. Cover, reduce the heat and simmer gently, stirring occasionally, for 15 minutes. Return the duck meat to the pan and simmer for a further 5 minutes. Season to taste with soy sauce, pepper and nutmeg and stir in half the cream. Ladle into warm bowls and add a swirl of the remaining cream to each bowl before serving.

Warming Duck Soup with Peas

SERVES 4

Duck Carcass Stock (page 61)
50 g/2 oz frozen peas
Gravy block or browning
30 ml/2 tbsp brandy
10 ml/2 tsp arrowroot
Salt and freshly ground black pepper

Prepare the Duck Carcass Stock. Strain and return to the rinsed-out saucepan. Pick all the meat off the carcass and add to the pan. Add the peas and simmer for 5 minutes. Stir in a little gravy block or browning to give a good, brown colour. Blend the brandy with the arrowroot and stir into the pan. Bring to the boil, stirring until slightly thickened. Taste and season, if necessary. Serve very hot.

Crunchy-topped Duck and Vegetable Soup

SERVES 4

1 carrot, coarsely grated
½ small swede (rutabaga), coarsely grated
1 potato, coarsely grated
1 celery stick, coarsely grated, discarding the strings
1 leek, coarsely grated
900 ml/1½ pts/3¾ cups chicken or duck stock
1 bay leaf
50 g/2 oz/⅓ cup red lentils
100 g/4 oz/1 cup cooked duck, chopped, all skin removed
15 ml/1 tbsp tomato purée (paste)
Salt and freshly ground black pepper
50 g/2 oz/¼ cup butter or margarine
75 g/3 oz/1½ cups breadcrumbs
25 g/1 oz/¼ cup Parmesan cheese, grated

Put the vegetables and stock in a saucepan with the bay leaf and lentils. Bring to the boil, part-cover, reduce the heat and simmer gently for 45 minutes. Add the duck, tomato purée and seasoning to taste. Simmer for a further 15 minutes. Meanwhile, melt the butter in a frying pan (skillet). Stir in the breadcrumbs and toss until golden. Mix in the cheese and tip into a small bowl. Ladle the soup into warm bowls, discarding the bay leaf. Serve with the crunchy topping handed separately.

Duck Giblet Soup

SERVES 4

Prepare as for Chicken Giblet Soup (page 56), but add half an orange to the soup while cooking and slice the remainder thinly to use for garnish. Flavour with 15 ml/1 tbsp orange liqueur or orange juice and add a little gravy block or browning before seasoning.

GAME

Game Carcass Stock

MAKES 900 ML/1½ PTS/3¾ CUPS

Prepare as for Chicken Carcass Stock (page 43), but use a game bird carcass and add the thinly pared rind of 1 small orange to the mixture.

Game Broth

SERVES 4–6

Game Carcass Stock, chilled
Salt and freshly ground black pepper
15 ml/1 tbsp chopped parsley
30 ml/2 tbsp tawny port (optional)

Remove all the fat from the stock. Reheat and season to taste. Stir in the parsley and flavour with tawny port, if liked.

Game Broth with Mushrooms

SERVES 4–6

Prepare as for Game Broth, but add 50 g/2 oz thinly sliced mushrooms to the stock before reheating and simmer for 2 minutes before seasoning.

Game Broth with Onion Croûtons

SERVES 4–6

Prepare as for Game Broth. Cut 2 slices of bread, crusts removed, into small cubes. Fry (sauté) in sunflower oil, tossing, until golden. Drain on kitchen paper (paper towels) and toss in 5 ml/1 tsp onion salt. Sprinkle on to the hot soup immediately before eating.

Game Soup

SERVES 6

Prepare as for Brown Turkey Pottage (page 59), but use a pheasant carcass instead of turkey. When cooked, purée the soup in a blender or food processor, then return to the pan, stir in 30 ml/2 tbsp port and reheat before serving.

Sparkling Pheasant Bortsch

SERVES 4–6

1 spring onion (scallion), very finely chopped
1 large cooked beetroot (red beet), grated
2 × 295 g/2 × 10½ oz/2 medium cans of condensed beef consommé
150 ml/¼ pt/⅔ cup water
100 g/4 oz/1 cup cooked pheasant, finely chopped, all skin removed
15 ml/1 tbsp white wine vinegar
60 ml/4 tbsp crème fraîche

Reserve a little of the chopped green top of the spring onion for garnish. Put the remainder in a saucepan with the beetroot, consommé, water, pheasant and vinegar. Bring to the boil and simmer gently for 5 minutes. Leave to cool, then chill. Spoon the jellied soup into cold bowls, top each with a spoonful of crème fraîche and sprinkle with the reserved spring onion before serving.

Pheasant Giblet Soup

SERVES 4–6

Prepare as for Chicken Giblet Soup (page 56), but flavour the soup with a sprig of sage and a celery stick instead of the bay leaf and parsley. After puréeing, add port instead of sherry, if liked, and colour with a little gravy block or browning before seasoning.

Light Bites

There are so many times when you need a light meal, whether it is an extra-special, tasty sandwich, a quick pan pizza or a jacket potato with a difference. Here you'll find a whole range of sumptuous ideas for nourishing snack meals, showing, yet again, how versatile poultry and game can be.

CHICKEN

Savoury Chicken Toasts

SERVES 4

75 g/3 oz button mushrooms, sliced
30 ml/2 tbsp water
30 ml/2 tbsp cornflour (cornstarch)
250 ml/8 fl oz/1 cup milk
A small knob of butter or margarine
Salt and freshly ground black pepper
15 ml/1 tbsp chopped parsley
15 ml/1 tbsp chopped thyme
175 g/6 oz/1½ cups cooked chicken, chopped, all skin removed
4 slices of bread
50 g/2 oz/½ cup Cheddar cheese, grated
Parsley sprigs, to garnish

Stew the mushrooms in the water until tender. Boil rapidly to evaporate the liquid. Blend the cornflour with a little of the milk, stir in the remaining milk and add to the pan with the butter or margarine. Bring to the boil and cook for 2 minutes, stirring all the time, until thick. Season to taste and stir in the parsley, thyme and chicken. Heat through. Toast the bread on both sides under a hot grill (broiler). Spoon the chicken mixture on top and cover with grated cheese. Return to the grill until the cheese melts and bubbles. Serve straight away, garnished with parsley sprigs.

Nutty Chicken Rarebit

SERVES 4

4 slices of bread
50 g/2 oz/½ cup Cheddar cheese, grated
75 g/3 oz/¾ cup cooked chicken, finely chopped
1 spring onion (scallion), finely chopped
50 g/2 oz/½ cup hazelnuts (filberts), chopped
15 g/½ oz/1 tbsp butter or margarine, softened
1.5 ml/¼ tsp ground cumin
Salt and freshly ground black pepper

Toast the bread on one side. Mix the remaining ingredients together well and spread over the untoasted sides of the bread. Place under a preheated grill (broiler) for 2–3 minutes until bubbling and lightly golden. Serve hot.

Chicken, Banana and Bacon Savoury

SERVES 4

4 rindless streaky bacon rashers (slices)
4 bananas, halved lengthways
40 g/1½ oz/3 tbsp butter or margarine, softened
75 g/3 oz/¾ cup Cheddar cheese, grated
75 g/3 oz/¾ cup cooked chicken, chopped, all skin removed
15 ml/1 tbsp dry vermouth
4 slices of toast, cut into triangles, to serve

Stretch the rashers with the back of a knife. Cut into halves. Wrap one half round each banana half. Grease a shallow ovenproof dish with 10 g/¼ oz/2 tsp of the butter or margarine. Arrange the wrapped bananas in the dish and dot with a further 10 g/¼ oz/2 tsp of the butter or margarine. Bake in a preheated oven at 200°C/400°F/gas mark 6 for 10 minutes. Mash together the rest of the butter or margarine and the remaining ingredients and spread over. Flash under a hot grill (broiler) until melted and bubbling. Serve with the toast triangles.

Crispy Chicken and Vegetable Rolls

MAKES 24

100 g/4 oz cabbage, shredded
1 onion, finely chopped
2 carrots, grated
100 g/4 oz/1 cup cooked chicken, finely chopped
50 g/2 oz/½ cup cooked long-grain rice
30 ml/2 tbsp soy sauce
5 ml/1 tsp light brown sugar
15 ml/1 tbsp medium-dry sherry
A pinch of ground ginger
A pinch of salt
A pinch of pepper
375 g/13 oz puff pastry (paste), thawed, if frozen
1 egg, beaten
Oil, for deep-frying

Mix together the cabbage, onion, carrots, chicken and rice in a bowl. Add the soy sauce, sugar, sherry, ginger, salt and pepper. Mix well. Roll out the pastry thinly on a floured surface to a 60 × 40 cm/24 × 16 in rectangle. Cut into 10 cm/4 in squares. Divide the filling between the centres of the pieces of pastry. Brush the edges with beaten egg. Fold in the two sides, then roll up each one in a sausage shape to enclose the filling. Heat the oil for deep-frying to 190°C/375°F or until a cube of day-old bread browns in 30 seconds. Fry (sauté) the rolls, a few at a time, until crisp and golden brown. Drain on kitchen paper (paper towels) and serve hot.

Butter Beanie

SERVES 2

425 g/15 oz/1 large can of butter (lima) beans, drained
A pinch of dried mixed herbs
A pinch of cayenne
100 g/4 oz/1 cup cooked chicken, chopped, all skin removed
Cheese Sauce (page 341)
30 ml/2 tbsp crushed cornflakes

Put the butter beans in a shallow dish. Add the herbs, cayenne and chicken and stir. Pour over the cheese sauce and sprinkle with the crushed cornflakes. Bake in a preheated oven at 190°C/375°F/gas mark 5 for about 25 minutes or until golden brown and hot through.

Quick Chicken Tikka Pizza

SERVES 1–2

100 g/4 oz/1 cup self-raising (self-rising) flour
A pinch of salt
40 g/1½ oz/3 tbsp butter or margarine
45 ml/3 tbsp tomato purée (paste)
100 g/4 oz/1 cup cooked chicken, diced, all skin removed
15 ml/1 tbsp plain yoghurt
10 ml/2 tsp curry paste
50 g/2 oz/½ cup Mozzarella cheese, grated
5 ml/1 tsp chopped coriander (cilantro)

Mix the flour and salt in a bowl. Rub in 25 g/1 oz/2 tbsp of the butter or margarine. Mix with enough water to form a soft but not sticky dough. Roll out to a round the size of the base of a medium frying pan (skillet). Heat the remaining butter or margarine in the pan and fry (sauté) the base for about 3 minutes until golden brown. Turn the base over. Spread the tomato purée on top. Mix the chicken with the yoghurt and curry paste and spread over. Sprinkle with the cheese, then the coriander. Cover with a lid or foil and cook over a gentle heat for about 10 minutes until the cheese has melted and the chicken is piping hot. Serve cut into wedges.

Quick Chicken and Pineapple Pizza

SERVES 1–2

Prepare as for Quick Chicken Tikka Pizza, but sprinkle the cooked chicken directly on top of the tomato purée (paste) and omit the yoghurt and curry paste. Scatter over 2 slices of canned pineapple, cut into small chunks. Sprinkle with 2.5 ml/½ tsp dried oregano and omit the coriander (cilantro), then add the cheese, cover and cook as before.

Chicken and Mushroom Pizza Special

SERVES 4

275 g/10 oz/1 packet of pizza base mix
60 ml/4 tbsp olive oil
1 large onion, chopped
100 g/4 oz button mushrooms, sliced
5 ml/1 tsp dried oregano
100 g/4 oz/1 cup cooked chicken, diced, all skin removed
Salt and freshly ground black pepper
225 g/8 oz/2 cups Mozzarella cheese, grated
5 ml/1 tsp capers
A few black olives

Make up the dough according to the packet directions. Place in an oiled plastic bag and leave in a warm place for about 45 minutes until doubled in size. Knead gently. Divide into quarters and roll out each to a round about 15 cm/6 in diameter. Place on two lightly oiled baking (cookie) sheets and brush with a little more oil. Cook the onion and mushrooms in the remaining oil, stirring, for 3 minutes. Stir in the oregano, chicken and some salt and pepper. Spoon over the pizza bases and top with the cheese. Garnish with the capers and olives. Bake one sheet above the other in a preheated oven at 190°C/375°F/gas mark 5 for 25 minutes, reversing the position of the baking sheets half-way through cooking. Serve hot.

Potato Pan Pizza

SERVES 4

225 g/8 oz potatoes, cut into even-sized pieces
Salt
15 g/½ oz/1 tbsp butter or margarine
75 g/3 oz/¾ cup plain (all-purpose) flour
A little milk
30 ml/2 tbsp sunflower oil
3 tomatoes, sliced
A good pinch of dried basil
100 g/4 oz/1 cup cooked chicken, chopped, all skin removed
75 g/3 oz/¾ cup Cheddar cheese, grated

Cook the potatoes in boiling salted water until tender. Drain and mash with the butter. Stir in the flour and mix with a little milk to form a firm dough. Knead gently on a lightly floured surface. Roll out to a round the size of the base of your frying pan (skillet). Heat half the oil in the pan. Add the potato base and fry (sauté) for 2 minutes until golden brown. Slide out of the pan on to a plate. Heat the remaining oil in the pan, then invert the base browned-side up. Top with the tomato slices and sprinkle the basil over. Add the chicken and top with the cheese. Cover with a lid and cook for 5 minutes over a gentle heat, then remove the lid and place the pan under a hot grill (broiler) for 2–3 minutes until the cheese is golden brown and bubbling. Serve hot cut into wedges.

Spicy Chicken and Potato Cakes

SERVES 4

225 g/8 oz potatoes, grated
1 small onion, grated
100 g/4 oz/1 cup cooked chicken, finely chopped
2.5 ml/½ tsp garam masala
1.5 ml/¼ tsp chilli powder
10 ml/2 tsp plain (all-purpose) flour
Salt and freshly ground black pepper
1 large egg, beaten
45 ml/3 tbsp sunflower oil
Shredded lettuce and mango chutney, to serve

Mix the potato with the onion, chicken and spices. Add the flour and a little salt and pepper. Mix with the egg to bind. Heat the oil in a frying pan (skillet), add spoonfuls of the mixture and fry (sauté) for about 2 minutes until golden brown underneath. Turn over and cook the other sides for 2–3 minutes until golden brown and cooked through. Drain on kitchen paper (paper towels). Serve on a bed of shredded lettuce with mango chutney.

Cheese Fondue with Chicken Bites

SERVES 4

350 g/12 oz/3 cups Cheddar cheese, grated
10 ml/2 tsp made English mustard
60 ml/4 tbsp white wine or cider
30 ml/2 tbsp milk
15 ml/1 tbsp Kirsch (optional)
16 frozen crumbed chicken bites
1 small baguette, cubed

Put all the ingredients except the chicken and bread in a saucepan or fondue pot. Heat gently, stirring, until melted. Meanwhile, grill (broil) or fry (sauté) the chicken bites according to the packet directions. Serve the fondue with the chicken and bread to dip in.

Chicken Stir-fry Sticks

Use any vegetables and salad stuffs you like.

SERVES 4

15 ml/1 tbsp sunflower oil
1 carrot, pared into ribbons with a potato peeler
1 celery stick, thinly sliced
5 cm/2 in piece of cucumber, thinly sliced
4 mushrooms, thinly sliced
2 tomatoes, chopped
½ green (bell) pepper, cut into very thin strips
1 garlic clove, crushed
75 g/3 oz/¾ cup cooked chicken, chopped, all skin removed
30 ml/2 tbsp soy sauce
A pinch of ground ginger
4 small baguettes

Heat the oil in a large frying pan (skillet) or wok. Add the prepared vegetables and stir-fry for 3 minutes. Add the chicken, soy sauce and ginger and toss for 2 minutes until piping hot. Cut along one side of each baguette and fill with the stir-fry mixture. Serve straight away.

Chicken, Mayo and Lettuce Baguette

SERVES 1

1 small baguette
Butter or margarine
75 g/3 oz/¾ cup cooked chicken, diced, all skin removed
30 ml/2 tbsp mayonnaise
Freshly ground black pepper
3 crisp lettuce leaves

Split the baguette along one edge and spread the inside with butter or margarine. Mix the chicken with the mayonnaise and season with pepper. Line the baguette with the lettuce and spoon in the chicken mixture.

Chicken, Egg and Tomato Baguette

SERVES 1

1 small baguette
Butter or margarine
1 hard-boiled (hard-cooked) egg, sliced
1 ripe tomato, sliced
50 g/2 oz/½ cup cooked chicken, chopped, all skin removed
10 ml/2 tsp mayonnaise
Freshly ground black pepper

Split the baguette along one edge and spread the inside with butter or margarine. Line with the egg slices and top with the tomato slices. Mix together the chicken and mayonnaise and spread inside. Season with pepper and serve.

Fragrant Chicken and Pesto Baguette

SERVES 1

1 small baguette
Butter or margarine
2 crisp lettuce leaves
15 ml/1 tbsp Pesto for Poultry (page 342 or use bought)
30 ml/2 tbsp mayonnaise
75 g/3 oz/¾ cup cooked chicken, chopped, all skin removed
15 ml/1 tbsp pine nuts, toasted

Split the baguette along one side and spread the inside with butter or margarine. Line with the lettuce leaves. Mix the pesto with the mayonnaise and stir in the chicken. Spread in the baguette and sprinkle with the pine nuts.

Italian Chicken Lunch

SERVES 1

7.5 cm/3 in hunk of ciabatta bread
1 or 2 thin slices of chicken breast
1 or 2 slices of Italian salami
2 slices of beefsteak tomato
4 torn basil leaves
15 ml/1 tbsp olive oil
Freshly ground black pepper

Split the bread along one side and gently open up slightly. Lay the chicken and salami in the bread. Top with the tomato slices and scatter the basil over. Drizzle with the olive oil and add a good grinding of black pepper.

Pimiento Chicken Sticks

SERVES 4

45 ml/3 tbsp plain yoghurt
15 ml/1 tbsp paprika
5 ml/1 tsp clear honey
200 g/7 oz/1 small can of pimientos, drained and chopped
175 g/6 oz/1½ cups cooked chicken, finely chopped, all skin removed
Salt and freshly ground black pepper
4 small baguettes
4 lettuce leaves

Mix the yoghurt with the paprika and honey. Stir in the pimientos and chicken and season with salt and pepper. Cut along one side of each baguette. Line with lettuce leaves, fill with the chicken mixture and serve.

Kentucky Fried Chicken Sandwich

SERVES 2

A little butter or margarine
4 slices of granary bread
2 slices of chicken breast
1 banana, sliced
2.5 ml/½ tsp ground cumin
2.5 ml/½ tsp dried onion granules
Salt and freshly ground black pepper
15 ml/1 tbsp chopped parsley

Thinly spread butter or margarine on one side of each slice of bread. Put the chicken on two of the slices, spread-sides down. Mash the banana and spread over. Mix together the cumin, onion granules, a little salt and pepper and the parsley and sprinkle over. Top with the remaining bread slices, buttered-sides up. Cook under a preheated grill (broiler), in a preheated frying pan (skillet), or in a sandwich toaster until golden on both sides. Cut into halves and serve.

Piperade with Chicken

SERVES 4

15 ml/1 tbsp olive oil
15 g/½ oz/1 tbsp butter or margarine
2 onions, sliced
2 green (bell) peppers, sliced
4 large tomatoes, quartered
1 garlic clove, crushed
100 g/4 oz/1 cup cooked chicken, diced
4 eggs, beaten
Salt and freshly ground black pepper
Crusty bread, to serve

Heat the oil and butter or margarine in a large frying pan (skillet). Add the prepared vegetables and garlic and stir-fry for 5 minutes until soft and lightly golden. Add the chicken and toss for 1 minute. Add the eggs, a little salt and lots of pepper. Cook, lifting and stirring gently, until the mixture has set. Serve straight from the pan with crusty bread.

Simple Chicken Omelette

SERVES 1

2 eggs
Salt and freshly ground black pepper
30 ml/2 tbsp water
50 g/2 oz/½ cup cooked chicken, cut into small pieces, all skin removed
A small knob of butter or 10 ml/2 tsp sunflower oil
10 ml/2 tsp chopped parsley, to garnish

Beat the eggs in a bowl with a little salt and pepper and the water. Stir in the chicken. Heat the butter or oil in a small omelette pan. When hot, pour in the egg mixture and cook, lifting and stirring gently, until the base is golden and the egg mixture is just set. Fold the omelette into three, then gently slide out of the pan on to a warm plate. Sprinkle with chopped parsley and serve straight away.

Simple Chicken and Mushroom Omelette

SERVES 1

Prepare as for Simple Chicken Omelette, but add 2 or 3 thinly sliced mushrooms with the chicken.

Simple Chicken and Prawn Omelette

SERVES 1

Prepare as for Simple Chicken Omelette, but add 30 ml/2 tbsp cooked, peeled prawns (shrimp), thawed and well drained on kitchen paper (paper towels), if frozen, with the chicken.

Simple Chicken and Chive Omelette

SERVES 1

Prepare as for Simple Chicken Omelette, but add 15 ml/1 tbsp snipped chives with the chicken and sprinkle with a few extra snipped chives instead of chopped parsley before serving.

Simple Chicken and Ham Omelette

SERVES 1

Prepare as for Simple Chicken Omelette, but use half chicken and half diced cooked ham instead of all chicken.

Chicken Soufflé Omelette

SERVES 1

2 eggs
5 ml/1 tsp lemon juice
50 g/2 oz/½ cup cooked chicken, chopped, all skin removed
Salt and white pepper
15 g/½ oz/1 tbsp butter
10 ml/2 tsp chopped parsley
Bread and butter, to serve

Separate one of the eggs. Beat the whole egg with the egg yolk. Add a little salt and pepper and stir in the chicken. Whisk the egg whites with the lemon juice until stiff. Fold into the yolk mixture with a metal spoon. Heat the butter in an omelette pan and add the egg mixture. Cook gently until the base is golden and the mixture is beginning to set. Place the pan under a preheated grill (broiler) until the top is puffy and golden and the omelette is just set. Slide out of the pan on to a plate, fold in half, if liked and sprinkle with chopped parsley before serving with bread and butter.

Chicken and Asparagus Soufflé Omelette

SERVES 1

Prepare as for Chicken Soufflé Omelette, but add 3 or 4 cooked asparagus spears, cut into short lengths, with the chicken.

Chicken and Sweetcorn Soufflé Omelette

SERVES 1

Prepare as for Chicken Soufflé Omelette, but add 30 ml/2 tbsp cooked sweetcorn (corn) with the chicken.

Chicken and Mushroom Soufflé Omelette

SERVES 1

Prepare as for Chicken Soufflé Omelette, but fry (sauté) 2 or 3 sliced button mushrooms in 15 g/½ oz/1 tbsp butter and remove from the pan. Then continue as before, adding the cooked mushrooms with the chicken.

Almost Instant Chicken Soufflé

SERVES 4

Butter or margarine, for greasing
175 g/6 oz/1½ cups cooked chicken, chopped
295 g/10½ oz/1 medium can of condensed cream of chicken soup
75 g/3 oz/¾ cup Cheddar cheese, grated
4 eggs, separated
Freshly ground black pepper

Lightly grease an 18 cm/7 in soufflé dish. Put the chicken in the base. Empty the soup into a bowl and whisk in the cheese and egg yolks. Season with pepper. Whisk the egg whites until stiff and fold in with a metal spoon. Spoon over the chicken. Bake in a preheated oven at 200°C/400°F/gas mark 6 for 25–30 minutes until well risen, golden and just set. Serve straight away.

Quick Chicken and Corn Soufflé

SERVES 4

Prepare as for Almost Instant Chicken Soufflé (page 71), but use only 100 g/4 oz/1 cup of cooked chicken and mix with 300 g/11 oz/1 medium can of creamed corn in the soufflé dish, then continue as before.

Quick Chicken and Bean Soufflé

SERVES 4

Prepare as for Almost Instant Chicken Soufflé (page 71), but put 400 g/ 14 oz/1 large can of baked beans in the base of the dish and use only 75 g/ 3 oz/¾ cup cooked chicken.

Quick Chicken and Asparagus Soufflé

SERVES 4

Prepare as for Almost Instant Chicken Soufflé (page 71), but put a drained 295 g/10½ oz/1 medium can of cut asparagus spears in the base and use only 100 g/4 oz/1 cup of cooked chicken. Substitute condensed asparagus soup for the chicken, if preferred.

Lemon Chicken Soufflé

SERVES 4

25 g/1 oz/¼ cup plain (all-purpose) flour
300 ml/½ pt/1¼ cups chicken stock
25 g/1 oz/2 tbsp butter or margarine, plus extra for greasing
4 eggs, separated
175 g/6 oz/1½ cups cooked chicken, chopped, all skin removed
Finely grated rind and juice of 1 lemon
Salt and freshly ground black pepper
15 ml/1 tbsp chopped parsley

Put the flour in a saucepan. Whisk in the stock until smooth. Add the butter or margarine. Bring to the boil and cook for 2 minutes, stirring, until very thick. Remove from the heat and cool slightly. Beat the egg yolks into the pan, then stir in the chicken and lemon rind. Season with salt and pepper and stir in the parsley. Whisk the egg whites with 5 ml/1 tsp of the lemon juice until stiff (use the remaining lemon juice for another recipe). Beat a spoonful of the egg white into the sauce mixture to slacken it slightly, then fold in the remainder with a metal spoon. Lightly grease a 1.2 litre/2 pt/5 cup soufflé dish. Spoon in the mixture. Bake in a preheated oven at 190°C/375°F/gas mark 5 for about 35 minutes until risen, golden and just set. Serve straight away.

Rosti with Chicken and Asparagus Rolls

SERVES 2

40 g/1½ oz/3 tbsp butter or margarine
450 g/1 lb potatoes, coarsely grated
1 onion, grated
1 garlic clove, crushed
Salt and freshly ground black pepper
275 g/10 oz/1 medium can of asparagus spears, drained
4 thin slices of chicken breast
Sweet pickle and tomatoes, to serve

Melt the butter or margarine in a large frying pan (skillet). Mix the potato, onion and garlic with a little salt and pepper. Add to the pan and press down well. Fry (sauté) over a moderate heat for about 8 minutes until golden brown underneath. Tip out of the pan on to a plate, then slide back in so the uncooked side is underneath. Continue cooking for a further 8–10 minutes until cooked through. Meanwhile, divide the asparagus spears between the chicken slices and roll up. Cut the rosti into quarters. Place two quarters on each of two serving plates. Put the chicken rolls to one side and serve with sweet pickle and tomatoes.

Spinach and Chicken Roulade

SERVES 4

Butter or margarine, for greasing
300 g/11 oz frozen chopped spinach, thawed
A pinch of grated nutmeg
4 eggs, separated
Salt and freshly ground black pepper
225 g/8 oz/1 medium can of chopped tomatoes, well drained
100 g/4 oz/1 cup cooked chicken, chopped, all skin removed
2.5 ml/½ tsp dried basil
30 ml/2 tbsp grated Parmesan cheese
Rolls and butter, to serve

Grease and line an 18 × 28 cm/7 × 11 in Swiss roll tin (jelly roll pan) and line with non-stick baking parchment. Squeeze the spinach well to remove excess moisture and place in a bowl. Add the nutmeg and egg yolks and beat well. Season with salt and pepper. Whisk the egg whites until stiff and fold in with a metal spoon. Turn into the prepared tin and level the surface. Bake in a preheated oven at 200°C/400°F/gas mark 6 for 20 minutes until risen, golden and just set.

Meanwhile, heat the tomatoes and chicken with the basil in a saucepan and season lightly. Place a clean sheet of baking parchment on a work surface and dust with half the Parmesan. Turn the cooked spinach mixture out on to the paper and remove the cooking paper. Spread the hot chicken mixture over and roll up from one of the short ends, using the baking parchment to help. Transfer to a warm serving dish, sprinkle with the remaining Parmesan cheese and serve hot with rolls and butter.

Quick Chinese Chicken Pittas

SERVES 4

175 g/6 oz/1½ cups cooked chicken, cut into neat pieces, all skin removed
425 g/15 oz/1 large can of stir-fry vegetables, rinsed and drained
15 ml/1 tbsp medium-dry sherry
15 ml/1 tbsp soy sauce
10 ml/2 tsp toasted sesame seeds
4 sesame seed pitta breads

Put the chicken, vegetables, sherry and soy sauce in a saucepan and heat through until piping hot, stirring all the time. Sprinkle in the sesame seeds. Warm the pitta breads either under the grill (broiler), in a toaster or in the microwave. Cut into halves and gently open up to form pockets. Fill with the chicken mixture and serve straight away.

Mustard Chicken, Carrot and Courgette Pittas

SERVES 4

60 ml/4 tbsp olive oil
30 ml/2 tbsp black mustard seeds
1 large carrot, coarsely grated
1 large courgette (zucchini), coarsely grated
175 g/6 oz/1½ cups cooked chicken, cut into small pieces, all skin removed
Lemon juice
Salt and freshly ground black pepper
4 pitta breads

Heat the oil in a large saucepan. Add the mustard seeds and cook until the seeds pop. Add the carrot, courgette and chicken. Toss over a moderate heat until piping hot. Spike with lemon juice and season with salt and pepper. Warm the pitta breads either under the grill (broiler), in a toaster or in the microwave. Gently cut a slit along one side of each pitta and open up to form a pocket. Spoon in the chicken mixture and serve straight away.

Curried Chicken and Peach Pittas

SERVES 4

5 ml/1 tsp curry paste
30 ml/2 tbsp crème fraîche
Salt and freshly ground black pepper
100 g/4 oz/1 cup cooked chicken, finely chopped, all skin removed
220 g/8 oz/1 small can of peach slices, drained and chopped
15 ml/1 tbsp chopped coriander (cilantro)
4 garlic pitta breads
4 crisp lettuce leaves

Mix together the curry paste and crème fraîche with a little salt and pepper. Stir in the chicken, peaches and coriander. Warm the pitta breads either under the grill (broiler), in a toaster or in the microwave. Gently cut a slit along one side of each pitta and open up to form a pocket. Line each with a crisp lettuce leaf, then fill with the curried chicken and peach mixture.

Chicken and Cashew Nut Pittas

SERVES 4

175 g/6 oz/1½ cups cooked chicken, diced, all skin removed
50 g/2 oz/½ cup salted cashew nuts
1 celery stick, chopped
30 ml/2 tbsp mayonnaise
5 ml/1 tsp soy sauce
100 g/4 oz black seedless grapes, halved
Salt and freshly ground black pepper
4 garlic pitta breads

Mix the chicken with the cashew nuts and celery. Mix in the mayonnaise and soy sauce, then fold in the grapes and season to taste. Warm the pitta breads either under the grill (broiler), in a toaster or in the microwave. Gently cut a slit along one side of each pitta and open up to form a pocket. Fill with the chicken mixture and serve straight away.

Chicken and Mushroom Muncher

SERVES 4

Butter or margarine
8 slices of wholemeal bread
4 slices of cooked chicken breast
215 g/7½ oz/1 small can of creamed mushrooms
A pinch of dried thyme
Freshly ground black pepper

Spread butter or margarine on one side of each bread slice. Lay a slice of chicken on four slices, buttered-side down. Top with the creamed mushrooms, thyme and a good grinding of pepper. Lay the other slices of bread on top, buttered-side up. Cook under a preheated grill (broiler), fry (sauté) in a preheated frying pan (skillet), pressing down with a fish slice during cooking, or use a sandwich toaster to cook the sandwiches until golden brown on both sides. Cut into halves and serve.

Chicken and Cress Butter Sandwiches

SERVES 4

1 bunch of watercress
75 g/3 oz/⅓ cup butter or margarine, softened
Freshly ground black pepper
¼ cucumber, thinly sliced
10 ml/2 tsp cider vinegar
8 slices of wholemeal bread
4 thin slices of chicken breast

Trim the feathery stalks off the watercress. Chop the remainder and place in a bowl. Add the butter or margarine and a good grinding of pepper and beat well. Mix the cucumber with the vinegar. Spread each slice of bread on one side with the cress butter. Top four slices with a slice of chicken breast, then drained cucumber slices. Invert the remaining bread slices on top and press together gently. Cut off the crusts, if liked, then cut into quarters diagonally. Serve straight away.

Chicken and Peanut Perfection

SERVES 4

8 slices of granary bread
Peanut butter
30 ml/2 tbsp mayonnaise
15 ml/1 tbsp redcurrant jelly (clear conserve)
100 g/4 oz/1 cup cooked chicken, chopped, all skin removed
Salt and freshly ground black pepper
4 lettuce leaves

Spread one side of each slice of bread with peanut butter. Mix together the mayonnaise and redcurrant jelly until blended. Fold in the chicken and season to taste. Spread on 4 slices of the bread and top with the lettuce leaves, then the remaining slices of bread, peanut-sides down. Cut into quarters and serve.

Thousand Island Chicken and Prawn Sandwiches

SERVES 4

75 g/3 oz cooked, peeled prawns (shrimp), thawed if frozen
8 slices of wholemeal bread
Butter or margarine
30 ml/2 tbsp mayonnaise
10 ml/2 tsp tomato ketchup (catsup)
5 ml/1 tsp Worcestershire sauce
2.5 ml/1 in piece of cucumber, finely chopped
75 g/3 oz/¾ cup cooked chicken, chopped, all skin removed
Salt and freshly ground black pepper

Drain the prawns thoroughly on kitchen paper (paper towels). Spread each slice of bread on one side with the butter or margarine. Mix the mayonnaise with the ketchup, Worcestershire sauce and cucumber. Stir in the chicken and prawns and season to taste. Spread on 4 slices of the bread and top with the remaining slices. Cut into quarters and serve.

Chicken and Avocado Coolers

SERVES 4

8 slices of granary bread
Butter or margarine
100 g/4 oz/1 cup cooked chicken, chopped, all skin removed
1 ripe avocado, peeled, stoned (pitted) and thinly sliced
5 ml/1 tsp lemon juice
Freshly ground black pepper

Spread one side of each slice of bread with butter or margarine. Top 4 slices with the chicken, then slices of avocado tossed in the lemon juice. Season well with pepper. Top with the remaining slices, cut into quarters and serve.

Chicken, Red Pepper and Chilli Sanwiches

SERVES 4

8 slices of white bread
100 g/4 oz/½ cup medium-fat soft cheese
100 g/4 oz/1 cup cooked chicken, diced, all skin removed
1 red (bell) pepper, thinly sliced
1 red onion, thinly sliced
Chilli relish

Spread one side of each slice of bread with the cheese. Top 4 of the slices with the chicken, then the pepper and onion slices. Spread the remaining slices with a little relish. Invert on to the chicken mixture. Press down lightly, cut into quarters and serve.

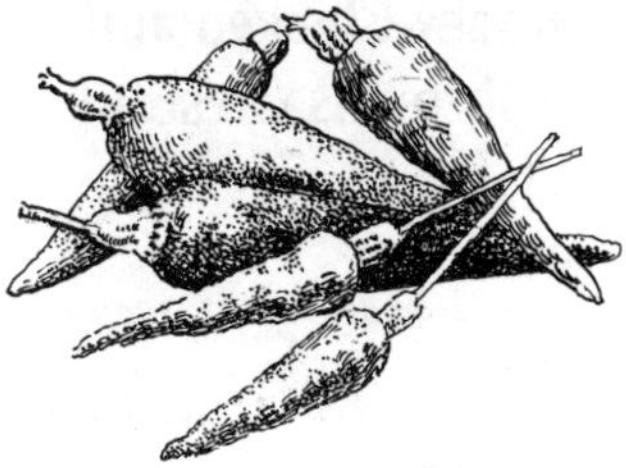

Curried Chicken and Fresh Mango Sandwiches

SERVES 4

8 slices of wholemeal bread
Butter or margarine
1 small fresh mango, peeled
30 ml/2 tbsp mayonnaise
10 ml/2 tsp curry paste
100 g/4 oz/1 cup cooked chicken, chopped, all skin removed
Salt and freshly ground black pepper

Spread one side of each slice of bread with butter or margarine. Cut all the mango flesh away from the stone (pit) and chop. Mix the mayonnaise with the curry paste. Stir in the chicken and mango. Season to taste. Spread on 4 slices of the bread and top with the remaining slices. Cut into quarters and serve.

Melting Crescents

SERVES 1

1 croissant
1 thin slice of cooked chicken breast
1 Gruyère or Emmental (Swiss) cheese slice
Tomato slices, to garnish

Split the croissant along one side. Fill with the folded chicken slice and the cheese slice. Place under a moderate grill (broiler) until the cheese melts, turning once. Serve garnished with tomato slices.

Gooey Chicken and Mushrooms Crescents

SERVES 2–4

4 croissants
215 g/7½ oz/1 small can of creamed mushrooms
4 thin slices of cooked chicken breast
8 basil leaves, torn
4 thin slices of Mozzarella cheese

Split the croissants along one side. Spread the creamed mushrooms in each. Push a slice of chicken into each croissant and add the basil and cheese. Grill (broil) under a moderate heat, turning once, until hot and the cheese has melted. Serve straight away.

Chicken and Bacon Stuffed Jackets

Cook the potatoes in the microwave, according to the manufacturer's instructions, if you prefer, and re-heat for 1–2 minutes.

SERVES 4

4 large potatoes, scrubbed
Sunflower oil
Salt and freshly ground black pepper
25 g/1 oz/2 tbsp butter or margarine
4 rindless streaky bacon rashers (slices), chopped
75 g/3 oz/¾ cup cooked chicken, diced, all skin removed
60 ml/4 tbsp crème fraîche

Scrub the potatoes, rub with oil and salt and prick all over with a fork. Place on a baking (cookie) sheet. Bake in a preheated oven at 190°C/375°F/gas mark 5 for 1 hour or until they feel soft when squeezed with an oven-gloved hand. Meanwhile, dry-fry the bacon until crisp. Cut a slice off the top of the potatoes and scoop out most of the potato into a bowl. Mash with the butter or margarine. Stir in the bacon and chicken and season with salt and pepper. Pile back into the skins and return to the oven for 10 minutes until piping hot. Serve topped with a spoonful of crème fraîche.

Chicken and Sweetcorn Jackets

SERVES 4

Prepare the potatoes as for Chicken and Bacon Stuffed Jackets, but omit the bacon and add a heated 200 g/7 oz/1 small can of drained sweetcorn (corn) to the mashed potato with the chicken.

Chicken and Chive Stuffed Jackets

SERVES 4

Prepare the potatoes as for Chicken and Bacon Stuffed Jackets, but omit the bacon and add 30 ml/2 tbsp snipped chives. Top with cottage cheese instead of crème fraîche.

Chicken, Ham and Pineapple Stuffed Jackets

SERVES 4

Prepare the potatoes as for Chicken and Bacon Stuffed Jackets, but omit the bacon and add 2 slices of canned pineapple, chopped, and 1 slice of ham, chopped.

Cooling Chicken Potato Toppers

SERVES 4

4 large potatoes
Sunflower oil
Salt and freshly ground black pepper
175 g/6 oz/¾ cup cottage cheese
100 g/4 oz/1 cup cooked chicken, chopped, all skin removed
15 ml/1 tbsp snipped chives

Scrub the potatoes, rub with oil and salt and prick all over with a fork. Either bake in a preheated oven at 190°C/375°F/gas mark 5 for 1 hour or until they feel tender when squeezed with an oven-gloved hand or cook in the microwave for about 4 minutes per potato, according to the manufacturer's instructions. Meanwhile, mix together the cheese, chicken and chives. Cut a cross in the top of each potato and squeeze gently. Place in shallow bowls. Spoon the topping over and add a good grinding of pepper.

Curried Chicken and Sultana Toppers

SERVES 4

4 large potatoes
Sunflower oil
Salt
30 ml/2 tbsp plain yoghurt
30 ml/2 tbsp mayonnaise
10 ml/2 tsp curry paste
15 ml/1 tbsp chopped coriander (cilantro)
15 ml/1 tbsp sultanas (golden raisins)
2.5 cm/1 in piece of cucumber, chopped
100 g/4 oz/1 cup cooked chicken, chopped, all skin removed

Cook the potatoes as for Cooling Chicken Potato Toppers. Meanwhile, mix together the yoghurt, mayonnaise and curry paste with the coriander, sultanas and cucumber. Mix in the chicken. Cut a cross in the top of each potato and squeeze gently. Place in bowls and top with the chicken mixture. Serve.

Mediterranean Potato Toppers

SERVES 4

4 large potatoes
Sunflower oil
Salt and freshly ground black pepper
225 g/8 oz/1 small can of chopped tomatoes
1 garlic clove, crushed
50 g/2 oz stoned (pitted) olives, sliced
4 basil leaves, chopped
100 g/4 oz/1 cup cooked chicken, chopped, all skin removed

Cook the potatoes as for Cooling Chicken Potato Toppers. Meanwhile, simmer the tomatoes with the garlic, olives and basil for 3–4 minutes until thick. Stir in the chicken and season with salt and pepper. Simmer for 2 minutes. Cut a cross in the top of each potato and squeeze gently. Spoon in the tomato filling and serve.

Chicken Livers, Bacon and Spinach

SERVES 2

225 g/8 oz chicken livers, trimmed and cut into bite-sized pieces, if necessary
25 g/1 oz/2 tbsp butter or margarine
A pinch of dried sage
Salt and freshly ground black pepper
4 back bacon rashers (slices), rinded
350 g/12 oz leaf spinach, well-washed
Crusty bread, to serve

Fry (sauté) the chicken livers in the butter or margarine with the sage for 5 minutes, stirring until just cooked and still pink. Season with salt and pepper. Meanwhile, grill (broil) the bacon until golden. Put the spinach in a saucepan and sprinkle with a little salt. Cover and cook for 5 minutes until tender. Drain and chop. Spoon the spinach on to warm plates. Spoon the chicken livers on top and put the bacon to one side. Serve with crusty bread.

Mumbled Eggs

SERVES 4

4 eggs
5 ml/1 tsp made English mustard
Salt and freshly ground black pepper
25 g/1 oz/2 tbsp butter or margarine
50 g/2 oz/¼ cup medium-fat soft cheese
25 g/1 oz button mushrooms, finely chopped
10 ml/2 tsp single (light) cream
4 slices of bread
50 g/2 oz smooth chicken liver pâté
20 ml/4 tsp chopped parsley

Beat the eggs with the mustard and a little salt and pepper. Melt the butter or margarine in a saucepan. Add the soft cheese, mushrooms and the egg mixture. Cook over a gentle heat, stirring, until the eggs are just set but still creamy. Do not allow the mixture to boil. Stir in the cream. Meanwhile, toast the bread on both sides. Spread with the pâté. Place on four warm plates and spoon the egg mixture over. Sprinkle with the chopped parsley and serve.

Speciality Chicken Liver Omelette

SERVES 4

15 ml/1 tbsp sunflower oil
1 small onion, finely chopped
1 garlic clove, crushed
100 g/4 oz chicken livers, trimmed and cut into neat strips
15 ml/1 tbsp brandy
150 ml/¼ pt/⅔ cup chicken stock
5 ml/1 tsp tomato purée (paste)
5 ml/1 tsp chopped sage
Salt and freshly ground black pepper
8 eggs
30 ml/2 tbsp single (light) cream
25 g/1 oz/2 tbsp butter or margarine
Fresh sage sprigs, to garnish

Heat the oil in a saucepan. Add the onion and garlic and fry (sauté) for 3 minutes. Add the livers and fry, stirring, for a further 2 minutes. Remove from the pan. Add the brandy, stock, tomato purée and sage. Bring to the boil and boil rapidly until reduced and syrupy. Return the onions and livers to the pan and season to taste. Keep warm over a very low heat. Beat the eggs with the cream and a little salt and pepper. Melt the butter or margarine in a large frying pan (skillet). Add the egg mixture and cook, lifting and stirring, until the omelette is golden underneath and the top almost set. Gently spread the chicken liver mixture over the egg. Fold it in thirds. Slide out on to a warm plate, cut into thick slices and serve hot, garnished with sage sprigs.

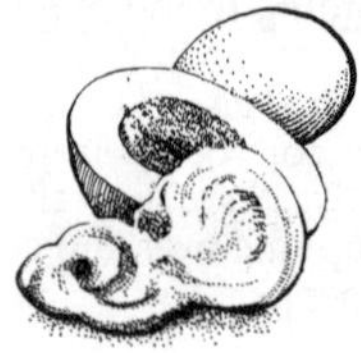

Pâté Fingers

SERVES 4

100 g/4 oz smooth chicken liver pâté
15 ml/1 tbsp brandy
1 hard-boiled (hard-cooked) egg, finely chopped
4 slices of wholemeal bread
Butter or margarine
30 ml/2 tbsp chopped parsley
15 ml/1 tbsp paprika

Beat the pâté with the brandy until smooth. Work in the egg. Toast the bread and spread with a little butter or margarine. Spread the pâté over and cut each into three fingers. Dip one end of each finger in the chopped parsley, the other in the paprika. Place on serving plates and serve straight away.

Herby Chicken Liver Toasts

SERVES 4

200 g/7 oz chicken livers
A knob of butter or margarine
5 ml/1 tsp chopped sage, plus extra to garnish
15 ml/1 tbsp chopped parsley
5 ml/1 tsp Worcestershire sauce
Salt and freshly ground black pepper
4 slices of granary bread, toasted

Trim any membranes from the livers and cut into bite-sized pieces. Melt the butter or margarine in a saucepan. Add the livers and toss over a gentle heat for 4–5 minutes until tender and just cooked. Do not overcook. Stir in the herbs, Worcestershire sauce, a little salt and lots of pepper. Pile on to the toast and sprinkle with a little extra chopped parsley before serving.

Chicken Liver Jackets

To cook the potatoes quicker, thread them on metal skewers to conduct the heat to their centres. Check for tenderness after 40 minutes.

SERVES 4

4 good-sized potatoes, scrubbed
Sunflower oil
Salt and freshly ground black pepper
75 g/3 oz/⅓ cup butter or margarine
30 ml/2 tbsp chopped parsley
8 chicken livers, trimmed

Rub the skins of the potatoes with a little oil, sprinkle with salt and prick all over with a fork. Place on a baking (cookie) sheet. Bake in a preheated oven at 190°C/375°F/gas mark 5 for about 1 hour or until tender when gently squeezed with an oven-gloved hand. Cut a slice lengthways off the top of each potato. Scoop out most of the flesh into a bowl. Mash well with the butter or margarine and a little seasoning, then work in the parsley. Pack about a third of the potato back into the shells. Put 2 chicken livers in each, season lightly, then pack the remaining potato on top. Rough up with a fork. Place on a baking sheet and bake for a further 30 minutes until golden on top.

Pâté Crunch

SERVES 4

4 small baguettes
100 g/4 oz smooth chicken liver pâté
100 g/4 oz/½ cup medium-fat soft cheese
15 ml/1 tbsp sunflower seeds
1 celery stick, finely chopped
5 cm/2 in piece of cucumber, sliced
2 tomatoes, sliced
Mustard and cress, to garnish

Cut along one edge of each baguette. Mash together the pâté, cheese, sunflower seeds and celery and spread in the baguettes. Fill with slices of cucumber and tomato and garnish with mustard and cress.

TURKEY

Californian Dreams

MAKES 30

15 stuffed green olives
15 ready-to eat prunes, stoned (pitted)
450 g/1 lb turkey sausages
50 g/2 oz/1 cup breadcrumbs
15 ml/1 tbsp paprika
1 egg, beaten
Oil, for deep-frying

Push an olive into the stone cavity of each prune. Skin the sausages and knead into a large sausage shape. Cut into 15 equal pieces and flatten each piece. Put a stuffed prune in the centre and wrap the sausagemeat around. Mix the breadcrumbs with the paprika. Roll the sausage balls in the egg, then in the breadcrumb mix to coat completely. Deep-fry for 8 minutes until cooked through and golden brown. Drain on kitchen paper (paper towels). Leave to cool. Cut into halves to serve.

Turkey Dogs

SERVES 2 OR 4

4 turkey sausages
1 onion, thinly sliced
15 g/½ oz/1 tbsp butter or margarine
2.5 ml/½ tsp chopped sage
4 finger rolls, split along one side
Tomato ketchup (catsup) and Dijon mustard, to serve

Grill (broil) or fry (sauté) the sausages until golden brown all over and cooked through. Drain on kitchen paper (paper towels). Meanwhile, cook the onion in the butter or margarine for about 5 minutes until soft and lightly golden. Stir in the sage and cook for a further minute. Warm the rolls either in the oven or the microwave. Put a sausage in each roll, top with the herby onions, a little ketchup and some Dijon mustard and serve very hot.

Super Sausage Rolls

MAKES 8

350 g/12 oz shortcrust pastry (basic pie crust)
Tomato relish
A little plain (all-purpose) flour
450 g/1 lb turkey sausages, skinned
Beaten egg, to glaze

Roll out the pastry to a 46 × 18 cm/18 × 7 in rectangle. Spread with tomato relish to within 2.5 cm/1 in of the long edge but right out to the shorter sides. With floured hands, shape the turkey sausagemeat into a 46 cm/18 in long roll. Place on the centre of the pastry. Brush the long edges of the pastry with water. Fold over the sausagemeat and press the long edges together to seal. Crimp between the finger and thumb. Cut into eight pieces and transfer to a baking (cookie) sheet. Brush with beaten egg to glaze. Bake in a preheated oven at 200°C/400°F/gas mark 6 for 30 minutes until the pastry is golden and the sausage is cooked. Serve hot or cold.

Turkey and Cranberry Sausage Rolls

MAKES 8

Prepare as for Super Sausage Rolls, but substitute cranberry sauce for the tomato relish and sprinkle it with 5 ml/1 tsp dried thyme before adding the sausagemeat.

Corny Turkey Sausage Rolls

MAKES 8

Prepare as for Super Sausage Rolls, but substitute corn relish for the tomato relish.

Cheese and Pickle Sausage Rolls

MAKES 8

Prepare as for Super Sausage Rolls, but substitute sweet sandwich pickle for the tomato relish and top with 75 g/ 3 oz/¾ cup strong Cheddar cheese, grated, before adding the sausagemeat.

Creamy Sausage and Mushroom Rolls

MAKES 8

Prepare as for Super Sausage Rolls, but spread the pastry with 185 g/6½ oz/ 1 small can of creamed mushrooms instead of the tomato relish and sprinkle with 5 ml/1 tsp dried oregano before adding the sausagemeat.

Crispy Turkey Rolls

MAKES 24

Prepare as for Crispy Chicken and Vegetable Rolls (page 66), but substitute cooked turkey for the chicken, shredded Brussels sprouts for the cabbage and chopped cooked Chinese egg noodles for the rice.

New Age BLTs

SERVES 2

4 slices of granary bread
Butter or margarine
4 turkey rashers (slices)
20 ml/4 tsp mayonnaise
1 large tomato, sliced
A few crisp lettuce leaves
Freshly ground black pepper

Spread the bread with butter or margarine. Grill (broil) or dry-fry the turkey rashers until crisp. Spread the mayonnaise on two slices of the bread. Top with the turkey rashers, cut to fit, then the tomato slices and some lettuce. Top with the remaining slices of bread. Cut into halves and serve straight away.

Avocado Rasher Grills

SERVES 4

4 turkey rashers (slices)
40 g/1½ oz/3 tbsp butter or margarine
4 long crusty rolls
2 ripe avocados, peeled, stoned (pitted) and sliced
10 ml/2 tbsp lemon juice
Dijon mustard
100 g/4 oz/1 cup Red Leicester cheese, grated
100 g/4 oz/1 cup mature Cheddar cheese, grated

Fry (sauté) the turkey rashers in half the butter or margarine until crisp. Meanwhile, split the rolls and open out flat. Toast the cut sides under the grill (broiler). Spread with the remaining butter or margarine. Toss the avocado slices in the lemon juice. Lay on the toasted sides of the rolls. Mash the mustard with the cheeses and spread over. Place under a hot grill (broiler) until melted. Top each with a chopped turkey rasher and serve hot.

Quick Macaroni Supper

SERVES 2

4 turkey rashers (slices)
100 g/4 oz quick-cook macaroni
100 g/4 oz/1 cup Shropshire Blue cheese, crumbled
25 g/1 oz/2 tbsp butter or margarine
10 ml/2 tsp Worcestershire sauce
Salt and freshly ground black pepper
1 tomato and a 2.5 cm/1 in piece of cucumber, chopped, to garnish

Grill (broil) or fry (sauté) the turkey rashers until fairly crisp. Cut into pieces. Meanwhile, cook the macaroni according to the packet directions. Drain and return to the pan. Stir in the turkey rashers, cheese, butter or margarine, Worcestershire sauce and a little seasoning and toss until the cheese and fat melt and the mixture is creamy. Pile on to warm plates and top with the chopped tomato and cucumber. Serve straight away.

Savoury Turkey Toasts

SERVES 2

Prepare as for Savoury Chicken Toasts (page 65), but substitute turkey for the chicken and spread each slice of toast with 5 ml/1 tsp cranberry sauce before adding the topping.

Turkey and Cranberry Toastie

SERVES 1

A little butter or margarine
2 slices of wholemeal bread
1 slice of turkey breast
10 ml/2 tsp cranberry sauce
15 ml/1 tbsp medium-fat soft cheese
15 ml/1 tbsp chopped parsley
A good pinch of dried thyme
Salt and freshly ground black pepper

Thinly spread butter or margarine on one side of each slice of bread. Put one slice, buttered-side down, on a board. Lay the turkey breast on top. Mash the cranberry sauce with the cheese, parsley, thyme and a little salt and pepper and spread on top of the turkey. Place the second slice of bread on top, buttered-side out. Cook under a preheated grill (broiler), in a preheated frying pan (skillet), or in a sandwich toaster until golden brown on both sides. Cut in half and serve hot.

Turkey Tartare Sandwiches

SERVES 4

40 g/1½ oz/3 tbsp butter or margarine, softened
50 g/2 oz/¼ cup medium-fat soft cheese
45 ml/3 tbsp tartare sauce from a jar
8 slices of wholemeal bread
100 g/4 oz/1 cup cooked turkey, chopped, all skin removed
Freshly ground black pepper

Mash the butter or margarine with the cheese and tartare sauce. Spread on one side of each slice of bread. Top 4 slices with a little of the cooked turkey and season with pepper. Invert the remaining slices of bread over and press together gently. Cut off the crusts, if preferred, then cut into quarters.

Piquant Turkey Specials

SERVES 4

8 slices of white bread
Butter or margarine
4 slices of turkey breast
4 cocktail gherkins (cornichons), chopped
1 tomato, finely chopped
8 fresh basil leaves, torn
Freshly ground black pepper

Spread the bread with butter or margarine. Lay a slice of turkey on 4 of the slices of bread. Top with the gherkins and tomato. Scatter the basil leaves over and season with a good grinding of pepper. Top with the remaining slices of bread, cut into quarters, and serve.

Turkey Mayo Sandwiches

SERVES 4

4 slices of wholemeal bread
4 slices of white bread
Butter or margarine
100 g/4 oz/1 cup cooked turkey, chopped, all skin removed
30 ml/2 tbsp mayonnaise
5 ml/1 tsp Dijon mustard
Salt and freshly ground black pepper
4 crisp lettuce leaves

Spread one side of each slice of bread with butter or margarine. Mix the turkey with the mayonnaise and mustard and season to taste. Spread on the wholemeal slices of bread. Top with the lettuce leaves, then the white slices. Cut into quarters and serve.

Chilli Turkey Sandwiches

SERVES 4

8 slices of wholemeal bread
Butter or margarine
100 g/4 oz/1 cup cooked turkey, chopped, all skin removed
2.5 cm/1 in piece of cucumber, finely chopped
30 ml/2 tbsp chilli relish
30 ml/2 tbsp mayonnaise
A few drops of Tabasco sauce

Spread one side of each slice of bread with butter or margarine. Mix the turkey with the cucumber, relish and mayonnaise. Add a few drops of Tabasco sauce. Spread over 4 slices of bread and top with the remaining slices. Cut into quarters and serve.

Creamy Cheese and Turkey Fruity

SERVES 4

8 slices of wholemeal bread
100 g/4 oz/½ cup medium-fat soft cheese
100 g/4 oz/1 cup cooked turkey, chopped, all skin removed
1 spring onion (scallion), chopped
6 ready-to-eat dried apricots, chopped
Freshly ground black pepper

Spread the bread with the cheese. Top four slices with turkey, then the spring onion, then the apricots. Season with pepper and top with the remaining slices, cheese-sides down. Cut into quarters and serve.

Bean and Sausage Toppers

SERVES 4

4 large potatoes
Sunflower oil
Salt
4 turkey sausages
400 g/14 oz/1 large can of baked beans
10 ml/2 tsp brown table sauce

Cook the potatoes as for Cooling Chicken Potato Toppers (page 77). Meanwhile, grill (broil) or fry (sauté) the sausages until golden brown and cooked through. Cut into small chunks. Heat the beans and stir in the sausages. Cut a cross in the top of each potato and squeeze gently. Spoon the beans and sausages over and top with a little brown sauce.

Ravishing Rasher Toppers

SERVES 4

4 large potatoes
Sunflower oil
Salt and freshly ground black pepper
4 turkey rashers (slices)
60 ml/4 tbsp soured (dairy sour) cream
2 spring onions (scallions), finely chopped
1 tomato, finely chopped

Cook the potatoes as for Cooling Chicken Potato Toppers (page 77). Meanwhile, fry (sauté) or grill (broil) the turkey rashers. Cut into small pieces. Mix with the soured cream, most of the spring onions, the tomato and a little salt and pepper. Cut a cross in the top of each potato and squeeze gently. Spoon in the topping and sprinkle with the reserved spring onions.

Turkey and Cranberry Toppers

SERVES 4

4 large potatoes
Sunflower oil
Salt and freshly ground black pepper
45 ml/3 tbsp mayonnaise
15 ml/1 tbsp cranberry sauce
50 g/2 oz cooked stuffing, chopped
100 g/4 oz/1 cup turkey, chopped, all skin removed
Chopped parsley, to garnish

Cook the potatoes as for Cooling Chicken Potato Toppers (page 77). Meanwhile, mix together the mayonnaise, cranberry sauce, stuffing and turkey. Season with salt and pepper. Cut a cross in the top of each potato and squeeze gently. Top with the turkey mixture and sprinkle with parsley.

Turkey and Stuffing Jackets

SERVES 4

4 large potatoes, scrubbed
Sunflower oil
Salt
25 g/1 oz/2 tbsp butter or margarine
75 g/3 oz/¾ cup cooked turkey, chopped, all skin removed
15 ml/1 tbsp cooked stuffing, chopped
Salt and freshly ground black pepper
20 ml/4 tsp redcurrant jelly (clear conserve)

Prick the potatoes all over and rub the skins with oil and salt. Place on a baking (cookie) sheet. Bake in a preheated oven at 190°C/375°F/gas mark 5 for 1 hour or until soft when squeezed with an oven-gloved hand. Cut a slice off the top of each potato and scoop out most of the potato into a bowl. Mash with the butter or margarine. Stir in the turkey and stuffing and season to taste. Pile back into the skins and return to the oven for 10 minutes. Top each with 5 ml/1 tsp redcurrant jelly and serve hot.

Cheesy Turkey Jackets

SERVES 4

Prepare as for Turkey and Stuffing Jackets, but omit the stuffing and stir 75 g/3 oz/¾ cup Cheddar cheese, grated, into the mixture. Then continue as before but top with sweet pickle instead of redcurrant jelly.

Curried Jackets

SERVES 4

Prepare as for Turkey and Stuffing Jackets, but omit the stuffing. Mash in 5–10 ml/1–2 tsp curry paste (or to taste) and 5 ml/1 tsp chopped coriander (cilantro). Top with mango chutney instead of redcurrant jelly.

Turkey and Kidney Bean Jackets

SERVES 4

Prepare as for Turkey and Stuffing Jackets, but omit the stuffing and redcurrant jelly and flavour the potato with chilli sauce, to taste. Stir in a drained 225 g/8 oz/1 small can of red kidney beans and a chopped spring onion (scallion). Top with 50 g/2 oz/½ cup Cheddar cheese, grated. Reheat as before.

Fast Macaroni Supper

SERVES 4

100 g/4 oz quick-cook macaroni
1 onion, chopped
1 small green (bell) pepper, chopped
25 g/1 oz/2 tbsp butter or margarine
100 g/4 oz/1 cup cooked turkey, chopped, all skin removed
4 eggs, beaten
Salt and freshly ground black pepper
3 tomatoes, sliced
15 ml/1 tbsp Worcestershire sauce
50 g/2 oz/½ cup Cheddar cheese, grated

Cook the macaroni according to the packet directions. Drain. Cook the onion and pepper in the butter or margarine for 3 minutes until softened. Stir in the turkey and cook, stirring, for 30 seconds. Season the eggs with salt and pepper and stir into the macaroni with the turkey mixture. Pour into a frying pan (skillet). Cook, lifting and stirring gently, until the omelette is golden brown underneath and almost set. Lay the tomato slices over the surface and drizzle with the Worcestershire sauce. Sprinkle evenly with the cheese. Place the pan under a preheated grill (broiler) until the cheese melts and bubbles. Serve straight away.

Turkey and Corn Scotch Pancakes

SERVES 4

90 ml/6 tbsp self-raising (self-rising) wholemeal flour
5 ml/1 tsp baking powder
2.5 ml/½ tsp garlic salt
Freshly ground black pepper
150 ml/¼ pt/⅔ cup plain yoghurt
3 eggs, separated
200 g/7 oz/1 small can of sweetcorn (corn) with (bell) peppers, drained
100 g/4 oz/1 cup cooked turkey, chopped, all skin removed
Sunflower oil, for shallow-frying
15 ml/1 tbsp snipped chives

Mix together the flour, baking powder, garlic salt and some pepper in a bowl. Add the yoghurt and egg yolks and mix until smooth. Stir in the corn and the turkey. Whisk the egg whites until stiff and fold in with a metal spoon. Heat a little oil in a large heavy frying pan (skillet). Pour off the excess. Drop spoonfuls of the mixture into the pan and fry (sauté) until golden underneath. Flip over and cook the other sides. Slide on to a warm plate and keep warm while cooking the remainder. Serve hot garnished with the chives.

Turkey Stuffed Pizzas

SERVES 4

2 pizza base mixes
225 g/8 oz/1 small can of chopped tomatoes, drained, reserving the juice
50 g/2 oz cooked French (green) beans, cut into small pieces
100 g/4 oz/1 cup cooked turkey, chopped, all skin removed
3 button mushrooms, thinly sliced
10 ml/2 tsp capers
60 ml/4 tbsp grated Mozzarella cheese
Salt and freshly ground black pepper
5 ml/1 tsp dried oregano
A little olive oil
Passata (sieved tomatoes)
2.5 ml/½ tsp dried basil
Grated Parmesan cheese, to serve

Make up the pizza dough and knead into one ball. Divide the dough into quarters. Roll out each piece to a 20 cm/8 in round. Divide the tomatoes, beans, turkey, mushrooms and capers between the centres of the rounds. Add the cheese and season with a little salt and pepper and the oregano. Brush all round the edges with water. Draw the dough up over the filling and press the edges well together to seal. Place sealed-sides down on an oiled baking (cookie) sheet. Brush with a little more oil. Bake in a preheated oven at 200°C/400°F/gas mark 6 for about 20 minutes until golden and cooked through. Meanwhile, make up the reserved tomato juice to 300 ml/½ pt/1¼ cups with passata. Add the basil. Heat through. Transfer the stuffed pizzas to warm plates. Spoon the passata over and sprinkle with grated Parmesan cheese before serving.

DUCK

Duck and Apple Sandwiches

SERVES 4

25 g/1 oz/2 tbsp butter or margarine, softened
5 ml/1 tsp dried sage
8 slices of granary bread
100 g/4 oz/1 cup cooked duck, finely chopped
30 ml/2 tbsp apple sauce
30 ml/2 tbsp mayonnaise
Salt and freshly ground black pepper

Mash the butter or margarine with the sage and spread thinly on one side of each slice of bread. Mix together the remaining ingredients and spread on 4 of the slices. Top with the remaining slices. Cut into triangles and serve.

GAME

Pheasant Mimosa

SERVES 4

4 hard-boiled (hard-cooked) eggs
100 g/4 oz/1 cup cooked pheasant, chopped, all skin removed
2 tomatoes, sliced
5 ml/1 tsp chopped basil
Salt and freshly ground black pepper
Cheese Sauce (page 341)
4 slices of granary bread
Butter or margarine

Shell the eggs, halve, remove the yolks and slice the whites. Place the egg whites in the base of a small ovenproof dish. Top with the pheasant and tomato slices and sprinkle with the basil. Season lightly. Spoon the Cheese Sauce over. Bake in a preheated oven at 200°C/400°F/gas mark 6 for 15–20 minutes until piping hot through and golden on top. Meanwhile toast the bread and spread with a little butter or margarine. Place the toast on four warm plates and spoon the baked mixture over. Pass the egg yolks through a sieve (strainer) over the top and serve hot.

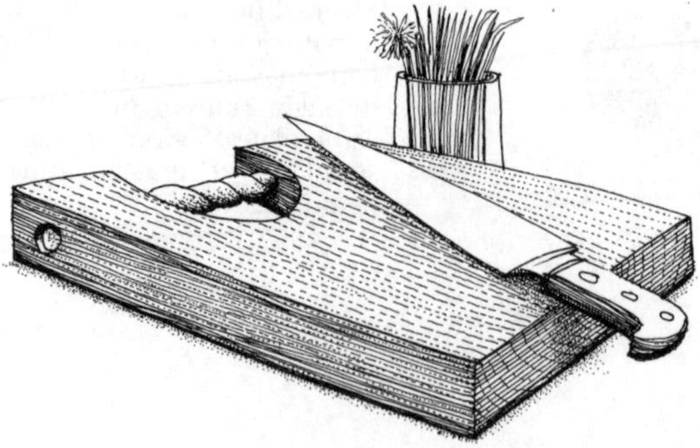

Pan-fried Specials

Chicken and all poultry is so easy to cook, it lends itself perfectly to being thrown in a frying pan (skillet) with any number of other exciting ingredients. It always produces quick, nutritious and mouth-watering meals, perfect for everyday eating or special occasions. For best results, use a good quality, heavy-based pan, preferably with a non-stick coating.

CHICKEN

Gorgeous Glazed Chicken

SERVES 4

4 skinless chicken breasts, about 175 g/6 oz each
25 g/1 oz/2 tbsp butter or margarine
120 ml/4 fl oz/½ cup dry vermouth
Salt and freshly ground black pepper
15 ml/1 tbsp chopped parsley
Speciality Creamed Potatoes (page 348) and French (green) beans, to serve

Brown the chicken breasts on both sides in the butter or margarine in a large frying pan (skillet). Add the vermouth and a little salt and pepper and cook for about 15–20 minutes, turning the chicken once during cooking, until the chicken is cooked through and stickily glazed. Throw in the parsley after 10 minutes cooking. Serve with Speciality Creamed Potatoes and French beans.

Creamy Cardamom Chicken

SERVES 4

4 skinless chicken breasts
Salt and freshly ground black pepper
50 g/2 oz/¼ cup butter or margarine
1 green (bell) pepper, thinly sliced
8 green cardamom pods, split
150 ml/¼ pt/⅔ cup dry white wine
5 ml/1 tsp soy sauce
300 ml/½ pt/1¼ cups crème fraîche
Watercress, to garnish
Wild Rice Mix (page 352), to serve

Season the chicken with salt and pepper. Fry (sauté) in the butter or margarine, turning occasionally, for about 20 minutes until cooked through. Remove from the pan and keep warm. Fry the pepper and cardamom pods in the pan for 2 minutes. Add the wine and stir, scraping up the sediment. Simmer until well reduced. Add the soy sauce and crème fraîche and cook for about 5 minutes until thickened. Taste and re-season, if necessary. Spoon over the chicken and garnish with watercress. Serve with Wild Rice Mix.

Spiced Creamy Chicken with Brandy

SERVES 4

50 g/2 oz/¼ cup butter or margarine
1.5 kg/3 lb oven-ready chicken, cut into 8 pieces (page 15)
2 onions, sliced
15 ml/1 tbsp curry powder
Salt and freshly ground black pepper
30 ml/2 tbsp plain (all-purpose) flour
60 ml/4 tbsp brandy
250 ml/8 fl oz/1 cup crème fraîche
15 ml/1 tbsp chopped mint
Buttered tagliatelle and a cucumber and tomato salad, to serve

Melt the butter or margarine in a frying pan (skillet). Add the chicken and brown all over. Remove from the pan. Add the onions and fry (sauté) for 2 minutes, stirring. Stir in the curry powder and cook for 1 minute. Return the chicken to the pan and season with salt and pepper. Cover with a lid or foil and cook gently for 30 minutes. Remove the chicken from the pan and keep warm. Stir the flour into the pan and cook for 1 minute. Blend in the brandy and crème fraîche and simmer for 3 minutes, stirring. Taste and re-season. Return the chicken to the pan, cover and simmer for a further 10 minutes. Transfer to warm serving plates, sprinkle with the mint and serve with buttered tagliatelle and a cucumber and tomato salad.

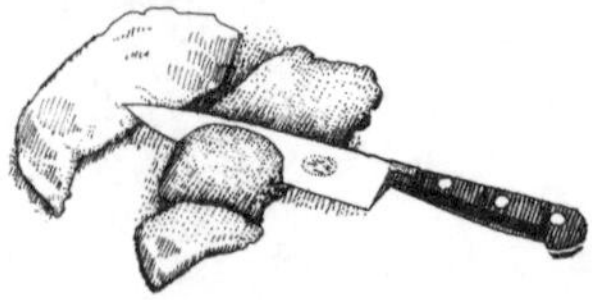

Scarborough Fair Chicken

SERVES 4

4 skinless chicken breasts
50 g/2 oz/¼ cup butter or margarine
1 garlic clove, crushed
15 ml/1 tbsp chopped parsley
5 ml/1 tsp chopped sage
10 ml/2 tsp chopped rosemary
5 ml/1 tsp chopped thyme
Salt and freshly ground black pepper
30 ml/2 tbsp white wine
150 ml/¼ pt/⅔ cup chicken stock
Speciality Creamed Potatoes (page 348) and French (green) beans, to serve

Wipe the chicken. Melt the butter or margarine in a large frying pan (skillet). Add the chicken and brown for 3 minutes. Turn over, add the garlic, herbs and a little salt and pepper and fry (sauté) for about 12 minutes, turning once or twice, until cooked through. Lift out of the pan and keep warm. Add the wine and stock. Bring to the boil and simmer, stirring, until slightly reduced and thickened. Transfer the chicken to warm serving plates. Spoon the pan juices over and serve hot with Speciality Creamed Potatoes and French beans.

Devils and Angels

SERVES 4

1.5 kg/3 lb ready-cooked chicken
50 g/2 oz/¼ cup butter or margarine
15 ml/1 tbsp Worcestershire sauce
15 ml/1 tbsp tomato ketchup (catsup)
5 ml/1 tsp soy sauce
2.5 ml/½ tsp anchovy essence (extract)
1.5 ml/¼ tsp made English mustard
A few drops of Tabasco sauce
Quick Béchamel Sauce (page 340)
4 rinded streaky bacon rashers (slices)
8 cherry tomatoes, halved
Chopped parsley, to garnish
Crusty bread and a green salad, to serve

Cut the legs off the chicken at the thigh joint and cut each into two pieces. Melt 15 ml/½ oz/1 tbsp of the butter or margarine in a frying pan (skillet) and stir in the Worcestershire sauce, ketchup, soy sauce, anchovy essence, mustard and a few drops of Tabasco sauce. Remove from the heat. Add the chicken legs and thighs and turn to coat completely in the mixture. Leave to marinate for 1 hour. Meanwhile, cut all the remaining meat off the carcass, discarding the skin. Cut into neat pieces and place in a saucepan with the Quick Béchamel Sauce. Heat through and keep hot. Stretch the bacon rashers with the back of a knife. Cut into halves and roll up. Heat the remaining butter or margarine in a frying pan (skillet) and fry (sauté) the bacon and tomatoes until cooked through, turning once. Place the pan of chicken legs and thighs over a high heat and fry until piping hot, turning and basting in the marinade until glazed. Pile the white chicken mixture in the centre of a large serving dish. Put the legs round the edge. Garnish with the bacon rolls and fried tomatoes and sprinkle with chopped parsley. Serve hot with crusty bread and a green salad.

Normandy Chicken

SERVES 4

75 g/3 oz/⅓ cup unsalted (sweet) butter
2 onions, thinly sliced
4 skinless chicken breasts
Salt and freshly ground black pepper
15 ml/1 tbsp plain (all-purpose) flour
10 ml/2 tsp curry powder
60 ml/4 tbsp water
60 ml/4 tbsp calvados
300 ml/½ pt/1¼ cups crème fraîche
1 green eating (dessert) apple, cored and cut into 4 rings
Chopped parsley, to garnish
French bread and a green salad, to serve

Melt 50 g/2 oz/¼ cup of the butter in a large heavy-based frying pan (skillet). Add the onions and chicken breasts. Season well. Brown quickly, then reduce the heat. Cover and cook gently for 15 minutes until the chicken and onions are tender. Transfer to a warmed dish with a draining spoon and keep warm. Blend together the flour, curry powder, water and calvados and stir into the pan juices. Stir in the crème fraîche and bring to the boil, stirring. Return the chicken and onions to the pan, cover and simmer for 10 minutes. Meanwhile, fry (sauté) the apple rings in the remaining butter until browned on both sides but still holding their shape. Transfer the chicken and sauce to warm plates. Put the apple rings to one side and sprinkle with parsley. Serve with lots of French bread and a green salad.

Bubble and Squeak Special

This is traditionally a leftover dish. To make sure you can make it, cook extra potatoes and cabbage when you have planned to serve them, then put to one side before dishing up so they don't get eaten anyway!

SERVES 4

450 g/1 lb cooked potatoes, chopped
225 g/8 oz cooked cabbage, chopped
Salt and freshly ground black pepper
50 g/2 oz/¼ cup butter or margarine
30 ml/2 tbsp sunflower oil
1 onion, chopped
100 g/4 oz/1 cup cooked chicken, roughly chopped, all skin removed
400 g/14 oz/1 large can of baked beans
10 ml/2 tsp Worcestershire sauce
15 ml/1 tbsp chopped parsley

Mix together the potatoes and cabbage and season well. Heat half the butter or margarine and all the oil in a large non-stick frying pan (skillet). Add the potato mixture and press down well. Fry (sauté) for about 10 minutes until richly brown and crisp underneath. Carefully slide out of the pan, invert into the pan and continue to fry for 5–10 minutes until the other side is well browned. Meanwhile, heat the remaining butter or margarine in a saucepan. Add the onion and cook gently for 4 minutes. Add the chicken, beans and Worcestershire sauce and heat gently for about 5 minutes, stirring, until piping hot. Spoon on to warm plates. Cut the bubble and squeak into quarters and place on top of the chicken mixture. Sprinkle with the parsley and serve piping hot.

Baby Chicken Fillets with Cognac

SERVES 4

700 g/1½ lb baby chicken fillets
30 ml/2 tbsp coarsely crushed black pepper
1.5 ml/¼ tsp salt
50 g/2 oz/¼ cup unsalted (sweet) butter
2 garlic cloves, crushed
60 ml/4 tbsp cognac
Speciality Creamed Potatoes (page 348) and broccoli, to serve

Coat the chicken fillets in the pepper and salt. Fry (sauté) them quickly in the butter with the garlic added for about 5 minutes until cooked through. Add the cognac to the pan and set alight. Shake the pan until the flames subside. Serve straight from the pan with Speciality Creamed Potatoes and broccoli.

Chicken Cordon Bleu

SERVES 4

4 skinless chicken breasts,
25 g/1 oz/2 tbsp butter or margarine
30 ml/2 tbsp sunflower oil
15 ml/1 tbsp chopped parsley
4 slices of ham
8 mushrooms, sliced
150 ml/¼ pt/⅔ cup chicken stock
4 slices of any quick-melting cheese
Super Sauté Potatoes with Garlic (page 349) and French (green) beans, to serve

Fry (sauté) the chicken in the butter or margarine and oil on each side to brown. Top each with a little parsley, a slice of ham and the mushrooms. Pour the stock around. Cover and simmer gently for 10 minutes until cooked through. Top each chicken breast with a slice of cheese. Cover and continue cooking until the cheese melts. Transfer the chicken to warm plates. Boil the liquid rapidly until well reduced and spoon over. Serve straight away with Super Sauté Potatoes with Garlic and French beans.

Simple Fried Chicken

SERVES 4

4 chicken portions
Milk
30 ml/2 tbsp plain (all-purpose) flour
Salt and freshly ground black pepper
75 g/3 oz/⅓ cup butter or margarine
30 ml/2 tbsp olive oil
15 ml/1 tbsp lemon juice
30 ml/2 tbsp chopped parsley
Super Sauté Potatoes (page 349) and a crisp salad, to serve

Wipe the chicken with kitchen paper (paper towels). Dip in milk. Mix the flour with a little salt and pepper and use to coat the chicken. Melt half the butter or margarine and all the oil in a large frying pan (skillet). Fry (sauté) the chicken on all sides to brown. With the skin sides up, cover the pan, reduce the heat and cook gently for about 20 minutes until the chicken is tender and cooked through. Transfer to warm serving plates. Add the remaining butter or margarine, the lemon juice and parsley to the pan and heat, stirring, until the fat has melted. Season lightly. Spoon over the chicken and serve straight away with Super Sauté Potatoes and a crisp salad.

Garlic Fried Chicken

SERVES 4

Prepare as for Simple Fried Chicken, but add 1 or 2 finely chopped garlic cloves to the browned chicken before covering and finishing cooking.

Fragrant Fried Chicken

SERVES 4

Prepare as for Simple Fried Chicken, but add 15 ml/1 tbsp chopped basil and 10 ml/2 tsp chopped sage with the parsley.

Spicy Fried Chicken

SERVES 4

Prepare as for Simple Fried Chicken (page 91), but add 2.5 ml/½ tsp chilli powder to the seasoned flour and add a seeded and chopped green chilli with the parsley. Serve with tomato relish on the side.

Fried Chicken Kiev

SERVES 4

100 g/4 oz/½ cup butter or margarine, softened
2 garlic cloves, crushed
30 ml/2 tbsp chopped parsley
Finely grated rind and juice of ½ lemon
Freshly ground black pepper
4 part-boned chicken breasts
25 g/1 oz/¼ cup plain (all-purpose) flour
1 egg, beaten
100 g/4 oz/2 cups white breadcrumbs
Oil, for deep-frying
Plain Boiled Rice (page 351) and broccoli, to serve.

Mash the butter or margarine with the garlic, parsley, lemon rind and juice and some black pepper. Wrap in greaseproof (waxed) paper and chill for at least 30 minutes until firm. Cut into four pieces. Wipe the chicken with kitchen paper (paper towels). Make a slit in the side of each breast and insert a piece of flavoured butter inside. Secure with wooden cocktail sticks (toothpicks). Dust with flour, then dip in the egg, then the breadcrumbs to coat completely. Chill for at least 1 hour. Heat the oil until a cube of day-old bread browns in 30 seconds. Deep-fry two kievs at a time for 15 minutes until crisp and golden. Drain on kitchen paper and keep warm while cooking the remainder. Remove the cocktail sticks before serving with Plain Boiled Rice and broccoli.

Cheesy Chicken Kiev

SERVES 4

Prepare as for Fried Chicken Kiev, but mash 75 g/3 oz/⅓ cup soft cheese with garlic and herbs with only 50 g/2 oz/¼ cup butter or margarine and omit the garlic, parsley and lemon. Continue as before.

Almond Chicken

SERVES 4

25 g/1 oz/2 tbsp butter or margarine
1 onion, finely chopped
50 g/2 oz button mushrooms, sliced
A pinch of ground ginger
A pinch of mace
A pinch of grated nutmeg
20 ml/4 tsp cornflour (cornstarch)
150 ml/¼ pt/⅔ cup chicken stock
30 ml/2 tbsp ground almonds
350 g/12 oz/3 cups cooked chicken, cut into neat pieces
150 ml/¼ pt/⅔ cup crème fraîche
1 egg
Salt and freshly ground black pepper
30 ml/2 tbsp toasted flaked (slivered) almonds
Plain Boiled Rice (page 351) and 60 ml/4 tbsp chopped parsley, to serve

Melt the butter or margarine in a frying pan (skillet). Add the onion and mushrooms and fry (sauté) for 3 minutes until lightly golden. Add the spices and cornflour and blend until smooth. Remove from the heat and stir in the stock and ground almonds. Return to the heat and bring to the boil, stirring, until thickened. Add the chicken, stir well and cook gently for 5 minutes. Beat together the crème fraîche and egg and stir into the mixture. Heat gently, stirring, until thickened but do not allow to boil again. Season well. Spoon on to warm plates, sprinkle with the flaked almonds and serve with Plain Boiled Rice with the chopped parsley stirred in.

Peppered Chicken

SERVES 4

25 g/1 oz/2 tbsp butter or margarine
4 skinless chicken breasts
1 garlic clove, crushed
100 g/4 oz button mushrooms, sliced
30 ml/2 tbsp pickled green peppercorns
30 ml/2 tbsp brandy
150 ml/¼ pt/⅔ cup dry white wine
150 ml/¼ pt/⅔ cup chicken stock
Salt
15 ml/1 tbsp cornflour (cornstarch)
30 ml/2 tbsp water
150 ml/¼ pt/⅔ cup double (heavy) cream
Speciality Creamed Potatoes (page 348) and broccoli, to serve

Melt the butter or margarine in a frying pan (skillet). Add the chicken breasts and brown all over. Add the garlic, mushrooms and peppercorns. Pour in the brandy and ignite. Shake the pan until the flames subside. Add the wine and stock and sprinkle with salt. Bring to the boil, cover, reduce the heat and simmer for about 20 minutes until the chicken is tender. Remove the chicken and keep warm. Blend the cornflour with the water and stir into the cooking juices. Bring to the boil, stirring. Add the cream and bring back to the boil, stirring all the time. Taste and add more salt, if necessary. Pour over the chicken and serve with Speciality Creamed Potatoes and broccoli.

Chicken and Ham Rolls with Pineapple Sauce

SERVES 4

4 skinless chicken breasts
4 slices of lean ham
25 g/1 oz/2 tbsp butter or margarine
1 small onion, finely chopped
1 garlic clove, crushed
75 ml/5 tbsp chicken stock
75 ml/5 tbsp medium-dry sherry
225 g/8 oz/1 small can of pineapple slices, drained, reserving the juice
10 ml/2 tsp cornflour (cornstarch)
Salt and freshly ground black pepper
2 glacé (candied) cherries, halved
Watercress, to garnish
Wild Rice Mix (page 352) and a green salad, to serve

Place the chicken breasts one at a time in a plastic bag and beat with a rolling pin or meat mallet to flatten. Remove from the bag. Place a slice of ham on each and roll up. Secure with wooden cocktail sticks (toothpicks). Melt the butter or margarine in a flameproof casserole (Dutch oven). Add the onion and garlic and fry (sauté) for 3 minutes, stirring. Add the chicken rolls and brown all over. Add the stock, sherry and 45 ml/3 tbsp of the reserved pineapple juice. Bring to the boil, reduce the heat, cover and simmer gently for 30 minutes. Remove the cocktail sticks. Keep the chicken rolls warm. Blend the cornflour with 15 ml/1 tbsp of the remaining pineapple juice. Stir into the juices in the casserole. Bring to the boil and cook for 1 minute, stirring. Taste and season with salt and pepper. Cut the chicken rolls into thick slices and arrange on warm serving plates. Spoon the sauce over. Put a pineapple slice to one side with half a glacé cherry in the centre of each and garnish with watercress. Serve hot with Wild Rice Mix and a green salad.

Cheesy Chicken Pancakes

SERVES 4

For the pancakes:
100 g/4 oz/1 cup plain (all-purpose) flour
A pinch of salt
1 egg
300 ml/½ pt/1¼ cups milk
Sunflower oil, for shallow-frying
For the filling:
25 g/1 oz/2 tbsp butter or margarine
1 bunch of spring onions (scallions), finely chopped
1 small red (bell) pepper, finely chopped
30 ml/2 tbsp cornflour (cornstarch)
300 ml/½ pt/1¼ cups chicken stock
5 ml/1 tsp Dijon mustard
175 g/6 oz/1½ cups cooked chicken, chopped, all skin removed
175 g/6 oz/1½ cups Cheddar cheese, grated
Salt and freshly ground black pepper
A sprig of parsley, to garnish
Tomato and onion salad, to serve

To make the pancakes, sift the flour and salt into a bowl. Make a well in the centre and add the egg and half the milk. Beat well to form a smooth batter. Stir in the remaining milk. Heat a lightly oiled medium frying pan (skillet). Add just enough batter to cover the base of the pan, tipping and swirling to coat it. Fry (sauté) until golden brown underneath. Toss or flip over with a fish slice and cook the other side. Slide out of the pan and make another seven pancakes.

To make the filling, melt the butter or margarine in a saucepan. Add the spring onions and chopped pepper and cook, stirring, for 3 minutes to soften. Remove from the heat and stir in the cornflour. Blend in the stock, bring to the boil and cook for 1 minute, stirring. Stir in the mustard and add the chicken and 100 g/4 oz/1 cup of the cheese. Season to taste. Divide the mixture between the pancakes, roll up and place in a shallow ovenproof dish. Sprinkle with the remaining cheese. Cover with foil and bake in a preheated oven at 180°C/350°F/gas mark 4 for about 20 minutes until piping hot. Garnish with a sprig of parsley and serve with a tomato and onion salad.

Curried Chicken Pancakes

SERVES 4

For the pancakes:
100 g/4 oz/1 cup plain (all-purpose) flour
A pinch of salt
1 egg
300 ml/½ pt/1¼ cups milk
Sunflower oil, for shallow-frying
For the filling:
15 g/½ oz/1 tbsp butter or margarine
1 onion, finely chopped
100 g/4 oz button mushrooms, sliced
225 g/8 oz/2 cups cooked chicken, chopped, all skin removed
15 ml/1 tbsp mango chutney, chopped
10 ml/2 tsp lemon juice
15 ml/1 tbsp mild curry paste
150 ml/¼ pt/⅔ cup crème fraîche
Salt and freshly ground black pepper
30 ml/2 tbsp chopped coriander (cilantro)

To make the pancakes, sift the flour and salt into a bowl. Make a well in the centre and add the egg and half the milk. Beat well to form a smooth batter. Stir in the remaining milk. Heat a lightly oiled medium frying pan (skillet). Add just enough batter to cover the base of the pan, tipping and swirling to coat it. Fry (sauté) until golden brown underneath. Toss or flip over with a fish slice and cook the other side. Slide out of the pan and keep warm while making another seven pancakes.

To make the filling, melt the butter or margarine in a saucepan. Add the onion and mushrooms and fry (sauté) for 4 minutes until softened and golden. Add the chicken and cook, stirring, for 1 minute. Add the remaining ingredients except the coriander and heat through. Divide between the pancakes and roll up. Serve on warm plates, sprinkled with the coriander.

Chicken Stroganoff

SERVES 4

40 g/1½ oz/3 tbsp butter or margarine
2 onions, sliced
100 g/4 oz button mushrooms, sliced
350 g/12 oz chicken stir-fry meat
30 ml/2 tbsp brandy
250 ml/8 fl oz/1 cup crème fraîche
Salt and freshly ground black pepper
Plain Boiled Rice (page 351) and a green salad, to serve

Melt the butter or margarine in a frying pan (skillet). Add the onions and mushrooms and fry (sauté), stirring, for 2 minutes. Add the chicken and continue to fry for a further 8 minutes until the chicken is tender. Add the brandy and ignite. Shake the pan until the flames subside. Stir in the crème fraîche and bring to the boil. Season to taste. Spoon over the Plain Boiled Rice and serve with a green salad.

Chicken Strips in Cantaloupes

SERVES 4

15 ml/1 tbsp olive oil
350 g/12 oz chicken stir-fry meat
1 yellow (bell) pepper, diced
1 bunch of spring onions (scallions), chopped
30 ml/2 tbsp soy sauce
15 ml/1 tbsp medium-dry sherry
A good pinch of ground ginger
Salt and freshly ground black pepper
2 ripe cantaloupe melons, halved and seeds removed
Lettuce leaves, to garnish

Heat the oil in a frying pan (skillet). Add the chicken, pepper and spring onions and stir-fry for 5–7 minutes until the chicken is tender. Add the soy sauce, sherry and ginger. Toss well and season to taste. Put the melons on serving dishes on a bed of lettuce leaves. Spoon in the chicken mixture and serve straight away.

Spinach Pancakes with Soft Cheese and Chicken

SERVES 4

For the pancakes:
100 g/4 oz frozen chopped spinach, thawed
100 g/4 oz/1 cup plain (all-purpose) flour
A pinch of salt
1 egg
175 ml/6 fl oz/¾ cup milk
Sunflower oil, for shallow-frying
For the filling:
100 g/4 oz/1 cup cooked chicken, chopped, all skin removed
225 g/8 oz/1 cup medium-fat soft cheese
1 small garlic clove, crushed
30 ml/2 tbsp chopped parsley
Freshly ground black pepper
150 ml/¼ pt/⅔ cup passata (sieved tomatoes)
30 ml/2 tbsp grated Parmesan cheese

To make the pancakes, purée the spinach in a blender or food processor. Sift the flour and salt into a bowl. Make a well in the centre and add the egg and the milk. Beat well to form a thick, smooth batter. Beat in the spinach purée. Heat a lightly oiled medium frying pan (skillet). Add just enough batter to cover the base of the pan, tipping and swirling to coat it. Fry (sauté) until golden brown underneath. Toss or flip over with a fish slice and cook the other side. Slide out of the pan and make another seven pancakes.

To make the filling, mix together the chicken, cheese, garlic and parsley with a little salt and pepper. Spread over the pancakes and roll up. Place in an ovenproof dish. Spoon the passata over and cover with foil. Bake in a preheated oven at 190°C/375°F/gas mark 5 for about 20 minutes until piping hot. Serve straight away, sprinkled with the Parmesan cheese.

Provençal Chicken Pancakes

SERVES 4

For the pancakes:
100 g/4 oz/1 cup plain (all-purpose) flour
A pinch of salt
1 egg
300 ml/½ pt/1¼ cups milk
Sunflower oil, for shallow-frying
For the filling:
Provençal Sauce (page 342)
175 g/6 oz/1½ cups cooked chicken, chopped, all skin removed
Cheese Sauce (page 341)
Green salad, to serve

Sift the flour and salt into a bowl. Make a well in the centre and add the egg and half the milk. Beat well to form a smooth batter. Stir in the remaining milk. Heat a lightly oiled medium frying pan (skillet). Add just enough batter to cover the base of the pan, tipping and swirling to coat it. Fry (sauté) until golden brown underneath. Toss or flip over with a fish slice and cook the other side. Slide out of the pan and make another seven pancakes.

Make the Provençal Sauce and stir in the chicken. Divide the mixture between the pancakes and roll up. Place in an ovenproof dish. Pour the Cheese Sauce over and bake in a preheated oven at 190°C/375°F/gas mark 5 for 30 minutes. Serve with a green salad.

Bacon, Chicken and Tomato Pancakes

SERVES 4

For the pancakes:
100 g/4 oz/1 cup plain (all-purpose) flour
A pinch of salt
1 egg
300 ml/½ pt/1¼ cups milk
Sunflower oil, for shallow-frying
For the filling:
1 onion, chopped
25 g/1 oz/2 tbsp butter or margarine
4 rindless streaky bacon rashers (slices), chopped
400 g/14 oz/1 large can of chopped tomatoes
15 ml/1 tbsp tomato purée (paste)
2.5 ml/½ tsp dried basil
A good pinch of caster (superfine) sugar
Salt and freshly ground black pepper
100 g/4 oz/1 cup cooked chicken, diced, all skin removed
75 g/3 oz/¾ cup Cheddar cheese, grated
Cucumber salad, to serve

To make the pancakes, sift the flour and salt into a bowl. Make a well in the centre and add the egg and half the milk. Beat well to form a smooth batter. Stir in the remaining milk. Heat a lightly oiled medium frying pan (skillet). Add just enough batter to cover the base of the pan, tipping and swirling to coat it. Fry (sauté) until golden brown underneath. Toss or flip over with a fish slice and cook the other side. Slide out of the pan and make another seven pancakes.

To make the filling, fry (sauté) the onion in the butter or margarine for 2 minutes. Add the bacon and cook for a further 2 minutes, stirring all the time. Add the tomatoes, purée, basil, sugar and a little salt and pepper. Bring to the boil and simmer for 5 minutes. Add the chicken and heat through. Divide the mixture between the pancakes. Roll up and place in an ovenproof dish. Sprinkle with the cheese and heat in a preheated oven at 190°C/375°F/gas mark 5 for about 20 minutes until the cheese is melted and golden and the pancakes are piping hot. Serve with a cucumber salad.

Savoury Dutch Pancakes

SERVES 4

For the pancakes:
100 g/4 oz/1 cup plain (all-purpose) flour
A pinch of salt
1 egg
300 ml/½ pt/1¼ cups milk
Sunflower oil, for shallow-frying
For the filling:
225 g/8 oz turkey rashers (slices), chopped
300 ml/½ pt/1¼ cups soured (dairy sour) cream
1 green (bell) pepper, finely chopped
1 garlic clove, crushed
30 ml/2 tbsp chopped parsley
Freshly ground black pepper
100 g/4 oz/1 cup Gouda (Dutch) cheese, grated
Tomato salad, to serve

To make the pancakes, sift the flour and salt into a bowl. Make a well in the centre and add the egg and half the milk. Beat well to form a smooth batter. Stir in the remaining milk. Heat a lightly oiled medium frying pan (skillet). Add just enough batter to cover the base of the pan, tipping and swirling to coat it. Fry (sauté) until golden brown underneath. Toss or flip over with a fish slice and cook the other side. Slide out of the pan and make another seven pancakes.

To make the filling, dry-fry the turkey rashers in a non-stick frying pan (skillet) until crisp. Stir in the cream, chopped pepper, garlic, parsley and a little salt and pepper. Divide the mixture between the pancakes. Roll up and place in an ovenproof dish. Sprinkle with the cheese. Cover with foil and bake in a preheated oven at 190°C/375°F/gas mark 5 for 10 minutes. Remove the foil and cook for a further 10 minutes until golden and bubbling. Serve with a tomato salad.

Piazzaiola Pancakes

SERVES 4

For the pancakes:
100 g/4 oz/1 cup plain (all-purpose) flour
A pinch of salt
1 egg
300 ml/½ pt/1¼ cups milk
Sunflower oil, for shallow-frying
For the filling:
Piazzaiola Sauce (page 335)
175 g/6 oz/1½ cups cooked chicken, chopped, all skin removed
75 g/3 oz/¾ cup Mozzarella cheese, grated
15 ml/1 tbsp olive oil
Freshly ground black pepper
A few basil leaves

To make the pancakes, sift the flour and salt into a bowl. Make a well in the centre and add the egg and half the milk. Beat well to form a smooth batter. Stir in the remaining milk. Heat a lightly oiled medium frying pan (skillet). Add just enough batter to cover the base of the pan, tipping and swirling to coat it. Fry (sauté) until golden brown underneath. Toss or flip over with a fish slice and cook the other side. Slide out of the pan and make another seven pancakes.

To make the filling, prepare the Piazzaiola Sauce and stir in the chicken. Heat through. Use the fill the pancakes and lay them in an ovenproof dish. Cover with the cheese, drizzle with the olive oil and season with a little black pepper. Place in a preheated oven at 190°C/375°F/gas mark 5 for 10 minutes or until piping hot and the cheese has melted and is just turning golden in a few places. Scatter the basil leaves over and serve.

Creamy Chicken with Mushrooms

SERVES 4

4 skinless chicken breasts
25 g/1 oz/2 tbsp butter or margarine
30 ml/2 tbsp olive oil
Salt and freshly ground black pepper
100 g/4 oz button mushrooms, sliced
30 ml/2 tbsp brandy
150 ml/¼ pt/⅔ cup double (heavy) cream
30 ml/2 tbsp chopped parsley
New potatoes and French (green) beans, to serve

Brown the chicken breasts in the butter or margarine and oil in a frying pan (skillet). Sprinkle with salt and pepper. Cover the pan, reduce the heat and cook gently for 20 minutes or until cooked through. Remove the chicken from the pan and keep warm. Add the mushrooms to the pan and cook, stirring, for 3 minutes. Add the brandy, ignite and shake the pan until the flames subside. Pour in the cream and bring to the boil, stirring. Season to taste. Stir in the parsley. Place the chicken breasts on warm plates. Spoon the sauce over and serve hot with new potatoes and French beans.

Chicken Burgers with Fresh Herbs

SERVES 4

900 g/2 lb minced (ground) chicken
30 ml/2 tbsp chopped parsley
15 ml/1 tbsp chopped thyme
1.5 ml/¼ tsp ground mace
Salt and freshly ground black pepper
1 egg, beaten
25 g/1 oz/2 tbsp unsalted (sweet) butter
Piazzaiola Sauce (page 335), jacket potatoes and coleslaw, to serve

Mix the chicken with the herbs, mace and a little salt and pepper. Mix in the egg. Shape into eight small cakes. Chill for 30 minutes while making the Piazzaiola Sauce. Keep the sauce warm over a gentle heat. Heat the butter in a large, non-stick frying pan (skillet). Fry (sauté) the burgers for about 4 minutes on each side until cooked through and golden brown. Transfer to warm plates. Spoon the Piazzaiola Sauce over and serve with jacket potatoes and coleslaw.

Sweet and Sour Chicken

SERVES 4

30 ml/2 tbsp sunflower oil
225 g/8 oz chicken stir-fry meat
1 carrot, cut into very thin matchsticks
5 cm/2 in piece of cucumber, cut into very thin matchsticks
1 small red (bell) pepper, cut into very thin strips
1 bunch of spring onions (scallions), cut into short lengths
320 g/12 oz/1 medium can of pineapple chunks
30 ml/2 tbsp tomato purée (paste)
45 ml/3 tbsp soy sauce
15 ml/1 tbsp cornflour (cornstarch)
30 ml/2 tbsp water
Special Egg Fried Rice (page 351), to serve

Heat the oil in a large frying pan (skillet). Add the chicken and vegetables and stir-fry for 6 minutes until the chicken is tender. Add the pineapple, tomato purée and soy sauce. Bring to the boil. Blend the cornflour with the water and stir into the sauce. Simmer for 2 minutes, stirring. Spoon on to the Special Egg Fried Rice and serve.

Sweet and Sour Chicken Balls

SERVES 4

100 g/4 oz/1 cup self-raising (self-rising) flour
2.5 ml/½ tsp salt
175 ml/6 fl oz/¾ cup water
175 g/6 oz/1½ cups cooked chicken, cut into small, bite-sized pieces
Oil, for deep-frying
Egg Fried Rice (page 351), to serve
Sweet and Sour Dipping Sauce (page 337)

Mix the flour with the salt. Beat in the cold water, adding a little more if necessary, to form a thick coating batter. Drop in the chicken. Heat the oil until a cube of day-old bread browns in 30 seconds. Using a spoon, drop in pieces of chicken coated in the batter, a few at a time, and cook for about 3 minutes until puffy and golden brown. Remove with a draining spoon, drain on kitchen paper (paper towels) and keep warm while cooking the remainder. Pile on to a bed of Egg Fried Rice and serve with the Sweet and Sour Dipping Sauce drizzled over.

Sesame Chicken and Broccoli Stir-fry

SERVES 4

30 ml/2 tbsp sunflower oil
15 ml/1 tbsp sesame oil
10 ml/2 tsp grated fresh root ginger
1 garlic clove, crushed
350 g/12 oz broccoli, cut into tiny florets
225 g/8 oz/2 cups cooked chicken, cut into neat pieces
120 ml/4 fl oz/½ cup chicken stock
10 ml/2 tsp soy sauce
15 ml/1 tbsp light brown sugar
Crispy Noodles (page 356), to serve
15 ml/1 tbsp toasted sesame seeds, to garnish

Heat the oils in a large frying pan (skillet) or wok. Add the ginger, garlic and broccoli and stir-fry for 3 minutes. Add all the remaining ingredients and simmer for about 3 minutes or until the broccoli is just tender but still has some bite. Spoon on to warm plates and lay the Crispy Noodles to the side. Sprinkle the broccoli mixture with the sesame seeds and serve.

Spicy Chinese Chicken

SERVES 4

1 large egg white
10 ml/2 tsp cornflour (cornstarch)
1 garlic clove, crushed
15 ml/1 tbsp grated fresh root ginger
3 skinless chicken breasts, cut diagonally into thin slices
60 ml/4 tbsp sunflower oil
15 ml/1 tbsp chilli oil
1 large onion, halved and thinly sliced
1 large green (bell) pepper, thinly sliced
1 green chilli, seeded and chopped
Dark Soy Dipping Sauce (page 337), uncooked
2 spring onions (scallions), chopped
Special Egg Fried Rice (page 351), to serve

Lightly beat the egg white with the cornflour, garlic and ginger. Add the chicken slices and toss to coat. Leave to stand for 15 minutes. Heat the oils in a wok or large frying pan (skillet). Lift the chicken out of the marinade and stir-fry for 3 minutes. Add the onion, pepper and chilli and stir-fry for 2 minutes. Stir in the Dark Soy Dipping Sauce and cook for 2 minutes. Sprinkle with the spring onions and serve with Special Fried Rice.

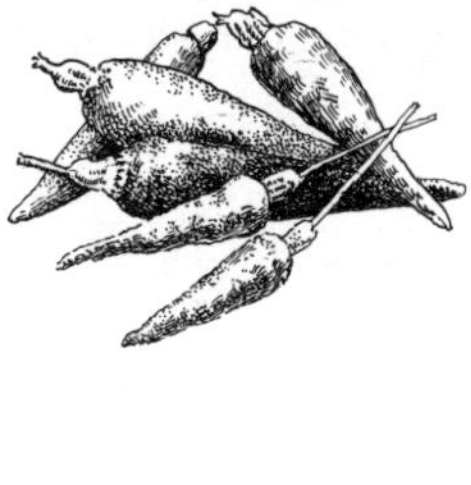

Chinese Chicken and Mushroom Stir-fry

SERVES 4

10 dried shiitake mushrooms, soaked and thinly sliced
350 g/12 oz chicken stir-fry meat
10 ml/2 tsp cornflour (cornstarch)
60 ml/4 tbsp sunflower oil
4 spring onions (scallions), cut diagonally into short lengths
1 large carrot, cut diagonally into very thin slices
1 courgette (zucchini), cut diagonally into very thin slices
1 garlic clove, crushed
50 g/2 oz/1 cup beansprouts
45 ml/3 tbsp soy sauce
15 ml/1 tbsp medium-dry sherry
A pinch of ground ginger
Plain Boiled Rice (page 351), to serve

Mix the mushrooms, with the chicken and toss in the cornflour. Heat the oil in a wok or large frying pan (skillet). Add the chicken mixture and stir-fry for 3 minutes. Add the prepared vegetables and beansprouts and stir-fry for a further 3 minutes. Add the soy sauce, sherry and ginger and toss thoroughly. Serve hot with Plain Boiled Rice.

Chinese Mushroom, Chicken and King Prawn Stir-fry

SERVES 4

Prepare as for Chinese Chicken and Mushroom Stir-fry, but use 175 g/6 oz chicken stir-fry meat and mix with 175 g/6 oz raw, peeled king prawns (jumbo shrimp), thawed if frozen.

Chinese Mushroom, Chicken and Pineapple Stir-fry

SERVES 4

Prepare as for Chinese Chicken and Mushroom Stir-fry, but use 225 g/8 oz chicken stir-fry meat and add 225 g/8 oz/1 medium can of pineapple pieces, drained. Substitute 15 ml/1 tbsp of the pineapple juice for the sherry.

Chicken with Mixed Peppers and Black Bean Sauce

SERVES 4

350 g/12 oz chicken stir-fry meat
20 ml/4 tsp cornflour (cornstarch)
60 ml/4 tbsp sunflower oil
1 green (bell) pepper, cut into neat squares
1 red pepper, cut into neat squares
1 bunch of spring onions (scallions), chopped
30 ml/2 tbsp black bean sauce
75 ml/5 tbsp soy sauce
5 ml/1 tsp grated fresh root ginger
1 garlic clove, crushed
30 ml/2 tbsp dry sherry
Crispy Noodles (page 356), to serve

Toss the chicken in the cornflour. Heat the oil in a wok or large frying pan (skillet). Stir-fry the chicken for 3 minutes. Add the peppers and spring onions and stir-fry for a further 3 minutes. Stir in the remaining ingredients and simmer for a further 2–3 minutes. Serve with Crispy Noodles.

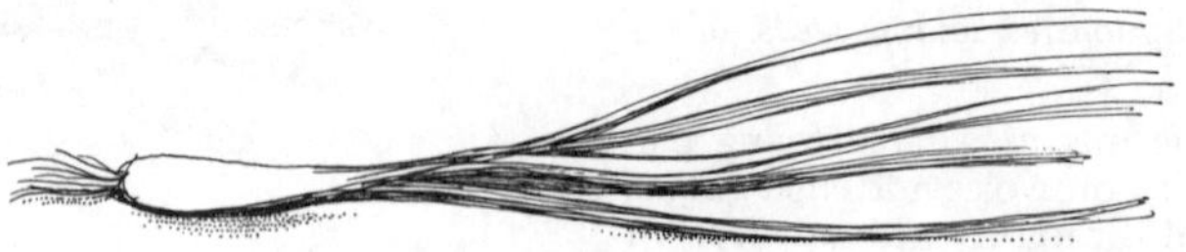

Szechuan Chicken

SERVES 4

60 ml/4 tbsp sunflower oil
3 large chicken breasts, thinly sliced
1 large green (bell) pepper, diced
1 large garlic clove, crushed
10 ml/2 tsp grated fresh root ginger
10 ml/2 tsp cornflour (cornstarch)
30 ml/2 tbsp water
30 ml/2 tbsp black bean sauce
30 ml/2 tbsp light brown sugar
30 ml/2 tbsp soy sauce
15 ml/1 tbsp sesame oil
Egg Fried Rice (page 351), to serve

Heat the oil in a wok or large frying pan (skillet). Add the chicken and stir-fry for 3 minutes. Add the pepper, garlic and ginger and stir-fry for a further 3 minutes. Blend the cornflour with the water and stir in the remaining ingredients. Add to the pan and cook for 2 minutes, stirring. Serve with Egg Fried Rice.

Mustard and Honey Chicken with Mangetout and Baby Corn

SERVES 4

100 g/4 oz mangetout (snow peas)
100 g/4 oz baby corn cobs
Salt and freshly ground black pepper
15 ml/1 tbsp sunflower oil
4 skinless chicken breasts
15 ml/1 tbsp clear honey
15 ml/1 tbsp apple juice
15 ml/1 tbsp orange juice
A squeeze of lemon juice
15 ml/1 tbsp soy sauce
10 ml/2 tsp wholegrain mustard
15 g/½ oz/1 tbsp unsalted (sweet) butter
2.5 ml/½ tsp chilli oil

Cook the mangetout and corn in lightly salted boiling water for 2 minutes. Drain and return to the saucepan. Heat the sunflower oil in a large frying pan (skillet). Add the chicken breasts and fry (sauté) for about 15 minutes, turning once or twice, until golden and cooked through. Remove from the pan and keep warm. Stir the honey, juices, soy sauce and mustard into the pan until bubbling. Whisk in the butter and season with pepper. Add the chilli oil to the mangetout and corn with a good grinding of pepper and a sprinkling of salt. Toss gently until hot. Put a chicken breast on each of four warm plates, carve in thick slices and fan out gently. Spoon the sauce over. Arrange a small pile of mangetout and corn to the side of each and serve.

Chicken and Mushrooms with Oyster Sauce

SERVES 4

1 onion
3 large chicken breasts, cut diagonally into thin slices
20 ml/4 tsp cornflour (cornstarch)
45 ml/3 tbsp sunflower oil
15 ml/1 tbsp sesame oil
1 large garlic clove, crushed
10 ml/2 tsp grated fresh root ginger
100 g/4 oz button mushrooms, sliced
90 ml/6 tbsp oyster sauce
20 ml/4 tsp light brown sugar
Plain Boiled Rice (page 351), to serve

Cut the onion in thin wedges, then separate into layers. Toss the chicken and onion in the cornflour. Heat the oils together in a wok or large frying pan (skillet). Add the chicken and onions and stir-fry for 3 minutes. Add the garlic, ginger and mushrooms and toss for a further 3 minutes. Stir in the oyster sauce and sugar and simmer for 2–3 minutes. Serve with Plain Boiled Rice.

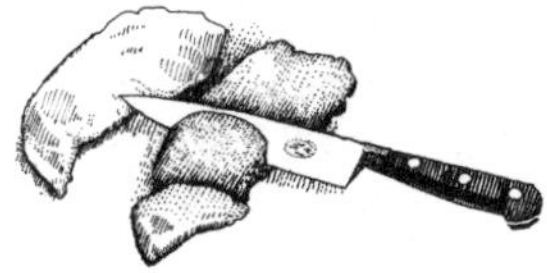

Cantonese-style Chicken

SERVES 4

8 baby chicken fillets
30 ml/2 tbsp soy sauce
75 g/3 oz/¾ cup plain (all-purpose) flour
5 ml/1 tsp salt
1.5 ml/¼ tsp dry mustard powder
15 ml/1 tbsp red wine vinegar
150 ml/¼ pt/⅔ cup water
Oil, for deep-frying
Sweet and Sour Dipping Sauce (page 337) and Egg Fried Rice (page 351), to serve

Place the chicken breasts one at a time in a plastic bag and beat with a rolling pin or meat mallet until flattened. Toss in the soy sauce. Mix the flour with the salt and mustard. Beat in the vinegar and water to form a smooth batter. Heat the oil until a cube of day-old bread browns in 30 seconds. Dip the chicken in the batter, then deep-fry, a few at a time, for about 5 minutes until crisp, golden and cooked through. Drain on kitchen paper (paper towels) and keep warm while cooking the remainder. Serve with the hot Sweet and Sour Dipping Sauce and Egg Fried Rice.

Stir-fry Chicken with Bamboo Shoots

SERVES 4

3 large chicken breasts, cut diagonally into thin slices
10 ml/2 tsp cornflour (cornstarch)
60 ml/4 tbsp sunflower oil
15 ml/1 tbsp grated fresh root ginger
2 garlic cloves, crushed
2 green (bell) peppers, cut diagonally into short strips
1 bunch of spring onions (scallions), cut diagonally into short lengths
185 g/6½ oz/1 small can of sliced bamboo shoots, drained
Tomato Dipping Sauce (page 337)
5 ml/1 tsp oyster sauce
Chinese egg noodles, to serve

Toss the chicken in the cornflour. Heat the oil in a wok or large frying pan (skillet). Add the chicken and stir-fry for 3 minutes. Add the ginger, garlic, peppers and onions and stir-fry for a further 3 minutes. Add the remaining ingredients and toss for a further 2 minutes. Serve hot with Chinese egg noodles.

Chinese Chicken Rissoles

SERVES 4

450 g/1 lb minced (ground) chicken
1 potato, grated
1 onion, grated
10 ml/2 tsp curry powder
1.5 ml/¼ tsp Chinese five spice powder
5 ml/1 tsp salt
50 g/2 oz/½ cup plain (all-purpose) flour
Oil, for deep-frying
Shredded lettuce
Tomato slices
Cucumber slices
Lemon wedges, to garnish
Chinese Curry Sauce (page 338), to serve

Mix together the chicken, potato, onion, curry powder, five spice powder, salt and flour thoroughly. Use your hands to shape the mixture into 16 small, flat cakes. Heat the oil until a cube of day-old bread browns in 30 seconds. Deep-fry the rissoles a few at a time for about 3 minutes until golden brown and cooked through. Drain on kitchen paper (paper towels). Keep warm while cooking the remainder. Serve on a bed of lettuce, tomato and cucumber, garnished with lemon wedges. Serve the Chinese Curry Sauce separately in little bowls.

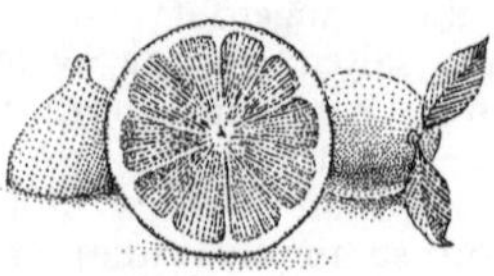

Chicken Stir-fry Scramble

SERVES 4

225 g/8 oz chicken stir-fry meat
30 ml/2 tbsp sunflower oil
1 bunch of spring onions (scallions), cut into short lengths
1 red chilli, seeded and chopped
1 garlic clove, crushed
1 aubergine (eggplant), halved and sliced
100 g/4 oz okra (ladies' fingers), each cut into 4 chunks
1 courgette (zucchini), sliced
2 potatoes, quartered and sliced
2 tomatoes, skinned, seeded and chopped
15 ml/1 tbsp tomato purée (paste)
300 ml/½ pt/1¼ cups chicken stock
5 ml/1 tsp red chilli sauce
Salt and freshly ground black pepper
2 eggs, beaten
Crusty bread, to serve

Stir-fry the chicken in the oil in a large wok or frying pan (skillet) for 3 minutes. Add the spring onions, chilli, garlic, aubergine, okra, courgette and potatoes and stir-fry for a further 2 minutes. Add the tomatoes, tomato purée and stock and bring to the boil. Reduce the heat and simmer for 15 minutes or until the vegetables are tender and most of the liquid has evaporated. Boil rapidly for a minute or two if necessary to remove the liquid. Stir in the chilli sauce and a little salt and pepper. Push all the ingredients to one side of the pan. Pour the eggs into the space left and stir over a moderate heat until the mixture begins to scramble, then gradually draw the remaining ingredients back into the egg, stirring gently. Pile on to hot plates and serve with crusty bread.

Chicken with Cashew Nuts and Noodles

SERVES 4

100 g/4 oz quick-cook Chinese egg noodles
30 ml/2 tbsp sunflower oil
225 g/8 oz chicken stir-fry meat
1 bunch of spring onions (scallions), cut into short lengths
1 carrot, grated
275 g/10 oz/5 cups beansprouts
25 g/1 oz/¼ cup cashew nuts
300 ml/½ pt/1¼ cups chicken stock
15 ml/1 tbsp cornflour (cornstarch)
15 ml/1 tbsp soy sauce

Cook the noodles according to packet directions. Drain. Heat the oil in a wok or large frying pan (skillet) and fry (sauté) the chicken, spring onions and carrots for 5 minutes, stirring. Add the beansprouts and cook for a further 3 minutes, stirring. Add the cashew nuts and stock. Blend the cornflour with the soy sauce and stir into the pan. Bring to the boil and cook for 2 minutes, stirring. Stir in the noodles and heat through. Serve piping hot.

Chicken Chéron

SERVES 6

6 skinless chicken breasts
15 g/½ oz/1 tbsp butter or margarine
Salt and freshly ground black pepper
425 g/15 oz/1 large can of artichoke bottoms
200 g/7 oz/1 small can of sweetcorn (corn) with (bell) peppers
1 carrot, grated
90 ml/6 tbsp dry white wine
1.5 ml/¼ tsp caster (superfine) sugar
Super Sauté Potatoes (page 349) and a mixed green salad, to serve

Fry (sauté) the chicken in the butter or margarine in a non-stick frying pan (skillet) for 3 minutes on each side to brown. Season with salt and pepper. Cover the pan and cook very gently for 15 minutes until tender and cooked through. Meanwhile, heat the artichokes, drain and keep warm. Heat the corn with the carrot until piping hot. When the chicken is cooked, remove from the pan and transfer to warm plates. Keep warm. Add the wine to the pan with the sugar. Bring to the boil and boil rapidly, stirring, until slightly reduced. Spoon over the chicken. Put the artichoke bottoms to one side of each chicken breast. Spoon the corn mixture on each and serve with Super Sauté Potatoes and a mixed green salad.

Peasant Chicken

SERVES 4

450 g/1 lb small new potatoes, scraped but left whole
25 g/1 oz/2 tbsp butter or margarine
30 ml/2 tbsp olive oil
4 chicken portions
100 g/4 oz button mushrooms
150 ml/¼ pt/⅔ cup chicken stock
Salt and freshly ground black pepper
2 garlic cloves, chopped
30 ml/2 tbsp chopped parsley
French bread and a mixed salad, to serve

Fry (sauté) the potatoes in a large frying pan (skillet) in half the butter or margarine and half the oil, turning until golden brown. Remove from the pan. Melt the remaining fat and oil and fry the chicken pieces on all sides to brown. Return the potatoes to the pan and add the mushrooms, stock and a little salt and pepper. Cover tightly, reduce the heat and cook very gently for about 40 minutes until the chicken and potatoes are tender. Sprinkle over the garlic and most of the parsley, re-cover and cook gently for a further 5 minutes. Transfer the chicken, potatoes and mushrooms to warm serving plates and keep warm. Boil the liquid rapidly, if necessary, to reduce a little. Taste and adjust the seasoning. Spoon over the chicken and vegetables and sprinkle with the remaining parsley. Serve with French bread and a mixed salad.

French-style Peasant Chicken

SERVES 4

Prepare as for Peasant Chicken, but use chanterelles instead of button mushrooms and add 30 ml/2 tbsp sliced stoned (pitted) black olives with the garlic and parsley.

Chicken Averone

SERVES 4

150 ml/¼ pt/⅔ cup chicken stock
1 bay leaf
1 small onion, halved
150 ml/¼ pt/⅔ cup red wine
40 g/1½ oz/3 tbsp butter or margarine
4 small skinless chicken breasts, about 150 g/5 oz each
25 g/1 oz/¼ cup plain (all-purpose) flour
150 ml/¼ pt/⅔ cup single (light) cream
75 g/3 oz/½ cup seedless red grapes, halved
Salt and freshly ground black pepper
Watercress, to garnish
New potatoes and Brussels sprouts, to serve

Put the stock, bay leaf, onion and wine in a saucepan. Bring to the boil and leave to infuse while cooking the chicken. Melt the butter or margarine in a large frying pan (skillet). Add the chicken and fry (sauté) on both sides for about 8–10 minutes until golden and cooked through. Remove from the pan and keep warm. Stir the flour into the pan and cook for 1 minute, stirring. Strain in the stock and wine, discarding the bay leaf and onion. Blend until smooth, then bring to the boil, stirring. Blend in the cream, grapes and salt and pepper to taste. Simmer for 2 minutes. Transfer the chicken to warm plates, spoon the sauce over and garnish with watercress. Serve with new potatoes and Brussels sprouts.

Creamy Tarragon Chicken

SERVES 4

4 skinless chicken breasts
25 g/1 oz/2 tbsp butter or margarine
10 ml/2 tsp plain (all-purpose) flour
15 ml/1 tbsp chopped tarragon
5 ml/1 tsp Dijon mustard
120 ml/4 fl oz/½ cup dry white wine
120 ml/4 fl oz/½ cup crème fraîche
Salt and freshly ground black pepper
Tarragon sprigs, to garnish
New potatoes and broccoli, to serve

Fry (sauté) the chicken in the butter or margarine in a frying pan (skillet) for about 15 minutes until golden brown on both sides and cooked through. Remove from the pan and keep warm. Stir the flour, tarragon, mustard and wine. Bring to the boil and boil for 3 minutes or until reduced by half. Stir in the crème fraîche and season to taste. Return the chicken to the pan with any juices and simmer gently for 5 minutes. Transfer to warm plates. Garnish with tarragon sprigs and serve with new potatoes and broccoli.

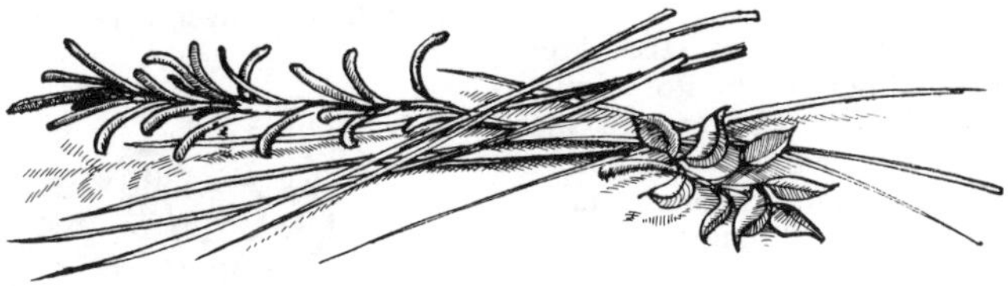

Chicken Burritos with Avocado, Tomato and Pineapple Salsa

SERVES 4

For the filling:
1 onion, finely chopped
1 garlic clove, crushed
350 g/12 oz minced (ground) chicken
15 ml/1 tbsp sunflower oil
400 g/14 oz/1 large can of chopped tomatoes
15 ml/1 tbsp tomato purée (paste)
2.5 ml/½ tsp ground cumin
2.5 ml/½ tsp chilli powder
2.5 ml/½ tsp dried oregano
Salt and freshly ground black pepper
1 large potato, finely diced
1 green (bell) pepper, finely diced
For the salsa:
1 large avocado
15 ml/1 tbsp lemon juice
1 red onion, finely chopped
275 g/10 oz/1 medium can of crushed pineapple, drained thoroughly
4 tomatoes, skinned and chopped
15 ml/1 tbsp chopped parsley
1 small green chilli, seeded and chopped
8 large flour tortillas and raw carrot, red and green pepper and cucumber strips, to serve

To make the filling, put the onion, garlic, chicken and oil in a non-stick saucepan. Cook, stirring, until the chicken is no longer pink and all the grains are separate. Add the tomatoes, tomato purée, cumin, chilli powder, oregano, some salt and pepper and the potato and diced pepper. Bring to the boil, stirring. Reduce the heat, part-cover and simmer for 20 minutes.

Meanwhile, to make the salsa, peel the avocado and remove the stone (pit). Cut into small dice and toss in the lemon juice. Mix with the remaining salsa ingredients and season to taste with salt and pepper. Chill until ready to serve. When the chicken mixture is cooked, warm the tortillas according to the packet directions. Divide the chicken mixture between them and roll up. Place on warm serving plates with a spoonful of salsa to the side and neat piles of the raw vegetables.

Sweet Barbecued Chicken Fillets

SERVES 4

Prepare as for Barbecued Turkey Steaks (page 115), but substitute skinless chicken breasts for the turkey.

Chinese Fire Chicken

SERVES 4

2 large skinless chicken breasts, cut into small chunks
8 button mushrooms, quartered
45 ml/3 tbsp cornflour (cornstarch)
45 ml/3 tbsp sunflower oil
2 garlic cloves, crushed
1 bunch of spring onions (scallions), cut into short lengths
1 red chilli, seeded and finely chopped
45 ml/3 tbsp soy sauce
120 ml/4 fl oz/½ cup apple juice
30 ml/2 tbsp white wine vinegar
Plain Boiled Rice (page 351), to serve
Cayenne, to garnish

Toss the chicken and mushrooms in the cornflour to coat completely. Heat the oil in a large frying pan (skillet) or wok and fry (sauté) the garlic and spring onions for 1 minute. Add the chicken mixture and cook, stirring, for 3 minutes. Stir in the remaining ingredients. Bring to the boil, stirring, reduce the heat and simmer for 4–5 minutes until the chicken is cooked through and coated in the sauce. Spoon on to a bed of plain boiled rice and sprinkle with cayenne before serving.

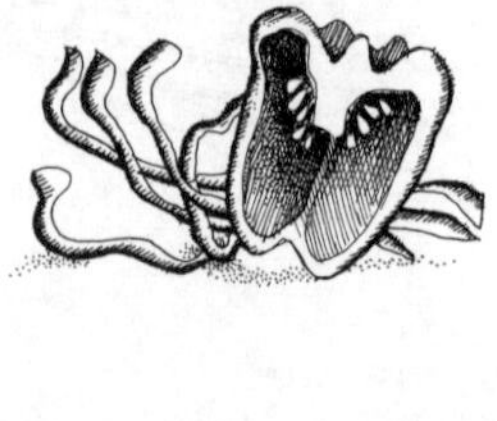

Chinese-style Chicken with Cashew Nuts and Rice

SERVES 4

225 g/8 oz/1 cup long-grain rice
25 g/1 oz/2 tbsp butter or margarine
225 g/8 oz boneless chicken thighs, skinned and cut into neat strips
300 g/11 oz/1 packet of ready-prepared stir-fry vegetables
25 g/1 oz/¼ cup raw cashew nuts
300 ml/½ pt/1¼ cups chicken stock
15 ml/1 tbsp cornflour (cornstarch)
15 ml/1 tbsp soy sauce

Boil the rice in lightly salted water according to the packet directions. Drain, rinse with boiling water and drain again. Meanwhile, melt the butter or margarine in a large frying pan (skillet) or wok. Add the chicken and stir-fry for 5 minutes. Add the stir-fry vegetables and cook, stirring, for 3 minutes. Add the cashew nuts and stock. Blend the cornflour with the soy sauce and stir in. Bring to the boil and cook for 2 minutes. Spoon the rice on to four warm serving plates. Spoon the chicken mixture to one side and serve straight away.

Golden Sweet and Sour Chicken Breasts

SERVES 4

4 skinless chicken breasts
30 ml/2 tbsp sunflower oil
1 onion, thinly sliced
1 orange (bell) pepper, halved and thinly sliced
1 large carrot, cut into matchsticks
1 garlic clove, crushed
410 g/14½ oz/1 large can of apricot halves in natural juice, drained, reserving the juice
150 ml/¼ pt/⅔ cup chicken stock
15 ml/1 tbsp light brown sugar
45 ml/3 tbsp cider vinegar
15 ml/1 tbsp soy sauce
A good pinch of ground ginger
175 g/6 oz/¾ cup long-grain rice
5 ml/1 tsp turmeric
200 g/7 oz/1 small can of sweetcorn (corn), drained
15 ml/1 tbsp cornflour (cornstarch)
15 ml/1 tbsp water
1 spring onion (scallion), finely chopped, to garnish

Brown the chicken breasts in the oil in a large frying pan (skillet). Remove from the pan. Add the onion, pepper, carrot and garlic and stir-fry for 3 minutes. Add the apricot juice, stock, sugar, vinegar, soy sauce and ginger. Return the chicken to the pan. Cover and simmer gently for 15 minutes until the chicken is tender. Meanwhile, cook the rice for 10 minutes in plenty of lightly salted boiling water to which the turmeric has been added. Drain and return to the saucepan. Add the sweetcorn, toss gently and keep hot. Lift the chicken out of the frying pan and keep warm. Blend the cornflour with the water and stir into the cooking liquid. Bring to the boil, stirring. Add the apricot halves and heat through for 1 minute. Spoon the rice and corn on to one side of 4 warm serving plates. Add the chicken breasts to the plates and spoon the sauce over. Sprinkle with the chopped spring onion and serve hot.

Japanese Peanut Chicken Stir-fry

SERVES 4

175 g/6 oz soba noodles
5 ml/1 tsp grated fresh root ginger
15 ml/1 tbsp sunflower oil
175 g/6 oz chicken stir-fry meat
1 red (bell) pepper, sliced
1 green pepper, sliced
1 yellow pepper, sliced
1 large carrot, cut into matchsticks
100 g/4 oz fresh shiitake mushrooms (or 50 g/2 oz dried, soaked), sliced
50 g/2 oz mangetout (snow peas)
100 g/4 oz/2 cups beansprouts
50 g/2 oz/½ cup roasted peanuts
Teriyaki sauce

Cook the noodles according to the packet directions. Drain and reserve. Meanwhile, fry (sauté) the ginger in the oil for 1 minute. Add the chicken and stir-fry for 3 minutes. Add the peppers, carrot and mushrooms and stir-fry for 2 minutes. Add the remaining ingredients except the teriyaki sauce. Stir-fry for 2 minutes. Add teriyaki sauce to taste, toss well and serve with the noodles.

Chicken Pesto

SERVES 4

4 boneless chicken breasts, about 175 g/6 oz each
25 g/1 oz/2 tbsp butter or margarine
1 bunch of spring onions (scallions), chopped
4 large, ripe tomatoes, skinned and chopped
300 ml/½ pt/1¼ cups dry white wine
15 ml/1 tbsp tomato purée (paste)
Salt and freshly ground black pepper
30 ml/2 tbsp Pesto for Poultry (page 342 or use bought)
30 ml/2 tbsp chopped parsley
30 ml/2 tbsp Mozzarella cheese, grated
Olive ciabatta bread and a crisp green salad, to serve

Fry (sauté) the chicken breasts in the butter or margarine for 5 minutes until golden on each side. Remove from the pan. Add the remaining ingredients except the pesto, parsley and cheese. Bring to the boil, stirring. Return the chicken to the pan and season. Cover and simmer for 15 minutes. Stir in the pesto and parsley. Cook, uncovered, for a further 5 minutes. Transfer to warm plates. Sprinkle the cheese over and flash under a hot grill (broiler) to melt the cheese. Serve with ciabatta bread and a crisp green salad.

Mixed Chicken and Vegetable Fritters with Aioli

SERVES 6

3 garlic cloves, crushed
175 ml/6 fl oz/¾ cup mayonnaise
30 ml/2 tbsp olive oil
Salt and freshly ground black pepper
1 aubergine (eggplant), sliced
1 courgette (zucchini), cut into chunks
2 carrots, cut into chunks
175 g/6 oz broccoli, cut into bite-sized florets
175 g/6 oz/1½ cups plain (all-purpose) flour
2 chicken breasts, cut into bite-sized pieces
250 ml/8 fl oz/1 cup tepid water
2 egg whites
Oil, for deep-frying
Crisp green salad with avocado, to serve

Mix the garlic with the mayonnaise and 15 ml/1 tbsp of the olive oil until well blended. Season to taste. Turn into a small bowl, cover and chill until required. Put the aubergine and courgette in a colander. Sprinkle with salt and leave to stand for 15 minutes. Rinse and dry thoroughly on kitchen paper (paper towels). Meanwhile, cook the carrots in boiling water for 4 minutes. Add the broccoli and cook for a further 2 minutes. Drain, rinse with cold water and drain again. Dry thoroughly on kitchen paper. Mix 25 g/1 oz/¼ cup of the flour with a little salt and pepper. Use to coat all the vegetables and the chicken. Sift the remaining flour with a pinch of salt into a bowl. Add the water and the remaining olive oil and beat to form a smooth batter. Whisk the egg whites until stiff and fold in with a metal spoon. Heat the oil for deep-frying until a cube of day-old bread browns in 30 seconds. Dip batches of pieces of vegetable or chicken at a time in the batter and deep-fry for about 5 minutes until crisp and golden brown. Drain on kitchen paper and keep warm while cooking the remainder. Serve with the aioli and a crisp green salad with avocado.

Chicken Fajitas

SERVES 4

1 garlic clove, crushed
15 ml/1 tbsp clear honey
150 ml/¼ pt/⅔ cup apple juice
150 ml/¼ pt/⅔ cup lager
60 ml/4 tbsp red wine vinegar
2.5 ml/½ tsp chilli powder
350 g/12 oz chicken stir-fry meat
100 g/4 oz button mushrooms, thickly sliced
25 g/1 oz/2 tbsp butter or margarine
1 bunch of spring onions (scallions), diagonally sliced
1 red (bell) pepper, cut into thin strips
1 green (bell) pepper, cut into thin strips
Salt and freshly ground black pepper
8 tortillas
Mixed salad, to serve

Put the garlic, honey, apple juice, lager, vinegar and chilli powder in a pan. Bring to the boil, reduce the heat and simmer for 5 minutes. Put the chicken and mushrooms in a shallow dish. Pour over the marinade and leave to marinate for 1 hour. Heat half the butter or margarine in a large frying pan (skillet). Add the spring onions and peppers and stir-fry for 4 minutes until softened. Remove from the pan and reserve. Add the remaining butter or margarine to the pan. Remove the chicken and mushrooms from the marinade and stir-fry for 5 minutes until cooked through. Return the spring onions and peppers to the pan with 60 ml/4 tbsp of the marinade and toss until piping hot and glazed. Season with salt and pepper. Warm the tortillas according to the packet directions. Divide the chicken mixture between the tortillas, roll up and serve with a mixed salad.

Spring Greens with Chicken, Bacon, Cumin and Eggs

SERVES 4

30 ml/2 tbsp sunflower oil
25 g/1 oz/2 tbsp butter or margarine
1 large onion, finely chopped
3 rindless streaky bacon rashers (slices), diced
5 ml/1 tsp cumin seeds, lightly crushed
700 g/1½ lb spring greens (collard greens), finely shredded
100 g/4 oz/1 cup cooked chicken, chopped, all skin removed
4 eggs
5 ml/1 tsp lemon juice
Crusty bread, to serve

Heat the oil and butter or margarine in a large saucepan. Fry (sauté) the onion and bacon for 5 minutes until golden brown and soft. Stir in the cumin seeds and cook for a further 2 minutes, stirring. Add the greens and continue to cook, tossing for about 5 minutes until the cabbage is just tender but has some bite. Add the chicken and cook, tossing, for 5 minutes. Meanwhile, poach the eggs in simmering water to which the lemon juice has been added for about 3 minutes until just set. Spoon the greens on to warm plates and top each with a poached egg. Serve straight away with crusty bread.

Chicken and Vegetable Fritters

SERVES 4

2 rindless streaky bacon rashers (slices), diced
1 onion, finely chopped
1 carrot, grated
15 g/½ oz/1 tbsp butter or margarine
100 g/4 oz/1 cup plain (all-purpose) flour
2 eggs, separated
150 ml/¼ pt/⅔ cup milk
225 g/8 oz/2 cups cooked chicken, diced, all skin removed
50 g/2 oz frozen peas, thawed
Salt and freshly ground black pepper
2.5 ml/½ tsp dried thyme
Oil, for deep-frying
Sweet and Sour Dipping Sauce (page 337) or Barbecue Sauce (page 336) and Plain Boiled Rice (page 351), to serve

Fry (sauté) the bacon, onion and carrot in the butter or margarine for 2 minutes. Leave to cool. Put the flour in a large bowl and add the egg yolks and milk. Beat well until smooth. Stir in the cooked onion mixture, the chicken and peas. Season well with salt and pepper and stir in the thyme. Whisk the egg whites until stiff and fold into the mixture with a metal spoon. Deep-fry spoonfuls of the mixture in hot oil for 2–3 minutes until golden brown, gently turning over in the oil if necessary halfway through cooking. Drain on kitchen paper (paper towels) and serve hot with Sweet and Sour Dipping Sauce or Barbecue Sauce and Plain Boiled Rice.

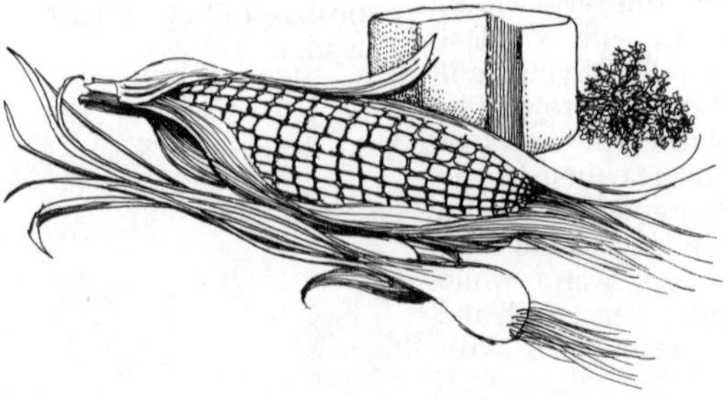

Livers in Cream and Sherry

SERVES 4

25 g/1 oz/2 tbsp butter or margarine
350 g/12 oz chicken livers, trimmed and cut into bite-sized pieces, if necessary
100 g/4 oz button mushrooms, sliced
2 onions, finely chopped
45 ml/3 tbsp double (heavy) cream
15 ml/1 tbsp medium-dry sherry
Salt and freshly ground black pepper
Chopped parsley, to garnish
Buttered tagliatelle and a green salad, to serve

Melt the butter or margarine in a frying pan (skillet). Add the livers, mushrooms and onions, cover and cook gently for 8 minutes, stirring occasionally until the livers are tender and cooked through but not hard. Stir in the cream and sherry and season to taste. Heat through. Spoon on to warm plates and sprinkle with chopped parsley. Serve with buttered tagliatelle and a green salad.

Chicken Liver Nests

SERVES 4

450 g/1 lb potatoes, cut into even-sized pieces
40 g/1½ oz/3 tbsp butter or margarine
15 ml/1 tbsp milk
2 onions, finely chopped
1 wineglass of dry vermouth
450 g/1 lb chicken livers, trimmed
5 ml/1 tsp chopped sage
Salt and freshly ground black pepper
350 g/12 oz frozen leaf spinach

Boil the potatoes in lightly salted water until tender. Drain and mash with 15 g/½ oz/1 tbsp of the butter or margarine and the milk. Spoon into four 'nests' on fireproof serving plates. Flash under a hot grill (broiler) to brown. Keep warm. Melt the remaining butter or margarine in a frying pan (skillet). Add the onions and fry (sauté), stirring for 4 minutes until golden and soft. Add the vermouth and boil until nearly all the liquid has evaporated. Stir in the chicken livers, sage and a little salt and pepper and cook, stirring, for about 5 minutes until the livers are brown but still tender. Taste and re-season, if necessary. Meanwhile, cook the spinach according to the packet directions. Drain. Spoon the hot livers into the 'nests' and surround with the spinach. Serve straight away.

Lemony Livers with White Beans

SERVES 4

1 onion, finely chopped
450 g/1 lb chicken livers, trimmed and cut into bite-sized pieces, if necessary
15 ml/1 tbsp sunflower oil
20 g/¾ oz/1½ tbsp unsalted (sweet) butter
1 garlic clove, crushed
Finely grated rind and juice of 1 small lemon
100 g/4 oz button mushrooms, halved
15 ml/1 tbsp brandy
Salt and freshly ground black pepper
2 × 425 g/2 × 15 oz/2 large cans of cannellini beans, drained
30 ml/2 tbsp chopped parsley
10 ml/2 tsp capers
Crusty bread and a green salad, to serve

Fry (sauté) the onion and chicken livers in the oil and butter for 4 minutes, stirring. Add the garlic, lemon rind and juice and mushrooms and cook for a further 2 minutes. Stir in the brandy and salt and pepper to taste. Add the beans and toss over a gentle heat until piping hot. Spoon into warm bowls and sprinkle with the parsley and capers. Serve with crusty bread and a green salad.

TURKEY

Turkey with Grape Juice and Grapes

SERVES 4

150 ml/¼ pt/⅔ cup chicken stock
150 ml/¼ pt/⅔ cup white grape juice
1 bouquet garni sachet
25 g/1 oz/2 tbsp butter or margarine
225 g/8 oz turkey stir-fry meat
25 g/1 oz/¼ cup plain (all-purpose) flour
100 g/4 oz seedless white grapes, halved
Salt and freshly ground black pepper
15 ml/1 tbsp chopped parsley
Speciality Creamed Potatoes (page 348) and broccoli, to serve

Put the stock and grape juice in a saucepan with the bouquet garni. Bring to the boil and leave to infuse for 10 minutes, then discard the bouquet garni. Meanwhile, heat the butter or margarine in a large frying pan (skillet). Add the turkey and stir-fry for 5 minutes. Add the flour and cook for 1 minute. Remove from the heat, then gradually blend in the infused stock and grape juice. Return to the heat, bring to the boil and cook for 2 minutes, stirring. Add the grapes and season to taste. Stir in the parsley. Serve on a pile of Speciality Creamed Potatoes with broccoli.

Peking-style Turkey

SERVES 4

1 bunch of spring onions (scallions)
¼ cucumber
350 g/12 oz turkey stir-fry meat
45 ml/3 tbsp soy sauce
5 ml/1 tsp grated fresh root ginger
1 garlic clove, crushed
10 ml/2 tsp red wine vinegar
Freshly ground black pepper
45 ml/3 tbsp plum jam (conserve)
5 ml/1 tsp lemon juice
8 Chinese pancakes or small tortillas
15 g/½ oz/1 tbsp butter or margarine

Cut the roots off the spring onions and cut off the green, leaving the onions about 7.5 cm/3 in long. Make a series of cuts through the white bulb to a depth of about 2.5 cm/1 in. Place in a bowl of cold water and chill to allow the ends to open out. Cut the cucumber into thin strips. Place in a serving bowl and chill. Put the turkey in a shallow dish. Mix together half the soy sauce and ginger and all the garlic, vinegar and a good grinding of pepper. Pour over the turkey and toss well. Leave to marinate for at least 1 hour to absorb the flavours.

Meanwhile, mix the plum jam with the remaining soy sauce and ginger and the lemon juice. Put in a small serving bowl. Warm the pancakes or tortillas according to the packet directions. Heat the butter or margarine in a large frying pan (skillet). Lift the turkey out of the marinade with a draining spoon and fry (sauté) for about 5 minutes until cooked through. Turn out on to a warm serving dish. To serve, use a spring onion 'brush' to dip in the plum sauce and spread over a pancake or tortilla. Add the spring onion, a spoonful of meat and some cucumber. Roll up and eat with the fingers.

Nutty Turkey Maryland Balls

SERVES 4

2 rindless streaky bacon rashers (slices), chopped
1 onion, chopped
25 g/1 oz/2 tbsp butter or margarine
150 g/5 oz/1¼ cups cooked turkey, chopped
200 g/7 oz/1 small can of sweetcorn (corn), drained
25 g/1 oz/¼ cup pecan nuts, finely chopped
175 g/6 oz/1½ cups plain (all-purpose) flour
A pinch of salt
250 ml/8 fl oz/1 cup tepid water
30 ml/2 tbsp sunflower oil, plus extra for deep-frying
2 egg whites
2 bananas, cut into chunks
Super Sauté Potatoes (page 349) and peas, to serve

Fry (sauté) the bacon and onion in half the butter or margarine for 3 minutes until lightly browned. Mix in the turkey, sweetcorn and nuts. Sift the flour and salt in a bowl. Add the water and oil and beat to a smooth batter. Stir in the turkey mixture. Whisk the egg whites until stiff and fold into the mixture with a metal spoon. Heat the oil for deep-frying until a cube of day-old bread browns in 30 seconds. Drop spoonfuls of the mixture into the oil and fry for 4–5 minutes until crisp and golden. Drain on kitchen paper (paper towels). Meanwhile, fry the bananas in the remaining butter or margarine in a frying pan (skillet) for 2–3 minutes until golden but still holding their shape. Drain on kitchen paper. Serve the balls with the bananas, Super Sauté Potatoes and peas.

Zingy Turkey Steaks

SERVES 4

4 turkey steaks, about 175 g/6 oz each
Salt and freshly ground black pepper
15 g/½ oz/1 tbsp butter or margarine
150 ml/¼ pt/⅔ cup ginger wine
10 ml/2 tsp lemon juice
1 piece of stem ginger in syrup, chopped
45 ml/3 tbsp soured (dairy sour) cream
450 g/1 lb baby new potatoes, quartered
450 g/1 lb spring greens (collard greens), shredded
Paprika, for dusting

Season the turkey steaks and fry (sauté) in the butter or margarine for about 8 minutes on each side until golden and cooked through. Remove from the pan and keep warm. Add the ginger wine to the pan. Bring to the boil and boil for 2–3 minutes. Stir in the lemon juice, ginger and soured cream. Bring to the boil and simmer for 2–3 minutes. Taste and re-season if necessary. Meanwhile, cook the potatoes in lightly salted boiling water for 4 minutes. Add the greens and continue boiling until both are tender. Drain thoroughly and add a good grinding of black pepper. Spread the potato and greens on to four warm plates. Top each with a turkey steak, then spoon the sauce over. Garnish with a dusting of paprika and serve straight away.

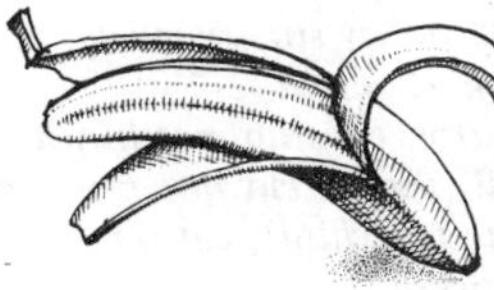

Turkey and Vegetables in Black Bean Sauce

SERVES 4

175 g/6 oz Chinese egg noodles
225 g/8 oz turkey stir-fry meat
45 ml/3 tbsp sunflower oil
225 g/8 oz thin French (green) beans, cut into short lengths
1 carrot, cut into very thin matchsticks
2 celery sticks, cut into very thin matchsticks
1 onion, chopped
100 g/4 oz cup mushrooms, thickly sliced
30 ml/2 tbsp soy sauce
15 ml/1 tbsp black bean sauce
10 ml/2 tsp cornflour (cornstarch)
30 ml/2 tbsp water

Cook the noodles according to the packet directions. Drain. Stir-fry the turkey in the oil in a wok or large frying pan (skillet) for 2 minutes. Add the beans, carrot, celery and onion and stir-fry for a further 3 minutes. Stir in the mushrooms and cook for 1 minute. Blend together the soy sauce, black bean sauce, cornflour and water. Stir into the pan and cook, stirring, for 2 minutes. Add the noodles, toss for 2 minutes and serve in bowls.

Turkey Stir-fry

SERVES 4

15 g/½ oz/1 tbsp butter or margarine
175 g/6 oz turkey stir-fry meat
1 onion, thinly sliced
1 large carrot, cut into matchsticks
1 red (bell) pepper, cut into thin strips
1 courgette (zucchini), cut into matchsticks
100 g/4 oz green cabbage, thinly shredded
50 g/2 oz frozen peas
100 g/4 oz/2 cups beansprouts
15 ml/1 tbsp soy sauce
1.5 ml/¼ tsp ground ginger
10 ml/2 tsp clear honey
30 ml/2 tbsp medium-dry sherry
Freshly ground black pepper
175 g/6 oz Chinese egg noodles

Heat the butter or margarine in a large frying pan (skillet). Add the turkey and stir-fry for 2 minutes. Add the onion and carrot and stir-fry for 2 minutes. Add the remaining vegetables and stir-fry for 3 minutes. Add the remaining ingredients except the noodles and toss for 2–3 minutes or until the vegetables are cooked to your liking. Meanwhile, cook the noodles according to the packet directions. Drain. Spoon into bowls and top with the turkey stir-fry.

Turkey and Lettuce Ribbon Stir-fry

SERVES 4

1 large carrot
1 large courgette (zucchini)
45 ml/3 tbsp sunflower oil
1 large garlic clove, crushed
10 ml/2 tsp grated fresh root ginger
4 spring onions (scallions), finely chopped
1 red (bell) pepper, cut into very thin strips
½ iceberg lettuce, shredded
100 g/4 oz/2 cups beansprouts
175 g/6 oz/1½ cups cooked turkey, cut into neat pieces
30 ml/2 tbsp oyster sauce
15 ml/1 tbsp mild chilli sauce

Pare the carrot and courgette into thin ribbons with a potato peeler. Heat the oil in a large frying pan (skillet) or wok. Add the garlic and ginger and stir-fry for 1 minute. Add the carrot, courgette, spring onions and pepper and stir-fry for 3 minutes. Add the remaining ingredients and stir-fry for a further 3 minutes. Spoon on to plates and serve.

Turkey, Broccoli and Bamboo Shoots with Yellow Bean Sauce

SERVES 4

1 onion
175 g/6 oz broccoli, cut into small florets
45 ml/3 tbsp sunflower oil
175 g/6 oz/1½ cups cooked turkey, cut into strips
10 ml/2 tsp cornflour (cornstarch)
30 ml/2 tbsp yellow bean sauce
15 ml/1 tbsp mild chilli sauce
5 ml/1 tsp ground ginger
185 g/6½ oz/1 small can of sliced bamboo shoots, drained
30 ml/2 tbsp soy sauce
Plain Boiled Rice (page 351), to serve

Cut the onion into small wedges and separate into layers. Stir-fry the broccoli and onion in the oil in a wok or large frying pan (skillet) for 3 minutes. Toss the turkey in the cornflour and add to the pan. Stir-fry for 1 minute. Add the remaining ingredients and stir-fry for a further 3 minutes. Serve in warm bowls on a bed of Plain Boiled Rice.

Turkey and Pineapple Stir-fry with Noodles

SERVES 4

225 g/8 oz turkey pieces
25 g/1 oz/2 tbsp butter or margarine
1 garlic clove, finely chopped
300 g/11 oz/1 packet of ready prepared fresh stir-fry mixed vegetables
100 g/4 oz button mushrooms, sliced
228 g/8 oz/1 small can of pineapple pieces in natural juice
175 g/6 oz/3 cups beansprouts
2 tomatoes, roughly chopped
30 ml/2 tbsp soy sauce
Salt and freshly ground black pepper
100 g/4 oz Chinese egg noodles
Prawn crackers, to serve

Trim the turkey pieces and cut into small, even-sized strips. Melt the butter or margarine in a large frying pan (skillet). Add the turkey and stir-fry for 3 minutes until browned and almost cooked through. Add the garlic, mixed vegetables and mushrooms and stir-fry for 3 minutes. Add the pineapple and its juice, the beansprouts, tomatoes, soy sauce and a little salt and pepper. Stir well, then cover and cook for 5 minutes. Meanwhile, cook the noodles according to the packet directions. Drain and add to the stir-fry. Mix well, then spoon on to warm plates and serve with prawn crackers.

Turkey and Apricot Stir-fry

SERVES 4

Prepare as for Turkey and Pineapple Stir-fry with Noodles, but substitute canned apricot halves, sliced, for the pineapple and use 225 g/8 oz/1 small can of bamboo shoots, drained, instead of the beansprouts.

Barbecued Turkey Steaks

SERVES 4

15 g/½ oz/1 tbsp butter or margarine
4 turkey breast steaks
15 ml/1 tbsp lemon juice
15 ml/1 tbsp malt vinegar
30 ml/2 tbsp tomato purée (paste)
15 ml/1 tbsp Worcestershire sauce
30 ml/2 tbsp clear honey
Super Sauté Potatoes (page 349) and mangetout (snow peas), to serve

Heat the butter or margarine in a large non-stick frying pan (skillet). Add the turkey and brown for 1 minute on each side. Mix together the remaining ingredients and spoon over. Cook for about 8 minutes over a gentle heat, turning occasionally, until cooked through and stickily glazed in the sauce. Serve with Super Sauté Potatoes and mangetout.

Fast Food Turkey Chow Mein

SERVES 4

250 g/9 oz/1 packet Chinese egg noodles
225 g/8 oz/2 cups cooked turkey, all skin removed, cut into strips
425 g/15 oz/1 large can of stir-fry mixed vegetables, drained
1 garlic clove, crushed
30 ml/2 tbsp soy sauce
30 ml/2 tbsp dry sherry
5 ml/1 tsp ground ginger
10 ml/2 tsp light brown sugar

Cook the noodles according to the packet directions. Drain. Put the turkey in a large frying pan (skillet). Rinse the vegetables under cold water, drain again and add to the chicken with the remaining ingredients. Heat through, stirring occasionally, until piping hot. Add the noodles and stir until well coated. Reheat and serve.

Oriental Turkey with Cashew Nuts and Mushrooms

SERVES 4

25 g/1 oz/2 tbsp butter or margarine
225 g/8 oz turkey stir-fry meat
1 bunch of spring onions (scallions), cut into short lengths
100 g/4 oz button mushrooms, sliced
225 g/8 oz/4 cups beansprouts
25 g/1 oz/¼ cup raw cashew nuts
300 ml/½ pt/1¼ cups chicken stock
15 ml/1 tbsp cornflour (cornstarch)
15 ml/1 tbsp soy sauce
Plain Boiled Rice (page 351), to serve

Heat the butter or margarine in a large frying pan (skillet) or wok. Add the turkey, onions and mushrooms and stir-fry for 5 minutes. Add the beansprouts and cook, stirring, for a further 2 minutes. Add the nuts and stock and bring to the boil. Blend together the cornflour and soy sauce, stir into the pan and cook, stirring, for 2 minutes. Spoon on to a bed of Plain Boiled Rice and serve.

Savoury Turkey Escalopes

SERVES 4

4 small turkey steaks, about 175 g/6 oz each
85 g/3½ oz/1 small packet of sage and onion stuffing mix
1 egg
15 ml/1 tbsp milk
Sunflower oil, for shallow-frying
Lemon wedges and sprigs of parsley or fresh sage, to garnish
Puréed Potatoes (page 350) and French (green) beans, to serve

Put the turkey steaks, one at a time, in a plastic bag and beat with a rolling pin or meat mallet until flattened and fairly thin. Put the stuffing mix in a shallow dish and beat the egg and milk in a separate dish. Dip the turkey in the beaten egg, then the stuffing to coat completely. Fry (sauté) the escalopes for 3–4 minutes until golden brown underneath. Turn over and fry the other sides until cooked through and golden. Drain on kitchen paper (paper towels). Garnish with lemon wedges and sprigs of parsley or fresh sage and serve with Puréed Potatoes and French beans.

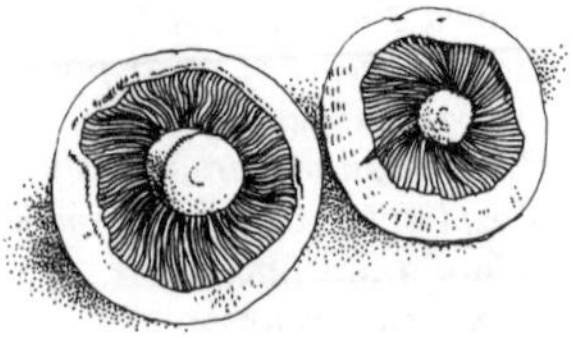

Turkey and Lentil Rissoles

SERVES 4

100 g/4 oz/⅔ cup brown or green lentils, soaked for 2 hours in boiling water
300 ml/½ pt/1¼ cups water
1 onion, quartered
175 g/6 oz/1½ cups cooked turkey
15 ml/1 tbsp tomato purée (paste)
5 ml/1 tsp dried oregano
Salt and freshly ground black pepper
1 egg, beaten
50 g/2 oz/1 cup breadcrumbs
Sunflower oil, for shallow-frying
Tomato wedges and parsley sprigs, to garnish
Sweet pickle, crusty bread and a mixed salad, to serve

Drain the lentils and place in a saucepan with the water. Bring to the boil, reduce the heat, cover and simmer gently for about 50 minutes until the liquid is absorbed and the lentils are soft and floury. Check once or twice during cooking and add a very little more water, if necessary. Mince (grind) or finely chop the onion and turkey in a food processor. Transfer to a bowl and add the cooked lentils, the tomato purée and oregano. Season with salt and pepper. Shape the mixture into 12 small, flat cakes. Dip in the egg, then the breadcrumbs to coat completely. Heat the oil in a large frying pan (skillet). Shallow-fry the rissoles, a few at a time, for 2 minutes on each side until crisp, golden and piping hot throughout. Drain on kitchen paper (paper towels) and keep warm while cooking the remainder. Serve hot, garnished with tomato wedges and parsley sprigs, with sweet pickle, crusty bread and a mixed salad.

DUCK

Duck Slivers with Orange

This is very rich, so half a large duck breast is enough for a portion.

SERVES 4

25 g/1 oz/2 tbsp butter or margarine
2 large duck breasts
Salt and freshly ground black pepper
15 ml/1 tbsp brandy
150 ml/¼ pt/⅔ cup chicken stock
5 ml/1 tsp light brown sugar
Finely grated rind and juice of 1 orange
15 ml/1 tbsp cornflour (cornstarch)
Watercress and 1 orange, sliced, to garnish
New potatoes and mangetout (snow peas), to serve

Heat the butter or margarine in a non-stick frying pan (skillet). Add the duck. Sprinkle with salt and pepper and fry (sauté) for 8 minutes, turn over, season again and cook for a further 7 minutes or until just pink in the centre. (Cook a little longer if you like your duck well done.) Remove from the pan and keep warm. Add the brandy to the pan and ignite. Shake the pan until the flames subside, then add the stock and sugar. Blend the orange rind and juice with the cornflour and stir into the pan. Cook, stirring, for 2 minutes until thickened and clear. Taste and re-season if necessary. Cut the duck into very thin slices and arrange on four serving plates. Spoon the sauce over and garnish with watercress and orange slices. Serve with new potatoes and mangetout.

Duck Slivers with Grapefruit

SERVES 4

Prepare as for Duck Slivers with Orange, but substitute the finely grated rind and juice of 1 pink grapefruit for the orange and use orange liqueur instead of the brandy for sweetness.

Duck with Ginger

SERVES 4

20 g/¾ oz/1½ tbsp butter or margarine
2 large duck breasts
Salt and freshly ground black pepper
150 ml/¼ pt/⅔ cup chicken stock
30 ml/2 tbsp ginger wine
15 ml/1 tbsp soy sauce
15 ml/1 tbsp cornflour (cornstarch)
Parsley sprigs, to garnish
Baby potatoes in their skins and braised celery, to serve

Heat the butter or margarine in a non-stick frying pan (skillet). Add the meat, season with salt and pepper and fry (sauté) for 8 minutes. Turn the duck over, season again and fry for a further 7 minutes or until just pink in the centre. (Cook a little longer if you like your duck well done.) Remove from the pan and keep warm. Add the stock and ginger wine to the pan and bring to the boil. Blend the soy sauce with the cornflour and stir into the pan. Bring to the boil and cook for 2 minutes, stirring, until thickened. Taste and re-season if necessary. Cut the duck into thin slices and arrange on four warm serving plates. Spoon the sauce over, garnish with parsley sprigs and serve with baby potatoes in their skins and braised celery.

Cantonese-style Duck

SERVES 4

Prepare as for Cantonese-style Chicken (page 102), but use 2 large duck fillets, each cut diagonally into four slices and beaten flat, instead of the chicken fillets, then continue as before.

Chinese Duck with Egg, Vegetables and Noodles

SERVES 4

175 g/6 oz Chinese egg noodles
45 ml/3 tbsp sunflower oil
2 duck breasts, cut into thin slivers
1 carrot, thinly sliced diagonally
1 bunch of spring onions (scallions), cut diagonally into short lengths
1 green (bell) pepper, cut into neat dice
100 g/4 oz cup mushrooms, thinly sliced
50 g/2 oz frozen peas
1 garlic clove, crushed
10 ml/2 tsp grated fresh root ginger
20 ml/4 tsp light brown sugar
30 ml/2 tbsp soy sauce
4 eggs, beaten

Cook the noodles according to the packet directions. Drain. Heat the oil in a wok or large frying pan (skillet). Add the duck and stir-fry for 3 minutes. Add the vegetables and stir-fry for a further 3 minutes. Add the garlic, ginger, sugar and soy sauce and cook for a further 2 minutes. Add the eggs and stir-fry until the mixture is just scrambled but still soft. Add the noodles and toss for 2 minutes. Serve piping hot.

Duck with Port and Redcurrant

SERVES 4

20 g/¾ oz/1½ tbsp butter or margarine
2 large duck breasts
Salt and freshly ground black pepper
150 ml/¼ pt/⅔ cup chicken stock
45 ml/3 tbsp port
15 ml/1 tbsp redcurrant jelly (clear conserve)
15 ml/1 tbsp cornflour (cornstarch)
15 ml/1 tbsp water
Parsley sprigs and 4 small bunches of redcurrants (optional), to garnish
New potatoes and French (green) beans, to serve

Heat the butter or margarine in a non-stick frying pan (skillet). Add the duck, season with salt and pepper and fry (sauté) for 8 minutes. Turn the duck over, season again and fry for a further 7 minutes or until just pink in the centre. (Cook a little longer if you like your duck well done.) Remove from the pan and keep warm. Add the stock, port and redcurrant jelly. Heat, stirring, until the jelly dissolves. Blend the cornflour with the water and stir in. Bring to the boil and cook for 2 minutes, stirring. Taste and re-season, if necessary. Cut the duck into thin slices and arrange on four serving plates. Spoon the sauce over. Garnish each with parsley sprigs and a small sprig of redcurrants, if using, and serve with new potatoes and French beans.

Blackcurrant Duck

SERVES 4

Prepare as for Duck with Port and Redcurrant, but substitute blackcurrant jelly (clear conserve) for the redcurrant and crème de cassis for the port. Garnish with small sprigs of blackcurrants or whitecurrants, if liked.

Duck with Raspberries

SERVES 4

Prepare as for Duck with Port and Redcurrant but add 15ml/1 tbsp raspberry vinegar to the sauce and toss in 75 g/3 oz raspberries just before serving. Omit the redcurrant garnish and serve with mixed salad leaves instead of French (green) beans.

Peppered Duck

SERVES 4

2 large duck breasts
30 ml/2 tbsp coarsely crushed black peppercorns
Salt
25 g/1 oz/2 tbsp butter or margarine
30 ml/2 tbsp brandy
150 ml/¼ pt/⅔ cup chicken stock
10 ml/2 tsp cornflour (cornstarch)
15 ml/1 tbsp water
150 ml/¼ pt/⅔ cup crème fraîche
15 ml/1 tbsp chopped parsley
Buttered noodles and broccoli, to serve

Coat the duck with the peppercorns and season with a little salt. Heat the butter or margarine in a non-stick frying pan (skillet) and fry (sauté) the duck for about 7 minutes on each side until just cooked through but slightly pink in the centre. (Cook a little longer if you like your duck well done.) Remove from the pan and keep warm. Add the brandy to the pan and ignite. Shake the pan until the flames subside, then add the stock and bring to the boil. Blend the cornflour with the water and stir in with the crème fraîche. Bring to the boil and cook for 2 minutes, stirring. Stir in the parsley. Cut the duck into thin slices and arrange on four warm plates. Spoon the sauce over and serve with buttered noodles and broccoli.

Duck and Avocado Pancakes

SERVES 4

2 duck breasts, cut into thin strips
30 ml/2 tbsp sunflower oil
1 garlic clove, crushed
1 red onion, thinly sliced
½ cucumber, cut into matchsticks
100 g/4 oz mangetout (snow peas)
100 g/4 oz/2 cups beansprouts
1 large avocado, sliced
15 ml/1 tbsp sesame oil
15 ml/1 tbsp soy sauce
15 ml/1 tbsp lemon juice
10 ml/2 tsp clear honey
12 Chinese pancakes or small flour tortillas, to serve

Stir-fry the duck in the sunflower oil for 4 minutes. Add the garlic, onion, cucumber and mangetout. Stir-fry for a further 4 minutes. Add the remaining ingredients, toss well and cook for 2 minutes. Spoon into the pancakes, roll up and serve.

GAME

Pheasant with Tomato and Cheese Cream

SERVES 4

1 large oven-ready pheasant, quartered (page 17)
15 ml/1 tbsp olive oil
15 g/½ oz/1 tbsp butter or margarine
15 ml/1 tbsp plain (all-purpose) flour
150 ml/¼ pt/⅔ cup chicken stock
6 ripe tomatoes, skinned, seeded and chopped
2.5 ml/½ tsp caster (superfine) sugar
150 ml/¼ pt/⅔ cup crème fraîche
50 g/2 oz/¼ cup Parmesan cheese, grated
Salt and freshly ground black pepper
Spaghetti, to serve

Fry (sauté) the pheasant in the oil and butter or margarine in a large frying pan (skillet) on all sides to brown. Cover, reduce the heat and continue to cook for about 30 minutes or until the pheasant is tender. Lift out of the pan and keep warm. Spoon off all but 15 ml/1 tbsp of the fat. Stir in the flour, blend in the stock and simmer, stirring, for 2 minutes. Add the tomatoes and sugar and simmer for 5 minutes. Stir in the crème fraîche, cheese and a little salt and pepper. Return the pheasant to the pan and simmer for about 5 minutes until bathed in the sauce. Taste and season if necessary. Serve on a bed of spaghetti.

Chinese Fried Pigeon

SERVES 4

2 plump oven-ready pigeons
45 ml/3 tbsp soy sauce
45 ml/3 tbsp dry sherry
5 ml/1 tsp grated fresh root ginger
Sunflower oil, for deep-frying
Salt
Lemon wedges, to garnish
Crispy Noodles (page 356) and a beansprout and green (bell) pepper salad, to serve

Cut the pigeons in quarters (page 17). Whisk together the soy sauce, sherry and ginger in a shallow dish. Add the pigeons and turn to coat completely. Leave to marinate for 1 hour. Heat the oil in a wok or large saucepan until a cube of bread browns in 30 seconds. Drain the pigeon quarters on kitchen paper (paper towels). Fry (sauté) a few at a time for 1 minute only. Remove from the oil with a draining spoon. Heat the oil again until almost smoking and a cube of bread browns in 20 seconds. Add the pigeons and fry for 4 minutes until crisp and brown. Drain on kitchen paper. Sprinkle with salt, place on a warm dish, garnish with lemon wedges and serve with Crispy Noodles and a beansprout and green pepper salad.

Italian-style Golden Fried Partridge

SERVES 4

2 oven-ready partridges, quartered (page 17)
2 lemons
1 small onion, finely chopped
90 ml/6 tbsp olive oil
Salt and freshly ground black pepper
50 g/2 oz/½ cup plain (all-purpose) flour
5 ml/1 tsp salt
2 eggs, beaten
100 g/4 oz/2 cups white breadcrumbs
50 g/2 oz/¼ cup unsalted (sweet) butter
Parsley sprigs and a few sliced stoned (pitted) olives, to garnish
Super Sauté Potatoes with Garlic (page 349) and a green salad, to serve

Wipe the partridges with kitchen paper (paper towels) and place in a shallow dish. Squeeze the juice from one of the lemons and mix with the onion, 30 ml/2 tbsp of the oil and a little salt and pepper. Pour over the birds. Turn to coat completely, then leave to marinate for 2 hours. Season the flour with a little salt and pepper. Drain the partridges on kitchen paper, then coat in the seasoned flour. Dip in the egg, then the breadcrumbs to coat completely. Heat the butter and remaining oil in a large, heavy-based frying pan (skillet). Fry (sauté) the partridges for about 8–10 minutes, turning occasionally, until golden brown and cooked through. Transfer to warm plates. Cut the remaining lemon into wedges and use with the olives and parsley sprigs to garnish the partridges. Serve with Super Sauté Potatoes with Garlic and a green salad.

Grills and Barbecues

Choose young birds for grilling (broiling) as they need to be very tender to take the fierce, fast cooking. All foods for grilling can be cooked on a barbecue and vice-versa. There are, however, a few recipes that have been specifically designed for the barbecue – just because the flavour is unmatchable.

CHICKEN

Plain Grilled Chicken in Butter

SERVES 4

4 chicken portions
50 g/2 oz/¼ cup butter, melted
10 ml/2 tsp lemon juice
5 ml/1 tsp dried mixed herbs
Salt and freshly ground black pepper
Super Sauté Potatoes (page 349) and a mixed salad, to serve

Wipe the chicken and place on a grill (broiler) rack. Mix the butter with the lemon juice, herbs and some salt and pepper. Brush all over the chicken. Grill (broil) for about 20 minutes, turning several times and brushing with the butter mixture until crisp on the outside, golden brown and cooked through. Serve with Super Sauté Potatoes and a mixed salad.

Plain Grilled Chicken with Garlic

SERVES 4

Prepare as for Plain Grilled Chicken in Butter, but add 1 or 2 crushed garlic cloves to the melted butter.

Sweet Spiced Chicken with Mint

SERVES 4

25 g/1 oz/2 tbsp butter or margarine
45 ml/3 tbsp chopped mint
2.5 ml/½ tsp ground cinnamon
2.5 ml/½ tsp grated nutmeg
15 ml/1 tbsp lemon juice
10 ml/2 tsp caster (superfine) sugar
4 skinless chicken breasts
1 lemon, sliced, and parsley sprigs, to garnish
New potatoes and a mixed salad, to serve

Mash the butter or margarine with the mint, spices, lemon juice and sugar. Spread all over the chicken. Place on foil on a grill (broiler) rack and grill (broil) for 6 minutes on each side or until golden brown and cooked through. Garnish with lemon slices and parsley sprigs and serve with new potatoes and a mixed salad.

Sweet Spiced Chicken with Coriander and Lemon

SERVES 4

Prepare as for Sweet Spiced Chicken with Mint, but substitute chopped coriander (cilantro) for the mint and add the finely grated rind of ½ lemon to the mixture.

Grilled Chicken with Hot Olive Sauce

SERVES 4

45 ml/3 tbsp olive oil
1 onion, finely chopped
2 garlic cloves, crushed
1 green (bell) pepper, chopped
400 g/14 oz/1 large can of chopped tomatoes
75 g/3 oz stuffed olives, sliced
2.5 ml/½ tsp cayenne
A few drops of Worcestershire sauce
Salt and freshly ground black pepper
4 chicken portions
Plain Boiled Rice (page 351), to serve

Heat 30 ml/2 tbsp of the oil in a saucepan and fry (sauté) the onion, garlic and pepper for 4 minutes until soft and lightly golden. Add the tomatoes, olives, cayenne and Worcestershire sauce and season lightly. Bring to the boil and simmer for 5 minutes until pulpy. Keep warm. Brush the chicken with the remaining oil. Place on a grill (broiler) rack. Season with salt and pepper and grill (broil) for about 20 minutes, turning often, until well-browned and cooked through, brushing with more oil as necessary. Transfer to warm plates and spoon the sauce over. Serve with Plain Boiled Rice.

Grilled Chicken with Corn Stuffing

SERVES 4

75 g/3 oz/1½ cups white breadcrumbs
200 g/7 oz/1 small can of sweetcorn (corn)
Salt and freshly ground black pepper
2.5 ml/½ tsp dried thyme
15 ml/1 tbsp chopped parsley
5 ml/1 tsp dried onion granules
75 g/3 oz/⅓ cup butter or margarine, melted
4 chicken portions
300 ml/½ pt/1¼ cups passata (sieved tomatoes)
2.5 ml/½ tsp dried basil
Green salad, to serve

Mix together the breadcrumbs, the contents of the can of corn (including any juice), a little salt and pepper, the thyme, parsley and onion granules. Add 50 g/2 oz/¼ cup of the butter or margarine and stir in. Place in a shallow, flameproof dish. Grill (broil) for 10 minutes until golden on the top. Keep warm in the oven at the lowest setting and warm some plates too. Place the chicken portions on foil on the grill (broiler) rack. Brush with the remaining butter and some seasoning. Grill for about 20 minutes, turning frequently, until cooked through and golden brown. Meanwhile, put the passata in a saucepan with the basil and heat through. Divide the stuffing between the four plates and top each with a chicken portion. Spoon a little passata over each and serve hot with a green salad.

Grilled Chicken Kiev

SERVES 4

4 skinless chicken breasts, about 175 g/6 oz each
50 g/2 oz/¼ cup butter or margarine
1 or 2 garlic cloves, crushed
30 ml/2 tbsp chopped parsley
Salt and freshly ground black pepper
A squeeze of lemon juice
Buttered Rice (page 351) and a mixed salad, to serve

Make a slit in the side of each chicken breast. Reserve 5 ml/1 tsp of the butter or margarine and mash the remainder with the garlic (more or less to taste), the parsley and a little salt and pepper. Spoon into the chicken breasts and secure thoroughly with cocktail sticks (toothpicks). Place on foil on the grill (broiler) rack. Smear the remaining butter or margarine over and add the lemon juice. Place under a hot grill (broiler) for about 15 minutes, turning once until cooked through. Transfer to warm plates immediately, remove the cocktail sticks and serve with Buttered Rice and a mixed salad.

Grilled Chicken Kiev with Lime and Coriander

SERVES 4

Prepare as for Grilled Chicken Kiev, but use chopped coriander (cilantro) instead of parsley and add the finely grated rind of ½ a lime to the mixture. Squeeze lime juice over the chicken before grilling (broiling) instead of lemon juice.

Cheat Chicken Maryland

SERVES 4

450 g/1 lb crumb-coated chicken breast pieces
4–8 rindless streaky bacon rashers (slices)
Watercress, to garnish
Super Sauté Potatoes (page 349), Fried Bananas (page 355) and Corn Fritters (page 355), to serve

Grill (broil) the chicken pieces according to the packet directions. Keep warm. Stretch the bacon rashers with the back of a knife. Cut into halves and roll up. Grill, turning once, for about 4 minutes until cooked through. Arrange the chicken and bacon rolls on four plates, garnish with watercress and serve with Super Sauté Potatoes, Fried Bananas and Corn Fritters.

Chicken with Curry Butter

SERVES 4

4 spring onions, (scallions), chopped
100 g/4 oz/½ cup unsalted (sweet) butter
15 ml/1 tbsp curry paste
5 ml/1 tsp lemon juice
Salt and freshly ground black pepper
4 skinless chicken breasts
Wild Rice Mix (page 352), to serve

Put the spring onions in a blender or food processor with the butter, curry paste and lemon juice. Run the machine until smooth. Season with salt and pepper and run the machine again. Place the chicken breasts on foil on the grill (broiler) rack. Spread with half the butter mixture. Grill (broil) for 8 minutes, basting frequently. Turn over and spread the other side of the chicken with the remaining curry butter. Grill for a further 8 minutes, basting frequently, until sizzling and cooked through. Serve with any of the buttery juices spooned over with Wild Rice Mix.

Chicken with Chinese Curry Butter

SERVES 4

Prepare as for Chicken with Curry Butter, but add 2.5 ml/½ tsp Chinese five spice powder to the curry paste and serve with Special Egg Fried Rice (page 351), instead of Wild Rice Mix.

Grilled Chicken with Chinese Five Spice Powder

SERVES 4

4 skinless chicken breasts
15 ml/1 tbsp Chinese five spice powder
30 ml/2 tbsp sesame oil
30 ml/2 tbsp sunflower oil
30 ml/2 tbsp lemon juice
100 g/4 oz/2 cups beansprouts
1 red (bell) pepper, shredded
2 spring onions (scallions), finely sliced
Soy sauce
Lemon wedges, to garnish
Egg Fried Rice (page 351), to serve

Wipe the chicken with kitchen paper (paper towels). Mix the spice powder with half the oils and half the lemon juice. Spread all over the chicken and leave to marinate for 2 hours in a shallow dish. Mix the beansprouts with the pepper and onions. Mix the remaining oils and lemon juice with soy sauce to taste. Place the chicken on foil on a grill (broiler) rack. Grill (broil) for about 15 minutes, turning occasionally and brushing with any marinade left in the dish until cooked through. Pour the soy sauce mixture over the beansprout mixture and toss. Transfer the chicken to warm serving plates. Spoon the salad to the side. Garnish with lemon wedges and serve with Egg Fried Rice.

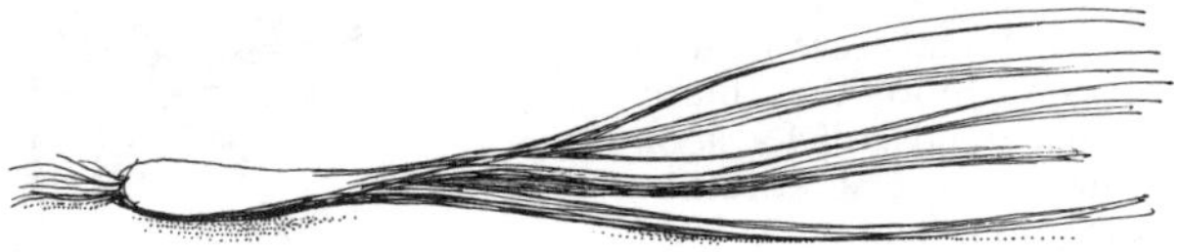

Grilled Spiced Chicken with Sweet Pepper Couscous

SERVES 6

6 skinless chicken breasts
90 ml/6 tbsp olive oil
1 garlic clove, crushed
5 ml/1 tsp ground coriander (cilantro)
5 ml/1 tsp ground cumin
5 ml/1 tsp paprika
2.5 ml/½ tsp ground cinnamon
Salt and freshly ground black pepper
10 ml/2 tsp lemon juice
1 red (bell) pepper, halved
1 green pepper, halved
1 orange pepper, halved
1 yellow pepper, halved
1 red onion, sliced and separated into rings
1 chicken stock cube
450 ml/¾ pt/2 cups boiling water
350 g/12 oz/2 cups couscous
15 ml/1 tbsp chopped mint
30 ml/2 tbsp chopped parsley
Lemon wedges and parsley sprigs, to garnish

Put the chicken breasts in a large shallow dish. Whisk half the oil with the garlic, spices, a little salt and pepper and half the lemon juice. Pour over the chicken, turn to coat completely, then leave to marinate for at least 2 hours. Preheat the grill (broiler) 30 minutes before the chicken has finished marinating. Lay the pepper halves and onion rings on the rack and brush with some of the remaining oil. Grill (broil) turning once, until slightly blackening in places and soft. Cut the peppers into strips and keep warm with the onion slices. Make up the chicken stock with the water. Pour over the couscous in a large bowl, stir well and leave to stand for 15 minutes. Remove the chicken from the marinade and grill for about 15 minutes, turning once and brushing with any remaining marinade, until cooked through and golden. Stir the peppers and onions into the couscous with the herbs, any remaining oil and the remaining lemon juice. Season to taste. Pile on to warm plates. Cut the chicken breasts into neat slices and fan out on top of the couscous. Serve straight away, garnished with lemon wedges and parsley sprigs.

Chicken with Mustard and Rosemary Rub

SERVES 4

2 large rosemary sprigs
1 garlic clove, crushed
5 ml/1 tsp black mustard seeds
15 ml/1 tbsp chopped parsley
1.5 ml/¼ tsp cayenne
2.5 ml/½ tsp celery salt
Freshly ground black pepper
4 skinless chicken breasts
30 ml/2 tbsp sunflower oil
Speciality Creamed Potatoes (page 348) and mangetout (snow peas), to serve

Strip the leaves off the rosemary sprigs. With the machine running, tip into a blender or food processor with the garlic, mustard seeds, parsley, cayenne and celery salt. Add a little pepper. Make several slashes on each side of the chicken. Rub this mixture well into the chicken on both sides and leave to marinate for about 2 hours. Brush with the oil and place on foil on a grill (broiler) rack. Grill (broil) for about 8 minutes on each side until cooked through and golden. Serve with Speciality Creamed Potatoes and mangetout.

Chicken, Ham and Tomato Grill

SERVES 4

4 skinless chicken breasts
30 ml/2 tbsp sunflower or olive oil
4 thin slices of lean ham
4 tomatoes, sliced
30 ml/2 tbsp grated Parmesan cheese
New potatoes and broccoli, to serve

Place the chicken breasts one at a time in a plastic bag and beat with a rolling pin or meat mallet to flatten. Brush with a little of the oil. Place under a hot grill (broiler) and grill (broil) for 3 minutes on each side. Top each with a slice of ham, then tomato slices. Brush with any remaining oil and sprinkle with the Parmesan. Grill until the tomatoes and ham are sizzling. Serve straight away with new potatoes and broccoli.

Gold-kissed Chicken Grill

SERVES 4

4 skinless chicken breasts, about 175 g/6 oz each
20 g/¾ oz/1½ tsp butter or margarine, melted
200g/7 oz/1 small can of sweetcorn (corn), drained
50 g/2 oz/½ cup Emmental (Swiss) or Cheddar cheese, grated
Watercress sprigs, to garnish
Mixed salad, to serve

Place the chicken breasts one at a time in a plastic bag and beat with a rolling pin or meat mallet to flatten. Brush with the butter or margarine and place on a grill (broiler) rack. Grill (broil) for 3 minutes on each side. Spoon the corn over and top with the cheese. Grill until the cheese is melted and golden. Garnish with watercress and serve straight away with a mixed salad.

Spicy Chicken Wings

SERVES 4

450 g/1 lb chicken wings, skin removed
For the marinade:
1 small onion, finely chopped
15 ml/1 tbsp clear honey
30 ml/2 tbsp Worcestershire sauce
15 g/½ oz/1 tbsp butter or margarine, melted
15 ml/1 tbsp paprika
5 ml/1 tsp cayenne
5 ml/1 tsp ground cumin
10 ml/2 tsp coarse sea salt
Freshly ground black pepper
Mixed salad leaves and tomato wedges, to garnish
Minted Yoghurt and Cucumber (page 339) and Perfect Potato Wedges (page 349), to serve

Put the chicken wings in a single layer in a roasting tin (pan). Mix together the marinade ingredients and pour over, rubbing the mixture into the flesh. Leave to marinate for 2 hours. Lift out of the marinade and grill (broil) for 15–20 minutes until cooked through and crispy, brushing with any remaining marinade during cooking. Garnish with mixed salad leaves and tomato wedges and serve with Minted Yoghurt and Cucumber and Perfect Potato Wedges.

Chicken Teriyaki Kebabs

SERVES 4

30 ml/2 tbsp soy sauce
30 ml/2 tbsp medium-dry sherry
1 garlic clove, crushed
A good pinch of ground ginger
10 ml/2 tsp clear honey
350 g/12 oz skinless chicken breasts, cubed
Egg Fried Rice (page 351), to serve

Mix the soy sauce with the sherry, garlic, ginger and honey. Add the chicken and toss well. Leave in a cool place to marinate for at least 2 hours. Thread on to soaked wooden skewers. Grill (broil) for about 8–10 minutes, turning occasionally and brushing occasionally with any remaining marinade, until tender and cooked through. Serve hot with Egg Fried Rice.

Chicken, Mushroom and Tomato Kebabs

SERVES 4

100 g/4 oz button mushrooms
350 g/12 oz skinless chicken breasts, cut into chunks
30 ml/2 tbsp olive oil
10 ml/2 tsp balsamic vinegar
1 garlic clove, crushed
Salt and freshly ground black pepper
8 cherry tomatoes
8 basil leaves
Tagliatelle tossed in Pesto for Poultry (page 342), to serve

Blanch the mushrooms in boiling water for 1 minute, then drain. Put the chicken in a shallow dish. Add the oil, vinegar and garlic and season with a little salt and pepper. Toss and leave to stand for 30 minutes. Thread on to skewers with the mushrooms, tomatoes and basil. Grill (broil) on foil on a grill (broiler) rack, turning occasionally, for about 8–10 minutes until the chicken is cooked through. Serve on a bed of tagliatelle tossed in Pesto for Poultry.

Chicken, Bacon and Corn Kebabs

SERVES 4

2 corn cobs
350 g/12 oz skinless chicken breasts, cut into chunks
30 ml/2 tbsp olive oil
15 ml/1 tbsp lemon juice
5 ml/1 tsp dried sage
Salt and freshly ground black pepper
4 rindless streaky bacon rashers (slices)
Melted butter, for brushing
Jacket-baked potatoes, topped with soured (dairy sour) cream and snipped chives, to serve

Cut each corn cob into 4 chunks and boil for 5 minutes in lightly salted water. Drain. Put the chicken in a dish and toss with the oil, lemon juice, sage and a little salt and pepper. Stretch the bacon with the back of a knife. Cut each in half and roll up. Thread the chicken, bacon rolls and corn cobs alternately on to skewers. Grill (broil) on foil on a grill (broiler) rack for about 8–10 minutes, turning and brushing with a little melted butter, until golden and cooked through. Serve with jacket-baked potatoes with soured cream and chives.

Spiced Yoghurt Chicken Kebabs

SERVES 4

60 ml/4 tbsp plain yoghurt
5 ml/1 tsp garam masala
5 ml/1 tsp ground cumin
1 garlic clove, crushed
5 ml/1 tsp light brown sugar
Salt and freshly ground black pepper
5 ml/1 tsp lemon juice
350 g/12 oz skinless chicken breasts, cut into chunks
Quick Pilau Rice (page 351), to serve
Lemon wedges and coriander (cilantro) leaves, to garnish

Mix everything but the chicken breasts together. Add the chicken and toss well. Leave to marinate for 2 hours. Thread on to skewers and grill (broil) on foil on a grill (broiler) rack for about 8–10 minutes, turning frequently, until golden and cooked through. Serve on a bed of Quick Pilau Rice, garnished with lemon wedges and coriander leaves.

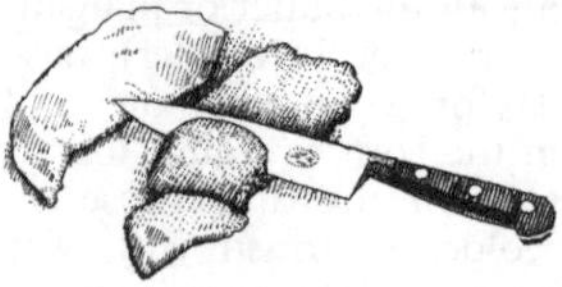

Greek-style Marinated Chicken Kebabs

SERVES 4

90 ml/6 tbsp olive oil
Finely grated rind and juice of 1 small lemon
15 ml/1 tbsp chopped oregano
1 garlic clove, crushed
Salt and freshly ground black pepper
450 g/1 lb chicken breasts, cut into bite-sized pieces
2 courgettes (zucchini), cut into chunks
2 red (bell) peppers, cut into chunks
4 stuffed olives
Buttered Rice (page 351) and a mixed salad, to serve

Whisk the oil in a shallow dish with the lemon rind and juice, the oregano, garlic and a little salt and pepper. Add the chicken, toss to coat completely and leave to marinate for 2 hours. Meanwhile, blanch the courgettes and peppers in boiling water for 3 minutes. Drain, rinse with cold water and drain again. Thread the chicken, courgettes and peppers on to four skewers and finish with a stuffed olive. Place on foil on a grill (broiler) rack and brush with any remaining marinade. Grill (broil) for about 8–10 minutes, turning once or twice, until golden brown and cooked through. Serve hot with Buttered Rice and mixed salad.

Turkish-style Marinated Chicken Kebabs

SERVES 4

Prepare as for Greek-style Marinated Chicken Kebabs, but add a chopped, seeded green chilli to the mixture and thread a stoned (pitted) black olive on the end of each skewer instead of a stuffed olive.

Chicken with Cointreau Sauce

SERVES 4

4 skinless chicken breasts, about 175 g/6 oz each
50 g/2 oz/¼ cup butter or margarine, melted
Salt and freshly ground black pepper
120 ml/4 fl oz/½ cup double (heavy) cream
60 ml/4 tbsp Cointreau
Grated rind and juice of 1 orange
1 egg
Chopped parsley, to garnish
Baby new potatoes and broccoli, to serve

Brush the chicken with a little of the butter or margarine and season lightly. Grill (broil) for about 6 minutes on each side or until golden and cooked through. Meanwhile, put the remaining butter or margarine in a saucepan with the remaining ingredients and whisk together thoroughly. Heat gently, whisking all the time, until thickened. Do not allow to boil. Season to taste. Spoon the sauce on to four warmed plates, top with a chicken breast and sprinkle with parsley. Serve with baby new potatoes and broccoli.

Chicken and Cheese Burgers

SERVES 4

Prepare as for Turkey and Cranberry Burgers (page 137), but substitute grated Cheddar cheese, pressed into 4 small balls, for the cranberry sauce.

Orchard Chicken

SERVES 4

1 small onion, finely chopped
1 garlic clove, crushed
5 ml/1 tsp caster (superfine) sugar
15 ml/1 tbsp Dijon mustard
250 ml/8 fl oz/1 cup apple juice
120 ml/4 fl oz/½ cup cider vinegar
15 ml/1 tbsp paprika
5 ml/1 tsp chilli powder
Salt and freshly ground black pepper
4 skinless chicken fillets, about 175 g/6 oz each
15 g/½ oz/1 tbsp butter or margarine, melted
Salt and freshly ground black pepper
15 ml/1 tbsp chopped parsley, to garnish
Jacket-baked potatoes and peas, to serve

Mix together all the ingredients except the chicken fillets, butter or margarine and seasoning in a shallow dish. Add the chicken and turn over in the marinade. Leave to marinate for 2 hours. Remove the chicken and place on a grill (broiler) rack. Brush with half the melted butter or margarine. Grill (broil) for 10–15 minutes, turning once and brushing with the remaining butter or margarine, until golden and cooked through. Meanwhile, boil the marinade until reduced and syrupy. Season to taste. Transfer the chicken to warm serving plates. Spoon the marinade over and serve each with a jacket-baked potato and peas.

Chicken Satay

SERVES 4

Prepare as for Simple Turkey Satay (page 139), but substitute cubed chicken breast for the turkey and lemon juice for the lime.

Rosemary Chicken with Wine-caramelled Onions

SERVES 4

8 small onions, peeled and halved
4 chicken portions
5 ml/1 tsp chopped rosemary
Salt and freshly ground black pepper
120 ml/4 fl oz/½ cup red wine
30 ml/2 tbsp light brown sugar
Jacket-baked potatoes and a green salad, to serve

Cook the onions in boiling water for 3 minutes. Drain. Put the chicken in a shallow pan. Sprinkle with the rosemary and salt and pepper. Arrange the onion halves around and pour the wine over. Cover and leave to marinate for at least 2 hours, turning occasionally. Lift the chicken out of the marinade and pat dry on kitchen paper (paper towels). Transfer the onions to a large sheet of foil, shiny side up. Add 90 ml/6 tbsp of the wine marinade and sprinkle with the sugar. Wrap up firmly. Put the onion parcel on the barbecue and cook for 10 minutes. Turn the parcel over. Add the chicken to the barbecue and cook with the onions for 30 minutes, turning the chicken occasionally and brushing with the remaining marinade, until the chicken is tender and cooked through and the onions are richly caramelised. Serve with jacket-baked potatoes and a green salad.

Spatchcock Poussin with Pesto

SERVES 2 OR 4

2 poussins (Cornish hens)
60 ml/4 tbsp Pesto for Poultry (page 342 or use bought)
30 ml/2 tbsp olive oil
Freshly ground black pepper
30 ml/2 tbsp clear honey
Olive focaccia, a rocket, grapefruit segment and walnut halves salad and French dressing, to serve

Spatchcock the poussins (page 18). From the neck end, carefully ease the skin away from the breast. Spoon half the pesto under the skin of each bird. Brush all over with some of the oil and sprinkle with pepper. Lay foil on the barbecue and brush with oil. Put the poussins skin-sides down on the foil and cook for 8 minutes. Turn over and brush the skin thoroughly with the honey. Continue to barbecue for about 20 minutes until cooked through. Transfer to serving plates and remove the skewers. Cut into halves, if liked. Spoon any juices on the foil over. Serve with olive focaccia and a rocket, grapefruit and walnut salad tossed in French dressing.

Spatchcock Poussin with Red Pesto

SERVES 4

Prepare as for Spatchcock Poussin with Pesto, but use Red Almond Pesto (page 342) instead of Pesto for Poultry.

Grilled Chicken with Basil and Anchovies

SERVES 4

50 g/2 oz/1 small can of anchovy fillets, drained
30 ml/2 tbsp milk
A good handful of basil
30 ml/2 tbsp balsamic vinegar
30 ml/2 tbsp lemon juice
10 ml/2 tsp Dijon mustard
120 ml/4 fl oz/½ cup olive oil, plus extra for brushing
4 chicken breasts with skin
1 small garlic clove, cut into 4 slivers
Buttered tagliatelle, to serve

Soak the anchovies in the milk for 30 minutes. Drain and place in a food processor or blender. Reserve 12 basil leaves and add the remainder to the anchovies with the vinegar, lemon juice and mustard. Run the machine until well blended, stopping and scraping down the sides of the machine, if necessary. With the machine running, gradually trickle in the oil, until the mixture forms a glossy sauce. Turn into a small serving bowl. Tuck the reserved basil leaves under the skin of each chicken breast with a sliver of garlic. Place skin-sides down on foil on the grill (broiler) rack. Brush with olive oil. Grill (broil) for 5 minutes. Turn the chicken over, brush again with oil and grill for about 5 minutes until golden brown and cooked through. Serve with the sauce and buttered tagliatelle.

Thai Grilled Chicken with Spiced Peaches

The stock from this recipe, strained, all fat removed then seasoned to taste and reheated, makes a delicious soup.

SERVES 4

1.5 kg/3 lb oven-ready chicken
1 chicken stock cube
1 bay leaf
1 onion, sliced
1 garlic clove, crushed
1 large carrot, chopped
5 ml/1 tsp dried basil
For the spiced peaches:
150 ml/¼ pt/⅔ cup dry white wine
15 ml/1 tbsp white wine vinegar
1 piece of cinnamon stick
6 black peppercorns
1 clove
5 ml/1 tsp light brown sugar
410 g/14½ oz/1 large can of peach slices, drained
40 g/1½ oz/3 tbsp butter or margarine, softened
1.5 ml/¼ tsp grated fresh root ginger
1.5 ml/¼ tsp turmeric
15 ml/1 tbsp mango chutney, chopped
A pinch of chilli powder
5 ml/1 tsp lemon juice
1 spring onion (scallion), chopped
5 cm/2 in piece of cucumber, chopped
Thai Fragrant Rice (page 351), to serve

Pull off any fat from just inside the body cavity of the chicken and discard. Wipe inside and out with kitchen paper (paper towels). Place in a large saucepan with the stock cube, bay leaf, onion, garlic, carrot and basil. Add just enough water to cover. Bring to the boil, skim the surface, part-cover, reduce the heat and simmer gently for 1 hour. Leave to cool in the liquid.

Meanwhile, to make the spiced peaches, put the wine, vinegar, spices and sugar in a saucepan. Bring to the boil. Add the peaches and bring back to the boil. Leave to cool in the liquid.

Carefully lift the chicken out of the cooking liquid and cut into quarters. Place on foil on a grill (broiler) rack. Mash the butter or margarine with the ginger, turmeric, chutney, chilli powder and lemon juice. Smear all over the chicken skin. Place under a preheated grill and grill (broil) until golden. Transfer to warm plates. Lift the spiced peaches out of the liquid and arrange alongside. Sprinkle with the chopped spring onion and cucumber and serve with Thai Fragrant Rice.

Thai Coconut Chicken

SERVES 4

50 g/2 oz creamed coconut
1 garlic clove, crushed
1 small green chilli, seeded and chopped
15 ml/1 tbsp chopped coriander (cilantro)
1 shallot, finely chopped
5 ml/1 tsp grated fresh root ginger
Finely grated rind and juice of 1 small lime
4 part-boned chicken breasts with skin
75 ml/5 tbsp sunflower oil
Freshly ground black pepper
Thai Fragrant Rice (page 351), to serve

Heat the coconut gently in a small saucepan until melted. Stir in the garlic, chilli, shallot, ginger and lime rind. Turn into a bowl and leave until cool and the mixture forms a thick paste. Gently pull back the skins from the chicken breasts to form a pocket. Using the fingers, smear the coconut mixture between the flesh and the skin. Secure with wooden cocktail sticks (toothpicks). Whisk the lime juice with the oil and a good grinding of pepper. Brush all over the chicken. Grill (broil) for about 30 minutes, turning occasionally, until crisp, golden and cooked through, brushing with the oil and lime juice once or twice during cooking. Remove the cocktail sticks and serve with Thai Fragrant Rice.

MacArthur Park Chicken

SERVES 6

12 boneless chicken thighs, skinned
5 ml/1 tsp garlic purée (paste)
15 ml/1 tbsp tomato purée
Freshly ground black pepper
100 g/4 oz Emmental (Swiss) cheese, cut into 12 cubes
12 rindless, extra-lean streaky bacon rashers (slices)
30 ml/2 tbsp sunflower oil

Open out the thighs on a board. Spread each with a very little of the garlic purée, then the tomato purée. Add a good grinding of pepper. Put a piece of cheese in the centre of each and re-shape. Stretch the bacon rashers slightly by scraping gently with the back of a knife. Wrap one rasher round each thigh to cover completely and secure with soaked wooden cocktail sticks (toothpicks). Brush with the oil and grill (broil) for about 25 minutes, turning frequently, until cooked through and the bacon is crisp and brown.

Barbecued Buffalo Wings

SERVES 6

2 shallots, finely chopped
1 large garlic clove, crushed
45 ml/3 tbsp sunflower oil
15 ml/1 tbsp clear honey
10 ml/2 tsp made English mustard
120 ml/4 fl oz/½ cup tomato ketchup (catsup)
90 ml/6 tbsp tomato purée (paste)
90 ml/6 tbsp red wine vinegar
15 ml/1 tbsp Worcestershire sauce
15 ml/1 tbsp soy sauce
A few drops of Tabasco sauce
24 chicken wings
Guacamole Relish (page 338), to serve

Fry (sauté) the shallots and garlic in the oil for 2 minutes, stirring. Blend in the remaining ingredients except the chicken wings. Cut the tips off the chicken wings at the first joint and discard. Add the chicken wings to the marinade and leave in a cool place for at least 1 hour. Thread the chicken wings on six long metal skewers. Grill (broil) or barbecue over hot coals for about 20 minutes, turning occasionally and brushing with any remaining marinade, until well browned and cooked through. Serve hot with Guacamole Relish.

All-weather Barbecue-spiced Drummers

SERVES 4

65 g/2½ oz/generous ¼ cup butter or margarine
8 chicken drumsticks
1 onion, finely chopped
150 ml/¼ pt/⅔ cup passata (sieved tomatoes)
30 ml/2 tbsp tomato ketchup (catsup)
15 ml/1 tbsp golden (light corn) syrup
60 ml/4 tbsp sweet brown table sauce
5 ml/1 tsp Worcestershire sauce
5 ml/1 tsp soy sauce
Freshly ground black pepper
Plain Boiled Rice (page 351) and a mixed salad, to serve

Melt half the butter or margarine in a roasting tin (pan). Add the chicken drumsticks and toss to coat completely. Roast in a preheated oven at 200°C/400°F/gas mark 6 for 15 minutes. Meanwhile, melt the remaining butter or margarine in a saucepan. Add the onion and fry (sauté) for 3 minutes, stirring, until lightly golden. Add the remaining ingredients and bring to the boil, stirring. Simmer for 5 minutes. Either continue to cook the chicken in the oven or transfer to the barbecue to finish cooking. Spoon the sauce over the chicken and cook for a further 20 minutes, turning and basting occasionally, until stickily glazed and cooked through. Serve hot with Plain Boiled Rice and a mixed salad.

Barbecued Spatchcock Baby Chicken

SERVES 4

4 poussins (Cornish hens)
5 ml/1 tsp made English mustard
40 g/1½ oz/3 tbsp butter or margarine
15 ml/1 tbsp Worcestershire sauce
10 ml/2 tsp cider vinegar
10 ml/2 tsp clear honey
Perfect Potato Wedges (page 349) and a mixed salad, to serve

Spatchcock the poussins (page 18). Wipe with kitchen paper (paper towels). Mix together the remaining ingredients and brush all over the poussins. Barbecue over hot coals, turning and basting several times, for about 30 minutes until cooked through and golden brown. Slide the birds off the skewers and serve with Perfect Potato Wedges and a mixed salad.

Spatchcocked Chicken with Lime

SERVES 4

4 poussins (Cornish hens)
60 ml/4 tbsp olive oil
Finely grated rind and juice of 1 lime
Salt and freshly ground black pepper
10 ml/2 tsp clear honey
Green salad, to serve

Spatchcock the poussins (page 18). Wipe all over with kitchen paper (paper towels). Lay the birds in a large shallow container. Mix together the remaining ingredients and spoon over, making sure the poussins are coated completely. Leave to marinate for 2 hours. Transfer to foil on a grill (broiler) rack. Grill (broil) for about 30 minutes, turning and basting with any remaining marinade, until cooked through and golden. Remove the skewers and serve with a green salad.

Spicy Yoghurt Chicken Breasts

SERVES 4

120 ml/4 fl oz/½ cup plain yoghurt
20 ml/4 tsp mild curry paste
20 ml/4 tsp desiccated (shredded) coconut
15 ml/1 tbsp light brown sugar
Salt and freshly ground black pepper
10 ml/2 tsp chopped coriander (cilantro)
4 chicken breasts
Plain Boiled Rice (page 351), to serve
Lemon wedges, shredded lettuce, cucumber slices and tomato slices, to garnish

Mix together the yoghurt, curry paste, coconut, sugar, a little salt and pepper and the coriander in a shallow dish. Add the chicken breasts and turn to coat completely. Leave to marinate for as long as possible (up to 12 hours). Remove from the marinade and place on a grill (broiler) rack. Grill (broil) for 10–15 minutes, turning occasionally and brushing with any remaining marinade until cooked through and golden. Serve on a bed of Plain Boiled Rice, garnished with lemon wedges, shredded lettuce and cucumber and tomato slices.

Plain Barbecued Chicken

SERVES 4

4 chicken portions
60 ml/4 tbsp olive oil
5 ml/1 tsp dried oregano
15 ml/1 tbsp balsamic vinegar
Salt and freshly ground black pepper
A selection of salads, to serve

Wipe the chicken with kitchen paper (paper towels) and place in a shallow dish. Whisk together the oil, oregano and vinegar with a little salt and pepper and pour over. Leave to marinate for 1–2 hours. Transfer to a hot barbecue and cook for 20 minutes, brushing occasionally with the marinade and turning two or three times, until well browned and cooked through. Serve with a selection of salads.

Grilled Italian Platter

SERVES 4

1 fennel bulb, cut lengthways into 5 mm/¼ in slices
2 small courgettes (zucchini), cut lengthways into 5 mm/¼ in slices
1 small aubergine (eggplant), cut lengthways into 5 mm/¼ in slices
2 onions, quartered
1 red (bell) pepper, quartered
4 large open mushrooms, peeled
4 small skinless chicken breasts
For the marinade:
60 ml/4 tbsp olive oil
1 garlic clove, crushed
Grated rind and juice of 1 lime
Salt and freshly ground black pepper
For the topping:
50 g/2 oz/1 small can of anchovies, drained
30 ml/2 tbsp milk
100 g/4 oz Mozzarella cheese, cut into 4 slices
15 ml/1 tbsp chopped parsley, to garnish
Ciabatta, to serve

Cook the fennel in lightly salted boiling water for 3 minutes. Drain, rinse with cold water and drain again. Arrange all the prepared vegetables in an even layer in the grill (broiler) pan with the chicken breasts. Mix together the marinade ingredients and drizzle over. Turn over gently and leave to marinate for 1 hour.

Soak the anchovies in the milk. Grill (broil) the chicken and vegetables, turning and brushing with any remaining marinade, for about 15 minutes until golden and tender. Lay a slice of Mozzarella on each of the mushrooms and the anchovy strips over the aubergines for the last minute or so of cooking until the anchovies are hot and the cheese is melting. Do not turn again. Transfer everything to warm serving plates, sprinkle with chopped parsley and serve with ciabatta.

Tandoori-style Grilled Chicken

SERVES 6

6 chicken breasts, skinned
150 ml/¼ pt/⅔ cup plain yoghurt
2 garlic cloves, crushed
15 ml/1 tbsp lemon juice
1.5 ml/¼ tsp chilli powder
5 ml/1 tsp ground cumin
2.5 ml/½ tsp ground allspice
30 ml/2 tbsp paprika
5 ml/1 tsp ground coriander (cilantro)
2.5 ml/½ tsp ground ginger
10 ml/2 tsp garam masala
Shredded lettuce, lemon wedges and onion rings, to garnish
Rice salad and Minted Yoghurt and Cucumber (page 339), to serve

Make several slashes in the chicken breasts with a sharp knife and place in a shallow dish. Mix together all the remaining ingredients and spoon over the chicken. Leave to marinate for at least 4 hours, preferably overnight. Drain from the marinade. Grill (broil) for 5–6 minutes on each side, turning occasionally and brushing with any remaining marinade, until cooked through and slightly blackened in places. Garnish with shredded lettuce, lemon wedges and onion rings and serve with a rice salad and Minted Yoghurt and Cucumber.

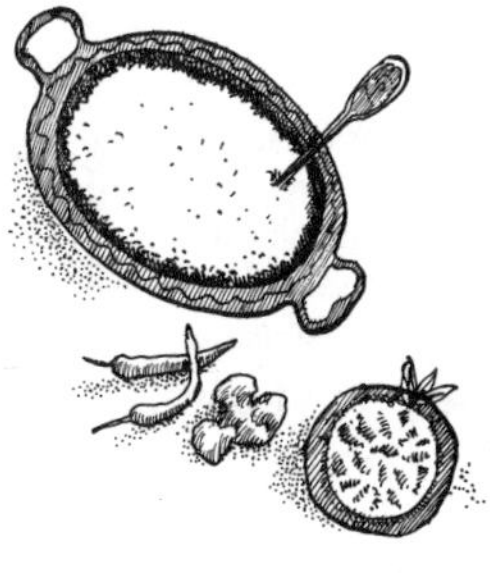

Basil and Lemon Barbecued Chicken

SERVES 4

Prepare as for Plain Barbecued Chicken (page 134), but add 1 finely chopped onion, 30 ml/2 tbsp chopped basil and the finely grated rind and juice of ½ lemon to the marinade.

Chilli Barbecued Chicken

SERVES 4

Prepare as for Plain Barbecued Chicken (page 134), but add 60 ml/4 tbsp mild chilli relish and Tabasco sauce to taste to the marinade.

Rosemary and Garlic Barbecued Chicken

SERVES 4

Prepare as for Plain Barbecued Chicken (page 134), but add 1 or 2 crushed garlic cloves and 15 ml/1 tbsp finely chopped rosemary to the marinade.

Lime and Green Peppercorn Barbecued Chicken

SERVES 4

Prepare as for Plain Barbecued Chicken (page 134), but omit the lemon juice and black pepper and add the finely grated rind and juice of 1 lime and 15 ml/2 tbsp crushed pickled green peppercorns to the marinade.

Oriental Barbecued Chicken

SERVES 4

Prepare as for Plain Barbecued Chicken (page 134), but omit the lemon juice and oregano. Use only 45 ml/3 tbsp olive oil and add 45 ml/3 tbsp soy sauce, 2 finely chopped spring onions (scallions), 2.5 ml/½ tsp ground ginger, 15 ml/1 tbsp clear honey and 15 ml/1 tbsp medium-dry sherry.

Buttered Barbecued Chicken

SERVES 4

Prepare as for Plain Barbecued Chicken (page 134), but after marinating quickly brown the chicken portions on the barbecue, then place each one on a large square of foil and add a good knob of butter or margarine to each. Wrap up securely and barbecue for 20 minutes, turning once, until cooked through. Open the foil parcels on plates to retain all the juices.

Buttered Flavoured Barbecued Chicken

SERVES 4

Prepare as for Buttered Barbecued Chicken, but use any of the other marinades suggested left.

Chicken Liver Brochettes

SERVES 4

8 chicken livers, trimmed and halved
30 ml/2 tbsp olive oil
Salt and freshly ground black pepper
5 ml/1 tsp lemon juice
2.5 ml/½ tsp dried sage
12 button (pearl) onions, peeled but left whole
4 rindless back bacon rashers (slices), cut into chunks
12 button mushrooms
Buttered Rice (page 351), to serve

Put the livers in a bowl and toss with the oil, a little salt and pepper, the lemon juice and sage. Leave to stand for 30 minutes. Meanwhile, boil the onions in water for 3 minutes. Drain. Thread the livers, onions, bacon and mushrooms on four skewers. Place on foil on a grill (broiler) rack. Grill (broil) for about 6 minutes, turning occasionally and brushing with any remaining marinade, until cooked through. Serve with Buttered Rice.

Chicken Liver Brochettes with Persimmons

SERVES 4

450 g/1 lb chicken livers, trimmed
1 onion, quartered and separated into layers
A small handful of sage leaves
75 g/3 oz/⅓ cup butter or margarine, melted
Salt and freshly ground black pepper
2 orange persimmons
4 long diagonal slices of French bread
Watercress, to garnish
Tomato and onion salad, to serve

Rinse the chicken livers and pat dry on kitchen paper (paper towels). Thread the chicken livers on soaked wooden skewers interspersed with the onion pieces and sage leaves. Brush all over with melted butter or margarine and season with salt and pepper. Cut the tops and bases off the persimmons and then cut into slices. Brush a sheet of foil with a little of the remaining butter or margarine. Add the persimmon slices in a single layer and brush with the butter or margarine. Brush the slices of bread with the remaining butter or margarine. Place everything on the grill (broiler rack) or barbecue and cook, turning once, until the bread is toasted on both sides, the chicken livers are just cooked but not hard and the persimmons are turning golden round the edges. Remove the bread, once toasted, and keep warm. Lay the toasted bread slices on serving plates. Slide the chicken liver brochettes off their skewers on top and place the persimmon slices to one side. Garnish with watercress and serve with a tomato and onion salad.

TURKEY

Turkey and Cranberry Burgers

SERVES 4

450 g/1 lb minced (ground) turkey
1 small onion, finely chopped
15 ml/1 tbsp chopped parsley
45 ml/3 tbsp fresh breadcrumbs
Grated rind of ½ lemon
2.5 ml/½ tsp dried thyme
1.5 ml/¼ tsp grated nutmeg
Salt and freshly ground black pepper
1 egg, beaten
40 ml/8 tsp cranberry sauce
4 small slices of bread
Butter or margarine
4 parsley sprigs
Super Sauté Potatoes (page 349) and mangetout (snow peas), to serve

Mix the turkey with the onion, parsley, breadcrumbs, lemon rind, thyme and nutmeg and season with salt and pepper. Mix with the egg to bind. Shape into eight flat cakes. Put 10 ml/ 2 tsp cranberry sauce on each of four of the patties. Top with the remaining ones and press the edges together well to seal. Grill (broil) for 5 minutes on each side until golden brown and cooked through. Meanwhile, cut large rounds from the slices of bread and spread very thinly on both sides with butter or margarine. Fry (sauté) in a frying pan (skillet) until golden brown on both sides. Transfer to four warm plates. Top each slice with a burger, garnish with a sprig of parsley and serve with Super Sauté Potatoes and mangetout.

Glazzwill Turkey Fillets

SERVES 4

4 turkey breast steaks
150 ml/¼ pt/⅔ cup dry white wine
15 g/½ oz/1 tbsp butter
Salt and freshly ground black pepper
150 ml/¼ pt/⅔ cup passata (sieved tomatoes)
30 ml/2 tbsp tomato purée (paste)
5 ml/1 tsp caster (superfine) sugar
16 basil leaves
4 slices of Parma ham
75 g/3 oz/¾ cup Mozzarella cheese, grated
Tagliatelle, to serve

Put the turkey, wine and butter in a saucepan. Season lightly. Bring to the boil, reduce the heat and simmer for 8–10 minutes until the turkey is tender. Do not over-cook. Lift out the turkey and transfer to foil on the grill (broiler) rack. Boil the wine rapidly until reduced by half. Stir in the passata, tomato purée and sugar. Bring to the boil and simmer for about 4 minutes, stirring, until slightly thickened. Chop 8 of the basil leaves and stir in. Season to taste. Top each turkey steak with a slice of Parma ham and cover with the grated cheese. Grill (broil) for a few minutes until the cheese melts and is just turning golden. Spoon the sauce on to four warm plates. Top each with a turkey steak and garnish with the remaining basil leaves. Serve with tagliatelle.

Grilled Turkey Wrapped in Bacon with Oriental Sauce

SERVES 4

4 turkey breast steaks
30 ml/2 tbsp soy sauce
8 rindless streaky bacon rashers (slices)
2.5 ml/½ tsp Chinese five spice powder
Sunflower oil
1 small onion, thinly sliced
1 small green (bell) pepper, cut into thin strips
1 carrot, cut into matchsticks
450 ml/¾ pt/2 cups unsweetened pineapple juice
15 ml/1 tbsp tomato ketchup (catsup)
15 ml/1 tbsp cornflour (cornstarch)
Freshly ground black pepper
Plain Boiled Rice (page 351), to serve

Place the steaks one at a time in a plastic bag and beat with a meat mallet or rolling pin to flatten slightly (not too thinly). Brush with a little of the soy sauce and roll up. Stretch the bacon rashers with the back of a knife. Wrap two round each steak to cover almost completely. Secure with cocktail sticks (toothpicks), if necessary. Brush with a little sunflower oil and sprinkle with the five spice powder. Place on foil on a grill (broiler) rack and grill (broil) for about 12–15 minutes, turning once or twice, until golden brown and cooked through. Meanwhile, heat 15 ml/1 tbsp oil in a saucepan. Add the onion, pepper and carrot and fry (sauté) gently for 5 minutes, stirring, until softened. Add the pineapple juice and ketchup and simmer for 4 minutes. Blend together the remaining soy sauce and cornflour and stir into the saucepan. Cook for 1 minute, stirring until thickened. Season with pepper. Transfer the turkey to warm plates, remove the cocktail sticks and spoon the sauce over. Serve with Plain Boiled Rice.

Turkey Pockets

SERVES 4

4 turkey breast steaks
5 ml/1 tsp paprika
Salt and freshly ground black pepper
60 ml/4 tbsp tomato ketchup (catsup)
100 g/4 oz Gruyère (Swiss) cheese, cut into 4 slices
30 ml/2 tbsp snipped chives
Olive oil, for brushing
Rigatoni pasta and Tomato Sauce (page 342), to serve

Place the steaks one at a time in a plastic bag and beat with a rolling pin or meat mallet to flatten. Season with the paprika and some salt and pepper. Spread with the ketchup, top with the cheese on one half of each turkey steak, then sprinkle with the chives. Fold in halves and secure with wooden cocktail sticks (toothpicks). Brush with the oil. Place on foil on the grill (broiler) rack. Grill (broil) for about 8 minutes on each side until cooked through, brushing once or twice with more oil. Remove the cocktail sticks. Serve straight away with rigatoni tossed in Tomato Sauce.

Grilled Turkey Wrapped in Parma Ham with Piazzaiola Sauce

4 turkey breast steaks
A few basil leaves
4 slices of Parma ham
15 ml/1 tbsp olive oil
10 ml/2 tsp lemon juice
Salt and freshly ground black pepper
Tagliatelle and Piazzaiola Sauce (page 335), to serve

Place the turkey fillets one at a time in a plastic bag and beat with a rolling pin or meat mallet to flatten. Lay one or two basil leaves on each steak and roll up. Wrap in the Parma ham and secure with cocktail sticks (toothpicks). Whisk the oil with the lemon juice and a little salt and pepper. Brush over the turkey on foil on a grill (broiler) rack. Grill (broil) for about 15 minutes, turning and brushing occasionally, until cooked through. Remove the cocktail sticks. Serve with tagliatelle and Piazzaiola Sauce.

Simple Turkey Satay

SERVES 4

1 shallot, finely chopped
1 large garlic clove, crushed
10 g/¼ oz/2 tsp butter or margarine
30 ml/2 tbsp smooth peanut butter
10 ml/2 tsp lime juice
15 ml/1 tbsp clear honey
15 ml/1 tbsp soy sauce
1.5 ml/¼ tsp chilli powder
120 ml/4 fl oz/½ cup milk
450 g/1 lb thick turkey breast steaks, diced
Thai Fragrant Rice (page 351), mangetout (snow peas) and baby corn cobs, to serve

Fry (sauté) the shallot and garlic in the butter or margarine for 2 minutes, stirring. Stir in the remaining ingredients except the milk and turkey. Bring to the boil, stirring. Blend in 90 ml/6 tbsp of the milk, reduce the heat and simmer for 2 minutes. Thread the turkey on to soaked wooden skewers and brush with a little of the sauce. Grill (broil) for about 8 minutes, turning occasionally, until tender and cooked through. Meanwhile, prepare and cook the Thai Fragrant Rice according to the recipe, adding the mangetout and baby corn cobs for the last 4 minutes. Drain. Reheat the remaining sauce with the remaining milk. Lay the kebabs on a bed of rice and vegetables, spoon the remaining sauce over and serve.

Tempting Turkey Fillets

SERVES 4

4 slices of turkey fillet, about 150 g/5 oz each
150 ml/¼ pt/⅔ cup cider
150 ml/¼ pt/⅔ cup passata (sieved tomatoes)
50 g/2 oz stoned (pitted) black olives, sliced
A pinch of caster (superfine) sugar
10 ml/2 tsp chopped sage
Salt and freshly ground black pepper
8 thin slices of liver sausage
50 g/2 oz/½ cup Bel Paese cheese, sliced
Spaghetti, to serve

Put the turkey and cider in a shallow pan. Bring to the boil, reduce the heat, cover and cook gently for about 8 minutes or until the turkey is tender. Remove the turkey and place on foil on a grill (broiler) rack. Boil the cider rapidly until reduced by half. Stir in the passata and add the olives and sugar. Bring to the boil and simmer for 4 minutes. Stir in half the sage. Season to taste. Put 2 slices of liver sausage on each turkey fillet and top with the cheese slices. Grill (broil) until the cheese melts and bubbles. Spoon the sauce on to four warm serving plates. Top each with a turkey fillet and scatter the remaining sage over. Serve with spaghetti.

Crunchy Meatballs with Tomato Barbecue Sauce

SERVES 6

For the meatballs:
700 g/1½ lb minced (ground) turkey
50 g/2 oz/1 cup fresh breadcrumbs
1 onion, finely chopped
2 celery sticks, finely chopped
50 g/2 oz/½ cup peanuts, chopped
5 ml/1 tsp ground cumin
5 ml/1 tsp dried oregano
Salt and freshly ground black pepper
1 small egg, beaten
For the sauce:
1 large onion, chopped
45 ml/3 tbsp olive oil
400 g/14 oz/1 large can of chopped tomatoes
15 ml/1 tbsp clear honey
30 ml/2 tbsp sweet pickle
15 ml/1 tbsp red wine vinegar
A few drops of Worcestershire sauce
Lemon wedges, to garnish
Plain Boiled Rice (page 351), to serve

Mix together all the meatball ingredients in a large bowl. Shape into golf ball-sized pieces around soaked wooden skewers, about four to a skewer.

To make the sauce, fry (sauté) the onion in 15 ml/1 tbsp of the oil for 3 minutes, stirring. Add the remaining sauce ingredients and simmer for 10 minutes until pulpy. Keep warm. Brush the meatballs with some of the remaining oil and grill (broil) for about 10 minutes, turning occasionally, until cooked through and golden brown, brushing with a little more oil during cooking. Garnish with lemon wedges and serve with the warm barbecue sauce and Plain Boiled Rice.

Mammoth Mushrooms

SERVES 4

4 large open mushrooms
225 g/8 oz turkey sausages
100 g/4 oz/½ cup medium-fat soft cheese
1 small red chilli, seeded and chopped
30 ml/2 tbsp chopped parsley
Freshly ground black pepper
Oil, for brushing
Super Sauté Potatoes (page 349) and a green salad, to serve

Peel the mushrooms. Remove the stems and chop finely. Remove the skin from the sausages and mash up the meat with the mushroom stalks. Dry-fry in a saucepan on the hob for about 3 minutes, stirring, until cooked through and crumbly. Remove from the heat and work in the cheese, chilli, parsley and some pepper. Brush the mushroom caps with oil and spoon in the sausage mixture. Grill (broil) for about 10 minutes until tender and sizzling. Serve with Super Sauté Potatoes and a green salad.

Turkey, Bacon and Pineapple Kebabs

SERVES 4

350 g/12 oz turkey steak
8 rindless streaky bacon rashers (slices)
225 g/8 oz/1 small can of pineapple chunks, drained, reserving the juice
30 ml/2 tbsp olive oil
5 ml/1 tsp dried mint
Salt and freshly ground black pepper
Egg Fried Rice (page 351), to serve

Cut the turkey into 16 cubes. Stretch the bacon rashers and cut each in half. Wrap one half round each turkey cube. Place in a shallow dish. Whisk the pineapple juice with the olive oil, mint and a little salt and pepper. Pour over the turkey and turn gently to coat in the marinade. Leave to stand for 1 hour. Thread with the pineapple cubes on skewers. Place on foil on the grill (broiler) rack and grill (broil) for about 10 minutes, turning occasionally and brushing with any remaining marinade, until cooked through and golden. Serve hot with Egg Fried Rice.

DUCK

Sweet and Spicy Duck

SERVES 4

120 ml/4 fl oz/½ cup dry sherry
120 ml/4 fl oz/½ cup strong black tea
120 ml/4 fl oz/½ cup soy sauce
1 garlic clove, crushed
30 ml/2 tbsp clear honey
5 ml/1 tsp ground cloves
Salt and freshly ground black pepper
4 small duck breasts, skin removed
15 g/½ oz/1 tbsp butter or margarine
Beansprouts, grated carrots and French dressing, to serve

Mix together the sherry, tea, soy sauce, garlic, honey, cloves and a little salt and pepper in a shallow dish. Add the duck and leave to marinate for 1 hour. Remove the duck from the marinade and place on a grill (broiler) rack. Boil the marinade until reduced by half. Stir in the butter or margarine. Brush all over the duck and grill (broil) for 10 minutes on each side, brushing regularly with the remaining marinade, until golden and cooked through. Serve with beansprouts and grated carrots tossed in French dressing.

Duck, Orange and Mushroom Kebabs

SERVES 4

45 ml/3 tbsp olive oil
2 oranges
15 ml/1 tbsp balsamic vinegar
Salt and freshly ground black pepper
1 garlic clove, crushed
2 large duck breasts, cut into bite-sized cubes
100 g/4 oz button mushrooms
12 button (pearl) onions
Crispy Noodle Cake (page 356), to serve

Put the oil in a shallow dish. Finely grate the rind and squeeze the juice of one of the oranges. Whisk into the oil with the balsamic vinegar, a little salt and pepper and the garlic. Add the duck cubes and the mushrooms. Toss gently and leave to marinate for 2–3 hours. Meanwhile, cook the onions in boiling water for 3 minutes. Drain. Thread the duck, mushrooms and onions on fine skewers. Grill (broil) on foil under a preheated grill (broiler) for about 12 minutes, turning occasionally and brushing with any remaining marinade, until golden and cooked through. Serve with Crispy Noodle Cake.

Duck, Orange and Chestnut Kebabs

SERVES 4

Prepare as for Duck, Orange and Mushroom Kebabs, but substitute canned chestnuts for the mushrooms, taking care when threading them on the skewers so they don't split.

Grilled Wild Duck

SERVES 2

2 oven-ready small mallard or widgeon
60 ml/4 tbsp apple juice
50 g/2 oz/¼ cup butter or margarine, melted
Salt and freshly ground black pepper
1 green eating (dessert) apple, cored and cut into 8 thin slices
Parsley Butter (page 343), to garnish
Super Sauté Potatoes (page 349) and peas, to serve

Halve the birds and place on foil in the grill (broiler) pan, skin sides down. Brush with a little of the apple juice, then a little melted butter or margarine and season well. Grill (broil) for 5 minutes. Turn over. Brush the skin with a little of the remaining apple juice and some more butter or margarine. Season again. Grill for 5 minutes and turn over again. Brush and grill for a further 10 minutes. Turn over so the skin is uppermost, brush again. Lay the apple slices along the side and brush with any remaining butter or margarine. Grill for a further 10 minutes until crisp and brown, turning the apple slices once and brushing frequently with any remaining apple juice and butter or margarine. Transfer the duck and apple slices to warm plates and spoon any juices over. Top each with a slice or two of Parsley Butter and serve with Super Sauté Potatoes and peas.

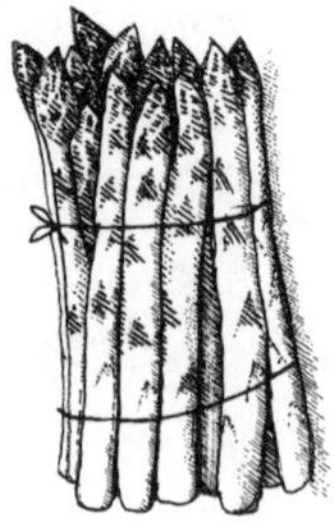

Roasts and Oven Bakes

There are many lovely roasting recipes in this chapter plus numerous ways to bake your birds in sauces, coatings or other flavourings. There are also basic roasting times for when you just want to roast a bird plainly and serve it with one of the gravies and the traditional accompaniments from the Sauces chapter (pages 333–346) and a selection of vegetables of your choice.

TO PLAIN ROAST YOUR BIRD

Prepare and cook according to the table below. In each case, remove the giblets if there are any and truss the bird (page 16), if necessary, before cooking. To check the bird is cooked, skewer the thickest part of the thigh and the juices should run clear. If not, continue cooking a little longer, then check again. Remember, if you are roasting two birds where the cooking time is calculated by weight (e.g. pheasant) you calculate the cooking time of one bird, not the two weights added together!

Bird	Preparation	Oven Temperature	Cooking Time
Capercaillie	Lay strips of fat bacon over the breast. Season inside and out. Put a knob of butter or margarine in the body cavity. Place in a roasting tin (pan). Baste often. Remove the bacon for the last 15 minutes and sprinkle the breast with plain (all-purpose) flour.	200°C/400°F/ gas mark 6	20 minutes per 450 g/1 lb
Capon	Stuff the neck end, if liked or place an onion or fresh herbs in the body cavity. Rub the skin with oil and sprinkle with salt. Place upside-down in a roasting tin (pan). Turn over half-way through cooking.	160°C/325°F/ gas mark 3	25 minutes per 450 g/1 lb plus 25 minutes
Chicken (up to 1.6 kg/3½ lb)	Prepare as for a capon, but cook right way up.	190°C/375°F/ gas mark 5	20 minutes per 450 g/1 lb plus 20 minutes
Chicken (1.75–2.75 kg 4–6 lb)	Prepare as for a capon.	160°C/325°F/ gas mark 3	25 minutes per 450 g/1 lb plus 25 minutes
Duck	Stuff the neck end if liked. Prick the skin all over with a fork and season with salt. Place in a roasting tin (pan).	200°C/400°F/ gas mark 6	20 minutes per 450 g/1 lb, then turn down the oven to 160°C/325°F/ gas mark 3 for a further 30 minutes
Goose	Prepare as for duck.	200°C/400°F/ gas mark 6	15 minutes per 450 g/1 lb plus 15 minutes
Grouse	Prepare as for capercaillie.	200°C/400°F/ gas mark 6	30–45 minutes
Guinea Fowl	Prepare as for a capon, but lay strips of bacon over the breast.	190°C/375°F/ gas mark 5	20 minutes per 450 g/1 lb plus 20 minutes

Bird	Preparation	Oven Temperature	Cooking Time
Mallard (wild duck)	Coat with softened butter or margarine and season. Place in a roasting tin (pan). Baste with a little port, orange liqueur or juice.	220°C/425°F/ gas mark 7	30 minutes
Ortolan	Prepare as for capercaillie.	220°C/425°F/ gas mark 7	20 minutes
Partridge	Prepare as for capercaillie.	200°C/400°F/ gas mark 6	30–45 minutes
Pheasant	Prepare as for capercaillie.	200°C/400°F/ gas mark 6	20 minutes per 450 g/1 lb
Pigeon	Prepare as for capercaillie.	220°C/425°F/ gas mark 7	20 minutes per 450 g/1 lb
Plover	Prepare as for capercaillie.	200°C/400°F/ gas mark 6	30–45 minutes
Poussin (Cornish hen)	Prepare as for capon but do not stuff.	200°C/400°F/ gas mark 6	40–50 minutes
Ptarmigan	Prepare as for capercaillie.	200°C/400°F/ gas mark 6	30–45 minutes
Quail	Prepare as for capercaillie.	220°C/425°F/ gas mark 7	20–25 minutes
Snipe	Prepare as for capercaillie.	220°C/425°F/ gas mark 7	20 minutes
Teal (wild duck)	Prepare as for mallard.	220°C/425°F/ gas mark 7	20 minutes
Turkey (up to 4.5 kg/ 10 lb)	Prepare as for capon but cover with foil. Remove the foil after the calculated time and continue cooking for 30 minutes.	190°C/375°F/ gas mark 5	15 minutes per 450 g/1 lb
Turkey (over 4.5 kg/ 10 lb)	Prepare as for capon but cover with foil. Remove the foil after the calculated time and continue cooking for 30 minutes.	190°C/375°F/ gas mark 5	10 minutes per 450 g/1 lb
Widgeon (wild duck)	Prepare as for mallard.	220°C/425°F/ gas mark 7	30 minutes
Woodcock	Prepare as for capercaillie.	220°C/425°F/ gas mark 7	20–25 minutes

CHICKEN

Butter Roast Chicken and Potatoes

SERVES 4

900 g/2 lb potatoes, peeled and cut into large chunks
1.5 kg/3 lb oven-ready chicken
Salt and freshly ground black pepper
15 ml/1 tbsp plain (all-purpose) flour
75 g/3 oz/⅓ cup butter or margarine, softened
Gravy (page 334) and mangetout (snow peas)

Cook the potatoes in lightly salted boiling water for 3 minutes. Drain. With the lid on the pan give the pan a good shake to rough up the edges of the potatoes. Remove the giblets from the chicken, if necessary. Wipe inside and out with kitchen paper (paper towels). Place the chicken in a roasting tin (pan) and season with salt and pepper. Sprinkle the breast with the flour. Smear all over the breast with 50 g/2 oz/¼ cup of the butter or margarine. Arrange the potatoes around the bird and dot with the remaining butter or margarine. Roast in a preheated oven at 190°C/375°F/gas mark 5 for 1½ hours, basting occasionally and turning the potatoes over half way through cooking. Serve with gravy and mangetout.

Garlic Butter Roast Chicken and Potatoes

SERVES 4

Prepare as for Butter Roast Chicken and Potatoes, but add 2 large garlic cloves to the body cavity of the chicken and add 30 ml/2 tbsp chopped parsley to the gravy.

Chicken Maryland

SERVES 6

6 chicken portions
Milk
90 ml/6 tbsp plain (all-purpose) flour
Salt and freshly ground black pepper
75 g/3 oz/1½ cups toasted breadcrumbs
75 g/3 oz/⅓ cup butter or margarine
30 ml/2 tbsp sunflower oil
Watercress sprigs, to garnish
Corn Fritters (page 355) and Fried Bananas (page 355), Brown Rice (page 351) and a green salad, to serve

Dip the chicken in milk, then coat in the flour seasoned with a little salt and pepper. Chill for 30 minutes. Dip in milk again, then coat in the breadcrumbs. Melt the butter or margarine with the oil in a large roasting tin (pan) in the oven at 190°C/375°F/gas mark 5. When sizzling, add the chicken and turn over in the fat to coat completely. Bake for 1 hour until golden brown and cooked through. Drain on kitchen paper (paper towels). Transfer to a large warm platter and garnish with watercress sprigs. Serve with Corn Fritters, Fried Bananas, Brown Rice and a green salad.

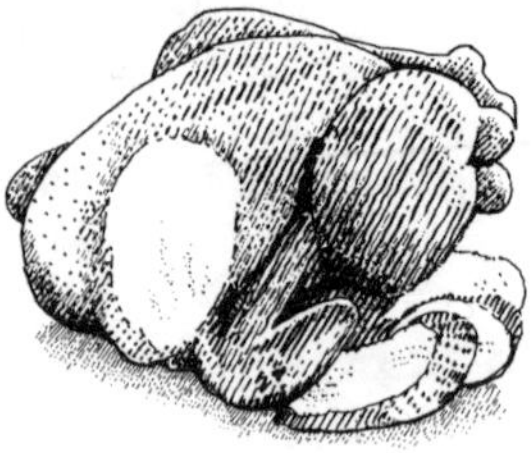

Roast Lemon Chicken and Vegetable Platter

SERVES 6

1.5 kg/3 lb oven-ready chicken
1 lemon
1 onion
1 garlic clove
A sprig of rosemary
A small knob of butter or margarine, softened
Salt and freshly ground black pepper
18 small new potatoes, scrubbed
350 g/12 oz French (green) beans
450 g/1 lb carrots, sliced
½ green cabbage, shredded
Chopped parsley
1 chicken stock cube
A pinch of caster (superfine) sugar (optional)

Pull off any excess fat inside the rim of the body cavity of the chicken and discard. Wipe inside and out with kitchen paper (paper towels). Place on a trivet (or an old upturned plate) in a roasting tin (pan). Squeeze the lemon, reserving the juice. Push the lemon shell inside the body cavity of the chicken with the onion, garlic and rosemary. Spread the butter or margarine over the breast, drizzle with some of the lemon juice and sprinkle with salt. Roast in a preheated oven at 190°C/375°F/gas mark 5 for 1 hour 20 minutes or until the juices run clear when a skewer is inserted in the thickest part of the thigh. Transfer to a carving dish and keep warm.

Meanwhile, boil the vegetables in separate pans in lightly salted water until tender. Drain, reserving the cooking water, and arrange on a serving platter. Sprinkle with chopped parsley and keep warm. Remove the trivet from the roasting tin and spoon off all but 15 ml/1 tbsp of the fat, leaving any cooking juices. Stir in 600 ml/1 pt/2½ cups of the vegetable cooking water and the stock cube. Bring to the boil and boil until reduced by about a quarter. Add a little more lemon juice and sweeten, if liked, with a little sugar. Season to taste with salt and pepper. Carve the chicken. Arrange on six warm plates and spoon a little of the gravy over. Pour the rest into a gravy boat. Serve with the hot vegetable platter.

Gooey Chicken Parcels

SERVES 4

4 chicken leg portions
Salt and freshly ground black pepper
1.5 ml/¼ tsp dried basil
25 g/1 oz/2 tbsp butter or margarine
4 slices of lean ham
20 ml/4 tsp Dijon mustard
4 slices of Gruyère (Swiss) cheese
Crusty bread and a green salad, to serve

Wipe the chicken with kitchen paper (paper towels). Season with salt and pepper and sprinkle with the basil. Grease four squares of foil, shiny-sides up. Put a chicken leg on each and wrap loosely but twist the edges together to seal. Place on a baking (cookie) sheet and roast in the oven at 180°C/350°F/gas mark 4 for 45 minutes. Meanwhile, spread the ham with the mustard. Carefully open up the parcels. Top each chicken portion with one of the ham slices, then a slice of cheese. Return, opened, to the oven and cook at 220°C/425°F/gas mark 7 for about 8 minutes until the cheese melts and bubbles. Serve straight away with crusty bread and a green salad.

Easy Roast Stuffed Chicken Breasts

SERVES 4

4 skinless chicken breasts
85 g/3½ oz/1 packet of parsley, thyme and lemon stuffing mix
Salt and freshly ground black pepper
15 g/½ oz/1 tbsp butter or margarine
20 ml/½ tbsp cornflour (cornstarch)
300 ml/½ pt/1¼ cups chicken stock
30 ml/2 tbsp chopped parsley
Royal Roast Potatoes (page 348) and a green vegetable, to serve

Make a slit in the side of each chicken breast with a sharp knife. Make up the stuffing according to the packet directions. Stuff the cavities in the chicken with the stuffing. Lightly grease four large squares of foil, shiny-sides up, with the butter or margarine. Put a chicken breast on each and wrap up. Place on a baking (cookie) sheet. Bake in a preheated oven at 190°C/375°F/gas mark 5 for about 30 minutes until cooked through. Meanwhile, blend the cornflour with a little of the stock in a small saucepan. Stir in the remaining stock and parsley. Bring to the boil and cook for 2 minutes, stirring, until thickened. When the chicken is cooked, open the parcels and pour any juices into the gravy. Put the chicken on warm plates and spoon the gravy over. Serve with Royal Roast Potatoes and a green vegetable.

Salt Roast Chicken with Potatoes, Garlic and Parsnips

SERVES 4-6

1.5 kg/3 lb oven-ready chicken
A sprig of sage
20 g/¾ oz/1½ tbsp unsalted (sweet) butter, melted
225 g/8 oz rock salt
450 g/1 lb baby potatoes, scrubbed but not peeled
2 large parsnips, cut into thumb-sized pieces
45 ml/3 tbsp sunflower oil
1 large garlic bulb
Cauliflower, coated in Cheese Sauce (page 341), to serve

Remove the giblets from the bird, if necessary. Wipe the chicken inside and out with kitchen paper (paper towels). Pull off any excess fat from just inside the body cavity and insert the sage. Brush all over with most of the melted butter, then cover liberally with the rock salt. Place the bird on a rack or upturned plate in a roasting tin (pan). Roast in the centre of a preheated oven at 220°C/425°F/gas mark 7 for 20 minutes, then reduce the heat to 190°C/375°F/gas mark 5 for a further 1½ hours until tender and cooked through. Meanwhile, boil the potatoes and parsnips in lightly salted water for 5 minutes. Drain well. Heat the oil in a roasting tin on the top shelf of the oven. When sizzling, add the potatoes and parsnips, toss well to coat in the oil, and roast on the top shelf for 1 hour until golden and cooked through, turning once. Also, brush the head of garlic with the remaining butter and wrap in foil. Place on the shelf with the chicken for 1 hour. To serve, remove the garlic from the oven. Open the foil and peel off the skin, leaving the roasted garlic cloves. Transfer the chicken to a carving dish, break the salt off the skin and discard. Carve the bird and serve with the garlic, roasted vegetables and cauliflower coated in Cheese Sauce.

Roast Part-boned Chicken with Lemon Grass and Rice Stuffing

SERVES 6

225 g/8 oz/1 cup wild rice mix
900 ml/1½ pts/3¾ cups chicken stock
1.5 g/3 lb oven-ready chicken
1 stem of lemon grass, finely chopped
1 large eating (dessert) apple, grated
15 ml/1 tbsp chopped spring onion (scallion)
Salt and freshly ground black pepper
A pinch of grated nutmeg
1 egg, beaten
25 g/1 oz/2 tbsp unsalted (sweet) butter, melted
Lemon juice (optional)
Gravy (see page 334), new potatoes and mangetout (snow peas), to serve

Cook the rice in the stock for about 20 minutes or until tender. Drain off any excess stock and reserve for the gravy. Remove the giblets from the chicken, if necessary. To part-bone the bird, make a slit along the backbone, then carefully scrape away each side of the rib cage until it is exposed on both sides. Cut through the joints at the wings and legs, but leave the limbs intact. Lift out the rib cage and backbone. Mix the rice with the lemon grass, apple, spring onion and a little salt and pepper. Stir in the nutmeg and the egg to bind. Pile the stuffing on the chicken where the bones were. Re-shape and sew up or secure with cocktail sticks (toothpicks). Place in a roasting tin (pan). Brush with melted butter and season lightly. Cover with foil. Roast at 190°C/375°F/gas mark 5 for 1½ hours, removing the foil for the last 30 minutes. Make gravy according to the recipe but using any reserved stock from cooking the rice and either giblet stock or vegetable water. Spike with lemon juice, if liked. Serve the chicken with the gravy, new potatoes and mangetout.

Fragrant Chicken Parcels

SERVES 4

15 g/½ oz/1 tbsp butter
2 leeks, sliced into rings
1 courgette (zucchini), thinly sliced
2 carrots, thinly sliced
4 chicken breasts
Salt and freshly ground black pepper
4 rosemary sprigs
150 ml/¼ pt/⅔ cup medium-dry white wine
16 small whole potatoes, scrubbed and threaded on metal skewers

Grease four large squares of foil with the butter. Divide the vegetables between the centres and top each with a chicken breast. Season. Add a sprig of rosemary to each and pour the wine over. Wrap loosely in the foil, twisting the edges together to seal well. Transfer to a baking (cookie) sheet. Place in a preheated oven with the potatoes and bake at 190°C/375°F/gas mark 5 for 45 minutes. Transfer the parcels to warm plates and serve with the potatoes.

Spicy Chicken Parcels

SERVES 4

Prepare as for Fragrant Chicken Parcels, but substitute 2 thinly sliced onions for the leeks and 1 green and 1 red (bell) pepper, thinly sliced, for the carrots. Omit the rosemary. Sprinkle with 1 seeded and chopped green chilli and add a halved cherry tomato to each chicken breast.

Baked Chicken with Prunes and Almonds

SERVES 4–6

1.5 kg/3 lb oven-ready chicken
175 g/6 oz/1 cup ready-to-eat prunes
Finely grated rind and juice of 1 orange
300 ml/½ pt/1¼ cups chicken stock
1 bouquet garni sachet
50 g/2 oz/½ cup blanched almonds
Salt and freshly ground black pepper
Oil, for greasing
2 rindless streaky bacon rashers (slices), grilled (broiled) until crisp
Speciality Creamed Potatoes (page 348) and broccoli, to serve

Remove the giblets from the bird, if necessary. Wipe the chicken inside and out with kitchen paper (paper towels). Pull off any excess fat from just inside the body cavity and discard. Put 50 g/2 oz/⅓ cup of the prunes in a blender or food processor with the orange rind and juice and the stock. Purée until smooth. Pour into an ovenproof dish, just large enough to take the chicken. Add the remaining prunes, the bouquet garni and the almonds. Top with the chicken and season with salt and pepper. Cover with lightly oiled foil and bake in the oven at 190°C/375°F/gas mark 5 for 1½ hours until the chicken is cooked through. Carefully remove the chicken and carve into neat pieces. Transfer to warm plates. Discard the bouquet garni, spoon off any fat from the sauce, taste and re-season the sauce if necessary. Spoon over the chicken and crumble the bacon over. Serve hot with Speciality Creamed Potatoes and broccoli.

Baked Chicken with Apricots and Walnuts

SERVES 4–6

Prepare as for Baked Chicken with Prunes and Almonds, but substitute ready-to-eat dried apricots for the prunes and walnuts for the almonds.

Pot Roast Paprika Chicken with Rice

SERVES 6

1.5 kg/3 lb oven-ready chicken
15 g/½ oz/1 tbsp butter or margarine
1 onion, finely chopped
1 green (bell) pepper, finely chopped
1 celery stick, chopped
225 g/8 oz/1 cup long-grain rice
400 g/14 oz/1 large can of chopped tomatoes
450 ml/¾ pt/2 cups chicken stock
1 bouquet garni sachet
Freshly ground black pepper
15 ml/1 tbsp paprika
200 g/7 oz/1 small can of sweetcorn (corn)

Remove the giblets from the bird, if necessary. Pull off any excess fat from just inside the body cavity and discard. Heat the butter or margarine in a large flameproof casserole (Dutch oven) and fry (sauté) the onion, pepper and celery for 2 minutes, stirring. Add the rice and stir for 1 minute. Add the tomatoes, stock, bouquet garni and season well with pepper. Top with the chicken and dust the flesh with the paprika. Bring to the boil, cover and place in a preheated oven at 190°C/375°F/gas mark 5. Cook for 1¼ hours. Discard the bouquet garni and stir in the sweetcorn. Re-cover and cook in the oven for a further 15 minutes. Carve the chicken and serve hot with the rice.

Pot Roast Chilli Chicken with Rice

SERVES 6

Prepare as for Pot Roast Paprika Chicken with Rice, but substitute a red (bell) pepper for the green, use half paprika and half chilli powder for dusting the chicken and add 225 g/8 oz frozen peas and sweetcorn instead of the can of corn.

Roasted Spiced Flower Chicken with Barley

SERVES 4

45 ml/3 tbsp olive oil
4 chicken breasts, cut into bite-sized pieces
225 g/8 oz broccoli, cut into small florets
1 small cauliflower, cut into small florets
5 ml/1 tsp coriander (cilantro) seeds
5 ml/1 tsp cumin seeds
Salt and freshly ground black pepper
350 g/12 oz/scant 2 cups pearl barley, soaked overnight in cold water and drained
900 ml/1½ pts/6 cups chicken stock
1 bay leaf
1 lemon, sliced
Parsley sprigs, to garnish

Brush a roasting tin (pan) with 15 ml/1 tbsp of the oil. Add the chicken, broccoli and cauliflower and drizzle with the remaining oil. Sprinkle with the coriander and cumin seeds and sprinkle with a little salt and pepper. Place on the shelf above the centre of the oven and roast, uncovered, for 30 minutes, tossing twice.

Meanwhile, put the pearl barley in a shallow flameproof dish. Add the stock, bay leaf and all but two slices of the lemon. Sprinkle with salt and pepper and bring to the boil. Transfer to the oven, just below the chicken and vegetables, and cook for 25 minutes or until tender and the barley has absorbed the liquid. Discard the bay leaf and lemon slices from the barley. Taste and re-season if necessary. Spoon the barley on to warm serving plates, pile the chicken and vegetable mixture on top and serve garnished with the reserved lemon slices and parsley sprigs.

Chicken and Cauliflower Cheese

SERVES 4

1 cauliflower, cut into florets
225 g/8 oz/2 cups cooked chicken, cut into bite-sized pieces
25 g/1 oz/2 tbsp butter or margarine
1 green (bell) pepper, chopped
1 onion, chopped
20 g/¾ oz/3 tbsp plain (all-purpose) flour
300 ml/½ pt/1¼ cups skimmed milk
50 g/2 oz/1 cup Cheddar cheese, grated
Salt and freshly ground black pepper
25 g/1 oz/½ cup bran flakes, crushed
1.5 ml/¼ tsp chilli powder
Crusty bread and a tomato salad, to serve

Cook the cauliflower in lightly salted boiling water until just tender. Drain and transfer to an ovenproof serving dish. Scatter the chicken over. Melt the butter or margarine in the cauliflower saucepan. Stir in the pepper and onion and cook, stirring, for 3 minutes. Stir in the flour. Remove from the heat and blend in the milk. Return to the heat and bring to the boil, stirring all the time. Cook for 2 minutes. Stir in the cheese and season to taste. Pour over the chicken and cauliflower. Mix the crushed bran flakes with the chilli powder and sprinkle over. Bake in a preheated oven at 190°C/375°F/gas mark 5 for 20 minutes. Serve hot with crusty bread and a tomato salad.

Chicken, Broccoli and Tomato Cheese

SERVES 4

Prepare as for Chicken and Cauliflower Cheese, but use broccoli instead of cauliflower and pour a drained 400 g/14 oz/1 large can of chopped tomatoes over the cooked broccoli before adding the cheese sauce.

Amazing Chicken and Broccoli Bake

SERVES 4–6

450 g/1 lb broccoli, cut into small florets
Salt
3 large skinless chicken breasts, cut into bite-sized pieces
300 ml/½ pt/1¼ cups chicken stock
295 g/10½ oz/1 medium can of condensed chicken soup
120 ml/4 fl oz/½ cup evaporated milk
150 ml/¼ pt/⅔ cup mayonnaise
15 ml/1 tbsp curry powder
15 ml/1 tbsp lemon juice
75 g/3 oz/¾ cup Cheddar cheese, grated
15 g/½ oz/1 tbsp butter, melted
25 g/1 oz/½ cup white breadcrumbs
3 tomatoes, sliced
Crusty rolls, to serve

Cook the broccoli in lightly salted boiling water until tender. Drain and place in an ovenproof dish. Poach the chicken in the stock in a saucepan for 8 minutes. Remove with a draining spoon and place on the broccoli. Boil the stock until reduced by half. Stir in the soup, milk, mayonnaise, curry powder and lemon juice. Add half the cheese and heat through, stirring. Pour over the chicken and broccoli. Mix the melted butter with the breadcrumbs and remaining cheese. Sprinkle over. Arrange the tomato slices round the edge and bake in a preheated oven at 190°C/375°F/gas mark 5 for about 30 minutes until golden and bubbling. Serve with crusty rolls.

Cheese and Chicken Fluff

SERVES 4

25 g/1 oz/2 tbsp butter or margarine
1 egg
300 ml/½ pt/1¼ cups milk
75 g/3 oz/1½ cups fresh breadcrumbs
100 g/4 oz/1 cup Cheddar cheese, grated
Salt and freshly ground black pepper
A pinch of cayenne
100 g/4 oz/1 cup cooked chicken, chopped, all skin removed
2 egg whites
Parsley sprigs, to garnish
Baked tomatoes, to serve

Lightly grease a 1.2 litre/2 pt/5 cup ovenproof dish. Beat together the egg and milk in a bowl. Stir in the breadcrumbs, cheese, some salt and pepper, the cayenne and the chicken. Leave to stand for 15 minutes. Whisk the egg whites until stiff and fold in with a metal spoon. Turn into the prepared dish and bake in a preheated oven at 200°C/400°F/gas mark 6 for 35 minutes until risen and golden brown. Remove from the oven and garnish with a parsley sprig. Serve hot with baked tomatoes.

Blue Cheese and Chicken Fluff

SERVES 4

Prepare as for Cheese and Chicken Fluff, but substitute half crumbled blue cheese for half the Cheddar and add 2 celery sticks, finely chopped, for added bite.

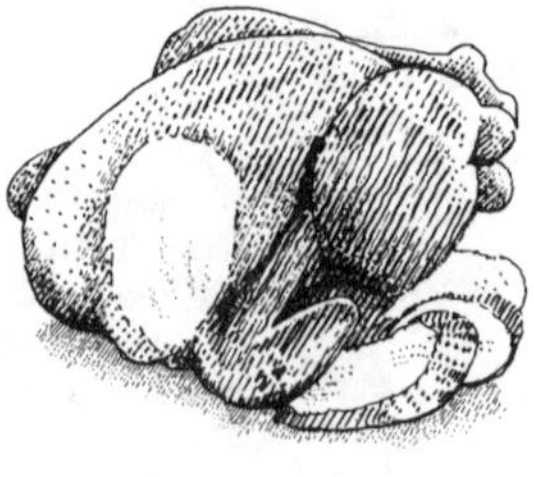

Traditional Sunday Roast Chicken

SERVES 4–6

1.75 g/4 lb oven-ready chicken
Sage and Onion Stuffing or Parsley and Thyme Stuffing (page 353)
Sunflower oil
Salt
Gravy (page 334), Royal Roast Potatoes (page 348), Bread Sauce (page 339), carrots and a green vegetable, to serve

Remove the giblets from the chicken, if necessary. Pull off any excess fat from just inside the body cavity and discard. Stuff the neck end with the stuffing and secure with a skewer. Place in a roasting tin (pan) and rub with oil. Sprinkle with salt. Roast in a preheated oven at 190°C/375°F/gas mark 5 for 1½ hours or until golden and the juices run clear when a skewer is inserted in the thickest part of the thigh. Leave to rest while making the gravy and serve with Royal Roast Potatoes, Bread Sauce, carrots and a green vegetable.

Thai Meat Balls

SERVES 4

450 g/1 lb minced (ground) chicken
100 g/4 oz/1 cup cooked Thai fragrant (or long-grain) rice
1 small onion, very finely chopped
1 egg, beaten
1 small green chilli, seeded and finely chopped
5 ml/1 tsp grated fresh root ginger
1 garlic clove, crushed
Salt and freshly ground black pepper
5 kaffir lime leaves, lightly bruised
Sunflower oil, for greasing
Thai Fragrant Rice (page 351) and Peanut Sauce (page 336), to serve
Coriander (cilantro) leaves, to garnish

Mix together all the ingredients except the lime leaves and shape into 12 small balls. Oil a shallow baking tin (pan) and arrange the leaves in the base. Top with the meat balls. Cover with foil and roast in a preheated oven at 200°C/400°F/gas mark 6 for 12–15 minutes until firm and cooked through. Transfer to a bed of Thai Fragrant Rice and serve with the Peanut Sauce spooned over, garnished with coriander leaves.

Chinese Chicken Burgers

SERVES 4

225 g/8 oz minced (ground) chicken
1 small onion, grated
30 ml/2 tbsp chopped coriander (cilantro)
10 ml/2 tsp soy sauce
Freshly ground black pepper
15 ml/1 tbsp curry powder
2.5 ml/½ tsp Chinese five spice powder
10 ml/2 tsp cold water
Sunflower oil, for brushing
Shredded lettuce, chopped tomatoes, cucumber and spring onions (scallions) and lemon wedges, to garnish
Tomato Dipping Sauce (page 337) and Crispy Noodles (page 356), to serve

Mix the chicken with the onion, coriander, soy sauce and a grinding of black pepper. Blend the curry and five-spice powders with the water. Stir into the meat mixture. Divide into quarters and shape each round an oiled metal skewer into a sausage shape. Line a roasting tin (pan) with foil and brush with a little oil. Lay the skewers in the tin and brush with oil. Bake in a preheated oven at 190°C/375°F/gas mark 5 for 20 minutes, turning once and brushing with more oil, until cooked through. Slide on to a bed of shredded lettuce, chopped tomatoes, cucumber and spring onions and the lemon wedges and serve with Tomato Dipping Sauce and Crispy Noodles.

Chicken and Vegetable Moussaka

SERVES 4

450 g/1 lb potatoes, sliced
2 courgettes (zucchini), sliced
1 aubergine (eggplant), sliced
1 red (bell) pepper, cut into strips
1 green pepper, cut into strips
1 large onion, chopped
4 tomatoes, chopped
2 large skinless chicken breasts, cut into small pieces
30 ml/2 tbsp olive oil
5 ml/1 tsp dried mixed herbs
12 stoned (pitted) black olives, sliced
30 ml/2 tbsp red wine
A good pinch of caster (superfine) sugar
Salt and freshly ground black pepper
150 ml/¼ pt/⅔ cup plain yoghurt
1 egg, beaten
75 g/3 oz/¾ cup Cheddar cheese, grated
Mixed salad, topped with olives and crumbled Feta cheese, to serve

Cook the potatoes in lightly salted boiling water for about 5 minutes or until just tender. Drain. Meanwhile, fry (sauté) the prepared vegetables and chicken in the olive oil, stirring, for 3 minutes. Add the herbs, olives, wine, sugar and a little salt and pepper. Reduce the heat, part cover and simmer for 10 minutes until tender. Layer the potatoes and vegetable mixture in a 1.5 litre/2½ pt/6 cup ovenproof dish, finishing with a layer of potatoes. Beat together the yoghurt and egg with a little salt and pepper and stir in the cheese. Spoon over the potatoes and bake in a preheated oven at 190°C/375°F/gas mark 5 for about 40 minutes until the topping is set and golden brown. Serve warm with a Greek-style mixed salad.

Chicken and Aubergine Moussaka

SERVES 4

1 large aubergine (eggplant), thinly sliced
1 onion, finely chopped
1 garlic clove, crushed
350 g/12 oz minced (ground) chicken
30 ml/2 tbsp olive oil
2.5 ml/½ tsp ground cinnamon
5 ml/1 tsp dried oregano
400 g/14 oz/1 large can of chopped tomatoes
15 ml/1 tbsp chopped parsley
Salt and freshly ground black pepper
1 egg
150 ml/¼ pt/⅔ cup plain yoghurt
50 g/2 oz/½ cup Cheddar cheese, grated
Mixed salad with cubed Feta cheese, to serve

Boil the aubergine in lightly salted water for about 5 minutes or until tender. Drain. Cook the onion, garlic and chicken in the oil in a saucepan for 5 minutes until the chicken is no longer pink and all the grains are separate. Stir in the cinnamon, oregano, tomatoes and parsley and season with salt and pepper. Simmer for 15 minutes. Layer the chicken mixture and aubergine slices in an ovenproof dish, finishing with a layer of aubergines. Beat the egg and yoghurt with the cheese and a little salt and pepper. Pour over. Bake in a preheated oven at 190°C/375°F/gas mark 5 for about 35 minutes until golden brown and set on top. Serve with a mixed salad with Feta cheese.

Chicken and Potato Moussaka

SERVES 4

Prepare as for Chicken and Aubergine Moussaka, but use 2 large potatoes, sliced, instead of the aubergine (eggplant).

Chicken and Courgette Moussaka

SERVES 4

Prepare as for Chicken and Aubergine Moussaka, but use 3 courgettes (zucchini), sliced, instead of the aubergine (eggplant).

Chicken Toad

SERVES 4

100 g/4 oz/1 cup plain (all-purpose) flour
A pinch of salt
2.5 ml/½ tsp dried sage
2 eggs
150 ml/¼ pt/⅔ cup milk
150 ml/¼ pt/⅔ cup water
45 ml/3 tbsp sunflower oil
1 onion, thinly sliced
225 g/8 oz/2 cups cooked chicken, cut into chunky pieces
Gravy (leftover or page 334) and a green vegetable, to serve

Sift the flour and salt into a bowl. Make a well in the centre. Add the sage and eggs. Mix together the milk and water. Add half to the bowl and beat well until a smooth batter is formed. Stir in the remaining milk and water. Pour the oil into a shallow baking tin (pan). Add the onion. Cook in a preheated oven at 220°C/425°F/gas mark 7 until sizzling. Add the chicken and heat again until sizzling. Pour in the batter. Cook towards the top of the oven for about 30 minutes until risen, crisp and golden. Serve cut into quarters with gravy and a green vegetable.

Chicken and Mushroom Toad

SERVES 4

Prepare as for Chicken Toad, but add 100 g/4 oz sliced mushrooms and reduce the quantity of chicken to 175 g/6 oz/1½ cups.

Chicken and Sweetcorn Toad

SERVES 4

Prepare as for Chicken Toad, but add 200 g/7 oz/1 small can of drained sweetcorn (corn) to the mixture and reduce the quantity of chicken to 175 g/6 oz/1½ cups.

Chicken and Vegetable Popovers

SERVES 4

Prepare as for Chicken Toad, but chop the onion and use only 100 g/4 oz/1 cup cooked chicken. Add 175 g/6 oz cold cooked vegetables, chopped. Heat the oil in 12 sections of a tartlet tin (patty pan) instead of a large tin. Continue as before, but cook for about 20 minutes until crisp, risen and golden. Serve 3 popovers per portion.

Chicken with Garlic and Lemon Butter

SERVES 4

4 skinless chicken breasts
40 g/1½ oz/3 tbsp butter or margarine
30 ml/2 tbsp chopped parsley
1 large garlic clove, crushed
Finely grated rind of ½ lemon
Freshly ground black pepper
Plain Boiled Rice (page 351) and a mixed green salad, to serve

Make a slit in the side of each chicken breast with a sharp knife to form a pocket. Mash the butter or margarine with the parsley, garlic, lemon rind and a good grinding of pepper. Divide the mixture between the pockets and secure the openings with cocktail sticks (toothpicks). Wrap in non-stick baking parchment, then foil, shiny-side in. Put on a baking (cookie) sheet. Bake in a preheated oven at 190°C/375°F/gas mark 5 for 30 minutes. Unwrap, remove the cocktail sticks and serve with Plain Boiled Rice and a mixed green salad.

Chicken with Garlic and Herb Butter

SERVES 4

Prepare as for Chicken with Garlic and Lemon Butter (page 155), but substitute 15 ml/1 tbsp chopped parsley and 15 ml/1 tbsp chopped basil for the lemon rind.

Chicken with Curried Butter

SERVES 4

Prepare as for Chicken with Garlic and Lemon Butter (page 155), but mash 15 ml/1 tbsp curry paste into the butter with 15 ml/1 tbsp chopped coriander (cilantro) instead of the parsley, garlic and lemon rind. Serve with mango chutney as well as the rice and salad.

Chicken Pesto Parcels

SERVES 4

Prepare as for Chicken with Garlic and Lemon Butter (page 155), but fill the chicken with pesto sauce from a jar or use Pesto for Poultry (page 342) instead of the butter mixture and serve with buttered tagliatelle instead of rice.

Chicken with Orange Butter

SERVES 4

Prepare as for Chicken with Garlic and Lemon Butter (page 155), but flavour the butter or margarine with the finely grated rind of ½ orange instead of lemon, omit the garlic and add 1.5 ml/¼ tsp ground cinnamon and 2.5 ml/½ tsp celery salt.

Baked Barbecued Chicken Drumsticks

SERVES 4

8 chicken drumsticks
40 g/1½ oz/3 tbsp butter or margarine
1 onion, finely chopped
2 garlic cloves, crushed
225 g/8 oz/1 small can of chopped tomatoes
30 ml/2 tbsp tomato ketchup (catsup)
30 ml/2 tbsp golden (light corn) syrup
15 ml/1 tbsp soy sauce
15 ml/1 tbsp red wine vinegar
Salt and freshly ground black pepper
Jacket potatoes and a mixed salad, to serve

Put the chicken drumsticks in a roasting tin (pan). Melt the butter or margarine in a saucepan and brush half of it over the chicken. Bake in a preheated oven at 190°C/375°F/gas mark 5 for 15 minutes. Meanwhile, add the onion and garlic to the remaining butter or margarine in the saucepan and fry (sauté) for 2 minutes, stirring. Add the remaining ingredients, bring to the boil and simmer for 3 minutes. Spoon over the chicken and cook for a further 10 minutes. Turn over the legs, baste with the sauce and cook for a further 15 minutes until cooked through and stickily glazed. Serve hot with jacket potatoes and a mixed salad.

Chicken and Leek Roulade with Mushroom Sauce

SERVES 6

1 very large potato, peeled and diced
1 leek, sliced
10 g/4 oz/1 cup self-raising (self-rising) flour
Salt and freshly ground black pepper
5 ml/1 tsp baking powder
75 g/3 oz/⅓ cup butter or margarine
2 eggs, separated
50 g/2 oz/¼ cup Cheddar cheese, grated
400 ml/14 fl oz/1¾ cups milk
For the filling:
350 g/12 oz/3 cups cooked chicken, chopped, all skin removed
400 g/14 oz/1 large can of chopped tomatoes
15 ml/1 tbsp tomato purée (paste)
2.5 ml/½ tsp dried basil
For the sauce:
1 small onion, finely chopped
75 g/3 oz button mushrooms, finely chopped
20 g/¾ oz/3 tbsp plain (all-purpose) flour
30 ml/2 tbsp chopped parsley
Mixed salad, to serve

Cook the potato and leek in lightly salted boiling water until tender. Drain and mash thoroughly together. Sift the self-raising flour with a little salt and pepper and the baking powder into a bowl. Rub in 50 g/2 oz/¼ cup of the butter or margarine. Stir in the potato and leek. Beat the egg yolks with the cheese and 120 ml/4 fl oz/½ cup of the milk. Add to the potato mixture and mix well. Whisk the egg whites until stiff and fold in with a metal spoon. Turn into a Swiss roll tin (jelly roll pan) lined with baking parchment and bake in a preheated oven at 200°C/400°F/gas mark 6 for about 15 minutes until risen, golden and the centre springs back when lightly pressed. Turn out on to clean baking parchment.

Meanwhile, put the chicken, tomatoes and tomato purée in a saucepan with the basil. Bring to the boil and simmer for 5 minutes, stirring occasionally, until pulpy. Season to taste. In a separate pan, heat the remaining butter or margarine and cook the onion and mushrooms, stirring, for 3 minutes until soft. Blend in the plain flour and cook for 1 minute. Stir in the remaining milk, bring to the boil and cook for 2 minutes, stirring. Add the parsley and season to taste. Spread the chicken mixture on the roulade. Roll up and transfer to a warm serving dish. Cut into slices and serve with the mushroom sauce and a salad.

Baked Chicken with Orange and Pine Nuts

SERVES 4

1 orange
4 skinless chicken breasts
25 g/1 oz/¼ cup pine nuts
45 ml/3 tbsp medium-dry sherry
15 ml/1 tbsp soy sauce
A pinch of chilli powder
A pinch of ground cinnamon
30 ml/2 tbsp clear honey
10 ml/2 tsp cornflour (cornstarch)
15 ml/1 tbsp water
30 ml/2 tbsp chopped parsley, to garnish
New potatoes, boiled in their skins, and peas, to serve

Thinly pare the rind from half the orange. Cut into thin strips and boil in water for 1 minute. Drain and reserve. Finely grate the remaining rind and squeeze the juice. Make several slashes in each chicken breast and lay in a flameproof casserole (Dutch oven). Mix the pine nuts and grated orange rind and juice with all the remaining ingredients, except the cornflour and water and pared orange rind, and spoon over the chicken. Chill for 1 hour to marinate. Bake in a preheated oven at 200°C/400°F/gas mark 6 for 35 minutes until cooked through. Lift the chicken out of the pan and transfer to warm plates. Blend the cornflour with the water and stir into the juices. Bring to the boil and cook for 1 minute, stirring. Cut the chicken into slices and fan out on the plates. Spoon the sauce over. Garnish with the orange rind and parsley. Serve with new potatoes in their skins and peas.

Dutch Roast

SERVES 4

1 thick slice of white bread, crusts removed
250 ml/8 fl oz/1 cup milk
450 g/1 lb minced (ground) chicken or turkey
1 egg, beaten
1 small onion, finely chopped
15 ml/1 tbsp chopped parsley
2.5 ml/½ tsp dried mixed herbs
Salt and freshly ground black pepper
75 g/3 oz/¾ cup browned breadcrumbs
250 ml/8 fl oz/1 cup chicken or turkey stock
15 ml/1 tbsp plain (all-purpose) flour
15 ml/1 tbsp water
Speciality Creamed Potatoes (page 348) and a green vegetable, to serve

Put the bread in a bowl. Bring the milk to the boil and pour over. Leave to soak for 30 minutes. Whisk with a fork to break up. Beat in the mince, egg, onion, herbs and a little salt and pepper. Shape into a rectangle in a roasting tin (pan) and coat in the breadcrumbs. Pour the stock around. Bake in a preheated oven at 180°C/350°F/gas mark 4 for 1 hour or until firm and spread slightly. Leave to stand for 5 minutes, then slice and transfer to warm plates. Keep warm. Quickly blend the flour with the water and stir into the juices in the pan. Bring to the boil, stirring, and season to taste, if necessary. Spoon over the roast and serve with Speciality Creamed Potatoes and a green vegetable.

Crunchy-coated Chicken

SERVES 4

8 chicken drumsticks
30 ml/2 tbsp plain (all-purpose) flour
Salt and freshly ground black pepper
1 egg, beaten
85 g/3½ oz/1 small packet of sage and onion stuffing mix
45 ml/3 tbsp sunflower or olive oil
Oven chips and French (green) beans, to serve

Pull all the skin off the chicken drumsticks and discard. Toss the drumsticks in the flour, mixed with a little salt and pepper. Dip in the egg, then in the stuffing mix to coat completely. Heat the oil in a non-stick baking tin (pan). Add the drumsticks and turn over in the oil. Bake in a preheated oven at 190°C/375°F/gas mark 5 for 20 minutes. Turn the legs over and bake for a further 20 minutes until crisp and golden brown. Drain on kitchen paper (paper towels) and serve hot or cold with oven chips and French beans.

Oven-crunched Sesame Chicken

SERVES 4

8 chicken drumsticks
30 ml/2 tbsp flour
85 g/3½ oz/1 packet of parsley and thyme stuffing mix
30 ml/2 tbsp sesame seeds
5 ml/1 tsp garlic salt
1 large egg, beaten
60 ml/4 tbsp sunflower oil
Salad-filled baguettes, to serve

Pull all the skin off the chicken drumsticks and discard. Dust the drumsticks with flour. Mix the stuffing with the sesame seeds and garlic salt. Dip the legs in the egg, then in the stuffing mixture. Pour the oil into a shallow baking tin (pan). Add the drumsticks. Bake in a preheated oven at 190°C/375°F/gas mark 5 for 20 minutes. Turn over and cook on the other side for a further 20 minutes until crisp and golden. Drain on kitchen paper (paper towels). Serve hot or cold with salad-filled baguettes.

Crunchy Lemon Chicken Legs

SERVES 4

Prepare as for Oven-crunched Sesame Chicken, but use parsley, thyme and lemon stuffing mix plus the finely grated rind of 1 lemon. Omit the sesame seeds and use celery salt instead of garlic salt.

Chicken Shack Pie

SERVES 4

1 onion, finely chopped
350 g/12 oz minced (ground) chicken
1 large carrot, grated
1 large turnip, grated
75 g/3 oz frozen peas
450 ml/¾ pt/2 cups chicken stock
2.5 ml/½ tsp dried mixed herbs
Salt and freshly ground black pepper
700 g/1½ lb potatoes, peeled and cut into even-sized pieces
45 ml/3 tbsp milk
15 g/½ oz/1 tbsp butter or margarine
5 ml/1 tsp Worcestershire sauce
30 ml/2 tbsp plain (all-purpose) flour
45 ml/3 tbsp cold water
2.5 ml/½ tsp paprika
Cabbage, to serve

Put the onion and mince in a large non-stick saucepan. Cook, stirring, for 5 minutes until the meat is browned and all the grains are separate. Spoon off any fat, but leave the juices. Add the carrot, turnip, peas and stock. Stir in the herbs, a little salt and lots of pepper. Bring to the boil, stirring occasionally, reduce the heat, part-cover and simmer very gently for 20 minutes. Meanwhile, cook the potatoes in boiling salted water until tender. Drain and mash with the milk, butter or margarine and Worcestershire sauce. Blend the flour with the water and stir into the chicken mixture. Bring to the boil and cook for 2 minutes, stirring, until thickened. Turn into an ovenproof dish. Spoon the potato on top and rough up with a fork. Dust with the paprika. Bake in a preheated oven at 200°C/400°F/gas mark 6 for 25 minutes until golden on top. Serve with cabbage.

Mighty Chicken Loaf

This could also be served cold with new potatoes and a salad.

SERVES 4

1 onion, quartered
225 g/8 oz/2 cups cooked chicken, roughly chopped
2 slices of lean cooked ham
25 g/1 oz/2 tbsp butter or margarine
30 ml/2 tbsp browned breadcrumbs
100 g/4 oz button mushrooms, chopped
2.5 ml/½ tsp dried mixed herbs
90 ml/6 tbsp medium oat bran
1 Weetabix, crushed
150 ml/¼ pt/⅔ cup milk
1 egg, beaten
A pinch of salt
Freshly ground black pepper
300 ml/½ pt/1¼ cups passata (sieved tomatoes)
2.5 ml/½ tsp dried basil
Royal Roast Potatoes (page 348) and curly kale, to serve

Mince (grind) the onion, chicken and ham or chop not too finely in a food processor. Use a little of the butter or margarine to lightly grease a 450 g/1 lb loaf tin (pan). Coat with the breadcrumbs. Melt the remaining butter or margarine in a saucepan. Add the mushrooms and herbs and fry (sauté) for 2 minutes, stirring. Sprinkle the oat bran over and stir for 1 minute. Add the Weetabix, milk and egg, then stir in the chicken mixture and season with the salt and some pepper. Turn into the prepared tin and smooth the surface. Cover with foil and stand the tin in a roasting tin (pan) containing 2.5 cm/1 in boiling water. Bake in a preheated oven at 180°C/350°F/gas mark 4 for 1 hour, then remove the foil and cook for a further 30 minutes until firm and cooked through. Meanwhile, warm the passata with the basil and a good grinding of pepper. Turn the loaf out on to a warm serving dish and serve sliced with the warm passata, Royal Roast Potatoes and curly kale.

Spinach, Chicken and Peanut Loaf

SERVES 4

225 g/8 oz frozen leaf spinach, thawed
1 large onion, quartered
2 boneless chicken thighs, skin removed
1 garlic clove
100 g/4 oz/1 cup salted peanuts
4 slices of bread
1 egg
5 ml/1 tsp yeast extract
Salt and freshly ground black pepper
2.5 ml/½ tsp dried mixed herbs
Royal Roast Potatoes (page 348) and carrots, to serve

Mince (grind) the spinach, onion, chicken, garlic, peanuts and bread. Beat together the egg and yeast extract and stir into the minced mixture. Season with salt, pepper and the herbs. Turn into a greased 450 g/1 lb loaf tin (pan). Cover with foil and bake in a preheated oven at 180°C/350°F/gas mark 4 for 1 hour or until firm. Leave to stand for 5 minutes. Loosen the edges, turn out and serve hot with Royal Roast Potatoes and carrots.

Chicken with Lime and Garlic

SERVES 4

4 small skinless chicken breasts
50 g/2 oz/¼ cup medium-fat soft cheese
1 large garlic clove, crushed
15 ml/1 tbsp chopped parsley
Grated rind and juice of 1 lime
Salt and freshly ground black pepper
30 ml/2 tbsp toasted desiccated (shredded) coconut
Thai Fragrant Rice (page 351) and a mixed salad, to serve

Make a slit in the side of each chicken breast to form a pocket. Mash the cheese with the garlic, parsley, lime rind and a little salt and pepper. Spoon into the chicken breasts. Place each on a square of foil and sprinkle with lime juice and a little more salt and pepper. Wrap up. Place on a baking (cookie) sheet and bake in a preheated oven at 190°C/375°F/gas mark 5 for 30 minutes, opening up the foil after 20 minutes to allow the chicken to brown. Sprinkle with the toasted desiccated coconut and serve with Thai Fragrant Rice and a mixed salad.

Chinese Chicken Wings

MAKES ABOUT 32

900 g/2 lb chicken wings (not portions, just the wings)
30 ml/2 tbsp wine vinegar
60 ml/4 tbsp sunflower oil
30 ml/2 tbsp soy sauce
1 large garlic clove, crushed
30 ml/2 tbsp golden (light corn) syrup
30 ml/2 tbsp tomato purée (paste)
30 ml/2 tbsp plum jam (jelly)
15 ml/1 tbsp lemon juice
5 ml/1 tsp ground ginger
Perfect Potato Wedges (page 349) and a mixed salad, to serve

Cut off and discard the wing tips. Cut the wings into two pieces at the next joint. Mix together the remaining ingredients in a large shallow baking tin (pan). Add the chicken and turn to coat in the mixture. Leave to marinate for at least 1 hour. Bake in a preheated oven at 180°C/350°F/gas mark 4 for about 1 hour, turning occasionally, until tender and coated in a sticky glaze. Serve warm or cold with Perfect Potato Wedges and a mixed salad.

Chicken and Mushroom Gougère

SERVES 4

Prepare as for Chicken Liver Gougère (page 164) but omit the livers and cook 100 g/4 oz sliced mushrooms with the bacon, onion and garlic. Stir 175 g/ 6 oz/1½ cups cooked, diced chicken into the sauce, then make the choux pastry and continue as before.

Chicken and Roast Vegetable Fajitas

SERVES 4

4 large chicken breasts
1 large garlic clove, crushed
Finely grated rind and juice of 1 lime
1 red chilli, seeded and finely chopped
15 ml/1 tbsp paprika
5 ml/1 tsp dried oregano
2.5 ml/½ tsp ground cumin
1.5 ml/¼ tsp ground cinnamon
45 ml/3 tbsp sunflower or olive oil
Salt and freshly ground black pepper
1 red (bell) pepper, cut into strips
1 green pepper, cut into strips
1 aubergine (eggplant), sliced
1 courgette (zucchini), diagonally sliced
12 flour tortillas
A small bowl of tomato or chilli relish
150 ml/¼ pt/⅔ cup crème fraîche
1 onion, finely chopped
A small bowl of finely shredded iceberg lettuce

Wipe the chicken with kitchen paper (paper towels) and slash in several places with a sharp knife. Place in a single layer in a shallow baking dish. Mix together the garlic, lime rind and juice, chilli, paprika, oregano, cumin and cinnamon with half the oil and season to taste. Pour over the chicken and leave to marinate for 2 hours. Arrange the prepared vegetables in a large shallow baking tin (pan) and drizzle with the remaining oil. Toss gently. Bake the chicken on the middle shelf and the vegetables on the top shelf of a preheated oven at 190°C/375°F/gas mark 5 for about 40 minutes until tender and cooked through, turning the vegetables and chicken once half-way through cooking.

Warm the tortillas in the microwave or between two plates over a pan of boiling water. Thinly slice the chicken breasts and place on large serving plates with the roasted vegetables and the tortillas. To serve, spread the tortillas with a little relish, add the vegetables and chicken, top with a little crème fraîche, chopped onion and shredded lettuce, roll up and eat with the fingers.

Baked Chinese Chicken

SERVES 4

30 ml/2 tbsp soy sauce
30 ml/2 tbsp clear honey
Grated rind and juice of 1 large orange
1 small garlic clove, crushed
10 ml/2 tsp chopped fresh root ginger
5 ml/1 tsp ground cumin
4 skinless chicken breasts, about 175 g/6 oz each
25 g/1 oz/2 tbsp butter or margarine, melted
To serve:
Plain Boiled Rice (page 351)
Chinese leaves (stem lettuce), shredded
A few spring onions (scallions), chopped
298 g/11 oz/1 medium can of mandarin oranges, drained
French dressing

Mix together all the ingredients except the chicken and butter or margarine in a shallow baking tin (pan). Add the chicken breasts, turn over in the marinade and leave to marinate for 3 hours or preferably overnight, turning occasionally. Drizzle the butter or margarine over, turn the chicken again and bake in a preheated oven at 180°C/350°F/gas mark 4 for 45 minutes until coated in sauce and cooked through. To serve, arrange the Plain Boiled Rice on four plates and lay a chicken breast on each. Mix together the Chinese leaves, spring onions and mandarins in a bowl and toss gently in the French dressing. Serve the salad separately.

Poussins à la Provençal

SERVES 6

6 poussins (Cornish hens)
25 g/1 oz/2 tbsp butter or margarine
60 ml/4 tbsp olive oil
1 onion, finely chopped
1 small garlic clove, crushed
12 stoned (pitted) black olives, sliced
450 ml/¾ pt/2 cups passata (sieved tomatoes)
30 ml/2 tbsp tomato purée (paste)
1 chicken stock cube
45 ml/3 tbsp red wine
15 ml/1 tbsp brandy
Salt and freshly ground black pepper
Chopped parsley, to garnish
French bread and a green salad, to serve

Wipe the poussins inside and out with kitchen paper (paper towels). Brown quickly in the butter or margarine and half the oil in a frying pan (skillet). Transfer to a large roasting tin (pan). Add the onion to the frying pan and fry (sauté) for 2 minutes, stirring. Add the remaining ingredients and bring to the boil. Pour around the poussins. Cover with foil and bake in a preheated oven at 180°C/350°F/gas mark 4 for 45 minutes. Transfer the birds to warm serving plates. Taste the sauce and re-season if necessary, then spoon over the birds. Sprinkle with chopped parsley and serve with French bread and a green salad.

Devilled Poussins

SERVES 4

4 poussins (Cornish hens)
25 g/1 oz/2 tbsp butter or margarine
15 ml/1 tbsp sunflower oil
300 ml/½ pt/1¼ cups double (heavy) cream
60 ml/4 tbsp Worcestershire sauce
30 ml/2 tbsp Dijon mustard
10 ml/2 tsp made English mustard
15 ml/1 tbsp tomato purée (paste)
5 ml/1 tsp soy sauce
A few drops of Tabasco sauce
Plain Boiled Rice (page 351) and a green salad, to serve

Wipe the poussins inside and out with kitchen paper (paper towels). Melt the butter or margarine with the oil in a flameproof dish. Add the birds and brown all over. Mix together the remaining ingredients and pour all over to coat completely. Bake in a preheated oven at 180°C/350°F/gas mark 4 for 45 minutes, basting occasionally. Serve with Plain Boiled Rice and a green salad.

Fragrant Herb Poussins with Lemon and Honey

SERVES 6

6 poussins (Cornish hens)
6 parsley sprigs
6 thyme sprigs
6 sage sprigs
6 rosemary sprigs
45 ml/3 tbsp clear honey
30 ml/2 tbsp lemon juice
25 g/1 oz/2 tbsp butter or margarine
Salt and freshly ground black pepper
90 ml/6 tbsp water
Lemon twists and parsley sprigs, to garnish
Cheese Potatoes (page 349) and mangetout (snow peas), to serve

Wipe the poussins inside and out with kitchen paper (paper towels). Push a sprig of each herb into each bird. Place breast-sides down in a large roasting tin (pan). Warm the honey, lemon juice and butter or margarine together with a little salt and pepper. Brush some over the birds. Roast in a preheated oven at 200°C/400°F/gas mark 6 for 25 minutes. Turn over, brush with the remaining honey mixture and continue roasting for a further 30–40 minutes until golden brown and the juices run clear when pierced at the thigh. Remove from the pan and keep warm. Spoon off any fat from the juices, add the water, bring to the boil and cook for 2 minutes, stirring. Season to taste. Transfer the poussins to warm serving plates and spoon the cooking juices over. Garnish with lemon twists and parsley sprigs and serve with Cheese Potatoes and mangetout.

Poussins Roasted with White Wine and Rosemary

SERVES 4

4 poussins (Cornish hens)
Salt and freshly ground black pepper
4 large rosemary sprigs
50 g/2 oz/¼ cup butter or margarine
1 wineglass of dry white wine
Rosemary sprigs, to garnish
Redcurrant jelly (clear conserve), new potatoes and French (green) beans, to serve

Wipe the poussins inside and out with kitchen paper (paper towels). Season inside and out with salt and pepper. Push rosemary sprig in each. Place in a roasting tin (pan) and smear liberally with the butter or margarine. Cover loosely with foil and roast in a preheated oven at 180°C/350°F/gas mark 4 for 30 minutes. Remove the foil, turn up the heat to 220°C/425°F/gas mark 7 and cook for a further 10–15 minutes, basting frequently, until cooked through and the skin is crisp. Lift the birds out of the pan and keep warm. Pour the wine into the pan. Bring to the boil and boil rapidly, scraping up any sediment, until slightly reduced. Season to taste. Spoon over the poussins and serve hot with redcurrant jelly, new potatoes and French beans.

Garlic and Lemon Chicken

SERVES 4

1.25 kg/2½ lb oven-ready chicken
Salt and freshly ground black pepper
1 large sprig of rosemary
2 garlic cloves, halved
30 ml/2 tbsp lemon juice
15 g/½ oz/1 tbsp butter or margarine
300 ml/½ pt/1¼ cups chicken stock
Rosemary sprigs and lemon twists, to garnish
Poppy Seed and Mustard Royal Roast Potatoes (page 348) and runner beans, to serve

Wipe the chicken inside and out with kitchen paper (paper towels). Remove any excess fat from around the body cavity. Season inside with a little salt and pepper and push in the rosemary sprig and garlic. Place in a flameproof casserole dish (Dutch oven). Sprinkle all over with the lemon juice and spread the butter or margarine over the breast. Season with a little salt. Pour the stock around and cook in a preheated oven at 190°C/375°F/gas mark 5 for 1¼ hours. Transfer the chicken to a carving dish. Spoon off any fat. Boil the juices rapidly until reduced by half. Season to taste. Cut the chicken into four portions, discarding the skin. Transfer to warm plates and spoon the pan juices over. Garnish with rosemary sprigs and lemon twists and serve with Poppy Seed and Mustard Royal Roast Potatoes and runner beans.

Crisp Baked Chicken

SERVES 4

8 chicken legs or thighs
75 g/3 oz/¾ cup plain (all-purpose) flour
10 ml/2 tsp paprika
2.5 ml/½ tsp mixed (apple-pie) spice
5 ml/1 tsp salt
5 ml/1 tsp coarse ground black pepper
2 eggs
120 ml/4 fl oz/½ cup milk
225 g/8 oz/2 cups dried breadcrumbs
Sunflower oil
Perfect Potato Wedges (page 349), soured (dairy sour) cream and a mixed salad, to serve

Remove the skin from the chicken, if preferred. Mix together the flour, spices, salt and pepper. Beat together the eggs and milk. Dip the chicken in the flour to coat, then in the egg mixture, then in the breadcrumbs. Heat 5 mm/¼ in oil in a large roasting tin (pan) in the oven at 220°C/425°F/gas mark 7 until sizzling. Add the chicken and bake in the oven for 30 minutes. Turn over in the oil and bake again for a further 20–30 minutes until crisp and cooked through. Drain on kitchen paper (paper towels) and serve hot with Perfect Potato Wedges, soured cream and a mixed salad.

Chicken Liver Gougère

SERVES 4

75 g/3 oz/⅓ cup butter or margarine
225 g/8 oz chicken livers, trimmed
100 g/4 oz smoked, rindless streaky bacon, diced
1 onion, finely chopped
1 garlic clove, crushed
90 g/3½ oz/scant 1 cup plain (all-purpose) flour
450 ml/¾ pt/2 cups tomato juice
15 ml/1 tbsp tomato purée (paste)
5 ml/1 tsp dried basil
5 ml/1 tsp caster (superfine) sugar
Salt and freshly ground black pepper
For the choux pastry (paste):
150 ml/¼ pt/⅔ cup water
2 eggs, beaten
50 g/2 oz/½ cup Cheddar cheese, grated
30 ml/2 tbsp breadcrumbs
Chopped parsley, to garnish
French (green) beans, to serve

Melt 25 g/1 oz/2 tbsp of the butter or margarine in a saucepan. Add the chicken livers, bacon, onion and garlic and fry (sauté) gently for 4 minutes, stirring. Stir in 25 g/1 oz/¼ cup of the flour and cook for 1 minutes, stirring. Remove from the heat and blend in the tomato juice, purée, basil, sugar and a little salt and pepper. Return to the heat, bring to the boil and cook for 2 minutes, stirring all the time. Leave to cool while making the choux pastry.

Sift the remaining flour and 5 ml/1 tsp salt on to a sheet of kitchen paper (paper towel). Put the remaining butter or margarine and the water in a saucepan. Heat until the fat melts. Add the flour all at once and beat with a wooden spoon until the mixture leaves the sides of the pan clean. Leave to cool slightly, then gradually beat in the eggs, a little at a time, beating well after each addition until the mixture is smooth and glossy but still holds its shape. Spoon round the edge of a lightly greased 1.75 litre/3 pt/7½ cup shallow ovenproof dish. Spoon the chicken liver mixture into the centre. Sprinkle the pastry with the cheese and breadcrumbs. Bake in a preheated oven at 200°C/400°F/gas mark 6 for 35 minutes until the pastry is risen, crisp and golden. Sprinkle with chopped parsley and serve hot with French beans.

Chunky Chicken Loaf

SERVES 4–6

450 g/1 lb chicken livers, cut into small pieces
225 g/8 oz lean minced (ground) chicken
2 onions, finely chopped
5 ml/1 tsp dried thyme
Salt and freshly ground black pepper
175 g/6 oz/3 cups soft breadcrumbs
1 egg, beaten
Jacket potatoes and baked tomatoes, to serve

Mix together all the ingredients and turn into a non-stick 900 g/2 lb loaf tin (pan), base-lined with non-stick baking parchment. Cover with foil and bake in a preheated oven at 190°C/375°F/gas mark 5 for 1½ hours. Cook for 5 minutes, then turn out, remove the paper and serve sliced with jacket potatoes and baked tomatoes.

Chicken and Carrot Tzimmes

SERVES 4

700 g/1½ lb carrots, sliced
2 large leeks, sliced
15 ml/1 tbsp light brown sugar
15 ml/1 tbsp golden (light corn) syrup
450 ml/¾ pt/2 cups chicken stock
225 g/8 oz chicken stir-fry meat
100 g/4 oz/1 cup self-raising (self-rising) flour
10 ml/2 tsp baking powder
A good pinch of salt
A good pinch of pepper
15 ml/1 tbsp chopped parsley
Cold milk, to mix
Mixed green salad, to serve

Cook the carrots and leeks in boiling water in a flameproof casserole (Dutch oven) for 4 minutes. Drain and return to the casserole. Stir in the sugar, syrup, stock and chicken. Cover and cook in a preheated oven at 150°C/300°F/gas mark 2 for 1½ hours. Mix together the flour, baking powder, salt, pepper and parsley. Just before the end of the cooking time, stir enough milk into the flour mixture to form a soft but not sticky dough. Roll the dough into eight small balls. Taste the carrot mixture and season, if necessary. Arrange the dumplings around the top of the carrot mixture. Re-cover, turn up the oven to 190°C/375°F/gas mark 5, and return the dish to the oven for a further 10 minutes. Remove the lid and cook for a further 10 minutes. Serve immediately with a mixed green salad.

Kentucky Baked Chicken

SERVES 4

Prepare as for Kentucky Baked Turkey (page 171), but use chicken breasts instead of turkey and serve with jacket-baked potatoes topped with soured (dairy sour) cream and a rasher (slice) or two of crisp bacon, crumbled, instead of the yoghurt and chives.

TURKEY

Turkey and Pumpkin Chermoula

SERVES 4

½ small pumpkin, diced
1 turnip, diced
1 onion, thinly sliced
400 g/14 oz/1 large can of chopped tomatoes
30 ml/2 tbsp tomato purée (paste)
150 ml/¼ pt/⅔ cup medium-dry white wine
1 garlic clove, crushed
15 ml/1 tbsp chopped parsley
15 ml/1 tbsp chopped coriander (cilantro)
5 ml/1 tsp ground cumin
A few drops of Tabasco sauce
Finely grated rind and juice of ½ lemon
5 ml/1 tsp caster (superfine) sugar
Salt and freshly ground black pepper
4 small turkey steaks, diced
350 g/12 oz/2 cups couscous
30 ml/2 tbsp olive oil
A few black olives and a sprig of coriander, to garnish

Boil the pumpkin, turnip and onion in water for 3 minutes. Drain. Empty the tomatoes into a large shallow baking dish. Blend the tomato purée with the wine and stir in the garlic, herbs, cumin, Tabasco sauce, lemon rind and juice, sugar and a little salt and pepper. Stir well. Add the turkey, pumpkin, turnip and onion, mix well, cover and leave to marinate in the fridge for several hours or overnight. When nearly ready to cook, put the couscous in a bowl and just cover with boiling water. Leave to stand for 10 minutes, then season to taste with salt and pepper. Spoon over the marinated turkey mixture and drizzle with the olive oil. Bake in a preheated oven at 180°C/350°F/gas mark 4 for about 45 minutes until cooked through and golden on top. Garnish with a few olives and a sprig of coriander and serve hot.

Turkey and Vegetable Parcels

SERVES 4

Prepare as for Fragrant Chicken Parcels (page 149), but substitute turkey breast steaks for the chicken, sage sprigs for the rosemary and add 100 g/4 oz sliced button mushrooms to the vegetables.

Golden Turkey and Sweetcorn Bake

SERVES 4–6

450 g/1 lb diced turkey thigh meat
75 g/3 oz/⅓ cup butter or margarine
30 ml/2 tbsp sunflower oil
1 onion, finely chopped
100 g/4 oz button mushrooms, thickly sliced
1 small green (bell) pepper, finely chopped
200 g/7 oz/1 small can of sweetcorn (corn), drained
450 g/1 lb potatoes, thinly sliced
45 ml/3 tbsp cornflour (cornstarch)
300 ml/½ pt/1¼ cups milk
50 g/2 oz/½ cup Cheddar cheese, grated
Salt and freshly ground black pepper
Crusty bread and a tomato salad, to serve

Fry (sauté) the turkey in half the butter or margarine and the oil in a saucepan for 3 minutes, stirring. Remove from the pan with a draining spoon and transfer to a large ovenproof dish. Add a further 15 g/½ oz/1 tbsp of the butter or margarine to the pan and fry the onion, mushrooms and pepper for 2 minutes, stirring. Spoon over the turkey. Spoon the corn over and arrange the potato slices in an even layer over the top. Blend the cornflour with the milk and add to the pan with the remaining butter or margarine. Bring to the boil and cook for 1 minute, stirring. Stir in the cheese and season to taste. Pour over the potatoes. Cover loosely with foil and bake in a preheated oven at 180°C/350°F/gas mark 4 for 40 minutes. Remove the foil and turn up the oven to 220°C/425°F/gas mark 7. Cook for a further 20 minutes or until the potato topping is cooked and golden and the turkey is tender. Serve hot with crusty bread and a tomato salad.

Redcurrant Roast Stuffed Turkey

SERVES 10–12

4.5 kg/10 lb oven-ready turkey
100 g/4 oz/1 cup cooked brown rice
100 g/4 oz/1 cup streaky bacon rashers (slices), rinded and finely chopped
200 g/7 oz/1 small can sweetcorn (corn), drained
2.5 ml/½ tsp dried mixed herbs
Salt and freshly ground black pepper
2.5 ml/½ tsp grated nutmeg
1 egg, beaten
40 g/1½ oz/3 tbsp butter or margarine
45 ml/3 tbsp redcurrant jelly (clear conserve)
Gravy (page 334)
15 ml/1 tbsp brandy
Royal Roast Potatoes (page 348), cauliflower and carrots, to serve

Wipe the turkey inside and out with kitchen paper (paper towels). Mix the rice with the bacon, corn, herbs, salt and pepper to taste and the nutmeg. Mix with the egg to bind. Stuff the neck end of the bird and secure the skin underneath with a skewer. Tuck the wing tips under and place upside-down in a lightly greased roasting tin (pan). Spread with half the remaining butter or margarine, then cover with foil, crimping it under the edges of the roasting tin. Roast for 1½ hours at 180°C/350°F/gas mark 4. Turn over, spread with the remaining butter or margarine, re-cover and roast for a further 1 hour. Remove the foil and drain off any cooking juices into a saucepan. Melt 30 ml/2 tbsp of the redcurrant jelly, brush over the breast and return to the oven for 15 minutes to glaze. Insert a skewer into the thickest part of the thigh. If the juices run clear, the turkey is cooked. If not, re-cover the breast and return to the oven for a further 10–15 minutes. Make gravy in your normal way or make Giblet Gravy (page 334) and add the remaining redcurrant jelly and the brandy. Serve with Royal Roast Potatoes, cauliflower and carrots.

Traditional Roast Turkey

You will see that the stuffing recipes tell you to double the quantities when stuffing a turkey, but for this recipe, use just one quantity as you are also stuffing the neck with sausagemeat.

SERVES 10–12

4.5 kg/10 lb oven-ready turkey
Sage and Onion or Parsley and Thyme Stuffing (page 353)
225 g/8 oz sausagemeat
Sunflower oil
Salt
Bacon-wrapped Chipolatas (page 354), Royal Roast Potatoes (page 348), Bread Sauce (page 339), Cranberry Sauce (page 339), Gravy (page 334), Brussels Sprouts with Chestnuts (page 350) and carrots

Remove the giblets from the bird, if necessary. Wipe the turkey inside and out with kitchen paper (paper towels). Make up the chosen stuffing. Use to fill half the neck end, and stuff the other half with sausagemeat, so they sit side by side. Secure the neck skin with a skewer. Truss in your usual way (or see page 16). Rub the breast with oil. Place upside-down in a roasting tin (pan) and rub oil over the base of the bird. Season with a little salt. Cover with foil and roast in a preheated oven at 190°C/375°F/gas mark 5 for 1½ hours. Turn the bird over and sprinkle with salt. Roast uncovered for a further 1½ hours until golden brown and the juices run clear when the thickest part of the thigh is pierced with a skewer. Transfer to a carving dish. Leave to rest for 10 minutes while making the gravy. Carve the bird and serve with Bacon-wrapped Chipolatas, Royal Roast Potatoes, Bread Sauce, Cranberry Sauce, Brussels Sprouts with Chestnuts and carrots and the gravy.

Roast Paprika Turkey

SERVES 10–12

4.5 kg/10 lb oven-ready turkey
2 quantities of Caraway Sausage Stuffing (page 354)
50 g/2 oz/¼ cup butter or margarine, softened
Salt
15 ml/1 tbsp paprika
Royal Roast Potatoes (page 348), carrots, broccoli and Gravy (page 334), to serve

Remove the giblets from the bird, if necessary. Wipe the turkey inside and out with kitchen paper (paper towels). Make up the stuffing and use to stuff the neck end of the bird. Secure the skin with a skewer. Truss if necessary. Smear with the butter or margarine and sprinkle with salt. Place upside-down in a roasting tin (pan). Roast in a preheated oven at 190°C/375°F/gas mark 5 for 2½ hours, turning over half-way through cooking. Remove the bird from the oven and sprinkle with the paprika, then return to the oven for 30 minutes. When cooked, transfer to a carving dish and allow to rest in a warm place for 15 minutes while making the gravy. Carve the turkey and serve with Royal Roast Potatoes, carrots, broccoli and the gravy.

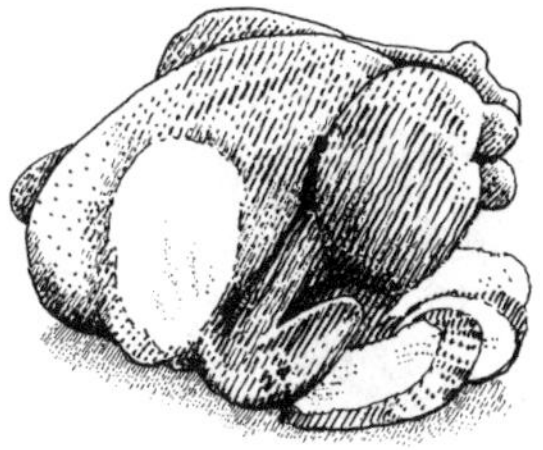

Californian-style Honey Roast Turkey

SERVES 12

4.5 kg/10 lb oven-ready turkey
2 quantities of Prune and Pecan Stuffing (page 354)
50 g/2 oz/¼ cup butter or margarine, softened
Salt
45 ml/3 tbsp clear honey
Gravy (page 334), Royal Roast Potatoes (page 348), carrots cooked in orange juice instead of water, and peas.

Remove the giblets from the bird, if necessary. Wipe the turkey inside and out with kitchen paper (paper towels). Make up the stuffing and use to stuff the neck end of the bird. Secure the skin with a skewer. Truss the bird, if necessary. Smear with the butter or margarine and season with a little salt. Place upside-down in a roasting tin (pan). Cover with foil and roast in a preheated oven at 190°C/375°F/gas mark 5 for 3 hours, turning the bird over half-way through cooking. Remove the foil and brush the bird with the honey. Cook, uncovered, for a further 15 minutes. To test if the bird is cooked, skewer the thickest part of the thigh and the juices should run clear. Leave to stand for 10 minutes while making the gravy. Transfer the bird to a carving dish. Carve the bird and serve with Royal Roast Potatoes, orange-flavoured carrots, peas and the gravy.

Thanksgiving Turkey

SERVES 12

4.5 kg/10 lb oven-ready turkey
1 onion, finely chopped
50 g/2 oz/¼ cup butter or margarine
350 g/12 oz/1 medium can of sweetcorn (corn), drained
200 g/7 oz/1 small can of pimientos, drained and chopped
Finely grated rind of 1 lemon
2.5 ml/½ tsp dried oregano
30 ml/2 tbsp chopped parsley
75 g/3 oz/1½ cups bran flakes, crushed
1 egg, beaten
Salt and freshly ground black pepper
100 g/4 oz streaky bacon rashers (slices)
Gravy (page 334)
30 ml/2 tbsp medium-dry sherry
30 ml/2 tbsp single (light) cream
Speciality Creamed Potatoes (page 348), mashed turnips, baby (pearl) onions and peas in white sauce, to serve

Remove the giblets from the bird, if necessary. Wipe the turkey inside and out with kitchen paper (paper towels). Fry (sauté) the onion in the butter or margarine for 2 minute, stirring. Add the corn, pimientos, lemon rind, oregano, parsley and bran flakes and mix well. Bind with the egg and season with salt and pepper. Use to stuff the neck end of the turkey. Secure the skin with a skewer. Place on a rack in a roasting tin (pan) and cover with the bacon rashers. Roast in a preheated oven at 190°C/375°F/gas mark 5 for 3 hours or until the juices run clear when a skewer is inserted in the thickest part of the thigh. Leave to stand for 10 minutes, then transfer to a carving dish. Make the gravy and stir in the sherry and cream. Serve the turkey with Speciality Creamed Potatoes, mashed turnips, baby onions with peas in white sauce and the gravy.

Sixteenth-century Roast Turkey

SERVES 12

4.5 kg/10 lb oven-ready turkey, with giblets
100 g/4 oz/2 cups white breadcrumbs
75 ml/5 tbsp milk
4 oysters (fresh, shelled or canned in brine), quartered
1 thin slice of smoked, cooked ham, finely chopped
1 small onion, very finely chopped
1 turkey liver, from the giblets, chopped
15 ml/1 tbsp chopped parsley
6 canned chestnuts, finely chopped
Salt and freshly ground black pepper
50 g/2 oz/¼ cup unsalted (sweet) butter, melted
150 ml/¼ pt/⅔ cup white wine
150 ml/¼ pt/⅔ cup chicken or turkey stock
Giblet Gravy (page 334)
30 ml/2 tbsp redcurrant jelly (clear conserve)
Bacon-wrapped Chipolatas (page 354), Bread Sauce (page 339), Royal Roast Potatoes (page 348) and a green vegetable, to serve

Remove the giblets and wipe the bird inside and out with kitchen paper (paper towels). Mix the breadcrumbs with the milk and leave to soak for 5 minutes. Stir in the oysters, ham, onion, turkey liver, parsley, chestnuts and a little salt and pepper. Use to stuff the neck end of the bird. Secure the skin with a skewer. Truss the bird if necessary. Brush all over with the melted butter. Place upside-down in a roasting tin (pan). Cover loosely with greaseproof (waxed) paper and roast in a preheated oven at 200°C/400°F/gas mark 6 for 1 hour. Turn the bird over. Reduce the oven temperature to 180°C/350°F/gas mark 4. Re-cover and return to the oven. Add the wine and stock and baste well. Cook for a further 1½ hours, basting every 30 minutes. Remove the greaseproof paper, sprinkle the breast with salt and pepper and cook, uncovered, for a further 30 minutes or until the juices run clear when a skewer is inserted in the thickest part of the thigh. Transfer to a carving dish and leave to rest. Make the Giblet Gravy, adding the juices from the roasting tin (pan) and stir in the redcurrant jelly. Carve and serve with Bacon-wrapped Chipolatas, Bread Sauce, Royal Roast Potatoes and a green vegetable.

Quick Turkey Loaf

SERVES 6

1 large onion, finely chopped
450 g/1 lb minced (ground) turkey
50 g/2 oz/1 cup wholemeal breadcrumbs
Salt and freshly ground black pepper
1 egg
360 ml/12½ fl oz/1 can of mixed vegetable juice
15 g/½ oz/1 tbsp butter or margarine
15 g/½ oz/2 tbsp plain (all-purpose) flour
A few drops of Worcestershire sauce
Cucumber twists, to garnish
Jacket-baked potatoes and peas, to serve

Mix the onion with the turkey, breadcrumbs and a little salt and pepper. Beat the egg with 60 ml/4 tbsp of the juice and stir into the mixture. Turn into a lightly greased 900 g/2 lb loaf tin (pan). Press down well. Bake in a preheated oven at 190°C/375°F/gas mark 5 for 1½ hours until firm to the touch. Meanwhile, melt the butter or margarine in a small saucepan. Blend in the flour and cook for 1 minute. Remove from the heat and blend in the remaining vegetable juice. Return to the heat, bring to the boil and cook for 2 minutes, stirring, until thickened and smooth. Season with Worcestershire sauce to taste. When the loaf is cooked, leave to cool in the tin for 5 minutes, then turn out on to a warm serving platter. Spoon a little sauce over and garnish with cucumber twists. Serve hot, cut into slices, with the remaining sauce, jacket-baked potatoes and peas.

Tempting Turkey Loaf

SERVES 4–6

Prepare as for Chunky Chicken Loaf (page 164), but use turkey livers and minced (ground) turkey instead of chicken. Add a crushed garlic clove and a small handful of chopped parsley to the mixture.

Turkey and Potato Pie

SERVES 4

Prepare as for Chicken Shack Pie (page 159), but substitute minced (ground) turkey for the chicken, a thinly sliced leek for the onion and ½ small swede (rutabaga), grated, for the turnip.

Light Turkey Pudding

SERVES 4

Butter or margarine, for greasing
4 slices of white bread, crusts removed
100 g/4 oz/1 cup cooked turkey, chopped, all skin removed
1 onion, grated
1.5 ml/¼ tsp dried sage
Salt and freshly ground black pepper
2 eggs
450 ml/¾ pt/2 cups milk
50 g/2 oz/½ cup Cheddar cheese, grated
Tomato chutney and a mixed salad, to serve

Grease a 1.5 litre/2½ pt/6 cup ovenproof dish. Break the bread into pieces and place in the dish. Add the turkey, onion, sage and some salt and pepper. Beat together the eggs and milk and pour into the dish. Stir, then leave to stand for 15 minutes. Break up with a fork, sprinkle with the cheese and bake in a preheated oven at 190°C/375°F/gas mark 5 for about 50 minutes until risen, golden and set. Serve hot with tomato chutney and a mixed salad.

Spicy Turkey Drummers

SERVES 4

75 g/3 oz/⅓ cup butter or margarine, softened
10 ml/2 tsp made English mustard
15 ml/1 tbsp tomato purée (paste)
2.5 ml/½ tsp cayenne
10 ml/2 tsp Worcestershire sauce
5 ml/1 tsp soy sauce
7.5 ml/1½ tsp light brown sugar
4 turkey drumsticks
90 ml/6 tbsp plain (all-purpose) flour
Minted Yoghurt and Cucumber (page 339) and Wild Rice Mix (page 352), to serve

Put the butter or margarine in a bowl and beat in the mustard, tomato purée, cayenne, Worcestershire and soy sauces and the sugar. Dust the drumsticks with the flour, spread with the butter or margarine mixture and place in a roasting tin (pan). Bake in a preheated oven at 180°C/350°F/gas mark 4 for 1 hour, turning once and basting with the melted mixture. Transfer the cooked drumsticks to foil on a grill (broiler) rack. Spoon the melted mixture from the roasting tin over. Grill (broil) for 10 minutes, turning once. Serve hot with Minted Yoghurt and Cucumber and Wild Rice Mix.

Kentucky Baked Turkey

SERVES 4

4 turkey steaks
5 ml/1 tsp coarse-ground black pepper
5 ml/1 tsp paprika
5 ml/1 tsp onion powder
1.5 ml/¼ tsp chilli powder
45 ml/3 tbsp sunflower or olive oil
4 small bananas
Jacket potatoes topped with plain yoghurt and a sprinkling of snipped chives and mixed peas and sweetcorn (corn), to serve

Place the turkey steaks one at a time in a plastic bag and beat briefly to flatten slightly and tenderise. Mix together the pepper, paprika and onion and chilli powders. Brush the turkey with a little of the oil. Dust with the pepper mixture on each side. Pour half the remaining oil in a roasting tin (pan) and heat in the oven at 200°C/400°F/gas mark 6 until sizzling. Remove from the oven and lay the turkey in it. Place in the oven on a shelf near the top. Peel and halve the bananas lengthways. Place in a small roasting tin with the remaining oil. Place on the shelf just under the turkey. Bake for about 20 minutes or until the turkey is tender and cooked through and the bananas have softened slightly. Serve the turkey and bananas with jacket potatoes topped with yoghurt and chives and peas and sweetcorn.

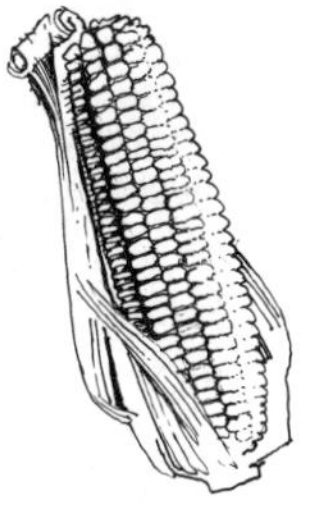

DUCK

Traditional Roast Duck

SERVES 2

2 kg/4½ lb oven-ready duck
1 small onion
A few sage leaves or 2.5 ml/½ tsp dried sage
Salt and freshly ground black pepper
Sage and Onion Stuffing (page 353)
Apple Sauce (page 340)
60 ml/4 tbsp plain (all-purpose) flour
600 ml/1 pt/2½ cups vegetable water or chicken stock, made with 1 stock cube
A little gravy block or browning
Royal Roast Potatoes (page 348), peas and carrots

Wipe the duck inside and out with kitchen paper (paper towels). Prick all over with a fork. Put the onion and sage leaves or dried sage in the body cavity. Place on a rack or small upturned plate in a roasting tin (pan). Sprinkle with salt. Roast in a preheated oven at 220°C/425°F/gas mark 7 for 1 hour, then turn down the heat to 180°C/350°F/gas mark 4 and cook for a further 30 minutes or until the duck is really tender. Meanwhile make the Stuffing and Apple Sauce.

Transfer the duck to a carving dish. Remove the trivet. Pour off all but 15 ml/1 tbsp of the fat but leave all the juices in the pan. Blend in the flour and cook over a moderate heat, stirring, for 2 minutes. Remove from the heat and gradually blend in the vegetable water or stock. Return to the heat, bring to the boil and cook for 2 minutes, stirring. Add gravy block or browning and season, to taste. Carve the duck and serve with the gravy, Royal Roast Potatoes, peas and carrots and the Stuffing and Apple Sauce.

Crusty Duck with Apricots

SERVES 4

2 kg/4½ lb oven-ready duck, with giblets
750 ml/1¼ pts/3 cups water
1 onion, quartered
1 carrot, sliced
15 ml/1 tbsp chopped sage
1 chicken stock cube
1 lemon, quartered
45 ml/3 tbsp plain (all-purpose) flour
Salt and freshly ground black pepper
15 ml/1 tbsp lemon marmalade
410 g/14½ oz/1 large can of apricot halves in natural juice, drained, reserving the juice
Watercress, to garnish
New potatoes, peas and broccoli, to serve

Remove the giblets from the duck and wipe inside and out with kitchen paper (paper towels). Chop the liver and reserve. Put the remaining giblets in a saucepan with the water, onion, carrot, sage and the stock cube. Bring to the boil, reduce the heat, part-cover and simmer for 1 hour.

Meanwhile, prick the duck all over with a fork. Place on a rack in a roasting tin (pan). Put the lemon inside the bird. Sprinkle the duck with 15 ml/1 tbsp of the flour and season with salt and pepper. Roast for 30 minutes at 200°C/400°F/gas mark 6, then reduce the heat to 180°C/350°F/ gas mark 4 and continue roasting for 1 hour until golden and tender.

Strain the stock into a measuring jug and reserve. Transfer the duck to a warm carving dish. Remove the rack from the tin. Pour off all but 15 ml/1 tbsp of the fat but reserve the juices. Add the liver and the remaining flour to the tin and cook over a moderate heat for 1 minute, stirring. Gradually blend in 450 ml/¾ pt/2 cups of the reserved stock and 150 ml/¼ pt/⅔ cup of the apricot juice. Add the marmalade. Bring to the boil and cook for 3 minutes, stirring. Season to taste and add the apricots. Heat through. Quarter the duck and place on warm serving plates. Arrange a few apricots to the side of each plate. Spoon a little of the gravy over and serve with new potatoes, peas, broccoli and the remaining gravy in a sauce boat.

Roast Duck with Cherries

SERVES 2

2 kg/4½ lb oven-ready duck
1 small onion
A sprig of mint or 2.5 ml/½ tsp dried mint
Salt
For the cherry sauce:
425 g/15 oz/1 large can of stoned (pitted) cherries
30 ml/2 tbsp cornflour (cornstarch)
30 ml/2 tbsp brandy
5 ml/1 tsp chopped fresh mint or 1.5 ml/¼ tsp dried mint
Royal Roast Potatoes (page 348), peas and carrots

Wipe the duck inside and out with kitchen paper (paper towels). Prick all over with a fork. Put the onion and sprig of mint or dried mint in the body cavity. Place on a rack or small upturned plate in a roasting tin (pan). Sprinkle with salt. Roast in a preheated oven at 220°C/425°F/gas mark 7 for 1 hour, then turn down the heat to 180°C/350°F/gas mark 4 and cook for a further 30 minutes or until the duck is really tender.

To make the cherry sauce, empty the contents of the can of cherries into a saucepan. Blend the cornflour with the brandy and stir into the cherries with the mint. Bring to the boil and cook for 1 minute, stirring, until thickened. Keep warm. Transfer the duck to a carving dish. Pour off all but 15 ml/1 tbsp of the fat and stir the pan juices into the cherry sauce. Carve the duck and serve with Royal Roast Potatoes, peas and carrots and the cherry sauce.

Honey Roast Duck

SERVES 4

2 kg/4½ lb oven-ready duck
1 small orange, halved
1 small onion, peeled and halved
Salt and freshly ground black pepper
225 g/8 oz/⅔ cup clear honey
25 g/1 oz/¼ cup cornflour (cornstarch)
300 ml/½ pt/1¼ cups pure orange juice
Finely grated rind and juice of 1 lemon
30 ml/2 tbsp snipped chives, to garnish
New potatoes in their skins and peas, to serve

Wipe the duck inside and out with kitchen paper (paper towels). Prick the skin all over with a fork. Push the orange and onion halves inside the body cavity. Place on a rack or small upturned plate in a roasting tin (pan) and season well. Pour over the honey to coat completely. Roast in a preheated oven at 220°C/425°F/gas mark 7 for 1 hour, basting occasionally. Turn down the oven to 180°C/350°F/gas mark 4 and continue cooking for 30 minutes.

Meanwhile, blend the cornflour with a little of the orange juice in a saucepan. Stir in the lemon rind and juice and a little salt and pepper. Bring to the boil and cook for 1 minute until thick and clear. When the duck is cooked, transfer to a carving dish and keep warm. Pour off all the fat from the roasting tin, then strain the juices into the orange and lemon sauce. Stir well. Cut the duck into quarters and transfer to warm serving plates. Spoon a little of the sauce over to glaze and sprinkle with the chives. Serve with new potatoes, peas and the remaining sauce.

Peking Duck

SERVES 4

900 ml/1½ pts/3¾ cups chicken stock
1 lemon, thinly sliced
45 ml/3 tbsp soy sauce
45 ml/3 tbsp clear honey
45 ml/3 tbsp dry sherry
1 small garlic clove, crushed
1.75 kg/4 lb oven-ready duck
12 spring onions (scallions)
12 Chinese pancakes or small flour tortillas
Hoisin sauce

Mix together the stock, lemon slices, soy sauce, honey, sherry and garlic in a saucepan. Bring to the boil and simmer for 30 minutes. Remove the giblets from the duck, if necessary. Wash the duck, dry inside and out with kitchen paper (paper towels) and prick all over with a fork. Place the duck upside-down on a rack in a roasting tin (pan). Spoon over some of the sauce, coating the underside. Turn over and coat the top with the remaining sauce. Leave to stand for 4 hours to dry out. Place in a preheated oven at 230°C/450°F/gas mark 8 for 20 minutes. Reduce the heat to 180°C/350°F/gas mark 4 and continue cooking for 2 hours or until the duck is really tender and the skin is crisp.

Meanwhile, trim the spring onions to about 7.5 cm/3 in from the white end, discarding the roots and the tough green ends. Make a series of cuts through the white bulb to a depth of about 2.5 cm/1 in. Place the onions in a bowl of cold water and chill so the white ends open out to form 'brushes'. Warm the pancakes or tortillas. Transfer the duck to a carving dish. Leave to stand for 10 minutes, then remove the skin and cut into strips. Remove the meat from the bones and using two forks pull apart into shreds. Pile the duck on to four plates with a small bowl of hoisin sauce on each. Lay the onion 'brushes' to one side. To eat, use an onion brush to dip in the sauce and spread some over a pancake. Lay the onion on top, add some duck and skin, roll up and eat with the fingers.

Chinese Tea-smoked Roast Duck

There are numerous recipes for this, some very complicated. Here is a simple, but nevertheless delicious, version.

SERVES 4

1.75 kg/4 lb oven-ready duck
1 orange
5 ml/1 tsp grated fresh root ginger
5 ml/1 tsp salt
15 ml/1 tbsp green peppercorns, crushed
30 ml/2 tbsp dry sherry
50 g/2 oz/¼ cup long-grain rice
50 g/2 oz/¼ cup Chinese green tea leaves
50 g/2 oz/¼ cup light brown sugar
12 ready-made Chinese pancakes
Hoisin sauce
1 bunch of spring onions (scallions), thinly shredded

Remove any giblets from the duck and use for stock for another recipe. Pull out any excess fat from just inside the body cavity and discard. Coarsely grate the rind from the orange and reserve. Halve the orange and place inside the duck with the ginger. Prick the duck all over with a fork. Mix together the salt, peppercorns and sherry and rub over the skin. Line a wok with a double thickness of foil. Mix the rice with the tea, sugar and orange rind and place in the wok. Lay a steaming rack over the tea mixture to come about 2.5 cm/1 in above the mixture. Put the duck on the rack and cover the wok with the lid. Put over a high heat until the mixture is smoking, then reduce the heat to moderate and continue to smoke the duck for 15 minutes. Turn off the heat (or remove if on an electric hob). Leave to stand without removing the lid for a further 15 minutes.

Transfer the duck, breast-side down, to a roasting tin (pan). Wrap the smoking mixture up in the foil and discard. Roast the duck in a preheated oven at 180°C/350°F/gas mark 4 for 1½ hours. Pour off the fat. Turn the bird over and roast for a further 1 hour. Pour off any more fat, then turn up the heat to 230°C/450°F/gas mark 8 and roast for a further 10 minutes until the skin is really crisp.

Meanwhile, warm the Chinese pancakes. Put some hoisin sauce in one bowl and the spring onions in another. When the duck is cooked, remove the crisp skin and cut into shreds. Pull all the meat from the bones and gently pull apart with two forks to shred. Pile the duck and skin separately on a warm plate and garnish with a little of the spring onion. To eat, spread the pancakes with a little hoisin sauce, top with duck and a little spring onion, roll up and eat with the fingers.

Sumptuous Duck and Apple Parcels

SERVES 4

Prepare as for Fragrant Chicken Parcels (page 149), but substitute duck breasts for the chicken, sprigs of sage for the rosemary, and add 2 eating (dessert) apples, skinned, cored and chopped, to the parcels.

Oriental Soy Duck with Apples

SERVES 4

1.75 kg/4 lb oven-ready duck
2 large cooking (tart) apples
3 onions, chopped
Salt and freshly ground black pepper
Soy sauce
15 g/½ oz/1 tbsp butter or margarine
30 ml/2tbsp apple juice
10 ml/2 tsp arrowroot
Plain Boiled Rice (page 351) and a beansprout and red (bell) pepper salad

Wipe the duck inside and out with kitchen paper (paper towels). Prick all over with a fork. Peel one of the apples and push inside the duck. Spread out one of the chopped onions in a roasting tin (pan) and place a rack on top. Put the duck on the rack and rub all over with salt, pepper and soy sauce. Roast in a preheated oven at 200°C/400°F/gas mark 6 for 20 minutes. Reduce the heat to 160°C/325°F/gas mark 3 and continue roasting for a further 1½ hours or until the duck is really tender. Peel and chop the remaining apple. Melt the butter or margarine in a saucepan. Add the remaining onion and apple and cook, stirring, for 4 minutes until golden. Add the apple juice and simmer for 5 minutes until pulpy. Lift the duck out on to a warm carving dish. Spoon off as much fat as possible from the roasting tin leaving the onion and juices. Blend the arrowroot with 15 ml/1 tbsp soy sauce and stir into the juices in the roasting tin. Add the apple and onion mixture and stir until thickened, adding a little more apple juice, if necessary, to form a thick but pourable sauce. Carve the duck, place on warm plates and spoon the sauce to one side. Serve with Plain Boiled Rice and a beansprout and red pepper salad.

GOOSE

Roast Goose in Cider

SERVES 8–10

4.5 kg/10 lb oven-ready goose, with giblets
600 ml/1 pt/2½ cups water
1 chicken stock cube
1 large onion, peeled but left whole
A sprig of sage
Salt and freshly ground black pepper
600 ml/1 pt/2½ cups cider
Butter or margarine, for greasing
25 g/1 oz/¼ cup plain (all-purpose) flour
A little gravy block or browning
Speciality Creamed Potatoes (page 348), buttered sprouts and Gooseberry Sauce (page 340), to serve

Remove the giblets and place in a saucepan with the water and the stock cube. Bring to the boil, reduce the heat, cover and simmer gently for 1 hour. Strain. Meanwhile, wipe the goose inside and out with kitchen paper (paper towels). Push the onion and sage inside the bird. Prick the skin all over with a fork and rub with salt. Place on a rack in a roasting tin (pan). Pour over all but 30 ml/2 tbsp of the cider. Cover loosely with lightly greased foil. Roast in a preheated oven at 190°C/375°F/gas mark 5 for 4 hours, basting every 30 minutes. Remove the foil after 2½ hours. When cooked, transfer the goose to a warm carving dish. Pour off as much fat as possible from the roasting tin. Blend the flour with a little of the giblet stock and stir into the roasting tin. Blend in the remaining stock and cider. Bring to the boil and cook for 2 minutes, stirring. Stir in a little gravy block or browning and season to taste. Carve the goose and serve with the gravy, Speciality Creamed Potatoes, buttered sprouts and Gooseberry Sauce.

Roast Goose with Sage, Apple and Calvados Stuffing

SERVES 8–10

4.5 kg/10 lb oven-ready goose, with giblets
900 ml/1½ pts/3¾ cups water
1 chicken stock cube
4 eating (dessert) apples, finely chopped
120 ml/4 fl oz/½ cup calvados
4 sage leaves, finely chopped
A good pinch of grated nutmeg
225 g/8 oz/4 cups fresh breadcrumbs
1 egg, beaten
Salt and freshly ground black pepper
25 g/1 oz/2 tbsp butter or margarine
Jerusalem Artichoke Purée (page 350) and broccoli, to serve

Remove the giblets from the bird and boil in a saucepan with the water and stock cube for 1 hour, then strain. Meanwhile, wipe the goose inside and out with kitchen paper (paper towels) and prick all over with a fork.

Mix the apples with 60 ml/4 tbsp of the calvados, the sage, nutmeg and breadcrumbs. Stir in the egg to bind, and season with salt and pepper. Pack some of the stuffing into the neck end of the goose. Secure with a skewer and place the bird on a rack in a roasting tin (pan). Rub the skin well with salt. Cover the breast with foil greased with a little of the butter or margarine. Put the remaining stuffing in a shallow, ovenproof dish, greased with a little of remaining butter or margarine. Dot with the remaining butter or margarine. Place the goose in a preheated oven at 180°C/350°F/gas mark 4 for 1 hour. Spoon off any fat in the roasting tin and pour the warmed stock over the bird. Baste the goose every 30 minutes after this. Continue to cook for a further 1½ hours. Remove the foil and add the dish of stuffing to the oven.

Continue to cook for a further 1 hour until the goose is tender with brown, crispy skin and the stuffing is well browned and cooked through. Transfer the goose to a warm carving dish. Spoon off as much fat as possible from the liquid left in the roasting tin and boil the liquid rapidly until slightly thickened. Taste and re-season, if necessary. Warm the remaining calvados in a small saucepan. Ignite and pour over the goose and leave until the flames subside. Carve and serve with the stuffing, gravy, Jerusalem Artichoke Purée and broccoli.

GAME

Fragrant Pheasant Hot-pot

SERVES 4

1 oven-ready pheasant, jointed (page 15)
15 ml/1 tbsp sunflower oil
2 large onions, sliced
2 large carrots, sliced
40 g/1½ oz/generous ⅓ cup pearl barley
1.5 ml/¼ tsp dried rosemary
2.5 ml/½ tsp dried sage
30 ml/2 tbsp chopped parsley
Salt and freshly ground black pepper
300 ml/½ pt/1¼ cups chicken stock
15 ml/1 tbsp redcurrant jelly (clear conserve)
1 kg/2¼ lb potatoes, sliced
15 g/½ oz/1 tbsp butter or margarine
A green vegetable, to serve

Brown the pheasant in the oil in a large frying pan (skillet). Transfer to a large ovenproof dish. Fry (sauté) the onions and carrots in the frying pan for 3 minutes until softened and lightly golden. Add to the pheasant. Add the barley, herbs and some salt and pepper. Stir the stock and redcurrant jelly together and pour over. Arrange the potatoes overlapping all over the top. Sprinkle with the little more salt and pepper and dot with the butter or margarine. Cover with foil and bake in a preheated oven at 160°C/325°F/gas mark 3 for 2½ hours, removing the foil for the last 40 minutes to brown the top. Serve hot with a green vegetable.

Victorian Roast Pheasant

It is traditional to garnish pheasant with a few of the beautiful tail feathers, pushed slightly into the body cavity. If you buy your bird from a butcher, you can ask for some feathers to use for this purpose. Wash the quills before using.

SERVES 4

1 oven-ready pheasant
1 small onion
1 clove
A 50 g/2 oz piece of braising steak
50 g/2 oz/¼ cup butter or margarine, softened
4 streaky bacon rashers (slices)
30 ml/2 tbsp plain (all-purpose) flour
A bunch of watercress, to garnish
Buttered Crumbs (page 352), Game Chips (page 348), Gravy (page 334), redcurrant jelly (clear conserve) and Jerusalem Artichoke Purée (page 350), to serve

Wipe the bird inside and out with kitchen paper (paper towels). Season inside and out. Stud the onion with the clove and place inside the bird with the piece of steak (the steak will keep the bird really moist and give it a great flavour). Truss if necessary. Place the bird in a roasting tin (pan) and smear the butter or margarine all over the breast. Lay the bacon rashers on top. Roast in a preheated oven at 200°C/400°F/gas mark 6 for 30 minutes. Remove the bacon and baste the breast with the juices and butter or margarine in the tin. Sprinkle the breast all over with the flour and baste with more butter or margarine. Return to the oven for a further 20–30 minutes until the breast is frothy and golden brown. Transfer to a serving dish and garnish with the watercress. Carve and serve with Buttered Crumbs, Game Chips, Gravy, redcurrant jelly and Jerusalem Artichoke Purée.

Pot Roast Pheasant with Parma Ham

SERVES 4

1 large oven-ready pheasant
4 wafer-thin slices of Parma or other raw cured ham
40 g/1½ oz/3 tbsp unsalted (sweet) butter, softened
15ml/1 tbsp olive oil
12 button (pearl) onions, peeled but left whole
16 baby carrots, scrubbed but left whole
30 ml/2 tbsp brandy
Salt and freshly ground black pepper
150 ml/¼ pt/⅔ cup chicken stock
Buttered tagliatelle and a green salad, to serve

Wipe the pheasant inside and out with kitchen paper (paper towels). Wrap completely in the Parma ham and tie securely. Melt half the butter and the oil in a flameproof casserole (Dutch oven). Add the pheasant and brown quickly on all sides. Remove from the pan. Add the onions and carrots and toss for 2 minutes, then push to one side of the pan. Return the pheasant to the pan. Warm the brandy in a soup ladle, ignite and pour over the bird. Shake the pan until the flames subside. Season with salt and pepper. Spread the bird with the remaining butter. Cover the casserole tightly with foil, then press a lid firmly on top to seal in all the steam. Roast in a preheated oven at 180°C/350°F/gas mark 4 for 1½ hours. Do not uncover during cooking. Remove from the oven, take off the lid and foil and transfer the bird, onions and carrots to a warm carving dish. Add the stock to the pan juices. Bring to the boil and boil for 1 minute. Taste and re-season, if necessary. Remove the ham from the bird and cut into pieces. Cut the bird into quarters (page 17). Transfer to warm plates with the onions and carrots. Spoon the sauce over, sprinkle with the Parma ham and serve with buttered tagliatelle.

Old Traditional Roast Partridge

SERVES 4

Prepare as for Victorian Roast Pheasant (page 177), but place 25 g/1 oz/2 tbsp butter or margarine inside each of four birds and a large sprig of thyme instead of the steak, onion and clove. Roast for 35 minutes. Serve with Bread Sauce (page 339), instead of Buttered Crumbs, but the same other accompaniments.

French-roast Partridge

SERVES 4

4 small oven-ready partridges
25 g/1 oz/2 tbsp unsalted (sweet) butter
4 orange slices
4 thyme sprigs
4–8 smoked streaky bacon slices (rashers)
4 slices of bread
Olive oil
30 ml/2 tbsp cornflour (cornstarch)
30 ml/2 tbsp orange liqueur
300 ml/½ pt/1¼ cups chicken stock
Salt and freshly ground black pepper
Watercress and orange slices, to garnish
New potatoes and a crisp green salad, to serve

Wipe the partridges inside and out with kitchen paper (paper towels). Place a quarter of the butter inside each bird with an orange slice and a sprig of thyme. Place in a roasting tin (pan) and lay the bacon rashers over each bird to cover the breasts completely. Roast in a preheated oven at 220°C/425°F/gas mark 7 for about 35 minutes or until tender. Meanwhile, cut the largest round possible out of each slice of bread. Fry (sauté) in olive oil until golden on both sides. Drain on kitchen paper. Remove the partridge from the roasting tin and keep warm. Spoon off the excess fat from the roasting tin, leaving the juices. Blend the cornflour with the orange liqueur and add to the juices with the stock. Bring to the boil and cook for 1 minute, stirring, until slightly thickened. Season to taste. Remove the orange slices and thyme from the partridges. Place a fried bread round on each of four warm serving plates. Top each with a partridge. Spoon a little of the sauce over. Garnish with watercress and orange slices and serve with the remaining sauce, new potatoes and a crisp green salad.

Roast Grouse with Onion Buttered Crumbs

SERVES 2

1 oven-ready grouse
40 g/1½ oz/3 tbsp butter or margarine
A thick slice of lemon
6 peppercorns
Salt and freshly ground black pepper
2 or 3 unsmoked streaky bacon rashers (slices)
2 slices of white bread, crumbed
5 ml/1 tsp onion powder
150 ml/¼ pt/⅔ cup chicken stock
Baby potatoes, mangetout (snow peas) and Cranberry Sauce (page 339 or use bought), to serve

Wipe the bird inside and out with kitchen paper (paper towels). Truss, if necessary. Put 25 g/1 oz/2 tbsp of the butter or margarine in the body cavity with the lemon slice and peppercorns. Place on a rack or an upturned saucer in a roasting tin (pan). Sprinkle the breast with salt, then lay the bacon rashers over. Roast in a preheated oven at 220°C/425°F/gas mark 7 for 35 minutes. Meanwhile, melt the remaining butter in a frying pan (skillet). Add the breadcrumbs and toss over a moderate heat until crisp and golden brown. Sprinkle the onion powder over and toss well. Remove from the heat and keep warm. Transfer the bird to a carving dish, draining off any juices back into the roasting tin (pan). Add the stock to the buttery juices. Bring to the boil, stirring, and boil rapidly until reduced. Taste and re-season if necessary. Cut the grouse in half and place on warm plates. Spoon the sauce over and put a pile of buttered crumbs to one side. Serve with baby potatoes, mangetout and Cranberry Sauce.

Roast Woodcock Rossini

SERVES 4

4 oven-ready woodcock
50 g/2 oz/¼ cup unsalted (sweet) butter
4 smoked streaky bacon rashers (slices)
Salt and freshly ground black pepper
4 slices of bread
100 g/4 oz smooth liver pâté
15 ml/1 tbsp cornflour (cornstarch)
Finely grated rind and juice of ½ small lemon
300 ml/½ pt/1¼ cups chicken stock
Game Chips (page 348) and broccoli, to serve

Truss the woodcock, if necessary. Using about half the butter, put a good knob in the body cavity of each. Place in a roasting tin (pan) and smear with the remaining butter. Halve the bacon rashers and put two halves over each woodcock breast. Sprinkle with a little salt and lots of pepper. Roast in a preheated oven at 220°C/425°F/gas mark 7 for about 35 minutes or until cooked through. Remove from the roasting tin and keep warm.

Meanwhile, cut the crusts off the bread, toast on each side and spread with the pâté. Spoon off all but 15 ml/1 tbsp of the fat from the roasting tin. Blend the cornflour with the lemon rind and juice and stir into the tin with the stock. Bring to the boil and cook for 1 minute, stirring. Season to taste. Transfer the toast to warm serving plates. Top each with a woodcock. Spoon a little of the gravy over and serve with Game Chips, broccoli and the remaining gravy handed separately.

Old English Roast Grouse

SERVES 4

Prepare as for Victorian Roast Pheasant (page 177), but use 2 oven ready grouse instead of the pheasant. Omit the steak and place 25 g/1 oz/2 tbsp butter or margarine inside each bird with a small onion and a clove. Roast for 45 minutes. Serve with Cranberry Sauce (page 339) instead of redcurrant jelly (clear conserve).

Honey and Mustard Glazed Guinea Fowl with Roasted Roots

SERVES 4

2 oven-ready guinea fowl
30 ml/2 tbsp clear honey
15 ml/1 tbsp wholegrain mustard
30 ml/2 tbsp pure orange juice
30 ml/2 tbsp chopped parsley
5 ml/1 tsp dried thyme
Salt and freshly ground black pepper
2 large parsnips
2 large carrots
2 beetroot (red beets)
2 turnips
60 ml/4 tbsp sunflower oil
5 ml/1 tsp cumin seeds, lightly crushed
25 g/1 oz/2 tbsp unsalted (sweet) butter, melted
60 ml/4 tbsp water
Coarse sea salt

Wipe the guinea fowl inside and out with kitchen paper (paper towels). Place in a roasting tin (pan). Whisk together the honey, mustard, orange juice, herbs and a little salt and pepper. Pour over the guinea fowl and leave to marinate for at least 30 minutes.

Meanwhile, peel and cut the vegetables into sticks about the size of an index finger. Boil in lightly salted water for 3 minutes, then drain. Heat the oil in a roasting tin. Add the vegetables and toss to coat in the oil. Sprinkle with the cumin seeds. Place in the top of a preheated oven at 190°C/375°F/gas mark 5. Cook for 10 minutes. Drizzle the melted butter over the guinea fowl, then place in the centre of the oven. Cook for about 50 minutes until tender, browned and cooked through. Toss the vegetables twice during cooking, and baste the birds. When cooked, transfer the birds to a carving dish and cut into halves. Place on warm plates. Stir the juices, add the water and boil, stirring, for 30 seconds. Taste and re-season if necessary. Spoon over the birds. Sprinkle the vegetables lightly with coarse sea salt, toss gently and spoon to the sides of the birds. Serve straight away.

Hunter's Squab

SERVES 6

3 oven-ready squab, halved
50 g/2 oz/¼ cup butter or margarine, softened
250 ml/8 fl oz/1 cup red wine
25 g/1 oz/¼ cup cashew nuts
15 ml/1 tbsp cranberry sauce
Salt and freshly ground black pepper
Chopped parsley, to garnish
Oven Pilaff (page 352), to serve

Wipe the birds inside and out with kitchen paper (paper towels). Cut each in half. Place in a roasting tin (pan) and smear with 40 g/1½ oz/3 tbsp of the butter or margarine. Pour in half the wine. Roast in a preheated oven at 200°C/400°F/gas mark 6 for 30 minutes. Meanwhile, fry (sauté) the cashews in the remaining butter or margarine in a frying pan (skillet) until golden. Drain on kitchen paper. Lift the birds out of the roasting tin and transfer to warm plates. Stir in the remaining wine and the cranberry sauce and bring the juices to the boil, stirring. Boil until reduced slightly and season to taste. Spoon over the birds and sprinkle with the cashews. Sprinkle with chopped parsley and serve with the Oven Pilaff.

Hunter's Pigeon

SERVES 6

Prepare as for Hunter's Squab, but use 6 oven-ready pigeons instead of squab and almonds instead of cashew nuts.

Roast Pigeons with Sherry Sauce

SERVES 4

4 oven-ready pigeons
Salt and freshly ground black pepper
150 g/5 oz/⅔ cup unsalted (sweet) butter
1 onion, very thinly sliced
4 slices of white bread, crusts removed
45 ml/3 tbsp plain (all-purpose) flour
300 ml/½ pt/1¼ cups chicken stock
15 ml/1 tbsp medium-dry sherry
10 ml/2 tsp tomato purée (paste)
A good pinch of light brown sugar
A little gravy block or browning
Watercress, to garnish
Game Chips (page 348) and peas, to serve

Wipe the pigeons inside and out with kitchen paper (paper towels). Season inside and out with salt and pepper. Put 15 g/½ oz/1 tbsp butter inside each bird. Melt 50 g/2 oz/¼ cup of the remaining butter in a roasting tin (pan). Add the onion and fry (sauté) for 3 minutes until lightly golden. Place the pigeons on top of the onion. Use a brush to coat the birds in the butter in the tin. Roast in a preheated oven at 200°C/400°F/gas mark 6 for 30 minutes, basting frequently. Meanwhile, spread the bread on both sides with the remaining butter and fry in a hot frying pan (skillet) until golden on both sides. Place on four warm plates. Transfer a pigeon to each piece of fried bread and keep warm. Pour off all but 15 ml/1 tbsp of the fat in the pan, but leave the juices and onion. Blend in the flour and cook for 1 minute, stirring. Remove from the heat and blend in the stock, sherry, tomato purée and the sugar. Return to the heat and bring to the boil, stirring. Add gravy block or browning and season to taste. Strain over the pigeons, garnish with watercress and serve hot with Game Chips and peas.

Snipe Parcels with Oyster Mushroom Sauce

SERVES 4

4 oven-ready snipe
75 g/3 oz/⅓ cup unsalted (sweet) butter
15 ml/1 tbsp olive oil
100 g/4 oz sweet-cured ham, diced
100 g/4 oz frozen peas
5 ml/1 tsp dried mint
Salt and freshly ground black pepper
150 ml/¼ pt/⅔ cup chicken stock
225 g/8 oz oyster mushrooms, chopped
120 ml/4 fl oz/½ cup dry white wine
75 ml/5 tbsp crème fraîche
Milk
New potatoes, sprinkled with chopped parsley, to serve

Wipe the snipe inside and out with kitchen paper (paper towels). Melt half the butter in a frying pan (skillet) with the oil and brown the birds on all sides. Remove from the pan. Cut four pieces of foil about 25 cm/10 in square. Melt half the remaining butter and brush all over the shiny side of the foil. Mix together the ham and peas with the mint and 30 ml/2 tbsp of the stock, and divide between the centres of the foil. Top each with a snipe. Season with salt and pepper. Wrap tightly in the foil and seal the edges well. Transfer to a baking (cookie) sheet. Roast in a preheated oven at 200°C/400°F/gas mark 6 for 30 minutes.

Meanwhile, melt the remaining butter in a saucepan. Add the mushrooms and fry (sauté) for 2 minutes. Stir in the wine and the remaining stock and simmer, uncovered, for 5 minutes. Purée in a blender or food processor and stir in the crème fraîche. Season to taste and thin with a little milk, if necessary. Return to the saucepan and reheat. Transfer the snipe parcels to warm plates. Open at the table to enjoy the fragrance and serve with the mushroom sauce and new potatoes, sprinkled with chopped parsley.

Quail Parcels with Oyster Mushroom Sauce

SERVES 4

Prepare as for Snipe Parcels with Oyster Mushroom Sauce, but use oven-ready quail instead of snipe, pancetta instead of sweet-cured ham, and baby broad (fava) beans instead of peas. Flavour with dried basil instead of mint.

Boned Stuffed Pigeons

SERVES 4

4 oven-ready pigeons, boned (page 15)
100 g/4 oz chicken liver pâté
50 g/2 oz/¼ cup butter or margarine
Salt and freshly ground black pepper
150 ml/¼ pt/⅔ cup medium-sweet cider
15 ml/1 tbsp brandy
15 ml/1 tbsp chopped parsley, to garnish
Speciality Creamed Potatoes (page 348) and French (green) beans, to serve

Wipe the boned pigeons with kitchen paper (paper towels). Spread with the pâté and roll up. Tie securely. Place in a flameproof casserole (Dutch oven). Smear with the butter or margarine and season lightly. Roast, uncovered, in a preheated oven at 190°C/375°F/gas mark 5 for 15 minutes. Pour the cider around and add the brandy. Cover and cook for a further 15–20 minutes until tender. Lift the pigeons out of the dish, place on warm serving plates and keep warm. Boil the juices until reduced and slightly thickened. Taste and re-season. Spoon over the pigeons and sprinkle with chopped parsley. Serve with Speciality Creamed Potatoes and French beans.

Roast Widgeon with Chicory and Orange Salad

SERVES 4

2 oven-ready widgeon
25 g/1 oz/2 tbsp butter or margarine
4 streaky bacon rashers (slices)
4 slices of white bread, crusts removed, toasted
Salt and freshly ground black pepper
10 ml/2 tsp plain (all-purpose) flour
2 oranges
2 heads of chicory
1 bunch of watercress
30 ml/2 tbsp olive oil
15 ml/1 tbsp lemon juice
10 ml/2 tbsp chopped parsley
5 ml/1 tsp Dijon mustard
5 ml/1 tsp caster (superfine) sugar
Orange Gravy (page 334) and Game Chips (page 348), to serve

Wipe the widgeon inside and out with kitchen paper (paper towels). Place a knob of the butter or margarine in each bird. Truss and tie 2 rashers of bacon over the breast of each bird. Smear with the remaining butter or margarine. Place on the slices of toast in a roasting tin (pan). Sprinkle with salt and pepper. Roast in a preheated oven at 200°C/400°F/gas mark 6 for 20 minutes. Remove the bacon, baste the breasts, then sprinkle with the flour. Baste again and return to the oven for 5 minutes until frothy.

Meanwhile, cut all the rind and pith from the oranges and cut the fruit into thin slices. Cut each slice in half. Cut a cone shaped core out of the base of each head of chicory. Cut the head into thick chunks and separate into leaves. Trim the feathery stalks off the watercress. Reserve a little watercress for garnish and mix the remaining watercress with the chicory. Place in four small salad bowls. Scatter the orange segments over. Whisk together the oil, lemon juice, parsley, mustard and sugar with a little salt and pepper. Spoon over the salads. Transfer the widgeon on their slices of toast to warm serving plates and remove the trussing string. Garnish with the reserved watercress. Serve with Orange Gravy, Game Chips and the salads.

Wild Duck with Blackberries

SERVES 6

1 brace of oven-ready wild duck (preferably mallards)
2 carrots, sliced
14 button (pearl) onions, peeled but left whole
1 bouquet garni sachet
1 orange, quartered
375 ml/13 fl oz/1½ cups red wine
Salt and freshly ground black pepper
50 g/2 oz/¼ cup butter or margarine
225 g/8 oz button mushrooms
50 g/2 oz/½ cup plain (all-purpose) flour
175 g/6 oz ripe blackberries
Caster (superfine) sugar
New potatoes and a green salad, to serve

Wipe the ducks inside and out with kitchen paper (paper towels). Place in a large flameproof casserole dish (Dutch oven). Add the carrots, two of the onions, the bouquet garni and the orange quarters. Pour the wine over. Add a little salt and pepper. Bring to the boil and transfer to a preheated oven at 160°C/325°F/gas mark 3 for 2½ hours or until the ducks are really tender and falling off the bones. Lift out of the casserole and take all the meat off the bones, discarding the skin. Place in a smaller casserole dish. Melt the butter or margarine in a saucepan. Add the remaining onions and the mushrooms and fry (sauté) for 2 minutes. Cover with a lid and cook gently for 5 minutes until tender. Blend in the flour. Strain the cooking liquid and pour into the pan. Bring to the boil, stirring, and simmer for 2 minutes. Stir in the blackberries and simmer for 1 minute. Taste and re-season with salt, pepper and sugar. Add to the duck and stir gently. Reheat in the oven at 180°C/350°F/gas mark 4 for 20 minutes. Serve with new potatoes and a green salad.

Pastry Dishes

All these dishes are encased in a dough of one sort or another, wrapping succulent, tasty fillings in crisp, melting baked crusts or light, soft, steamed ones. Some are elegant and impressive, others practical and cheap for a simple family meal. All are utterly delicious!

CHICKEN

Creamy Chicken Pie

SERVES 6

1.5 kg/3 lb oven-ready chicken, cut into quarters
2 onions, finely chopped
2 carrots, finely chopped
2 celery sticks, finely chopped
1 litre/1¾ pts/4¼ cups water
1 chicken stock cube
40 g/1½ oz/3 tbsp butter or margarine
40 g/1½ oz/⅓ cup plain (all-purpose) flour
60 ml/4 tbsp dried milk powder (non-fat dry milk)
60 ml/4 tbsp double (heavy) cream
Salt and freshly ground black pepper
375 g/13 oz/1 block of puff pastry (paste), thawed if frozen
Beaten egg, to glaze
Carrots and peas, to serve

Put the chicken in a saucepan with the onions, carrots and celery. Add the water and stock cube. Bring to the boil, reduce the heat, skim the surface, part-cover and simmer gently for 1¼ hours or until the chicken is really tender. Lift the chicken out of the pan, discard the skin and bones and cut the meat into neat pieces. Strain the stock and reserve the vegetables.

Melt the butter or margarine in the rinsed-out saucepan. Add the flour and cook, stirring, for 1 minute. Remove from the heat and blend in 450 ml/¾ pt/2 cups of the stock and the milk powder. Return to the heat, bring to the boil and cook for 2 minutes, stirring. Add the chicken, vegetables and cream. Season to taste. Turn into a 1.2 litre/2 pt/5 cup pie dish. Put a pie funnel in the centre. Roll out the pastry to slightly larger than the pie dish. Cut a strip off all round. Brush the edge of the pie dish with water and lay the strip on top. Brush with water. Lay the pastry on top. Press the edges together to seal, then trim. Knock up and flute with the back of a knife. Make a hole in the centre to allow the funnel to poke through. Make leaves out of the trimmings. Brush the pastry with beaten egg. Add the leaves and brush again. Place on a baking (cookie) sheet. Bake in a preheated oven at 220°C/425°F/gas mark 7 for about 25–30 minutes until golden brown and cooked through. Serve hot with carrots and peas.

Chicken, Spinach and Pecan Pies

SERVES 4

2 chicken breasts, cut into small pieces
225 g/8 oz frozen leaf spinach, thawed
100 g/4 oz/½ cup cottage cheese
25 g/1 oz/¼ cup pecan nuts, chopped
A good pinch of grated nutmeg
Freshly ground black pepper
A pinch of salt
4 large filo pastry (paste) sheets
15 g/½ oz/1 tbsp butter or margarine, melted
150 ml/¼ pt/⅔ cup passata (sieved tomatoes)
Baby carrots and peas, to serve

Put the chicken in a bowl. Squeeze out all the excess moisture from the spinach, chop then add to the chicken with the cheese, nuts, nutmeg, a good grinding of pepper and just a pinch of salt. Mix thoroughly. Lay a sheet of filo pastry on the work surface and brush very lightly with a little of the melted butter or margarine. Fold the pastry in half to form a square. Brush with a little more melted fat and fold in half again. Add a quarter of the chicken mixture, then fold the pastry over the filling to form a neat parcel. Transfer to a non-stick baking (cookie) sheet and repeat with the remaining ingredients. Brush each parcel with any remaining butter or margarine. Bake in a preheated oven at 190°C/375°F/gas mark 5 for 30 minutes until golden and cooked through. Meanwhile, heat the passata in a small saucepan or in a bowl in the microwave. Spoon on to warm plates. Top each with a pie and serve with baby carrots and peas.

Chicken and Egg Pie

SERVES 6

30 ml/2 tbsp sunflower oil
Salt and freshly ground black pepper
100 g/4 oz/½ cup long-grain rice
3 eggs, scrubbed under the cold tap
350 g/12 oz/3 cups wholemeal flour
175 g/6 oz/¾ cup hard block margarine, cut into small pieces
1 bunch of spring onions (scallions), finely chopped
350 g/12 oz minced (ground) chicken
45 ml/3 tbsp tomato chutney
30 ml/2 tbsp plain (all-purpose) flour
1 egg, beaten, to glaze
Mixed salad, to serve

Line a 900 g/2 lb loaf tin (pan) with a double thickness of foil, standing 5 cm/2 in above the rim. Brush the foil with some of the oil. Bring a saucepan of water to the boil and add a little salt. Pour in the rice and stir, bring back to the boil, drop in the eggs in their shells and cook together for 10 minutes, Drain, rinse well with cold water and drain again. Remove the eggs from the rice. Mix the wholemeal flour with 1.5 ml/¼ tsp salt. Add the margarine and rub in with the fingertips until the mixture resembles breadcrumbs. Mix with enough cold water to form a firm dough. Knead gently on a lightly floured surface. Cut off about a quarter of the dough and reserve. Roll out the remainder and use to line the loaf tin, pressing it gently into the corners, making sure there are no cracks.

Fry (sauté) the spring onions in the remaining oil for 2 minutes until soft but not brown. Stir in the chicken and cook until it is no longer pink and all the grains are separate. Stir in the chutney, rice and a little salt and pepper. Shell the eggs and toss in the flour. Spoon half the chicken mixture into the dough-lined tin. Top with the eggs in a line. Top with the remaining chicken mixture and press down gently. Roll out the remaining pastry and use as a lid. Brush the edges of the pie with water and place the lid in position. Press well together and trim the edges. Crimp the edges between the finger and thumb. Makes some leaves out of any trimmings. Brush the top with beaten egg, put the leaves in position and brush with more egg. Make a hole in the centre to allow the steam to escape. Place on a baking (cookie) sheet. Bake in a preheated oven at 200°C/400°F/gas mark 6 for 20 minutes, then reduce the heat to 180°C/350°F/gas mark 4 for a further 1 hour until cooked through and golden brown. Cover the top with foil if the pie is over browning. Remove from the oven and leave to cool in the tin for 30 minutes. Loosen the edge and carefully lift out using the foil to help. Place on a wire rack and ease the foil down the sides. Leave to cool completely. Chill until ready to serve.

Spicy Chicken and Pease Pudding Crisp

SERVE 4

425 g/15 oz/1 large can of pease pudding
150 ml/¼ pt/⅔ cup coconut milk
100 g/4 oz whole button mushrooms
350 g/12 oz cooked chicken tikka, separated into pieces
30 ml/2 tbsp chopped coriander (cilantro)
3 sheets of filo pastry (paste)
40 g/1½ oz/3 tbsp oil
2.5 ml/½ tsp cayenne
10 ml/2 tsp black mustard seeds
Green salad, to serve

Empty the pease pudding into an ovenproof dish and stir in the coconut milk until well blended. Fold in the mushrooms, chicken and coriander. Lay the filo sheets on top of each other and cut into 7.5 cm/3 in squares. Pinch the centre of each square to form a bunch of pastry. Lay these bunches all over the surface of the mixture and brush with oil. Dust with the cayenne and sprinkle with the mustard seeds. Bake in a preheated oven at 200°C/400°F/gas mark 6 for 20 minutes. Lay a sheet of foil over the top to prevent over-browning and cook for a further 20 minutes until piping hot throughout. Serve with a green salad.

Chicken and Parsley Quiche

SERVES 4

175 g/6 oz/1½ cups plain (all-purpose) flour
A pinch of salt
75 g/3 oz/⅓ cup hard block margarine, cut into pieces
1 onion, finely chopped
15 ml/1 tbsp sunflower oil
175 g/6 oz/1½ cups cooked chicken, chopped, all skin removed
Freshly ground black pepper
50 g/2 oz/½ cup Cheddar cheese, grated
30 ml/2 tbsp chopped parsley
2 eggs
300 ml/½ pt/1¼ cups milk
Salad, to serve

Sift the flour and salt into a bowl. Add the margarine and rub in with the fingertips until the mixture resembles fine breadcrumbs. Mix with enough cold water to form a firm dough. Knead gently on a lightly floured surface. Roll out and use to line a 20 cm/8 in flan dish (pie pan). Prick the base with a fork and fill with crumpled foil. Bake in a preheated oven at 200°C/400°F/gas mark 6 for 10 minutes. Remove the foil and cook for a further 5 minutes to dry out. Meanwhile, fry (sauté) the onion in the oil for 2 minutes. Tip into the flan and scatter the chicken over. Season with salt and pepper and add the cheese and parsley. Beat the eggs and milk together and pour into the flan. Place on a baking (cookie) sheet. Bake in the oven at 190°C/375°F/gas mark 5 for about 30 minutes or until just set and golden brown on top. Serve hot or cold with salad.

Chicken and Sweetcorn Quiche

SERVES 4

Prepare as for Chicken and Parsley Quiche, but use only 100 g/4 oz/1 cup of cooked chicken and add 200 g/7 oz/1 small can of sweetcorn (corn), drained. Omit the parsley.

Chicken, Sweetcorn and Pepper Quiche

SERVES 4

Prepare as for Chicken and Sweetcorn Quiche, but arrange a sliced green or red (bell) pepper in overlapping circles over the cheese before baking.

Chicken and Ham Quiche

SERVES 4

Prepare as for Chicken and Parsley Quiche, but add a good pinch of dried sage to the onion when frying (sautéing) and use only 75 g/3 oz/¾ cup chicken but add 75 g/3 oz/¾ cup cooked ham, diced.

Chicken and Mushroom Quiche

SERVES 4

Prepare as for Chicken and Parsley Quiche, but add 100 g/4 oz sliced button mushrooms when cooking the onions and use only 100 g/4 oz/1 cup cooked chicken. Flavour with snipped chives instead of parsley.

Chicken and Prawn Quiche

SERVES 4

Prepare as for Chicken and Parsley Quiche, but use only 75 g/3 oz/¾ cup cooked chicken and add 75 g/3 oz cooked, peeled prawns (shrimp), thawed and thoroughly drained if frozen, and beat in 5 ml/1 tsp soy sauce with the eggs and milk.

Chicken and Broccoli Quiche

SERVES 4

Prepare as for Chicken and Parsley Quiche, but use only 100 g/4 oz/1 cup cooked chicken and add 100 g/4 oz tiny broccoli florets, first cooked for 3 minutes in lightly salted boiling water and drained. Omit the parsley.

Chicken and Potato Quiche

SERVES 4

Prepare as for Chicken and Parsley Quiche, but use only 100 g/4 oz/ 1 cup cooked chicken and add 1 large cooked potato, cut into small dice. Sprinkle with 5 ml/1 tsp caraway seeds, if liked, before adding the cheese.

Chicken and Asparagus Quiche

SERVES 4

Prepare as for Chicken and Parsley Quiche, but omit the parsley and arrange 300 g/11 oz/1 medium can of asparagus spears, well-drained, in a starburst pattern over the cheese before adding the eggs and milk.

Chicken and Tomato Quiche

SERVES 4

Prepare as for Chicken and Parsley Quiche, but omit the parsley and arrange 2 sliced tomatoes around the top of the cheese before adding the milk and sprinkle with a few torn basil leaves.

Chicken and Vegetable Pasties

MAKES 8

175 g/6 oz chicken stir-fry meat, chopped
100 g/4 oz frozen peas
1 large potato, diced
1 large carrot, diced
Salt and freshly ground black pepper
1 chicken stock cube
15 ml/1 tbsp chopped parsley
10 ml/2 tsp chopped thyme
225 g/8 oz/1 cup soft tub margarine
350 g/12 oz/3 cups plain (all-purpose) flour
30 ml/2 tbsp cold water
1 egg, beaten
Pickles, to serve

Mix the chicken with the peas, potato and carrots. Season with salt and pepper and crumble in the stock cube. Stir in the herbs and mix well. Put the margarine in a bowl with 225 g/8 oz/ 2 cups of the flour, a pinch of salt and the water. Beat until smooth, then work in the remaining flour and knead gently. Roll out on a lightly floured surface and cut into 8 rounds using a small tea plate as a guide. Divide the chicken mixture between the rounds. Brush the edges with beaten egg and draw up over the filling, pinching firmly together to seal. Crimp the edges between the finger and thumb. Transfer to a lightly greased baking (cookie) sheet. Brush with beaten egg to glaze. Bake in a preheated oven at 220°C/425°F/gas mark 7 for 10 minutes. Reduce the heat to 180°C/ 350°F/gas mark 4 and cook for a further 30 minutes or until the pasties are golden brown and the filling is cooked through. Serve hot or cold with pickles.

Chicken Parcels with Cranberry

SERVES 4

4 sheets of filo pastry (paste)
50 g/2 oz/¼ cup butter or margarine, melted
425 g/15 oz/1 large can of chicken chunks in white sauce
5 ml/1 tsp dried mixed herbs
60 ml/4 tbsp cranberry sauce
15 ml/1 tbsp port
Finely grated rind of ½ lemon
Parsley sprigs, to garnish
New potatoes and asparagus, to serve

Lay a pastry sheet on the work surface. Brush with a little of the fat and fold in half. Brush again. Put a quarter of the chicken in the centre of the pastry and sprinkle with a quarter of the herbs. Draw the pastry over the filling to form a pouch. Transfer to a greased baking (cookie) sheet. Repeat with the remaining pastry and filling. Brush all four parcels with the remaining fat. Bake in a preheated oven at 200°C/400°F/gas mark 6 for 10–15 minutes until golden brown. Meanwhile, heat the cranberry sauce, port and lemon rind in a small saucepan. Transfer the parcels to warm plates. Put a spoonful of the sauce to the side of each, garnish with parsley and serve with new potatoes and asparagus.

Chicken and Spring Vegetable Jalousie

SERVES 6

For the filling:
100 g/4 oz fresh, shelled or frozen peas
100 g/4 oz fresh, shelled or frozen broad (fava) beans
1 bunch of spring onions (scallions), chopped
2 young carrots, finely diced
100 g/4 oz spring greens (collard greens), shredded
25 g/1 oz/¼ cup plain (all-purpose) flour
300 ml/½ pt/1¼ cups milk
25 g/1 oz/2 tbsp butter or margarine
100 g/4 oz/1 cup Cheddar cheese, grated
175 g/6 oz/1½ cups cooked chicken, diced, all skin removed
Salt and freshly ground black pepper
For the pastry (paste):
275 g/10 oz/2½ cups self-raising (self-rising) flour
75 g/3 oz/¾ cup shredded vegetable suet
175 ml/6 fl oz/¾ cup water, to mix
1 egg, beaten
Beetroot and onion salad, to serve

To make the filling, cook all the prepared vegetables in boiling salted water for 4 minutes. Drain, rinse with cold water and drain again. Whisk together the plain flour and milk in a saucepan until smooth. Add the butter or margarine. Bring to the boil and cook for 2 minutes, stirring all the time until thickened and smooth. Stir in 50 g/ 2 oz/½ cup of the cheese and the chicken and vegetables. Season to taste with salt and pepper.

To make the pastry, sift the self-raising flour and a pinch of salt into a bowl. Add the suet and remaining cheese and mix with the water to form a firm dough, adding a little more water, if necessary. Knead gently on a lightly floured surface. Cut into half. Roll out one half to a rectangle, about 20 cm × 30 cm/8 in × 12 in. Place on a lightly greased baking (cookie) sheet. Roll out the remaining pastry to the same size. Fold lightly in half lengthways and make a series of cuts along the length of the folded side to within 1 cm/½ in of the open long edges. Gently open out. Spoon the filling over the rectangle of pastry on the baking sheet to within 1 cm/½ in of the edges all round. Brush the edges with the egg. Carefully lift the cut rectangle over the top and press the edges well together to seal. Knock up the edges all round. Brush with egg to glaze. Cook in a preheated oven at 200°C/ 400°F/gas mark 6 for about 25 minutes until the pastry is golden and the filling is piping hot. Serve hot or leave until cold and cut into six squares. Serve with a beetroot and onion salad.

Chicken Florentine

SERVES 4

375 g/13 oz/1 block of frozen puff pasty (paste), thawed
4 small skinless chicken breasts
350 g/12 oz spinach, cooked and chopped
2 tomatoes, skinned and sliced
175 g/6 oz Mozzarella cheese, thinly sliced
Grated nutmeg
Salt and freshly ground black pepper
1 egg, beaten
Grated celeriac (celery root) and carrots tossed in olive oil and vinegar, to serve

Cut the pastry into quarters and roll out each quarter to a thin square. Place a chicken breast on each. Top with the spinach, then tomato slices, then the Mozzarella cheese. Sprinkle with nutmeg, salt and pepper. Brush the edges with the egg, then fold over the pastry to form neat parcels. Transfer to a dampened baking (cookie) sheet, sealed-sides down. Make two small slits in the top of each parcel to allow steam to escape. Brush the surface with the egg. Bake in a preheated oven at 200°C/ 400°F/gas mark 6 for 35 minutes until golden and cooked through. Transfer to warm plates and serve with a celeriac and carrot salad.

Chicken in Filo Pastry with Asparagus Sauce

SERVES 4

4 skinless chicken breasts
50 g/2 oz/¼ cup butter or margarine, melted
4 sheets of filo pastry (paste)
40 ml/8 tsp redcurrant jelly (clear conserve)
5 ml/1 tsp dried thyme
Salt and freshly ground black pepper
300 g/11 oz/1 medium can of cut asparagus spears, drained, reserving the liquid
30 ml/2 tbsp crème fraîche
A pinch of grated nutmeg
Parsley sprigs, to garnish
New potatoes and broccoli, to serve

Fry (sauté) the chicken breasts in half the butter or margarine for 5 minutes, turning once, until golden and almost cooked. Lay the pastry sheets on the work surface. Brush with a little of the remaining butter or margarine, fold into halves and brush again. Put 10 ml/2 tsp redcurrant jelly in the centre of each piece of pastry. Top each with a chicken breast and sprinkle with the thyme and a little salt and pepper. Fold the pastry over the filling to cover completely. Transfer, folded-sides down, to a greased baking (cookie) sheet. Bake in a preheated oven at 200°C/400°F/gas mark 6 for 15 minutes until golden brown. Meanwhile, purée the asparagus in a blender or food processor. Turn into a small saucepan and stir in the crème fraîche. Thin with a little of the reserved asparagus liquid. Season with the nutmeg and a little salt and pepper. Heat through. Transfer the chicken parcels to warm serving plates. Spoon a little sauce over, garnish with parsley and serve hot with new potatoes and broccoli.

Chicken and Leek Pie

SERVES 6

450 g/1 lb leeks
4 streaky bacon rashers (slices), rinded and diced
176 g/6 oz chicken stir-fry meat
300 ml/½ pt/1¼ cups chicken stock
1 bouquet garni sachet
Salt and freshly ground black pepper
1 egg
45 ml/3 tbsp crème fraîche
225 g/8 oz puff pastry (paste), thawed, if frozen
Pickles, to serve

Trim the leeks, slit them almost through from the green end to the root end and rinse thoroughly under cold running water. Slice fairly thickly. Drain and place in a 1.5 litre/2½ pt/6 cup pie dish. Add the bacon and chicken and mix well. Add the stock, bouquet garni and some salt and pepper. Cover loosely with foil and bake in a preheated oven at 150°C/300°F/gas mark 2 for about 1½ hours until most of the liquid has evaporated. Remove the bouquet garni. Beat the egg with 30 ml/2 tbsp of the crème fraîche and stir into the pie. Roll out the pastry to just larger than the pie dish. Cut a strip off the pastry. Dampen the edge of the dish with water and place the strip of pastry round the rim. Brush again with water. Put the pastry lid in position, press the edges well together to seal, knock up and flute with the back of a knife. Make a slit in the centre to allow steam to escape and brush all over with the remaining crème fraîche. Turn the oven up to 200°C/400°F/gas mark 6 and cook for about 30 minutes until risen and golden brown. Serve hot or cold with pickles.

Welsh Cream of Chicken Pie

SERVES 6

1.5 kg/3 lb oven-ready chicken
1 large onion
1 clove
1 bouquet garni sachet
Salt and freshly ground black pepper
2 large leeks, sliced
2 potatoes, sliced
100 g/4 oz/1 cup plain (all-purpose) flour
100 g/4 oz/1 cup wholemeal flour
100 g/4 oz/½ cup butter or block margarine, diced
Beaten egg, to glaze
150 ml/¼ pt/⅔ cup double (heavy) cream
Peas and carrots, to serve

Put the chicken in a saucepan. Stud the onion with the clove and add with the bouquet garni. Just-cover with cold water and add a little salt and pepper. Part-cover, bring to the boil, reduce the heat and simmer for 1 hour. Remove from the heat and leave the chicken to cool in the liquid. Skim the surface to remove the fat. Remove the chicken, reserving the cooking liquid, and take all the meat off the bones, discarding the skin. Cut into large, neat pieces. Meanwhile, part-cook the leeks and potatoes in lightly salted boiling water for 3 minutes. Drain.

Mix the flours and 2.5 ml/½ tsp salt in a bowl. Add the butter or margarine and rub in with the fingertips until the mixture resembles fine breadcrumbs. Mix with enough cold water of form a firm dough. Wrap in clingfilm (plastic wrap) and chill for 30 minutes.

Layer the chicken, leeks and potatoes in a 1.5 litre/2½ pt/6 cup pie dish. Pour in 300 ml/½ pt/1¼ cups of the stock the chicken was cooked in. Knead the pastry (paste) gently on a lightly floured surface. Roll out to just larger than the pie dish. Trim. Roll out the trimmings and cut a strip to fit all round the rim. Dampen the rim with water and place the pastry strip in position. Lay the pastry lid in position, press the edges well together to seal, knock up and flute with the back of a knife. Make a fairly large hole in the middle to allow steam to escape. Make a rose to go over the hole and some leaves out of the trimmings. Brush all over with beaten egg and bake in a preheated oven at 190°C/375°F/gas mark 5 for 30 minutes, then reduce the heat to 160°C/325°F/gas mark 3 and cook for a further 15 minutes. Carefully remove the rose and pour the cream in through the hole. Replace the rose and return to the oven for 5 minutes. Serve hot with peas and carrots.

Picnic Pies

SERVES 4

225 g/8 oz shortcrust pastry (basic pie crust)
100 g/4 oz/1 cup cooked chicken, diced, all skin removed
1 potato, finely chopped
1 carrot, finely chopped
1 spring onion (scallion), chopped
1.5 ml/¼ tsp dried oregano
Salt and freshly ground black pepper
60 ml/4 tbsp chicken gravy, to moisten
Beaten egg, to glaze
Coleslaw, to serve

Roll out the pastry fairly thinly and cut into 7.5 cm/3 in rounds with a biscuit (cookie) cutter. Re-knead the trimmings and cut again to make 16 circles. Place eight circles on a baking (cookie) sheet. Mix together the chicken, vegetables, oregano, a little salt and pepper and the gravy. Divide the chicken mixture between the centres of the pastry rounds and brush the edges with water. Top with the second circles and crimp the edges between the finger and thumb. Brush with beaten egg and make a hole in the centre of the top of each to allow steam to escape. Bake in a preheated oven at 220°C/425°F/gas mark 7 for 20–25 minutes until golden and cooked through. Serve with coleslaw.

Smoked Chicken and Ham Vol-au-vent

SERVES 4

375 g/13 oz/1 block of puff pastry (paste), thawed if frozen
1 egg, beaten
100 g/4 oz chestnut mushrooms, sliced
2 spring onions (scallions), finely chopped
40 g/1½ oz/3 tbsp butter or margarine
40 g/1½ oz/scant ⅓ cup plain (all-purpose) flour
450 ml/¾ pt/2 cups milk
175 g/6 oz/1½ cups smoked chicken, diced
50 g/2 oz/½ cup smoked cooked ham, diced
30 ml/2 tbsp chopped parsley
Salt and freshly ground black pepper
Crisp green salad, to serve

Cut the pastry in half. Roll out one half and cut into an 18 cm (7 in) diameter round, using a plate as a guide. Place on a dampened baking (cookie) sheet. Roll out the second piece of pastry to the same size. Place a 15 cm/6 in saucer in the centre of the second piece of pastry and cut round the edge, almost through the pastry. Brush the border of the pastry on the baking sheet with the egg. Carefully lift the second piece of pastry on top so it fits exactly. Mark in a criss-cross pattern with the back of a knife and brush with egg to glaze. Bake in a preheated oven at 220°C/425°F/gas mark 7 for 10–15 minutes or until risen and golden brown. Carefully transfer the pastry to a serving plate. Carefully loosen, then remove the round from the top of the pastry and reserve. Scoop out any uncooked dough in the centre.

Cook the mushrooms and spring onions gently in the butter or margarine for 3–4 minutes until soft but not brown. Stir in the flour and cook for 1 minute. Remove from the heat and gradually blend in the milk. Return to the heat, bring to the boil and cook for 2 minutes, stirring. Stir in the chicken, ham and parsley. Season to taste. Heat until piping hot. Spoon into the pastry case, top with the reserved lid and serve warm or cold with a crisp green salad.

Creamy Chicken Vol-au-vents

SERVES 4

225 g/8 oz frozen puff pastry (paste), thawed
Beaten egg, to glaze
½ quantity of Quick Béchamel Sauce (page 340)
175 g/6 oz/1½ cups cooked chicken, diced, all skin removed
15 ml/1 tbsp double (heavy) cream
15 ml/1 tbsp chopped parsley
Salt and freshly ground black pepper

Roll out the pastry as directed on the packet and cut into four rounds using a 9 cm/3½ in fluted biscuit (cookie) cutter. Place upside-down on a dampened baking (cookie) sheet. Using a 4 cm/1½ in biscuit cutter, mark a circle in the centre of the pastry cutting only half-way through the pastry. Brush with beaten egg and leave to rest for 30 minutes. Bake in a preheated oven at 220°C/425°F/gas mark 7 for 12–15 minutes until risen, golden and crisp. Carefully lift out the centres of the pastry cases and reserve. Scoop out any uncooked pastry from inside, taking care not to damage the shells. Return to the switched-off oven with the door slightly ajar for 10 minutes to dry out. Meanwhile, to make the sauce, stir together the chicken, cream and parsley and season to taste. Heat through gently. Spoon into the hot pastry cases, top with the lids and serve hot.

Creamy Chicken and Mushroom Vol-au-vents

SERVES 4

Prepare as for Creamy Chicken Vol-au-vents, but cook 50 g/2 oz chopped button mushrooms in 30 ml/2 tbsp water and 5 ml/1 tsp lemon juice until soft. Boil rapidly to evaporate any liquid, then mix with just 100 g/4 oz/1 cup of chicken and continue as before.

Creamy Chicken and Prawn Vol-au-vents

SERVES 4

Prepare as for Creamy Chicken Vol-au-vents (page 191), but use half the quantity of cooked chicken and half small cooked, peeled prawns (shrimp), well-drained on kitchen paper (paper towels) before adding to the sauce. Spike the sauce with lemon juice before heating.

Creamy Chicken and Ham Vol-au-vents

SERVES 4

Prepare as for Creamy Chicken Vol-au-vents (page 191), but use half cooked chicken and half cooked ham, diced, then continue as before, adding 1.5 ml/¼ tsp Dijon mustard to the sauce, if liked.

Creamy Chicken and Sweetcorn Vol-au-vents

SERVES 4

Prepare as for Creamy Chicken Vol-au-vents (page 191), but use only 100 g/4 oz/1 cup cooked chicken and add 50 g/2 oz cooked frozen sweetcorn (corn) to the sauce.

Creamy Chicken and Avocado Vol-au-vents

SERVES 4

Prepare as for Creamy Chicken Vol-au-vents (page 191), but use ½ a ripe avocado, diced and tossed in lemon juice, and only half the quantity of chicken. Continue as before.

Cheesy Chicken and Chive Plait

SERVES 4

225 g/8 oz/2 cups cooked chicken, diced, all skin removed
50 g/2 oz/½ cup Cheddar cheese, grated
120 ml/4 fl oz/½ cup cottage cheese and chives
Salt and freshly ground black pepper
25 g/1 oz/½ cup wholemeal breadcrumbs
375 g/13 oz/1 block of frozen puff pastry (paste), thawed
Beaten egg, to glaze
30 ml/2 tbsp grated Parmesan cheese
300 ml/½ pt/1¼ cups passata (sieved tomatoes)
30 ml/2 tbsp snipped chives
New potatoes and a green salad, to serve

Mix together the chicken, cheeses, a little salt and pepper and the breadcrumbs. Roll out the pastry to a large rectangle and spoon the filling down the centre. Make diagonal cuts down the length of the pastry on either side of the filling at 2 cm/¾ in intervals. Brush with water. Fold the ends over the filling, then wrap the strips alternately over the filling to form a plait. Carefully transfer the plait to a dampened baking (cookie) sheet and brush with egg to glaze. Bake in a preheated oven at 200°C/400°F/gas mark 6 for about 30 minutes until golden, puffy and piping hot. Meanwhile, heat the passata and chives together with a little salt and pepper. Spoon on to a large platter and top with the plait. Serve hot with new potatoes and a green salad.

Chicken and Mushroom Flan

SERVES 4

For the pastry (paste):
200 g/7 oz/1¾ cups plain (all-purpose) flour
Salt and freshly ground black pepper
1.5 ml/¼ tsp turmeric
100 g/4 oz/½ cup butter or block margarine
1 egg yolk
15 ml/1 tbsp cold water
For the filling:
2 chicken portions
300 ml/½ pt/1¼ cups chicken stock
1 bay leaf
1 small green (bell) pepper, halved and thinly sliced
50 g/2 oz button mushrooms, sliced
150 ml/¼ pt/⅔ cup milk
150 ml/¼ pt/⅔ cup single (light) cream
1 hard-boiled (hard-cooked) egg, finely chopped and 30 ml/2 tbsp chopped parsley, to garnish
New potatoes and a tomato salad, to serve

To make the pastry, sift 175 g/6 oz/ 1½ cups of the flour with a pinch of salt and the turmeric into a bowl. Cut 75 g/3 oz/⅓ cup of the butter or margarine into small pieces, add to the flour and rub in with the fingertips until the mixture resembles fine breadcrumbs. Mix together the egg yolk and water and stir unto the mixture to form a firm dough. Knead gently on a lightly floured surface, roll out and use to line a 20 cm/ 8 in square, shallow ovenproof dish. Prick the base with a fork. Fill with crumpled foil and bake in a preheated oven at 200°C/400°F/gas mark 6 for 10 minutes. Remove the foil and return to the oven for 5 minutes to dry out.

Meanwhile, to make the filling, put the chicken in a saucepan with the stock, bay leaf and a little pepper. Bring to the boil, reduce the heat, part-cover and simmer gently for 25 minutes until the chicken is really tender. Lift out of the pan, reserving the stock, discard the skin and cut all the meat off the bones. Cut into neat pieces. Strain the stock into a measuring jug. Melt the remaining butter in a saucepan. Add the green pepper and cook, stirring, for 3–4 minutes. Add the mushrooms and continue cooking for 2 minutes until both are soft. Stir in the remaining flour and cook for 1 minute. Remove from the heat and blend in 150 ml/¼ pt/⅔ cup of the reserved chicken stock and the milk. Return to the heat, bring to the boil and cook for 2 minutes, stirring. Blend in the cream and add the cooked chicken. Season to taste. Turn into the flan case (pie shell). Garnish attractively with the chopped egg and parsley and either serve warm or leave until cold and chill before serving with new potatoes and a tomato salad.

Deep-fried Chicken Parcels

SERVES 4–6

225 g/8 oz/2 cups plain (all-purpose) flour
Salt and freshly ground black pepper
100 g/4 oz/½ cup hard block margarine, diced
175 g/6 oz/1½ cups cooked chicken, finely chopped, all skin removed
15 ml/1 tbsp mayonnaise
15 ml/1 tbsp tomato relish
Oil, for deep-frying
Speciality Creamed Potatoes (page 348) and peas, to serve

Mix the flour and a pinch of salt in a bowl. Add the margarine and rub in with the fingertips until the mixture resembles fine breadcrumbs. Mix with enough cold water to form a firm dough. Knead gently on a lightly floured surface. Roll out to 5 mm/¼ in thick. Cut into 12 squares. Mix the chicken with the mayonnaise, relish and salt and pepper to taste. Divide the mixture between the centres of the pastry (paste). Brush the edges with water. Fold the pastry over the filling and press the edges well together to seal. Pinch all round between the finger and thumb to decorate and further seal. Deep-fry for about 7 minutes until crisp and golden brown. Drain on kitchen paper (paper towels). Serve hot with Speciality Creamed Potatoes and peas.

Arabic Chicken Bloomer

This isn't technically a pastry (paste) dish, but it is a pie of sorts!

SERVES 4

4 small chicken breasts, diced
Juice of ½ lime
300 ml/½ pt/1¼ cups chicken stock
5 ml/1 tsp turmeric
1 green cardamom pod, split
2.5 ml/½ tsp ground cumin
425 g/15 oz/1 large can of chick peas (garbanzos), drained
1 garlic clove, crushed
15 ml/1 tbsp raisins
15 ml/1 tbsp pine nuts
15 ml/1 tbsp chopped mint
15 ml/1 tbsp chopped parsley
Salt and freshly ground black pepper
1 small sesame-seeded bloomer loaf
Tomato, onion and green olive salad, to serve

Put the chicken, lime juice, stock and spices in a saucepan. Bring to the boil, reduce the heat, part-cover and simmer gently for 10 minutes or until the chicken is tender and cooked through. Lift the chicken out of the stock with a draining spoon and reserve. Add the chick peas to the stock with the garlic and raisins and boil rapidly until the liquid has almost evaporated. Stir in the chicken, pine nuts and herbs and season to taste. Cut a thick slice off the top of the loaf and gently pull out some of the soft interior to form a boat. Spoon the hot chicken and chick pea mixture into the bread and replace the lid. Wrap in foil and bake in a preheated oven at 200°C/400°F/gas mark 6 for 5 minutes. Cut into thick chunks and serve with a tomato, onion and green olive salad.

Japanese Chicken Dumplings

SERVES 4

225 g/8 oz/2 cups plain (all-purpose) flour
A pinch of salt
120 ml/4 fl oz/½ cup warm water
450 g/1 lb Chinese leaves (stem lettuce), chopped
225 g/8 oz chicken stir-fry meat, very finely chopped
6 spring onions (scallions), finely chopped
2.5 ml/½ tsp grated fresh root ginger
Soy sauce
15 ml/1 tbsp dry sherry
15 ml/1 tbsp sesame oil
Hot chilli sauce, to serve

Sift the flour and salt into a bowl. Gradually work in the water to form a dough. Knead gently on a lightly floured surface until smooth and elastic and no longer sticky. Cover and leave to rest for 30 minutes. Meanwhile, cook the Chinese leaves in lightly salted boiling water for 3 minutes. Drain and dry on kitchen paper (paper towels). Mix with the chicken, spring onion, ginger, 15 ml/1 tbsp soy sauce, the sherry and oil. Roll out the dough into a long sausage shape. Cut into 50 equal pieces and flatten each, then roll into a 6 cm/2½ in round. Put a small spoonful of filling in the centre of each round. Dampen the edges, fold over and press well together to seal. Drop into a large pan of boiling water, bring to the boil and cook for 5 minutes. Remove from the pan with a draining spoon. Serve with a bowl of soy sauce and a bowl of hot chilli sauce.

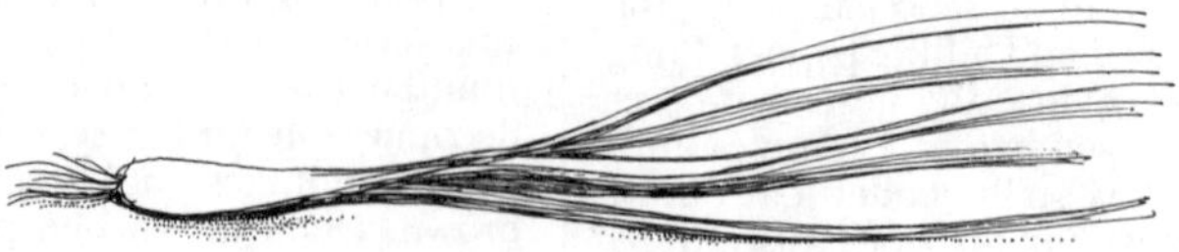

Chicken Liver Morsels

SERVES 4–6

100 g/4 oz/½ cup butter or margarine
100 g/4 oz chicken livers, trimmed and chopped
3 rindless streaky bacon rashers (slices), chopped
1 small onion, finely chopped
25 g/1 oz/¼ cup chopped mixed nuts
2.5 ml/½ tsp dried mixed herbs
30 ml/2 tbsp red wine
50 g/2 oz frozen peas
Salt and freshly ground black pepper
12 sheets of filo pastry (paste)
Parsley sprigs, to garnish

Melt 25 g/1 oz/2 tbsp of the butter or margarine in a saucepan. Add the livers, bacon and onion and fry (sauté) for 2 minutes. Stir in the nuts, herbs, wine and peas and simmer until the liquid has almost evaporated. Season to taste. Melt the remaining butter or margarine. Place the pastry sheets on a work surface. Brush each with a little melted butter or margarine. Fold into halves lengthways and brush again. Spoon the filling towards one end of the strips. Fold the pastry over and over to form rectangular parcels, tucking in the ends. Place on a lightly greased baking (cookie) sheet and brush with any remaining butter or margarine. Bake in a preheated oven at 190°C/375°F/gas mark 5 for about 20 minutes until golden. Serve warm, garnished with parsley.

TURKEY

Boxing Day Pie

SERVES 4–6

225 g/8 oz puff pastry (paste), thawed if frozen
225 g/8 oz/2 cups cooked turkey, diced, all skin removed
100 g/4 oz cooked sausagemeat, cut into pieces
100 g/4 oz cooked stuffing
100g/4 oz button mushrooms, sliced
295 g/10½ oz/1 medium can of condensed mushroom soup
45 ml/3 tbsp Cranberry Sauce (page 339), or use bought)
Freshly ground black pepper
Beaten egg or single (light) cream, to glaze
Royal Roast Potatoes (page 348) and French (green) beans, to serve

Roll out the pastry to slightly larger than the top of a 1.2 litre/2 pt/5 cup pie dish. Put a pie funnel or eggcup in the centre of the dish. Put the turkey, sausagemeat, stuffing and mushrooms in the dish and mix well. Spoon the soup and cranberry sauce over. Cut a strip off the pastry. Dampen the edge of the dish and lay the strip of pastry round the edge. Lay the pastry lid in position, pressing the edge well to seal. Trim, knock up and flute with the back of a knife. Make a slit in the centre to allow steam to escape. Decorate with leaves made out of pastry trimmings. Brush with beaten egg or cream to glaze. Lay the leaves in position and brush again. Bake in a preheated oven at 200°C/400°F/gas mark 6 for about 35 minutes or until puffy, golden brown and piping hot. Serve with Royal Roast Potatoes and French beans.

Turkey Christmas Parcel

SERVES 4–6

For the rough puff pastry (paste):
225 g/8 oz/2 cups plain (all-purpose) flour
A good pinch of salt
1.5 ml/¼ tsp cayenne
15 ml/1 tbsp paprika
100 g/4 oz/1 cup Cheddar cheese, grated
100 g/4 oz/½ cup hard block margarine, cut into chunks
150 ml/¼ pt/⅔ cup ice-cold water
For the filling:
Basic Quick White Sauce (page 340)
5 ml/1 tsp lemon juice
2.5 ml/½ tsp dried thyme
175 g/6 oz/1½ cups cooked turkey, diced, all skin removed
175 g/6 oz cold cooked vegetables, diced
Freshly ground black pepper
1 egg, beaten
Pickles, to serve

To make the pastry, sift the flour, salt, cayenne and paprika into a bowl. Stir in the cheese. Add the lumps of margarine. Using a knife, mix with the cold water to form a very lumpy dough. Use the hands to stick the dough together. Roll out on a lightly floured surface to a rectangle about 2.5 cm/1 in thick. Fold the bottom third up over the pastry, then the top third down over. Press the edges together with the rolling pin to seal then give the dough a quarter turn. Repeat the rolling and folding twice more. Wrap in clingfilm (plastic wrap) and chill for 30 minutes.

Meanwhile, make the filling. Prepare the sauce. Stir in the lemon juice, thyme, turkey and vegetables and season with pepper. Roll and fold the pastry once more, then roll out and trim to a 30 cm/12 in square. Pile the filling in the centre then brush the edges with beaten egg. Fold the pastry over the filling as you would wrap a parcel. Invert on a baking (cookie) sheet. Roll out the trimmings and lay on the parcel to represent ribbon or string. Brush all over with beaten egg and bake in a preheated oven at 220°C/425°F/gas mark 7 for 20 minutes, then reduce the heat to 180°C/350°F/gas mark 4 and continue cooking for 15 minutes until risen, crisp and golden. Transfer to a warm serving plate and serve hot with pickles.

Tempting Turkey Vol-au-vents

SERVES 4

225 g/8 oz frozen puff pastry (paste), thawed
Beaten egg, to glaze
½ quantity of Quick Béchamel Sauce (page 340)
175 g/6 oz/1½ cups cooked turkey, diced, all skin removed
15 ml/1 tbsp crème fraîche
A pinch of dried thyme
15 ml/1 tbsp chopped parsley
Salt and freshly ground black pepper

Roll out the pastry as directed on the packet and cut into four rounds using a 9 cm/3½ in fluted biscuit (cookie) cutter. Place upside-down on a dampened baking (cookie) sheet. Using a 4 cm/1½ in biscuit cutter, mark a circle in the centre of the pastry, cutting only half-way through the pastry. Brush with egg and leave to rest for 30 minutes. Bake in a preheated oven at 220°C/425°F/gas mark 7 for 12–15 minutes until risen, golden and crisp. Carefully lift out the centres of the pastry cases and reserve. Scoop out any uncooked pastry from inside, taking care not to damage the shells. Return to the switched-off oven with the door slightly ajar for 10 minutes to dry out. Meanwhile, to make the sauce, stir together the turkey, crème fraîche, thyme and parsley and season to taste. Heat through gently. Spoon into the hot pastry cases, top with the lids and serve hot.

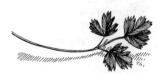

Turkey, Bacon and Egg Pie

SERVES 10–12

700 g/1½ lb lean bacon joint, rind and fat removed and cubed
700 g/1½ lb diced turkey meat
A good pinch of grated nutmeg
Freshly ground black pepper
15 ml/1 tbsp chopped parsley
15 ml/1 tbsp snipped chives
350 g/12 oz/3 cups plain (all-purpose) flour
1.5 ml/¼ tsp salt
175 g/6 oz/¾ cup hard block margarine, diced
60 ml/4 tbsp cold water
6 hard-boiled (hard-cooked) eggs, shelled
1 egg, beaten
300 ml/½ pt/1¼ cups chicken stock
10 ml/2 tsp powdered gelatine

Mix together the bacon and turkey with the nutmeg, a good grinding of pepper and the herbs. Sift the flour and salt into a bowl. Add the margarine and rub in with the fingertips until the mixture resembles fine breadcrumbs. Mix with the water to form a firm dough. Knead gently on a lightly floured surface. Cut the dough in half. Roll out one half and use to line a 1.75 litre/3 pt/7½ cup rectangular ovenproof dish. Put half the meat mixture in the dish. Arrange the hard-boiled eggs in two rows down the length of the dish and cover with the remaining meat mixture. Roll out the remaining pastry (paste) to a rectangle and lay on top for a lid. Trim the edges, knock up and flute with the back of a knife. Make some leaves out of the pastry trimmings and use to decorate the top of the pie. Brush all over with beaten egg to glaze. Make a hole in the centre to allow steam to escape.

Place the pie on a baking (cookie) sheet. Bake in a preheated oven at 200°C/400°F/gas mark 6 for 15 minutes. Reduce the heat to 180°C/350°F/gas mark 4 and cook for a further 45 minutes. Leave to cool. Put 30 ml/2 tbsp of the stock in a small bowl. Sprinkle the gelatine over and leave to soften for 5 minutes. Stand the bowl in a pan of hot water or heat briefly in the microwave to dissolve the gelatine completely. Stir into the remaining stock in a measuring jug. Leave until cold but not set. Carefully and slowly pour the cold stock through the hole in the top of the pie. Chill for at least 3 hours or overnight to set the jelly. Serve cold, cut into thick slices.

Turkey and Stuffing Vol-au-vents

SERVES 4

Prepare as for Tempting Turkey Vol-au-vents, but use 100 g/4 oz/1 cup cooked turkey and 50 g/2 oz chopped cooked stuffing from the bird. Omit the thyme.

Turkey and Cranberry Vol-au-vents

SERVES 4

Prepare as for Tempting Turkey Vol-au-vents, but add 15 ml/1 tbsp cranberry sauce and omit the crème fraîche.

Turkey, Bacon and Mushroom Vol-au-vents

SERVES 4

Prepare as for Tempting Turkey Vol-au-vents, but dry-fry (sauté) 1 rasher (slice) of streaky bacon, finely chopped, and 4 button mushrooms, finely chopped, until tender and use only 100 g/4 oz/1 cup of cooked turkey. Then continue as before, but omit the thyme.

GAME

Pheasant and Steak Pudding

Once you have taken off the meat, use the pheasant carcass for stock for this recipe or Game Soup (page 63).

SERVES 6–8

1 small oven-ready pheasant
225 g/8 oz braising steak, all fat removed
350 g/12 oz/3 cups self-raising (self-rising) flour
Salt and freshly ground black pepper
175 g/6 oz/1½ cups shredded suet
1 onion, thinly sliced
100 g/4 oz button mushrooms, sliced
2.5 ml/½ tsp dried mixed herbs
300 ml/½ pt/1½ cups red wine
15 ml/1 tbsp brandy
300 ml/½ pt/1¼ cups pheasant, beef or chicken stock
Broccoli and baby carrots, to serve

Cut all the meat off the pheasant and cut into neat pieces, discarding the skin. Cut the steak into strips. Sift the flour with 5 ml/1 tsp salt in a bowl. Stir in the suet. Mix with enough cold water to form a soft but not sticky dough. Knead gently on a lightly floured surface. Cut off a third and reserve for a lid. Roll out the remainder and use to line a 1.75 litre/3 pt/7½ cup pudding basin. Put a layer of half the steak in the pudding basin. Top with half the onion slices, then half the pheasant, then half the mushrooms, seasoning with a little salt and pepper between each layer. Sprinkle with half the herbs. Repeat the layers and seasoning. Pour in the wine and brandy. Add enough of the stock to just cover the ingredients. Roll out the remaining dough, dampen the edge and place in position, pressing the edges together to seal. Cover with a double thickness of greased greaseproof (waxed) paper, with a pleat in the middle to allow for rising, twisting and folding under the rim to secure. Steam for 3 hours, topping up with boiling water as necessary. Remove the paper. Either tie a napkin round the basin and serve, or loosen the edges and turn the pudding out on to a shallow serving dish. Serve with fresh broccoli and baby carrots.

Game Pie

SERVES 4–6

85 g/3½ oz/1 packet of parsley and thyme stuffing mix
For the pastry (paste):
225 g/8 oz/2 cups plain (all-purpose) flour
Salt and freshly ground black pepper
100 g/4 oz/½ cup butter or margarine, diced
For the filling:
225 g/8 oz/2 cups cooked pheasant, diced, all skin removed
225 g/8 oz/2 cups cooked turkey or chicken, diced, all skin removed
4 streaky bacon rashers (slices), rinded and diced
100 g/4 oz button mushrooms, sliced
300 ml/½ pt/1¼ cups gravy or chicken stock
15 ml/1 tbsp cornflour (cornstarch)
15 ml/1 tbsp redcurrant jelly (clear conserve)
Beaten egg, to glaze
New potatoes and a mixed salad, to serve

Make up the stuffing mix with boiling water according to the packet directions. When cool enough to handle, shape into 12 small balls. To make the pastry, sift the flour and a pinch of salt into a bowl. Add the butter or margarine and rub in with the fingertips until the mixture resembles fine breadcrumbs. Mix with enough water to form a firm dough. Knead gently on a lightly floured surface. Cut into halves. Roll out one half and use to line a 23 cm/9 in pie dish. Put a pie funnel or upturned egg cup in the centre.

Put half the pheasant and turkey in the dish. Scatter with half the bacon and mushrooms. Arrange the stuffing balls in a layer over. Top with the remaining pheasant, turkey, bacon and mushrooms. Blend the gravy or stock with the cornflour and redcurrant jelly. Pour into the dish and season well with pepper. Roll out the remaining pastry. Brush the edges with water and place the pastry lid in position, pressing the edges well together to seal. Trim, knock up and flute with the back of a knife. Make a slit in the centre to allow steam to escape and make a rose and leaves out of pastry trimmings. Brush the top of the pie with egg. Put the rose and leaves in the centre and brush these with egg. Bake in a preheated oven at 200°C/400°F/gas mark 6 for about 40 minutes until golden brown and piping hot throughout. Serve with new potatoes and a mixed salad.

Raised Game Pie

SERVES 6–8

For the hot water pastry (paste):
350 g/12 oz/3 cups plain (all-purpose) flour
2.5 ml/½ tsp salt
1 egg yolk
60 ml/4 tbsp milk
60 ml/4 tbsp water
100 g/4 oz/½ cup white vegetable fat
For the filling:
225 g/8 oz pork sausagemeat
450 g/1 lb game (pheasant, partridge, pigeon etc., or a mixture), boned
350 g/12 oz frying (sautéing) steak, diced
100 g/4 oz raw ham, diced
1 onion, chopped
1.5 ml/¼ tsp dried sage
1.5 ml/¼ tsp dried thyme
30 ml/2 tbsp chopped parsley
Salt and freshly ground black pepper
300 ml/½ pt/1¼ cups Game Carcass Stock, made with the bones (page 63)
Beaten egg, to glaze
10 ml/2 tsp powdered gelatine
Pickles and salads, to serve

To make the pastry, sift the flour and salt into a bowl. Make a well in the centre. Beat the egg yolk and 15 ml/1 tbsp of the milk together and pour in. Warm the remaining milk, water and fat in a saucepan until the fat melts. Bring to the boil. Pour into the flour. Work with a wooden spoon until the mixture forms a dough. Knead gently on a lightly floured surface. Place in a plastic bag and leave to stand for 30 minutes.

Roll out two-thirds of the pastry and use to line a raised pie mould or an 18 cm/7 in loose-bottomed cake tin (pan). Press out the sausagemeat to a suitable size and place in the lined tin. Mix the other meats with the onion and herbs, season with a very little salt and a good grinding of pepper and place in the tin. Add half the Game Carcass Stock. Roll out the remaining pastry to the right shape to use as a lid. Brush the edges with water. Press the lid in position and trim. Crimp between finger and thumb. Brush all over the top with beaten egg. Decorate with leaves made out of the trimmings and brush again. Make a hole in the centre to allow steam to escape. Place on a baking (cookie) sheet and bake in a preheated oven at 200°C/ 400°F/gas mark 6 for 30 minutes until lightly browned. Reduce the heat to 180°C/350°F/gas mark 4 and continue cooking for 2 hours. Cover the top lightly with foil if over-browning. Remove from the oven.

Sprinkle the gelatine over the remaining stock in a measuring jug. Leave to soften for 5 minutes, then stand the bowl in a pan of hot water or heat briefly in the microwave until dissolved. Carefully pour the stock through the hole in the centre of the pie. Leave in the tin to cool completely, then chill overnight. Remove the mould or tin and serve sliced with pickles and salads.

Yorkshire Pigeon Pie

SERVES 6

2 oven-ready pigeons, quartered (page 17)
1 small gammon steak, about 100 g/ 4 oz, cut into thin strips
225 g/8 oz lean sirloin steak, thinly sliced
2 hard-boiled (hard-cooked) eggs, quartered
Salt and freshly ground black pepper
450 ml/¾ pt/2 cups chicken or game stock
5 ml/1 tsp beef extract
15 ml/1 tbsp brandy
15 ml/1 tbsp chopped parsley
375 g/13 oz/1 block of frozen puff pastry (paste), thawed
Beaten egg, to glaze
Speciality Creamed Potatoes (page 348), buttered Brussels sprouts and redcurrant jelly (clear conserve), to serve

Layer the pigeons, meats and eggs in a pie dish, seasoning between each layer. Blend the stock with the beef extract, brandy and parsley and pour over. Roll out the pastry to just larger than the pie dish. Cut a strip off the edge. Brush the edge of the dish with water and lay the strip in position. Brush again with water. Top with the pastry lid. Knock up, trim and flute with the back of a knife. Make a hole in the centre to allow steam to escape. Mark the top gently with the back of a knife in a criss-cross pattern. Transfer the pie on a baking (cookie) sheet and brush with egg to glaze. Bake in a preheated oven at 200°C/400°F/gas mark 6 for 25 minutes until golden. Reduce the heat to 150°C/300°F/gas mark 2 and cook for a further 1½ hours, covering the top loosely with foil if over-browning. Serve hot with Speciality Creamed Potatoes, buttered sprouts and redcurrant jelly.

Saxon Partridge and Oyster Pudding

SERVES 4–6

225 g/8 oz/2 cups self-raising (self-rising) flour
Salt and freshly ground black pepper
100 g/4 oz/1 cup shredded suet
1 large oven-ready partridge, cut into 6 pieces (page 15)
175 g/6 oz rump steak, diced
15 ml/1 tbsp cornflour (cornstarch)
6 fresh oysters
15 ml/1 tbsp chopped parsley
15 ml/1 tbsp chopped thyme
1 wineglass of ruby port
300 ml/½ pt/1¼ cups chicken stock
Plain boiled potatoes and sugar snap peas, to serve

Sift the flour and a good pinch of salt into a bowl. Add the suet. Mix with enough cold water to form a soft but not sticky dough. Knead gently on a lightly floured surface. Cut off a third to use as a lid. Roll out the remainder and use to line a 1.2 litre/2 pt/5 cup pudding basin. Dust the partridge and steak with the cornflour mixed with a little salt and pepper. Carefully open the oysters, reserving the juice. Layer the steak and partridge in the basin with the oysters and their juice. Add the herbs and season lightly. Pour on the port and enough of the stock to fill the basin. Roll out the remaining dough to use as a lid. Brush with water and place in position, pressing the edges well together to seal. Cover with a double thickness of greased greaseproof (waxed) paper, with a pleat in the centre to allow for rising, twisting and folding under the rim to secure. Steam for 3 hours, topping up with boiling water as necessary. Loosen the edge, turn out and serve with plain boiled potatoes and sugar snap peas.

Saxon Partridge and Mushroom Pudding

SERVES 4–6

Prepare as for Saxon Partridge and Oyster Pudding, but substitute halved mushrooms for the oysters and a full-bodied red wine for the port.

Pigeon Pie

Use the carcasses for Game Soup (page 63)

SERVES 4

4 oven-ready pigeons
225 g/8 oz pork shoulder steak
1 onion, chopped
25 g/1 oz/2 tbsp butter or margarine
2 hard-boiled (hard-cooked) eggs, quartered
100 g/4 oz/1 cup cooked ham pieces, cut into neat pieces, all gristle removed
30 ml/2 tbsp plain (all-purpose) flour
300 ml/½ pt/1¼ cups pork or chicken stock
30 ml/2 tbsp redcurrant jelly (clear conserve)
2.5 ml/½ tsp dried sage
Salt and freshly ground black pepper
225 g/8 oz puff pastry (paste), thawed if frozen
Beaten egg, to glaze
Mangetout (snow peas), to serve

Cut as much meat as possible off the pigeons, discarding any sinews. Cut into chunks. Cut the pork into bite-sized chunks. Brown the onion in the butter or margarine in a frying pan (skillet). Remove from the pan with a draining spoon and place in a 1.2 litre/2 pt/5 cup pie dish. Brown the pigeon and pork in the butter or margarine, then transfer to the dish. Add the eggs and ham. Blend the flour into the remaining butter or margarine in the pan. Gradually stir in the stock and redcurrant jelly. Bring to the boil and cook for 2 minutes, stirring. Pour into the dish and season with the sage and a little salt and pepper. Brush the edge of the dish with water. Roll out the pastry. Cut off a strip and lay it around the edge of the dish. Brush with water again. Top with the pastry, trim, knock up and flute with the back of a knife. Make a slit in the centre to allow steam to escape. Make some shapes out of the trimmings and use to decorate the pie. Brush all over with beaten egg. Bake in a preheated oven at 200°C/400°F/gas mark 6 for 30 minutes, then reduce the heat to 180°C/350°F/gas mark 4 and bake for a further 30 minutes or until the pigeons and pork are tender. Serve hot with mangetout.

Squab Pie

SERVES 4

Prepare as for Pigeon Pie, but substitute 4 oven-ready squab for the pigeons.

Casseroles

Casseroles were traditionally cooked in the oven, often using tougher cuts of meat, requiring long, slow cooking. But today a casserole can be any dish cooked in a sauce in a casserole dish (Dutch oven), whether on top of the stove or in the oven. Here is a selection of good, old-fashioned casseroles – which you can't beat for richness of flavour – and some of the much quicker, modern-style top-of-the-stove recipes. Don't forget, if you are cooking it on top of the stove, the casserole dish must be flameproof not just ovenproof.

CHICKEN

Lemon Chicken

SERVES 4

4 skinless chicken breasts
300 ml/½ pt/1¼ cups chicken stock
Finely grated rind and juice of 1 small lemon
30 ml/2 tbsp clear honey
1 bay leaf
Salt and freshly ground black pepper
15 ml/1 tbsp cornflour (cornstarch)
15 ml/1 tbsp cold water
30 ml/2 tbsp double (heavy) cream
30 ml/2 tbsp chopped parsley
Wild Rice Mix (page 352) and leaf spinach, to serve

Put the chicken breasts in a flameproof casserole (Dutch oven). Add the stock, lemon rind and juice, honey, bay leaf, salt and lots of pepper. Bring to the boil, reduce the heat, cover and cook very gently for 15 minutes. Remove the bay leaf, then carefully lift out the chicken breasts. Blend the cornflour with the water and stir into the cooking juices. Bring to the boil and cook for 1 minute, stirring. Stir in the cream. Return the chicken to the sauce and heat through. Sprinkle the parsley over and serve with Wild Rice Mix and leaf spinach.

Pink Grapefruit and Chive Chicken

SERVES 4

Prepare as for Lemon Chicken, but substitute the finely grated rind and juice of ½ pink grapefruit for the lemon and snipped chives for the parsley. Serve with Speciality Creamed Potatoes (page 348) and mangetout (snow peas).

White Chicken and Bacon Casserole

SERVES 4

4 chicken portions
50 g/2 oz/¼ cup butter or margarine
15 ml/1 tbsp sunflower oil
3 large onions, thinly sliced
4 rindless streaky bacon rashers (slices), diced
40 g/1½ oz/⅓ cup plain (all-purpose) flour
600 ml/1 pt/2½ cups milk
1 chicken stock cube
1 bouquet garni sachet
Salt and freshly ground black pepper
100 g/4 oz small button mushrooms
30 ml/2 tbsp double (heavy) cream
30 ml/2 tbsp chopped parsley, to garnish
Speciality Creamed Potatoes (page 348) and peas, to serve

Wipe the chicken portions with kitchen paper (paper towels). Melt half the butter or margarine and the oil in a frying pan (skillet). Add the chicken and brown on all sides. Remove the chicken and place in a flameproof casserole (Dutch oven). Add the onions and bacon and fry (sauté) gently for 2 minutes. Add to the chicken. Melt the remaining butter or margarine in the frying pan. Add the flour and cook for 1 minute. Remove from the heat. Gradually blend in the milk. Return to the heat, crumble in the stock cube and add the bouquet garni. Bring to the boil, stirring. Season to taste and pour over the chicken. Add the mushrooms to the casserole. Cover and cook in a moderate oven at 180°C/ 350°F/gas mark 4 for 1 hour. Stir in the cream and bring to the boil again. Remove the bouquet garni. Taste and re-season. Sprinkle with the parsley and serve with Speciality Creamed Potatoes and peas.

Pot Roast Chicken with Orange and Pecans

SERVES 4

1 bunch of spring onions (scallions), chopped
2 carrots, sliced
15 ml/1 tbsp sunflower oil
4 chicken portions
Finely grated rind and juice of 1 orange
300 ml/½ pt/1¼ cups chicken stock
50 g/2 oz/½ cup pecan nuts
1 bouquet garni sachet
Salt and freshly ground black pepper
10 ml/2 tsp cornflour (cornstarch)
15 ml/1 tbsp brandy or water
Jacket-baked potatoes and peas, to serve

Fry (sauté) the spring onions and carrots in the oil in a flameproof casserole (Dutch oven) for 2 minutes. Top with the chicken portions. Blend the orange rind and juice with the stock and pour over. Add the pecans and bouquet garni. Season lightly. Cover and cook in a preheated oven at 190°C/375°F/gas mark 5 for 1 hour. Discard the bouquet garni. Lift the chicken out of the casserole and transfer to warm plates. Keep warm. Blend the cornflour with the brandy or water and stir into the casserole. Bring to the boil and cook for 1 minute, stirring. Taste and re-season if necessary. Spoon the sauce over and serve with jacket-baked potatoes and peas.

Pot Roast Chicken with Tomatoes and Cashew Nuts

SERVES 4

Prepare as for Pot Roast Chicken with Orange and Pecans, but substitute 2 beefsteak tomatoes, skinned, seeded and chopped, for the orange rind and juice and raw cashew nuts for the pecans. Use medium-dry sherry instead of brandy to mix with the cornflour.

Chilli con Pollo

SERVES 4

225 g/8 oz minced (ground) chicken
1 large onion, chopped
30 ml/2 tbsp sunflower oil
5 ml/1 tsp chilli powder
5 ml/1 tsp ground cumin
5 ml/1 tsp dried oregano
450 ml/¾ pt/2 cups passata (sieved tomatoes)
2 × 425 g/2 × 15 oz/2 large cans of red kidney beans, drained
15 ml/1 tbsp tomato purée (paste)
Salt and freshly ground black pepper
Plain Boiled Rice (page 351), shredded lettuce and grated Cheddar cheese, to serve

Fry (sauté) the chicken and onion in the oil, stirring, for 5 minutes until the chicken is no longer pink and all the grains are separate. Stir in the chilli, cumin and oregano and cook for a further 1 minute. Stir in the passata, beans, tomato purée and a little salt and pepper. Simmer for 20 minutes, stirring occasionally. Serve on a bed of Plain Boiled Rice with shredded lettuce and grated Cheddar cheese.

Enchiladas

SERVES 4

Prepare as for Chilli con Pollo, but roll up the chilli mixture in 8 large flour tortillas and lay them in an ovenproof dish. Sprinkle liberally with grated Cheddar cheese, cover with foil and bake in a preheated oven at 190°C/375°F/gas mark 5 for 20 minutes. Serve with shredded lettuce and chilli relish.

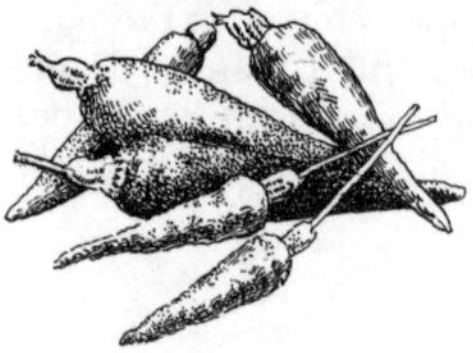

Crispy Tacos

SERVES 4

1 quantity of Chilli con Pollo
1 box of crispy corn tacos
Shredded lettuce, chopped tomato, cucumber and onion, soured (dairy sour) cream and grated Cheddar cheese, to serve

Prepare the Chilli con Pollo. Warm the tacos as directed on the packet. Fill with the chilli and top with a little lettuce, chopped tomato, cucumber and onion, a small spoonful of soured cream and a little grated cheese.

Chicken Veronique

SERVES 4

4 chicken portions
45 ml/3 tbsp plain (all-purpose) flour
Salt and freshly ground black pepper
15 g/½ oz/1 tbsp unsalted (sweet) butter
15 ml/1 tbsp sunflower oil
1 onion, finely chopped
300 ml/½ pt/1¼ cups medium-dry white wine
15 ml/1 tbsp chopped tarragon
150 ml/¼ pt/⅔ cup single (light) cream
100 g/4 oz seedless white grapes, halved
A sprig of tarragon, to garnish
Speciality Creamed Potatoes (page 348), baby carrots and baby corn cobs, to serve

Wipe the chicken with kitchen paper (paper towels), then toss in 15 ml/1 tbsp of the flour, seasoned with a little salt and pepper. Heat the butter and oil in a flameproof casserole (Dutch oven) and brown the chicken on all sides. Remove from the dish. Add the onion and cook gently for 3 minutes until a pale golden brown. Add the remaining flour and cook, stirring, for 1 minute. Remove from the heat and gradually blend in the wine. Return to the heat, bring to the boil and cook for 1 minute, stirring. Add the tarragon. Return the chicken to the pan and season with salt and pepper. Cover and cook in a preheated oven at 190°C/375°F/gas mark 5 for 1 hour until the chicken is tender. Transfer the chicken with a draining spoon to a warm serving dish. Stir the cream into the casserole with most of the grapes. Heat through but do not boil. Taste and re-season, if necessary. Pour over the chicken and garnish with the remaining grapes and a sprig of tarragon. Serve with Speciality Creamed Potatoes, baby carrots and baby corn cobs.

Chicken Averonique

SERVES 4

Prepare as for Chicken Veronique, but use red wine instead of white and red grapes instead of white. Flavour with 2.5 ml/½ tsp dried mixed herbs instead of the tarragon and garnish with watercress instead of the tarragon sprig.

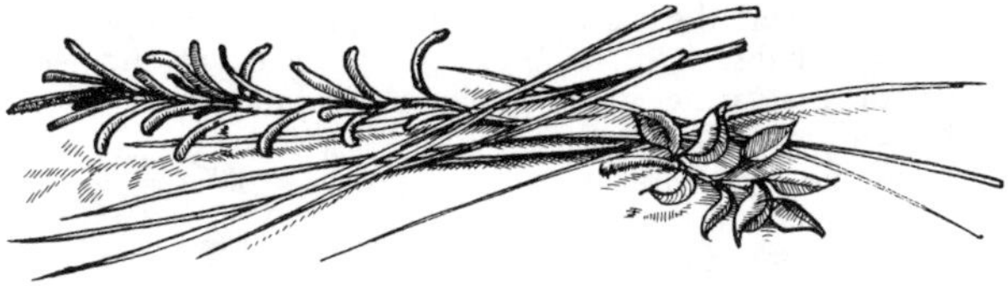

Chicken Fricassee

SERVES 4

40 g/1½ oz/3 tbsp butter or margarine
15 ml/1 tbsp sunflower oil
4 chicken portions, each cut into 2 pieces, all skin removed
2 onions, chopped
2 celery sticks, chopped
1 large turnip, diced
7.5 ml/1½ tsp dried thyme
Finely grated rind and juice of 1 small lemon
600 ml/1 pt/2½ cups chicken stock
30 ml/2 tbsp plain (all-purpose) flour
Salt and white pepper
75 g/3 oz/1½ cups white breadcrumbs
30 ml/2 tbsp chopped parsley
1 egg, beaten
45 ml/3 tbsp crème fraîche
Speciality Creamed Potatoes (page 348) and carrots, to serve

Melt 25 g/1 oz/2 tbsp of the butter or margarine and the oil in a large frying pan (skillet). Add the chicken and cook quickly on all sides to seal without browning. Transfer to a large casserole (Dutch oven). Add one of the onions to the frying pan with the celery and turnip, cover and cook gently for 5 minutes until soft but not brown. Add to the chicken. Sprinkle with half the thyme, half the lemon rind and all the lemon juice. Blend a little of the stock with the flour until smooth, add the remaining stock and pour into the frying pan. Bring to the boil, stirring. Pour over the chicken. Season with salt and pepper. Cover and cook in a preheated oven at 180°C/350°F/gas mark 4 for 45 minutes. Meanwhile, mix the breadcrumbs with the remaining onion, remaining thyme, the parsley and some seasoning. Mix with the egg to bind. Shape into small balls. Melt the remaining butter or margarine in a frying pan and brown the stuffing balls quickly all over. Stir the crème fraîche into the casserole, top with the stuffing balls, re-cover and cook for a further 30 minutes. Serve hot with Speciality Creamed Potatoes and carrots.

Blanquette of Chicken

SERVES 4

1.5 kg/3 lb oven-ready chicken
300 ml/½ pt/1¼ cups chicken stock
300 ml/½ pt/1¼ cups milk
100 g/4 oz rindless streaky bacon, diced
1 large onion
2 cloves
A good pinch of grated nutmeg
1 bouquet garni sachet
Salt and white pepper
25 g/1 oz/2 tbsp butter or margarine, softened
25 g/1 oz/¼ cup plain (all-purpose) flour
2 egg yolks
10 ml/2 tsp lemon juice
Chopped parsley and lemon twists, to garnish
Plain boiled potatoes, to serve

Cut the chicken into quarters, then each quarter into two pieces (page 15). Remove as much skin as possible. Put the pieces in a large flameproof casserole (Dutch oven) with the stock, milk and bacon. Stud the onion with the cloves and add to the pan with the nutmeg and bouquet garni. Season with a little salt and pepper. Bring to the boil, reduce the heat, cover and simmer gently for 1¼ hours until the chicken is really tender. Lift the chicken out of the cooking liquid and keep warm in a shallow serving dish. Mash the butter or margarine with the flour until smooth. Gradually whisk into the cooking liquid over a moderate heat until thickened and boiling, whisking all the time. Leave to cool slightly. Lightly beat the egg yolks with the lemon juice. Whisk into the sauce but do not boil again. Taste and re-season. Pour over the chicken and sprinkle with chopped parsley. Add a few lemon twists and serve hot with plain boiled potatoes.

Coq au Vin

SERVES 4

4 chicken portions
45 ml/3 tbsp olive oil
15 g/½ oz/1 tbsp unsalted (sweet) butter
100 g/4 oz rindless streaky bacon, diced
12 button (pearl) onions
25 g/1 oz/¼ cup plain (all-purpose) flour
300 ml/½ pt/1¼ cups red wine
150 ml/¼ pt/⅔ cup chicken stock
100 g/4 oz button mushrooms
Salt and freshly ground black pepper
15 ml/1 tbsp brandy
1 bouquet garni sachet
2 slices of white bread, crusts removed
Watercress sprigs, to garnish
French bread and a crisp green salad, to serve

Wipe the chicken with kitchen paper (paper towels). Heat 15 ml/1 tbsp of the oil with the butter in a large flameproof casserole (Dutch oven). Brown the chicken portions on all sides and remove. Add the bacon and onions and brown quickly. Remove from the pan with a draining spoon. Blend the flour into the cooking juices and cook for 1 minute, stirring. Remove from the heat and gradually blend in the wine and stock. Return to the heat and bring to the boil, stirring. Return the chicken, onions and bacon to the casserole and add the mushrooms. Season and add the brandy and bouquet garni. Cover and cook in a preheated oven at 180°C/350°F/gas mark 4 for 1 hour. Meanwhile, cut each bread slice into four triangles. Fry (sauté) the bread in a frying pan (skillet) in the remaining oil until golden brown on both sides. Drain on kitchen paper. When the chicken is cooked, stir gently, remove the bouquet garni sachet, taste and re-season if necessary. Arrange the fried bread triangles around the edge of the casserole, garnish with watercress sprigs and serve hot with French bread and a crisp green salad.

Coq au Vin Blanc

SERVES 4

Prepare as for Coq au Vin, but use a fruity white wine instead of red, thin strips of salami instead of the bacon and 50 g/2 oz stoned (pitted) black olives, sliced, instead of the mushrooms.

Quick Italian Chicken Casserole

SERVES 4

4 skinless chicken breasts
295 g/10½ oz/1 medium can of condensed cream of tomato soup
2.5 ml/½ tsp dried basil
Freshly ground black pepper
Buttered noodles and broccoli, to serve

Put the chicken breasts in a flameproof casserole (Dutch oven). Spoon over the soup. Half-fill the can with water and pour over. Add the basil and lots of pepper. Bring to the boil, reduce the heat, cover and cook gently for 20 minutes, stirring gently occasionally, until the chicken is cooked through and is bathed in a rich tomato sauce. Serve the chicken with buttered noodles and broccoli.

Quick French Chicken Casserole

SERVES 4

Prepare as for Quick Italian Chicken Casserole, but use a can of condensed mushroom soup instead of the tomato, add 15 ml/1 tbsp brandy and dried mixed herbs instead of basil. Add a few sliced mushrooms, too, if liked.

Chicken Crumble Casserole

SERVES 4

10 g/¼ oz/2 tsp butter or margarine
4 skinless chicken breasts
200 g/7 oz/1 small can of sweetcorn (corn)
295 g/10½ oz/1 medium can of condensed chicken soup
15 ml/1 tbsp lemon juice
30 ml/2 tbsp water
85 g/3½ oz/1 small packet of parsley and thyme stuffing mix
1 small red (bell) pepper, cut into thin strips
Plain boiled potatoes and French (green) beans, to serve

Heat the butter or margarine in a flameproof casserole (Dutch oven) and brown the chicken on both sides. Pour off any remaining fat. Mix the contents of the can of corn with the soup, lemon juice and water. Pour over the chicken. Bring to the boil, cover, reduce the heat and simmer for 15–20 minutes until the chicken is tender. Meanwhile, make up the stuffing mix with enough boiling water to form a moist crumble. Scatter over the chicken and arrange the pepper strips in a criss-cross pattern on top. Place under a moderate grill (broiler) for about 10 minutes until golden. Serve hot with plain boiled potatoes and French beans.

Chicken, Aubergine and Pine Nut Casserole

SERVES 4

1 large aubergine (eggplant), sliced
4 chicken portions
30 ml/2 tbsp olive oil
1 onion, finely chopped
50 g/2 oz/½ cup pine nuts
15 ml/1 tbsp tomato purée (paste)
15 ml/1 tbsp lemon juice
300 ml/½ pt/1¼ cups chicken stock
2.5 ml/½ tsp dried oregano
5 ml/1 tsp clear honey
Salt and freshly ground black pepper
Plain Boiled Rice (page 351), to serve

Boil the aubergine in lightly salted water for 3 minutes or until almost tender. Drain. Meanwhile, brown the chicken in the olive oil in a flameproof casserole (Dutch oven). Remove from the pan with a draining spoon. Fry (sauté) the onion in the casserole for 2 minutes to soften. Add the aubergine, then the remaining ingredients. Bring to the boil, stirring. Return the chicken to the pan, cover and cook in a preheated oven at 180°C/350°F/gas mark 4 for 1½ hours until the chicken is really tender. Serve with Plain Boiled Rice.

Mediterranean Chicken Casserole

SERVES 4

1 onion, thinly sliced
1 aubergine (eggplant), sliced
1 green (bell) pepper, sliced
2 courgettes (zucchini), sliced
1 large garlic clove, crushed
30 ml/2 tbsp olive oil
400 g/14 oz/1 large can of chopped tomatoes
Salt and freshly ground black pepper
1 bouquet garni sachet
250 ml/8 fl oz/1 cup red wine
15 ml/1 tbsp tomato purée (paste)
4 skinless chicken breasts
Plain boiled potatoes and a green salad, to serve

Fry (sauté) the onion, aubergine, green pepper, courgettes and garlic in the oil in a large flameproof casserole (Dutch oven) for 5 minutes, stirring all the time. Add the tomatoes, some salt and pepper, the bouquet garni, wine and tomato purée. Stir well. Tuck the chicken breasts into the mixture so they are completely covered. Cover and cook over a gentle heat for 40 minutes. Remove the bouquet garni, taste and re-season if necessary. If there is too much liquid, boil rapidly for a few minutes to reduce slightly, then serve with plain boiled potatoes and a green salad.

Brittany Chicken

SERVES 4

8 chicken drumsticks, skin removed, if preferred
20 g/¾ oz/1½ tbsp unsalted (sweet) butter
15 ml/1 tbsp olive oil
1 onion, chopped
25 g/1 oz/¼ cup plain (all-purpose) flour
30 ml/2 tbsp tomato purée (paste)
150 ml/¼ pt/⅔ cup medium-sweet cider
150 ml/¼ pt/⅔ cup chicken stock
400 g/14 oz/1 large can of chopped tomatoes
425 g/15 oz/1 large can of artichoke hearts, drained and halved
25 g/1 oz stoned (pitted) green olives
Salt and freshly ground black pepper
A few sprigs of flatleaf parsley, to garnish
Brown Rice (page 351), to serve

Brown the chicken in the butter and oil in a flameproof casserole (Dutch oven). Remove from the pan. Add the onion to the casserole and cook for 3 minutes until lightly browned. Stir in the flour and cook for 1 minute. Remove from the heat and blend in the tomato purée, cider, stock and tomatoes. Return to the heat and bring to the boil, stirring. Return the chicken to the pan and add the artichokes and olives. Season to taste. Cover and cook in a preheated oven at 180°C/350°F/gas mark 4 for 1½ hours until the chicken is really tender. Spoon on to a bed of Brown Rice and garnish with flatleaf parsley before serving.

Herb-stuffed Chicken Rolls

SERVES 4

40 g/1½ oz/¾ cup white breadcrumbs
30 ml/2 tbsp chopped parsley
15 ml/1 tbsp chopped basil
15 ml/1 tbsp chopped thyme
Salt and freshly ground black pepper
1 egg, beaten
4 small skinless chicken breasts
300 ml/½ pt/1¼ cups chicken stock
15 ml/1 tbsp cornflour (cornstarch)
30 ml/2 tbsp single (light) cream
New potatoes, courgettes (zucchini) and carrots, to serve

Mix the breadcrumbs with the herbs and some salt and pepper. Stir in the egg to bind. Halve each chicken breast lengthways with a sharp knife to make eight thin slices. Spread the stuffing over each slice and roll up. Secure with cocktail sticks (toothpicks). Place in a flameproof casserole (Dutch oven) and add the stock. Bring to the boil, reduce the heat, cover and cook for 15 minutes or until cooked through. Drain, place on warm serving plates and remove the cocktail sticks. Keep warm. Blend the cornflour with the cream and stir into the stock. Bring to the boil and simmer for 2 minutes. Taste and add more seasoning if necessary. Pour over the chicken and serve with new potatoes, courgettes and carrots.

Polonaise Chicken

SERVES 4

4 chicken portions
60 ml/4 tbsp plain (all-purpose) flour
Salt and freshly ground black pepper
45 ml/3 tbsp olive oil
1 onion finely chopped
1 garlic clove, crushed
100 g/4 oz button mushrooms, sliced
300 ml/½ pt/1¼ cups dry white wine
150 ml/¼ pt/⅔ cups chicken stock
5 ml/1 tsp saffron powder
1 bouquet garni sachet
30 ml/2 tbsp breadcrumbs, toasted
30 ml/2 tbsp chopped parsley
1 hard-boiled (hard-cooked) egg, chopped
Buttered noodles and a green salad, to serve

Toss the chicken portions in half the flour, seasoned with a little salt and pepper. Heat 30 ml/2 tbsp of the oil in a flameproof casserole (Dutch oven). Brown the chicken on all sides and remove. Heat the remaining oil in the casserole and fry (sauté) the onion, garlic and mushrooms for 2 minutes. Stir in any remaining flour. Pour in the wine and stir well. Return the chicken to the casserole dish. Blend the stock with the saffron and pour over. Add the bouquet garni and season lightly. Bring to the boil, stir, cover and transfer to a preheated oven at 180°C/350°F/gas mark 4 for 1½ hours. Stir well, remove the bouquet garni, taste and re-season, if necessary. Transfer the chicken and sauce to four serving plates. Mix together the breadcrumbs, parsley and egg and sprinkle over. Serve straight away with buttered noodles and a green salad.

Chicken Paprika

SERVES 4

2 onions, sliced
25 g/1 oz/2 tbsp butter or margarine
4 skinless chicken breasts, about 175 g/6 oz each
30 ml/2 tbsp paprika
400 g/14 oz/1 large can of chopped tomatoes
228 g/8 oz/1 small can of pimientos, drained and chopped
Salt and freshly ground black pepper
45 ml/3 tbsp thick plain yoghurt
Chopped parsley, to garnish
Buttered noodles, sprinkled with caraway seeds, and a green salad, to serve

Fry (sauté) the onions in the butter or margarine in a flameproof casserole (Dutch oven) for 2 minutes. Add the chicken breasts and fry on each side to brown. Add the remaining ingredients except the yoghurt. Bring to the boil, reduce the heat, part-cover and simmer for 10 minutes. Remove the lid and simmer for a further 10 minutes. Taste and re-season if necessary. Remove the chicken and transfer to warm serving plates. Stir the yoghurt into the sauce. Do not re-boil. Spoon over, garnish with chopped parsley and serve with buttered noodles sprinkled with caraway seeds and a green salad.

Braised Chicken in Black Bean Sauce

SERVES 4

350 g/12 oz chicken stir-fry meat
10 ml/2 tsp cornflour (cornstarch)
30 ml/2 tbsp black bean sauce
1 large garlic clove, crushed
2.5 cm/1 in piece of fresh root ginger, grated
60 ml/4 tbsp soy sauce
60 ml/4 tbsp medium-dry sherry
45 ml/3 tbsp clear honey
45 ml/3 tbsp sunflower oil
300 ml/½ pt/1¼ cups chicken stock
100 g/4 oz closed-cup mushrooms, thickly sliced
5 cm/2 in piece of cucumber, finely chopped, to garnish
Plain Boiled Rice (page 351) and Chinese Chilli Dipping Sauce (page 337), to serve

Mix the chicken with the remaining ingredients except the oil, stock and mushrooms. Leave to marinate for 1 hour. Heat the oil in a flameproof casserole (Dutch oven). Add the chicken and fry (sauté), stirring, for 3 minutes. Add the stock and mushrooms. Bring to the boil, cover and simmer gently for 30 minutes. Spoon on to a bed of Plain Boiled Rice in warm bowls. Sprinkle with the cucumber and drizzle with a little Chilli Dipping Sauce before serving.

Chicken Pimenton

You can use paprika if you cannot find pimenton spice locally.

SERVES 4

4 chicken portions
50 g/2 oz/¼ cup butter or margarine
1 onion, chopped
60 ml/4 tbsp flaked (slivered) almonds
30 ml/2 tbsp plain (all-purpose) flour
15 ml/1 tbsp pimenton
200 ml/7 fl oz/scant 1 cup chicken stock
300 ml/½ pt/1¼ cups soured (dairy sour) cream
Salt and freshly ground black pepper
1 red (bell) pepper, cut into thin strips
Plain Boiled Rice (page 351), sprinkled with fennel seeds, to serve

Brown the chicken portions in half the butter or margarine in a flameproof casserole (Dutch oven). Remove from the pan. Melt the remaining butter or margarine and add the onion. Fry (sauté) for 2 minutes, then add the nuts and continue frying until golden. Immediately stir in the flour and pimenton and cook for 1 minute. Remove from the heat and gradually blend in the stock. Bring to the boil. Stir in the cream. Return the chicken to the pan and season with salt and pepper. Cover and cook in a preheated oven at 180°C/350°F/gas mark 4 for 1½ hours. Taste and re-season if necessary. Meanwhile, cook the red pepper strips in boiling water for 3 minutes. Drain, rinse with cold water and drain again. Arrange in a lattice pattern over the chicken and serve hot with Plain Boiled Rice sprinkled with fennel seeds.

Dry Martini Chicken

Use another dry vermouth if you prefer.

SERVES 4

4 chicken portions
20 g/¾ oz/1½ tbsp unsalted (sweet) butter
30 ml/2 tbsp sunflower oil
1 large garlic clove, crushed
120 ml/4 fl oz/½ cup dry Martini
150 ml/¼ pt/⅔ cup chicken stock
10 ml/2 tsp gin
15 ml/1 tbsp pickled green peppercorns
10 ml/2 tsp caster (superfine) sugar
1 bunch of watercress, trimmed and chopped
Finely grated rind and juice of ½ lemon
Salt
15 ml/1 tbsp cornflour (cornstarch)
15 ml/1 tbsp water
30 ml/2 tbsp double (heavy) cream
Buttered noodles and cooked broccoli florets, to serve

Brown the chicken in the butter and oil in a flameproof casserole (Dutch oven). Add the garlic, Martini, stock, gin, peppercorns, sugar, half the watercress and the lemon rind and juice. Bring to the boil and add salt to taste. Cover and cook in a preheated oven at 180°C/350°F/gas mark 4 for 1 hour. Lift out the chicken and keep warm. Blend the cornflour with the water and stir into the casserole with the remaining watercress. Bring to the boil on top of the stove and cook for 2 minutes, stirring. Stir in the cream. Taste and re-season if necessary. Spoon over the chicken and serve with buttered noodles tossed with cooked broccoli florets.

Chicken with Water Chestnuts

SERVES 4

4 chicken portions
15 ml/1 tbsp medium-dry sherry
5 ml/1 tsp light brown sugar
30 ml/2 tbsp sunflower oil
1 bunch of spring onions (scallions), cut into diagonal pieces
175 g/6 oz button mushrooms, quartered
225 g/8 oz/1 small can of water chestnuts, quartered
600 ml/1 pt/2½ cups chicken stock
15 ml/1 tbsp soy sauce
30 ml/2 tbsp cornflour (cornstarch)
Plain Boiled Rice (page 351), to serve

Place the chicken in a shallow dish. Drizzle with the sherry and add the sugar. Toss to coat and leave to marinate for 2 hours. Heat the oil in a flameproof casserole (Dutch oven). Add the chicken and brown on all sides. Remove from the pan with a draining spoon. Add the spring onions and mushrooms and cook, stirring, for 2 minutes. Add the water chestnuts, stock and soy sauce. Return the chicken to the pan and bring to the boil. Cover and transfer to a preheated oven at 180°C/350°F/gas mark 4 for 1½ hours or until really tender. Transfer the chicken to warm plates and keep warm. Blend the cornflour with a little water and stir into the cooking liquid. Bring to the boil and cook for 2 minutes, stirring. Spoon over the chicken and serve with Plain Boiled Rice.

Nutty Chicken with Water Chestnuts

SERVES 4

Prepare as for Chicken with Water Chestnuts, but add 75 g/3 oz raw cashew nuts to the casserole before cooking.

Jamaican Chicken

SERVES 4

450 g/1 lb uncooked diced chicken
1 large onion, sliced
1 large garlic clove, crushed
1 green chilli, seeded and chopped
30 ml/2 tbsp sunflower oil
200 g/7 oz/1 packet of creamed coconut, cut into small pieces
300 ml/½ pt/1¼ cups chicken stock
1 small fresh pineapple, rinded and diced, discarding any hard core
15 ml/1 tbsp chopped thyme
Salt and freshly ground black pepper
15 ml/1 tbsp chopped coriander (cilantro) and a few toasted coconut flakes, to garnish
Plain Boiled Rice (page 351), tossed with a diced avocado, to serve

Brown the chicken, onion, garlic and chilli in the oil in a flameproof casserole (Dutch oven) for 3 minutes, stirring. Add the remaining ingredients and bring to the boil gently, stirring all the time, until the coconut melts. Cover and cook in a preheated oven at 180°C/350°F/gas mark 4 for 50 minutes or until the chicken is really tender. Taste and re-season if necessary. Serve garnished with the coriander and toasted coconut on a bed of Plain Boiled Rice tossed with diced avocado.

Tropical Chicken

SERVES 4

Prepare as for Jamaican Chicken, but substitute a large green banana, cut into chunks, for the pineapple and spike the mixture with freshly squeezed lime juice to taste.

Fijian Chicken

SERVES 4

4 chicken portions
25 g/1 oz/2 tbsp butter or margarine
425 g/15 oz/1 large can of pineapple pieces in natural juice, drained, reserving the juice
15 ml/1 tbsp soy sauce
4 celery sticks, sliced
1 carrot, chopped
1 green (bell) pepper, cut into thin strips
3 tomatoes, quartered
Salt and freshly ground black pepper
15 ml/1 tbsp cornflour (cornstarch)
30 ml/2 tbsp water
Plain Boiled Rice (page 351) and chopped melon and cucumber, tossed in French dressing, to serve

Brown the chicken in the butter or margarine in a flameproof casserole (Dutch oven). Remove from the pan with a draining spoon. Make the pineapple juice up to 300 ml/½ pt/1¼ cups with water. Add to the casserole with the soy sauce, celery and carrot. Add the chicken. Bring to the boil, reduce the heat, cover and simmer for 20 minutes. Add the pineapple pieces, green pepper, tomatoes and a little salt and pepper and cook for a further 20 minutes. Lift out the chicken and transfer to warm plates. Blend the cornflour with the water and stir into the pan. Bring to the boil and cook for 1 minute, stirring. Taste and re-season if necessary. Spoon over the chicken and serve with Plain Boiled Rice and the melon and cucumber salad.

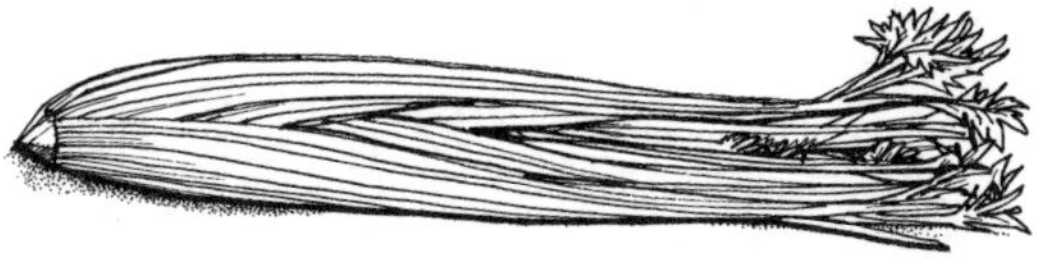

Hot Peanut Chicken

SERVES 4

2 red chillies
8 chicken drumsticks, skin removed, if preferred
30 ml/2 tbsp sunflower oil
1 large garlic clove, crushed
25 g/1 oz/¼ cup plain (all-purpose) flour
600 ml/1 pt/2½ cups chicken stock
100 g/4 oz/½ cup smooth peanut butter
30 ml/2 tbsp tomato purée (paste)
100 g/4 oz/1 cup roasted peanuts, chopped
5 ml/1 tsp red hot chilli sauce
Salt and freshly ground black pepper
15 ml/1 tbsp chopped coriander (cilantro)
Thai Fragrant Rice (page 351), to serve

Chop the chillies and remove the seeds if you can't stand the heat! Brown the drumsticks in the oil in a flameproof casserole (Dutch oven). Remove from the casserole. Stir in the garlic, chillies and flour and cook for 1 minute. Remove from the heat and gradually blend in the stock. Return to the heat and bring to the boil, stirring. Stir in the peanut butter, tomato purée and 75 g/3 oz/¾ cup of the peanuts. Return the chicken to the pan. Cover and cook in a preheated oven at 180°C/350°F/gas mark 4 for 1 hour. Add the chilli sauce, taste and add salt and pepper if necessary. Sprinkle with the remaining nuts and the coriander and serve with Thai Fragrant Rice.

Zesty Chicken and Vegetable Casserole

SERVES 4

4 chicken portions
4 rindless streaky bacon rashers (slices), diced
2 onions, chopped
100 g/4 oz button mushrooms, quartered
2 celery sticks, chopped
40 g/1½ oz/3 tbsp butter or margarine
450 g/1 lb baby potatoes, scrubbed
2 turnips, cut into large dice
2 large carrots, thickly sliced
400 g/14 oz/1 large can of chopped tomatoes
1 wineglass of white wine
1 bay leaf
Salt and freshly ground black pepper
½ small green cabbage, shredded
Finely grated rind of 1 lemon
30 ml/2 tbsp chopped parsley
Crusty bread, to serve

Cut each chicken portion into two pieces. Fry (sauté) the bacon, onions, mushrooms and celery in a flameproof casserole (Dutch oven) in half the butter or margarine until golden. Remove from the pan and reserve. Add the remaining butter or margarine and fry the chicken pieces on all sides to brown. Return the bacon and cooked vegetables to the pan and arrange the potatoes, turnips and carrots around. Spoon over the tomatoes and add the wine, bay leaf and some salt and pepper. Cover tightly and cook in a preheated oven at 180°C/350°F/gas mark 4 for 1¼ hours. Stir in the cabbage, re-cover and cook in the oven for a further 30 minutes. Stir well, remove the bay leaf, taste and re-season if necessary. Mix together the lemon rind and parsley and sprinkle over. Serve with lots of crusty bread.

Sherried Chicken Casserole

SERVES 4

4 chicken portions
25 g/1 oz/2 tbsp butter or margarine
1 large onion, finely chopped
100 g/4 oz button mushrooms, quartered
400 g/14 oz/1 large can of chopped tomatoes
1 sherry glass of medium-dry sherry
30 ml/2 tbsp tomato purée (paste)
1 bouquet garni sachet
Salt and freshly ground black pepper
A few snipped chives, to garnish
Jacket-baked potatoes and peas, to serve

Brown the chicken portions in the butter or margarine in a flameproof casserole (Dutch oven). Remove from the pan with a draining spoon. Add the onion and fry (sauté) for 2 minutes, stirring. Add the mushrooms and cook for 1 minute. Return the chicken to the pan. Add the can of tomatoes. Blend the sherry with the tomato purée and stir in. Add the bouquet garni and some salt and pepper. Bring to the boil. Cover and cook in a preheated oven at 180°C/350°F/gas mark 4 for 1½ hours or until the chicken is really tender. Spoon off any fat and remove the bouquet garni. Garnish with snipped chives and serve with jacket-baked potatoes and peas.

Citrus Chicken

SERVES 4

1 large orange
4 chicken portions
45 ml/3 tbsp plain (all-purpose) flour
Salt and freshly ground black pepper
25 g/1 oz/2 tbsp butter or margarine
2 leeks, sliced
1 small onion, sliced
1 chicken stock cube
175 g/6 oz button mushrooms
5 ml/1 tsp dried thyme
Lemon juice, to taste
Chopped parsley, to garnish
Royal Roast Potatoes (page 348) and baby carrots, to serve

Thinly pare the rind from the orange. Cut into thin strips and reserve. Halve the orange and squeeze all the juice. Make up to 600 ml/1 pt/2½ cups with water. Toss the chicken in the flour with a little salt and pepper. Melt the butter or margarine in a flameproof casserole (Dutch oven), add the chicken and brown all over. Remove from the pan with a draining spoon. Add the leeks and onion and fry (sauté) quickly to brown. Blend any remaining flour with a little of the orange juice and water. Stir in the remainder and add to the pan. Crumble in the stock cube. Bring to the boil, stirring. Return the chicken to the pan. Add the mushrooms, half the orange rind, the thyme and a little more salt and pepper. Cover and cook in a preheated oven at 180°C/350°F/gas mark 4 for 1½ hours or until the chicken is really tender. Add lemon juice and more seasoning to taste. Sprinkle over the remaining orange rind and chopped parsley and serve with Royal Roast Potatoes and baby carrots.

Brown Rice and Chicken Slow-Pot

SERVES 4

1.25 kg/2½ lb oven-ready chicken
225 g/8 oz/1 cup brown long-grain rice
8 button (pearl) onions, peeled but left whole
2 carrots, cut into chunks
2 turnips, cut into chunks
A pinch of grated nutmeg
5 ml/1 tsp chopped sage
Salt and freshly ground black pepper
600 ml/1 pt/2½ cups hot chicken stock
60 ml/4 tbsp single (light) cream
A few sage sprigs, to garnish
Spring greens (collard greens), to serve

Wipe the chicken inside and out with kitchen paper (paper towels). Pull off any excess fat from around the body cavity and discard. Place in a casserole (Dutch oven). Wash the rice thoroughly in several changes of water. Drain and surround the chicken. Add the vegetables, nutmeg, sage and a little salt and pepper. Pour the hot stock over. Cover tightly and cook in a preheated oven at 140°C/275°F/gas mark 1 for 2 hours. Check and add a little more stock if the rice is becoming too dry. Re-cover and continue cooking for a further 2 hours. Turn up the heat to 200°C/400°F/gas mark 6 and cook for a further 30 minutes, adding a little more stock if necessary. Remove the chicken and ease it apart into portions. Stir the cream into the rice. Taste and add more seasoning if necessary. Spoon on to warm plates, top with the chicken and serve with spring greens.

Chicken Goulash

SERVES 4

1 onion, chopped
2 carrots, diced
15 ml/1 tbsp paprika
15 ml/1 tbsp sunflower or olive oil
225 g/8 oz chicken stir-fry meat
400g/14 oz/1 large can of chopped tomatoes
15 ml/1 tbsp tomato purée (paste)
150 ml/¼ pt/⅔ cup chicken stock
Salt and freshly ground black pepper
275 g/10 oz/1 medium can of cut green beans, drained
15 ml/1 tbsp cornflour (cornstarch)
30 ml/2 tbsp water
Buttered noodles, to serve
Crème fraîche and caraway seeds, to garnish

Fry (sauté) the onion, carrots and paprika in the oil, stirring, for 2 minutes in a flameproof casserole (Dutch oven). Add the chicken and fry for 1 minute. Stir in the tomatoes, purée and stock. Season to taste with salt and pepper. Bring to the boil, reduce the heat, cover and simmer gently for 20 minutes. Add the beans to the goulash. Blend the cornflour with the water and stir in. Bring back to the boil and cook for 2 minutes, stirring gently, until thickened. Taste and re-season, if necessary. Arrange the buttered noodles on warm serving plates and spoon the goulash to one side. Top the goulash with a spoonful of crème fraîche and sprinkle with caraway seeds before serving.

Chicken Gumbo

SERVES 4

15 g/½ oz/1 tbsp butter or margarine
450 g/1 lb skinless chicken meat, diced
12 button (pearl) onions, peeled but left whole
1 extra-lean back bacon rasher (slice), finely diced
5 ml/1 tsp turmeric
5 ml/1 tsp ground coriander (cilantro)
2.5 ml/½ tsp chilli powder
225 g/8 oz okra (ladies' fingers), trimmed
1 red (bell) pepper, sliced
1 green pepper, sliced
225 g/8 oz/1 small can of chopped tomatoes
15 ml/1 tbsp tomato purée (paste)
1 large bay leaf
2.5 ml/½ tsp dried oregano
600 ml/1 pt/2½ cups chicken stock, made with 2 stock cubes
Freshly ground black pepper
15 ml/1 tbsp chopped parsley
Plain Boiled Rice (page 351), to serve

Heat the butter or margarine in a large flameproof casserole (Dutch oven). Add the chicken and brown for 3 minutes, stirring. Add the onions, bacon and spices and cook, stirring, for a further 1 minute. Add the remaining ingredients except the parsley. Bring to the boil, reduce the heat, cover and simmer very gently for 1 hour. Remove the bay leaf. Sprinkle with the parsley and serve spooned over Plain Boiled Rice in large soup bowls.

New Orleans Chicken Gumbo

SERVES 6

40 g/1½ oz/3 tbsp butter or margarine
15 ml/1 tbsp sunflower oil
30 ml/2 tbsp plain (all-purpose) flour
1 litre/1¾ pts/4¼ cups chicken stock
2 thick belly pork rashers (slices), rinded and diced
1 onion, chopped
2 celery sticks, chopped
2 garlic cloves, crushed
450 g/1 lb okra (ladies' fingers), trimmed and sliced
400 g/14 oz/1 large can of chopped tomatoes
225 g/8 oz cooked, peeled prawns (shrimp)
450 g/1 lb/4 cups cooked chicken, diced, all skin removed
50 g/2 oz frozen peas
Tabasco sauce
Salt and freshly ground black pepper
Plain Boiled Rice (page 351), to serve

Melt half the butter or margarine in a large pan with the oil. Add the flour and stir until lightly browned. Gradually blend in the stock and bring to the boil, stirring. Remove from the heat. Brown the pork in the remaining butter or margarine in a large flameproof casserole (Dutch oven) until the fat runs. Stir in the onion, celery and garlic and fry (sauté) for 2 minutes. Add the okra and fry for 5 minutes, stirring. Stir in the tomatoes and simmer for 10–15 minutes. Stir in the slightly thickened stock, bring to the boil, reduce the heat, cover and simmer gently for 1 hour. Add the prawns, chicken and peas and cook for 5 minutes. Season with Tabasco, salt and pepper to taste. Serve the gumbo in bowls with a spoonful of Plain Boiled Rice on top.

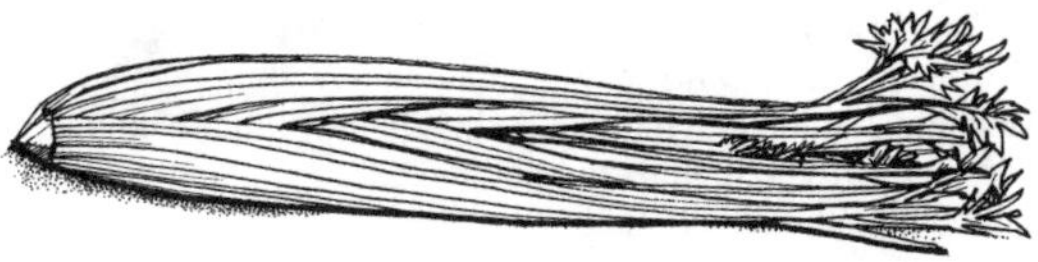

Bridgetown Chicken with Yam Muffins

SERVES 4

For the muffins:
425 g/15 oz/1 large can of yams, drained
Salt and freshly ground black pepper
100 g/4 oz/1 cup plain (all-purpose) flour
5 ml/1 tsp baking powder
2 eggs, separated
45 ml/3 tbsp milk
For the casserole:
1 large onion, chopped
4 chicken portions, each cut into two pieces
30 ml/2 tbsp olive oil
2 garlic cloves, crushed
5 ml/1 tsp grated fresh root ginger
1 green chilli, seeded and chopped
400 g/14 oz/1 large can of chopped tomatoes
300 ml/½ pt/1¼ cups chicken stock
5 cm/2 in piece of cinnamon stick
1 small lime
5 ml/1 tsp light brown sugar
A few coriander (cilantro) leaves, to garnish

To make the muffins, place the yams in a bowl and mash well with a little salt and pepper. Sift the flour and baking powder over and mix with the egg yolks and milk. Whisk the egg whites until stiff and fold in with a metal spoon. Turn into the 12 sections of an oiled tartlet tin (patty pan). Bake in a preheated oven at 200°C/400°F/gas mark 6 for about 20 minutes or until risen, golden and firm to the touch. Turn out on to a wire rack to cool.

Meanwhile, brown the onion and chicken in the oil in a flameproof casserole (Dutch oven). Add the garlic, ginger, chilli, tomatoes, stock and cinnamon stick. Bring to the boil. Thinly pare the rind off the lime and squeeze the juice. Add the lime juice and the sugar to the casserole and season to taste. Stir well. Cover and cook in a preheated oven at 180°C/350°F/gas mark 4 for 1 hour or until the chicken is tender and bathed in sauce. Taste and re-season if necessary. Meanwhile, cut the pared lime rind into thin strips and boil in water for 2 minutes. Drain, rinse with cold water and drain again. Sprinkle the lime rind and a few coriander leaves over the casserole and serve with the yam muffins.

Spiced Chicken Casserole

SERVES 4

4 chicken portions
30 ml/2 tbsp plain (all-purpose) flour
Salt and freshly ground black pepper
5 ml/1 tsp paprika
25 g/1 oz/2 tbsp butter or margarine
5 ml/1 tsp curry powder
295 g/10½ oz/1 medium can of condensed mushroom soup
Lemon wedges and gherkin (cornichon) 'fans', to garnish
Oven Pilaf (page 352), to serve

Toss the chicken portions in the flour, seasoned with a little salt and pepper and the paprika. Melt the butter or margarine in a flameproof casserole (Dutch oven) and brown the chicken on all sides. Remove from the pan. Drain off any excess fat. Sprinkle the curry powder into the casserole and add the soup. Add a little more pepper. Bring to the boil, stirring. Add the chicken, cover and cook in a preheated oven at 180°C/350°F/gas mark 4 for 1½ hours. Spoon on to warm plates, garnish with lemon wedges and gherkin fans and serve with Oven Pilaf.

Curried Chicken and Mushroom Casserole

SERVES 4

1 onion, finely chopped
15 g/½ oz/1 tbsp butter or margarine
75 g/3 oz button mushrooms, sliced
15 ml/1 tbsp curry powder
295 g/10½ oz/1 medium can of condensed mushroom soup
8 skinless chicken thighs
Jacket-baked potatoes and a tossed green salad, to serve

Fry (sauté) the onion in the butter or margarine in a flameproof casserole (Dutch oven) for 2 minutes, stirring. Add the mushrooms, cover, reduce the heat and cook for a further 3 minutes to soften. Add the curry powder and cook for 30 seconds, stirring. Stir in the soup until well blended. Add the chicken and spoon the soup mixture over them. Cover with a lid and cook in a preheated oven at 180°C/350°F/gas mark 4 for 1¼ hours until tender and bathed in a rich sauce. Serve with jacket-baked potatoes and a tossed green salad.

Curried Chicken and Celery Casserole

SERVES 4

Prepare as for Curried Chicken and Mushroom Casserole, but substitute celery soup for the mushroom soup and 2 finely chopped celery sticks for the mushrooms.

Winter Chicken Pot

SERVES 4

4 chicken portions
25 g/1 oz/2 tbsp butter or margarine
1 onion, sliced
4 carrots, sliced
1 small swede (rutabaga), sliced
100 g/4 oz/generous ½ cup pearl barley
900 ml/1½ pts/3¾ cups chicken stock
Salt and freshly ground black pepper
3 potatoes, scrubbed and cut into bite-sized pieces
1 small green cabbage, shredded

Brown the chicken portions in the butter or margarine in a large flameproof casserole (Dutch oven). Remove from the pan with a draining spoon. Add the onion, carrots and swede and fry (sauté) for 2 minutes, stirring. Add the barley and stock and return the chicken to the pan. Season to taste. Bring to the boil, reduce the heat, cover and simmer for 45 minutes. Add the potatoes and cabbage, cover and continue cooking for 20 minutes or until everything is tender. Serve in large open soup bowls.

Winter Chicken and Lentil Pot

SERVES 4

Prepare as for Winter Chicken Pot, but substitute a sliced turnip and a sliced parsnip for the swede (rutabaga) and soaked green lentils for the pearl barley.

Cassoulet

SERVES 6

225 g/8 oz/1⅓ cups dried haricot (navy) beans, soaked overnight
450 g/1 lb belly pork, boned, rinded and diced
2 garlic cloves, crushed
1 carrot, diced
2 celery sticks, diced
2 onions, chopped
15 ml/1 tbsp black treacle (molasses)
10 ml/2 tsp caster (superfine) sugar
1 bouquet garni sachet
10 ml/2 tsp Dijon mustard
Salt and freshly ground black pepper
6 chicken thighs, all skin removed
1 smoked pork ring, cut into chunks

Drain the beans and place in a large flameproof casserole (Dutch oven). Cover with water. Bring to the boil and boil rapidly for 10 minutes. Add all the remaining ingredients except the chicken and pork ring. Just-cover with cold water. Bring to the boil, cover and transfer to a preheated oven at 180°C/350°F/gas mark 4 for 2 hours. Add the chicken and sausage pieces, pushing them well down in the bean mixture. Add a little more water if the mixture is becoming too dry. Re-cover reduce the heat to 160°C/325°F/gas mark 3 and continue cooking for a further 2½ hours until the beans are really tender and bathed in a rich sauce. Remove the bouquet garni sachet, taste and re-season if necessary. Serve in warm bowls.

Chicken Harcouet

SERVES 4

4 chicken portions
50 g/2 oz/¼ cup unsalted (sweet) butter
30 ml/2 tbsp olive oil
4 streaky bacon rashers (slices), rinded and chopped
1 onion, chopped
1 carrot, finely chopped
1 celery stick, chopped
60 ml/4 tbsp calvados
250 ml/8 fl oz/1 cup medium-dry cider
Salt and freshly ground black pepper
150 ml/¼ pt/⅔ cup double (heavy) cream
1 red eating (dessert) apple, peeled, cored and sliced into rings
1 green eating apple, peeled, cored and sliced into rings
Boiled potatoes in their skins and peas, to serve

Brown the chicken in all but 15 g/1½ oz/1 tbsp of the butter and all the oil in a flameproof casserole (Dutch oven). Remove from the pan with a draining spoon. Add the bacon, onion, carrot and celery and fry (sauté) for 2 minutes, stirring. Add the calvados. Ignite and shake the pan until the flames subside. Add the cider. Return the chicken to the pan and bring to the boil. Season. Cover and cook in a preheated oven at 180°C/ 350°F/gas mark 4 for 1½ hours. Remove the chicken from the pan, transfer to warm serving plates and keep warm. Stir in the cream, bring to the boil and simmer for 3 minutes until slightly thickened. Taste and re-season if necessary. Meanwhile, fry the apple slices in the remaining butter until lightly golden on each side. Spoon the sauce over the chicken, garnish with the apple slices and serve with potatoes boiled in their skins and peas.

TURKEY

Tangy Turkey Wings with Ginger

SERVES 4

4 turkey wings
45 ml/3 tbsp sunflower oil
2 onions, chopped
1 garlic clove, crushed
2 oranges
300 ml/½ pt/1¼ cups chicken stock
45 ml/3 tbsp sweet sherry
5 ml/1 tsp grated fresh root ginger
Salt and freshly ground black pepper
20 ml/4 tsp cornflour (cornstarch)
30 ml/2 tbsp water
4 parsley sprigs
Speciality Creamed Potatoes (page 348) and shredded spring greens (collard greens), to serve

Cut off and discard the turkey wing tips, then cut the wings into two pieces at the first joint. Wipe with kitchen paper (paper towels). Heat the oil in a flameproof casserole (Dutch oven). Brown the wing joints on all sides and remove from the pan. Add the onions and garlic and fry (sauté) for 3 minutes until softened and lightly golden. Return the turkey to the pan. Cut two slices off one of the oranges, halve each and reserve for garnish. Finely grate the rind from the remaining oranges and squeeze the juice. Add to the casserole with the stock, sherry, ginger and a little salt and pepper. Bring to the boil, cover and transfer to a preheated oven at 160°C/325°F/gas mark 3 for 1½ hours or until the turkey is really tender. Lift the wings out of the casserole and transfer to warm serving plates. Keep warm. Blend together the cornflour and water and stir into the casserole. Cook on top of the stove for 2 minutes until thickened and bubbling. Taste and re-season if necessary. Spoon over the turkey, garnish each with half a slice of orange and a parsley sprig and serve with Speciality Creamed Potatoes and shredded spring greens.

Turkey Cassoulet

SERVES 6

Prepare as for Cassoulet, but substitute 350 g/12 oz turkey casserole meat for the chicken thighs and 225 g/8 oz turkey sausages, cut into chunks, for the smoked pork ring.

Braised Turkey with Bacon and Vegetables

SERVES 10

1 small oven-ready turkey, about 2.75 kg/6 lb
25 g/1 oz/2 tbsp butter or margarine
10 onions, peeled but left whole
4 large carrots, thickly sliced
½ swede (rutabaga), cut into chunks
3 celery sticks, cut into chunks
750 g/1¾ lb lean unsmoked gammon joint, soaked in cold water, if necessary
1 bay leaf
Salt and freshly ground black pepper
1.2 litres/2 pts/6 cups chicken stock
Parsley Sauce (page 341) and plain boiled potatoes, to serve

Remove the giblets if necessary. Wipe the bird inside and out and truss if necessary. Melt the butter or margarine in a very large flameproof casserole (Dutch oven) and brown the bird on all sides. Remove from the pan. Add the vegetables and toss quickly to brown lightly for 2 minutes. Return the turkey to the pan and add the gammon joint. Add the bay leaf and season lightly. Pour on the stock. Bring to the boil, cover tightly and transfer to a preheated oven at 180°C/350°F/gas mark 4 for 2½ hours or until the turkey and gammon are really tender. Carefully lift the bird and gammon out of the liquid and place on a large carving dish. Lift out the vegetables and keep warm. Boil the stock rapidly until reduced by a third. Discard the bay leaf. Taste and re-season, if necessary. Carve the turkey and gammon. Serve some of each with the cooked vegetables, the broth poured over, with lots of Parsley Sauce and plain boiled potatoes.

Somerset Turkey Pot Roast with Dumplings

SERVES 4

2 carrots, cut into chunks
1 parsnip, cut into chunks
2 onions, quartered
2 turnips, cut into chunks
1 boneless turkey roast
150 ml/¼ pt/⅔ cup chicken stock
300 ml/½ pt/1¼ cups medium-sweet cider
Salt and freshly ground black pepper
1 small bay leaf
8 even-sized potatoes, scrubbed
100 g/4 oz/1 cup self-raising (self-rising) flour
50 g/2 oz/½ cup shredded vegetable suet
5 ml/1 tsp dried rosemary, crushed
15 ml/1 tbsp cornflour (cornstarch)
30 ml/2 tbsp water
30 ml/2 tbsp crème fraîche
30 ml/2 tbsp chopped parsley

Place the prepared vegetables in a large flameproof casserole (Dutch oven). Place the turkey roast on top of the vegetables. Add the stock and cider, season with a little salt and pepper and add the bay leaf. Arrange the potatoes around the meat. Cover and cook in a preheated oven at 160°C/325°F/gas mark 3 for 1½ hours.

About 20 minutes before the end of cooking time, sift the self-raising flour and a pinch of salt into a bowl. Stir in the suet and rosemary. Mix with enough cold water to form a soft but not sticky dough. Shape into eight small balls and arrange around the turkey. Re-cover and cook in the oven for a further 15 minutes until the dumplings are fluffy and cooked through. Lift the turkey out of the casserole on to a warm serving dish. Remove the inner wrapper and carve the meat. Arrange the dumplings and vegetables around. Blend the cornflour with the water and stir into the juices. Bring to the boil and cook for 1 minute, stirring. Stir in the crème fraîche and re-season if necessary. Pour a little sauce over the turkey, sprinkle with the chopped parsley and serve hot with the remaining sauce.

Turkey Pot Roast with Wine and Two Cheeses

SERVES 4

Prepare as for Somerset Turkey Pot Roast with Dumplings, but use white wine instead of cider. Add 50 g/2 oz/ ½ cup Cheddar cheese, grated, and 15 ml/1 tbsp chopped parsley to the dumplings instead of the rosemary and stir in fromage frais instead of crème fraîche.

Tender Turkey Steaks in Smooth Cider Sauce

SERVES 4

4 turkey steaks
150 ml/¼ pt/⅔ cup medium-sweet cider
150 ml/¼ pt/⅔ cup chicken stock
2.5 ml/½ tsp dried basil
2.5 ml/½ tsp dried oregano
Salt and freshly ground black pepper
20 ml/4 tsp cornflour (cornstarch)
30 ml/2 tbsp milk
150 ml/¼ pt/⅔ cup single (light) cream
15 ml/1 tbsp chopped parsley
Speciality Creamed Potatoes (page 348), runner beans and baby carrots, to serve

Place the turkey steaks in a flameproof casserole (Dutch oven) and add the cider, stock, herbs and a little salt and pepper. Bring to the boil, reduce the heat, cover and cook gently for about 10–15 minutes until really tender. Remove from the pan with a draining spoon and keep warm. Blend the cornflour with the milk. Stir into the pan and bring to the boil, stirring. Simmer for 1 minute. Blend in the cream, taste and re-season. Heat through. Garnish with the parsley and serve with Speciality Creamed Potatoes, runner beans and baby carrots.

Creamed Turkey Grand Marnier

SERVES 4

Prepare as for Tender Turkey Steaks in Smooth Cider Sauce, but use 90 ml/ 6 tbsp dry white wine and 60 ml/4 tbsp Grand Marnier instead of the cider and use crème fraîche instead of the single cream. Garnish with parsley and some orange twists.

Tyrolean Turkey

SERVES 4

4 turkey steaks
25 g/1 oz/2 tbsp butter or margarine
1 onion, finely chopped
1 garlic clove, crushed
1 small white cabbage, finely shredded
15 ml/1 tbsp caraway seeds
Salt and freshly ground black pepper
2 large potatoes, thinly sliced
300 ml/½ pt/1¼ cups chicken stock

Brown the turkey in the butter or margarine in a flameproof casserole (Dutch oven). Remove from the pan. Add the onion and garlic and fry (sauté), stirring, for 1 minute. Add the cabbage and cook, stirring, for 2 minutes until the cabbage begins to soften slightly. Sprinkle with the caraway seeds and a little salt and pepper. Return the turkey to the pan and top with the potato slices. Pour over the stock and season lightly again with salt and pepper. Cover with a lid or foil and bake in a preheated oven at 160°C/ 325°F/gas mark 3 for 1 hour. Remove the lid, turn up the heat to 190°C/ 375°F/gas mark 5 and cook for a further 30 minutes until the potatoes are browning. Serve hot.

Turkey and Spring Vegetable Casserole with Bay

SERVES 4

50 g/2 oz thin French (green) beans, cut into short lengths
100 g/4 oz baby corn cobs, halved
100 g/4 oz baby carrots, scrubbed but left whole
2 small courgettes (zucchini), cut into chunks
50 g/2 oz shelled broad (fava) beans
450 g/1 lb diced turkey meat
12 button (pearl) onions, peeled but left whole
1 garlic clove, crushed
25 g/1 oz/2 tbsp unsalted (sweet) butter
20 g/¾ oz/3 tbsp plain (all-purpose) flour
300 ml/½ pt/1½ cups chicken stock
150 ml/¼ pt/⅔ cup apple juice
1 bay leaf
Salt and freshly ground black pepper
15 ml/1 tbsp chopped parsley
Baby new potatoes, to serve

Blanch the beans, corn, carrots, courgettes and broad beans in boiling water for 2 minutes. Drain, rinse with cold water and drain again. Brown the turkey, onions and garlic in the butter in a flameproof casserole (Dutch oven) for 2 minutes, stirring. Stir in the flour and cook for 1 minute. Remove from the heat and gradually blend in the stock and apple juice. Return to the heat and bring to the boil, stirring. Add the bay leaf and a little salt and pepper. Stir in the blanched vegetables. Cover and cook in a preheated oven at 180°C/ 350°F/gas mark 4 for 45 minutes or until everything is tender. Taste and re-season if necessary. Sprinkle with chopped parsley and serve with baby new potatoes.

Turkey Herb Crumble

SERVES 4

4 thin turkey steaks
295 g/10½ oz/1 medium can of condensed celery soup
15 ml/1 tbsp lemon juice
30 ml/2 tbsp water
Freshly ground black pepper
85 g/3½ oz/1 small packet of sage and onion stuffing mix
Shredded white cabbage tossed in French dressing, to serve

Place the turkey steaks one at a time in a plastic bag and beat to flatten slightly. Quickly brown on both sides in a flameproof casserole (Dutch oven). Mix the soup with the lemon juice and water and pour over the turkey. Add a good grinding of pepper. Cover with a lid and simmer gently for 15 minutes until the turkey is tender and cooked through. Meanwhile, make up the stuffing mix with enough boiling water to form a moist crumble and scatter over the surface. Grill (broil) under a moderate heat for about 10 minutes until crisp and golden. Serve with shredded cabbage salad.

Three-herb Turkey Casserole

SERVES 4

4 turkey breast steaks
30 ml/2 tbsp sunflower oil
1 garlic clove, crushed
15 ml/1 tbsp chopped parsley
15 ml/1 tbsp chopped basil
15 ml/1 tbsp chopped oregano
2.5 ml/½ tsp paprika
30 ml/2 tbsp tomato purée (paste)
1 wineglass of dry white wine
Salt and freshly ground black pepper
Plain Boiled Rice (page 351) and broccoli, to serve

Brown the turkey quickly on both sides in a flameproof casserole (Dutch oven). Mix together the remaining ingredients and pour over. Cover and cook in a preheated oven at 190°C/350°F/gas mark 4 for about 40 minutes until the turkey is tender. Taste and re-season if necessary. Serve with Plain Boiled Rice and broccoli.

Braised Turkey with Redcurrant and Mushrooms

SERVES 4

4 turkey breast steaks
45 ml/3 tbsp sunflower oil
2 onions, sliced
1 carrot, thinly sliced
100 g/4 oz button mushrooms, sliced
600 ml/1 pt/2½ cups chicken stock
Salt and freshly ground black pepper
5 ml/1 tsp dried mixed herbs
30 ml/2 tbsp redcurrant jelly (clear conserve)
15 ml/1 tbsp plain (all-purpose) flour
15 ml/1 tbsp soy sauce
15 ml/1 tbsp water
15 ml/1 tbsp chopped parsley
New potatoes and broccoli, to serve

Brown the turkey steaks quickly in the oil in a large flameproof casserole (Dutch oven). Remove from the pan with a draining spoon. Add the onions and carrot and fry (sauté) quickly for 2 minutes. Add the mushrooms and fry for a further 1 minute. Lay the turkey on top of the vegetables and pour over the stock. Season with salt and pepper and the herbs. Cover, bring to the boil, reduce the heat and simmer gently for 30–40 minutes until the turkey and vegetables are tender. Carefully lift the turkey out of the casserole and transfer to warm serving plates. Keep warm. Stir the redcurrant jelly into the cooking liquid. Blend the flour with the soy sauce and water and stir in. Bring to the boil and cook for 2 minutes, stirring all the time. Taste and re-season if necessary. Spoon over the turkey and sprinkle with the parsley. Serve with new potatoes and broccoli.

DUCK

Moroccan-style Duck

SERVES 4

2 large duck breasts, cut into bite-sized pieces
15 ml/1 tbsp olive oil
15 g/½ oz/1 tbsp unsalted (sweet) butter
12 button (pearl) onions, peeled but left whole
1 large garlic clove, crushed
5 ml/1 tsp ground cumin
1 red (bell) pepper, halved and cut into thin strips
1 green pepper, halved and cut into thin strips
1 orange pepper, halved and cut into thin strips
1 yellow pepper, halved and cut into thin strips
2 large carrots, cut into chunks
1 large courgette (zucchini), cut into chunks
2 beefsteak tomatoes, skinned and finely chopped
350 ml/12 fl oz/1⅓ cups chicken stock
30 ml/2 tbsp chopped coriander (cilantro)
15 ml/1 tbsp cornflour
15 ml/1 tbsp water
30 ml/2 tbsp toasted pine nuts, to garnish
Plain cooked couscous, to serve

Brown the duck in the oil and butter on all sides in a flameproof casserole (Dutch oven). Remove from the casserole with a draining spoon. Add the onions and garlic and fry (sauté) for 2 minutes, stirring. Add the cumin and remaining vegetables and fry for a further 2 minutes. Return the duck to the casserole and add the stock and half the coriander. Bring to the boil, cover and transfer to a preheated oven at 180°C/350°F/gas mark 4 and cook for 1½ hours until really tender. Blend the cornflour with the water and stir into the casserole. Cook on top of the stove for 2 minutes, stirring, until thickened. Sprinkle with the remaining coriander and the pine nuts and serve hot with couscous.

French-style Duck Casserole

SERVES 4

1.75 kg/4 lb oven-ready duck
25 g/1 oz/2 tbsp butter or margarine
12 button (pearl) onions, peeled but left whole
600 ml/1 pt/2½ cups duck or chicken stock
Salt and freshly ground black pepper
225 g/8 oz frozen peas
15 ml/1 tbsp chopped mint
15 ml/1 tbsp chopped oregano
15 ml/1 tbsp chopped parsley
1.5 ml/¼ tsp grated nutmeg
1 round lettuce, shredded
45 ml/3 tbsp plain (all-purpose) flour
Mint sprigs, to garnish
Plain boiled potatoes, to serve

Remove the giblets (use for the stock, page 61, if liked). Wipe inside and out with kitchen paper (paper towels). Prick all over with a fork. Melt the butter or margarine in a flameproof casserole (Dutch oven) and brown the duck on all sides. Remove the duck and brown the onions. Pour off any fat. Return the duck to the pan. Add the stock and a little salt and pepper. Bring to the boil, cover and transfer to a preheated oven at 200°C/400°F/gas mark 6 for 30 minutes. Skim the surface of any fat. Add the remaining ingredients except the flour and water. Reduce the heat to 180°C/350°F/gas mark 4 and cook for a further 1½ hours. Remove the duck and keep warm. Skim off any fat. Blend the cornflour with a little water to make a paste. Stir into the casserole, place on top of the stove and simmer for 3 minutes, stirring. Taste and re-season, if necessary. Carve the duck, discarding the skin. Transfer to warm plates. Spoon the pea sauce over each portion, garnish with mint sprigs and serve with plain boiled potatoes.

Salted Casseroled Duck

SERVES 4

1.75 kg/4 lb oven-ready duck, with giblets
225 g/8 oz sea salt
750 ml/1¼ pts/3 cups water
1 chicken stock cube
2 large leeks, thinly sliced
Freshly ground black pepper
300 ml/½ pt/1¼ cups apple juice
15 ml/1 tbsp brandy
New potatoes, peas and Onion Sauce (page 0341), to serve

Remove the giblets from the duck and wipe inside and out with kitchen paper (paper towels). Place the bird in a large dish and rub half of the salt into the skin. Cover loosely with foil and place in the fridge overnight. Put the giblets in a saucepan with the water and stock cube. Bring to the boil, reduce the heat, cover and simmer for 1 hour. Strain, leave to cool, then chill.

Next day, turn the duck and rub with the remaining salt. Re-cover and chill for a further day.

Rinse the duck thoroughly and wipe dry with kitchen paper. Place the leeks in a casserole (Dutch oven) and top with the duck. Season with pepper. Add the stock, apple juice and brandy. Bring to the boil, cover and transfer to a preheated oven at 180°C/350°F/gas mark 4 for 2½ hours. Transfer the duck to a warm serving dish and cut into quarters. Place on serving plates and keep warm. Spoon off any fat from the cooking liquid, strain into a saucepan and boil rapidly until reduced and slightly thickened. Spoon over the duck and serve with new potatoes, peas and Onion Sauce.

Old English Country Duck

SERVES 4

1 1.75 kg/4 lb oven-ready duck
25 g/1 oz/2 tbsp butter or margarine
2 onions, sliced
2 streaky bacon rashers (slices), rinded and diced
1 carrot, finely diced
600 ml/1 pt/2½ cups duck or chicken stock
Salt and freshly ground black pepper
1 bouquet garni sachet
45 ml/3 tbsp port
450 g/1 lb baby turnips, peeled but left whole
Jacket-baked potatoes and mangetout (snow peas), to serve

Remove the giblets from the duck (use for the stock, page 61, if liked). Wipe inside and out with kitchen paper (paper towels). Prick all over with a fork. Melt the butter or margarine in a flameproof casserole (Dutch oven). Brown the duck all over. Remove from the pan. Add the onions, bacon and carrot and fry (sauté), stirring, for 2 minutes. Remove from the pan with a draining spoon and drain off all the fat. Return the duck to the pan with the onion mixture. Pour on the stock. Add a little salt and pepper, the bouquet garni and the port. Surround with the turnips. Bring to the boil, cover and transfer to a preheated oven at 180°C/350°F/gas mark 4. Cook for 2 hours or until the duck and turnips are tender. Remove the duck and turnips from the casserole and keep warm. Discard the bouquet garni. Skim the surface again. Boil rapidly until the sauce has reduced by half. Taste and re-season if necessary. Carve the duck and arrange on warm plates. Spoon a little of the sauce over and arrange the turnips to one side. Serve with the remaining sauce, jacket-baked potatoes and mangetout.

Casseroled Duck with Turnips and Carrots

SERVES 6

6 duck portions
50 g/2 oz/½ cup plain (all-purpose) flour
Salt and freshly ground black pepper
30 ml/2 tbsp sunflower oil
1 large onion, halved and thinly sliced
450 g/1 lb carrots, diced
450 g/1 lb turnips, diced
600 ml/1 pt/2½ cups chicken stock
1 satsuma, clementine or similar fruit
1 bay leaf
Parsley sprigs, to garnish
Royal Roast Potatoes (page 348) and peas, to serve

Wipe the duck with kitchen paper (paper towels). Season the flour with some salt and pepper and use to coat the duck. Heat the oil in a flameproof casserole (Dutch oven). Brown the duck quickly on all sides and remove from the casserole. Add the onion, carrots and turnips to the casserole and fry (sauté) for 4 minutes, stirring. Pour off any remaining fat. Return the duck to the pan and pour over the stock. Finely grate the rind from the satsuma or other fruit and add to the casserole with the bay leaf. Cover and cook in a preheated oven at 180°C/350°F/gas mark 4 for 1 hour. Remove the lid and continue cooking for a further 40 minutes until the duck skin is crisp.

Remove the duck from the casserole, transfer to a warm serving dish and keep warm. Spoon off any fat from the surface of the casserole and discard the bay leaf. Purée the contents of the casserole in a blender or food processor and return to the dish. Reheat. Taste and re-season, if necessary. Peel the satsuma and remove all the pith. Separate into segments. Spoon the sauce over the duck and garnish with the satsuma segments and parsley sprigs. Serve hot with Royal Roast Potatoes and peas.

Salmi de Canard

SERVES 4

2 kg/4½ lb oven-ready duck, with giblets
3 onions, sliced
3 large carrots, sliced
2 celery sticks, chopped
1 bay leaf
1 clove
1 chicken stock cube
600 ml/1 pt/2½ cups water
1 slice of lemon
2 smoked streaky bacon rashers (slices)
50 g/2 oz button mushrooms, very finely chopped
25 g/1 oz/¼ cup plain (all-purpose) flour
45 ml/3 tbsp port
Salt and freshly ground black pepper
8 stoned (pitted) green olives
French bread and a green salad, to serve

Put the duck giblets in a saucepan with one of the onions, one of the carrots, one of the celery sticks, the bay leaf, clove and stock cube. Add the water. Bring to the boil, skim the surface, reduce the heat, part-cover and simmer gently for 30 minutes. Meanwhile, put the slice of lemon in the body cavity of the duck. Put the remaining vegetables in a roasting tin (pan) and lay the duck on top. Cover the breast with the bacon. Roast in a preheated oven at 200°C/400°F/gas mark 6 for 30 minutes. Remove the duck, discard the bacon and cut the bird into quarters. Place in a casserole dish (Dutch oven). Spoon off the excess fat from the roasting tin. Stir in the mushrooms. Sprinkle the flour over the vegetables and stir well. Strain the stock and gradually blend into the vegetables. Bring to the boil, stirring. Stir in the port and season to taste. Pour over the duck. Cover and cook in the oven at 180°C/350°F/gas mark 4 for 1 hour or until the duck is really tender. Add the olives, taste and re-season if necessary. Serve hot with lots of French bread and a green salad.

GAME

Pheasant with Celery and Walnuts

SERVES 4

2 oranges
1 onion, thinly sliced
2 celery sticks, chopped
50 g/2 oz/½ cup walnuts,
50 g/2 oz/¼ cup unsalted (sweet) butter
1 oven-ready cock pheasant, quartered (page 17)
4 unsmoked streaky bacon rashers (slices), rinded and diced
100 ml/3½ fl oz/scant ½ cup chicken stock
75 ml/5 tbsp red vermouth
Salt and freshly ground black pepper
15 ml/1 tbsp cornflour (cornstarch)
Jacket-baked potatoes and peas, to serve

Pare the rind off one of the oranges. Cut into thin strips and boil in water for 3 minutes. Drain, rinse with cold water, drain again and reserve. Squeeze the juice from both oranges. Fry (sauté) the onion, celery and walnuts in half the butter in a flameproof casserole (Dutch oven) for 3 minutes, stirring. Remove from the pan with a draining spoon. Brown the pheasant and bacon in the remaining butter. Return the celery mixture to the pan and pour on the orange juice, stock, vermouth and a little salt and pepper. Bring to the boil, cover and cook in a preheated oven at 180°C/350°F/gas mark 4 for 1½ hours or until the pheasant is really tender. Transfer the bird to warm serving plates. Blend the cornflour with a little water and stir into the cooking liquid. Bring to the boil and cook for 1 minute, stirring, until slightly thickened. Taste and re-season, if necessary. Spoon over the pheasant and serve with jacket-baked potatoes and peas.

Pheasant with Celeriac and Carrot

SERVES 4

Prepare as for Pheasant with Celery and Walnuts, but omit the oranges. Use ½ celeriac (celery root), cut into very thin matchsticks, instead of the celery and 1 large carrot, cut into thin matchsticks, instead of the walnuts. Add an extra 50 ml/2 fl oz/¼ cup chicken stock instead of the orange juice and add 30 ml/2 tbsp single (light) cream after thickening the juices.

Casserole of Pheasant with Chestnuts and Oranges

SERVES 4

1 oven-ready pheasant, quartered (page 17)
25 g/1 oz/2 tbsp butter or margarine
2 onions, thinly sliced
300 g/11 oz/1 medium can of chestnuts
45 ml/3 tbsp plain (all-purpose) flour
450 ml/¾ pt/2 cups chicken or game stock
30 ml/2 tbsp redcurrant jelly (clear conserve)
3 oranges
Salt and freshly ground black pepper
Watercress, to garnish
Jacket-baked potatoes and peas, to serve

Wipe the pheasant all over with kitchen paper (paper towels). Brown in the butter or margarine in a flameproof casserole (Dutch oven), then remove. Add the onions and chestnuts and fry (sauté) for 2 minutes, stirring. Stir in the flour and cook for 1 minute. Blend in the stock and redcurrant jelly and bring to the boil. Finely grate the rind and squeeze the juice from 1 of the oranges. Add to the casserole. Return the pheasant to the casserole and add a little salt and pepper. Cover and transfer to a preheated oven at 180°C/350°F/gas mark 4 for 1½ hours. Meanwhile, cut all the rind and pith off the other two oranges and separate into segments by cutting either side of each membrane. When the pheasant is tender, remove from the oven, taste the sauce and re-season if necessary. Transfer the portions to warm serving plates. Spoon the sauce over. Garnish with the orange segments and watercress. Serve with jacket-baked potatoes and peas.

Forestry Pheasant

SERVES 4

1 oven-ready pheasant
25 g/1 oz/2 tbsp butter or margarine
12 button (pearl) onions, peeled but left whole
4 rindless streaky bacon rashers (slices), diced
4 chipolata sausages, halved
150 ml/¼ pt/⅔ cup chicken or game stock
150 ml/¼ pt/⅔ cup red wine
100 g/4 oz small button mushrooms
Salt and freshly ground black pepper
Jacket-baked potatoes and leaf spinach, to serve

Wipe the pheasant inside and out with kitchen paper (paper towels). Brown in the butter or margarine in a flameproof casserole (Dutch oven). Remove from the casserole. Add the onions, bacon and sausages and fry (sauté) for 3 minutes. Stir in the stock, wine and mushrooms. Return the bird to the casserole and season lightly. Cover and place in a preheated oven at 180°C/350°F/gas mark 4 for 1½ hours. Lift the pheasant out on to a warm carving dish. Cut into quarters and transfer to warm serving plates. Lift out the sausages, onions and mushrooms with a draining spoon and add to the plates. Keep warm. Spoon off as much fat as possible from the cooking juices, then boil rapidly until reduced by half. Taste and re-season, if necessary. Spoon over the pheasant and serve with jacket-baked potatoes and leaf spinach.

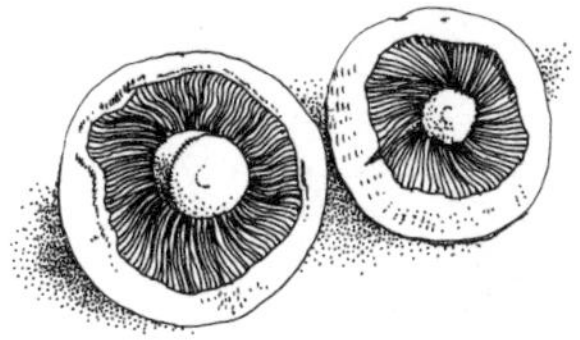

Pheasant with Cider and Pears

SERVES 4

1 oven-ready pheasant, quartered (page 17)
40 g/1½ oz/3 tbsp butter or margarine
2 large cooking pears, thinly sliced
Salt and freshly ground black pepper
15 ml/1 tbsp brandy
150 ml/¼ pt/⅔ cup medium-sweet cider
8 baby onions, peeled but left whole
30 ml/2 tbsp crème fraîche
Chopped parsley, to garnish
Speciality Creamed Potatoes (page 348) and peas, to serve

Rinse the pheasant under cold running water and dry on kitchen paper (paper towels). Melt half the butter or margarine in a flameproof casserole (Dutch oven) and brown the pheasant all over. Remove with a draining spoon. Put half the pears in the base of the casserole and toss in the juices. Lay the pheasant on top and season well. Add the remaining pear slices. Mix together the brandy and cider and pour over. Cover tightly and cook in a preheated oven at 180°C/350°F/gas mark 4 for 1 hour. Meanwhile, boil the onions in water for 5 minutes. Drain, dry on kitchen paper and fry (sauté) in the remaining butter or margarine to brown. Arrange round the top of the casserole and return to the oven for 15 minutes. Remove the pheasant, onions and pears and transfer to a warm serving dish. Boil the juices until well reduced and stir in the crème fraîche. Spoon over the pheasant and sprinkle with chopped parsley. Serve with Speciality Creamed Potatoes and peas.

Pheasant with White Wine and Apples

SERVES 4

Prepare as for Pheasant with Cider and Pears, but substitute eating (dessert) apples for the pears and a fruity white wine for the cider.

Casseroled Pheasant with Italian Sauce

SERVES 4

1 oven-ready cock pheasant, quartered (page 17)
25 g/1 oz/2 tbsp butter or margarine
15 ml/1 tbsp plain (all-purpose) flour
150 ml/¼ pt/⅔ cup chicken stock
6 tomatoes, skinned, seeded and chopped
5 ml/1 tsp caster (superfine) sugar
150 ml/¼ pt/⅔ cup double (heavy) cream
50 g/2 oz/½ cup Parmesan cheese, grated
Salt and freshly ground black pepper
Basil leaves, to garnish
New potatoes and a mixed leaf salad, to serve

Fry (sauté) the pheasant in the butter or margarine in a flameproof casserole (Dutch oven) on all sides to brown. Cover, reduce the heat and cook gently for 40 minutes or until tender (depending on the toughness of the bird). Remove from the pan and keep warm. Drain off the fat. Blend the flour with the stock and stir into the pan. Bring to the boil, stirring. Add the tomatoes, sugar, cream and cheese and simmer for 3 minutes, stirring. Season to taste. Return the pheasant to the pan and simmer for a further 5 minutes. Transfer to warm plates. Scatter a few basil leaves over and serve with new potatoes and a mixed leaf salad.

Salmi of Pheasant

SERVES 4

Espagnole Sauce (page 335)
45 ml/3 tbsp port
15 ml/1 tbsp redcurrant jelly (clear conserve)
1 oven-ready pheasant, quartered (page 17)
Salt and freshly ground black pepper
25 g/1 oz/2 tbsp butter or margarine
100 g/4 oz button mushrooms, left whole
2 slices of white bread, crusts removed
30 ml/2 tbsp olive oil
30 ml/2 tbsp chopped parsley
New potatoes, to serve

Make the Espagnole sauce and stir in the port and redcurrant jelly. Wipe the pheasant quarters with kitchen paper (paper towels). Season lightly. Brown in the butter or margarine in a flameproof casserole (Dutch oven). Cover with a lid and cook gently for 20 minutes. Pour over the sauce. Add the mushrooms. Bring to the boil. Reduce the heat, cover and simmer very gently for 1 hour until the pheasant is really tender. Meanwhile, fry (sauté) the bread in the olive oil until golden on both sides. Drain on kitchen paper and cut into triangles. When the pheasant is cooked, lift it out on to warm plates, spoon the sauce over, garnish with the fried bread triangles and the parsley and serve with new potatoes.

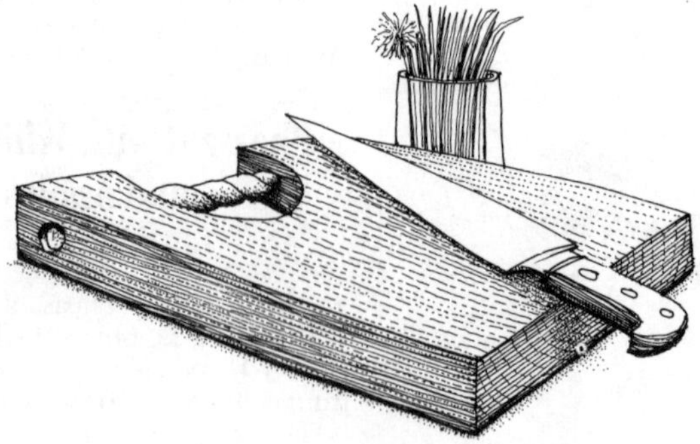

Pheasant with Artichokes and Chestnuts

SERVES 4

1 large oven-ready pheasant, quartered (page 17)
300 ml/½ pt/1¼ cups dry white wine
300 ml/½ pt/1¼ cups chicken stock
15 ml/1 tbsp brandy
350 g/12 oz/1 medium can of unsweetened chestnut purée (paste)
30 ml/2 tbsp crème fraîche
425 g/15 oz/1 large can of artichoke hearts, drained and very finely chopped
Salt and freshly ground black pepper
A pinch of grated nutmeg
25 g/1 oz/2 tbsp unsalted (sweet) butter, diced
100 g/4 oz baby button mushrooms, trimmed
30 ml/2 tbsp water
Parsley sprigs, to garnish
Plain boiled potatoes, to serve

Wipe the pheasant with kitchen paper (paper towels). Place in a flameproof casserole (Dutch oven) and add the wine, stock and brandy. Bring to the boil, reduce the heat and simmer gently for 1 hour or until the pheasant is really tender. Lift the bird out of the pan with a draining spoon. Place on a warm serving dish and keep warm. Boil the liquid until reduced to about 300 ml/½ pt/1¼ cups. Stir in the chestnut purée, crème fraîche, artichokes, a little salt and pepper and the nutmeg. Bring to the boil, stirring. Whisk in the butter a piece at a time. Taste and re-season, if necessary. Meanwhile, cook the mushrooms in the water until tender. Boil rapidly to evaporate the liquid. Spoon the sauce over the pheasant, garnish with the mushrooms and parsley sprigs and serve hot with plain boiled potatoes.

Taunton Grouse

SERVES 4

2 oven-ready grouse, halved (page 17)
40 g/1½ oz/3 tbsp butter or margarine
30 ml/2 tbsp sunflower oil
1 large onion, finely chopped
2 turnips, finely chopped
4 streaky bacon rashers (slices), rinded and diced
25 g/1 oz/2 tbsp plain (all-purpose) flour
300 ml/½ pt/1¼ cups chicken stock
450 ml/¾ pt/2 cups medium-sweet cider
1 bouquet garni sachet
Salt and freshly ground black pepper
2 slices of bread, each cut into 4 triangles
15 ml/1 tbsp chopped parsley
Speciality Creamed Potatoes (page 348) and shredded cabbage, to serve

Brown the grouse in 25 g/1 oz/2 tbsp of the butter or margarine and 15 ml/1 tbsp of the oil in a flameproof casserole (Dutch oven). Remove from the pan. Add the onion, turnips and bacon and fry (sauté) for 2 minutes, stirring. Stir in the flour and cook, stirring, for 1 minute. Remove from the heat and blend in the stock and cider. Return to the heat and bring to the boil, stirring. Return the grouse to the casserole. Add the bouquet garni and some salt and pepper. Cover and cook in a preheated oven at 180°C/350°F/gas mark 4 for 1½ hours. Remove the bouquet garni. Meanwhile, fry the bread in the remaining butter or margarine and oil until golden brown on both sides. Spoon the grouse on to warm plates with the sauce and arrange two triangles of fried bread to the side of each. Sprinkle the grouse with the parsley and serve with Speciality Creamed Potatoes and shredded cabbage.

Grouse in Lager

SERVES 4

Prepare as for Taunton Grouse, but use lager instead of cider and add 15 ml/1 tbsp clear honey (or to taste) to the sauce.

Marinated Grouse of the Ancient Romans

The Ancient Romans didn't have powdered gelatine, but it makes the dish much simpler to make!

SERVES 4

2 oven-ready grouse
2 shallots, finely chopped
150 ml/¼ pt/⅔ cup white wine
30 ml/2 tbsp olive oil
15 ml/1 tbsp clear honey
1 large bay leaf
2 carrots, diced
1 turnip, diced
2 celery sticks, sliced
600 ml/1 pt/2½ cups chicken stock
2.5 ml/½ tsp anchovy essence (extract)
1 bouquet garni sachet
Salt and freshly ground black pepper
10 ml/2 tsp powdered gelatine
30 ml/2 tbsp chopped parsley
Fresh bay leaves, to garnish
Buttered toast, to serve

Skin the birds and wipe inside and out with kitchen paper (paper towels). Place in shallow container with a lid. Mix together the shallots, wine, half the oil and the honey and pour over. Turn to coat the birds completely. Add the bay leaf, torn in half. Cover and leave in the fridge to marinate for 2 days.

When ready to cook, brown the prepared vegetables in the remaining oil in a flameproof casserole (Dutch oven). Top with the birds and pour over the marinade, discarding the bay leaf. Add the stock, anchovy essence, bouquet garni and a little salt and pepper. Bring to the boil, reduce the heat, cover and cook very gently for 1 hour until the birds are really tender. Leave to cool in the liquid. Remove any fat, lift the birds out and place on a plate. Boil the liquid until it is reduced by half. Stir in the gelatine until completely dissolved and add the parsley. Taste and re-season, if necessary. Pour into a lightly oiled ring mould. Leave until cold, then chill. Meanwhile, remove all the meat from the grouse and chill. When ready to serve, turn the jellied vegetables out on to a serving plate. Place the grouse in the centre and garnish with fresh bay leaves before serving with buttered toast.

Victorian Grouse Fricassee

SERVES 4

2 oven-ready grouse
1 large onion
1 clove
A pinch of grated nutmeg
Salt and white pepper
Milk, if necessary
25 g/1 oz/2 tbsp butter or margarine
175 g/6 oz button mushrooms, halved
25 g/1 oz/¼ cup plain (all-purpose) flour
1 slice of smoked ham, diced
2 hard-boiled (hard-cooked) eggs
150 ml/¼ pt/⅔ cup double (heavy) cream
30 ml/2 tsp chopped parsley
Plain Boiled Rice (page 351) and buttered carrots, to serve

Wipe the grouse inside and out with kitchen paper (paper towels) and place in a large saucepan. Peel the onion and stud with the clove. Add to the pan with the nutmeg and 5 ml/1 tsp salt. Add just enough water to cover the birds. Bring to the boil, skim the surface, reduce the heat, cover and simmer gently for 1 hour. Lift out the grouse. Remove the skin and cut all the meat off the bones. Cut into neat pieces. Skim the surface of the cooking liquid to remove as much fat as possible and measure 600 ml/1 pt/2½ cups into a measuring jug, topping up with milk, if necessary. Remove the clove from the onion and chop the onion. Melt the butter or margarine in a saucepan. Add the onion and mushrooms and cook for 2 minutes, stirring. Stir in the flour and cook for 1 minute, stirring. Blend in the measured stock, bring to the boil and cook for 2 minutes, stirring. Add the grouse, ham, eggs and cream and season with salt and pepper and stir in the parsley. Simmer gently for 5 minutes. Spoon on to a bed of Plain Boiled Rice and serve with buttered carrots.

Salmi of Grouse

SERVES 4

Prepare as Salmi of Pheasant (page 230), but use two grouse, halved. Use 30 ml/2 tbsp whisky instead of the port and sweeten the sauce with 5 ml/ 1 tsp clear honey. Cook in the butter or margarine for 12 minutes instead of 20 minutes, then continue as before.

Braised Pigeons with Red Cabbage

SERVES 6

6 oven-ready pigeons
400 ml/14 fl oz/1¾ cups red wine
1 carrot
2 onions
1 garlic clove, crushed
1 bouquet garni sachet
Salt and freshly ground black pepper
Finely grated rind of ½ lemon
50 g/2 oz/¼ cup unsalted (sweet) butter
1 small red cabbage, shredded
1 eating (dessert) apple, cored and sliced
50 g/2 oz/⅓ cup sultanas (golden raisins)
30 ml/2 tbsp red wine vinegar
45 ml/3 tbsp light brown sugar
30 ml/2 tbsp water
100 g/4 oz smooth chicken liver pâté with garlic
Lemon wedges and watercress sprigs, to garnish
Jacket-baked potatoes with soured (dairy sour) cream flavoured with snipped chives, to serve

Wash the pigeons and dry with kitchen paper (paper towels). Place in a dish in a single layer. Pour over the wine. Chop the carrot and one of the onions and add to the dish with the garlic, bouquet garni, a little salt and pepper and the lemon rind. Cover and leave to marinate overnight.

When ready to cook, remove the birds from the marinade. Heat the butter in a flameproof casserole (Dutch oven). Brown the birds on all sides. Pour on the marinade and bring to the boil. Cover and cook in a preheated oven at 150°C/300°F/gas mark 2 for 2½–3 hours.

When the birds are in the oven, peel and thinly slice the remaining onion. Mix with the cabbage, apple, sultanas, vinegar and sugar in a second casserole dish. Season with salt and pepper and add the water. Cover and place in the oven with the pigeons for the remaining cooking time. Cook until the pigeons are really tender. Lift the pigeons out of the liquid and keep warm. Gradually whisk the pâté into the cooking liquid, over a gentle heat until thickened and well-flavoured. Taste and re-season if necessary. Transfer the pigeons to warm serving plates. Spoon a little of the sauce over each. Garnish with lemon wedges and watercress and serve with the cabbage mixture and jacket-baked potatoes, topped with soured cream and chives.

Braised Squab with White Cabbage and Caraway

SERVES 4

Prepare as for Braised Pigeons with Red Cabbage, but use squab instead of pigeons, white cabbage instead of red, white wine vinegar instead of red wine vinegar and add 10 ml/2 tsp caraway seeds to the mixture.

Casserole of Pigeons with Baby Onions and Mushroom Stuffing Balls

SERVES 4

4 small oven-ready pigeons
50 g/2 oz/¼ cup unsalted (sweet) butter
100 g/4 oz pancetta, diced
12 button (pearl) onions, peeled but left whole
30 ml/2 tbsp plain (all-purpose) flour
450 ml/¾ pt/2 cups chicken stock
15 ml/1 tbsp brandy
1 bay leaf
1 lemon slice
Salt and freshly ground black pepper
100 g/4 oz/2 cups wholemeal breadcrumbs
50 g/2 oz button mushrooms, finely chopped
5 ml/1 tsp Worcestershire sauce
30 ml/2 tbsp chopped parsley
Finely grated rind of ½ lemon
1 large egg, beaten
Chopped parsley, to garnish
Plain boiled potatoes, to serve

Wipe the pigeons inside and out with kitchen paper (paper towels). Melt half of the butter in a large flameproof casserole (Dutch oven). Add the pigeons and brown on all sides. Remove from the casserole. Add the pancetta and onions and fry (sauté) for 1 minute, stirring. Stir in the flour. Remove from the heat and gradually blend in the stock and brandy. Return to the heat, bring to the boil and cook for 2 minutes, stirring all the time. Return the pigeons to the casserole and turn over in the liquid. Add the bay leaf and lemon slice, a little salt and a good grinding of pepper. Cover and place in a preheated oven at 180°C/350°F/gas mark 4 for 1 hour. Meanwhile, mix the breadcrumbs with the mushrooms, Worcestershire sauce, parsley and lemon rind. Add a little salt and lots of pepper. Melt the remaining butter and stir in with the egg to bind. Shape into 12 small balls. Arrange the stuffing balls around the pigeons in the casserole. Cover again and return to the oven for a further 30 minutes. Discard the bay leaf and lemon slice. Taste the liquid and re-season, if necessary. Sprinkle with chopped parsley and serve with plain boiled potatoes.

Creamy Pigeons with Redcurrant

SERVES 4–6

4 oven-ready pigeons
Salt and freshly ground black pepper
4 small rosemary sprigs
75 g/3 oz/⅓ cup butter or margarine
150 ml/¼ pt/⅔ cup crème fraîche
15 ml/1 tbsp redcurrant jelly (clear conserve)
Rosemary sprigs, to garnish
Plain boiled potatoes and a crisp green salad, to serve

Wipe the pigeons inside and out with kitchen paper (paper towels). Season inside and out with salt and pepper and push a small rosemary sprig inside each bird. Melt the butter or margarine in a large flameproof casserole (Dutch oven). Brown the pigeons on all sides. Cover with a lid and cook very gently for 45 minutes, turning twice. Transfer the pigeons to warm serving plates and keep warm. Add the crème fraîche and redcurrant jelly to the juices in the pan and bring to the boil, stirring, until thickened and the jelly has dissolved. Season to taste. Spoon over the pigeons, garnish each with a rosemary sprig and serve hot with plain boiled potatoes and a crisp green salad.

Spatchcocked Pigeons in Red Wine

SERVES 4

4 oven-ready pigeons, spatchcocked (page 18)
Salt and freshly ground black pepper
50 g/2 oz/¼ cup butter or margarine
30 ml/2 tbsp sunflower oil
1 small onion, grated
20 g/¾ oz/3 tbsp plain (all-purpose) flour
300 ml/½ pt/1¼ cups chicken stock
120 ml/4 fl oz/½ cup red wine
15 ml/1 tbsp brandy
15 ml/1 tbsp tomato purée (paste)
4 slices of wholemeal bread, crusts removed
100 g/4 oz baby button mushrooms
Chopped parsley, to garnish
Speciality Creamed Potatoes (page 348) and baby carrots with peas, to serve

Wipe the pigeons with kitchen paper (paper towels). Season with salt and pepper. Brown the pigeons in half the butter or margarine and oil in a large flameproof casserole (Dutch oven) until golden brown. Remove from the pan. Add the onion and fry (sauté) for 1 minute, stirring. Stir in the flour and cook for a further 1 minute. Remove from the heat and blend in the stock and wine. Return to the heat and bring to the boil, stirring. Stir in the brandy and tomato purée and season to taste. Return the pigeons to the casserole. Cover and simmer very gently for 45 minutes until the pigeons are tender.

Meanwhile, fry the bread in the remaining butter or margarine and oil until golden on both sides. Drain on kitchen paper. Place a slice of fried bread on four warm serving plates. Top each with a spatchcocked pigeon and spoon the sauce over. Meanwhile, simmer the mushrooms in a little water, salt and pepper for 3–4 minutes until cooked through. Transfer with a draining spoon to beside the pigeons, sprinkle with chopped parsley and serve with Speciality Creamed Potatoes and baby carrots with peas.

Partridge in Milk

SERVES 4

2 oven-ready partridges, halved (page 17)
1 onion, chopped
2 rindless streaky bacon rashers (slices), diced
1 carrot, thinly sliced
1 turnip, thinly sliced
600 ml/1 pt/2½ cups milk
Salt and white pepper
1.5 ml/¼ tsp ground mace
15 g/½ oz/2 tbsp cornflour (cornstarch)
15 g/½ oz/1 tbsp unsalted (sweet) butter
15 ml/1 tbsp chopped parsley, to garnish
New potatoes and French (green) beans, to serve

Wipe the birds with kitchen paper (paper towels). Place in a casserole (Dutch oven). Add the onion, bacon, carrot and turnip. Pour in all but 30 ml/2 tbsp of the milk. Season with salt and white pepper and add the mace. Bring just to the boil. Cover and transfer to a preheated oven at 180°C/350°F/gas mark 4 and cook for 1 hour or until the partridges are really tender. Carefully lift the birds out of the pan and keep warm. Blend the cornflour with the remaining milk. Stir into the cooking liquid, bring to the boil and cook for 1 minute, stirring. Whisk in the butter in small pieces and simmer for 2 minutes. Taste and re-season, if necessary. Pour over the partridges, garnish with the parsley and serve with new potatoes and French beans.

Partridge with Olives

SERVES 4

2 oven-ready partridges
15 ml/1 tbsp plain (all-purpose) flour
Salt and freshly ground black pepper
25 g/1 oz/2 tbsp butter or margarine
1 onion, finely chopped
4 rindless streaky bacon rashers (slices), chopped
300 ml/½ pt/1¼ cups chicken or game stock
200 ml/7 fl oz/scant 1 cup red wine
5 ml/1 tsp tomato purée (paste)
1 small bay leaf
50 g/2 oz stoned (pitted) black olives, halved
Watercress, to garnish
Plain boiled potatoes, to serve

Wipe the partridges inside and out with kitchen paper (paper towels), then cut into halves. Mix the flour with a little salt and pepper and sprinkle all over the birds. Melt the butter or margarine in a flameproof casserole (Dutch oven) and brown the partridge all over. Remove from the pan. Add the onion and bacon and fry (sauté) for 2 minutes. Stir in the stock, wine and tomato purée. Bring to the boil. Return the partridge to the pan. Add the bay leaf. Cover and cook in a preheated oven at 180°C/350°F/gas mark 4 for 1 hour. Remove the partridge and transfer to warm serving plates. Boil the sauce rapidly until reduced by half. Taste and re-season. Stir in the olives. Spoon over the partridge and garnish with watercress. Serve with plain boiled potatoes.

Salmi of Partridge

SERVES 4

Prepare as for Salmi of Pheasant (page 230), but use 2 partridges instead of the pheasant. Flavour the Espagnole Sauce with medium-dry sherry instead of port and continue as before.

Country Partridge Casserole

SERVES 4

2 oven-ready partridges, quartered (page 17)
25 g/1 oz/2 tbsp butter or margarine
2 onions, sliced
2 carrots, sliced
1 small parsnip, sliced
225 g/8 oz pork chipolatas, cut into chunks
2 rindless streaky bacon rashers (slices), chopped
300 ml/½ pt/1¼ cups chicken or game stock
1 bouquet garni sachet
30 ml/2 tbsp raisins
25 g/1 oz/¼ cup walnut halves, roughly chopped
Salt and freshly ground black pepper
15 ml/1 tbsp plain (all-purpose) flour
15 ml/1 tbsp water
30 ml/2 tbsp chopped parsley
Redcurrant jelly (clear conserve) and jacket-baked potatoes, to serve

Wipe the partridges with kitchen paper (paper towels). Brown in the butter or margarine in a flameproof casserole (Dutch oven). Remove from the pan. Add the prepared vegetables, the sausages and bacon and fry (sauté) for 3 minutes, stirring. Pour off any excess fat. Add the stock, bouquet garni, raisins and walnuts. Return the birds to the pan and season lightly. Bring to the boil, cover and place in a preheated oven at 180°C/350°F/gas mark 4 for 1 hour. Remove the birds from the pan. Blend the flour with the water until smooth. Stir in a little of the hot stock, then pour back into the pan. Stir well. Bring to the boil and cook for 2 minutes, stirring. Return the partridges to the pan. Taste and re-season, if necessary. Sprinkle with chopped parsley and serve with redcurrant jelly and jacket-baked potatoes.

Guinea Fowl in White Bordeaux

SERVES 4

2 oven-ready guinea fowl, each cut into 4 pieces (page 17)
75 ml/5 tbsp plain (all-purpose) flour
Salt and freshly ground black pepper
100 g/4 oz belly pork, rinded and diced
18 button (pearl) onions, peeled but left whole
75 g/3 oz/⅓ cup unsalted (sweet) butter
30 ml/2 tbsp brandy
600 ml/1 pt/2½ cups white Bordeaux
1 bouquet garni sachet
15 ml/1 tbsp clear honey
175 g/6 oz whole button mushrooms
Chopped parsley, to garnish
Baby new potatoes, baby sweetcorn and baby carrots, to serve

Toss the guinea fowl joints in 30 ml/2 tbsp of the flour seasoned with a little salt and pepper. Cook the pork in a flameproof casserole (Dutch oven) until the fat runs and the pork is beginning to brown, tossing all the time. Remove from the casserole with a draining spoon. Add the onions and brown in the pork fat. Remove from the casserole. Melt 25 g/1 oz/2 tbsp of the butter in the pan and brown the birds on all sides. Return the pork and onions to the pan. Add the brandy and ignite. Shake the pan until the flames subside. Add the wine, bouquet garni, honey, mushrooms and a little salt and pepper. Bring to the boil, cover and cook gently for about 45 minutes or until the birds are tender.

Remove the bouquet garni. Mash together the remaining butter and flour until smooth. Remove the guinea fowl, onions and mushrooms from the pan with a draining spoon and keep warm. Gradually whisk the butter mixture into the liquid in the pan over a moderate heat until thickened and smooth. Continue cooking for 2 minutes, stirring all the time. Taste and re-season if necessary. Return the guinea fowl, onions and mushrooms to the sauce. Sprinkle with chopped parsley and serve with baby new potatoes, baby corn cobs and baby carrots.

Cumberland Casseroled Quail

SERVES 4

1 orange
4 oven-ready quail
25 g/1 oz/2 tbsp butter or margarine
90 ml/6 tbsp port
300 ml/½ pt/1¼ cups chicken stock
45 ml/3 tbsp redcurrant jelly (clear conserve)
Salt and freshly ground black pepper
1 piece of cinnamon stick
10 ml/2 tsp lemon juice
Speciality Creamed Potatoes (page 348) and buttered shredded cabbage, to serve

Thinly pare the rind from the orange. Cut into thin strips. Boil in water for 3 minutes, drain, rinse with cold water, drain again and reserve. Squeeze the orange juice. Wipe the quail inside and out with kitchen paper (paper towels). Brown in the butter or margarine in a flameproof casserole (Dutch oven). Add the remaining ingredients except the lemon juice and bring to the boil. Cover and place in a preheated oven at 200°C/400°F/gas mark 6 for 25 minutes. Stir in the lemon juice, taste and re-season, if necessary. Serve hot with Speciality Creamed Potatoes and buttered shredded cabbage.

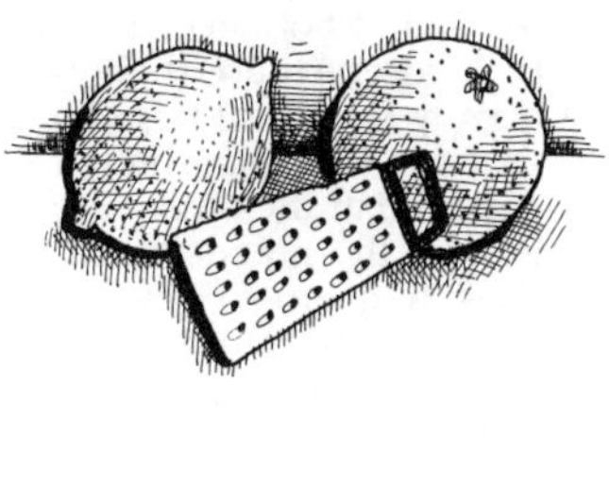

Quail Ragout with Mushroom Selection

You can buy packs of oyster, chanterelle, morel and chestnut mushrooms in supermarkets. Use any varieties you like.

SERVES 4

4 oven-ready quail, halved (page 17)
60 ml/4 tbsp plain (all-purpose) flour
Salt and freshly ground black pepper
Finely grated rind of ½ orange
2 fat, rindless, streaky bacon rashers (slices), diced
30 ml/2 tbsp olive oil
1 leek, thinly sliced
1 small garlic clove, crushed
30 ml/2 tbsp calvados or brandy
100 g/4 oz mixed mushrooms, sliced
450 ml/¾ pt/2 cups chicken stock
1 bouquet garni sachet
Chopped parsley, to garnish
Hot French bread, to serve

Wipe the quail with kitchen paper (paper towels). Mix the flour with a little salt and pepper and the orange rind. Use to coat the quail. Dry-fry the bacon in a large flameproof casserole (Dutch) oven until the fat runs. Remove from the pan with a draining spoon. Add the oil, then the quail and brown on all sides. Remove from the pan. Stir in the leek and garlic and fry (sauté) for 1 minute, stirring. Return the bacon and quail to the pan. Add the calvados or brandy and ignite. Shake the pan until the flames subside. Add the mushrooms, stock and bouquet garni. Bring to the boil, cover, reduce the heat and simmer gently for 25–30 minutes until the quail are really tender. Discard the bouquet garni. Lift the birds out of the casserole. Boil the liquid rapidly until reduced by a quarter. Taste and re-season, if necessary. Return the quail to the casserole, sprinkle with chopped parsley and serve with hot French bread.

Spiced Salmi of Snipe

SERVES 4

1 lemon
4 oven-ready snipe
4 streaky bacon rashers (slices)
15 ml/1 tbsp olive oil
1 onion, finely chopped
1 carrot, finely chopped
150 ml/¼ pt/⅔ cup chicken stock
150 ml/¼ pt/⅔ cup white wine
15 ml/1 tbsp tomato purée (paste)
1.5 ml/¼ tsp cayenne
1.5 ml/¼ tsp ground ginger
Salt and freshly ground black pepper
4 slices of white bread, crusts removed
25 g/1 oz/2 tbsp butter or margarine
5 ml/1 tsp caster (superfine) sugar
Watercress sprigs, to garnish
Baby new potatoes, baby carrots, baby corn and thin French (green) beans, to serve

Cut four slices from the lemon and reserve for garnish. Squeeze the juice from the remainder. Wipe the snipe inside and out with kitchen paper (paper towels). Wrap a rasher of bacon round each and secure. Heat the oil in a flameproof casserole (Dutch oven). Add the onion and carrot and fry (sauté) for 3 minutes. Add the birds. Cover and roast in a preheated oven at 220°C/425°F/gas mark 7 for 15 minutes. Lift the birds out of the casserole to remove and discard the bacon. Return the birds to the casserole. Blend the stock with the wine and tomato purée. Add to the pan with the cayenne, ginger and a little salt and pepper. Bring to the boil, cover, reduce the heat and simmer for 10–15 minutes until tender. Meanwhile, fry the bread in the butter or margarine until golden and crisp on both sides. Drain on kitchen paper. Remove the birds from the casserole, stir in the lemon juice and boil the liquid until reduced by half. Add the sugar, taste and re-season, if necessary. Place a snipe on a slice of fried bread on four warm plates. Strain the sauce over and garnish with watercress sprigs. Serve hot with baby new potatoes, baby carrots, baby corn cobs and thin French beans.

Pasta and Rice Meals

Pasta and rice are rapidly becoming as much a staple part of our diet as potatoes. Both are highly nutritious and very versatile and can be the base of a huge choice of fantastic poultry and game recipes.

CHICKEN

Chicken Ravioli

SERVES 4–6

For the sauce:
30 ml/2 tbsp olive oil
15 g/½ oz/1 tbsp butter or margarine
1 garlic clove, crushed
750 ml/1½ pts/3 cups passata (sieved tomatoes)
45 ml/3 tbsp tomato purée (paste)
5 ml/1 tsp dried basil
5 ml/1 tsp dried rosemary, crushed
Salt and freshly ground black pepper
For the filling:
100 g/4 oz minced (ground) pork
1 garlic clove, crushed
175 g/6 oz/1½ cups cooked chicken, finely chopped
50 g/2 oz/½ cup cooked ham, finely chopped
30 ml/2 tbsp chopped parsley
1 egg, beaten
For the pasta:
450 g/1 lb/4 cups plain (all-purpose) flour
2 eggs
250 ml/8 fl oz/1 cup water
Grated Parmesan cheese, to serve

To make the sauce, heat the oil and butter or margarine in a pan and fry (sauté) the garlic for 1 minute. Add the passata, tomato purée, basil and rosemary. Season to taste. Bring to the boil, cover, reduce the heat to as low as possible and simmer for 20 minutes.

To make the filling, dry-fry the pork with the garlic, stirring, until the pork is no longer pink and all the grains are separate. Remove from the heat and stir in the remaining meats and the parsley. Season lightly and mix in the egg to bind.

To make the pasta, sift the flour and a pinch of salt into a large bowl. Make a well in the centre. Add the eggs and half the water. Gradually work in the flour, adding more water as necessary to form a firm dough. Knead gently on a lightly floured surface. Cut the dough in half. Roll out each half to a large, thin square. Place small spoonfuls of the chicken mixture at regular intervals in rows across one sheet of dough. Brush between each mound with water. Lay the second sheet over the top and gently press between each mound to seal the edges. Cut into small cushions, using a pastry (paste) cutter or a sharp knife. Bring a large pan of lightly salted water to the boil. Drop in the ravioli and cook in batches for about 4 minutes until they rise to the surface and are just cooked. Remove with a draining spoon and keep warm while cooking the remainder. Add to the tomato sauce and simmer for 5 minutes. Serve hot, sprinkled with grated Parmesan cheese.

Chicken Tetrazzini

SERVES 4

350 g/12 oz spaghetti
25 g/1 oz/2 tbsp unsalted (sweet) butter
1 onion, finely chopped
175 g/6 oz button mushrooms, sliced
1 celeriac (celery root), grated
1 carrot, grated
15 ml/1 tbsp plain (all-purpose) flour
150 ml/¼ pt/⅔ cup chicken stock
150 ml/¼ pt/⅔ cup single (light) cream
225 g/8 oz/2 cups cooked chicken, diced, all skin removed
Milk
50 g/2 oz/½ cup Parmesan cheese, grated
30 ml/2 tbsp flaked (slivered) almonds
15 ml/1 tbsp chopped parsley

Cook the spaghetti according to the packet directions. Drain. Meanwhile, melt the butter and cook the onion, mushrooms, celeriac and carrot for 4 minutes, stirring, until soft but not brown. Blend in the flour and cook for 1 minute. Stir in the stock and cream. Bring to the boil and simmer for 2 minutes. Add the chicken and heat through. Stir in the spaghetti and thin with a little milk, if necessary. Toss over a gentle heat. Pile into a flameproof dish. Sprinkle with the Parmesan, almonds and parsley and flash under a hot grill (broiler) until bubbling and the almonds are toasted.

Chicken and Ricotta Ravioli

SERVES 4–6

Prepare the sauce and pasta dough as for Chicken Ravioli, but omit the pork and mix 100 g/4 oz/½ cup ricotta cheese into the filling ingredients after frying (sautéing).

Chicken, Spinach and Ricotta Ravioli

SERVES 4–6

Prepare the sauce and pasta dough as for Chicken Ravioli, but for the filling mix 100 g/4 oz/1 cup of cooked, finely chopped chicken, 100 g/4 oz/½ cup ricotta cheese and 100 g/4 oz cooked chopped spinach, very well drained, instead. Flavour with a good pinch of nutmeg and some salt and pepper and bind with the egg. Then continue as before.

Pasta Soufflé Sensation

SERVES 4

Butter or margarine, for greasing
425 g/15 oz/1 large can of pasta in tomato sauce
295 g/10½ oz/1 medium can of condensed cream of chicken soup
75 g/3 oz/¾ cup Cheddar cheese, grated
4 eggs, separated
Freshly ground black pepper

Grease a 20 cm/8 in round soufflé dish. Empty the contents of the can of pasta into the dish. Put the soup in a bowl. Whisk in the cheese and egg yolks and season with pepper. Whisk the egg whites until stiff and fold into the soup mixture with a metal spoon. Turn into the soufflé dish and bake in the hot oven at 200°C/400°F/gas mark 6 for about 25–30 minutes until well risen and golden. Serve straight away.

Sun-kissed Tagliatelle

SERVES 4

285 g/10½ oz/1 small jar of sun-dried tomatoes, drained, reserving the oil
Olive oil
100 g/4 oz/1 cup Parmesan cheese, grated
50 g/2 oz/½ cup chopped mixed nuts
50 g/2 oz/½ cup chopped parsley
2 garlic cloves
4 skinless chicken breasts
Salt and freshly ground black pepper
225 g/8 oz tagliatelle
Lemon wedges and parsley sprigs, to garnish

Put the tomatoes in a blender or food processor. Make up the reserved tomato oil to 300 ml/½ pt/1¼ cups with olive oil. Add the oil to the blender with the remaining ingredients except the chicken, seasoning and pasta. Run the machine until the mixture forms a smooth paste, stopping the machine and scraping down the sides from time to time. If the paste is a too thick, add a little hot water. Lay the chicken breasts on foil on the grill (broiler) rack. Brush with a little olive oil and season with salt and pepper. Grill (broil) for about 12 minutes, turning once or twice and brushing with oil, until cooked through and golden. Meanwhile, cook the pasta according to the packet directions. Drain and return to the saucepan. Add the sun-dried tomato paste and heat gently, tossing, until every strand is coated. Pile on to warm plates, place a chicken breast to one side and garnish with lemon wedges and parsley sprigs.

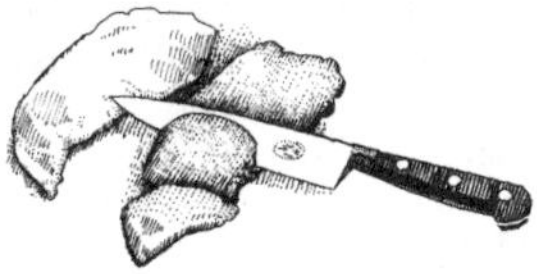

Gnocchi alla Romana con Pollo

SERVES 6

900 ml/1½ pts/3¾ cups milk
1 sprig of rosemary
225 g/8 oz/1⅓ cups semolina (cream of wheat)
100 g/4 oz/½ cup unsalted (sweet) butter
175 g/6 oz/1½ cups Parmesan cheese, grated
Salt and freshly ground black pepper
3 large eggs, beaten
Freshly grated nutmeg
4 chicken portions
30 ml/2 tbsp olive oil
1 garlic clove, crushed
Chopped parsley, to garnish
Green salad, to serve

Put the milk in a saucepan with the rosemary. Bring to the boil, remove from the heat and leave to infuse for 15 minutes. Remove the rosemary. Stir in the semolina and bring to the boil, stirring all the time. Cook for 3 minutes, remove from the heat and stir in half the butter and 100g/4 oz/1 cup of the cheese. Season well with salt and pepper. Gradually beat the eggs into the mixture. Turn into a greased shallow baking tin (pan) and chill for 2 hours until firm. Cut into squares, then roll into walnut-sized balls with lightly floured hands. Use a little of the remaining butter to grease an ovenproof dish. Arrange the gnocchi in a single layer in the dish. Sprinkle with a little more salt and pepper and some freshly grated nutmeg. Melt the remaining butter and drizzle over the surface. Sprinkle with the remaining cheese. Put the chicken in a small roasting tin (pan). Mix the oil with the garlic and some salt and pepper and drizzle over the chicken. Put the gnocchi in the middle of the oven and the chicken on the shelf above and bake at 180°C/350°F/gas mark 4 for about 40 minutes until golden brown and the chicken is cooked through. Transfer the chicken to warm plates and spoon the juices over. Sprinkle with parsley and serve with the gnocchi and a green salad.

Grilled Chicken with Pasta

SERVES 4

225 g/8 oz fresh pasta
50 g/2 oz/¼ cup unsalted (sweet) butter
Freshly ground black pepper
50 g/2 oz/½ cup Parmesan cheese, freshly grated
Plain Grilled Chicken in Butter (page 123)
Lemon wedges, to garnish
Green salad, to serve

Cook the pasta in boiling salted water for about 4 minutes until just tender. Drain. Melt the butter in the saucepan. Add the pasta and lots of pepper and toss well with two forks over a gentle heat. Pile on to a serving dish and top with the cheese before serving with the chicken, garnished with lemon wedges, and a green salad.

Chicken and Tarragon Peppered Tagliatelle

SERVES 4

225 g/8 oz tagliatelle
25 g/1 oz/2 tbsp butter or margarine
1 small onion, finely chopped
30 ml/2 tbsp chopped tarragon
30 ml/2 tbsp white wine vinegar
30 ml/2 tbsp dry white wine
175 g/6 oz/1½ cups cooked chicken, cut into small pieces, all skin removed
150 g/5 oz/⅔ cup soft cheese with black pepper
150 ml/¼ pt/⅔ cup single (light) cream
A few tarragon sprigs
Crisp green salad, to serve

Cook the tagliatelle according to the packet directions. Drain and return to the pan. Melt the butter or margarine in a saucepan. Add the onion and cook gently for 2 minutes until softened but not browned. Add the tarragon, vinegar and wine and boil rapidly until well reduced and thickened. Stir in the chicken, cheese and cream and heat through gently for 2–3 minutes. Add to the pasta and toss lightly. Pile on to serving plates, garnish with tarragon sprigs and serve with a green salad.

Spaghetti with Chicken, Ricotta and Broccoli

SERVES 4–6

450 g/1 lb broccoli, cut into tiny florets
75 g/3 oz/⅓ cup butter or margarine
175 g/6 oz/¾ cup Ricotta cheese
50 g/2 oz/½ cup Parmesan cheese, grated
175 g/6 oz/1½ cups cooked chicken, diced
60 ml/4 tbsp chopped parsley
1.5 ml/¼ tsp cayenne
Salt and freshly ground black pepper
350 g/12 oz spaghetti
Hot Herb Bread (page 357), to serve

Steam the broccoli or boil in lightly salted water until just tender. Drain. Melt all but 15 g/½ oz/1 tbsp of the butter or margarine in a saucepan. Add the cheeses, chicken and parsley and heat through, stirring. Add the broccoli and heat through. Season to taste with the cayenne and a little salt and pepper. Meanwhile, cook the spaghetti according to the packet directions. Drain and toss in the remaining butter. Pile on to warm plates and top with the sauce. Serve with Hot Herb Bread.

Austrian Schinkenfleckerl

SERVES 4

10 ml/2 tsp olive oil, plus extra for greasing (optional)
30 ml/2 tbsp dried breadcrumbs
225 g/8 oz/2 cups short-cut macaroni
1 small onion, finely chopped
50 g/2 oz/¼ cup butter or margarine
250 ml/8 fl oz/1 cup soured (dairy sour) cream
2 eggs
100 g/4 oz/1 cup lean cooked ham, finely diced
100 g/4 oz/1 cup cooked chicken, diced
50 g/2 oz/½ cup Emmental (Swiss) cheese, grated
Salt and freshly ground black pepper
3 tomatoes
6 open mushrooms

Grease a 15 cm/6 in round, deep cake tin (pan) with the oil and coat with the breadcrumbs. Cook the macaroni according to the packet directions. Drain, rinse with cold water and turn into a large bowl. Fry (sauté) the onion gently in the butter or margarine for 3 minutes until soft but not brown. Stir into the pasta. Whisk the cream and eggs together. Add to the pasta with the ham, chicken and cheese. Mix well and season to taste. Spoon into the prepared tin and level the surface. Stand in a roasting tin (pan) with enough cold water to come a third of the way up the tin. Bake in the oven at 200°C/400°F/gas mark 6 for 30 minutes or until set and the top is golden brown. Remove from the baking tin and allow to cool for 5 minutes. Meanwhile grill (broil) the tomatoes and mushrooms, brushed with a little olive oil, if liked. Turn the schinkenfleckerl out on to a serving dish and garnish with the tomatoes and mushrooms before serving.

Italian Lunchtime Fettuccine

SERVES 4

450 g/1 lb fettuccine
100 g/4 oz/½ cup unsalted (sweet) butter
300 ml/½ pt/1¼ cups double (heavy) cream
Salt and freshly ground black pepper
Plain Grilled Chicken with Garlic (page 123)
Crusty bread and green olives, to serve

Cook the fettuccine according to the packet directions. Drain and return to the saucepan. Cut the butter into flakes and add to the pan with the cream. Stir over a gentle heat until well coated. Season thoroughly with a little salt and lots of black pepper. Serve with the chicken and crusty bread and a bowl of green olives.

Spaghetti all'Uova

SERVES 4–6

450 g/1 lb spaghetti
2 chicken stock cubes
225 g/8 oz/1 cup unsalted (sweet) butter
75 g/3 oz/¾ cup Pecorino cheese, grated
6 eggs, beaten
Salt and freshly ground black pepper
Crisp green salad

Cook the spaghetti in boiling water to which the stock cubes have been added for 10 minutes. Drain in a colander. Cut half the butter into small pieces and place in the same saucepan. Return the spaghetti to the saucepan. Sprinkle with half the cheese, add the eggs, a little salt and lots of pepper. Toss over a very gentle heat until thoroughly blended and the eggs have just set. Turn into warm serving bowls, dot with flakes of the remaining butter and sprinkle with the remaining cheese. Serve with a crisp green salad.

Savoury Chicken and Egg Pasta

SERVES 4

225 g/8 oz wholewheat pasta shapes
30 ml/2 tbsp olive oil
1 onion, chopped
1 garlic clove, crushed
225 g/8 oz spring greens (collard greens), shredded
400 g/14 oz/1 large can of chopped tomatoes
15 ml/1 tbsp chopped sun-dried tomatoes
2.5 ml/½ tsp dried mixed herbs
Salt and freshly ground black pepper
100 g/4 oz/1 cup cooked chicken, chopped
2 hard-boiled (hard-cooked) eggs, chopped
50 g/2 oz/1 cup breadcrumbs
50 g/2 oz/½ cup Cheddar cheese, grated
15 g/½ oz/1 tbsp butter or margarine

Cook the pasta according to the packet directions. Drain. Meanwhile, heat the oil in a large saucepan. Add the onion and garlic and cook for 2 minutes until softened but not browned. Add the greens and cook for 1 minute until beginning to wilt. Add the tomatoes, sun-dried tomatoes, herbs, a little salt and lots of pepper. Cover and cook gently for 5 minutes. Stir in the cooked pasta, chicken and eggs. Turn into a 1.2 litre/2 pt/5 cup ovenproof dish. Mix together the breadcrumbs and cheese and sprinkle over. Dot with the butter or margarine and bake at 190°C/375°F/gas mark 5 for about 20 minutes until the top is golden brown and the mixture is piping hot.

Cheese and Chicken Gnocchi

SERVES 4

600 ml/1 pt/2½ cups milk
1 onion
2 cloves
1 bay leaf
100 g/4 oz/⅔ cup semolina (cream of wheat)
175 g/6 oz/1½ cups Cheddar cheese, grated
75 g/3 oz/¾ cup cooked chicken, finely chopped
30 ml/2 tbsp chopped parsley
Salt and freshly ground black pepper
Tabasco sauce
1 egg, beaten
100 g/4 oz/1 cup dried breadcrumbs
Oil, for deep-frying
Tomato Sauce (page 342), to serve

Put the milk in a saucepan. Stud the onion with the cloves and place in the milk with the bay leaf. Bring to the boil, remove from the heat and leave to infuse for 15 minutes. Strain and return to the saucepan. Blend in the semolina. Bring to the boil, stirring all the time, and cook for about 5 minutes until thick. Remove from the heat and stir in half the cheese, the chicken and parsley. Season well with salt and pepper and a few drops of Tabasco sauce. Spread the mixture on to a wetted cold dinner plate to make a round and chill for 2 hours. Cut into wedges, dip in the egg, then the breadcrumbs and deep-fry in hot oil until crisp and golden. Drain on kitchen paper (paper towels) and serve hot with Tomato Sauce.

Chicken and Tarragon Meatballs with Spicy Spaghetti

SERVES 4

350 g/12 oz minced (ground) chicken
2 garlic cloves, crushed
15 ml/1 tbsp chopped tarragon
100 g/4 oz/2 cups white breadcrumbs
Salt and freshly ground black pepper
1 egg, beaten
1 onion, finely chopped
15 ml/1 tbsp olive oil
400 g/14 oz/1 large can of chopped tomatoes
15 ml/1 tbsp tomato purée (paste)
5 ml/1 tsp caster (superfine) sugar
350 g/12 oz spaghetti
30 ml/2 tbsp chilli oil
Green salad, to serve

Mix the chicken with one of the garlic cloves, the tarragon, 75 g/3 oz/1½ cups of the breadcrumbs and some salt and pepper. Add the egg and mix together to bind. Shape into 12 small balls, then roll in the remaining breadcrumbs. Place on a sheet of foil on a grill (broiler) rack. Grill (broil), turning once or twice, for about 10 minutes until browned and cooked through. Meanwhile, cook the onion in the oil in a saucepan for 2 minutes. Add the remaining garlic, the tomatoes, purée and sugar. Simmer for 5 minutes and season to taste. Add the meatballs to the sauce and simmer for a further 10 minutes. Meanwhile, cook the spaghetti according to the packet directions. Drain, return to the pan and toss in the chilli oil. Pile the spaghetti on to warm plates, top with the meatballs and sauce and serve with a green salad.

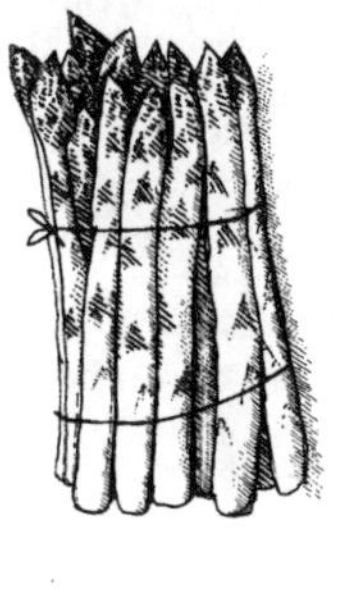

Chicken and Asparagus Bake

SERVES 4

225 g/8 oz conchiglie or other pasta shapes
295 g/10½ oz/1 small can of asparagus spears, drained
225 g/8 oz/2 cups cooked chicken, cut into bite-sized pieces, all skin removed
Salt and freshly ground black pepper
A pinch of grated nutmeg
295 g/10½ oz/1 small can of condensed cream of chicken soup
120 ml/4 fl oz/½ cup milk
150 ml/¼ pt/⅔ cup crème fraîche
50 g/2 oz/½ cup Cheddar cheese, grated
50 g/2 oz/1 cup breadcrumbs
15 g/½ oz/1 tbsp butter or margarine, melted
Parsley sprigs, to garnish
Garlic Bread (page 357) and young spinach leaves, tossed in French dressing and sprinkled with crisp, crumbled bacon, to serve

Cook the pasta according to the packet directions. Drain and transfer to a large ovenproof dish. Top with the drained asparagus, then the chicken. Season lightly with salt, pepper and the nutmeg. Blend the soup with the milk, crème fraîche and cheese. Spoon over. Mix the breadcrumbs with the butter or margarine and sprinkle over. Bake in a preheated oven at 190°C/375°F/gas mark 5 for about 35 minutes until piping hot and golden on top. Serve with Garlic Bread and a spinach and bacon salad.

Chicken and Celery Bake

SERVES 4

Prepare as for Chicken and Asparagus Bake, but use a can of chopped celery instead of asparagus. Spoon 228 g/8 oz/1 small can of chopped tomatoes over the celery before adding the soup mixture and omit the nutmeg.

Chicken and Sweetcorn Bake

SERVES 4

Prepare as for Chicken and Asparagus Bake (page 245), but use 350 g/12 oz/1 medium can of sweetcorn (corn) with (bell) peppers instead of the asparagus spears.

Lasagne al Forno

SERVES 4

1 large onion, finely chopped
1 garlic clove, crushed
350 g/12 oz extra-lean minced (ground) chicken
1 celery stick, finely chopped
100 g/4 oz button mushrooms, sliced
400 g/14 oz/1 large can of chopped tomatoes
30 ml/2 tbsp dry white vermouth (optional)
15 ml/1 tbsp tomato purée (paste)
2.5 ml/½ tsp dried oregano
A pinch of salt
Freshly ground black pepper
6 sheets no-need-to-precook wholewheat lasagne
2 quantities of Cheese Sauce (page 341)
Dressed green salad, to serve

Put the onion, garlic, chicken and celery in a large non-stick saucepan. Cook, stirring, for 5 minutes until the meat is brown and all the grains are separate. Add the mushrooms, tomatoes, vermouth, if using, the tomato purée, oregano, salt and lots of pepper. Bring to the boil, stirring, then reduce the heat and simmer for 15 minutes, stirring occasionally, until the meat is bathed in a rich sauce. Spoon a little of the meat sauce in the base of fairly shallow ovenproof dish. Top with a layer of lasagne, breaking it to fit. Layer the meat and lasagne in the dish, finishing with a layer of lasagne. Spoon the Cheese Sauce over. Bake in a preheated oven at 190°C/375°F/gas mark 5 for 40 minutes until cooked through and golden on top. Serve hot with a dressed green salad.

Lasagne with Chicken and Artichokes

SERVES 4

Prepare as for Lasagne al Forno, but substitute 425 g/15 oz/1 large can of artichoke hearts, drained and quartered, for the mushrooms, red wine for the vermouth and plain or egg lasagne for wholemeal.

Chicken and Red Wine Pasta

SERVES 4

1 large onion, finely sliced
1 garlic clove, crushed
25 g/1 oz/2 tbsp butter or margarine
4 skinless chicken breasts, about 175 g/6 oz each
Salt and freshly ground black pepper
400 g/14 oz/1 large can of chopped tomatoes
90 ml/6 tbsp red wine
30 ml/2 tbsp chopped parsley
A good pinch of caster (superfine) sugar
175 g/6 oz rigatoni
15 ml/1 tbsp chopped basil
Lollo rosso lettuce, onion and cucumber salad, to serve

Fry (sauté) the onion and garlic in half the butter or margarine for 3 minutes, stirring, until softened and lightly golden. Remove from the pan with a draining spoon. Brown the chicken in the remaining butter or margarine in the same pan. Return the onions and garlic to the pan with the remaining ingredients except the pasta and basil. Bring to the boil, reduce the heat and simmer for 15–20 minutes, stirring occasionaly, until the chicken is cooked and the sauce is pulpy. Meanwhile, cook the pasta according to the packet directions. Drain. When the chicken is cooked, lift out of the pan and transfer to four warm serving plates. Mix the cooked pasta with the sauce and spoon to one side of the chicken. Sprinkle with the basil and serve with a lollo rosso lettuce, onion and cucumber salad.

Chicken and Cider Quills

SERVES 4

Prepare as for Chicken and Red Wine Pasta, but substitute cider for the red wine, penne for the rigatoni and chopped parsley for the basil. Stir 30 ml/2 tbsp double (heavy) cream into the sauce.

Fragrant Chicken with Spaghetti

SERVES 4

1 large onion, finely chopped
1 garlic clove, crushed
25 g/1 oz/2 tbsp butter or margarine
30 ml/2 tbsp olive oil
4 skinless chicken breasts, cut into chunks
30 ml/2 tbsp chopped basil
30 ml/2 tbsp chopped parsley
1 large rosemary sprig
1 small bay leaf
1 green chilli, seeded and chopped
250 ml/8 fl oz/1 cup chicken stock
1 wineglass of white wine
Salt and freshly ground black pepper
350 g/12 oz spaghetti
Tomato salad, to serve

Fry (sauté) the onion and garlic in the butter or margarine and oil for 2 minutes, stirring, until lightly golden. Add the chicken and cook, stirring, for a further 2 minutes. Add all the herbs, the chilli, stock and wine and season with salt and pepper. Bring to the boil, reduce the heat, part-cover and simmer gently, stirring occasionally, for 45 minutes. Meanwhile, cook the spaghetti according to the packet directions. Drain and return to the pan. Remove the rosemary and bay leaf from the chicken mixture. Add the chicken mixture to the spaghetti and toss thoroughly. Taste and re-season if necessary. Pile on to warm plates and serve with a tomato salad.

Glazed Chicken Quills

SERVES 4

25 g/1 oz/2 tbsp butter or margarine, melted
45 ml/3 tbsp clear honey
15 ml/1 tbsp soy sauce
2.5 ml/½ tsp ground ginger
4 chicken portions
75 ml/5 tbsp dry white wine
Salt and freshly ground black pepper
225 g/8 oz penne pasta
100 g/4 oz dwarf beans, cut into short lengths
200 g/7 oz/1 small can of pimiento caps, drained and cut into thin strips
30 ml/2 tbsp olive oil

Mix the melted butter or margarine with the honey, soy sauce and ginger. Place the chicken portions in a roasting tin (pan) and brush the honey glaze over. Turn over so the skin is facing down and brush again. Pour the wine around and season the chicken lightly with salt and pepper. Bake at 220°C/425°F/gas mark 7 for 20 minutes. Turn the chicken over, baste with the juices and any remaining glaze. Return to the oven and cook for a further 15–20 minutes, basting twice. Meanwhile, cook the pasta according to the packet directions, adding the beans for the last 5 minutes cooking. Drain and return to the pan. Add the pimiento strips and olive oil and toss lightly over a gentle heat. Pile on to a warm serving dish. Place the chicken on top and keep warm. Boil the juices rapidly in the pan until syrupy. Spoon over the chicken and serve straight away.

Cannelloni Bolognese

SERVES 4

Prepare as for Chicken Lasagne Bolognese (page 248), but instead of layering with lasagne sheets, use the meat mixture to fill 8–12 no-need-to-pre-cook cannelloni tubes. Place in a lightly oiled ovenproof dish and cover with the Cheese Sauce. Bake as before.

Chicken Lasagne Bolognese

SERVES 4

1 onion, chopped
1 garlic clove
1 carrot, finely chopped
30 ml/2 tbsp sunflower oil
350 g/12 oz minced (ground) chicken
400 g/14 oz/1 large can of chopped tomatoes
30 ml/2 tbsp tomato purée (paste)
150 ml/¼ pt/⅔ cup red wine or chicken stock
1 small bay leaf
1 slice of lemon
Salt and freshly ground black pepper
5 ml/1 tsp caster (superfine) sugar
6–8 sheets of no-need-to-precook lasagne
2 quantities of Cheese Sauce (page 341)
Green salad and Garlic Bread (page 357), to serve

Cook the onion, garlic and carrot in the oil for 2 minutes, stirring, in a saucepan. Stir in the chicken and fry (sauté) until the chicken is no longer pink and all the grains are separate. Stir in the tomatoes, purée, wine or stock, bay leaf and slice of lemon. Season with salt and pepper and add the sugar. Bring to the boil, part-cover and simmer gently for 20 minutes until a rich sauce is formed. Discard the bay leaf and lemon. Spoon a little into the base of a shallow, ovenproof dish. Put a layer of lasagne sheets on top, breaking to fit if necessary. Top with half the meat sauce. Repeat the layers, finishing with a layer of lasagne. Spoon the Cheese Sauce over the top. Bake in a preheated oven at 190°C/375°F/gas mark 5 for about 35–40 minutes until golden on top and the lasagne feels tender when a knife is inserted down through the centre. Serve hot with a green salad and Garlic Bread.

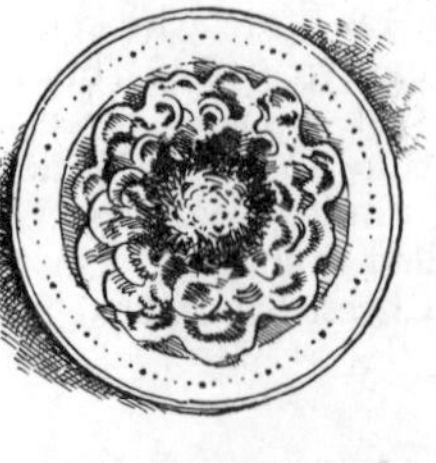

Spaghetti Bolognese

SERVES 4

Prepare as for Chicken Lasagne Bolognese, but omit the lasagne and when the meat sauce is simmering, cook 350 g/12 oz spaghetti according to the packet directions and drain. Pile on to plates, spoon the Bolognese sauce over and sprinkle with grated Parmesan cheese. Omit the Cheese Sauce.

Baked Pasta Bolognese

SERVES 4

Prepare as for Chicken Lasagne Bolognese, but omit the lasagne and when the meat sauce is cooking, cook 225 g/8 oz pasta shapes according to the packet directions. Drain and stir into the cooked meat sauce. Turn into an ovenproof dish and top with the Cheese Sauce. Bake in a preheated oven at 190°C/375°F/gas mark 5 for about 20 minutes until the sauce is browning.

Simple Pasta Bake

SERVES 4

225 g/8 oz pasta shapes
1 onion, chopped
15 ml/1 tbsp sunflower oil
225 g/8 oz minced (ground) chicken
400 g/14 oz/1 large can of chopped tomatoes
2.5 ml/½ tsp dried mixed herbs
Salt and freshly ground black pepper
75 g/3 oz/¾ cup Cheddar cheese, grated
Hot Herb Bread (page 357) and a mixed salad, to serve

Cook the pasta according to the packet directions. Drain. Meanwhile, fry (sauté) the onion in the oil for 2 minutes. Add the chicken and cook, stirring, until the chicken is no longer pink and all the grains are separate. Stir in the tomatoes, herbs and some salt and pepper and simmer for 10 minutes. Add the cooked pasta and toss. Turn into an ovenproof dish and sprinkle with the cheese. Bake in a preheated oven at 190°C/375°F/gas mark 5 for about 20 minutes until golden brown.

Peasant Chicken Pasta

SERVES 4

4 chicken portions
30 ml/2 tbsp olive oil
25 g/1 oz/2 tbsp butter or margarine
Salt and freshly ground black pepper
100 g/4 oz button mushrooms
45 ml/3 tbsp chopped parsley
2 garlic cloves, chopped
150 ml/¼ pt/⅔ cup chicken stock
225 g/8 oz conchiglie or rigatoni

Brown the chicken portions in the oil and butter or margarine in a large frying pan (skillet). Season with salt and pepper. Cover and cook gently for 20 minutes. Add the mushrooms and cook for 10 minutes. Sprinkle the chicken with the parsley and garlic, cover and cook for 4 minutes. Lift the chicken out of the pan and keep warm. Add the stock to the juices in the pan and boil, stirring, until slightly reduced. Meanwhile, cook the pasta in plenty of boiling salted water for 10 minutes until just tender. Drain. Stir the pasta into the juices in the pan. Top with the chicken and serve straight away.

French Peasant Chicken Pasta

SERVES 4

Prepare as for Peasant Chicken Pasta, but use chanterelles instead of cultivated button mushrooms and add 15 ml/1 tbsp brandy with the chicken stock.

Chicken and Spinach Lasagne

SERVES 6

30 ml/2 tbsp olive oil
1 large onion, finely chopped
1 garlic clove, crushed
225 g/8 oz/2 cups cooked chicken, diced, all skin removed
200 g/7 oz chicken livers, trimmed and chopped
100 g/4 oz button mushrooms, sliced
5 ml/1 tsp dried thyme
2.5 ml/½ tsp ground mace
65 g/2½ oz/generous ½ cup plain (all-purpose) flour
300 ml/½ pt/1¼ cups chicken stock
225 g/8 oz frozen chopped spinach, thawed
Salt and freshly ground black pepper
300 ml/½ pt/1¼ cups milk
50 g/2 oz/¼ cup butter or margarine
50 g/2 oz/½ cup Cheddar cheese, grated
8 no-need-to-precook lasagne sheets
30 ml/2 tbsp Parmesan cheese, grated

Heat the oil in a large pan. Add the onion and garlic and fry (sauté) for 2 minutes. Add the chicken and cook, stirring, for 1 minute. Stir in the chicken livers, mushrooms, thyme and mace and cook for 30 seconds. Stir in 15 ml/1 tbsp of the flour and cook for 1 minute. Blend in the stock, bring to the boil, reduce the heat, cover and simmer for 5 minutes. Squeeze out all the moisture from the spinach, stir into the chicken mixture and season to taste. Meanwhile, whisk the milk with the remaining flour in a saucepan. Stir in the butter or margarine and bring to the boil, stirring all the time. Simmer for 2 minutes, then stir in the Cheddar cheese and season to taste. Spoon a very thin layer of the chicken mixture into a greased 2 litre/3½ pt/8 cup ovenproof dish. Top with a layer of lasagne. Add a layer of half the remaining chicken, then a third of the cheese sauce, then a layer of lasagne. Add the rest of the chicken, half the remaining cheese sauce and all the remaining lasagne. Top with the remaining cheese sauce. Sprinkle with the Parmesan and bake at 190°C/375°F/gas mark 5 for 40 minutes.

Somerset Chicken Bake

SERVES 4–5

225 g/8 oz rotelli
2 onions, finely sliced
450 g/1 lb cooking (tart) apples, sliced
75 g/3 oz/⅓ cup butter or margarine
350 g/12 oz chicken stir-fry meat
300 ml/½ pt/1¼ cups dry cider
50 g/2 oz/⅓ cup raisins
5 ml/1 tsp dried thyme
1 chicken stock cube
10 ml/2 tsp cornflour (cornstarch)
15 ml/1 tbsp water
Salt and freshly ground black pepper

Cook the pasta according to the packet directions. Drain. Meanwhile, fry (sauté) the onions and half the apples in a third of the butter or margarine until soft and lightly golden. Remove from the pan with a draining spoon. Melt half the remaining butter or margarine in the pan. Add the chicken and cook, stirring, for 5 minutes. Stir in the cider, raisins, thyme and stock cube and bring to the boil, stirring. Blend the cornflour with the water and stir into the pan. Bring to the boil, stirring, until thickened. Return the onion and apple mixture to the pan and season to taste. Put half the pasta in an ovenproof dish. Top with half the chicken mixture, then repeat the layers. Top with a layer of the remaining apple slices. Melt the remaining butter or margarine and brush over. Bake at 180°C/350°F/gas mark 4 for about 25 minutes until piping hot and the apples on top are tender and lightly golden.

Chicken Tuscany

SERVES 4

40 g/1½ oz/3 tbsp butter or margarine
1 onion, finely chopped
2 garlic cloves, crushed
1 green (bell) pepper, chopped
1 red pepper, chopped
400 g/14 oz/1 large can of chopped tomatoes
75 g/3 oz/½ cup green olives, stoned (pitted) and chopped
2.5 ml/½ tsp cayenne
A few drops of Worcestershire sauce
Salt and freshly ground black pepper
4 skinless chicken breasts, about 175 g/6 oz each
225 g/8 oz tagliatelle
Crisp green salad, to serve

Melt 15 g/½ oz/1 tbsp of the butter or margarine in a saucepan. Add the onion, garlic and peppers and fry (sauté) fairly gently for 5 minutes until soft but not brown. Add the tomatoes, olives, cayenne, Worcestershire sauce and a little salt and pepper. Bring to the boil, reduce the heat and simmer for 10 minutes. Meanwhile, melt half the remaining butter or margarine. Brush over the chicken and place on a grill (broiler) rack. Grill (broil) for about 8 minutes until golden on both sides and cooked through. Meanwhile, cook the pasta according to the packet directions. Drain and toss with the remaining butter or margarine. Transfer the chicken to warm plates and spoon the sauce over. Spoon the pasta to one side and serve with a crisp green salad.

Chicken, Leek and Walnut Vermicelli

SERVES 4

2 small leeks, thinly sliced
15 ml/1 tbsp walnut oil
15 ml/1 tbsp olive oil
50 g/2 oz/½ cup walnuts, chopped
2 chicken breast fillets, finely diced
150 ml/¼ pt/⅔ cup medium-dry white wine
150 ml/¼ pt/⅔ cup crème fraîche
Salt and freshly ground black pepper
350 g/12 oz vermicelli
15 ml/1 tbsp chopped parsley

Fry (sauté) the leeks in the two oils for 2 minutes until slightly softened. Add the walnuts, cover with a lid, reduce the heat and cook gently for 5 minutes until soft. Add the chicken and wine, re-cover and simmer gently for 10 minutes until the chicken is tender. Stir in the crème fraîche and season to taste. Meanwhile, cook the vermicelli according to the packet directions. Drain and pile on to warm serving plates. Spoon the hot sauce over and garnish with chopped parsley.

Sweet and Sour Chicken Delight

SERVES 4

15 ml/1 tbsp sunflower oil
2 chicken breast fillets, cut into small, thin strips
1 carrot, cut into matchsticks
1 small red (bell) pepper, cut into thin strips
¼ cucumber, diced
430 g/15½ oz/1 large can of pineapple pieces
30 ml/2 tbsp tomato purée (paste)
15 ml/1 tbsp clear honey
45 ml/3 tbsp soy sauce
2.5 ml/½ tsp ground ginger
60 ml/4 tbsp malt vinegar
10 ml/2 tsp cornflour (cornstarch)
15 ml/1 tbsp water
250 g/9 oz vermicelli

Heat the oil in a large saucepan. Fry (sauté) the chicken in the oil for 4 minutes until cooked through. Remove from the pan. Add the remaining ingredients except the cornflour, water and vermicelli. Bring to the boil and boil for 5 minutes. Blend the cornflour with the water and stir into the sauce. Cook, stirring, until thickened and clear. Return the chicken to the sauce and heat through. Meanwhile, cook the vermicelli according to the packet directions. Drain. Add to the sweet and sour sauce and toss well.

Spaghetti with Chicken and Sage

SERVES 4

350 g/12 oz spaghetti
75 ml/5 tbsp olive oil
225 g/8 oz minced (ground) chicken
100 g/4 oz button mushrooms, finely chopped
1 onion, finely chopped
1 garlic clove, crushed
10 ml/2 tsp chopped sage
150 ml/¼ pt/⅔ cup chicken stock
Salt and freshly ground black pepper
6 stoned (pitted) black or green olives, sliced
30 ml/2 tbsp chopped parsley
Grated Parmesan cheese, to garnish
Mixed salad, to serve

Cook the spaghetti according to the packet directions. Drain and return to the pan. Meanwhile, heat the oil in another pan. Add the chicken, mushrooms, onion and garlic and cook, stirring, for about 5 minutes until the chicken grains are separate and no longer pink. Add the sage, stock and seasoning, cover and simmer gently for a further 5–10 minutes. Add to the spaghetti and toss over a gentle heat. Stir in the olives and parsley. Pile on to warm plates, garnish with Parmesan cheese and serve with a mixed salad.

Spaghetti with Chicken and Mushrooms

SERVES 4

40 g/1½ oz/3 tbsp butter or margarine
225 g/8 oz boneless chicken, skinned and diced
2 carrots, finely chopped
1 celery stick, finely chopped
1 large onion, finely chopped
1 garlic clove, crushed
175 g/6 oz button mushrooms, sliced
6 tomatoes, skinned and chopped
50 g/2 oz frozen peas
Salt and freshly ground black pepper
5 ml/1 tsp dried mixed herbs
350 g/12 oz spaghetti
20 ml/4 tsp Parmesan cheese, grated
Crisp green salad, to serve

Melt the butter or margarine in a saucepan. Add the remaining ingredients except the spaghetti and Parmesan and fry (sauté), stirring, for 3 minutes. Reduce the heat, cover and simmer gently for 15 minutes until the vegetables and chicken are tender. Meanwhile, cook the spaghetti according to the packet directions. Drain and return to the pan. Add the chicken mixture and toss well. Pile on to warm plates and sprinkle with the Parmesan. Serve with a crisp green salad.

Creamy Chicken and Almond Pasta

SERVES 4

350 g/12 oz rigatoni
225 g/8 oz chestnut mushrooms, sliced
15 ml/1 tbsp lemon juice
50 g/2 oz/¼ cup butter or margarine
2.5 ml/½ tsp dried oregano
175 g/6 oz/1½ cups cooked chicken, cut into bite-sized pieces, all skin removed
90 ml/6 tbsp crème fraîche
Salt and freshly ground black pepper
50 g/2 oz/½ cup toasted flaked (slivered) almonds
Mixed salad, to serve

Cook the pasta according to the packet directions. Drain and return to the saucepan. Meanwhile, put the mushrooms, lemon juice, butter or margarine and oregano in a saucepan. Cover and cook gently for 5 minutes until tender. Add the chicken, cover and heat through for 4 minutes. Tip into the pasta and stir in the crème fraîche. Season to taste and heat through. Pile on to warm plates, scatter the almonds over and serve piping hot with a mixed salad.

Creamy Chicken with Peas and Hazelnuts

SERVES 4

Prepare as for Creamy Chicken and Almond Pasta, but substitute frozen peas for the mushrooms, dried mint for the oregano and toasted hazelnuts (filberts) for the almonds.

Anchovy and Pâté Eggs with Vermicelli

SERVES 4

300 ml/½ pt/1¼ cups milk
25 g/1 oz/¼ cup plain (all-purpose) flour
75 g/3 oz/⅓ cup unsalted (sweet) butter
Salt and freshly ground black pepper
75 g/3 oz/¾ cup Parmesan cheese, grated
4 hard-boiled (hard-cooked) eggs
30 ml/2 tbsp anchovy essence (extract)
50 g/2 oz smooth chicken liver pâté
90 ml/6 tbsp double (heavy) cream
350 g/12 oz vermicelli
10 ml/2 tsp capers, chopped
15 ml/1 tbsp chopped parsley

Blend a little of the milk with the flour in a saucepan. Stir in the remaining milk and add 25 g/1 oz/2 tbsp of the butter. Bring to the boil and cook for 2 minutes, stirring all the time. Season with salt and pepper and stir in the cheese. Halve the eggs and mash the yolks in a bowl. Beat in half the remaining butter, the anchovy essence, pâté and the cream. Season to taste. Pipe or spoon the mixture into the egg whites and place in an ovenproof dish. Cover with foil and heat through in the oven at 160°C/325°F/gas mark 3 for about 10 minutes or until piping hot. Meanwhile cook the vermicelli according to the packet directions. Drain and return to the saucepan. Add the remaining butter in small flakes, add a good grinding of pepper, the capers and parsley and toss well. Pile on to serving plates and put two egg halves to one side of each serving.

Chicken Liver and Hazelnut Cannelloni

SERVES 4

45 ml/3 tbsp olive oil
1 onion, finely chopped
1 garlic clove, crushed
450 g/1 lb chicken livers, finely chopped or minced (ground)
5 ml/1 tsp dried oregano
225 g/8 oz/1 small can of chopped tomatoes
30 ml/2 tbsp tomato purée (paste)
50 g/2 oz/½ cup hazelnuts (filberts), roughly chopped
Salt and freshly ground black pepper
8 no-need-to-precook cannelloni tubes
1½ quantities of Cheese Sauce (page 341)
30 ml/2 tbsp Parmesan cheese, grated

Heat the oil in a saucepan. Add the onion and garlic and fry (sauté), stirring, for 2 minutes. Add the chicken livers, oregano, tomatoes, tomato purée, nuts and a little salt and pepper. Cook gently for 5 minutes, stirring occasionally. Spoon into a piping (pastry) bag fitted with a large plain tube. Use to fill the cannelloni tubes. Arrange in a single layer in a greased ovenproof dish. Pour the Cheese Sauce over and sprinkle with the Parmesan. Bake at 190°C/375°F/gas mark 5 for about 35 minutes or until the cannelloni is tender and the top is golden brown.

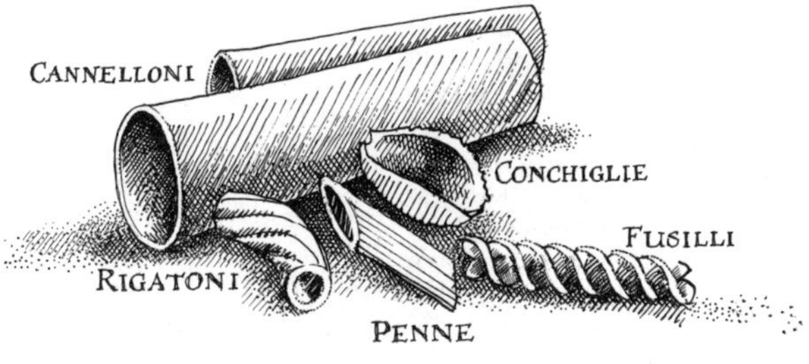

Sherried Chicken Liver Lasagne

SERVES 4

1 large onion, finely chopped
1 garlic clove, crushed
75 g/3 oz/⅓ cup butter or margarine
100 g/4 oz streaky bacon, rinded and diced
200 g/7 oz chicken livers, trimmed and chopped
175 g/6 oz button mushrooms, chopped
450 ml/¾ pt/2 cups chicken stock
50 g/2 oz/½ cup plain (all-purpose) flour
45 ml/3 tbsp medium-dry sherry
Salt and freshly ground black pepper
300 ml/½ pt/1¼ cups milk
75 g/3 oz/¾ cup Cheddar cheese, grated
6–8 wholemeal no-need-to-precook lasagne sheets

Fry (sauté) the onion and garlic in 50 g/2 oz/¼ cup of the butter or margarine for 3 minutes until softened and lightly golden. Stir in the bacon and chicken livers and cook, stirring, for 2 minutes. Stir in the mushrooms and cook for a further 1 minute. Add the stock, bring to the boil, reduce the heat, cover and simmer for 10 minutes. Blend half the flour with the sherry. Stir into the pan and bring to the boil, stirring, until thickened. Season to taste. Meanwhile, melt the remaining butter or margarine in a saucepan. Stir in the remaining flour and the milk until smooth. Bring to the boil and cook for 2 minutes, stirring all the time, until thickened. Season to taste and stir in half the cheese. Put a thin layer of the chicken liver mixture in the base of a large shallow ovenproof dish. Top with a layer of lasagne. Add half the remaining chicken liver mixture, then another layer of lasagne. Repeat the layers. Top with the cheese sauce and sprinkle with the remaining cheese. Bake at 190°C/375°F/gas mark 5 for about 40 minutes or until the lasagne is tender when a knife is inserted down through the centre and the top is golden brown.

Piquant Chicken Liver Farfalle

SERVES 4

225 g/8 oz farfalle
1 bunch of spring onions (scallions), finely chopped
25 g/1 oz/2 tbsp butter or margarine
15 ml/1 tbsp olive oil
1 wineglass of red vermouth
450 g/1 lb chicken livers, trimmed and chopped
5 ml/1 tsp chopped sage
Salt and freshly ground black pepper
30 ml/2 tbsp chopped parsley

Cook the pasta according to the packet directions. Drain and return to the saucepan. Meanwhile, fry (sauté) the spring onions in the butter or margarine and oil until soft but not brown. Add the vermouth and simmer until reduced by half. Add the chicken livers and sage and cook quickly for about 2–3 minutes, until brown but not dry. Season to taste. Add to the cooked farfalle, toss well and sprinkle with chopped parsley before serving.

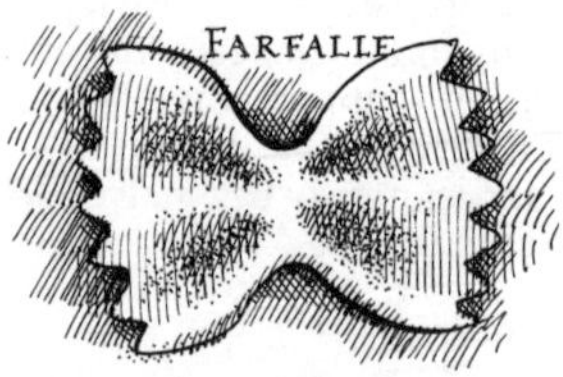

Paella Valencia

SERVES 6

1.5 kg/3 lb oven-ready chicken, cut into 8 pieces (page 15)
60 ml/4 tbsp olive oil
1 onion, finely chopped
1 red (bell) pepper, diced
1 green pepper, diced
350 g/12 oz/1½ cups bomba or risotto rice
450 g/1 lb mussels in their shells, scrubbed and beards removed
Chicken stock
5 ml/1 tsp saffron powder
225 g/8 oz tomatoes, skinned, seeded and chopped
175 g/6 oz frozen peas
Salt and freshly ground black pepper
1 bay leaf
1 sprig of marjoram
100 g/4 oz chorizo sausage, sliced
100 g/4 oz cooked, peeled prawns (shrimp)
400 g/14 oz/1 large can of artichoke hearts, drained and halved
Lemon wedges
6 whole cooked, unpeeled prawns
30 ml/2 tbsp chopped parsley

Brown the chicken pieces in the oil in a paella pan or very large frying pan (skillet) for 10 minutes. Remove from the pan. Add the onion and fry (sauté) for 3 minutes until softened and lightly browned. Add the peppers and rice and cook, stirring for 1 minute. Return the chicken to the pan. Add the mussels and enough chicken stock to cover the ingredients. Stir in the saffron, tomatoes, peas and a little salt and pepper and add the bay leaf and marjoram. Bring to the boil, reduce the heat, cover and simmer gently for 20 minutes or until the rice is cooked and has absorbed most of the liquid. Add a little more stock during cooking if necessary.

Remove the mussels. Snap off the top shells and discard with any unopened mussels. Keep the mussels warm in the bottom shells. Stir the chorizo, prawns and artichokes into the rice mixture and heat through. Return the mussels to the pan. Garnish with the lemon wedges, whole prawns and parsley.

Italian-style Savoury Rice Cake

SERVES 4

450 ml/¾ pt/2 cups milk
Salt and freshly ground black pepper
225 g/8 oz/1 cup risotto rice
25 g/1 oz/2 tbsp unsalted (sweet) butter
75 ml/5 tbsp freshly Parmesan cheese, grated
175 g/6 oz/1½ cups cooked chicken, chopped, all skin removed
4 eggs, separated
Chopped parsley, to garnish

Bring the milk to the boil with a pinch of salt and pepper. Add the rice, cover and simmer gently for 15 minutes or until the milk is absorbed and the rice is just tender. Remove from the heat and stir in half the butter, the cheese, chicken and egg yolks. Mix thoroughly and re-season. Use the remaining butter to grease a 1.5 litre/2½ pt/6 cup soufflé dish. Whisk the egg whites until stiff and fold into the rice with a metal spoon. Turn into the prepared dish and bake in the oven at 180°C/350°F/gas mark 4 for about 30 minutes until golden and just set. Loosen the edge of the cake and turn out on to a serving plate. Garnish with parsley and serve straight away.

Risotto al Forno

SERVES 4

60 ml/4 tbsp olive oil
1 small onion, finely chopped
2 large chicken breasts, cut into chunks
450 g/1 lb/2 cups risotto rice
1.2 litres/2 pts/5 cups hot chicken stock
Salt and freshly ground black pepper
15 g/½ oz/1 tbsp unsalted (sweet) butter
Tomato Sauce (page 341)
Parmesan cheese, grated

Heat the oil in a flameproof casserole (Dutch oven). Add the onion and chicken and fry (sauté) for 2 minutes. Stir in the rice and cook for 1 minute. Stir in the stock, season well and bring to the boil. Cover tightly and bake in the oven at 180°C/350°F/gas mark 4 for 1 hour. Stir in the butter and re-season if necessary. Serve with Tomato Sauce and grated Parmesan cheese.

Creamy Chicken, Ham and Mushroom Risotto

SERVES 6

50 g/2 oz/1 cup dried porcini mushrooms
25 g/1 oz/2 tbsp unsalted (sweet) butter
30 ml/2 tbsp olive oil
1 small onion, finely chopped
450 g/1 lb/2 cups risotto rice
1.2 litres/2 pts/5 cups hot chicken stock
Salt and freshly ground black pepper
100 g/4 oz/1 cup cooked ham, diced
100 g/4 oz/1 cup cooked chicken, diced
120 ml/4 fl oz/½ cup single (light) cream
Chopped parsley
100 g/4 oz/1 cup Parmesan cheese, grated

Soak the mushrooms in hot water for 1 hour. Drain and wash thoroughly under running water. Pat dry on kitchen paper (paper towels), then slice. Heat the butter and oil in a large flameproof casserole (Dutch oven) and fry (sauté) the onion and mushrooms for 2 minutes. Add the rice and cook for 1 minute, stirring. Add 2 ladlefuls of the stock and simmer until it is absorbed. Continue this way until the rice is just tender. Season to taste. Stir in the ham, chicken and cream and heat through for 2–3 minutes. Spoon on to warm plates, sprinkle with parsley and the cheese and serve hot.

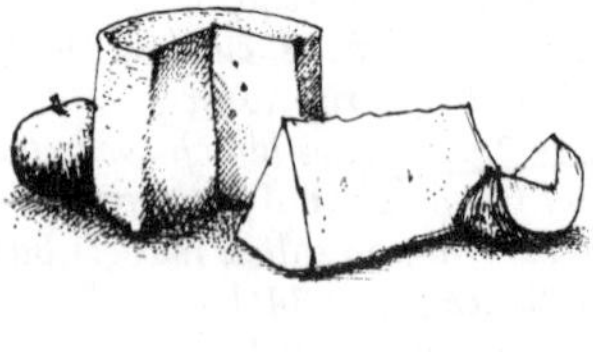

Risotto Bianco con Pollo

SERVES 4–6

75 g/3 oz/⅓ cup unsalted (sweet) butter
15 ml/1 tbsp olive oil
1 large chicken breast, cut into small pieces
1 onion, finely chopped
1 garlic clove, crushed
225 g/8 oz/1 cup risotto rice
900 ml/1½ pts/3¾ cups hot chicken stock
Salt and freshly ground black pepper
100 g/4 oz/1 cup Parmesan cheese, grated

Heat 50 g/2 oz/¼ cup of the butter in a large saucepan with the oil. Add the chicken, onion and garlic and fry (sauté) for 3 minutes until softened and lightly golden. Stir in the rice and cook, stirring, for 1 minute until glistening with the oil and butter. Add a third of the stock. Bring to the boil, reduce the heat, cover and simmer until the stock has been absorbed. Gradually stir in the remaining stock, bring to the boil, reduce the heat, re-cover and simmer gently for about 15 minutes until all the stock has been absorbed and the rice is creamy. Boil rapidly, if necessary to evaporate any remaining stock. Season well with salt and lots of pepper and stir in the remaining butter. Spoon into a warm serving dish and sprinkle with Parmesan cheese before serving

Risotto Bianco di Napoli

SERVES 4

Prepare as for Risotto Bianco con Pollo, but stir in 100 g/4 oz/1 cup Mozzarella cheese, grated, just before serving and garnish with green olives.

Rich and Creamy Risotto

SERVES 4

15 g/½ oz/1 tbsp unsalted (sweet) butter
1 small onion, finely chopped
100 g/4 oz/1 cup pancetta, finely diced
2 skinless chicken breasts, cut into small pieces
450 g/1 lb/2 cups risotto rice
1.2 litres/2 pts/5 cups hot chicken stock
120 ml/4 fl oz/½ cup double (heavy) cream
Salt and freshly ground black pepper
100 g/4 oz/1 cup Parmesan cheese, grated

Heat the butter in a flameproof casserole (Dutch oven). Add the onion, pancetta and chicken and fry (sauté) for 3 minutes until the onion is golden and the pancetta has lost its pink colour. Stir in the rice and cook for 1 minute. Blend in 2 ladlefuls of the stock and simmer until it has been absorbed. Repeat, adding a little stock at a time, for about 15 to 20 minutes, until the rice is just tender. Stir in the cream, season to taste and add the Parmesan. Serve straight away.

Parmesan Rice with Chicken, Tomatoes and Basil

SERVES 4

30 ml/2 tbsp olive oil
1 onion, finely chopped
1 large skinless chicken breast, chopped
225 g/8 oz/1 cup risotto rice
600 ml/1 pt/2½ cups hot chicken stock
50 g/2 oz/½ cup chopped basil
50 g/2 oz/½ cup chopped parsley
2 large ripe tomatoes, skinned, seeded and chopped
Salt and freshly ground black pepper
100 g/4 oz/1 cup Parmesan cheese, grated

Heat the oil in a large saucepan. Add the onion and chicken and fry (sauté) for 2 minutes. Stir in the rice and cook for 1 minute. Add 2 ladlefuls of the stock and simmer until it is absorbed. Repeat for about 15 minutes until the rice is tender and creamy. Stir in the herbs, tomatoes, some salt and pepper and half the cheese. Stir for 1 minute to heat the tomatoes. Pile on to a warm serving dish and sprinkle the remaining cheese over.

Extra-fragrant Parmesan Rice

SERVES 4

Prepare as for Parmesan Rice with Chicken, Tomatoes and Basil, but add a large sprig of rosemary and a bay leaf to the rice while cooking. Discard before serving.

Riso Pecorino Romano con Pollo

SERVES 4

350 g/12 oz/1½ cups risotto rice
4 skinless chicken breasts
60 ml/4 tbsp olive oil
Salt and freshly ground black pepper
6 basil leaves, finely chopped
75 ml/5 tbsp grated Pecorino cheese
3 tomatoes, cut into wedges
Parsley sprigs, to garnish

Cook the rice in plenty of boiling salted water for 18 minutes. Drain well and return to the saucepan. Meanwhile, brush the chicken with some of the oil. Season with salt and pepper and grill (broil) for about 12 minutes, turning once or twice, until golden and cooked through, brushing with a little more oil from time to time. Stir the basil, cheese and 30 ml/2 tbsp olive oil into the hot rice. Season to taste. Press into four individual moulds and immediately turn out on to hot serving plates. Garnish with the tomatoes and parsley and serve straight away with the chicken breasts.

Gorgonzola Speciality

SERVES 4–6

75 g/3 oz/⅓ cup unsalted (sweet) butter
175 g/6 oz/1½ cups Gorgonzola cheese, crumbled
120 ml/4 fl oz/½ cup crème fraîche
120 ml/4 fl oz/½ cup dry white wine
Salt and freshly ground black pepper
350 g/12 oz/1½ cups risotto rice
15 ml/1 tbsp lemon juice
4 skinless chicken breasts
A few basil leaves
Green salad, to serve

Melt 50 g/2 oz/¼ cup of the butter in a saucepan. Stir in the cheese until melted. Blend in the crème fraîche and wine. Heat, stirring, for about 1½ minutes until thickened. Season lightly. Cook the rice in plenty of boiling salted water for about 18 minutes, until just tender. Drain and turn into a hot serving dish. Meanwhile, melt the remaining butter with the lemon juice and a little salt and pepper. Brush all over the chicken. Place on foil on the grill (broiler) rack and grill (broil) for about 12 minutes, turning occasionally, until cooked through. Reheat the sauce if necessary and drizzle over the rice. Place the chicken on warm plates, garnish with basil leaves and serve with the hot rice and a green salad.

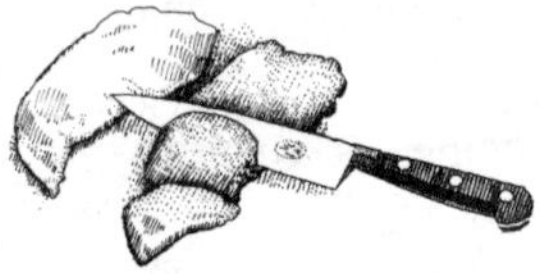

Cottage Rice Casserole

SERVES 4–6

350 g/12 oz/1½ cups long-grain rice
50 g/2 oz/¼ cup butter or margarine, plus extra for greasing
1 large onion, finely chopped
175 g/6 oz minced (ground) chicken
450 ml/¾ pt/2 cups soured (dairy sour) cream
225 g/8 oz/1 cup cottage cheese
15 ml/1 tbsp snipped chives
Salt and freshly ground white pepper
2 green chillies, seeded and chopped
225 g/8 oz/2 cups Cheddar cheese, grated
Crisp green salad, to serve

Cook the rice in plenty of boiling salted water for 10 minutes or until tender. Drain. Meanwhile, melt the butter or margarine in a pan and fry (sauté) the onion and chicken until the grains of chicken are brown and separate. Stir into the cooked rice with the cream, cottage cheese, chives and a little salt and pepper. Spoon half this mixture into a greased ovenproof dish. Sprinkle with half the chillies and half the grated cheese. Repeat the layers. Bake in the oven at 190°C/375°F/gas mark 5 for about 25 minutes or until the top is golden brown. Serve with a crisp green salad.

Savoury Egg Rice

SERVES 4

1 packet of savoury rice with (bell) peppers
100 g/4 oz/1 cup cooked chicken, chopped
4 eggs
Garlic Bread (page 357), to serve

Empty the rice into a large frying pan (skillet) and add water as directed on the packet. Bring to the boil, reduce the heat, cover and simmer for 15 minutes. Remove the lid and stir in the chicken. Make four wells in the rice mixture and break an egg into each. Cover and continue cooking over a gentle heat for 5 minutes or until eggs are set to your liking. Serve straight from the pan with Garlic Bread.

Chicken and Egg Fried Rice with Bacon

SERVES 6

3 onions, thinly sliced
4 rindless streaky bacon rashers (slices), cut into thin strips
30 ml/2 tbsp sunflower oil
100 g/4 oz frozen peas
100 g/4 oz/1 cup cooked chicken, chopped
50 g/2 oz/¼ cup unsalted (sweet) butter
4 eggs, beaten
Salt and freshly ground black pepper
350 g/12 oz/3 cups cooked long-grain rice

Fry (sauté) the onion and bacon in the oil for 2 minutes, stirring. In a separate pan, cook the peas and chicken for 2 minutes in the butter. Add the eggs to the bacon and onion. Swirl the pan so the egg covers the base. Cook gently until the egg sets, then scramble lightly but don't break up the egg too much. Stir in the rice, chicken and peas, season to taste and heat through, tossing gently, so the rice grains stay separate. Serve straight away.

Eastern Rice with Egg

SERVES 6

450 g/1 lb/2 cups basmati rice
1 litre/1¾ pts/4½ cups water
A pinch of salt
60 ml/4 tbsp sunflower oil
2 onions, thinly sliced
225 g/8 oz minced (ground) chicken
2.5 ml/½ tsp turmeric
1.5 ml/¼ tsp chilli powder
8 hard-boiled (hard-cooked) eggs, shelled
15 ml/1 tbsp water
30 ml/2 tbsp chopped coriander (cilantro)
Brinjals (page 338), to serve

Wash the rice and drain it thoroughly. Place in a large heavy-based saucepan with the water and salt. Bring to the boil, reduce the heat, cover and simmer gently for 15 minutes or until the rice is almost tender and has absorbed all the liquid. Meanwhile, heat the oil in a separate pan. Add the onions and chicken and fry (sauté), stirring, until the chicken is no longer pink and all the grains are separate. Stir in the turmeric and chilli powder and fry for 1 minute, stirring. Add the eggs and cook, stirring gently, for 3 minutes until the eggs are golden. Add the rice to the eggs with the water. Cover tightly and cook very gently for 5 minutes until piping hot. Stir in the chopped coriander and serve hot with Brinjals.

Ceylonese Rice

SERVES 4

225 g/8 oz/1 cup long-grain rice
75 ml/5 tbsp sunflower oil
1 large chicken breast, cut diagonally into thin strips
3 leeks, sliced
1 green chilli, seeded and chopped
1 small onion, thinly sliced
4 eggs, beaten
Salt and freshly ground black pepper

Cook the rice in plenty of boiling salted water for 10 minutes or until just tender. Drain, rinse with boiling water and drain again. Meanwhile, heat the oil in a large frying pan (skillet) and fry (sauté) the chicken, leeks, chilli and onion for about 5–8 minutes until tender but not brown. Add the eggs and a little salt and pepper and fry, stirring, until the eggs begin to scramble. Add the rice a spoonful at a time, stirring well. Pile on to a warm serving dish and serve hot.

Rice with Eggs and Chicken

SERVES 4

350 g/12 oz/1½ cups risotto rice
175 g/6 oz/1½ cups cooked chicken, cut into small pieces
2 egg yolks, lightly beaten
20 g/¾ oz/1½ tbsp unsalted (sweet) butter
Salt and freshly ground black pepper
45 ml/3 tbsp chopped parsley
50 g/2 oz/½ cup Parmesan cheese, grated

Cook the rice in plenty of boiling salted water for about 16–18 minutes until just tender. Drain thoroughly. Return to the pan over a gentle heat. Add the cooked chicken. Pour the egg yolks over the rice and stir vigorously until well mixed and set. Stir in the butter and season with salt and pepper. Stir in the parsley and cheese and serve.

Creamed Risotto with Chicken and Lemon

SERVES 4

50 g/2 oz/¼ cup unsalted (sweet) butter
1 large skinless chicken breast, chopped
100 g/4 oz button mushrooms, sliced
350 g/12 oz/1½ cups risotto rice
1 litre/1¾ pts/4¼ cups hot chicken stock
15 ml/1 tbsp plain (all-purpose) flour
Salt and freshly ground black pepper
Grated rind and juice of 1 lemon
75 ml/5 tbsp double (heavy) cream
Broccoli, to serve

Melt half the butter in a heavy-based pan. Add the chicken, mushrooms and rice and cook, stirring, for 1 minute. Add 2 ladlefuls of the stock and simmer until it has been absorbed. Repeat the process for about 15–20 minutes until the rice is just tender. Melt the remaining butter in a saucepan. Stir in the flour, then blend in the remaining stock. Bring to the boil and cook for 2 minutes until thickened. Season to taste and stir in the lemon rind and juice and the cream. Pile the rice into a warmed serving dish, pour the sauce over, stir lightly and serve with broccoli.

Risotto with Chicken, Cheese and Wine

SERVES 4

30 ml/2 tbsp olive oil
2 onions, finely chopped
1 large skinless chicken breast, cut into tiny pieces
450 g/1 lb/2 cups risotto rice
1 litre/1¾ pts/4¼ cups hot chicken stock
250 ml/8 fl oz/1 cup Italian white wine
15 g/½ oz/1 tbsp unsalted (sweet) butter
60 ml/4 tbsp freshly Parmesan cheese, grated
Salt and freshly ground black pepper

Heat the oil in a flameproof casserole (Dutch oven). Add the onions and chicken and cook, stirring, for 2 minutes. Stir in the rice and cook for 1 minute. Add 250 ml/8 fl oz/1 cup of the stock, bring to the boil and simmer until the stock is absorbed. Repeat for about 15–20 minutes until the rice is just tender and the risotto creamy. Add half the wine after 10 minutes cooking. Stir in the butter, remaining wine and the cheese. Simmer for 2 minutes. Taste and season, if necessary. Serve straight away.

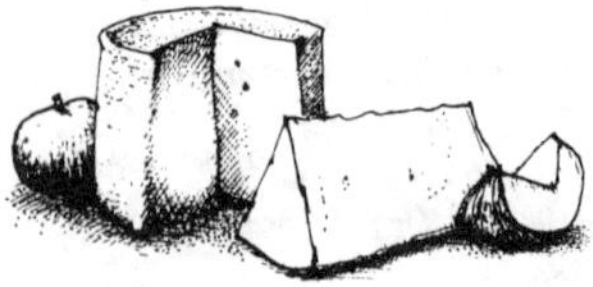

Tuscan Risotto with Chicken, Spices and Raisins

SERVES 4

45 ml/3 tbsp seedless raisins
45 ml/3 tbsp olive oil
1 whole garlic clove
1 large skinless chicken breast, cut into very small pieces
A pinch of ground cloves
A pinch of grated nutmeg
450 g/1 lb/2 cups risotto rice
1.2 litres/2 pts/5 cups hot chicken stock
50 g/2 oz/½ cup chopped parsley
Salt and freshly ground black pepper
50 g/2 oz Parmesan cheese, shaved into flakes

Soak the raisins in boiling water for 30 minutes. Drain and pat dry on kitchen paper (paper towels). Heat the oil in a flameproof casserole (Dutch oven). Add the garlic clove and fry (sauté) until golden, then discard. Add the chicken and spices and fry for 1 minute. Add the rice and cook for 1 minute. Stir in 250 ml/8 fl oz/1 cup of the stock and simmer until the stock is absorbed. Repeat twice more. Stir in the raisins and continue adding stock for about 15–20 minutes until the rice is just tender and the risotto creamy. Stir in the parsley and season with salt and pepper. Scatter the flakes of Parmesan over the surface and serve.

Arancini Siciliani

SERVES 6

225 g/8 oz/1 cup risotto rice
50 g/2 oz/½ cup Parmesan cheese, grated
2 eggs, beaten
300 ml/½ pt/1¼ cups passata (sieved tomatoes)
Salt and freshly ground black pepper
50 g/2 oz/½ cup Mozzarella, finely diced
50 g/2 oz/½ cup cooked chicken, finely diced
50 g/2 oz/1 cup breadcrumbs
Oil, for deep-frying
15 ml/1 tbsp chopped basil
6 small basil sprigs

Cook the rice in plenty of boiling salted water for 15 minutes. Drain, rinse with cold water and drain again. Turn into a bowl and stir in the Parmesan, eggs, 15 ml/1 tbsp of the passata and a little salt and pepper. Mix well. Put the Mozzarella cheese and chicken in a separate bowl with 15 ml/1 tbsp of the passata and season lightly. Divide the cold rice mixture into 12 portions. Using well floured hands, shape each into a ball. Make a hollow in the centre and add a small spoonful of the cheese and chicken mixture. Re-shape into a ball, adding a little more rice if necessary. Repeat with each portion of rice. Roll each thickly in breadcrumbs. Chill for 30 minutes.

Deep-fry, a few at a time, until crisp and golden brown. Drain on kitchen paper (paper towels). Meanwhile, warm the remaining passata with the chopped basil and a little salt and pepper. When all the balls are cooked, spoon a little passata on six serving plates. Place two balls on each plate and top each with a sprig of basil.

Chicken, Hazelnut and Vegetable Rice

SERVES 4

1 onion, finely chopped
1 garlic clove, crushed
50 g/2 oz button mushrooms, thinly sliced
15 ml/1 tbsp sunflower oil
225 g/8 oz/1 cup brown long-grain rice
600 ml/1 pt/2½ cups chicken stock
1 carrot, finely chopped
225 g/8 oz French (green) beans, cut into short lengths
1 red (bell) pepper, diced
100 g/4 oz/1 cup blanched hazelnuts (filberts)
175 g/6 oz/1½ cups cooked chicken, diced, all skin removed
Salt and freshly ground black pepper
Chopped parsley, to garnish
Tomato salad, to serve

Cook the onion, garlic and mushrooms in the oil in a large saucepan for 3 minutes, stirring. Add the rice and stir for 1 minute. Add the stock, bring to the boil, reduce the heat, cover and simmer very gently for 35–40 minutes, adding a little more stock if necessary, until just tender and the rice has absorbed the liquid. Add the carrot, beans and pepper after 25 minutes' cooking time. Meanwhile, toast the hazelnuts in a frying pan (skillet), tossing until golden brown. Remove from the pan immediately. Cut the nuts in half and add to the cooked rice with the chicken. Toss over a gentle heat for 5 minutes. Season to taste. Pile on to warm plates, sprinkle with parsley and serve with a tomato salad.

Iranian Shireen Polow

SERVES 6

Thinly pared rind of 2 oranges
225 g/8 oz carrots, cut into matchsticks
75g/3 oz/¾ cup flaked (slivered) almonds
75 g/3 oz/¾ cups shelled pistachio nuts
120 ml/4 fl oz/½ cup water
100 g/4 oz/½ cup granulated sugar
Salt and freshly ground black pepper
450 g/1 lb/4 cups chicken meat, diced
5 ml/1 tsp saffron powder
30 ml/2 tbsp boiling water
450 g/1 lb/2 cups long-grain rice
150 ml/¼ pt/⅔ cup groundnut (peanut) or sunflower oil
5 ml/1 tsp ground cinnamon
15 ml/1 tbsp melted butter or margarine

Cut the orange rind into thin strips and boil in water for 3 minutes. Drain, rinse with cold water and drain again. Place in a pan with the carrots, nuts, water and sugar. Season with salt and pepper. Bring to the boil and simmer for 3 minutes. Place the chicken in a separate pan with just enough water to cover. Bring to the boil and simmer for 8 minutes. Dissolve the saffron the boiling water. Stir half the saffron into the chicken and set aside. Cook the rice in plenty of boiling salted water until just tender. Drain. Pour the oil into a large heavy-based pan. Put a layer of the nut mixture in the base. Add a layer of chicken and dust with cinnamon. Add a layer of rice. Repeat the layers until all the ingredients are used. Cover and cook over a very gentle heat for 40 minutes. Mix the remaining saffron with the melted butter or margarine and drizzle over the surface before serving.

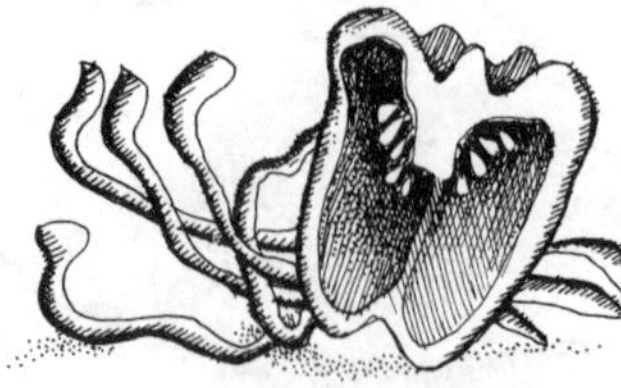

Chicken and Prawn Risotto

SERVES 4

175 g/6 oz chicken stir-fry meat
1 small green (bell) pepper, diced
1 small red pepper, diced
1 onion, finely chopped
25 g/1 oz/2 tbsp butter or margarine
225 g/8 oz/1 cup risotto rice
600 ml/1 pt/2½ cups chicken stock
5 ml/1 tsp saffron powder
100 g/4 oz frozen peas
100 g/4 oz cooked, peeled prawns (shrimp)
Salt and freshly ground black pepper
4 stoned (pitted) black olives, sliced
15 ml/1 tbsp chopped parsley

Fry (sauté) the chicken, peppers and onion in the butter or margarine in a large frying pan (skillet) for 4 minutes, stirring. Add the rice and cook for 1 minute. Add 150 ml/¼ pt/⅔ cup of the stock and the saffron. Cook, stirring, until the liquid has been absorbed. Add another 150 ml/¼ pt/⅔ cup of the stock and cook again until absorbed. Add the remaining stock, the peas, prawns and some salt and pepper. Cover, reduce the heat and simmer gently for about 10 minutes or until the rice has absorbed the liquid and the mixture is creamy but still has some bite. Stir in the olives, taste and re-season if necessary. Spoon on to plates and sprinkle with the parsley before serving.

Chicken and Clam Risotto

SERVES 4

Prepare as for Chicken and Prawn Risotto, but substitute 2 courgettes (zucchini) for the red and green (bell) peppers and add 298 g/10½ oz/1 medium can clams, drained. Omit the prawns (shrimp).

Spanish Rice

SERVES 4

175 g/6 oz boneless chicken meat, diced
1 onion, chopped
1 small green (bell) pepper, diced
1 small red pepper, diced
25 g/1 oz/2 tbsp butter or margarine
225 g/8 oz/1 cup long-grain rice
5 ml/1 tsp turmeric or saffron powder
600 ml/1 pt/2½ cups chicken stock
2 tomatoes, roughly chopped
100 g/4 oz frozen peas
100 g/4 oz cooked, peeled prawns (shrimp)
Salt and freshly ground black pepper
4 black olives, halved and stoned (pitted) and chopped parsley, to garnish
Mixed leaf salad, to serve

Fry (sauté) the chicken, onion and peppers in the butter or margarine, stirring, for 4 minutes. Stir in the rice and cook for 1 minute. Add the turmeric or saffron and the stock, bring to the boil, stirring, cover and simmer for 10 minutes. Stir in the tomatoes, peas, prawns and a little salt and pepper. Cover and continue cooking for a further 10 minutes over a low heat until the rice is cooked and has absorbed all the liquid. Fluff up with a fork, spoon on to warm plates and garnish each with halved olives and chopped parsley before serving with a mixed leaf salad.

Bangkok Supper

SERVES 4

225 g/8 oz/1 cup long-grain rice
50 g/2 oz frozen peas
2 onions, sliced
40 g/1½ oz/3 tbsp butter or margarine
15 ml/1 tbsp curry powder
2.5 ml/½ tsp ground cinnamon
175 g/6 oz chicken stir-fry meat
50 g/2 oz/½ cup cooked ham, diced
Salt and freshly ground black pepper
1 egg
30 ml/2 tbsp water
30 ml/2 tbsp chopped coriander (cilantro)
Orange and Mango Salsa (page 336), to serve

Cook the rice according to the packet directions, adding the peas for the last 5 minutes' cooking time. Drain, rinse with cold water and drain again. Meanwhile, fry (sauté) the onions in 25 g/1 oz/2 tbsp of the butter or margarine in a large frying pan (skillet) or wok for 2 minutes until softened but not browned. Add the curry powder, cinnamon and chicken and stir-fry for 5 minutes until the chicken is tender and cooked through. Add the ham, rice and peas and toss over a gentle heat for 4 minutes. Season to taste. Meanwhile, beat the eggs and water with a little salt and pepper and stir in the coriander. Melt the remaining butter or margarine in an omelette pan and fry the egg mixture until set underneath. Turn over and cook the other side. Roll up and cut into shreds. Pile the rice mixture on to four warm plates and top with the shredded omelette. Serve with Orange and Mango Salsa.

Malaysian Chicken Rice

SERVES 4

225 g/8 oz/1 cup long-grain rice
50 g/2 oz frozen peas
1 bunch of spring onions (scallions), chopped
45 ml/3 tbsp sunflower oil
5 ml/1 tsp ground cumin
2.5 ml/½ tsp ground cinnamon
1 small green chilli, seeded and chopped
175 g/6 oz chicken stir-fry meat
Salt and freshly ground black pepper
4 hard-boiled (hard-cooked) eggs, sliced
30 ml/2 tbsp water
30 ml/2 tbsp chopped coriander (cilantro)
Fresh beansprouts mixed with grated cucumber and flavoured to taste with lemon juice, soy sauce and a pinch of light brown sugar, to serve

Cook the rice according to the packet directions, adding the peas for the last 5 minutes' cooking time. Drain, rinse with boiling water and drain again. Meanwhile, fry (sauté) the spring onions in the oil in a large frying pan (skillet) or wok for 2 minutes until softened but not browned. Add the cumin, cinnamon, chilli and chicken and stir-fry for 5 minutes until the chicken is tender and cooked through. Add the rice and peas and toss over a gentle heat for 4 minutes. Season to taste. Lay the egg slices over, cover and heat through for 2–3 minutes. Sprinkle with the coriander and serve straight from the pan with the beansprout and cucumber salad.

Chicken and Tarragon Risotto

SERVES 4

45 ml/3 tbsp olive oil
2 onions, finely chopped
2 garlic cloves, crushed
2 celery sticks, chopped
1 red (bell) pepper, chopped
1 green pepper, chopped
100 g/4 oz button mushrooms, quartered
275 g/10 oz/1¼ cups risotto rice
750 ml/1¼ pts/3 cups hot chicken stock
350 g/12 oz/3 cups cooked chicken, diced
Salt and freshly ground black pepper
Grated rind and juice of ½ small lemon
30 ml/2 tbsp chopped tarragon

Heat the oil in a large frying pan (skillet). Add the onions, garlic and celery and cook, stirring, for 2 minutes. Add the peppers and mushrooms and stir for 1 minute. Add the rice and stir until all the grains are coated in the oil. Stir in the stock, bring to the boil, reduce the heat, cover and cook gently for 15 minutes. Stir, add the chicken, a little salt and pepper, the lemon rind and juice and the tarragon. Re-cover and cook for a further 5 minutes or until the rice has absorbed all the liquid and is tender. Serve hot straight from the pan.

Chicken, Chive and Pineapple Risotto

SERVES 4

Prepare as for Chicken and Tarragon Risotto, but add a 225 g/8 oz/1 small can of pineapple pieces, drained, instead of the mushrooms and substitute snipped chives for the tarragon.

Speciality Chicken Risotto

SERVES 6

1.25 kg/2½ lb oven-ready chicken
1 celery stick, chopped
1 large carrot, chopped
30 ml/2 tbsp olive oil
1 onion, finely chopped
450 g/1 lb/2 cups risotto rice
375 ml/13 fl oz/1½ cups dry white wine
400 g/14 oz/1 large can of chopped tomatoes
Salt and freshly ground black pepper
100 g/4 oz/1 cup Parmesan cheese, freshly grated
A few celery leaves, to garnish

Wipe the chicken inside and out with kitchen paper (paper towels). Place in a large pot. Cover with water and add the celery and carrot. Bring to the boil, reduce the heat, cover and simmer gently for 1½ hours until the chicken is really tender and falling off the bones. Remove from the stock, cool slightly, then take all the meat off the bones, discarding the skin. Dice the meat. Put the bones back in the stock and simmer for a further 1 hour. Strain and leave to cool, then skim the surface of any fat. Measure 900 ml/1½ pts/3¾ cups to use for the recipe and freeze the remainder.

Heat the oil in a large flameproof casserole (Dutch oven). Add the onion and fry (sauté) for 2 minutes. Stir in the rice and cook for 1 minute. Stir in the wine and tomatoes and simmer until the wine is absorbed. Stir in a quarter of the stock and simmer, stirring, until it has been absorbed. Repeat the process once more, then add the chicken and the remaining stock and simmer, stirring, until the rice is just tender and has absorbed the liquid. Season to taste and serve hot with the cheese sprinkled over and garnished with celery leaves.

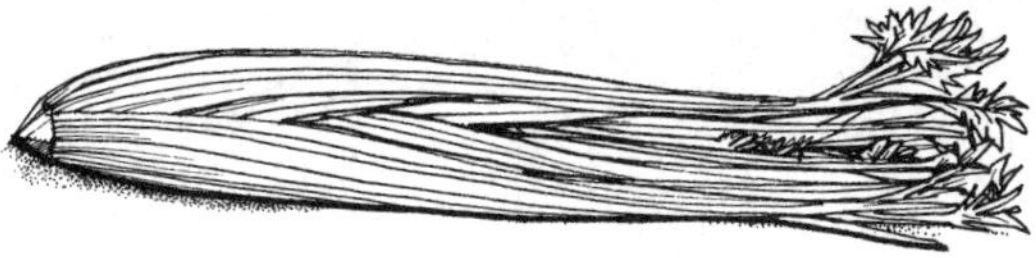

Syrian Chicken Dome

SERVES 6

1.5 kg/3 lb oven-ready chicken, cut into portions (page 15)
10 ml/2 tsp dried onion flakes
2.5 ml/½ tsp allspice
2.5 ml/½ tsp turmeric
Salt and freshly ground black pepper
25 g/1 oz/2 tbsp butter or margarine, plus extra for greasing
1.2 litres/2 pts/5 cups boiling water
100 g/4 oz frozen peas
450 g/1 lb/2 cups long-grain rice
25 g/1 oz/¼ cup toasted flaked (slivered) almonds

Put the chicken portions in a dish. Sprinkle with the onion flakes, spices and a little salt and pepper and leave to stand for 30 minutes. Melt the butter or margarine in a large saucepan or flameproof casserole (Dutch oven). Add the chicken and brown on all sides. Pour the water over, bring to the boil again, cover and simmer for about 30 minutes until the chicken is tender. Remove the chicken with a draining spoon. Add the peas and rice to the cooking liquid. Bring to the boil, reduce the heat, cover and simmer gently until the rice is tender and has absorbed the liquid. Top up with a little water, if necessary, during cooking. Season to taste. Meanwhile, cut all the chicken meat off the bones, discarding the skin. Cut into neat pieces. Grease a large warmed soufflé dish or mould. Sprinkle the nuts over the base, then lay the chicken on top. Cover with the hot rice mixture and press down firmly. Leave in a warm place for 3 minutes, then turn out and serve.

Indian Chicken and Mushroom Pilau

SERVES 2–4

150 ml/¼ pt/⅔ cup long-grain rice
30 ml/2 tbsp sunflower oil
1 onion, chopped
1 garlic clove, chopped
100 g/4 oz button mushrooms, sliced
5 ml/1 tsp garam masala
5 ml/1 tsp grated fresh root ginger
400 ml/14 fl oz/1¾ cups hot chicken stock
175 g/6 oz/1½ cups cooked chicken, diced, all skin removed
Salt and freshly ground black pepper
30 ml/2 tbsp chopped coriander (cilantro)
Minted Yoghurt and Cucumber (page 339), to serve

Measure the rice in a measuring jug. Rinse thoroughly with cold water in a sieve (strainer). Drain well. Heat the oil in a saucepan. Add the onion and garlic and fry (sauté) for about 5 minutes until well browned. Stir in the mushrooms and cook for a further minute. Add the rice, garam masala and ginger until coated with the oil. Pour on the stock and stir well. Add the chicken and sprinkle with salt and pepper. Cover tightly with foil, then a lid and turn down the heat as low as possible. Leave undisturbed for 20 minutes. Turn off the heat and leave for 5 minutes. Remove the foil and lid and fluff up with a fork. Sprinkle with the coriander and serve with Minted Yoghurt and Cucumber.

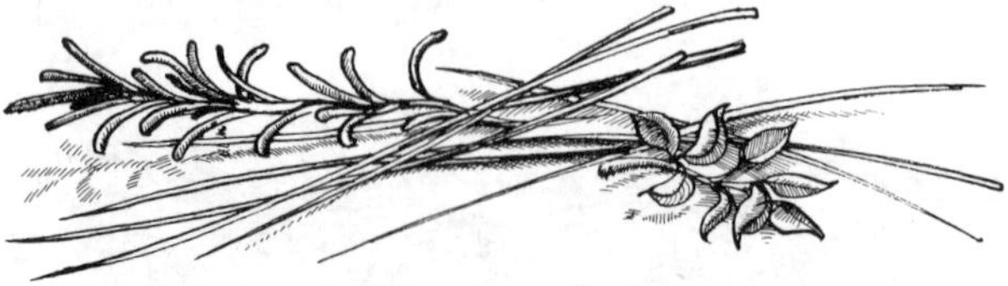

Chicken, Corn and Mushroom Pilaf

SERVES 6

1 large onion, finely chopped
1 garlic clove, crushed
100 g/4 oz/½ cup unsalted (sweet) butter
350 g/12 oz/1½ cups long-grain rice
1 litre/1¾ pts/4¼ cups chicken stock
225 g/8 oz button mushrooms, sliced
2.5 ml/½ tsp saffron powder
Salt and freshly ground black pepper
225 g/8 oz/2 cups cooked chicken, cut into bite-sized pieces
200 g/7 oz/1 small can of sweetcorn (corn), drained
4 tomatoes, skinned, seeded and chopped

Fry (sauté) the onion and garlic in the butter in a large flameproof casserole (Dutch oven) until soft but not brown. Stir in the rice and cook for 2 minutes until transparent and glistening. Add the stock, mushrooms and saffron. Season with salt and pepper, stir well and bring to the boil. Stir again, cover and transfer to the oven at 180°C/350°F/gas mark 4. Cook for 40 minutes, then stir in the chicken, corn and tomatoes. Return to the oven and cook for about 25 minutes until the rice is cooked and has absorbed all the liquid. Add a little more stock or water when you add the chicken if the rice is already looking dry.

Piquant Chicken Bake

SERVES 4–6

225 g/8 oz/1 cup long-grain rice
600 ml/1 pt/2½ cups hot chicken stock
1 red (bell) pepper, diced
30 ml/2 tbsp chopped parsley
Salt and freshly ground black pepper
25 g/1 oz/2 tbsp butter or margarine
5 ml/1 tsp onion salt
5 ml/1 tsp celery salt
10 ml/2 tsp paprika
1.5 kg/3 lb oven-ready chicken, cut into 8 pieces (page 15)
15 ml/1 tbsp chopped gherkins (cornichons)
50 g/2 oz/⅓ cup stuffed olives, sliced
10 ml/2 tsp lemon juice

Mix together the rice, stock, red pepper, parsley and a little salt and pepper in a large flameproof casserole (Dutch oven). Stir well. Blend the butter or margarine, onion and celery salt and paprika together and rub over the chicken. Lay on top of the rice and bring to the boil. Cover and bake in the oven at 180°C/ 350°F/gas mark 4 for about 45 minutes or until the chicken and rice are tender. Stir the gherkins, olives and lemon juice into the rice. Taste and re-season if necessary. Leave to stand, covered, for 5 minutes, then serve.

Washday Rice

SERVES 4

350 g/12 oz/1½ cups long-grain rice
30 ml/2 tbsp olive oil
4 eggs, beaten
100 g/4 oz/1 cup cooked chicken, diced, all skin removed
5 cm/2 in piece of cucumber, chopped
4 spring onions (scallions), chopped
50 g/2 oz mushrooms, sliced
15 ml/1 tbsp soy sauce
Salt and freshly ground black pepper

Cook the rice in plenty of boiling salted water until tender. Drain, rinse with cold water and drain again. Heat half the oil in a frying pan (skillet) and fry (sauté) half the egg until just beginning to set. Stir in the cooked rice, the chicken, cucumber, onions, mushrooms and soy sauce. Cook, stirring, until piping hot. Season to taste. Meanwhile, in a separate small frying pan, heat the remaining oil and make an omelette using the remaining beaten egg, seasoned with salt and pepper. Pile the rice mixture on to a warmed serving dish, slice the omelette and scatter on top.

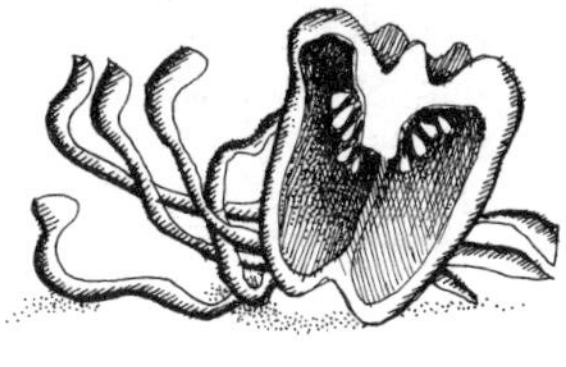

Indonesian Chicken, Prawn and Egg Rice

SERVES 6–8

1 small oven-ready chicken
3 onions
2 cloves
1 bay leaf
3 parsley sprigs
6 peppercorns
Salt and freshly ground black pepper
450 g/1 lb/2 cups basmati rice
45 ml/3 tbsp olive oil
30 ml/2 tbsp peanut butter
5 ml/1 tsp chilli powder
100 g/4 oz cooked, peeled prawns (shrimp)
100 g/4 oz/1 cup cooked ham, diced
5 ml/1 tsp ground cumin
5 ml/1 tsp ground coriander (cilantro)
1 garlic clove, crushed
A little grated nutmeg
30 ml/2 tbsp toasted cashew nuts
12 cooked, unpeeled prawns (shrimp)
2 hard-boiled (hard-cooked) eggs, quartered

Wipe the chicken inside and out with kitchen paper (paper towels). Place in a saucepan. Stud one of the onions with the cloves and add to the pan with the bay leaf, parsley, peppercorns and a little salt. Add enough water to cover the bird. Bring to the boil, reduce the heat, cover and simmer for 1 hour or until the chicken is tender. Leave to cool slightly, then lift out the chicken. Strain the stock and return to the pan. Bring to the boil, add the rice and simmer for 10 minutes or until the rice is tender. Drain, if necessary and keep warm, covered with a cloth to absorb any remaining moisture. Cut all the chicken off the bones, discarding the skin. Cut into neat pieces. Thinly slice the remaining onions. Heat the oil in a large pan. Add the onions and fry (sauté) until soft and lightly golden. Stir in the peanut butter and chilli powder (add less if you don't like food too hot). Add the prawns, ham, chicken and rice. Continue frying, tossing gently, until the rice is lightly golden. Stir in the cumin, coriander, garlic and nutmeg. Toss gently until well blended, then season to taste. Pile on to a hot serving dish. Sprinkle with the toasted cashews and garnish with the unpeeled prawns and quartered eggs.

Arroz con Pollo

SERVES 4 OR 8

1.5 kg/3 lb oven-ready chicken, cut into 8 pieces (page 15)
45 ml/3 tbsp olive oil
1 large onion, sliced
1 red (bell) pepper, thinly sliced
100 g/4 oz button mushrooms, sliced
4 plum tomatoes, skinned, seeded and roughly chopped
12 stoned (pitted) green olives
15 ml/1 tbsp capers
Salt and freshly ground black pepper
350 g/12 oz/1½ cups long-grain rice
750 ml/1¼ pts/3 cups hot chicken stock
4 stoned (pitted) black olives, sliced, and 15 ml/1 tbsp chopped parsley, to garnish
Green salad, to serve

Wipe the chicken pieces with kitchen paper (paper towels). Brown in the oil in a large flameproof casserole (Dutch oven). Remove from the pan with a draining spoon. Add the onion and fry (sauté) for 3 minutes, stirring. Add the pepper, mushrooms, tomatoes, green olives and capers. Season lightly and stir well. Top with the chicken. Cover and cook gently for 30 minutes, stirring occasionally to prevent sticking. Meanwhile, wash the rice in several changes of cold water. Drain well and stir into the casserole. Pour on the hot stock and bring to the boil. Cover, reduce the heat and simmer gently for 15–20 minutes until the rice is tender and has absorbed all the liquid. Stir two or three times and add a little boiling water if necessary. Serve piping hot, garnished with the black olives and parsley, with a green salad.

Chicken Jambalaya

SERVES 6

1 oven-ready poussin (Cornish hen), cut into 6 pieces (page 15)
120 ml/4 fl oz/½ cup olive oil
1 large red onion, finely chopped
2 garlic cloves, crushed
2 celery sticks, chopped
1 green (bell) pepper, diced
450 g/1 lb/2 cups risotto rice
225 g/8 oz/2 cups cooked ham, diced
350 g/12 oz raw, peeled king prawns (jumbo shrimp)
225 g/8 oz chorizo sausage, thickly sliced
200 g/7 oz/1 small can of chopped tomatoes
60 ml/4 tbsp tomato purée (paste)
2 sun-dried tomatoes, finely chopped
1 bouquet garni sachet
A pinch of ground cloves
1.5 ml/¼ tsp cayenne
Salt and freshly ground black pepper
1.2 litres/2 pts/5 cups chicken stock
90 ml/6 tbsp dry white wine
15 ml/1 tbsp chopped parsley
6 cooked, unpeeled king prawns (jumbo shrimp)
A few black olives

Brown the poussin pieces in half the oil in a large frying pan (skillet). Remove from the pan. Heat the remaining oil and fry (sauté) the onion, garlic, celery and pepper for 2 minutes until softened but not browned. Add the rice and stir over a gentle heat for 1 minute. Return the chicken to the pan with all the remaining ingredients except the parsley, unshelled prawns and olives. Bring to the boil, stirring, reduce the heat, cover and simmer gently for 15–20 minutes, adding a little more stock or wine if the rice is becoming too dry. Stir gently, taste and add a little more seasoning if necessary. Discard the bouquet garni, garnish with the parsley, prawns and olives and serve straight away.

Louisiana Jambalaya

SERVES 4

4 chicken portions
30 ml/2 tbsp sunflower oil
225 g/8 oz smoked pork sausage, sliced
1 onion, chopped
2 celery sticks, chopped
2 garlic cloves, crushed
1 green (bell) pepper, cut into strips
1 carrot, chopped
750 ml/1¼ pts/3 cups chicken stock
225 g/8 oz/1 cup long-grain rice
10 ml/2 tsp paprika
2 beefsteak tomatoes, skinned, seeded and chopped
Tabasco sauce
1 bunch of spring onions (scallions), chopped
Salt and freshly ground black pepper

Brown the chicken in the oil. Add the sausage and fry (sauté) for 3 minutes. Remove from the pan with a draining spoon and keep warm. Add the prepared vegetables and fry for 2–3 minutes, stirring. Return the chicken and sausage to the pan. Add the stock, cover and simmer gently for 15 minutes. Add the rice, paprika, tomatoes, a few drops of Tabasco sauce and half the spring onions. Cover and cook gently for a further 15 minutes or until the rice is tender and has absorbed the liquid. Taste and season if necessary. Sprinkle with the remaining spring onions before serving.

Quick Rice Supper

SERVES 2

1 packet of savoury mushroom or vegetable rice
175 g/6 oz/1½ cups cooked chicken, chopped
50 g/2 oz/½ cup Mozzarella or Cheddar cheese, grated

Prepare the rice according to the packet directions. Stir in the chicken and heat through for 3–4 minutes. Spoon into shallow flameproof dishes. Top with the cheese and flash under a hot grill (broiler).

Chicken and Mussel Risotto

SERVES 4

25 g/1 oz/2 tbsp butter or margarine
1 onion, chopped
225 g/8 oz/1 cup long-grain rice
250 g/9 oz/1 medium can of mussels in brine (not vinegar)
Chicken stock
225 g/8 oz/2 cups cooked chicken, diced, all skin removed
Salt and freshly ground black pepper
30 ml/2 tbsp chopped parsley
45ml/3 tbsp single (light) cream
Finely grated rind of 1 lemon
Green salad, to serve

Melt the butter or margarine in a large frying pan (skillet). Add the onion and fry (sauté) for 3 minutes until soft and lightly golden. Stir in the rice and stir until glistening. Drain the liquid from the can of mussels into a measuring jug and make up to 600 ml/1 pt/2½ cups with stock. Pour half into the pan. Bring to the boil and cook, stirring, until absorbed. Add the mussels and chicken and season with salt and pepper. Pour in the remaining stock. Cover and cook over a gentle heat for about 10–15 minutes until the rice is tender and has absorbed the liquid, stirring occasionally and adding a little more stock, if necessary. Stir in the parsley and cream and heat through. Spoon on to warm plates, sprinkle with the lemon rind and serve with a green salad.

Japanese-style Sesame Chicken

SERVES 4

175 g/6 oz/¾ cup long-grain rice
50 g/2 oz/½ cup plain (all-purpose) flour
Salt and freshly ground black pepper
15 ml/1 tbsp sesame seeds
4 skinless chicken breasts
50 g/2 oz/¼ cup butter or margarine
15 ml/1 tbsp sesame oil
300 ml/½ pt/1¼ cups chicken stock
45 ml/3 tbsp rice wine or dry white wine
2.5 ml/½ tsp ground coriander (cilantro)
1.5 ml/¼ tsp ground ginger
1.5 ml/¼ tsp chilli powder
300 ml/½ pt/1¼ cups double (heavy) cream

Cook the rice in plenty of boiling salted water until tender. Drain, rinse with boiling water, drain again and return to the pan. Meanwhile, mix the flour with a little salt and pepper and the sesame seeds. Use to coat the chicken breasts. Melt half the butter or margarine with the oil in a large frying pan (skillet). Fry (sauté) the chicken breasts for 3 minutes on each side until golden. Drain off any excess oil in the frying pan. Add the stock and wine, bring to the boil, reduce the heat, cover and simmer for 10–15 minutes or until the chicken is cooked through. Stir the remaining butter or margarine into the cooked rice with a little salt and pepper. Mix the spices together and sprinkle over. Toss well and heat through gently. Pile on to a serving dish. Remove the chicken breasts from the cooking liquid and arrange on the rice. Keep warm. Stir the cream into the cooking liquid and simmer, stirring, until slightly thickened. Pour over the chicken and serve straight away.

Andalusian Rice

SERVES 4

175 g/6 oz/1½ cups diced boneless chicken meat
1 small green (bell) pepper, diced
1 small red pepper, diced
30 ml/2 tbsp olive oil
225 g/8 oz/1 cup risotto or long-grain rice
600 ml/1 pt/2½ cups chicken stock
100 g/4 oz frozen peas and sweetcorn (corn)
100 g/4 oz cooked, peeled prawns (shrimp)
Salt and freshly ground black pepper
A few green olives, to garnish

Fry (sauté) the chicken and peppers in the oil for 4 minutes, stirring. Add the rice and cook for 1 minute, stirring. Pour on the stock, bring to the boil, cover and simmer for 10 minutes. Add the peas and sweetcorn and prawns, re-cover and cook very gently for a further 10 minutes until the rice is cooked and has absorbed nearly all the liquid. Season to taste and stir lightly. Garnish with a few green olives before serving.

Savoury Chicken Liver Risotto

SERVES 4–6

40 g/1½ oz/¾ cup dried porcini mushrooms
45 ml/3 tbsp olive oil
1 whole garlic clove
50 g/2 oz/1 small can of anchovies, drained and chopped
450 g/1 lb/2 cups risotto rice
1.2 litres/2 pts/5 cups hot chicken stock
200 g/7 oz chicken livers, trimmed and cut into pieces
Freshly ground black pepper

Soak the mushrooms in boiling water for 30 minutes. Drain, rinse thoroughly then cut into bite-sized pieces. Heat the oil in a flameproof casserole (Dutch oven). Add the garlic clove, fry (sauté) until golden, then discard. Stir in the mushrooms, anchovies and rice. Cook for 1 minute. Add 250 ml/8 fl oz/1 cup of the stock, bring to the boil and simmer, stirring, until the stock is absorbed. Repeat with 2 more cups of stock. Add the chicken livers and continue adding the stock for about 15–20 minutes, until the rice is just tender and creamy. Serve straight away with a good grinding of black pepper.

Chicken Liver and Rice-stuffed Peppers

SERVES 4

75 g/3 oz/⅓ cup long-grain rice
4 large red or green (bell) peppers
25 g/1 oz/2 tbsp butter or margarine
1 onion, finely chopped
50 g/2 oz button mushrooms, chopped
175 g/6 oz chicken livers, trimmed and chopped
2.5 ml/½ tsp dried sage
30 ml/2 tbsp chopped parsley
Salt and freshly ground black pepper
1 egg, beaten
25 g/1 oz/¼ cup Cheddar cheese, finely grated
Tomato Sauce (page 342), and crusty bread, to serve

Cook the rice in plenty of lightly salted boiling water for 10 minutes. Drain. Meanwhile, cut a slice off the stalk end of each pepper and remove the seeds and white membranes. Plunge the peppers into boiling water and simmer for 3 minutes. Drain, rinse with cold water and drain again. Melt the butter or margarine in a saucepan. Add the onion and cook for 2 minutes, stirring. Add the mushrooms and livers and cook for a further 2 minutes, stirring. Stir in the cooked rice, the sage, parsley and some salt and pepper. Mix with the egg to bind. Spoon into the peppers and top each with a quarter of the cheese. Place in a roasting tin (pan) and add 45 ml/3 tbsp water to the tin. Bake in a preheated oven at 180°C/350°F/gas mark 4 for about 40 minutes or until the peppers are tender and the tops are golden brown. Serve hot with Tomato Sauce and crusty bread.

TURKEY

Leicester Macaroni

SERVES 4

225 g/8 oz short-cut macaroni
450 ml/¾ pt/2 cups milk
25 g/1 oz/¼ cup plain (all-purpose) flour
50 g/2 oz/¼ cup butter or margarine
175 g/6 oz/1½ cups Red Leicester cheese, grated
400 g/14 oz/1 large can of chopped tomatoes, drained
100 g/4 oz/1 cup cooked turkey, diced
100 g/4 oz/1 cup cooked ham, diced
Salt and freshly ground black pepper
45 ml/3 tbsp crushed cornflakes
Sweet pickle, to serve

Cook the macaroni according to the packet directions. Drain. Meanwhile, blend a little of the milk in a saucepan with the flour. Add the remaining milk and half the butter or margarine. Bring to the boil and cook for 2 minutes, stirring all the time. Stir in 100 g/4 oz/1 cup of the cheese, the tomatoes, turkey, ham and a little salt and pepper. Fold in the macaroni. Turn into a shallow ovenproof dish. Mix the remaining cheese with the cornflakes and sprinkle over. Dot with the remaining butter or margarine and bake in the oven at 200°C/400°F/gas mark 6 for about 20 minutes or until bubbling and golden brown. Serve with sweet pickle.

Turkish Ravioli

SERVES 4–6

1 egg
1 egg yolk
350 g/12 oz/3 cups plain (all-purpose) flour
100 ml/3½ fl oz/6½ tbsp water
Salt and freshly ground black pepper
225 g/8 oz/2 cups cooked turkey, finely chopped
1 onion, grated
5 ml/1 tsp dried oregano
450 ml/¾ pt/2 cups plain yoghurt
4 garlic cloves, crushed
100 g/4 oz/½ cup unsalted (sweet) butter
450 ml/¾ pt/2 cups passata (sieved tomatoes)

Beat together the whole egg and egg yolk. Put the flour in a bowl. Make a well in the centre and add the eggs, water and 5 ml/1 tsp salt. Gradually work the mixture into a dough, then knead gently until smooth. Wrap in clingfilm (plastic wrap) and leave to stand for at least 30 minutes.

Cut the dough in half. Keep one half covered and roll out the other as thinly as possible on a lightly floured surface to a square. Keep the other half covered. Mix the turkey with the onion, a little salt and pepper and the oregano. Cut the dough into 4 cm/1½ in squares. Put a tiny bit of filling on each and fold over to form a triangle. Place on a floured baking (cookie) sheet. Repeat with the remaining dough. Drop the triangles into a large pan of boiling water, a few at a time, and cook for about 4 minutes until they rise to the surface. Remove with a draining spoon and keep warm in a large serving dish while cooking the remainder. Mix together the yoghurt and garlic. Melt the butter, stir in the passata and boil until the mixture thickens. When all the ravioli is cooked, spoon the garlic yoghurt, then the hot tomato sauce over and serve straight away.

Mountain Special

SERVES 4

350 g/12 oz spaghetti
120 ml/4 fl oz/½ cup olive oil
2 garlic cloves, crushed
4 turkey rashers (slices), chopped
4 ripe tomatoes, diced
Salt and freshly ground black pepper
20 basil leaves, torn into small pieces
50 g/2 oz/½ cup goat's cheese, roughly crumbled
A few black olives
Green salad, to serve

Cook the spaghetti according to the packet directions. Drain. Meanwhile, heat the oil in a saucepan. Add the garlic and cook gently for 1 minute. Add the turkey rashers and fry (sauté) for 2 minutes. Add the tomatoes and a little salt and pepper and cook gently for 1–2 minutes, stirring, until heated through but the tomatoes are still in pieces. Add the basil and toss gently. Add the cooked spaghetti and toss well. At the last minute, add the cheese, toss again and serve immediately with a few olives scattered over and a green salad.

Fettuccine with Turkey and Jalopeño Pepper Cream

SERVES 4–6

350 g/12 oz turkey breast steaks, cut diagonally into thin strips
15 ml/1 tbsp olive oil
15 g/½ oz/1 tbsp butter or margarine
120 ml/4 fl oz/½ cup white wine vinegar
2.5 ml/½ tsp salt
1 small onion, finely chopped
1 jalopeño pepper, seeded and chopped
600 ml/1 pt/2½ cups double (heavy) cream
30 ml/2 tbsp chopped coriander (cilantro)
Salt and freshly ground black pepper
350 g/12 oz fettuccine

Toss the turkey in the hot oil and butter for 3 minutes. Put the vinegar, salt, onion and chilli in a saucepan. Bring to the boil and boil rapidly for about 5 minutes until the mixture is reduced by a half. Add the cream, bring to the boil and boil rapidly until the mixture is well reduced and thickened. Add half the coriander and the contents of the turkey pan and stir well. Season to taste. Meanwhile, cook the pasta according to the packet directions. Drain. Add the cream sauce, toss well and sprinkle with the remaining coriander before serving.

Salsa Alfredo for Fresh Pasta

SERVES 4

350 g/12 oz any fresh pasta
450 ml/¾ pt/2 cups double (heavy) cream
50 g/2 oz/¼ cup unsalted (sweet) butter
175 g/6 oz/1½ cups Parmesan cheese, freshly grated
Freshly ground black pepper
4 turkey rashers (slices), grilled (broiled) until crisp, crumbled
Ciabatta bread, to serve

Cook the pasta according to the packet directions. Drain. Meanwhile, bring the cream and butter to the boil in a saucepan. Reduce the heat and simmer for 1 minute. Add half the cheese and some pepper and whisk until smooth. Add to the cooked pasta with the remaining cheese and toss over a gentle heat. Pile on to warm plates, add a good grinding of pepper and serve topped with the crumbled turkey rashers.

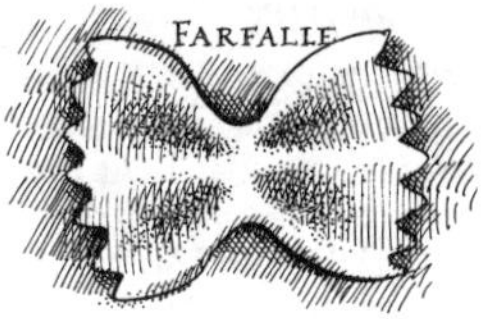

Spaghetti with Turkey Carbonara

SERVES 4

350 g/12 oz spaghetti
4 turkey rashers (slices), chopped
75 g/3 oz/⅓ cup butter or margarine
5 eggs
30 ml/2 tbsp chopped parsley
Salt and freshly ground black pepper
50 g/2 oz/½ cup Parmesan cheese, grated
Green salad, to serve

Cook the spaghetti according to the packet directions. Drain and return to the saucepan. Meanwhile, fry (sauté) the turkey in the butter or margarine until browned. Beat the eggs with the parsley, a little salt and lots of pepper and the cheese. Add the hot turkey rashers and the juices to the spaghetti and toss. Add the egg mixture and stir and toss until the mixture is creamy and piping hot. Do not allow to scramble completely. Serve immediately with a green salad.

Wraysbury Carbonara

SERVES 4

350 g/12 oz spaghetti
60 ml/4 tbsp olive oil
4 turkey rashers (slices), diced
1 onion, finely chopped
1 garlic clove, crushed
100 g/4 oz button mushrooms, sliced
Salt and freshly ground black pepper
2 eggs
60 ml/4 tbsp milk
30 ml/2 tbsp chopped parsley
Parmesan cheese, grated
Mixed salad, to serve

Cook the spaghetti according to the packet directions. Drain and return to the pan. Meanwhile, heat the oil in a small saucepan. Add the turkey rashers, onion and garlic and fry (sauté) for 1 minute, stirring. Add the mushrooms and cook for 2 minutes. Add a little salt and a good grinding of pepper, cover and cook over a gentle heat while the pasta cooks. Add the mixture to the cooked spaghetti and toss well. Beat the eggs with the milk and add to the pan with half the parsley. Stir and toss over a gentle heat until lightly scrambled but still very creamy. Spoon on to hot plates, garnish with the parsley and lots of grated Parmesan cheese and serve with a mixed salad.

Christmas Turkey Lasagne

SERVES 4

1 onion, chopped
1 garlic clove, crushed
30 ml/2 tbsp sunflower oil
400 g/14 oz/1 large can of chopped tomatoes
15 ml/1 tbsp tomato purée (paste)
100 g/4 oz button mushrooms, sliced
175 g/6 oz/1½ cups cooked turkey, diced, all skin removed
75 ml/5 tbsp red or white wine
Salt and freshly ground black pepper
2.5 ml/½ tsp dried oregano
2.5 ml/½ tsp caster (superfine) sugar
2 quantities of Quick Béchamel Sauce (page 340)
6–8 no-need-to-precook green lasagne sheets
45 ml/3 tbsp Parmesan cheese, grated
Green salad, to serve

Fry (sauté) the onion and garlic in the oil in a saucepan for 2 minutes, stirring. Stir in the tomatoes, purée and mushrooms and simmer gently for 5 minutes. Stir in the turkey and wine and season with salt and pepper, the oregano and sugar. Spoon a little of the Quick Béchamel Sauce into the base of a shallow ovenproof dish. Top with a layer of lasagne sheets, breaking to fit if necessary. Spread over half the turkey mixture. Repeat the layers of lasagne and turkey, finishing with a layer of lasagne. Top with the remaining Quick Béchamel Sauce and sprinkle with the Parmesan. Bake in a preheated oven at 190°C/375°F/gas mark 5 for about 35 minutes until the top is brown and the lasagne feels tender when a knife is inserted down through the centre. Serve hot with a green salad.

Spaghetti with Turkey and Oyster Mushrooms

SERVES 4

60 ml/4 tbsp olive oil
175 g/6 oz/1½ cups diced turkey meat
1 carrot, finely chopped
1 celery stick, finely chopped
1 garlic clove, crushed
100 g/4 oz oyster mushrooms, sliced
50 g/2 oz frozen peas
300 ml/½ pt/¼ cups passata (sieved tomatoes)
5 ml/1 tsp caster (superfine) sugar
2.5 ml/½ tsp dried basil
350 g/12 oz spaghetti
Salt and freshly ground black pepper
Parmesan cheese, grated, to serve

Heat the oil in a large pan. Add all the ingredients except the spaghetti, seasoning and cheese and fry (sauté), stirring, for 3 minutes. Reduce the heat, cover and cook gently for 10 minutes, stirring occasionally. Meanwhile cook the spaghetti in plenty of boiling salted water for 10 minutes or according to the packet directions. Drain and add to the turkey mixture. Season to taste, toss lightly and serve hot with grated Parmesan cheese.

Tagliatelle alla Panna

SERVES 4

350 g/12 oz green tagliatelle
40 g/1½ oz/3 tbsp unsalted (sweet) butter
75 ml/5 tbsp double (heavy) cream
100 g/4 oz/1 cup cooked ham, cut into thin strips
100 g/4 oz/1 cup cooked turkey, cut into thin strips
Salt and freshly ground black pepper
Freshly grated nutmeg
Grated Parmesan cheese, to garnish
Grated carrot and courgette (zucchini), tossed in French dressing, to serve

Cook the tagliatelle according to the packet directions. Drain and return to the pan. Add the butter, cream, ham, turkey, a sprinkling of salt, a good grinding of pepper and lots of grated nutmeg and toss over a gentle heat until piping hot and well mixed. Serve garnished with lots of grated Parmesan cheese and a carrot and courgette salad.

Turkey with Grapes, Olives and Pasta

SERVES 4

300 ml/½ pt/1¼ cups chicken stock
1 bay leaf
40 g/1½ oz/3 tbsp butter or margarine
225 g/8 oz turkey stir-fry meat
25 g/1 oz/¼ cup plain (all-purpose) flour
5 ml/1 tsp grated lemon rind
150 ml/¼ pt/⅔ cup single (light) cream
75 g/3 oz seedless black grapes, halved
75 g/3 oz stoned (pitted) green olives, halved
Salt and freshly ground black pepper
350 g/12 oz green tagliatelle
30 ml/2 tbsp chopped parsley, to garnish

Put the stock in a pan. Add the bay leaf. Bring to the boil and leave to infuse while preparing the rest of the sauce. Melt the butter or margarine in a separate pan. Add the turkey and cook, stirring, for 4–5 minutes until cooked through. Add the flour and cook, stirring, for 1 minute. Discard the bay leaf, then gradually blend the stock into the turkey mixture, stirring all the time. Add the lemon rind. Bring to the boil and cook for 3 minutes, stirring. Stir in the cream, add the grapes and olives and season to taste. Meanwhile, cook the pasta according to the packet directions. Drain and return to the pan. Add the sauce, toss well, pile on to warm plates and garnish with chopped parsley.

Four-cheese Melting Moments with Crunchy Turkey

SERVES 4

4 turkey breast steaks
1 egg, beaten
100 g/4 oz/2 cups fresh breadcrumbs
Salt and freshly ground black pepper
Sunflower oil, for shallow-frying
350 g/12 oz tagliatelle
25 g/1 oz/¼ cup plain (all-purpose) flour
600 ml/1 pt/2½ cups milk
25 g/1 oz/2 tbsp butter or margarine
1 bay leaf
50 g/2 oz/½ cup Emmental (Swiss) cheese, grated
50 g/2 oz/½ cup Fontina cheese
50 g/2 oz/½ cup Mozzarella cheese, grated
50 g/2 oz/½ cup Pecorino cheese, grated
Parsley sprigs and lemon wedges, to garnish
Tomato salad, to serve

Place the turkey steaks, one at a time, in a plastic bag and beat with a rolling pin or meat mallet to flatten. Dip in the egg, then the breadcrumbs seasoned with a little salt and pepper. Fry (sauté) in hot oil for about 3 minutes on each side until golden brown and cooked through. Drain on kitchen paper (paper towels) and keep warm. Meanwhile, cook the pasta according to the packet directions. Drain. Whisk together the flour and milk in a saucepan until smooth. Add the butter or margarine and bay leaf and bring to the boil, whisking all the time, until thickened and smooth. Simmer for 2 minutes, stirring. Remove the bay leaf. Stir in the cheeses and a little seasoning. Heat through until melted. Add to the cooked pasta and toss well. Pile on to warm plates. Put a turkey steak to one side of each, garnish with lemon wedges and parsley and serve with a tomato salad.

Turkey and Basil Lasagne

SERVES 4

Prepare as for Lasagne as Forno (page 246), but substitute minced (ground) turkey for the minced chicken, white wine for the vermouth and 30 ml/2 tbsp chopped basil for the dried oregano. Use green lasagne sheets instead of wholemeal.

Creamed Baked Rice with Cheese

SERVES 4–6

450 g/1 lb/2 cups risotto rice
25 g/1 oz Fontina cheese, thinly sliced
25 g/1 oz/2 tbsp unsalted (sweet) butter
Salt and freshly ground black pepper
60 ml/4 tbsp double (heavy) cream
100 g/4 oz/1 cup Parmesan cheese, grated
4 turkey rashers (slices), chopped

Cook the rice in plenty of boiling salted water for about 15 minutes until almost tender. Drain thoroughly. Spread half the rice in a shallow ovenproof dish. Cover with half the Fontina cheese, dot with butter and season lightly. Drizzle over half the cream. Repeat the layers and top it all with the grated Parmesan. Bake at 180°C/350°F/gas mark 4 for about 20 minutes until golden on top. Meanwhile, fry (sauté) the turkey rashers. Scatter over the top and serve straight away.

Suppli al Telefono

When the balls are pulled apart the cheese should stretch into long threads, like telephone wires, hence the name.

SERVES 6

1 onion, finely chopped
50 g/2 oz/¼ cup butter or margarine
225 g/8 oz/1 cup risotto rice
400 g/14 oz/1 large can of tomato juice
150 ml/¼ pt/⅔ cup chicken stock
30 ml/2 tbsp Parmesan cheese, grated
Salt and freshly ground black pepper
1.5 ml/¼ tsp cayenne
2 eggs, beaten
4 turkey rashers (slices)
100 g/4 oz Mozzarella cheese, cut into 12 cubes
75 g/3 oz/1½ cups breadcrumbs
Oil, for deep-frying

Fry (sauté) the onion in the butter or margarine for 2 minutes until softened and turning golden. Stir in the rice and cook for 1 minute. Stir in the tomato juice and stock. Bring to the boil, reduce the heat, cover and cook gently for 15–20 minutes until the rice is cooked and has absorbed all the liquid. If there is any left, boil rapidly for a few minutes, stirring all the time. Remove from the heat and stir in the Parmesan. Season with salt, pepper and the cayenne. Stir in the eggs. Turn the mixture into a bowl, leave to cool, then chill until fairly firm. Meanwhile, grill (broil) the turkey rashers until cooked, then finely chop. With floured hands, take a good spoonful of the rice mixture and flatten in the palm. Place a cube of cheese and a twelfth of the chopped turkey rashers in the centre. Top with another spoonful of the rice mixture and shape into a ball. Roll in the breadcrumbs. Repeat with the remaining ingredients. Chill again for 30 minutes. Deep-fry, a few at a time, until crisp and golden. Drain on kitchen paper (paper towels) and serve straight away.

Arroz Poblano

SERVES 6

350 g/12 oz/1½ cups long-grain rice
60 ml/4 tbsp sunflower oil
2 green chillies, seeded and chopped
1 small onion, finely chopped
1 garlic clove, crushed
225 g/8 oz turkey breast steak, cut into very thin strips
1.75 litres/3 pts/7½ cups chicken stock
Salt and freshly ground black pepper
100 g/4 oz/1 cup Cheddar cheese, grated
Tomato and onion salad, to serve

Fry (sauté) the rice in the oil until golden, stirring all the time. Add the chillies, onion, garlic and turkey and cook for 1 minute, stirring. Stir in the stock and a little salt and pepper. Bring to the boil, reduce the heat, cover and cook gently for about 20 minutes, stirring occasionally, until the rice is tender and has absorbed the liquid. Add a little more stock if drying out too quickly. Pile into a flameproof serving dish, top with the cheese and flash under a hot grill (broiler) until the cheese melts. Serve straight away with a tomato and onion salad.

Dolcelatte, Turkey and Watercress Mould

SERVES 4–6

Prepare as for Gorgonzola Speciality (page 258), but substitute Dolcelatte cheese for the Gorgonzola. After cooking the rice, add 1 chopped bunch of watercress and 175 g/6 oz/1¼ cups finely chopped cooked turkey instead of the chicken. Heat through for 3 minutes, stirring. Press the rice mixture into a hot mould. Immediately turn out on to a serving dish and pour the sauce over. Serve with a tomato salad.

Turkey and Tomato Rice

SERVES 4

175 g/6 oz/¾ cup long-grain rice
1 onion, thinly sliced
1 green (bell) pepper, thinly sliced
25 g/1 oz/2 tbsp unsalted (sweet) butter
400 g/14 oz/1 large can of chopped tomatoes
10 ml/2 tsp caster (superfine) sugar
Salt and freshly ground black pepper
1 bay leaf
175 g/6 oz/1½ cups cooked turkey, diced, all skin removed
25 g/1 oz/¼ cup Parmesan cheese, freshly grated
Mixed green salad, to serve

Cook the rice in plenty of boiling salted water for 10 minutes. Drain. Fry (sauté) the onion and pepper in the butter for 1 minute. Cover and cook gently for a further 4 minutes until soft. Add the rice, tomatoes, sugar, a little salt and pepper and the bay leaf. Bring to the boil, reduce the heat and simmer gently for 10 minutes, stirring occasionally. Add the turkey and cook for a further 5 minutes. Remove the bay leaf. Spoon on to warm plates and sprinkle liberally with the Parmesan cheese before serving with a mixed green salad.

Savoury Cheese Timbale

SERVES 4

350 g/12 oz/1½ cups risotto rice
40 g/1½ oz/3 tbsp unsalted (sweet) butter
60 ml/4 tbsp Parmesan cheese, grated
175 g/6 oz Fontina cheese, thinly sliced
175 g/6 oz Gruyere (Swiss) cheese, thinly sliced
75 g/3 oz/¾ cup cooked ham, chopped
75 g/3 oz/¾ cup cooked turkey, chopped
Watercress, to garnish
Crusty bread and Fresh Sweet Chutney (page 338), to serve

Cook the rice in plenty of boiling salted water for 18 minutes. Drain thoroughly and return to the saucepan. Grease a large ring mould with a little of the butter. Stir the remaining butter and the Parmesan into the rice. Spoon a third of the rice into the mould and press down well. Top with a third of the sliced cheeses, ham and turkey. Repeat the layers twice more until all the ingredients are used. Bake for 10–15 minutes at 180°C/350°F/gas mark 4 to melt the cheeses and heat the ham and turkey through. Loosen the edge of the mould and turn out on to a serving dish. Serve straight away, garnished with watercress, with crusty bread and Fresh Sweet Chutney.

Rice Dream

SERVES 4–6

350 g/12 oz/1½ cups risotto rice
225 g/8 oz Mozzarella cheese, cubed
100 g/4 oz cooked ham in a piece, cubed
100 g/4 oz/1 cup cooked turkey, diced
2 large egg yolks, lightly beaten
30 ml/2 tbsp freshly grated Parmesan cheese
Salt and freshly ground black pepper
Parsley sprigs, to garnish
Mixed salad, to serve

Cook the rice in plenty of boiling salted water for 18 minutes. Drain thoroughly and return to the saucepan. Add the remaining ingredients. Toss over a moderate heat for 4–5 minutes until well combined and piping hot. Pile on to serving plates, garnish with parsley and serve immediately with a mixed salad.

Turkey and Tomato Rice with Sweetcorn and Peas

SERVES 4

Prepare as for Turkey and Tomato Rice, but add 175 g/6 oz/1½ cups frozen peas and sweetcorn (corn) with the turkey and use a bouquet garni sachet instead of the bay leaf.

Turkey Liver and Pea Risotto

SERVES 6

1 large onion, finely chopped
4 rindless streaky bacon rashers (slices), chopped
1 large garlic clove, crushed
50 g/2 oz/¼ cup unsalted (sweet) butter
15 ml/1 tbsp olive oil
450 g/1 lb turkey livers, trimmed and roughly chopped
100 g/4 oz button mushrooms, sliced
225 g/8 oz/1 cup long-grain rice
600 ml/1 pt/2½ cups chicken stock
Salt and freshly ground black pepper
225 g/8 oz frozen peas
2.5 ml/½ tsp dried oregano
Chopped parsley, to garnish
Parmesan cheese, grated, to serve

Fry (sauté) the onion, bacon and garlic in the butter and oil for 2 minutes. Add the livers and fry for 4 minutes, stirring. Stir in the mushrooms and rice and cook for 1 minute. Add the stock and some salt and pepper. Bring to the boil, stirring. Part-cover and simmer gently for 12 minutes. Stir in the peas and oregano, cover and cook for a further 10 minutes or until the rice is tender and has absorbed the liquid. Stir well. Taste and re-season, if necessary. Pile on to plates, sprinkle with parsley and serve with grated Parmesan cheese.

DUCK

Watercress, Duck and Egg Pasta

SERVES 4

1 bunch of watercress
30 ml/2 tbsp chopped parsley
30 ml/2 tbsp lemon juice
6 eggs
100 g/4 oz/½ cup unsalted (sweet) butter, melted
Salt and freshly ground black pepper
225 g/8 oz penne pasta
2 spring onions, very finely chopped
100 g/4 oz/1 cup cooked duck, finely chopped
Cayenne, for dusting

Chop the watercress, discarding the feathery stalks. Mix with the parsley. Whisk all but 5 ml/1 tsp of the lemon juice with 2 of the eggs in a saucepan. Gradually whisk in 75 g/3 oz/⅓ cup of the melted butter and whisk over a very gentle heat until thickened. Do not boil or the mixture will scramble. Stir in the watercress and parsley and season to taste. Cook the penne according to the packet directions. Drain. Fry (sauté) the spring onions in the remaining butter in the pasta saucepan for 3 minutes until softened and lightly golden. Stir in the duck and toss over a gentle heat for a further 2 minutes, until hot. Add the pasta and toss again until well mixed and very hot. Divide between four individual dishes. Meanwhile, poach the remaining eggs in a pan of gently simmering water to which the remaining lemon juice has been added. Remove with a draining spoon and place on top of the pasta. Spoon the warm watercress sauce over and flash under a hot grill (broiler) to glaze. Serve straight away, dusted with a little cayenne.

Duck Breasts with Dolcelatte Dream

SERVES 4

4 small duck breasts
Salt and freshly ground black pepper
2 celery sticks, finely chopped
25 g/1 oz/2 tbsp butter
75 g/3 oz Dolcelatte cheese, diced
50 g/2 oz/¼ cup medium-fat soft cheese
90 ml/6 tbsp single (light) cream
15 ml/1 tbsp chopped parsley
350 g/12 oz tagliatelle
45 ml/3 tbsp pure orange juice
1 bunch of watercress
Green salad, to serve

Season the duck breasts with a little salt and pepper. Place skin-sides down in a frying pan (skillet). Fry (sauté) for about 5 minutes until the fat is running, turn over and continue cooking for about 10 minutes, turning once or twice, until the duck is tender and cooked through. Meanwhile, put the celery and butter in a double saucepan or in a bowl over a pan of gently simmering water. Cover and cook gently for about 8 minutes or until softened. Add the cheeses and cook, stirring, until smooth and melted. Stir in the cream. Add plenty of pepper and stir well. Stir in the parsley. Cook the tagliatelle according to the packet directions. Drain. Remove the duck breasts from the pan and transfer to warm plates. Cut into diagonal slices and fan out gently. Add the orange juice to the pan. Bring to the boil, stirring, until slightly thickened, scraping up the sediment. Season very lightly and drizzle over the duck. Add the pasta to the sauce, toss well and spoon on to the plates. Trim the watercress and use to garnish generously. Serve straight away with a green salad.

Duck Liver, Pine Nut and Spinach Cannelloni

SERVES 4

Prepare as for Chicken Liver and Hazelnut Cannelloni (page 253), but substitute 225 g/8 oz duck livers for chicken and pine nuts for the hazelnuts (filberts). Add 225 g/8 oz chopped, cooked spinach to the liver mixture.

Risotto with Cheese, Duck, Garlic and Parsley

SERVES 4

45 ml/3 tbsp olive oil
3 garlic cloves, finely chopped
1 large duck breast, skinned and finely diced
450 g/1 lb/2 cups risotto rice
1.2 litres/2 pts/5 cups hot chicken stock
100 g/4 oz/1 cup chopped parsley
75 g/5 tbsp Parmesan cheese, grated
Salt and freshly ground black pepper

Heat the oil in a heavy-based saucepan. Add the garlic and duck and fry (sauté) gently for 2 minutes. Stir in the rice and cook for 1 minute. Add 250 ml/8 fl oz/1 cup of the stock and simmer until is has been absorbed. Repeat the process until the rice is just tender and the risotto creamy. Stir in the parsley, cheese and salt and pepper to taste. Serve hot.

Duck with Orange Rice

SERVES 6

100 g/4 oz/½ cup unsalted (sweet) butter
1 onion, finely chopped
3 celery sticks, chopped
Grated rind and juice of 2 large oranges
900 ml/1½ pts/3¾ cups chicken stock
450 g/1 lb/2 cups long-grain rice
Salt and freshly ground black pepper
1 bouquet garni sachet
3 large or 6 small duck breasts
Watercress sprigs, to garnish

Heat 50 g/2 oz/¼ cup of the butter in a large, heavy-based saucepan. Add the onion and celery and fry (sauté) gently, stirring, for 2 minutes until soft but not brown. Stir in the orange rind and juice and the stock. Bring to the boil. Stir in the rice and add some salt and pepper and the bouquet garni sachet. Bring back to the boil, reduce the heat, part-cover and simmer gently for about 20 minutes, stirring occasionally, until the rice is cooked and has absorbed all the liquid. Remove the bouquet garni.

Meanwhile season the duck breasts with salt and pepper. Heat the remaining butter in a large frying pan (skillet). Fry (sauté) the duck breasts for about 12 minutes until cooked but still slightly pink in the centre, turning twice. Remove from the pan and leave to rest in a warm place until the rice is cooked. When ready to serve, cut the duck breasts in thick, diagonal slices. Arrange on warm serving plates and spoon any juices over. Put a pile of the orange rice to one side. Garnish with watercress.

Duck Shoot Rice

SERVES 4

2 kg/4½ lb oven-ready duck
Salt and freshly ground black pepper
75 g/3 oz/¼ cup apricot jam (conserve)
75 g/3 oz/¼ cup orange marmalade
30 ml/2 tbsp light brown sugar
Grated rind and juice of 1 lemon
150 ml/¼ pt/⅔ cup orange juice
225 g/8 oz/1 cup wild rice mix
½ celeriac (celery root), grated
600 ml/1 pt/2½ cups water
90 ml/6 tbsp redcurrant jelly (clear conserve)
15 ml/1 tbsp Worcestershire sauce
5 ml/1 tsp soy sauce
15 ml/1 tbsp Dijon mustard

Clean the duck inside and out with a damp cloth. Prick all over with a fork. Place on a rack over a roasting tin and rub with salt and pepper. Roast at 230°C/450°F/gas mark 8 for 15 minutes. Pour off the fat and remove the rack. Mix together the jam, marmalade, sugar, lemon rind and juice and 45 ml/3 tbsp of the orange juice. Spread all over the duck and roast for 15 minutes until a rich, deep brown. Reduce the heat to 180°C/350°F/gas mark 4 and continue cooking for 1 hour or until the duck is tender. Cut into four portions. Meanwhile, cook the rice and celeriac in the water for about 20 minutes or until just tender and the water is absorbed, stirring occasionally. Heat the remaining orange juice with the redcurrant jelly, Worcestershire sauce, soy sauce and Dijon mustard until smooth and hot. Pile the rice on to warmed serving plates. Top each with a duck portion and serve hot with the sauce.

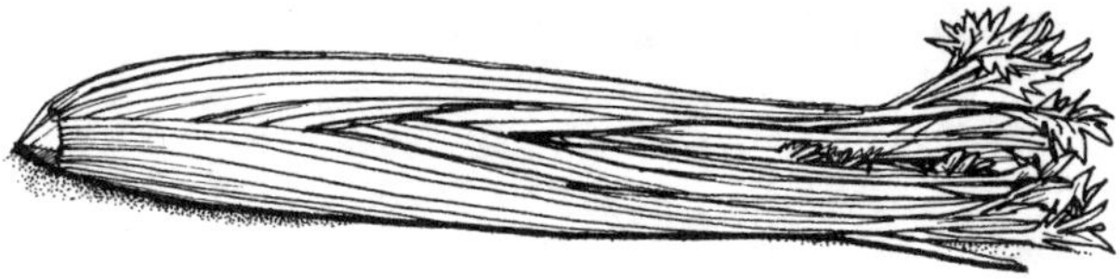

Creamy Champagne and Duck Risotto

SERVES 4

25 g/1 oz/2 tbsp unsalted (sweet) butter
1 small onion, finely chopped
1 large duck breast, skinned and finely chopped
450 g/1 lb/2 cups risotto rice
½ bottle dry champagne
750 ml/1¼ pts/3 cups hot chicken stock
120 ml/4 fl oz/½ cup double (heavy) cream
75 ml/5 tbsp freshly Parmesan cheese, grated
Salt
Watercress and orange salad, to serve

Melt the butter in a flameproof casserole (Dutch oven). Add the onion and duck and fry (sauté) for 2 minutes. Stir in the rice and cook for 1 minute. Add half the champagne, bring to the boil and simmer until it has been absorbed. Add a third of the stock and simmer until it is absorbed. Repeat the process with the champagne and stock for about 15–20 minutes, until the rice is just tender and creamy. Warm the cream in a small saucepan. When the rice is cooked, stir in the cream and cheese and season with salt. Serve straight away with a watercress and orange salad.

Duck Liver and Apple-stuffed Peppers

SERVES 4

Prepare as for Chicken Liver and Rice-stuffed Peppers (page 271), but substitute duck livers for chicken and a chopped eating (dessert) apple for the mushrooms. Serve with Espagnole Sauce (page 335) instead of the tomato sauce.

GAME

Hunter's Spaghetti

SERVES 4

1 large oven-ready cock pheasant
15 ml/1 tbsp olive oil
100 g/4 oz streaky bacon rashers (slices), rinded and diced
1 garlic clove, crushed
1 onion, finely chopped
2 celery sticks, finely chopped
2 carrots, finely chopped
100 g/4 oz cup mushrooms, chopped
45 ml/3 tbsp plain (all-purpose) flour
120 ml/4 fl oz/½ cup port
450 ml/¾ pt/2 cups chicken stock
Salt and freshly ground black pepper
1 bouquet garni sachet
Grated rind and juice of 1 lemon
350 g/12 oz spaghetti
Grated Parmesan cheese, to garnish

Cut all the meat off the pheasant and remove any tendons. Cut into small pieces, discarding the skin. Heat the oil in a large pan and fry (sauté) the bacon, garlic, onion, celery and carrots for 5 minutes, stirring, until golden brown. Add the mushrooms and pheasant meat and cook, stirring, for 2 minutes. Stir in the flour and cook for 2–3 minutes, stirring, until browned. Remove from the heat and blend in the port and stock. Return to the heat and bring to the boil, stirring, until thickened. Add salt and pepper to taste and the bouquet garni. Cover, reduce the heat and simmer gently for 1 hour, stirring occasionally. Add the lemon rind, salt and pepper and lemon juice to taste. Meanwhile, cook the spaghetti according to the packet directions. Pile into shallow bowls and spoon the pheasant sauce on top. Garnish with Parmesan cheese before serving.

Giant Game Cushions

SERVES 4–6

For the pasta:
350 g/12 oz/3 cups strong plain (bread) flour
1.5 ml/¼ tsp salt
5 eggs, beaten
5 ml/1 tsp olive oil
For the filling and sauce:
1 oven-ready pheasant
2 onions, quartered
1 large carrot, roughly chopped
2 garlic cloves, crushed
40 g/1½ oz/3 tbsp unsalted (sweet) butter
600 ml/1 pt/2½ cups water
1 bouquet garni sachet
Salt and freshly ground black pepper
120 ml/4 fl oz/½ cup white wine
2 tomatoes, skinned, seeded and finely chopped
15 ml/1 tbsp tomato purée (paste)
15 ml/1 tbsp brandy
15 ml/1 tbsp sunflower oil
3 smoked rindless streaky bacon rashers (slices), diced
50 g/2 oz chestnut mushrooms
15 ml/1 tbsp grated Parmesan cheese, plus extra to garnish
30 ml/3 tbsp double (heavy) cream
15 ml/1 tbsp chopped parsley
Crusty bread and a green salad, to serve

To make the pasta, sift the flour and salt into a bowl. Add the eggs and oil and work until smooth with a wooden spoon, then knead on a floured surface until shiny and elastic. Alternatively place in a food processor and run the machine until smooth and elastic. Place in a plastic bag and chill for several hours.

To make the filling and sauce, cut all the meat off the pheasant, discarding the skin and any tendons. Wrap in clingfilm (plastic wrap) and chill until ready to use. Break up the carcass and place in a saucepan with one of the onions, the carrot and garlic. Add half the butter and fry (sauté), stirring, for 5 minutes until browned. Add the water, bouquet garni and some salt and pepper. Bring to the boil, reduce the heat, part-cover and simmer gently for 1 hour. Strain and return to the pan. Add all but 15 ml/1 tbsp of the wine, the tomatoes, tomato purée and brandy. Bring to the boil and boil rapidly until reduced by about a third and slightly thickened. Taste and re-season, if necessary.

Brown the pheasant meat in the remaining butter and the sunflower oil for 3 minutes, stirring. Remove from the pan with a draining spoon and place in a food processor. Roughly chop the remaining onion and add to the pan with the bacon and mushrooms. Fry for 2 minutes, stirring. Add to the pheasant with the Parmesan, the remaining wine and the cream. Run the machine until the mixture forms a paste. Season well.

Cut the chilled dough in half. Roll out each half to a rectangle, 5 mm/¼ in thick. Spoon the filling at 5 cm/2 in intervals in rows on one sheet of the dough. Brush in between each one with water. Lay the second sheet on top and press gently between each mound to seal the dough. Using a pastry cutter or sharp knife, cut between each mound to form large cushions of pasta.

Bring a large pan of lightly salted water to the boil. Drop in the pasta cushions and cook for 3–4 minutes or until they rise to the surface of the pan and feel tender. Lift out of the pan with a draining spoon and transfer to large, open soup plates. Spoon the reheated sauce over and sprinkle with grated Parmesan and the parsley. Serve with crusty bread and a green salad.

Spaghetti with Ricotta, Pheasant and Asparagus

SERVES 4

Prepare as for Spaghetti with Chicken, Ricotta and Broccoli (page 243), but substitute pheasant for the chicken and asparagus for the broccoli. To cook the asparagus, trim the stalks, lay in a steamer and steam for about 10 minutes, until tender. Cut into short lengths.

Cheese, Pheasant and Rice Croquettes

SERVES 4–6

225 g/8 oz/1 cup long-grain rice
30 ml/2 tbsp lemon juice
2 chicken stock cubes
75 g/3 oz/¾ cup Gruyere (Swiss) cheese, grated
100 g/4 oz/1 cup cooked pheasant, finely chopped, all skin removed
25 g/1 oz/2 tbsp unsalted (sweet) butter
Salt and freshly ground black pepper
2 eggs
100 g/4 oz/2 cups white breadcrumbs
Oil, for deep-frying
Tomato relish and a green salad, to serve

Cook the rice in plenty of boiling water to which the lemon juice and stock cubes have been added for 10 minutes or until just tender. Drain. Transfer to a mixing bowl and stir in the cheese, pheasant, butter, a little salt and lots of pepper. Beat one of the eggs and stir in. Using the fingers, shape into small sausage shapes. Beat the second egg. Dip the rolls in the breadcrumbs, then the egg, then in the breadcrumbs again. Chill until firm. Deep-fry in hot oil a few at a time until crisp and golden brown. Drain on kitchen paper (paper towels) and serve with tomato relish and a green salad.

Risotto with Pheasant, Cheese and Mixed Herbs

SERVES 4

Prepare as for Risotto with Cheese, Duck, Garlic and Parsley (page 280), but use just 1 garlic clove and fry (sauté) for 1 minute only, then stir in 175 g/6 oz cooked pheasant, cut into small pieces and all skin removed, instead of the duck. Add 15 ml/1 tbsp each of chopped thyme, oregano and basil with the parsley.

Risotto con le Quaglie

SERVES 4

4 oven-ready quail
Salt and freshly ground black pepper
4 thin slices of pancetta or streaky bacon
15 ml/1 tbsp olive oil
375 ml/13 fl oz/1½ cups dry white wine
25 g/1 oz/2 tbsp unsalted (sweet) butter
1 small onion, finely chopped
450 g/1 lb/2 cups risotto rice
1.2 litres/2 pts/5 cups hot chicken stock
Freshly ground black pepper
100 g/4 oz/1 cup Parmesan cheese, freshly grated
15 ml/1 tbsp chopped parsley

Wipe the quail inside and out with kitchen paper (paper towels). Season with salt and wrap each in a slice of pancetta. Heat the oil in a large frying pan (skillet) and fry (sauté) the quail on all sides for about 15 minutes until brown and almost tender. Add the wine and simmer until it has almost evaporated. Leave in the pan and keep warm. Meanwhile, melt half the butter in a large flameproof casserole (Dutch oven). Add the onion and fry for 2 minutes. Stir in the rice and cook for 1 minute. Add about a quarter of the stock and simmer, stirring, until it has been absorbed. Repeat the process, stirring, for about 15–20 minutes, until the rice is just tender. Remove from the heat, stir in the remaining butter, a little salt and pepper and the cheese. Quickly pack into a large ring mould and press down firmly. Invert on a serving plate and place the quail in the centre. Spoon any cooking juices over and sprinkle with the parsley.

Braised Quail in Hock with Seasoned Rice

SERVES 6

350 g/12 oz/1½ cups long-grain rice
6 oven-ready quail
50 g/2 oz/¼ cup butter or margarine
30 ml/2 tbsp olive oil
25 g/1 oz/¼ cup shelled pistachio nuts
25 g/1 oz/¼ cup pine nuts
2 red onions, finely chopped
150 ml/¼ pt/⅔ cup hock or similar medium white wine
600 ml/1 pt/2½ cups chicken stock
Grated rind and juice of 1 orange
15 ml/1 tbsp redcurrant jelly (clear conserve)
Salt and freshly ground black pepper
Chopped parsley, to garnish

Wash the rice well in several changes of cold water, then leave to drain. Wipe the quail inside and out with kitchen paper (paper towels). Heat half the butter or margarine and oil in a large flameproof casserole (Dutch oven) and fry (sauté) the quail on all sides to brown. Remove from the casserole. Add the pistachios and pine nuts and fry until turning lightly golden. Remove from the pan and drain on kitchen paper. Add the onion to the casserole and fry until soft and lightly golden. Return the quail to the pan, add the wine and 150 ml/¼ pt/⅔ cup of the stock, the orange rind and juice, the redcurrant jelly and a little salt and pepper. Bring to the boil, reduce the heat, cover very tightly (with foil first, if necessary, then the lid) and simmer very gently for 30–40 minutes until the quail are tender. Meanwhile, heat the remaining butter or margarine and oil in a saucepan. Add the rice and fry for 2 minutes, stirring. Add the remaining stock and a little salt and pepper. Simmer for 15 minutes until the rice is tender, adding more stock or water if necessary. Pile the rice on to serving plates and top with the quail. Spoon the juices over and garnish with the fried nuts and chopped parsley.

Pheasant, Chicken Liver and Broccoli Risotto

SERVES 4

175 g/6 oz chicken livers
100 g/4 oz broccoli, cut into tiny florets
40 g/1½ oz/3 tbsp butter or margarine
2 onions, chopped
2 garlic cloves, crushed
2 rindless extra-lean back bacon rashers (slices), diced
2 carrots, chopped
225 g/8 oz/1 cup long-grain rice
175 g/6 oz/1½ cups cooked pheasant, diced, all skin removed
600 ml/1 pt/2½ cups chicken stock
2.5 ml/½ tsp dried sage
Salt and freshly ground black pepper
15 ml/1 tbsp chopped parsley
30 ml/2 tbsp Parmesan cheese, grated
Mixed green salad, to serve

Trim the chicken livers and cut into bite-sized pieces, if necessary. Blanch the broccoli in boiling water for 2 minutes, then drain. Melt the butter or margarine in a heavy-based saucepan. Add the onions, garlic, bacon and carrots and fry (sauté), stirring, for 3 minutes. Add the livers and cook for a further 3 minutes or until browned but still very soft. Stir in the rice and pheasant, then add the stock, sage and a little salt and pepper. Bring to the boil, reduce the heat, cover and simmer very gently for 15 minutes. Add the broccoli and cook for a further 10 minutes or until the rice is tender and has absorbed the liquid. Spoon on to warm plates and sprinkle with the parsley and Parmesan cheese. Serve hot with a mixed green salad.

Curries

This chapter has curries from all over the world, some authentic and traditional, others quick and convenient. You will see that virtually all the curries are for chicken as it is the favourite bird for this treatment – somehow Pheasant Vindaloo doesn't have quite the same ring to it! But there is nothing stopping you experimenting with turkey or other birds for any of them!

CHICKEN

Tandoori Chicken Drummers

SERVES 4

8 chicken drumsticks, all skin removed
300 ml/½ pt/1¼ cups plain yoghurt
1 small garlic clove, crushed
15 ml/1 tbsp tandoori powder
5 ml/1 tsp chopped coriander (cilantro)
Salt and freshly ground black pepper
Shredded lettuce, lemon wedges, tomato wedges and coriander sprigs, to garnish
Plain Boiled Rice (page 351)and mango chutney or lime pickle, to serve

Make several slashes in the flesh of the chicken legs. Mix together the remaining ingredients in a large, shallow dish. Add the chicken and rub the mixture well into the slits. When well coated, leave to marinate for at least 3 hours. Place the chicken in a baking tin (pan) and spoon any remaining marinade over. Cover with foil and bake in a preheated oven at 200°C/400°F/gas mark 6 for 45 minutes. Remove the foil, pour off any liquid and bake uncovered for 15 minutes until browned and cooked through. Garnish with shredded lettuce, lemon and tomato wedges and coriander sprigs and serve with boiled rice and mango chutney or lime pickle.

Monday Chicken Curry

SERVES 4

1 onion, chopped
1 garlic clove, crushed
30 ml/2 tbsp sunflower oil
175 g/6 oz button mushrooms, halved
15 ml/1 tbsp curry paste
450 ml/¾ pt/2 cups chicken stock
100 g/4 oz creamed coconut, cut into chunks
45 ml/3 tbsp raisins
225 g/8 oz/2 cups cooked chicken, cut into large bite-sized piece
175 g/6 oz cooked leftover vegetables, chopped if necessary
Salt and freshly ground black pepper
30 ml/2 tbsp chopped coriander (cilantro)
Naan bread, to serve

Cook the onion and garlic in the oil for 3 minutes until lightly golden. Add the mushrooms and cook for 1 minute. Add the curry paste and stock. Bring to the boil and stir in the coconut and raisins. Cook until the coconut dissolves. Add the chicken and vegetables and simmer very gently for 10 minutes. Season to taste and stir in the coriander. Serve with naan bread.

Dry Chicken Curry

SERVES 4

5 ml/1 tsp fenugreek seeds, crushed
15 ml/1 tbsp ground coriander (cilantro)
15 ml/1 tbsp ground cumin
5 ml/1 tsp turmeric
2 red chillies, seeded and finely chopped
40 g/1½ oz/3 tbsp butter or margarine
1 onion, thinly sliced
5 ml/1 tsp black mustard seeds
1.5 kg/3 lb oven-ready chicken, cut into 8 pieces (page 15)
15 ml/1 tbsp desiccated (shredded) coconut
5 ml/1 tsp tamarind pulp
120 ml/4 fl oz/1 cup water
Salt and freshly ground black pepper
Naan bread, mango chutney and Brinjals (page 338), to serve

Mix the spices together. Melt the butter or margarine in a saucepan and add the onion. Fry (sauté) for 3 minutes until lightly browned. Add the spices and fry for 1 minute, stirring. Add the mustard seeds and chicken and brown on all sides. Add the remaining ingredients, cover and cook very gently for about 45 minutes until the chicken is really tender and the liquid has evaporated. Cook quickly for a few minutes at the end if any liquid remains. Serve with naan bread, mango chutney and Brinjals.

Indian Fried Chicken

SERVES 4

1.5 kg/3 lb oven-ready chicken, cut into 8 pieces (page 15)
2.5 ml/½ tsp ground cardamom
5 ml/1 tsp ground cinnamon
10 ml/2 tsp ground coriander (cilantro)
2.5 ml/½ tsp chilli powder
2.5 ml/½ tsp turmeric
5 ml/1 tsp grated fresh root ginger
15 ml/1 tbsp water
2 garlic cloves, crushed
Salt and freshly ground black pepper
40 g/1½ oz/3 tbsp butter or margarine
2 large onions, thinly sliced
400 g/14 oz/1 large can of coconut milk
Quick Pilau Rice (page 351), to serve

Wipe the chicken all over with kitchen paper (paper towels). Make several slashes in the fleshy parts of the chicken. Mix the spices with the water to form a paste. Stir the garlic and some salt and pepper into the spice paste and rub all over the chicken pieces. Melt the butter or margarine in a flameproof casserole (Dutch oven). Fry (sauté) the onions for 3 minutes until lightly golden. Add the chicken and fry on all sides to brown. Add the coconut milk, part-cover and simmer gently for about 45 minutes or until the chicken is tender and bathed in sauce. Taste and re-season if necessary. Serve with Quick Pilau Rice.

Indian Chicken

SERVES 4

10 ml/2 tsp tamarind pulp
250 ml/8 fl oz/1 cup water
4 chicken portions
30 ml/2 tbsp sunflower oil
2 large onions, finely chopped
1 green (bell) pepper, finely chopped
10 ml/2 tsp ground cumin
10 ml/2 tsp ground coriander (cilantro)
5 ml/1 tsp chilli powder
5 ml/1 tsp turmeric
2.5 ml/½ tsp ground cardamom
50 g/2 oz creamed coconut
2 large tomatoes, skinned and chopped
30 ml/2 tbsp chopped coriander
Plain Boiled Rice (page 351) and Fresh Sweet Chutney (page 338), to serve

Infuse the tamarind pulp in the water while preparing the rest of the dish. Wipe the chicken with kitchen paper (paper towels). Brown all over in the oil in a flameproof casserole (Dutch oven). Remove from the pan with a draining spoon. Add the onions and pepper and fry (sauté) for 3 minutes. Add the spices and fry for 1 minute, stirring. Add the tamarind mixture and the creamed coconut and stir until the coconut melts. Return the chicken to the pan. Bring to the boil, cover, reduce the heat and cook for 20 minutes. Add the tomatoes and continue cooking for 10–15 minutes until the chicken is tender and bathed in a rich sauce. Transfer to warm plates, sprinkle with the coriander and serve with Plain Boiled Rice and Fresh Sweet Chutney.

Chicken Tikka

SERVES 6

5 ml/1 tsp grated fresh root ginger
2 garlic cloves, crushed
2.5 ml/½ tsp salt
5 ml/1 tsp ground black pepper
2.5 ml/½ tsp ground mace
2.5 ml/½ tsp ground cumin
2.5 ml/½ tsp ground coriander (cilantro)
1 egg, beaten
50 g/2 oz/½ cup Cheddar cheese, grated
2 green chillies, seeded and chopped
30 ml/2 tbsp chopped coriander
150 ml/¼ pt/⅔ cup double (heavy) cream
45 ml/3 tbsp cornflour (cornstarch)
30 ml/2 tbsp sunflower oil
8 chicken breasts, cut into bite-sized pieces
Lemon wedges, to garnish
Quick Pilau Rice (page 351) and Minted Yoghurt and Cucumber (page 339), to serve

Mix together everything except the chicken in a container with a lid. Add the chicken, mix well, cover and chill overnight. Thread the chicken on six skewers and lay on a rack in a baking tin (pan). Cook in a preheated oven at 180°C/350°F/gas mark 4 for 15 minutes, turning occasionally and basting with any remaining marinade, until cooked through and golden brown. Serve on a bed of Pilau Rice, garnished with lemon wedges, with Minted Yoghurt and Cucumber.

Mild Chicken Curry

SERVES 4

4 chicken portions, each cut into 2 pieces
2 onions, roughly chopped
90 ml/6 tbsp plain yoghurt
2.5 ml/½ tsp ground ginger
2.5 ml/½ tsp ground cumin
5 ml/1 tsp turmeric
A pinch of chilli powder
25 g/1 oz/2 tbsp butter or margarine
2 potatoes, quartered
Salt
Plain Boiled Rice (page 351) and mango chutney, to serve

Wipe the chicken with kitchen paper (paper towels) and place in a shallow dish. Purée the onions with the yoghurt and spices in a blender or food processor. Pour over the chicken and turn the pieces over to cover completely. Leave to marinate for 30 minutes. Heat the butter or margarine in a flameproof casserole (Dutch oven). Add the chicken mixture and fry (sauté) for 3 minutes. Arrange the potato pieces over and season with a little salt. Cover and cook in a preheated oven at 180°C/350°F/gas mark 4 for 1 hour. Stir well, then serve with Plain Boiled Rice and mango chutney.

Chicken Palak

SERVES 4

2 large onions, finely chopped
40 g/1½ oz/3 tbsp butter or margarine
2 garlic cloves, crushed
2.5 cm/1 in piece of cinnamon stick
10 ml/2 tsp coriander (cilantro)
5 ml/1 tsp grated fresh root ginger
1.5 kg/3 lb oven-ready chicken, cut into 8 pieces (page 15)
2 beefsteak tomatoes, skinned and chopped
350 g/12 oz young leaf spinach, well washed
Salt and freshly ground black pepper
Plain Boiled Rice (page 351) and Minted Yoghurt and Cucumber (page 339), to serve

Fry (sauté) the onions in the butter or margarine for 2 minutes, stirring. Add the garlic and spices and fry for a further minute. Add the chicken and brown on all sides. Remove the chicken and add the tomatoes and spinach. Season lightly. Cook, stirring, for 4 minutes until the spinach wilts. Return the chicken to the pan, cover and cook gently for 45 minutes or until everything is tender. Taste and re-season, if necessary. Serve with Plain Boiled Rice and Minted Yoghurt and Cucumber.

Balti Chicken

SERVES 4

450 g/1 lb tomatoes, roughly chopped
1 large green (bell) pepper, chopped
2 green chillies, seeded and chopped
45 ml/3 tbsp sunflower oil
1.5 kg/3 lb oven-ready chicken, cut into 8 pieces (page 15) and skinned
6 cardamom pods, split
5 ml/1 tsp light brown sugar
1.5 ml/¼ tsp turmeric
2.5 ml/½ tsp coarsely ground black pepper
Salt
250 ml/8 fl oz/1 cup chicken stock
2.5 cm/1 in piece of cinnamon stick
Plain Boiled Rice (page 351), to serve

Purée the tomatoes, pepper and chillies in a blender or food processor. Heat the oil in a flameproof casserole (Dutch oven). Add the chicken and brown all over. Remove from the pan. Add the cardamom pods and fry (sauté) for 2 minutes. Add the tomato and pepper mixture. Stir in the sugar, turmeric, pepper and a little salt. Bring to the boil and simmer gently, stirring occasionally, until the oil rises to the surface. Stir in the stock, add the cinnamon stick and return the chicken to the pan. Cover and simmer gently for 45 minutes until the chicken is really tender and bathed in a rich sauce. Discard the cinnamon stick. Heat a balti dish until really hot. Tip in the curry and it should sizzle. Serve straight away with Plain Boiled Rice.

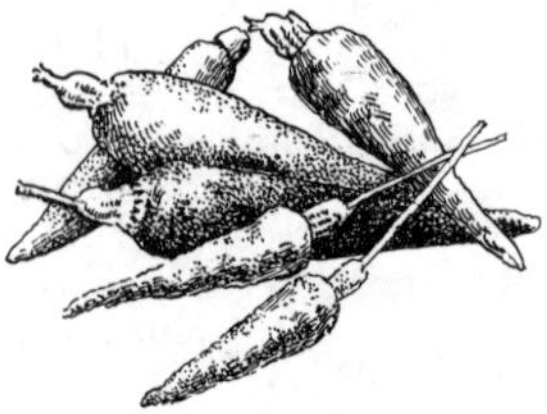

Chicken Korma

SERVES 4

4 large onions
2 green chillies, seeded and chopped
5 ml/1 tsp grated fresh root ginger
1 garlic clove, crushed
5 ml/1 tsp turmeric
15 ml/1 tbsp black mustard seeds
100 g/4 oz creamed coconut, cut into chunks
45 ml/3 tbsp sunflower oil
1.5 kg/3 lb oven-ready chicken, quartered, each cut into 2 pieces
5 cm/2 in piece of cinnamon stick
2 cardamom pods, split
2 cloves
Salt and freshly ground black pepper
300 ml/½ pt/1¼ cups plain yoghurt
1 lemon, cut into 5 wedges
Plain Boiled Rice (page 351), to serve

Roughly chop two of the onions and purée in a blender or food processor with the chillies, ginger, garlic, turmeric, mustard seeds and the pieces of creamed coconut. Slice the remaining onions. Heat the oil in a saucepan. Add the sliced onions and fry (sauté) for 3 minutes, stirring. Add the spice purée and stir for 3 minutes. Add the chicken and fry for 1 minute. Turn over the pieces and fry for a further minute. Add the cinnamon, cardamom and cloves, season with some salt and pepper and stir in the yoghurt. Cover tightly and simmer very gently for 1 hour. Check from time to time and add a little water if becoming too dry. Squeeze one of the lemon wedges over the surface and serve hot with Plain Boiled Rice, garnished with the remaining lemon wedges.

Chicken Dhansak

SERVES 4

50 g/2 oz/⅓ cup brown lentils, soaked overnight
50 g/2 oz/⅓ cup red lentils, soaked overnight
50 g/2 oz /⅓ cup green split peas, soaked overnight
2 onions, roughly chopped
2 potatoes, roughly chopped
1 aubergine (eggplant), roughly chopped
1 large courgette (zucchini), roughly chopped
1.5 kg/3 lb oven-ready chicken, quartered, each cut into 2 pieces
Salt
30 ml/2 tbsp sunflower oil
4 spring onions (scallions), chopped
3 garlic cloves, crushed
5 ml/1 tsp fenugreek seeds
10 ml/2 tsp grated fresh root ginger
5 ml/1 tsp ground cumin
5 ml/1 tsp ground coriander (cilantro)
2.5 ml/½ tsp turmeric
15 ml/1 tbsp water
15 ml/1 tbsp chopped coriander, to garnish
Quick Pilau Rice (page 351), chopped cucumber, tomatoes and banana, and lime pickle, to serve

Drain the lentils and split peas and place in a saucepan with the onions, potatoes, aubergine and courgette. Top with the chicken. Add just enough water to cover the ingredients and sprinkle with salt. Bring to the boil, cover, reduce the heat and simmer for 1½ hours or until the chicken and vegetables are really tender. Carefully lift out the chicken and reserve. Purée the remaining contents of the saucepan in a blender or food processor. Meanwhile, heat the oil in the rinsed-out pan and fry (sauté) the spring onions and garlic until softened and lightly golden. Take out half and reserve for garnish. Add the fenugreek seeds to the pan and fry until they 'pop'. Stir in the remaining spices and the water and fry for 2 minutes, stirring. Add to the purée and stir well. Return the chicken to the pan, bring to the boil and simmer for 15 minutes. Sprinkle with the remaining spring onions and the chopped coriander and serve with Quick Pilau Rice, chopped cucumber, tomatoes and banana, and lime pickle.

Cheat Chicken Dhansak

SERVES 4

100 g/4 oz/⅔ cup green lentils, soaked overnight
1 garlic clove, crushed
385 g/13½ oz/1 large can of curry cook-in sauce
4 chicken portions, all skin removed
225 g/8 oz/1 cup long-grain rice
2.5 ml/½ tsp turmeric
2.5 ml/½ tsp salt
3 cardamom pods, split (optional)
2 hard-boiled (hard-cooked) eggs, sliced
2 bananas, sliced and tossed in lemon juice
2 tomatoes, sliced
½ cucumber, sliced
50 g/2 oz/½ cup salted peanuts
Minted Yoghurt and Cucumber (page 339), to serve

Drain the lentils and place them in a casserole (Dutch oven). Stir in the garlic and curry sauce. Add the chicken and spoon the sauce over. Cover and cook in a preheated oven at 180°C/350°F/gas mark 4 for 1½ hours until the chicken and lentils are tender. Meanwhile, cook the rice in plenty of boiling water to which the turmeric, salt and cardamom pods, if using, have been added for about 10 minutes until just tender. Drain and fluff up with a fork. Spoon the rice in a ring on four warm serving plates. Spoon the chicken and sauce into the centre. Arrange all the sliced ingredients attractively round the edge and sprinkle the curry with the peanuts. Serve with Minted Yoghurt and Cucumber.

Chicken Bhuna Masala

SERVES 4

15 ml/1 tbsp sunflower oil
25 g/1 oz/2 tbsp butter or margarine
10 ml/2 tsp ground cardamom
1.5 ml/¼ tsp ground cloves
5 ml/1 tsp ground ginger
2.5 ml/½ tsp turmeric
2 green chillies, seeded and chopped
2 large onions, finely chopped
1 large garlic clove, crushed
3 beefsteak tomatoes, skinned and chopped
Salt and freshly ground black pepper
4 skinless chicken breasts
60 ml/4 tbsp water
30 ml/2 tbsp chopped coriander (cilantro)
Naan bread and Minted Yoghurt and Cucumber (page 339), to serve

Heat the oil and butter or margarine in a large pan. Add the spices, onions and garlic and fry (sauté) for 2 minutes, stirring. Add the tomatoes and cook until pulpy. Season to taste. Add the chicken breasts and cook for 2 minutes on each side. Pour in the water, cover and simmer very gently for 45 minutes. Taste and re-season, if necessary. Sprinkle with the chopped coriander. Serve with naan bread and Minted Yoghurt and Cucumber.

Chicken Seek Kebabs

SERVES 4

1 onion, roughly chopped
15 ml/1 tbsp grated fresh root ginger
10 ml/2 tsp ground cinnamon
5 ml/1 tsp ground cumin
2.5 ml/½ tsp chilli powder
450 g/1 lb minced (ground) chicken
10 ml/2 tsp lemon juice
30 ml/2 tbsp plain yoghurt
30 ml/2 tbsp gram flour
30 ml/2 tbsp chopped coriander (cilantro)
Salt and freshly ground black pepper
Plain Boiled Rice (page 351), shredded lettuce, tomato slices, cucumber slices and mango chutney, to serve

Put the onion and spices in a mortar or small bowl. Pound with a pestle or the end of a rolling pin until the mixture forms a smooth paste. Mix with the chicken, lemon juice, yoghurt, flour, coriander and 2.5 ml/½ tsp salt until thoroughly blended. With floured hands, divide the mixture into 8 pieces and shape each piece into a sausage shape around a skewer. Lay on foil on a grill (broiler) rack. Grill (broil) for about 15 minutes, turning once or twice, until golden brown and cooked through. Serve hot on a bed of Plain Boiled Rice with shredded lettuce, tomato and cucumber slices and mango chutney.

Chicken Moghlai

SERVES 4

2 large onions, chopped
1 green (bell) pepper, chopped
2 green chillies, seeded and chopped
25 g/1 oz/2 tbsp butter or margarine
15 ml/1 tbsp sunflower oil
8 skinless chicken thighs
60 ml/4 tbsp plain yoghurt
60 ml/4 tbsp double (heavy) cream
4 garlic cloves, crushed
30 ml/2 tbsp cashew nut butter
Salt and freshly ground black pepper
1 lime
Torn coriander (cilantro) leaves, to garnish
Plain Boiled Rice (page 351), to serve

Fry (sauté) the onions, pepper and chillies in the butter or margarine and oil for 3 minutes, stirring. Add the chicken and fry for 2 minutes, turning once. Blend together the yoghurt, cream, garlic and cashew nut butter and stir into the pan. Season with a little salt and pepper. Cover tightly and simmer gently for 45 minutes or until the chicken is really tender and bathed in a thick sauce. Slice half the lime thinly and reserve. Squeeze the juice from the remainder and stir into the curry. Taste and re-season if necessary. Spoon on to warm plates, garnish with limes slices and torn coriander leaves, and serve with Plain Boiled Rice.

Chicken Dopiaza

SERVES 4

30 ml/2 tbsp sunflower oil
25 g/1 oz/2 tbsp butter or margarine
1.5 kg/3 lb oven-ready chicken, cut into 8 pieces (page 15)
4 onions, sliced
4 beefsteak tomatoes, skinned and chopped
3 large garlic cloves, crushed
3 red chillies, seeded and chopped
15 ml/1 tbsp ground coriander (cilantro)
15 ml/1 tbsp ground cumin
10 ml/2 tsp grated fresh root ginger
2.5 ml/½ tsp turmeric
600 ml/1 pt/2½ cups water
Salt and freshly ground black pepper
12 baby potatoes
Naan bread, to serve

Heat the oil and butter or margarine in a large saucepan. Brown the chicken on all sides and remove from the pan with a draining spoon. Add the onions and fry (sauté) for 3 minutes, stirring, until golden. Add the tomatoes, garlic and spices and simmer for about 10 minutes until pulpy. Stir in the water and some salt and pepper and return the chicken to the pan. Bring to the boil, reduce the heat, part-cover and simmer for 45 minutes. Add the potatoes, re-cover and simmer for a further 15 minutes or until the potatoes and chicken are tender and bathed in a rich sauce. Taste and re-season, if necessary. Serve with naan bread.

Thai Chicken Curry

SERVES 4

4 small skinless chicken breasts, about 150 g/5 oz each
60 ml/4 tbsp lime juice
10 ml/2 tsp curry powder
175 ml/6 fl oz/¾ cup canned coconut milk
75 g/3 oz/⅓ cup peanut butter
30 ml/2 tbsp white wine vinegar
15 ml/1 tbsp soy sauce
10 ml/2 tsp cornflour (cornstarch)
1 small green chilli, seeded and finely chopped
Light brown sugar
30 ml/2 tbsp sunflower oil
Torn coriander (cilantro) leaves, to garnish
Thai Fragrant Rice (page 351), shredded Chinese leaves (stem lettuce) and slices of fresh mango, to serve

Cut the chicken into bite-sized pieces. Place in a shallow dish and sprinkle with the lime juice and half the curry powder. Leave to marinate for at least 1 hour, stirring occasionally. Put the coconut milk, peanut butter, vinegar, soy sauce, cornflour, remaining curry powder and chilli in a saucepan. Heat gently, stirring, until melted, then bring to the boil and simmer for 3 minutes, stirring. Sweeten to taste with light brown sugar. Thread the chicken on to soaked wooden skewers. Brush with oil and grill (broil) for 8–10 minutes until tender and cooked through. Transfer to warm plates. Spoon a little sauce over and sprinkle with torn coriander leaves. Serve with Thai Fragrant Rice, shredded Chinese leaves and slices of mango and the remaining sauce.

Chicken Vindaloo

SERVES 4

10 ml/2 tsp chilli powder
10 ml/2 tsp ground cumin
5 ml/1 tsp turmeric
10 ml/2 tsp ground mustard seeds
5 ml/1 tsp ground coriander (cilantro)
2.5 cm/1 in piece of fresh root ginger, grated
2.5 ml/½ tsp salt
150 ml/¼ pt/⅔ cup white wine vinegar
1 large onion, finely chopped
1 large garlic clove, crushed
1.5 kg/3 lb oven-ready chicken, cut into 8 pieces (page 15), skinned
50 g/2 oz/¼ cup butter or margarine
Quick Pilau Rice (page 351) and Minted Yoghurt and Cucumber (page 339)

Mix the spices with the salt and vinegar in a large shallow dish. Stir in the onion and garlic. Add the chicken pieces and toss in the mixture to coat completely. Cover well and chill overnight to marinate. Melt the butter or margarine in a flameproof casserole (Dutch oven). Add the chicken mixture. Bring to the boil, reduce the heat, cover and simmer for 45 minutes until the chicken is tender, stirring once or twice. Serve with Quick Pilau Rice and Minted Yoghurt and Cucumber.

Oriental Chicken Curry

SERVES 4

100 g/4 oz creamed coconut, cut into chunks
600 ml/1 pt/2½ cups boiling water
45 ml/3 tbsp curry powder
5 ml/1 tsp Chinese five spice powder
10 ml/2 tsp grated fresh root ginger
450 g/1 lb chicken breasts, diced
60 ml/4 tbsp sunflower oil
2 garlic cloves, crushed
Salt
30 ml/2 tbsp chopped coriander (cilantro)
Plain Boiled Rice (page 351), to serve

Put the coconut in a bowl and stir in the boiling water. When dissolved, stir in the spices. Leave to cool. Add the chicken and leave to marinate for 1 hour. Heat the oil in a wok or large frying pan (skillet). Add the garlic and stir-fry for 1 minute. Lift the chicken out of the marinade and stir-fry for 5 minutes. Add the marinade and cook for a further 15–20 minutes, stirring. Season with salt to taste and stir in the coriander. Spoon on to a bed of Plain Boiled Rice and serve.

Chicken Kashmir

SERVES 4

15 ml/1 tbsp sunflower oil
25 g/1 oz/2 tbsp butter or margarine
1 large onion, thinly sliced
5 cm/2 in piece of cinnamon stick
2 cloves
4 cardamom pods, split
4–6 chicken breasts, cut into bite-sized pieces
12 raw cashew nuts, split in halves
30 ml/2 tbsp raisins
120 ml/4 fl oz/½ cup plain yoghurt
120 ml/4 fl oz/½ cup double (heavy) cream
2.5 ml/½ tsp saffron powder
Salt and freshly ground black pepper
30 ml/2 tbsp chopped coriander (cilantro)
1 green chilli, seeded and finely chopped
Plain Boiled Rice (page 351), to serve

Heat the oil and butter or margarine in a saucepan. Add the onion and fry (sauté), stirring, for 3 minutes, until lightly golden. Add the spices and fry for a further minute, stirring. Add the chicken and toss over a moderate heat for 2 minutes. Just-cover with water, bring to the boil and simmer for 30 minutes until the liquid has evaporated. Stir in the nuts, raisins, yoghurt, cream, saffron and a little salt and pepper. Add half the coriander and heat gently, stirring, until piping hot and thick. Taste and re-season, if necessary. Serve garnished with the remaining coriander and the chopped chilli, with Plain Boiled Rice.

Aru Murgh

SERVES 4

1 onion, finely chopped
40 g/1½ oz/3 tbsp butter or margarine
1.5 kg/3 lb oven-ready chicken, cut into 8 pieces (page 15)
1 garlic clove, crushed
1 green chilli, finely chopped
5 ml/1 tsp ground cumin
2 beefsteak tomatoes, skinned and chopped
175 g/6 oz ready-to-eat dried apricots, halved
150 ml/¼ pt/⅔ cup water
Salt and freshly ground black pepper
15 ml/1 tbsp desiccated (shredded) coconut
15 ml/1 tbsp chopped coriander (cilantro)
Naan bread, to serve

Fry (sauté) the onion in the butter or margarine for 3 minutes. Add the chicken and brown on all sides. Remove from the pan and stir in the spices. Cook for 1 minute, then add the tomatoes, apricots and water. Return the chicken to the pan and season lightly. Cover and cook very gently for 1 hour. Taste and re-season, sprinkle with the desiccated coconut and coriander and serve with naan bread.

Chinese Curried Meatballs

SERVES 4

450 g/1 lb minced (ground) chicken
10 ml/2 tsp curry powder
1.5 ml/¼ tsp Chinese five spice powder
5 ml/1 tsp soy sauce
5 ml/1 tsp ground ginger
1 egg, beaten
450 ml/¾ pt/2 cups chicken stock
Chinese Curry Sauce (page 338)
175 g/6 oz Chinese egg noodles, cooked
Lemon wedges, to garnish

Mix the chicken with the curry and five spice powders, the soy sauce and ginger. Mix with the egg to bind. Bring the stock to the boil in a saucepan, then reduce to a simmer. Shape the chicken mixture into 20 small balls. Drop into the simmering stock and cook for 5 minutes. Heat the Chinese Curry Sauce. Lift the balls out of the pan and place on a bed of Chinese egg noodles. Drizzle the sauce over and serve straight away, garnished with lemon wedges.

Cardamom Chicken

SERVES 4

4 chicken portions
45 ml/3 tbsp sunflower oil
2 large onions
2 garlic cloves, crushed
2.5 cm/1 in piece of fresh root ginger, grated
5 ml/1 tsp chilli powder
5 ml/1 tsp ground cinnamon
10 ml/2 tsp turmeric
10 ml/2 tsp ground cumin
5 ml/1 tsp ground coriander (cilantro)
1.5 ml/¼ tsp ground cloves
6 green cardamom pods, split
1 small bay leaf
300 ml/½ pt/1¼ cups water
300 ml/½ pt/1¼ cups plain yoghurt
10 ml/2 tsp garam masala
Salt and freshly ground black pepper
Plain Boiled Rice (page 351) and mango chutney, to serve

Brown the chicken in half the oil in a flameproof casserole (Dutch oven). Remove from the pan. Grate one of the onions and chop the other. Fry (sauté) the chopped onion in the remaining oil in the casserole until golden. Stir in the grated onion, the garlic and all the spices. Cook, stirring, for 1 minute. Add the bay leaf, water and yoghurt and stir well to blend. Return the chicken to the pan and push down in the sauce so it is coated completely. Bring to the boil, cover, reduce the heat and simmer for 1 hour, stirring occasionally. Stir in the garam masala and season to taste with salt and pepper. Discard the bay leaf. Serve with Plain Boiled Rice and mango chutney.

Chicken Massage

SERVES 4

350 g/12 oz boneless chicken meat, diced
1 onion, chopped
1 small green (bell) pepper, diced
15 ml/1 tbsp curry paste
30 ml/2 tbsp sunflower oil
450 ml/¾ pt/2 cups chicken stock
½ block of creamed coconut, cut into chunks
225 g/8 oz/1 small can of pease pudding
15 ml/1 tbsp raisins
Salt and freshly ground black pepper
15 ml/1 tbsp chopped coriander (cilantro)
Shredded lettuce, tomato wedges and lemon wedges, to garnish
Plain Boiled Rice (page 351), to serve

Fry (sauté) the chicken, onion, pepper and curry paste in the oil for 4 minutes, stirring. Add the stock, coconut, pease pudding and raisins. Bring to the boil, stirring, reduce the heat and simmer gently for 10 minutes, stirring, to prevent sticking. Season to taste and stir in the coriander. Spoon on to warm plates, garnish with shredded lettuce, tomato and lemon wedges and serve with Plain Boiled Rice.

Chicken Saag

SERVES 4

2.5 ml/½ tsp ground cinnamon
2.5 ml/½ tsp ground cumin
2.5 ml/½ tsp ground coriander (cilantro)
2.5 ml/½ tsp chilli powder
1 garlic clove, crushed
30 ml/2 tbsp water
30 ml/2 tbsp sunflower oil
2 onions, halved and thinly sliced
60 ml/4 tbsp chopped coriander
1 large tomato, finely chopped
Salt
5 ml/1 tsp caster (superfine) sugar
175 g/6 oz frozen leaf spinach, thawed
225 g/8 oz/2 cups cooked chicken, diced, all skin removed
4 cooked potatoes, cut into small chunks
Naan bread, to serve

Put the spices in a cup and mix with the water. Heat the oil and fry (sauté) the onions for 3 minutes, stirring. Add the spices from the cup, the coriander and tomato and season lightly with salt. Fry for 1 minute. Add the sugar, spinach, chicken and potatoes stir well, cover and cook gently for 8 minutes. Serve with naan bread.

Chicken and Lentil Curry

SERVES 4

4 chicken portions
45 ml/3 tbsp sunflower oil
1 large onion, finely chopped
1 garlic clove, crushed
1 carrot, finely chopped
1 green (bell) pepper, finely chopped
5 ml/1 tsp chilli powder
5 ml/1 tsp turmeric
5 ml/1 tsp grated fresh root ginger
10 ml/2 tsp ground cumin
5 ml/1 tsp salt
15 ml/1 tbsp tomato purée (paste)
450 ml/¾ pt/2 cups chicken stock
225 g/8 oz/1⅓ cups green lentils, soaked overnight in cold water
Lime pickle and naan bread, to serve

Brown the chicken in half the oil in a flameproof casserole (Dutch oven). Remove from the pan. Add the remaining oil, then brown the onion, garlic, carrot and pepper for 2 minutes, stirring. Stir in all the spices and cook for 30 seconds, stirring. Blend in the salt, tomato purée and stock. Drain the lentils and stir in. Bring to the boil, stir again, and add the chicken. Cover and cook in a preheated oven at 180°C/350°F/gas mark 4 for 1½ hours until the chicken and lentils are tender. Stir well. Serve with lime pickle and lots of naan bread.

Mild Curried Banana Chicken

SERVES 6

6 chicken portions, all skin removed
30 ml/2 tbsp mild curry paste
50 g/2 oz/¼ cup unsalted (sweet) butter
30 ml/2 tbsp sunflower oil
2 onions, thinly sliced
1 large garlic clove, crushed
45 ml/3 tbsp plain (all-purpose) flour
600 ml/1 pt/2½ cups chicken stock
4 slightly green bananas
Salt and freshly ground black pepper
350 g/12 oz/1½ cups long-grain brown rice
45 ml/3 tbsp currants
15 ml/1 tbsp paprika
15 ml/1 tbsp desiccated (shredded) coconut

Rub the chicken all over with half the curry paste. Cover and leave in a cool place to marinate for 2 hours. Melt half the butter and half the oil in a large flameproof casserole (Dutch oven). Add the onions and garlic and fry (sauté) for 3 minutes, stirring, until lightly golden. Add the remaining curry paste and fry for 1 minute. Stir in the flour and cook for a further minute. Remove from the heat and gradually blend in the stock. Return to the heat, bring to the boil, and cook for 2 minutes, stirring. Peel and thinly slice one of the bananas and add to the sauce. Add the chicken portions and push down well into the sauce. Bring to the boil, then transfer to a preheated oven at 190°C/375°F/gas mark 5 for 1 hour. Season to taste.

Meanwhile, cook the rice in plenty of lightly salted boiling water for about 35 minutes or until cooked but still 'nutty'. Drain and stir in the currants. Heat the remaining butter and oil in a frying pan (skillet). Peel the remaining bananas. Cut into halves, then split the halves to make a total of 12 pieces. Fry in the butter and oil for 1–2 minutes each side until lightly golden but still holding their shape. Spoon the rice on to six warm plates and make into nests. Put the chicken and sauce in the centre. Arrange two pieces of banana on each plate. Mix the paprika with the coconut and sprinkle over. Serve hot.

Punjabi Butter Chicken

SERVES 4

60 ml/4 tbsp plain yoghurt
Juice of 1 small lime
1 large garlic clove, crushed
5 ml/1 tsp grated fresh root ginger
2 green chillies, seeded and chopped
2.5 ml/½ tsp ground coriander (cilantro)
2.5 ml/½ tsp ground cumin
Salt and freshly ground black pepper
1.5 kg/3 lb oven-ready chicken, cut into 8 pieces (page 15), skinned
25 g/1 oz/2 tbsp butter or margarine
4 large tomatoes, quartered
30 ml/2 tbsp chopped coriander
1.5 ml/¼ tsp turmeric
30 ml/2 tbsp tomato purée (paste)
5 ml/1 tsp caster (superfine) sugar
175 ml/6 fl oz/¾ cup double (heavy) cream
2.5 ml/½ tsp garam masala
2.5 ml/½ tsp chilli powder
Plain Boiled Rice (page 351) and lime pickle, to serve

Mix together the yoghurt, lime juice, garlic, ginger, chillies, coriander, cumin and 5 ml/1 tsp salt in a large, shallow dish. Make several slashes in each piece of chicken. Place in the marinade and turn to coat completely. Cover and chill to marinate for several hours or overnight. Melt the butter or margarine in a flameproof casserole (Dutch oven). Add the contents of the dish and cook, stirring, over a moderate heat for 30 minutes or until the chicken is tender and the liquid has evaporated. Meanwhile, purée the tomatoes in a blender or food processor and blend in the chopped coriander, turmeric, tomato purée, sugar and a little salt and pepper. Stir in half the cream. Add to the chicken and simmer gently until the fat rises to the top, adding a little water if the mixture is getting too dry. Taste and re-season. Stir in the remaining cream. Sprinkle with the garam masala and chilli powder and serve with Plain Boiled Rice and lime pickle.

Chicken Biryani

SERVES 4

1 onion, sliced
10 ml/2 tsp sunflower oil
225 g/8 oz chicken stir-fry meat
12.5 ml/2½ tsp turmeric
1 garlic clove, crushed
2.5 ml/½ tsp ground ginger
2.5 ml/½ tsp ground cumin
2.5 ml/½ tsp ground coriander (cilantro)
150 ml/¼ pt/⅔ cup plain yoghurt
Salt and freshly ground black pepper
225 g/8 oz/1 cup long-grain rice
30 ml/2 tbsp currants
30 ml/2 tbsp flaked (slivered) almonds
Shredded lettuce and cucumber and tomato slices, to serve

Fry (sauté) the onion in the oil for 3 minutes. Add the chicken and fry for 3 minutes, stirring. Add 7.5 ml/1½ tsp of the turmeric and the remaining ingredients except the rice, currants and almonds. Bring to the boil, then reduce the heat and simmer for about 20 minutes, stirring occasionally, until almost dry (the mixture will curdle at first). Meanwhile, cook the rice in plenty of boiling salted water to which the remaining turmeric has been added for 10 minutes or until the grains are just tender but still have some bite. Drain. Dry-fry the currants and almonds in a frying pan (skillet) until the nuts are golden, stirring all the time. Remove from the heat immediately to prevent over-browning. Spoon the rice on to warm serving plates. Pile the chicken mixture on top and sprinkle with the nuts and currants. Serve with a side salad of lettuce, tomatoes and cucumber.

Leftover Chicken Biryani

SERVES 4

225 g/8 oz/1 cup basmati rice
50 g/2 oz frozen peas
25 g/1 oz/2 tbsp butter or margarine
2 onions, thinly sliced
1 clove
5 cardamom pods, split
2.5 cm/1 in piece of cinnamon stick
10 ml/2 tsp curry paste
15 ml/1 tbsp water
175 g/6 oz/1½ cups cooked chicken, diced, all skin removed
15 ml/1 tbsp chopped coriander (cilantro)
30 ml/2 tbsp sultanas (golden raisins)
30 ml/2 tbsp flaked (slivered) almonds, toasted

Cook the rice in plenty of lightly salted boiling water for 10 minutes, adding the peas after 5 minutes. Drain, rinse with boiling water and drain again. Meanwhile, heat the butter or margarine in a saucepan and fry (sauté) the onions until golden brown, stirring all the time. Add the spices, curry paste and water and cook for 1 minute, stirring. Add the chicken and heat through for 2–3 minutes, stirring gently. Fold in the rice, coriander, sultanas and almonds. Toss gently. Remove the whole spices, if liked, before serving.

Chicken Tikka Biryani

SERVES 4

Prepare as for Leftover Chicken Biryani, but substitute bought chicken tikka for the cooked chicken.

Egg Vindaloo Basmati

SERVES 4

2 onions, finely chopped
30 ml/2 tbsp sunflower oil
10 ml/2 tsp curry powder
2.5 ml/½ tsp chilli powder
30 ml/2 tbsp plain (all-purpose) flour
150 ml/¼ pt/⅔ cup cider vinegar
450 ml/¾ pt/2 cups chicken stock
1 bay leaf
1 small piece of cinnamon stick
2.5 ml/½ tsp dried thyme
Salt and freshly ground black pepper
6 hard-boiled (hard-cooked) eggs
175 g/6 oz/1½ cups cooked chicken, cut into bite-sized pieces
225 g/8 oz/1 cup basmati rice
5 ml/1 tsp garam masala
60 ml/4 tbsp desiccated (shredded) coconut
Plain yoghurt, to garnish

Fry (sauté) the onions in the oil in a saucepan for 3 minutes until softened and lightly golden. Add the curry and chilli powders and fry for 1 minute. Stir in the flour and cook for 2 minutes, stirring. Remove from the heat and gradually blend in the vinegar and stock. Return to the heat and bring to the boil, stirring. Add the bay leaf, cinnamon stick and thyme and season to taste with salt and pepper. Reduce the heat, cover and simmer very gently for 45 minutes, stirring occasionally to prevent sticking. Remove the bay leaf and cinnamon. Halve the eggs and add to the sauce with the chicken. Heat gently for 8–10 minutes. Meanwhile, cook the rice in plenty of boiling salted water for 10 minutes, drain and return to the pan. Sprinkle over the garam masala and half the coconut. Stir in lightly but evenly. Pile the rice on to warm serving plates, spoon 3 egg halves and some sauce over each and garnish with a swirl of yoghurt and a dusting of the remaining coconut.

Chicken Tikka Masala

SERVES 4

1 garlic clove, crushed
Finely grated rind and juice of 1 small lime
2.5 ml/½ tsp chilli powder
5 ml/1 tsp ground ginger
Salt and freshly ground black pepper
6 chicken breasts, cut into bite-sized pieces
45 ml/3 tbsp sunflower oil
3 large onions, thinly sliced
1 bay leaf
5 cm/2 in piece of cinnamon stick
5 ml/1 tsp turmeric
250 ml/8 fl oz/1 cup plain yoghurt
30 ml/2 tbsp chopped coriander (cilantro)
1 large green chilli, seeded and finely chopped
Quick Pilau Rice (page 351) and Mushrooms Bhajis (page 355), to serve

Mix together the garlic, lime rind and juice, the chilli powder, ginger and some salt and pepper. Add the chicken pieces and toss well to coat. Leave to marinate for 3 hours. Thread on to skewers and place on a rack in a baking tin (pan). Cook in a preheated oven at 180°C/350°F/gas mark 4 for 15 minutes until cooked through. Meanwhile, heat the oil in a saucepan. Add the onions, bay leaf and cinnamon and fry (sauté) for 5 minutes, stirring, until browned. Add the turmeric and cook for a further minute. Remove from the heat and stir in the yoghurt, coriander, chilli and sugar. Return to the heat and simmer for about 10 minutes until thick (the mixture will look watery at first). Remove the chicken from the skewers and add to the sauce. Simmer gently for a further 10 minutes. Serve with Quick Pilau Rice and Mushroom Bhajis.

Chicken Jalfrezi

SERVES 4

2 large or 4 small skinless chicken breasts, cubed
10 ml/2 tsp garlic powder
5 ml/1 tsp chilli powder
5 ml/1 tsp ground ginger
25 g/1 oz/2 tbsp butter or margarine
1 onion, very finely chopped
30 ml/2 tbsp curry paste
2 green (bell) peppers, cut into thin strips
30 ml/2 tbsp water
4 mild green chillies, seeded and chopped
60 ml/4 tbsp chopped coriander (cilantro)
A little salt
A little sugar
Plain Boiled Rice (page 351), to serve

Put the meat in a shallow dish and sprinkle with the garlic and chilli powders and the ground ginger. Heat the butter or margarine in a large frying pan (skillet). Add the onion and fry (sauté), stirring, for 2 minutes. Add the curry paste, chicken and peppers and stir-fry for 6 minutes. Add the water, chillies and coriander and toss for 2 minutes. Season to taste with salt and sugar. Serve on a bed of Plain Boiled Rice.

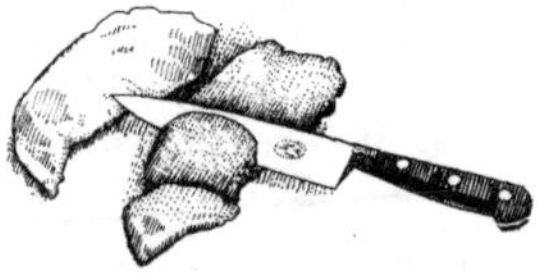

Chicken Pal

This is a fiery dish – not for the faint-hearted!

SERVES 4

1 onion, finely chopped
2 large garlic cloves, crushed
10 ml/2 tsp grated fresh root ginger
30 ml/2 tbsp sunflower oil
15 g/½ oz/1 tbsp butter or margarine
15 ml/1 tbsp chilli powder
2.5 ml/½ tsp ground coriander (cilantro)
5 ml/1 tsp ground cumin
5 ml/1 tsp garam masala
30 ml/2 tbsp water
400 g/14 oz/1 large can of chopped tomatoes
30 ml/2 tbsp tomato purée (paste)
6 green chillies, seeded and chopped
1.5 kg/3 lb oven-ready chicken, cut into 8 pieces (page 15), skinned
Salt and freshly ground black pepper
Plain Boiled Rice (page 351), Minted Yoghurt and Cucumber (page 339) and Onion Bhajis (page 355), to serve

Fry (sauté) the onion, garlic and ginger in half the oil and the butter or margarine in a flameproof casserole (Dutch oven) for 3 minutes, stirring. Mix the spices to a paste with the water. Stir into the onions and cook for 5 minutes, stirring. Add the tomatoes, purée and chillies and cook for 5 minutes until pulpy. Meanwhile, fry the chicken in the remaining oil in a frying pan (skillet) until browned all over. Add to the curry mixture. Season lightly. Cover and transfer to a preheated oven at 200°C/400°F/gas mark 6. Cook for 1 hour. Taste and re-season, if necessary. Serve with Plain Boiled Rice, Minted Yoghurt and Cucumber and Onion Bhajis.

Chicken Breasts Masala

SERVES 4

150 ml/¼ pt/⅔ cup plain yoghurt
1 garlic clove, crushed
5 ml/1 tsp ground ginger
5 ml/1 tsp chilli powder
5 ml/1 tsp ground cumin
5 ml/1 tsp garam masala
5 ml/1 tsp salt
5 ml/1 tsp ground black pepper
4 skinless chicken breasts
Shredded lettuce and tomato and cucumber slices, to garnish
Quick Pilau Rice (page 351), to serve

Mix the yoghurt with the garlic, spices, salt and pepper in a shallow dish. Add the chicken, turn over to coat completely, cover and chill to marinate for several hours or overnight. Place on a baking (cookie) sheet and bake in a preheated oven at 190°C/375°F/gas mark 5 for about 30 minutes until cooked through, turning once half-way through cooking. Alternatively grill (broil) for about 8 minutes on each side. Garnish with lettuce, tomato and cucumber and serve on a bed of Quick Pilau Rice.

TURKEY

Turkey Keema

SERVES 4

1 large onion, finely chopped
30 ml/2 tbsp sunflower oil
450 g/1 lb minced (ground) turkey
30 ml/2 tbsp curry powder
300 ml/½ pt/1¼ cups chicken stock
2 garlic cloves, crushed
2.5 cm/1 in piece of fresh root ginger, grated
15 ml/1 tbsp tomato purée (paste)
Salt and freshly ground black pepper
Plain Boiled Rice (page 351) and mango chutney, to serve

Fry (sauté) the onion gently in the oil for 3 minutes until softened but not browned. Add the turkey and fry, stirring, until the meat is no longer pink and all the grains are separate. Stir in the curry powder and cook for a further 3 minutes. Add the stock, garlic, ginger and tomato purée. Simmer for 15–20 minutes until the mixture is fairly dry. Season to taste. Serve on a bed of Plain Boiled Rice with mango chutney.

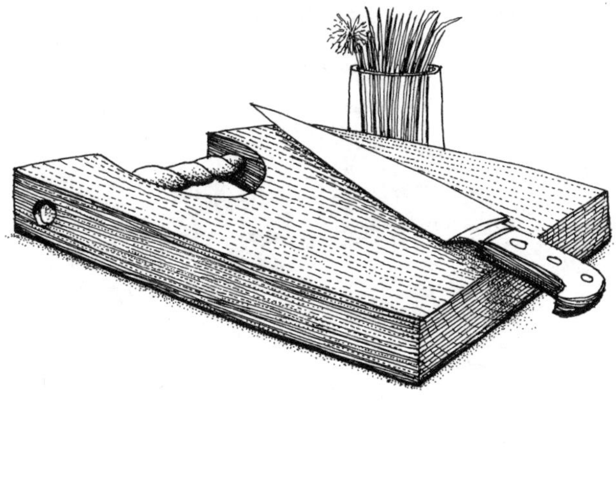

GAME

Game Curry

SERVES 4

20 g/¾ oz/1½ tbsp butter or margarine
15 ml/1 tbsp sunflower oil
2 onions, finely chopped
1 garlic clove, crushed
15 ml/1 tbsp curry paste
15 ml/1 tbsp plain (all-purpose) flour
30 ml/2 tbsp mango chutney, chopped if necessary
15 ml/1 tbsp lemon juice
30 ml/2 tbsp sultanas (golden raisins)
450 ml/¾ pt/2 cups chicken stock
Salt and freshly ground black pepper
5 ml/1 tsp garam masala
350 g/12 oz/3 cups cooked game, cut into neat pieces, all skin removed
Plain Boiled Rice (page 351) and Popadoms (page 355), to serve

Put the butter or margarine and oil in a saucepan. Add the onions and garlic and fry (sauté) for 2 minutes, stirring. Stir in the curry paste and flour and stir for 1 minute. Blend in the remaining ingredients except the garam masala and game, seasoning to taste with salt and pepper. Bring to the boil, reduce the heat and simmer for 30 minutes, stirring occasionally. Add the garam masala and game, cover and simmer gently for a further 15 minutes until hot throughout and tender. Serve on a bed of Plain Boiled Rice with Popadoms.

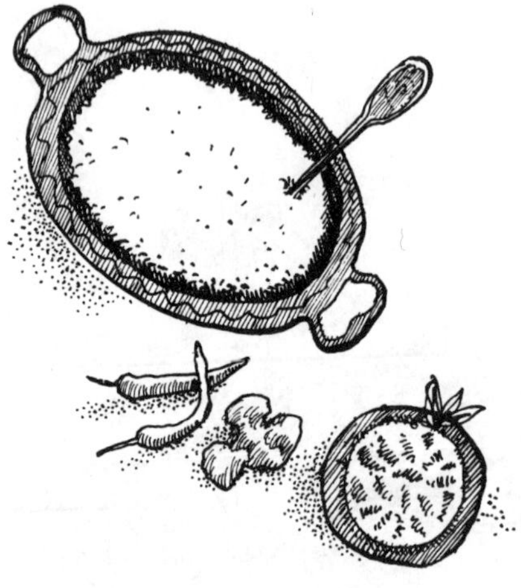

Salads

We tend to think of salad days as being hot, balmy, long and summery. But salads make delicious, sometimes extremely impressive meals all year round. And, if you're a chilly mortal, start with one of the heart-warming recipes from the Soup chapter (pages 42–63).

Minted Brown Rice Ring

SERVES 6

225 g/8 oz/1 cup brown rice
50 g/2 oz frozen peas
3 ripe tomatoes, seeded and diced
30 ml/2 tbsp currants
50 g/2 oz/½ cup pine nuts
25 g/1 oz/¼ cup toasted flaked (slivered) almonds
30 ml/2 tbsp sunflower oil
15 ml/1 tbsp white wine vinegar
Salt and freshly ground black pepper
5 ml/1 tsp caster (superfine) sugar
15 ml/1 tbsp chopped mint
175 g/6 oz/1½ cups cooked chicken
30 ml/2 tbsp mayonnaise
15 ml/1 tbsp plain yoghurt
1 bunch of watercress

Cook the rice according to the packet directions, adding the peas for the last 5 minutes of cooking. Drain, rinse with cold water and drain again. Add the tomatoes, currants, pine nuts and almonds and mix well. Whisk the oil and vinegar with a little salt, plenty of pepper, the sugar and mint. Pour over the rice mixture and toss well. Pack into a 1.2 litre/2 pt/5 cup ring mould. Chill. Mix the chicken with the mayonnaise and yoghurt and season with salt and pepper. Turn out on to a serving dish, fill the centre with the chicken mixture and garnish with watercress.

Party Rice Salad

SERVES 10

275 g/10 oz/1¼ cups long-grain rice
100 g/4 oz frozen peas
50 g/2 oz/⅓ cup sultanas (golden raisins)
25 g/1 oz/¼ cup toasted flaked (slivered) almonds
4 celery sticks, chopped
45 ml/3 tbsp olive oil
15 ml/1 tbsp white wine vinegar
A pinch of caster (superfine) sugar
A pinch of salt
2.5 ml/½ tsp made English mustard
Freshly ground black pepper
Cold cooked chicken and salami platter, to serve

Cook the rice in plenty of boiling, salted water for 10 minutes, adding the peas half-way through cooking. Drain, rinse with cold water and drain again. Mix with the sultanas, nuts and celery in a large salad bowl. Blend together the remaining ingredients with a good grinding of black pepper. Pour over the salad and toss well. Serve with a cold cooked chicken and salami platter.

Greek Chicken and Mushroom Salad

SERVES 6

1 onion, chopped
90 ml/6 tbsp olive oil
300 ml/½ pt/1¼ cups dry white wine
Salt and freshly ground black pepper
1 bouquet garni sachet
1 garlic clove, crushed
225 g/8 oz/1 small can of chopped tomatoes
350 g/12 oz button mushrooms, quartered
225 g/8 oz/1 cup long-grain rice
175 g/6 oz/1½ cups cooked chicken, diced
1 green (bell) pepper, chopped
50 g/2 oz stoned (pitted) black olives
Chopped parsley, to garnish

Fry (sauté) the onion in two thirds of the oil for 3 minutes until softened but not browned. Add the remaining ingredients except the rice, chicken, green pepper and olives. Bring to the boil, reduce the heat and simmer for about 15 minutes until the mushrooms are cooked and the liquid is reduced and thickened. Remove the bouquet garni, taste and re-season if necessary. Leave to cool, then chill. Meanwhile cook the rice in plenty of boiling salted water until just tender. Drain, rinse with cold water and drain again. Stir in the chicken, pepper and olives and season to taste. Make nests of the rice on serving plates. Spoon the chilled mushrooms in the centre and sprinkle with chopped parsley.

Apple Harvest Salad

SERVES 4

225 g/8 oz/1 cup long-grain rice
1 large green eating (dessert) apple, diced
Juice of 2 lemons
6 pecan halves, roughly chopped
100 g/4 oz/1 cup cooked chicken, diced
175 g/6 oz/1½ cups cooked ham, diced
45 ml/3 tbsp olive oil
15 ml/1 tbsp Worcestershire sauce
Salt and freshly ground black pepper

Cook the rice in plenty of boiling salted water until just tender. Drain, rinse with cold water and drain again. Place in a large salad bowl. Toss the apple in a little of the lemon juice to prevent browning. Add to the rice with the nuts, chicken and ham and toss gently. Whisk together the olive oil, remaining lemon juice and Worcestershire sauce with a little salt and pepper and pour over the salad. Toss gently until completely coated, then serve.

Californian Fruit and Rice for Poultry or Game

SERVES 6

425 g/15 oz/1 large can of crushed pineapple, drained, reserving the juice
300 g/11 oz/1 small can of mandarin oranges, drained, reserving the juice
1 packet of lemon jelly (jello)
2 carrots, grated
50 g/2 oz/⅓ cup seedless raisins
2 spring onions (scallions), finely chopped
225 g/8 oz/2 cups cooked long-grain rice
Cos (romaine) lettuce leaves
Cold cooked poultry or game, to serve

Put the juice from the pineapple and mandarins in a measuring jug. Use to dissolve the jelly according to the packet directions, adding water if necessary. Mix together the pineapple, mandarins, carrots, raisins and spring onions in a large jelly mould. Pour over half the jelly and chill until set. Mix the remaining jelly with the cooked rice. Spoon over the set fruit and chill again until set. To serve, dip briefly in hot water and turn out on to a serving dish. Garnish with cos lettuce leaves and serve with any cold cooked poultry or game.

Swiss Chicken Salad

SERVES 4

4 skinless chicken breasts
45 ml/3 tbsp sunflower oil
Salt and freshly ground black pepper
100 g/4 oz/1 cup pine nuts
1 fennel bulb, sliced, reserving the green fronds for garnish
100 g/4 oz/1 cup Emmental (Swiss) cheese, cubed
1 red eating (dessert) apple, diced
100 g/4 oz seedless green grapes, halved
45 ml/3 tbsp soured (dairy sour) cream
45 ml/3 tbsp mayonnaise
15 ml/1 tbsp white wine vinegar
5 ml/1 tsp clear honey
30 ml/2 tbsp chopped parsley
1 round lettuce

Brush the chicken breasts with 15 ml/1 tbsp of the oil. Place on foil on a grill (broiler) rack and season with salt and pepper. Grill (broil), turning once, for about 12 minutes until tender, lightly golden and cooked through. Meanwhile, dry-fry the pine nuts in a frying pan (skillet) for a few minutes, tossing, until lightly toasted. Remove from the pan straight away and reserve. Mix the fennel with the cheese, apple and grapes. Blend together the cream, mayonnaise, vinegar and honey and season to taste with salt and pepper. Add to the cheese mixture and toss gently with half the parsley. Arrange the lettuce leaves on four plates and spoon the vegetable and fruit mixture on top. Carve the chicken into thick slices and arrange attractively to one side. Sprinkle with the remaining parsley and serve.

Marinated Chinese Chicken Salad

SERVES 4

1 garlic clove, crushed
1.5 ml/¼ tsp Chinese five spice powder
5 ml/1 tsp grated fresh root ginger
90 ml/6 tbsp pure orange juice
90 ml/6 tbsp apple juice
30 ml/2 tbsp lemon juice
60 ml/4 tbsp cider vinegar
10 ml/2 tsp clear honey
60 ml/4 tbsp soy sauce
4 skinless chicken breasts
100 g/4 oz baby corn cobs
100 g/4 oz/2 cups beansprouts
15 ml/1 tbsp sesame oil
15 ml/1 tbsp sesame seeds
½ small head of Chinese leaves (stem lettuce), shredded
1 bunch of spring onions (scallions), cut into short lengths
1 carrot, thinly pared with a potato peeler
5 cm/2 in piece of cucumber, thinly pared with a potato peeler

Put the garlic, five spice powder, ginger, fruit juices, vinegar, honey and soy sauce in a large, shallow container and mix well. Make several slashes in each chicken breast and place in the marinade. Turn over to coat completely, cover and leave in a cool place for 4 hours or overnight to marinate. Cook the corn cobs in lightly salted boiling water for 4 minutes. Drain, rinse with cold water and drain again. Cut in short lengths and mix with the beansprouts. Heat the oil in a large frying pan (skillet) or wok. Cook the chicken breasts for about 6 minutes on each side until tender and cooked through. Add the marinade and simmer for a further 2–3 minutes. Remove from the heat and leave to cool slightly. Toast the sesame seeds in a frying pan until golden, tossing all the time. Tip out of the pan immediately so they don't over-brown. Mix the Chinese leaves and spring onions with the carrot, cucumber, beansprouts and corn. Arrange on four plates. Slice the chicken thickly and arrange on top. Spoon the warm marinade over and sprinkle with the sesame seeds before serving.

Stir-fry Chicken and Vegetable Salad

SERVES 4

75 g/3 oz/1 slab of Chinese egg noodles
45 ml/3 tbsp sunflower oil
175 g/6 oz chicken stir-fry meat
1 bunch of spring onions (scallions), cut into diagonal pieces
1 garlic clove, crushed
1 red (bell) pepper, cut into strips
2 celery sticks, cut into matchsticks
1 large carrot, cut into matchsticks
1 courgette (zucchini), cut into matchsticks
7.5 cm/3 in piece of cucumber, cut into matchsticks
50 g/2 oz button mushrooms, sliced
15 ml/1 tbsp white wine vinegar
2.5 ml/½ tsp ground ginger
30 ml/2 tbsp soy sauce
5 ml/1 tsp caster (superfine) sugar
15 ml/1 tbsp dry sherry
Salt and freshly ground black pepper
Prawn (shrimp) crackers, to serve

Cook the noodles according to the packet directions. Drain, rinse with cold water and drain again. Heat the oil in a wok or large frying pan (skillet). Stir-fry the chicken for 2 minutes. Add the onions and garlic and stir-fry for 1 minute. Add the remaining vegetables and stir-fry for 3 minutes until slightly softened but still with bite. Remove from the heat. Add the remaining ingredients and the cooked noodles and toss well. Leave to cool. Pile into bowls and serve with prawn crackers.

Warm Chicken, Carrot, Courgette and Wild Rice Salad

SERVES 6

100 g/4 oz/½ cup wild rice mix
175 g/6 oz/1½ cups cooked chicken, shredded
225 g/8 oz carrots, grated
225 g/8 oz courgettes (zucchini), grated
Salt and freshly ground black pepper
90 ml/6 tbsp sunflower oil
30 ml/2 tbsp mustard seeds
30 ml/2 tbsp lemon juice

Cook the wild rice mix according to the packet directions. Drain, rinse with cold water and drain again. Place in a bowl and add the chicken, carrots and courgettes. Season. Heat the oil in a frying pan (skillet). Add the mustard seeds and fry (sauté) quickly until they begin to pop. Stir in the lemon juice, pour over the salad, toss quickly and serve straight away.

Fragrant Stuffed Tomatoes

SERVES 4

8 large tomatoes
1 small onion, finely chopped
25 g/1 oz/2 tbsp butter or margarine
50 g/2 oz/¼ cup brown rice
150 ml/¼ pt/⅔ cup chicken stock
Salt and freshly ground black pepper
50 g/2 oz/½ cup cooked chicken, finely chopped
15 g/½ oz/2 tbsp chopped pistachio nuts
15 ml/1 tbsp currants
2 rosemary sprigs

Cut a slice off the rounded ends of the tomatoes and reserve for 'lids'. Scoop out the seeds and reserve. Fry (sauté) the onion in the butter or margarine for 2 minutes until softened but not browned. Stir in the rice, stock and a little salt and pepper. Bring to the boil, reduce the heat, cover and simmer gently for 30 minutes. Stir in the chicken, nuts, currants and rosemary and cook for a further 15 minutes or until the rice is really tender and has absorbed all the liquid. Remove the rosemary, taste and re-season if necessary. Stir in the tomato seeds. Pack into the tomatoes, top with the lids and chill until ready to serve.

American-style Hot Chicken Salad

SERVES 6

175 g/6 oz/¾ cup long-grain rice
450 g/1 lb/4 cups cooked chicken, chopped
½ bunch of spring onions (scallions), finely chopped
1 canned pimiento, chopped
275 g/10 oz/1 medium can of cream of chicken soup
275 g/10 oz/1 medium can of cream of mushroom soup
100 ml/3 fl oz/6½ tbsp mayonnaise
Salt and freshly ground black pepper
2 celery sticks, chopped
1 carrot, grated
50 g/2 oz/½ cup toasted flaked (slivered) almonds
50 g/2 oz/½ cup Cheddar cheese, grated
50 g/2 oz/1 cup cornflakes

Cook the rice in plenty of boiling salted water until tender. Drain. Mix with the remaining ingredients except the cornflakes. Turn into a large ovenproof dish. Crush the cornflakes over the top and bake at 180°C/350°F/gas mark 4 for 30 minutes.

Hawaiian Chicken

SERVES 4

300 g/11 oz/1 medium can of pineapple chunks, drained
175 g/6 oz/1½ cups cooked long-grain rice
175 g/6 oz/1½ cups cooked chicken, diced
200 g/7 oz/1 small can of sweetcorn (corn) with (bell) peppers, drained
30 ml/2 tbsp mayonnaise
Lettuce leaves
Tomato wedges, to garnish

Mix together all the ingredients except the lettuce leaves in a bowl. Fold in gently until well combined. Pile on to a bed of lettuce and garnish with tomato wedges before serving.

Continental Chicken and Vegetable Salad

SERVES 4

225 g/8 oz/1 cup risotto rice
45 ml/3 tbsp olive oil
Juice of 3 lemons
200 g/7 oz/1¾ cups cooked chicken, diced
1 yellow (bell) pepper, diced
2 tomatoes, diced
3 hard-boiled (hard-cooked) eggs, cut into chunks
175 g/6 oz Gruyere (Swiss) cheese, cubed
60 ml/4 tbsp chopped parsley
4 basil leaves, finely chopped
Salt and freshly ground black pepper
A few stoned (pitted) green olives, quartered, to garnish

Cook the rice in plenty of boiling salted water for 15–20 minutes until just tender but still with some texture. Drain, rinse with cold water and drain again. Place in a bowl and drizzle with the oil and lemon juice. Add all the remaining ingredients and toss lightly. Pack into a large mould and chill for 1 hour. Turn out on to a serving plate and garnish with the olive quarters.

Umbrian Chicken and Pea Salad

SERVES 4

225 g/8 oz/1 cup risotto or long-grain rice
A large sprig of mint
225 g/8 oz frozen peas
200 g/7 oz/1¾ cups cooked chicken, finely chopped
3 stoned (pitted) green olives, finely chopped
60 ml/4 tbsp olive oil
Juice of 1 lemon
Salt and freshly ground black pepper
Lettuce leaves
2 hard-boiled (hard-cooked) eggs, sliced

Cook the rice in plenty of boiling salted water with the mint added for 15 minutes or until just tender, adding the peas for the last 5 minutes' cooking time. Drain, rinse with cold water and drain again. Remove the mint. Place the rice and peas in a bowl. Add the chicken and olives, oil and lemon juice. Season well, then toss. Press into a mould and chill for at least 1 hour, then turn out on to a bed of lettuce. Garnish with the sliced eggs and serve.

Simple Curried Chicken Mayonnaise

SERVES 4

1 packet of savoury rice with mushrooms
½ cooked chicken
45 ml/3 tbsp mayonnaise
20 ml/4 tsp mango chutney
10 ml/2 tsp curry paste
Paprika, for dusting
Bite-sized popadoms, to serve

Cook the rice according to the packet directions. Drain, spoon into a ring on a large serving plate and leave until cold. Pick all the meat off the chicken and cut into bite-sized pieces. Mix the mayonnaise with the chutney and curry paste. Fold in the chicken and pile into the centre of the cold rice. Dust with paprika and serve with bite-sized popadoms.

Chicken and Vegetable Cassata

SERVES 4–6

350 g/12 oz/1½ cups risotto rice
225 g/8 oz shelled, fresh, young peas, cooked if preferred
100 g/4 oz/1 cup cooked chicken, shredded
3 thick slices of ham, cut into thin strips
4 stoned (pitted) black olives, chopped
4 basil leaves, chopped
75 ml/5 tbsp olive oil
30 ml/2 tbsp balsamic vinegar
Salt and freshly ground black pepper
Lettuce leaves
3 hard-boiled (hard-cooked) eggs, cut into wedges

Cook the rice in plenty of boiling salted water for 15–20 minutes until just tender but still with some bite. Drain, rinse with cold water and drain again. Place in a large bowl and add all the remaining ingredients except the lettuce and eggs. Mix gently, then pack into a large, lightly oiled pudding basin. Press down well, then chill for at least 1 hour. Loosen the edge, then turn out on to a bed of lettuce and garnish with the wedges of hard-boiled egg.

Curried Rice, Chicken and Cheese Salad

SERVES 4

225 g/8 oz/1 cup long-grain rice
400 g/14 oz/1 large can of baked beans
10 ml/2 tsp curry powder
15 ml/1 tbsp salad cream
30 ml/2 tbsp sultanas (golden raisins)
75 g/3 oz Cheddar cheese, cubed
75 g/3 oz/¾ cup cooked chicken, cubed
Lettuce leaves
Chopped parsley, to garnish

Cook the rice in plenty of boiling salted water until tender. Drain, rinse with cold water and drain again. Place in a bowl with the beans, curry powder, salad cream, sultanas, cheese and chicken. Toss well. Pile on to a bed of lettuce and serve garnished with parsley.

Warm Brown Rice, Chicken and Nut Salad

SERVES 4

225 g/8 oz/1 cup brown rice
750 ml/1¼ pts/3 cups chicken stock
1 large skinless chicken breast, diced
1 onion, chopped
3 celery sticks, chopped
1 garlic clove, crushed
1 green (bell) pepper, chopped
30 ml/2 tbsp olive oil
Salt and freshly ground black pepper
100 g/4 oz/1 cup mixed nuts, chopped
A squeeze of lemon juice

Cook the rice in the stock for about 45 minutes or until tender and the stock is absorbed, stirring occasionally and adding the chicken after 30 minutes. Remove from the heat, turn into a serving dish and leave to cool slightly. Fry (sauté) the onion, celery, garlic and pepper in the oil for 1 minute, until slightly softened. Add to the cooked rice with a little salt and pepper and the nuts and toss well. Add a good squeeze of lemon juice and serve warm.

English Country Chicken Salad

SERVES 4–6

350 g/12 oz/1½ cups long-grain rice
225 g/8 oz/2 cups cooked chicken, diced
1 cucumber, thinly sliced
2 hard-boiled (hard-cooked) eggs, sliced
2 tomatoes, halved, seeded and cut into chunks
45 ml/3 tbsp olive oil
Juice of 1 lemon
Salt and freshly ground black pepper
Lettuce leaves

Cook the rice in plenty of boiling salted water until tender. Drain, rinse with cold water and drain again. Place in a large bowl and gently mix in all the remaining ingredients except the lettuce. Turn into a large, lightly oiled pudding basin and press down firmly. Chill for at least 1 hour. Loosen the edge, then turn out on to a bed of lettuce and serve. Alternatively, simply toss gently and serve with the lettuce.

Caribbean Pasta Salad

SERVES 6

100 g/4 oz conchiglie pasta
1 oakleaf lettuce
½ small iceberg lettuce
4 celery sticks, chopped
4 carrots, grated
200 g/7 oz/1 small can of pineapple chunks, drained
75 g/3 oz/½ cup stoned (pitted) dates, chopped
175 g/6 oz/1½ cups cooked chicken, diced
45 ml/3 tbsp mayonnaise
Finely grated rind and juice of 1 lime
90 ml/6 tbsp sunflower oil
Salt and freshly ground black pepper
50 g/2 oz/½ cup walnut halves, chopped

Cook the pasta according to the packet directions. Drain, rinse with cold water and drain again. Line a salad bowl with the lettuce leaves. Mix together all the remaining ingredients except the walnuts and toss lightly. Pile on to the bed of lettuce and sprinkle with the walnuts before serving.

Chinese Chicken, Prawn and Beansprout Salad

SERVES 4

100 g/4 oz Chinese egg noodles, cooked
100 g/4 oz cooked, peeled prawns (shrimp)
100 g/4 oz/1 cup cooked chicken, diced
100 g/4 oz/2 cups beansprouts
45 ml/3 tbsp sunflower oil
15 ml/1 tbsp sherry vinegar
15 ml/1 tbsp soy sauce
A pinch of ground ginger
1 red (bell) pepper, cut into thin strips
2.5 cm/1 in piece of cucumber, cut into thin strips
4 spring onions (scallions), chopped

Mix together all the ingredients in a bowl. Toss well and chill before serving.

Oriental Green Bean, Chicken and Peanut Salad

SERVES 4–6

250 g/9 oz/1 packet of Chinese egg noodles
225 g/8 oz thin French (green) beans, cut into short lengths
90 ml/6 tbsp peanut butter
30 ml/2 tbsp caster (superfine) sugar
150 ml/¼ pt/⅔ cup chicken stock
30 ml/2 tbsp soy sauce
175 g/6 oz/1½ cups cooked chicken, cut into chunks

Cook the noodles according to the packet directions. Drain, rinse with cold water and drain again. Cook the beans in boiling salted water for 5 minutes until just tender. Drain, rinse with cold water and drain again. Blend together the peanut butter, sugar, stock and soy sauce in a bowl. Add the chicken, beans and noodles, toss well and serve straight away.

Curried Chicken Pasta Salad

SERVES 4

225 g/8 oz pasta shapes
60 ml/4 tbsp mayonnaise
30 ml/2 tbsp curried peach chutney
2 dried peaches, chopped
10 ml/2 tsp curry paste
175 g/6 oz/1½ cups cooked chicken, chopped
Lettuce leaves
Lemon wedges

Cook the pasta according to the packet directions. Drain, rinse with cold water and drain again. Blend the mayonnaise in a bowl with the chutney, peaches and curry paste. Fold in the chicken and pasta and chill. Serve on a bed of lettuce, garnished with lemon wedges.

Chicken Chaudfroid

Use the chicken cooking water for soup or for any recipe requiring chicken stock.

SERVES 6

6 part-boned chicken breasts
1 onion
1 chicken stock cube
1 carrot
300 ml/½ pt/1¼ cups milk
1 bay leaf
8 peppercorns
1.5 ml/¼ tsp salt
25 g/1 oz/2 tbsp butter or margarine
25 g/1 oz/¼ cup plain (all-purpose) flour
1 sachet of aspic jelly powder to make 300 ml/½ pt/1¼ cups aspic
10 ml/2 tsp powdered gelatine
1 small red (bell) pepper
A piece of cucumber skin
Baby new potatoes and a mixed salad, to serve

Put the chicken in a saucepan. Halve the onion and add half to the pan with the stock cube. Cut off a quarter of the carrot and add. Just-cover with water. Bring to the boil, reduce the heat, part-cover and simmer gently for 40 minutes until tender and succulent. Leave to cool, then remove with a draining spoon and drain on kitchen paper (paper towels). Meanwhile, put the remaining onion half in a saucepan with the milk, bay leaf, peppercorns and salt. Bring to the boil, remove from the heat and leave to infuse for 30 minutes. Strain.

Melt the butter or margarine in a saucepan. Stir in the flour and cook, stirring, for 1 minute. Remove from the heat and gradually blend in the strained milk. Return to the heat, bring to the boil and cook for 2 minutes, stirring, until thick and smooth. Cover with a circle of wet greaseproof (waxed) paper and leave to cool.

Make up the aspic jelly according to the packet directions. Stir in the gelatine until completely dissolved. Leave until the consistency of egg white, then stir half into the cold white sauce.

Pull all the skin off the chicken and discard. Place the chicken on a wire rack with a large plate underneath to catch the drips. Spoon the jellied white sauce over each portion to coat completely and leave for 15 minutes to set. Cut small, attractive shapes out of the remaining carrot, the pepper and cucumber. Arrange over the coated chicken. If the clear aspic jelly has set, warm slightly, then leave until the consistency of egg white again. Spoon all over the chicken to glaze. Chill until ready to serve with baby new potatoes and a mixed salad.

Chicken and Tuna Niçoise

SERVES 4

225 g/8 oz French (green) beans, cut into short lengths
225 g/8 oz cooked new potatoes, diced
2 hard-boiled (hard-cooked) eggs, roughly chopped
1 small onion, sliced into rings
4 tomatoes, roughly diced
185 g/6½ oz/1 small can of tuna, drained
175 g/6 oz/1½ cups cooked chicken, diced
50 g/2 oz/1 small can of anchovies, drained and cut into thin slivers
90 ml/6 tbsp olive oil
30 ml/2 tbsp red wine vinegar
Salt and freshly ground black pepper
Cos (romaine) lettuce leaves
A few black olives, to garnish

Cook the beans in boiling water for 5 minutes until just tender. Drain, rinse with cold water and drain again. Place in a bowl with the remaining ingredients except the lettuce and season with a little salt and lots of black pepper. Toss very gently so as not to break up the tuna too much. Pile on to a bed of lettuce and scatter the olives over.

Hindle Wakes

SERVES 6–8

1.75 g/4 lb oven-ready chicken
100 g/4 oz ready-to-eat prunes
50 g/2 oz/1 cup breadcrumbs
25 g/1 oz/¼ cup chopped mixed nuts
15 ml/1 tbsp chopped parsley
15 ml/1 tbsp dried thyme
175 ml/6 fl oz/¾ cup white wine vinegar
Salt and white pepper
40 g/1½ oz/3 tbsp butter or margarine
30 ml/2 tbsp light brown sugar
1 chicken stock cube
1 lemon
25 g/1 oz/¼ cup cornflour (cornstarch)
2 large eggs
Parsley sprigs, to garnish
Baby new potatoes and a beetroot (red beet), orange and watercress salad, to serve

Remove the giblets from the chicken, if necessary and wipe inside and out with kitchen paper (paper towels). Reserve 6 prunes for garnish, chop the remainder and place in a bowl. Mix with the breadcrumbs, nuts, herbs, 10 ml/2 tsp of the vinegar and a little salt and white pepper. Melt 20 g/¾ oz/1½ tbsp of the butter or margarine and stir into the stuffing. Use to stuff the neck end of the bird and secure the skin with a skewer. Truss the bird, if necessary and place in a flameproof casserole (Dutch oven). Add just enough water to cover, the remaining vinegar and the sugar. Add the giblets if you have them and crumble in the stock cube. Bring to the boil, reduce the heat, part-cover and simmer gently for 1 hour. Remove from the heat and leave to cool in the liquid overnight.

Skim off any fat from the surface, then remove the chicken and place on a large serving plate. Remove any string and the skewer. Measure 450 ml/¾ pt/2 cups of the stock. (Reserve the remainder for another recipe.)

Thinly pare the rind from the lemon, cut into thin strips, then boil in water for 3 minutes. Drain, rinse with cold water and drain again. Squeeze the lemon juice. Melt the remaining butter or margarine in a saucepan. Blend in the cornflour (cornstarch) and cook, stirring, for 1 minute. Remove from the heat and blend in the measured stock. Return to the heat and bring to the boil, stirring until thickened. Simmer for 2 minutes. Beat the eggs in a small bowl. Whisk 60 ml/4 tbsp of the hot sauce into the eggs, then return this mixture to the remaining sauce and cook very gently, stirring, until the mixture coats the back of a spoon. Do not allow the mixture to boil. Whisk the lemon juice into the sauce. Cover with a circle of wet greaseproof (waxed) paper to prevent a skin forming and leave to cool.

Remove as much skin as possible from the bird and discard. Spoon half the cold sauce over to coat completely. Leave to stand for 30 minutes to set, then spoon the remaining sauce over. Clean the dish round the bird with kitchen paper (paper towels). Arrange parsley sprigs and the reserved prunes around and sprinkle the lemon rind over the breast. Serve cold with baby new potatoes and a beetroot, orange and watercress salad.

Sunny Chicken Salad

SERVES 4

175 g/6 oz pasta shapes
175 g/6 oz/1½ cups cooked chicken, diced
30 ml/2 tbsp chopped parsley
200 g/7 oz/1 small can of sweetcorn (corn), drained
30 ml/2 tbsp olive oil
15 ml/1 tbsp lemon juice
½ bunch of spring onion (scallions), chopped
Lettuce leaves

Cook the pasta according to the packet directions. Drain, rinse with cold water and drain again. Mix with the remaining ingredients except the lettuce. To serve, toss gently and pile on to a bed of lettuce leaves.

Mediterranean Jellied Chicken

SERVES 4

15 ml/1 tbsp powdered gelatine
300 ml/½ pt/1¼ cups chicken stock
45 ml/3 tbsp lemon juice
75 ml/5 tbsp mayonnaise
1 spring onion (scallion), finely chopped
3 celery sticks, chopped
1 green (bell) pepper, chopped
1 red pepper, chopped
5 cm/2 in piece of cucumber, chopped
5 ml/1 tsp chopped basil
6 stuffed olives, sliced
350 g/12 oz/3 cups cooked chicken, chopped, all skin removed
Salt and freshly ground black pepper
Lollo rosso lettuce leaves
A sprig of basil
New potatoes and a mixed salad, to serve

Dissolve the gelatine in the stock according to the packet directions. Stir in the lemon juice. Leave to cool. When cold, whisk in the mayonnaise and chill until the consistency of egg white. Fold in the prepared vegetables, the basil, olives and chicken. Season to taste. Turn into a fluted mould and chill until set. Loosen the edges and turn out on to a bed of lollo rosso leaves. Garnish with a sprig of basil and serve with new potatoes and a mixed salad.

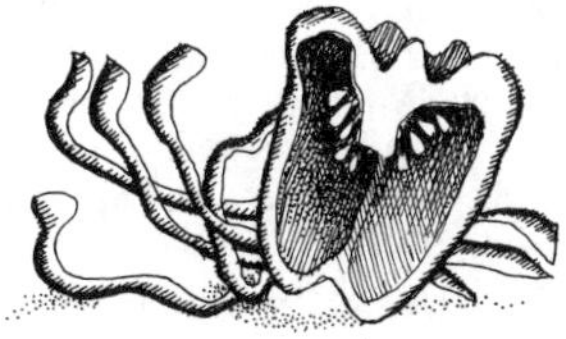

Poached Chicken with Summer Fruit and Vegetable Salad

SERVES 4

4 skinless chicken breasts
450 ml/¾ pt/2 cups chicken stock
Salt and freshly ground black pepper
1 carrot, cut into matchsticks
1 raw beetroot (red beet), cut into matchsticks
1 celery stick, cut into matchsticks
100 g/4 oz radishes, thinly sliced
1 courgette (zucchini), cut into matchsticks
1 turnip, cut into matchsticks
1 yellow (bell) pepper, cut into matchsticks
100 g/4 oz baby strawberries, sliced
100 g/4 oz raspberries
15 ml/1 tbsp tarragon vinegar
15 ml/1 tbsp raspberry vinegar
30 ml/2 tbsp Dijon mustard
30 ml/2 tbsp olive oil
A good pinch of caster (superfine) sugar
30 ml/2 tbsp snipped chives, to garnish
Crusty bread, to serve

Put the chicken breasts in a shallow pan. Add the stock and a little salt and pepper. Bring to the boil, reduce the heat, cover and poach gently for 8 minutes. Remove from the pan and leave to cool. Boil the stock rapidly until reduced by half. Arrange neat piles of the different vegetables and fruits around the edges of four large plates. Place a chicken breast in the centre of each. Whisk the vinegars, mustard and oil into the reduced stock. Sweeten with sugar and season with salt and pepper. Spoon a little over each pile of vegetable and fruit and spoon the remainder over the chicken. Sprinkle the chicken with snipped chives and serve cold with crusty bread.

Packed with Plenty Salad

SERVES 6

225 g/8 oz wholewheat pasta shapes
175 g/6 oz cherry tomatoes, halved
1 green (bell) pepper, diced
200 g/7 oz/1 small can of sweetcorn (corn) drained
175 g/6 oz/1½ cups cooked chicken, diced, all skin removed
175 g/6 oz Cheddar cheese, diced
60 ml/4 tbsp olive oil
25 ml/1½ tbsp lemon juice
5 ml/1 tsp Dijon mustard
10 ml/2 tsp chopped parsley
Salt and freshly ground black pepper

Cook the pasta according to the packet directions. Drain, rinse with cold water and drain again. Place in a large salad bowl and add the tomatoes, green pepper, corn, chicken and cheese. Whisk together the remaining ingredients, adding a good pinch of salt and pepper, and pour over the salad. Toss gently and chill for at least 1 hour to allow the flavours to develop.

Curried Chicken and Pasta Salad

SERVES 4

175 g/6 oz pasta shapes
225 g/8 oz cooked chicken, cut into neat pieces, all skin removed
45 ml/3 tbsp mayonnaise
5 ml/1 tsp curry paste
225 g/8 oz/1 small can of curried baked beans
1 green (bell) pepper, diced
Lettuce leaves
30 ml/2 tbsp whole almonds
5 ml/1 tsp mixed (apple-pie) spice
Sliced tomatoes and chopped spring onions (scallions), tossed in French dressing, to serve

Cook the pasta according to the packet directions. Drain, rinse with cold water and drain again. Add the chicken. Mix the mayonnaise with the curry paste and baked beans. Add to the chicken and pasta with the green pepper and toss gently. Pile on to a bed of lettuce leaves. Dry-fry the almonds in a frying pan (skillet) until golden and toss in the mixed spice. Scatter over the salad and serve with the tomato and spring onion salad.

Chicken Supreme Salad

SERVES 4

4 small skinless chicken breasts
300 ml/½ pt/1¼ cups chicken stock
Salt and freshly ground black pepper
175 g/6 oz/¾ cup long-grain rice
½ cucumber, diced
2 red eating (dessert) apples, diced
5 ml/1 tsp lemon juice
120 ml/4 fl oz/½ cup plain yoghurt
75 ml/5 tbsp mayonnaise
5 ml/1 tsp curry paste
10 ml/2 tsp curried fruit chutney
Torn coriander (cilantro) leaves, to garnish
Crisp green salad, to serve

Put the chicken in a saucepan with the stock. Bring to the boil, reduce the heat and poach gently for about 10–15 minutes until the chicken is tender. Remove from the pan with a draining spoon and leave until cold. Meanwhile, make the stock up to 600 ml/1 pt/2½ cups with water. Bring to the boil, add a little salt and the rice and cook for about 10 minutes until tender. Drain, rinse with cold water, drain again and leave until cold. Mix in the cucumber and apple. Pile on to four serving plates and place a cold chicken breast on the top of each. Mix the yoghurt with the mayonnaise and curry paste. Stir in the chutney and season to taste. Spoon over the chicken and garnish with a few torn coriander leaves. Serve with a crisp green salad.

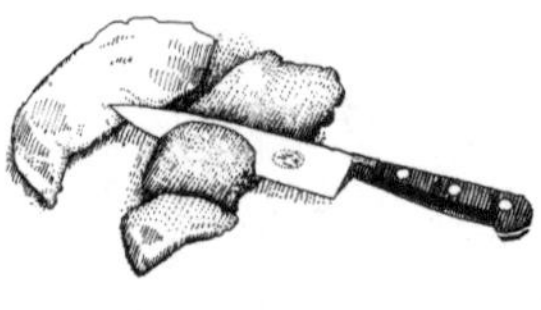

Chicken, Blue Cheese and Pear Salad

SERVES 4

100 g/4 oz/½ cup brown rice
50 g/2 oz frozen peas
50 g/2 oz/⅓ cup currants
1 bunch of radishes, trimmed and sliced
2 celery sticks, sliced
100 g/4 oz blue Shropshire cheese, cubed
2 ripe pears
15 ml/1 tbsp lemon juice
225 g/8 oz/2 cups cooked chicken, cut into neat pieces, all skin removed
1 bunch of watercress, separated into sprigs
45 ml/3 tbsp plain yoghurt
45 ml/3 tbsp mayonnaise
15 ml/1 tbsp milk
Salt and freshly ground black pepper
4 cherry tomatoes, to garnish

Cook the rice in plenty of lightly salted boiling water for about 30 minutes or until tender, adding the peas for the last 5 minutes. Drain, rinse with cold water and drain again. Tip into a bowl. Add the currants, radishes, celery and cheese. Dice the pears, but do not peel. Toss in the lemon juice, then add to the bowl with the chicken. Toss all together gently. Spoon on to four serving plates and tuck the watercress sprigs in around. Whisk together the yoghurt, mayonnaise and milk with a little salt and pepper and drizzle over. Cut a cross down through each tomato from the rounded end towards the stalk end. Gently peel back the red flesh leaving the seeds in the centre to represent lilies. Arrange one to the side of each plate and serve.

Chicken and Spiced Almond Salad

SERVES 4

1.25 kg/2½ lb oven-ready chicken
1 garlic clove
25 g/1 oz/2 tbsp butter or margarine
Salt and freshly ground black pepper
For the sauce:
75 ml/5 tbsp mayonnaise
75 ml/5 tbsp plain yoghurt
15 ml/1 tbsp tomato purée (paste)
5 ml/1 tsp Worcestershire sauce
5 cm/2 in piece of cucumber, chopped
50 g/2 oz/½ cup blanched almonds
1.5 ml/¼ tsp chilli powder
1.5 ml/¼ tsp mixed (apple-pie) spice
1 small lollo rosso lettuce
Lemon wedges, to garnish
Cold cooked long-grain rice, tossed with a handful of currants, a little chopped parsley and French dressing, to serve

Wipe the chicken inside and out with kitchen paper (paper towels). Pull off any excess fat round the body cavity and discard. Place in a roasting tin (pan) and put the garlic clove inside. Spread half the butter or margarine over and sprinkle with a little salt and pepper. Cover and roast in a preheated oven at 190°C/375°F/gas mark 5 for 1¼ hours or until the juices run clear when a skewer is inserted in the thickest part of the thigh. Remove from the pan and drain on kitchen paper. Leave to cool a little.

To make the sauce, mix the mayonnaise with the yoghurt, tomato purée and Worcestershire sauce. Season lightly. Stir in the cucumber. Melt the remaining butter or margarine in a frying pan (skillet). Fry (sauté) the almonds until golden brown. Sprinkle with the spices and toss well. Drain on kitchen paper. Carve the chicken. Lay the lettuce leaves on four plates and top each with warm chicken pieces. Spoon the sauce over and scatter the almonds over. Garnish with the lemon wedges and serve with a rice, currant and parsley salad.

Coronation Chicken

There are many variations on this dish but this recipe is my favourite.

SERVES 6

450 g/1 lb/2 cups long-grain rice
100 g/4 oz frozen peas
15 ml/1 tbsp sunflower oil
1 large onion, finely chopped
15 ml/1 tbsp curry powder
5 ml/1 tsp tomato purée (paste)
150 ml/¼ pt/⅔ cup red wine
150 ml/¼ pt/⅔ cup chicken stock, made with ½ stock cube
1 bay leaf
15 ml/1 tbsp mango chutney, chopped if necessary
450 ml/¾ pt/2 cups mayonnaise
White pepper
200 g/7 oz/1 small can of sweetcorn (corn), drained
Round lettuce leaves
450 g/1 lb/4 cups cooked chicken, cut into neat pieces, all skin removed
30 ml/2 tbsp toasted flaked (slivered) almonds

Cook the rice in plenty of boiling salted water for about 10 minutes or until tender, adding the peas after 5 minutes. Drain, rinse with cold water and drain again. Meanwhile, heat the oil in a saucepan. Add the onion and fry (sauté) gently for 3 minutes until softened but not browned. Stir in the curry powder and cook for 1 minute. Add the tomato purée, wine, stock and bay leaf. Bring to the boil, reduce the heat and simmer for 10 minutes. Remove from the heat, then leave to cool. Discard the bay leaf and stir in the chutney and mayonnaise. Season with pepper. Mix the corn with the rice and peas. Arrange the lettuce leaves on a large platter and spoon the rice mixture over. Pile the chicken in the centre and spoon the sauce over. Sprinkle with the flaked almonds and serve cold.

Fast Chicken and Spiced Hazelnuts

SERVES 4

A 1.5 kg/3 lb cooked chicken
150 ml/¼ pt/⅔ cup mayonnaise
15 ml/1 tbsp milk
15 ml/1 tbsp tomato purée (paste)
5 ml/1 tsp Worcestershire sauce
5 cm/2 in piece of cucumber, chopped
50 g/2 oz/½ cup blanched hazelnuts (filberts)
15 g/½ oz/1 tbsp butter or margarine
1.5 ml/¼ tsp chilli powder
1.5 ml/¼ tsp ground cinnamon
Lettuce leaves
New potatoes, to serve

Carve the bird (page 17). Blend the mayonnaise with the milk, tomato purée, Worcestershire sauce and cucumber. Fry (sauté) the nuts in the butter or margarine until golden. Sprinkle with the spices, toss well and drain on kitchen paper (paper towels). Place the lettuce on a large serving platter. Arrange the chicken attractively on top, spoon the mayonnaise mixture over and sprinkle with the nuts. Serve with new potatoes.

Summer Paella

SERVES 6

450 g/1 lb mussels in their shells
1.2 litres/2 pts/5 cups chicken stock
1.25 kg/2½ lb chicken, jointed into 6 pieces (page 15)
Salt and freshly ground black pepper
90 ml/6 tbsp olive oil
1 Spanish onion, finely chopped
1 garlic clove, crushed
4 baby squid, cleaned and sliced into rings
450 g/1 lb/2 cups risotto rice
15 ml/1 tbsp paprika
5 ml/1 tsp saffron powder
1 bay leaf
1 red (bell) pepper, sliced
1 green pepper, sliced
4 tomatoes, skinned and chopped
100 g/4 oz shelled fresh or frozen peas
12 cooked, unpeeled prawns (shrimp)
6 black olives
Lemon wedges and chopped parsley, to garnish
Focaccia and a green salad, to serve

Scrub the mussels, discarding any that are damaged or won't close when sharply tapped. Remove the beards. Place in a saucepan with half the stock. Bring to the boil, cover and cook for a few minutes, shaking the pan occasionally, until the mussels have opened. Leave to cool. Wipe the chicken with kitchen paper (paper towels) and season with a little salt and pepper. Heat the oil in a large paella pan or frying pan (skillet). Fry (sauté) the chicken on all sides to brown. Reduce the heat and cook for a further 10 minutes. Remove from the pan. Add the onion and garlic and fry for 2 minutes until slightly softened. Add the squid and cook for 1 minute. Stir in the rice and cook, stirring, for 1 minute until coated with oil. Strain the mussel liquor into the pan and add the remaining stock. Stir in the paprika, saffron and bay leaf and return the chicken to the pan. Bring to the boil, cover with a lid or foil, reduce the heat and simmer gently for 15 minutes. Add the peppers, tomatoes and peas and cook for a further 10 minutes until the rice is just tender and has absorbed nearly all the liquid and the chicken is cooked through. Season to taste and stir gently. Remove from the heat and leave to cool. Fork through and arrange the mussels, still in their shells (or break off the top shells if liked) over the top, discarding any that have not opened. Add the prawns and olives. Garnish with lemon wedges and sprinkle with chopped parsley. Chill, if liked. Serve with focaccia and a green salad.

Biryani Salad

SERVES 4

200 g/7 oz/1 packet of pilau rice
175 g/6 oz/1½ cups cooked chicken, diced, all skin removed
430 g/15½ oz/1 large can of chick peas (garbanzos), drained
1 small green (bell) pepper, diced
2 tomatoes, diced
1 bunch of spring onions (scallions), chopped
90 ml/6 tbsp coconut milk
90 ml/6 tbsp plain yoghurt
1 small green chilli, finely chopped, or chilli powder to taste
For the dressing:
30 ml/2 tbsp sunflower oil
10 ml/2 tsp lemon juice
20 ml/4 tsp smooth mango chutney
Salt and freshly ground black pepper
30 ml/2 tbsp currants
30 ml/2 tbsp toasted flaked (slivered) almonds

Cook the rice according to the packet directions. Drain, rinse with cold water and drain again. Place in a salad bowl and add the remaining ingredients. Toss gently. Whisk together the dressing ingredients with a little salt and pepper. Pour over the salad and toss gently. Turn into serving bowls and garnish each with the currants and toasted almonds.

Poussins with Warm Vegetable Salad

SERVES 4

4 poussins (Cornish hens)
2 garlic cloves, halved
4 small bay leaves
45 ml/3 tbsp olive oil
Salt and freshly ground black pepper
1 large carrot, cut into matchsticks
75 g/3 oz French (green) beans, cut into short lengths
75 g/3 oz mangetout (snow peas)
1 large courgette (zucchini), cut into matchsticks
1 red (bell) pepper, cut into thin strips
15 ml/1 tbsp white wine vinegar
5 ml/1 tsp Dijon mustard
5 ml/1 tsp caster (superfine) sugar
15 ml/1 tbsp chopped parsley

Wipe the poussins inside and out with kitchen paper (paper towels). Place in a roasting tin (pan). Put half a garlic clove and a small bay leaf in the body cavity of each. Brush with 15 ml/1 tbsp of the olive oil and sprinkle with salt and pepper. Roast in a preheated oven at 190°C/375°F/gas mark 5 for about 45 minutes or until the juices run clear when pierced at the thickest part of the thigh. Remove from the tin and reserve. Meanwhile, cook the vegetables all together in lightly salted boiling water for 3 minutes. Drain and place in a bowl. Strain the juices from the chicken into a jug. Whisk in the remaining oil, the vinegar, mustard and sugar. Season to taste. Pour over the vegetables and toss gently. Pile on to four plates, top each with a poussin and sprinkle with the parsley. Serve warm.

Smoked Chicken, Ham and Walnut Salad

SERVES 4

350 g/12 oz baby new potatoes
100 g/4 oz/1 cup lean smoked ham, cut into thin strips
100 g/4 oz/1 cup walnuts, roughly chopped
½ iceberg lettuce, shredded
½ curly endive (frisée lettuce), cut into small pieces
1 red onion, thinly sliced
175 g/6 oz/1½ cups smoked chicken, cut into thin strips
15 ml/1 tbsp clear honey
45 ml/3 tbsp olive oil
45 ml/3 tbsp white wine vinegar
2.5 ml/½ tsp ground cumin
Salt and freshly ground black pepper

Boil the potatoes in their skins until just tender. Drain and leave to cool. Dry-fry the ham until crisp and reserve. Mix together the potatoes, walnuts, lettuces, onion and chicken in a salad bowl. Whisk together the remaining ingredients, adding salt and pepper to taste. Pour over the salad. Toss gently and sprinkle with the crisp ham.

Layered Chicken Pâté with Sweet Pepper Salad

SERVES 8

450 g/1 lb chicken livers, trimmed
100 g/4 oz rindless streaky bacon, diced
1 garlic clove, crushed
100 g/4 oz/½ cup butter or margarine
100 g/4 oz/2 cups breadcrumbs
25 g/1 oz/¼ cup shredded (chopped) vegetable suet
15 ml/1 tbsp chopped parsley
5 ml/1 tsp dried thyme
5 ml/1 tsp dried sage
Salt and freshly ground black pepper
2 eggs, beaten
350 g/12 oz chicken stir-fry meat
2 red (bell) peppers, halved and sliced
2 green peppers, halved and sliced
2 yellow peppers, halved and sliced
60 ml/4 tbsp olive oil
30 ml/2 tbsp white wine vinegar
5 ml/1 tsp caster (superfine) sugar
2.5 ml/½ tsp Dijon mustard
1 round lettuce
Crusty bread, to serve

Line the base of an 18 cm/7 in deep round, loose-bottomed cake tin (pan) with non-stick baking parchment. Fry (sauté) the chicken livers, bacon and garlic in the butter or margarine in a saucepan for 2–3 minutes, stirring. Purée in a blender or food processor. Mix the breadcrumbs with the suet, herbs and some salt and pepper. Stir in the eggs to bind. Put a layer of half the chicken liver mixture in the prepared tin. Cover with half the chicken meat. Cover with all the stuffing, then a layer of the remaining chicken meat and top with the remaining chicken liver mixture. Cover securely with foil and place the tin in a roasting tin containing 2.5 cm/1 in boiling water. Cook in a preheated oven at 180°C/350°F/gas mark 4 for 1½ hours until set and the mixture is shrinking from the sides of the tin. The pâté mixture will look pink.

Remove from the roasting tin and cover with clean foil, then a small plate. Weigh down with weights or cans of food. Leave until cold, then chill overnight. Put the prepared peppers in a bowl. Whisk together the oil, vinegar, sugar, mustard and some salt and pepper and pour over. Toss and leave to marinate for at least 30 minutes. Arrange the lettuce leaves on a serving plate. Turn out the pâté on to the plate and serve with the pepper salad and crusty bread.

Oriental Chicken and Beansprout Salad

SERVES 4

225 g/8 oz/1 medium can of pineapple rings, drained, reserving the juice
100 g/4 oz/2 cups beansprouts
175 g/6 oz/1½ cups cooked chicken, cut into bite-sized pieces, all skin removed
1 green (bell) pepper, halved and thinly sliced
1 onion, halved and thinly sliced
15 ml/1 tbsp soy sauce
15 ml/1 tbsp sunflower oil
5 ml/1 tsp tomato purée (paste)
Salt and freshly ground black pepper
Prawn (shrimp) crackers, to serve

Cut the pineapple rings into chunks and mix with the beansprouts, chicken, green pepper and onion. Whisk the pineapple juice with the remaining ingredients. Pour over the salad and toss well. Leave to stand for 30 minutes, then toss again and serve in bowls with prawn crackers.

TURKEY

Stilton, Turkey and Walnut Salad

SERVES 4

225 g/8 oz pasta shapes
225 g/8 oz/2 cups cooked turkey, diced
50 g/2 oz/½ cup Stilton cheese, crumbled
150 ml/¼ pt/⅔ cup plain yoghurt
A little milk
A good pinch of sugar
A good pinch of mustard powder
A good pinch of salt
A good pinch of pepper
50 g/2 oz/½ cup chopped walnuts
Mixed lettuce leaves
Chopped parsley

Cook the pasta according to the packet directions. Drain, rinse with cold water and drain again. Stir in the turkey. Mash the cheese with the yoghurt and thin with a little milk if necessary. Add the sugar, mustard, salt and pepper and mix again. Fold in the walnuts. Add to the pasta and toss. Pile the pasta on to a bed of mixed lettuce leaves, sprinkle with parsley and serve chilled.

Beetroot Layer

SERVES 6

4 cooked beetroot (red beets), sliced
1 bunch of spring onions (scallions), chopped
225 g/8 oz/2 cups cooked turkey, diced
100 g/4 oz/1 cup cooked long-grain rice
30 ml/2 tbsp sliced gherkins (cornichons)
50 g/2 oz/½ cup walnuts, chopped
45 ml/3 tbsp French dressing or 2 parts oil to 1 part vinegar and a little salt, pepper and sugar

Layer the beetroot, onions, turkey, rice, gherkins and walnuts in a glass serving dish. Spoon the dressing over and chill for at least 30 minutes before serving.

Curried Turkey and Rice Salad

SERVES 4

225g/8 oz/1 cup long-grain rice
50 g/2 oz frozen peas
25 g/1 oz/⅙ cup currants
15 ml/1 tbsp toasted flaked (slivered) almonds
60 ml/4 tbsp mayonnaise
15 ml/1 tbsp mild curry paste
30 ml/2 tbsp curried fruit chutney
5 ml/1 tsp lemon juice
225 g/8 oz/2 cups cold cooked turkey, diced
425 g/15 oz/1 large can of haricot (navy) beans, drained
2 tomatoes, cut into wedges

Cook the rice in plenty of boiling salted water for 10 minutes or until just tender, adding the peas after 5 minutes' cooking. Drain, rinse with cold water and drain again. Stir in the currants and nuts and spoon the mixture into a border on a large serving plate. Mix the mayonnaise with the curry paste and chutney. Stir in the lemon juice. Fold in the turkey and beans and pile the mixture into the centre of the rice. Garnish with tomato wedges before serving.

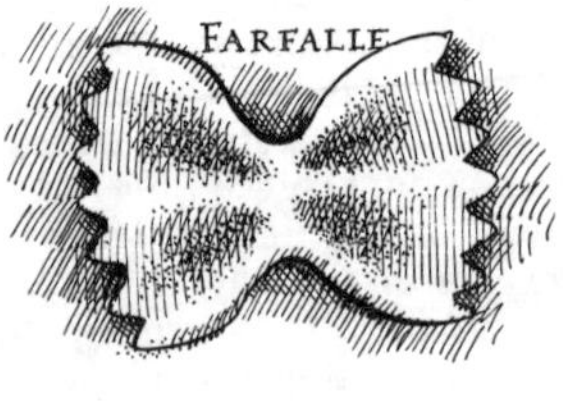

Sunny Smoked Turkey and Nectarine Munch

SERVES 4

4 ripe nectarines, skinned, stoned (pitted) and sliced
175 g/6 oz/1½ cups smoked turkey breast, cut into thin strips
250 g/9 oz/1 large packet of fresh beansprouts
4 spring onions (scallions), diagonally sliced
1 green (bell) pepper, cut into thin strips
2 celery sticks, sliced
30 ml/2 tbsp sunflower seeds
45 ml/3 tbsp sunflower oil
15 ml/1 tbsp orange juice
10 ml/2 tsp lemon juice
5 ml/1 tsp caster (superfine) sugar
5 ml/1 tsp Dijon mustard
2 slices of bread, crusts removed, cubed
1 garlic clove, chopped

Put the first seven ingredients in a bowl and toss gently. Whisk together 30 ml/2 tbsp of the oil, the orange juice, lemon juice, sugar and mustard. Fry (sauté) the bread cubes in the remaining oil with the garlic added until golden brown. Drain on kitchen paper (paper towels). When ready to serve, pour the dressing over the salad. Toss gently, pile into bowls and garnish with the garlic croûtons.

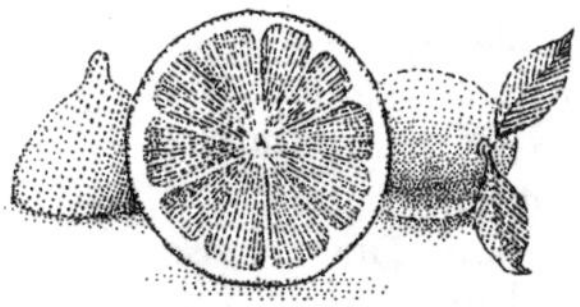

Jellied Turkey Mayonnaise

SERVES 6

300 ml/½ pt/1¼ cups chicken stock
15 ml/1 tbsp powdered gelatine
1 small red (bell) pepper, finely diced
3 black stoned (pitted) olives, halved
50 g/2 oz frozen peas, cooked
1 celery stick, chopped
1 spring onion (scallion), finely chopped
225 g/8 oz/2 cups cooked turkey meat, chopped, all skin removed
90 ml/6 tbsp mayonnaise
Finely grated rind and juice of ½ lemon
Salt and freshly ground black pepper
Round lettuce leaves and cucumber slices, to garnish
Hot French bread, to serve

Pour 45 ml/3 tbsp of the stock into a small bowl. Sprinkle the gelatine over and leave to soften for 5 minutes. Stand the bowl in a pan of hot water or heat briefly in the microwave until completely dissolved. Stir in the remaining stock and leave until cold. Arrange a few pieces of pepper and the olives in the base of a lightly oiled 900 ml/1½ pt/3¾ cup mould. Pour on just enough cold stock to cover and leave until set. Meanwhile mix the remaining pepper with the peas, celery, spring onion and turkey. Blend the mayonnaise with the lemon rind and juice and fold in. When the remaining stock is the consistency of egg white, fold into the mixture. Season to taste. Turn into the prepared mould and chill until set. When ready to serve, loosen the edge slightly and turn out on to lettuce leaves on a serving plate. Garnish all round with cucumber slices and serve with hot French bread.

Magnificent Turkey Centrepiece

SERVES 12

5.5 kg/12 lb oven-ready turkey
2 quantities of forcemeat stuffing (see Forcemeat Balls, page 354)
30 ml/2 tbsp sunflower oil
Salt
65 g/2½ oz aspic jelly powder
750 ml/1¼ pts/3 cups mayonnaise
1 small green (bell) pepper, cut into diamond shapes
1 small red pepper, cut into diamond shapes
Watercress, to garnish
Jacket-baked potatoes and a selection of salads, to serve

Remove the giblets from the bird and wipe inside and out with kitchen paper (paper towels). Make up the stuffing but instead of shaping into balls use to stuff the neck end of the bird. Secure the skin with a skewer, then truss if necessary. Weigh the bird and calculate the cooking time allowing 15 minutes per 450 g/1 lb plus 30 minutes over. Place upside-down in a roasting tin (pan). Rub the skin with the oil and season with salt. Cover with foil and roast in a preheated oven at 190°C/375°F/gas mark 5 for the calculated cooking time. Turn over half-way through cooking. Remove from the oven, leave to cool in the tin for 30 minutes, then transfer to a wire rack set over a tray to cool completely. Make up the aspic according to the packet directions but using only half the quantity of water advised. Leave until cold.

Meanwhile, pull off as much skin as possible from the turkey and discard. When the aspic is the consistency of egg white, reserve 60 ml/4 tbsp in a separate bowl and fold the mayonnaise into the remainder in a large bowl. Spoon some of this into a small jug and place the bowl of the rest of the mixture over a pan of warm water to prevent it setting. Quickly spoon the mayonnaise from the jug over the turkey to coat completely, replenishing from the bowl as you go. Allow any drips to fall on the tray. When the turkey is completely coated, leave to set completely. Remove the warmed mayonnaise mixture from the pan of water and leave until on the point of setting again and quickly spoon all over the turkey. Arrange the pepper diamonds attractively over the breast and leave to set. Melt the reserved aspic again. When on the point of setting, lightly brush all over the turkey to give a shiny glaze. When completely set, carefully transfer to a serving dish, garnish with watercress and serve with jacket-baked potatoes and a selection of salads.

Sausage Salad Supreme

SERVES 4–6

100 g/4 oz/½ cup wild rice mix
4 slices white bread, cubed
45 ml/3 tbsp sunflower oil
8 thick turkey sausages, cooked and sliced
325 g/11½ oz/1 medium can of sweetcorn (corn) with (bell) peppers, drained
430 g/15½ oz/1 large can of butter (lima) beans, drained
½ cucumber, diced
1 bunch of radishes, trimmed and quartered
1 garlic clove, crushed
150 ml/¼ pt/⅔ cup thick plain yoghurt
30 ml/2 tbsp snipped chives

Cook the rice according to the packet directions. Drain, rinse with cold water and drain again. Fry (sauté) the bread in the oil until golden. Drain on kitchen paper (paper towels). Mix the rice with the sausages, corn, butter beans, cucumber and radishes. Mix the garlic with the yoghurt and chives. Just before serving, stir the fried bread into the salad, divide between serving plates and top each with a spoonful of the dressing.

Turkey, Melon and Raisin Salad

SERVES 4

2 turkey breast steaks, about 350 g/12 oz in all
1 onion, chopped
1 carrot, chopped
1 bouquet garni sachet
300 ml/½ pt/1¼ cups chicken stock
Salt and freshly ground black pepper
75 g/3 oz/½ cup large stoned (pitted) raisins (not the smaller seedless variety)
60 ml/4 tbsp mayonnaise
Lemon juice
A few drops of Tabasco sauce
½ small honeydew melon
½ curly endive (frisée lettuce)
200 g/7 oz/1 small can of pimientos, drained and cut into thin strips

Place the turkey steaks, one at a time, in a plastic bag and lightly beat with a rolling pin or meat mallet to flatten slightly. Place in a frying pan (skillet) with the onion, carrot, bouquet garni and stock. Season lightly. Bring to the boil, reduce the heat cover with a lid or foil and poach gently for about 10 minutes until the turkey is tender. Lift out of the pan and reserve. Remove the bouquet garni. Boil the liquid rapidly until well reduced and syrupy. Stir in the raisins and leave to cool. When cold, stir in the mayonnaise and flavour to taste with lemon juice and Tabasco sauce. Cut the turkey steaks into thin strips. Scoop the melon into balls using a melon baller or cut off the rind and dice the flesh. Add to the dressing with the turkey and toss gently. Place the curly endive leaves on serving plates, top with the turkey and melon mixture and arrange the pimiento strips in a lattice pattern over the top. Serve straight away.

Turkey Caesar Salad

SERVES 4

25 g/1 oz/2 tbsp butter or margarine
4 turkey rashers (slices)
2 slices of bread, crusts removed, cubed
1 small cos (romaine) lettuce, torn into pieces
1 garlic clove, crushed
45 ml/3 tbsp olive oil
15 ml/1 tbsp white wine vinegar
5 ml/1 tsp Dijon mustard
5 ml/1 tsp caster (superfine) sugar
2.5 ml/½ tsp dried oregano
Salt and freshly ground black pepper
30 ml/2 tbsp Parmesan cheese, grated
30 ml/2 tbsp chopped parsley

Melt the butter or margarine in a frying pan (skillet). Add the turkey rashers and fry (sauté) until crisp. Drain on kitchen paper (paper towels) and cut into pieces. Fry the bread in the pan until golden all over. Drain on kitchen paper. Place the lettuce in a large salad bowl. Add the turkey rashers. Whisk the garlic, oil, vinegar, mustard, sugar and oregano with some salt and pepper. Pour into the bowl and toss well. Scatter with the croûtons, Parmesan and parsley and serve.

Turkey and Avocado Platter with Mushroom Dressing

SERVES 6

1 turkey breast joint
1 garlic clove
75 ml/5 tbsp olive oil
2.5 ml/½ tsp dried oregano
Salt and freshly ground black pepper
2 large avocados
Lemon juice
30 ml/2 tbsp balsamic vinegar
5 ml/1 tsp Dijon mustard
75 g/3 oz button mushrooms, finely chopped
2 spring onion (scallions), finely chopped
Parsley sprigs, to garnish
Hot Potato Salad (page 350), to serve

Weigh the joint and calculate the cooking time, allowing 20 minutes per 450 g/1 lb plus 20 minutes over. Cut the garlic clove into thin slivers. Gently loosen the skin of the joint and slide the slivers underneath. Alternatively, halve the garlic clove and rub all over the skin, then discard. Brush with a little of the oil and place in a roasting tin (pan). Sprinkle with the oregano and a little salt and pepper. Roast in a preheated oven at 180°C/350°F/gas mark 4 for the calculated cooking time. Remove from the tin and leave to cool. Strain the cooking liquid and reserve.

Meanwhile, halve and peel the avocados, remove the stones (pits), then cut into neat slices. Toss in a little lemon juice. Whisk the remaining olive oil with the cooking juices, the vinegar and mustard. Whisk in lemon juice to taste. Stir in the mushrooms and spring onions and leave to stand for at least 30 minutes to allow the flavours to develop. Carve the turkey breast into neat slices. Arrange attractively on a large platter with the avocado slices. Drizzle the dressing over and garnish with parsley sprigs. Serve with Hot Potato Salad.

Curried Turkey and Butter Bean Salad

SERVES 4

225 g/8 oz/1 cup long-grain rice
Salt
50 g/2 oz frozen peas
30 ml/2 tbsp sultanas (golden raisins)
1 red eating (dessert) apple, chopped
10 ml/2 tsp lemon juice
225 g/8 oz/2 cups cooked turkey, diced
75 ml/5 tbsp mayonnaise
15 ml/1 tbsp curry paste
30 ml/2 tbsp peach chutney
425 g/15 oz/1 large can of butter (lima) beans, drained
1 peach, 1 tomato and a 5 cm/2 in piece of cucumber, sliced, to garnish

Cook the rice in plenty of lightly salted boiling water for 10 minutes, adding the peas after 5 minutes. Drain, rinse with cold water and drain again. Stir in the sultanas. Put the apple in a bowl and toss in the lemon juice. Add the turkey. Blend the mayonnaise with the curry paste and chutney. Stir into the turkey and apple and add the beans. Mix gently. Spoon the rice in a border on a large serving platter and spoon the curry mixture into the centre. Garnish with the peach, tomato and cucumber slices and serve.

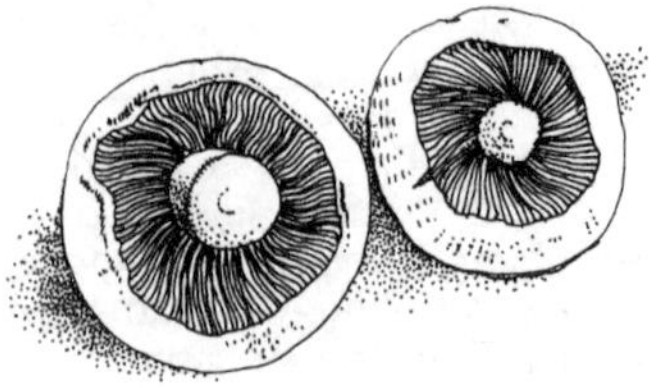

Turkey Ballantine

SERVES UP TO 20 PEOPLE

1 large onion, finely chopped
225 g/8 oz button mushrooms, finely chopped
1 large garlic clove, crushed
100 g/4 oz/½ cup butter or margarine
700 g/1½ lb pork sausagemeat
75 g/3 oz/¾ cup pistachio nuts
100 g/4 oz/2 cups fresh breadcrumbs
60 ml/4 tbsp chopped parsley
30 ml/2 tbsp chopped thyme
30 ml/2 tbsp Dijon mustard
Finely grated rind and juice of 1 lemon
Salt and freshly ground black pepper
1 egg, beaten
5.5 kg/12 lb turkey, boned (page 15)
450 g/1 lb smoked pork loin, in one piece
A selection of salads, to serve

Fry (sauté) the onion, mushrooms and garlic in half the butter or margarine for 3 minutes, stirring. Turn into a bowl and leave to cool. Work in the sausagemeat, pistachio nuts, breadcrumbs, herbs, mustard, lemon rind and juice and a little salt and pepper. Mix with the egg to bind. Lay the boned turkey on a board, skin-side down. Spread the stuffing over. Cut the pork loin in half lengthways, if necessary, and lay them down the centre of the turkey. Fold the turkey round the stuffing to completely enclose. Either sew up or secure with fine skewers. Place in a roasting tin (pan). Spread the remaining butter or margarine all over the skin. Sprinkle with salt. Roast in a preheated oven at 180°C/350°F/gas mark 4 for 2½ hours or until the juices run clear when a skewer is inserted gently. Transfer to a serving plate and leave to cool, then chill before serving in thick slices with a selection of salads.

Turkey Scotch Egg Salad

SERVES 4

225 g/8 oz turkey sausages
4 hard-boiled (hard-cooked) eggs, shelled
Plain (all-purpose) flour
1 egg, beaten
85 g/3½ oz/1 small packet of parsley, thyme and lemon stuffing mix
Oil for deep-frying
Ready-made coleslaw, to garnish
Lettuce, tomatoes, cucumber and spring onions (scallions) and made English mustard, to serve

Remove the skin from the sausages and divide the sausagemeat into four equal pieces. Flatten each piece to about 10 cm/4 in diameter rounds. Dust the eggs with flour. Wrap one in each piece of sausagemeat to cover completely. Roll in the egg, then the stuffing mix. Deep-fry in hot oil for about 4 minutes until golden brown. Drain on kitchen paper (paper towels) and leave to cool. Halve. Place on plates, garnish with a spoonful of coleslaw and serve with a salad of lettuce, tomatoes, cucumber and spring onions and English mustard handed separately.

Turkey and Cranberry Pâté Layer

SERVES 6–8

100 g/4 oz/½ cup butter or margarine
450 g/1 lb turkey or chicken livers, chopped
100 g/4 oz streaky bacon, diced
1 garlic clove, crushed
5 ml/1 tsp juniper berries, crushed
15 ml/1 tbsp port
Salt and freshly ground black pepper
100 g/4 oz/2 cups breadcrumbs
30 ml/2 tbsp chopped parsley
15 ml/1 tbsp chopped sage
1 small onion, finely chopped
2 eggs, beaten
2 turkey breast fillets, cut into neat pieces
185 g/6½ oz/1 small jar of cranberry sauce
Colourful mixed pickles, a green salad and focaccia with olives or sun-dried tomatoes, to serve

Line a 900 g/2 lb loaf tin (pan) with non-stick baking parchment. Melt the butter or margarine in a saucepan. Add the livers, bacon, garlic and juniper berries and fry (sauté), stirring, for 2 minutes. Purée in a blender or food processor with the port and season well. Mix the breadcrumbs with the herbs, onion and a little salt and pepper. Mix with the eggs to bind. Place half the turkey liver mixture in the tin. Top with half the turkey meat, then half the breadcrumb mixture. Add a layer of half the cranberry sauce, then the remaining breadcrumb mixture, then the remaining turkey meat, then, lastly the rest of the liver mixture. Cover the tin with foil, twisting and folding under the rim to secure. Stand it in a roasting tin containing 2.5 cm/1 in boiling water. Bake in a preheated oven at 180°C/350°F/gas mark 4 for 1½ hours until just set and shrinking from the sides of the tin. (Don't worry if it looks pink and moist). Remove from the oven, cover with clean foil and place two saucers on top. Weigh down with weights or cans of food. Leave until cold, then chill. Turn out on to a board, cut into slices and serve with colourful mixed pickles, a green salad and focaccia with olives or sun-dried tomatoes.

Around the World Warm Salad

SERVES 4

225 g/8 oz conchiglie pasta
225 g/8 oz French (green) beans, cut into 3 pieces
30–45 ml/2–3 tbsp Pesto for Poultry (page 342 or use bought)
4 eggs
1 Spanish onion, halved and thinly sliced
1 garlic clove, finely chopped
45 ml/3 tbsp olive oil
4 turkey rashers (slices), chopped
15 ml/1 tbsp red wine vinegar
Salt and freshly ground black pepper
100 g/4 oz/½ cup Feta cheese, crumbled

Cook the pasta according to the packet directions, adding the beans half-way through cooking. Drain and return to the saucepan. Add the pesto to taste and toss gently to coat. Poach the eggs in water for 3–5 minutes or to your liking. Drain and place in cold water to prevent further cooking. Meanwhile, fry (sauté) the onion and garlic in the oil for 3 minutes until soft but not brown. Add the turkey rashers and fry for a further 2 minutes, stirring. Add the contents of the pan to the cooked pasta and beans with the vinegar, a little salt and pepper and the cheese. Toss gently. Pile on to serving plates and top each with a poached egg. Serve straight away.

Warm Turkey Liver and Asian Pear Salad

SERVES 4

2 Asian pears
10 ml/2 tsp lemon juice
450 g/1 lb turkey livers, trimmed and cut into bite-sized pieces
90 ml/6 tbsp olive oil
15 ml/1 tbsp cider vinegar
5 ml/1 tsp wholegrain mustard
15 ml/1 tbsp whisky
5 ml/1 tsp clear honey
Salt and freshly ground black pepper
175 g/6 oz mixed salad leaves
10 ml/2 tsp chopped tarragon
Baby new potatoes, to serve

Peel, core and cut the pears into neat pieces. Toss in the lemon juice. Rinse the turkey livers and pat dry on kitchen paper (paper towels). Heat half the oil in a large frying pan (skillet). Fry (sauté) the turkey livers for 4–5 minutes, tossing gently, until cooked but still soft and slightly pink. Remove from the pan. Stir the remaining oil, the vinegar, mustard, whisky and honey into the juices in the pan and season to taste with salt and pepper. Pile the salad leaves and pear pieces on to four serving plates. Return the livers to the pan and toss gently to heat through. Spoon on top of the salad and sprinkle with the tarragon. Serve straight away with baby new potatoes.

DUCK

Nutty Apricot and Duck Cooler

SERVES 4

175 g/6 oz pasta shapes
100 g/4 oz/⅔ cup ready-to-eat dried apricots, quartered
50 g/2 oz/½ cup pine nuts
12 stoned (pitted) black olives, halved
1 cucumber, diced
175 g/6 oz/1½ cups cooked duck, diced
150 ml/¼ pt/⅔ cup soured (dairy sour) cream
Grated rind and juice of 1 lime
15 ml/1 tbsp clear honey
Salt and freshly ground black pepper
15 ml/1 tbsp snipped chives
Curly endive (frisée lettuce) leaves
Cayenne

Cook the pasta according to the packet directions. Drain, rinse with cold water and drain again. Place in a bowl and add the apricots, pine nuts, olives, cucumber and duck. Blend the cream with the lime rind and juice, honey, a little salt and pepper and the chives. Mix thoroughly, then pour over the salad and toss well. Chill for at least 1 hour to allow the flavours to develop, then pile on to a bed of curly endive and sprinkle with cayenne before serving.

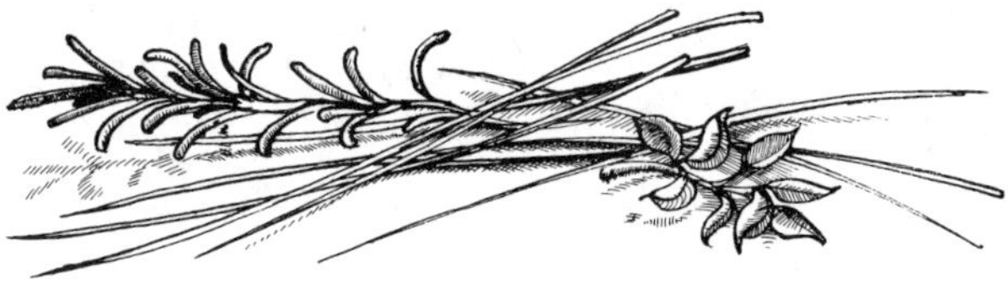

Tangy Duck, Watercress and Orange Salad

SERVES 4

450 g/1 lb new potatoes, boiled
225 g/8 oz/2 cups cooked duck, diced
2 bunches of watercress
2 oranges
20 ml/4 tsp snipped chives
45 ml/3 tbsp olive oil
15 ml/1 tbsp lemon juice
Grated rind of ½ lemon
10 ml/2 tsp clear honey
2.5 ml/½ tsp Dijon mustard
Salt and freshly ground black pepper

Place the potatoes and duck in a serving bowl. Trim the watercress and separate into small sprigs. Add to the bowl. Holding the oranges over the bowl to catch the juice, pare off all the rind and pith and separate the flesh into segments. Add to the bowl and squeeze over any juice left in the membranes. Add the chives. Mix together the oil, lemon juice, lemon rind, honey, mustard and a little salt and pepper until thoroughly blended. Pour over the salad and toss well before serving.

Saffron Rice and Duck Salad

SERVES 4

225 g/8 oz/1 cup long-grain rice
225 g/8 oz frozen peas
2 carrots, roughly chopped
2 courgettes (zucchini), roughly chopped
1.5 ml/¼ tsp saffron powder
25 ml/1½ tbsp olive oil
Salt and freshly ground black pepper
60 ml/4 tbsp mayonnaise
60 ml/4 tbsp Apple Sauce (page 340 or use bought)
225 g/8 oz/2 cups cooked duck, diced
Fresh basil leaves

Cook the rice in plenty of boiling salted water for 12 minutes, adding the peas, carrots and courgettes half-way through cooking. Drain, rinse with cold water and drain again. Stir in the saffron and olive oil and season to taste. Pack into a lightly oiled ring mould and chill for at least 1 hour. Turn out on to a serving plate. Mix together the mayonnaise, Apple Sauce and duck and season to taste. Spoon the mayonnaise mixture into the centre of the rice and scatter with torn basil leaves before serving.

Chilled Tomato and Cardamom Rice with Duck

SERVES 4

15 ml/1 tbsp sunflower oil
6 cardamom pods, split
5 ml/1 tsp cumin seeds
225 g/8 oz/1 cup basmati rice
45 ml/3 tbsp tomato juice
15 ml/1 tbsp tomato purée (paste)
1.5 ml/¼ tsp salt
Grated rind and juice of 1 orange
Approx. 600 ml/1 pt/2½ cups water
175 g/6 oz /1½ cups cooked duck, cut into neat pieces
4 tomatoes, cut into wedges
1 orange, cut into small wedges

Heat the oil in a pan. Add the cardamom and cumin and fry (sauté), stirring, until the seeds pop. Stir in the rice, tomato juice, purée, salt and orange rind and juice. Pour over enough water to cover by 2.5 cm/1 in. Bring to the boil, reduce the heat, cover and simmer gently for 20 minutes or until the rice is tender and has absorbed all the liquid. Allow to cool. Mix in the duck, then chill. Pile on to a serving dish and garnish with tomato and orange wedges before serving.

Speciality Duck Platter

SERVES 8

1.75 kg/4 lb oven-ready duck, boned (page 15)
1.25 kg/2½ lb oven-ready chicken, boned (page 15)
For the stuffing:
100 g/4 oz/2 cups breadcrumbs
Grated rind and juice of 1 orange
45 ml/3 tbsp redcurrant jelly (clear conserve)
15 ml/1 tbsp chopped thyme
15 ml/1 tbsp chopped parsley
100 g/4 oz/1 cup pine nuts
1 egg, beaten
Salt and freshly ground black pepper
2 large carrots, coarsely grated
15 ml/1 tbsp olive oil
For the potato salad:
900 g/2 lb baby new potatoes
30 ml/2 tbsp mayonnaise
30 ml/2 tbsp plain yoghurt
5 ml/1 tsp grated onion
Orange slices and thyme sprigs, to garnish
Chicory (Belgian endive), watercress and fresh, stoned (pitted) cherries tossed in French dressing, to serve

Mix together the stuffing ingredients except the carrots, seasoning well. Lay the duck skin-side down on a board. Carefully remove the skin from the chicken. Lay the chicken on top of the duck with the leg meat at opposite ends from the duck leg meat. Season. Spread half the stuffing down the length of the chicken and cover with the grated carrot. Top with the remaining stuffing. Wrap up the duck over the stuffing, tucking in the ends and overlapping along its back to form a neat parcel. Sew up with a trussing needle and string or secure firmly with cocktail sticks (toothpicks). Weigh and calculate the cooking time, allowing 25 minutes per 450 g/1 lb. Place in a roasting tin (pan). Brush with the olive oil and sprinkle with salt. Roast in a preheated oven at 190°C/375°F/gas mark 5 for the calculated time. Remove from the tin and leave to cool. Remove the string or cocktail sticks and wrap in foil. Chill until ready to serve.

Meanwhile, cook the potatoes in lightly salted boiling water until tender. Drain. While still warm, mix in the mayonnaise, yoghurt and onion and season to taste with salt and pepper. Carve the stuffed duck into thick slices. Pile the potatoes in the centre of a large platter and arrange the duck slices around. Garnish with orange slices and thyme sprigs and serve with a dressed salad of chicory, watercress and cherries.

Spiced Duck with Lime and Potato Salad

SERVES 4

1.75 kg/4 lb oven-ready duck
2 limes
Salt and freshly ground black pepper
450 g/1 lb baby new potatoes, scrubbed
30 ml/2 tbsp sunflower oil
15 ml/1 tbsp red wine vinegar
15 ml/1 tbsp lime marmalade
5 ml/1 tsp garam masala
1 bunch of watercress, trimmed

Prick the duck all over with a fork. Place in a roasting tin (pan). Cut one of the limes in half and place inside the bird. Sprinkle the skin with salt and pepper. Roast in a preheated oven at 180°C/350°F/gas mark 4 for 2 hours or until a rich brown and very tender. Meanwhile, cook the potatoes in lightly salted water for about 10 minutes or until tender but still holding their shape. Drain and keep warm. When the duck is cooked, remove from the tin and cut off the breast skin and reserve. Remove all the meat from the carcass and shred by pulling apart with two forks. Keep warm. Place the skin under a preheated grill (broiler) and grill (broil) until crisp. Drain on kitchen paper (paper towels) and cut into strips. Pour off all but 15 ml/1 tbsp of the fat in the roasting tin. Stir in the oil, vinegar, marmalade and garam masala and heat until the marmalade dissolves. Taste and re-season. Cut the remaining lime into eight wedges. Place the watercress on four serving plates and top with the potatoes. Pile the duck on top and spoon the warm dressing over. Top with the strips of duck skin and serve warm, garnished with the lime wedges.

GAME

Partridge and Pear Salad

SERVES 4

2 oven-ready partridges
1 lemon, halved
Salt and freshly ground black pepper
30 ml/2 tbsp quince or redcurrant jelly (clear conserve)
6 unsmoked, fat streaky bacon rashers (slices)
400 g/14 oz/1 large can of vine leaves
300 ml/½ pt/1¼ cups medium-sweet cider
2 chicken stock cubes
3 ripe pears
1 bunch of watercress, trimmed
½ round lettuce, separated into leaves and torn
1 bunch of spring onions (scallions), finely chopped
45 ml/3 tbsp olive oil
15 ml/1 tbsp cider vinegar
30 ml/2 tbsp apple juice
5 ml/1 tsp Dijon mustard
100 g/4 oz cherry tomatoes
New potatoes and quince or redcurrant jelly, to serve

Wash the partridges and dry well with kitchen paper (paper towels). Push half a lemon inside each and a spoonful of quince or redcurrant jelly. Season with salt and pepper. Wrap the bacon round each bird, then wrap completely in vine leaves. Tie securely with string. Place in a large saucepan and add the cider. Add just enough water to cover the birds and crumble in the stock cubes. Bring to the boil, reduce the heat, cover and simmer very gently for 1½ hours. Lift the birds out of the cooking liquid and immediately plunge into iced water to cool quickly.

When completely cold, remove from the water, dry thoroughly on kitchen paper and unwrap. Cut each bird in half. Peel the pears, halve, remove the cores and slice neatly. Arrange the watercress and torn lettuce leaves on a large platter and lay the partridges on top. Arrange the pear slices attractively around and scatter with the spring onions. Whisk together the remaining ingredients and drizzle over the salad. Serve with new potatoes and quince or redcurrant jelly.

Pheasant and Five Bean Salad

SERVES 4

100 g/4 oz frozen broad (fava) beans
100 g/4 oz French (green) beans, each cut into 3 pieces
425 g/15 oz/1 large can of red kidney beans, rinsed and drained
425 g/15 oz/1 large can of butter (lima) beans, rinsed and drained
425 g/15 oz/1 large can of flageolet beans, rinsed and drained
175 g/6 oz/1½ cups cooked pheasant meat
1 small red onion, finely chopped
1 garlic clove, crushed
45 ml/3 tbsp sunflower oil
15 ml/1 tbsp red wine vinegar
10 ml/2 tsp balsamic vinegar
5 ml/1 tsp caster (superfine) sugar
Salt and freshly ground black pepper
2 hard-boiled (hard-cooked) eggs, cut into wedges
A small sprig of parsley, to garnish

Cook the broad and French beans together in lightly salted water for 5 minutes. Drain, rinse with cold water and drain again. Place in a bowl with the canned beans and the pheasant. Add all but 5 ml/1 tsp of the onion. Whisk the garlic with the oil, vinegars, sugar and some salt and pepper. Pour over the salad and toss gently. Pile into a large salad bowl and arrange the egg wedges in a starburst pattern on top. Put the remaining onion in the centre. Add the sprig of parsley and chill for 30 minutes, if time, before serving.

Dutch Rice Ring

SERVES 4

175 g/6 oz/¾ cup long-grain rice
100 g/4 oz/1 cup frozen diced mixed vegetables
30 ml/2 tbsp olive oil
15 ml/1 tbsp white wine vinegar
Salt and freshly ground black pepper
A pinch of grated nutmeg
2 ripe pears, diced
100 g/4 oz Edam cheese, diced
100 g/4 oz/1 cup cooked pheasant or other game bird, diced
1 head of Florence fennel, chopped, reserving the green fronds
45 ml/3 tbsp plain yoghurt
15 ml/1 tbsp snipped chives

Cook the rice and mixed vegetables in plenty of boiling salted water for 10 minutes. Drain, rinse with cold water and drain again. Whisk together the oil, vinegar, a little salt and pepper and the nutmeg and pour over the rice. Toss well. Spoon the mixture into an oiled 1.5 litre/2½ pt/6 cup ring mould. Press down well and chill while preparing the filling. Mix the pears, cheese, pheasant, fennel and yoghurt with a little salt and pepper and the chives. Turn out the rice ring on to a serving plate. Spoon the cheese filling into the middle and garnish with the fennel fronds.

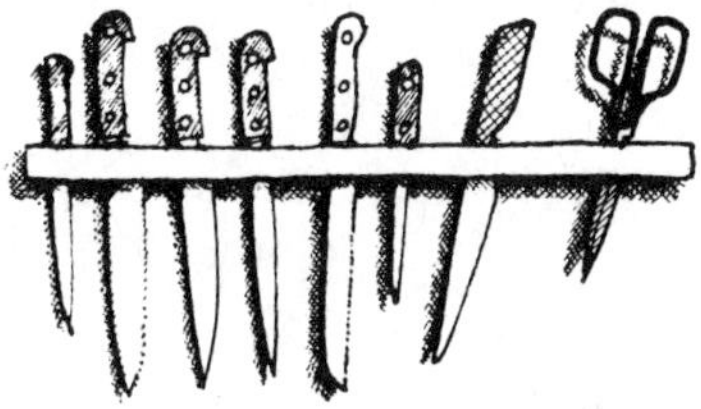

Partridge with Bresaola in Vine Leaves with Waldorf Salad

Use vacuum-packed, canned or fresh, blanched vine leaves for this dish. The stock can be used for soup or other game recipes.

SERVES 4

4 small oven-ready partridge
4 slices of bresaola (raw, cured beef)
Salt and freshly ground black pepper
8 large vine leaves
1 chicken stock cube
1 red eating (dessert) apple
1 green eating apple
15 ml/1 tbsp lemon juice
3 celery sticks, chopped
½ white cabbage, finely shredded
25 g/1 oz/2 tbsp walnut halves
30 ml/2 tbsp sultanas (golden raisins)
45 ml/3 tbsp mayonnaise
15 ml/1 tbsp olive oil
30 ml/2 tbsp snipped chives

Wipe the birds inside and out with kitchen paper (paper towels). Lay a slice of bresaola over the breast of each and season with salt and pepper. Wrap a vine leaf securely round each and tie well with string. Pack in a single layer in a large flameproof casserole (Dutch oven). Pour over enough water to cover and add the stock cube. Bring to the boil, cover, reduce the heat and simmer for 35 minutes. Remove from the heat and leave to cool in the liquid. Meanwhile, core and chop the apples but do not peel. Place in a bowl and add the lemon juice. Toss. Mix in the celery, cabbage, walnuts and sultanas. Blend the mayonnaise with the olive oil and stir in to coat completely. Lift the partridge out of the cold stock and drain on kitchen paper. Remove the string. Transfer to serving plates. Put a pile of Waldorf Salad to one side and sprinkle with the chives to garnish.

Edwardian Rum Partridge with Grape, Lettuce and Watercress Salad

SERVES 4

4 small partridge, freshly roasted (page 145) and quartered (page 17)
150 ml/¼ pt/⅔ cup dark rum
Juice of ½ lemon
2 little gem lettuces
1 bunch of watercress
45 ml/3 tbsp olive oil
15 ml/1 tbsp white wine vinegar
5 ml/1 tsp Dijon mustard
30 ml/2 tbsp chopped parsley
A good pinch of caster (superfine) sugar
A good pinch of salt
A good pinch of freshly ground black pepper
100 g/4 oz seedless black grapes, halved
Hot Potato Salad (page 350), to serve

Place the quartered, roasted birds in a casserole dish (Dutch oven) while still hot and pour the rum over. Cover and leave until cold, turning occasionally. Chill in the fridge overnight. Turn occasionally until ready to serve. Separate the lettuces into leaves and tear into small pieces. Trim the stalks off the watercress and separate into small sprigs. Place in a bowl. Whisk together the oil, vinegar, mustard and parsley and season with the sugar, salt and pepper. Pour over the lettuce mixture and toss well. Pile on to serving plates and scatter with the grapes. Drain the partridge on kitchen paper (paper towels) and arrange over the salads. Serve with Hot Potato Salad.

Valencian Pheasant

SERVES 4

1 oven-ready pheasant
25 g/1 oz/2 tbsp butter or margarine
Salt and freshly ground black pepper
1 bunch of spring onions (scallions), chopped
2 celery sticks, sliced
90 ml/6 tbsp olive oil
45 ml/3 tbsp red wine vinegar
2.5 ml/½ tsp dried rosemary, crushed
4 oranges
1 round lettuce
16 stoned (pitted) black olives
Hot Potato Salad (page 350), to serve

Wipe the bird inside and out with kitchen paper (paper towels). Place in a roasting tin (pan). Smear with the butter or margarine and season with salt and pepper. Roast in a preheated oven at 190°C/ 375°F/gas mark 5 for 1 hour. Remove from the oven and leave until cold. Carve the cold bird and place in a shallow dish. Sprinkle with the onions and celery. Whisk together the oil, vinegar, rosemary and some salt and pepper. Spoon about half over the pheasant and leave to marinate for 1 hour. Cut all the peel and pith off the oranges and slice the flesh. Lay the lettuce leaves on a large platter and arrange the pheasant attractively on top. Place the orange slices all round the edge of the dish and garnish with the olives. Spoon the remaining dressing over the oranges and serve with Hot Potato Salad.

Sauces

This chapter embraces every sauce, relish or savoury butter you could ever wish for to accompany your poultry and game.

GRAVIES

Giblet Gravy

You can increase the quantity of flour and add vegetable cooking water as well to make a larger quantity of gravy.

MAKES 450 ML/¾ PT/2 CUPS

Giblets from the bird being roasted
1 onion
1 clove
1 small bay leaf
600 ml/1 pt/2½ cups water
45 ml/3 tbsp plain (all-purpose) flour
Gravy block or browning
Salt and freshly ground black pepper

Put the giblets in a saucepan with the onion, clove, bay leaf and water. Bring to the boil, reduce the heat, cover and simmer gently for 1 hour. Strain. When the bird is cooked, spoon off all but 15 ml/1 tbsp of the fat from the roasting tin (pan) but leave all the juices. Blend in the flour and cook over a moderate heat for 1 minute, stirring. Remove from the heat and gradually blend in the stock. Return to the heat, bring to the boil and cook for 2 minutes, stirring. Add gravy block or browning as required and season to taste with salt and pepper. Pour into a warm gravy boat and serve hot.

Vegetable Water Gravy

Fresh birds may not have any giblets, so use this gravy instead. You can increase the quantity of flour and water to make more gravy. If you run out of vegetable water, use chicken or vegetable stock: 1 stock cube to every 300–450 ml/½–¾ pt/1¼–2 cups water.

MAKES 450 ML/¾ PT/2 CUPS

45 ml/3 tbsp plain (all-purpose) flour
450 ml/¾ pt/2 cups vegetable cooking water (some from each of the vegetables cooked to serve with the meal)
Gravy block or browning
Salt and freshly ground black pepper

Spoon off all but 15 ml/1 tbsp of the fat from the roasting tin (pan) but leave all the juices. Stir in the flour and cook on top of the stove for 1 minute. Remove from the heat and gradually blend in the vegetable water. Return to the heat, bring to the boil and cook for 2 minutes, stirring. Add gravy block or browning to taste and season well. Pour into a warm gravy boat and serve hot.

Orange Gravy

SERVES 4

1 small onion, finely chopped
15 g/½ oz/1 tbsp butter or margarine
5 ml/1 tsp light brown sugar
Thinly pared rind and juice of 1 orange
200 ml/⅓ pt/scant 1 cup chicken or game stock
60 ml/4 tbsp port
Salt and freshly ground black pepper
5 ml/1 tsp cornflour (cornstarch)
10 ml/2 tsp water

Fry (sauté) the onion in the butter or margarine for about 5 minutes until richly browned, adding the sugar after 3 minutes. Add the orange rind and juice and the stock. Bring to the boil, cover and simmer gently for 10 minutes. Remove the orange rind. Stir in the port and season to taste. Blend the cornflour with the water and stir in. Bring to the boil and simmer for 1 minute. Strain into a sauceboat and serve.

SAUCES

Piazzaiola Sauce

Ideal with chicken burgers or any grilled (broiled) or fried (sautéed) poultry or game.

SERVES 4–6

2 onions, finely chopped
2 garlic cloves, crushed
1 green (bell) pepper, diced
1 red pepper, diced
15 ml/1 tbsp olive oil
50 g/2 oz button mushrooms, chopped
400 g/14 oz/1 large can of chopped tomatoes
15 ml/1 tbsp tomato purée (paste)
Tabasco sauce
5 ml/1 tsp dried oregano
Salt and freshly ground black pepper

Put the onions, garlic and peppers in a saucepan with the oil. Cook gently, stirring, for about 5 minutes until lightly golden. Add the mushrooms and stir for 1 minute. Add the tomatoes and purée. Simmer for 10 minutes until pulpy and the vegetables are tender. Season well with Tabasco sauce and add the oregano and a little salt and pepper. Use as required.

Espagnole Sauce

SERVES 4

1 onion, roughly chopped
1 celery stick, chopped
1 carrot, chopped
1 bacon rasher (slice), cut up
15 g/½ oz/1 tbsp butter or margarine
10 ml/2 tsp sunflower oil
25 g/1 oz/¼ cup plain (all-purpose) flour
450 ml/¾ pt/2 cups chicken stock
10 ml/2 tsp tomato purée (paste)
1 bouquet garni sachet
Gravy block or browning
Salt and freshly ground black pepper

Cook the onion, celery, carrot and bacon in the butter or margarine and oil gently for about 8 minutes, stirring, until well browned. Add the flour and cook, stirring, for 1 minute. Remove from the heat and blend in the stock. Bring to the boil, stirring, until thickened. Stir in the tomato purée and add the bouquet garni sachet. Cover and simmer gently for 30 minutes. Strain the sauce and return to the pan. Add a little gravy block or browning if necessary to give a good, rich colour, then season to taste. Use as required.

Bigarde Sauce

SERVES 4–6

1 quantity of Espagnole Sauce
Thinly pared rind and juice of 1 Seville or sweet orange
15 ml/1 tbsp lemon juice
30 ml/2 tbsp port

Prepare and strain the Espagnole Sauce. Return to the saucepan. Meanwhile, cut the orange rind into very thin strips and boil in water for 5 minutes. Drain. Add to the sauce with the strained orange juice, the lemon juice and port. Reheat thoroughly.

Barbecue Sauce

SERVES 4–6

1 garlic clove, crushed
1 small onion, very finely chopped
10 ml/2 tsp sunflower oil
100 g/4 oz tomato purée (paste)
300 ml/½ pt/1¼ cups fruity, dry white wine
10 ml/2 tsp soy sauce
30 ml/2 tbsp clear honey
30 ml/2 tbsp white wine vinegar
A few drops of Tabasco sauce
Salt and freshly ground black pepper

Put the garlic, onion and oil in a small saucepan. Cook for 2 minutes, stirring, until the onion is softened. Add the remaining ingredients, bring to the boil, reduce the heat and simmer for about 20 minutes until thick. Taste and re-season if necessary. Serve with any grilled (broiled) or barbecued meats, fish or vegetables.

Peanut Sauce

SERVES 4

100 ml/3½ fl oz/scant ½ cup water
3 spring onions (scallions), finely chopped
225 g/8 oz/1 cup crunchy peanut butter
15 ml/1 tbsp clear honey
30 ml/2 tbsp soy sauce
A few drops of Tabasco sauce

Put the water in a small saucepan with 2 of the spring onions. Bring to the boil and simmer for 3 minutes. Stir in the peanut butter, honey, soy sauce and Tabasco sauce to taste. Stir until smooth. Thin with a little more water, if necessary. Spoon into a small bowl and sprinkle with the remaining spring onion.

Orange and Mango Salsa

SERVES 4–6

1 large just-ripe mango
4–6 spring onions (scallions), finely chopped
2 oranges
1 small red chilli, seeded and chopped
15 ml/1 tbsp chopped mint
2.5 ml/½ tsp grated fresh root ginger
A pinch of salt
Freshly ground black pepper
5 ml/1 tsp lemon juice

Peel the mango and cut all the fruit off the stone (pit). Cut into small dice and place in a bowl. Add the spring onions. Finely grate the rind from one of the oranges. Cut off all the peel and pith from both. Slice the fruit, then cut into small pieces. Add to the mango and onion. Add the remaining ingredients and mix well. Cover and chill for at least 1 hour to allow the flavours to develop.

Orange and Pineapple Salsa

SERVES 4

Prepare as for Orange and Mango Salsa, but use 300 g/11 oz/1 medium can of crushed pineapple, well drained, instead of the mango.

Brown Onion Salsa

SERVES 4–6

450 g/1 lb onions, chopped
25 g/1 oz/2 tbsp butter or margarine
30 ml/2 tbsp light brown sugar
Salt and freshly ground black pepper

Cook the onions in the butter or margarine, stirring, for 5 minutes until softened. Add the sugar, turn up the heat and continue cooking until a rich golden brown, stirring frequently. Purée in a blender or food processor and season to taste. Reheat gently, if liked.

Dark Soy Dipping Sauce

SERVES 4

60 ml/4 tbsp dark soy sauce
30 ml/2 tbsp medium-dry sherry
1 sliver of garlic
30 ml/2 tbsp light brown sugar
120 ml/4 fl oz/½ cup chicken stock
20 ml/1½ tbsp cornflour (cornstarch)
30 ml/2 tbsp water

Put the soy sauce, sherry, garlic, sugar and stock in a saucepan. Blend the cornflour with the water and stir in. Bring to the boil, stirring, until slightly thickened. Turn into a small bowl and leave to cool. Discard the garlic. Chill until required.

Light Soy Dipping Sauce

SERVES 4

30 ml/2 tbsp soy sauce
60 ml/4 tbsp pale dry sherry
20 ml/4 tsp caster (superfine) sugar
1 thin sliver of fresh root ginger
10 ml/2 tsp cornflour (cornstarch)
30 ml/2 tbsp water

Put the soy sauce, sherry and sugar in a saucepan. Add the ginger. Blend the cornflour with the water and stir in. Bring to the boil, stirring, until thickened. Pour into a small bowl and leave to cool. Discard the ginger. Chill until required.

Sweet and Sour Dipping Sauce

SERVES 4

30 ml/2 tbsp soy sauce
45 ml/3 tbsp tomato ketchup (catsup)
90 ml/6 tbsp clear honey
60 ml/4 tbsp malt vinegar
60 ml/4 tbsp pineapple juice
60 ml/4 tbsp orange juice
30 ml/2 tbsp cornflour (cornstarch)
30 ml/2 tbsp water

Blend together the soy sauce, ketchup, honey, vinegar and fruit juices. Blend the cornflour with the water and stir in. Bring to the boil and cook for 1 minute until thickened and clear. Serve hot.

Chinese Chilli Dipping Sauce

For a hotter sauce, add more chilli powder or a few drops of Tabasco sauce.

SERVES 4

2 spring onions (scallions), finely chopped
10 ml/2 tsp grated fresh root ginger
1 garlic clove, crushed
60 ml/4 tbsp medium-dry sherry
20 ml/4 tsp caster (superfine) sugar
30 ml/2 tbsp tomato purée (paste)
2.5 ml/½ tsp chilli powder
A good pinch of Chinese five spice powder
60 ml/4 tbsp chicken stock
10 ml/2 tsp cornflour (cornstarch)
15 ml/1 tbsp water

Mix together all the ingredients except the cornflour and water in a saucepan. Blend the cornflour with the water and stir in. Bring to the boil and cook for 1 minute, stirring. Leave until cold, then use as required.

Tomato Dipping Sauce

SERVES 4

90 ml/6 tbsp red wine vinegar
45 ml/3 tbsp tomato ketchup (catsup)
15 ml/1 tbsp tomato purée (paste)
90 ml/6 tbsp caster (superfine) sugar
5 ml/1 tsp soy sauce
10 ml/2 tsp cornflour (cornstarch)
15 ml/1 tbsp water

Put the vinegar, ketchup, tomato purée, sugar and soy sauce in a saucepan. Stir until the sugar has dissolved. Blend the cornflour with the water and stir in. Bring to the boil and cook for 1 minute, stirring. Leave to cool and use as required.

Chinese Curry Sauce

SERVES 4

30 ml/2 tbsp curry powder
2.5 ml/½ tsp Chinese five spice powder
2 onions, grated
1 garlic clove, crushed
30 ml/2 tbsp sunflower oil
10 ml/2 tsp caster (superfine) sugar
120 ml/4 fl oz/½ cup chicken stock
Salt

Fry (sauté) the curry powder and five spice powder with the onions and garlic in the oil for 4 minutes, stirring. Add the sugar and stock. Bring to the boil, reduce the heat and simmer gently for about 10 minutes until slightly thickened. Season to taste with salt. Use as required.

Fresh Sweet Chutney

This is good with curries and all cold poultry and game. It will keep in a sealed container in the fridge for up to 2 weeks.

SERVES 4–6

1 large cooking (tart) apple, quartered
1 small onion, quartered
1 red (bell) pepper, quartered
1 beefsteak tomato, skinned and seeded
2 celery sticks, cut into chunks
30 ml/2 tbsp sultanas (golden raisins)
5 ml/1 tsp grated fresh root ginger
15 ml/1 tbsp chopped mint
15 ml/1 tbsp light brown sugar
30 ml/2 tbsp cider vinegar
5 ml/1 tsp salt
1 garlic clove, crushed

Put the apple, onion, pepper, tomato and celery in a food processor and chop finely (or do it by hand if necessary). Place in a saucepan with the remaining ingredients. Bring to the boil and cook for 3 minutes, stirring. Turn into a bowl and leave to cool, then chill.

Guacamole Relish

SERVES 6

2 large ripe avocados
15 ml/1 tbsp lemon juice
1 shallot, grated
90 ml/6 tbsp sunflower oil
15 ml/1 tbsp Worcestershire sauce
A few drops of Tabasco sauce
2 tomatoes, seeded and finely chopped
2.5 cm/1 in piece cucumber, finely chopped

Halve the avocados, remove the stones (pits) and scoop the flesh out of the skins into a bowl. Mash well with a fork, then mash in the lemon juice and shallot. Gradually beat in the oil, a few drops at a time, until thick and fairly smooth. (If the mixture curdles, gradually beat it into 30 ml/2 tbsp mayonnaise.) Flavour to taste with the Worcestershire sauce and Tabasco sauce. Fold in the tomato and cucumber just before serving.

Brinjals

Ideal with all the dishes in the curry chapter (pages 286–302) or any spiced dish.

SERVES 4–6

1 large aubergine (eggplant)
1 onion
1 green chilli, seeded and chopped
Salt
Caster (superfine) sugar
Juice of 1 small lemon

Cut the stalk off the aubergine, then cook whole in boiling water for about 10 minutes or until tender. Drain, rinse with cold water and drain again. Cut in half and scoop out the softened pulp into a bowl. Cut a few thin rings off the onion and reserve for garnish, then finely chop the remainder. Beat into the aubergine with the chilli. Season to taste with salt, sugar and lemon juice. Turn into a small serving dish and arrange the onion rings on top to garnish. Chill until ready to serve.

Minted Yoghurt and Cucumber

Serve this with curries (as raita) or as a dip (like tzaziki).

SERVES 4

½ cucumber, finely chopped or coarsely grated
15 ml/1 tbsp dried mint
1 small garlic clove, crushed (optional)
150 ml/¼ pt/⅔ cup thick plain yoghurt
Salt and freshly ground black pepper

Gently squeeze the cucumber to remove excess moisture. Place in a bowl. Add the mint, garlic, if using, and the yoghurt and mix well. Season to taste and leave to stand for at least 30 minutes to allow the flavours to develop.

Rouille

SERVES 4–6

1 red chilli, seeded and chopped
1 red (bell) pepper, chopped
2 large garlic cloves, crushed
1 slice of white bread, crusts removed
1 egg yolk
Salt and white pepper
75 ml/5 tbsp sunflower oil
75 ml/5 tbsp olive oil

Put the chilli, red pepper, garlic, bread and egg yolk in a blender. Add a sprinkling of salt and pepper. Run the machine until smooth, stopping and scraping down the sides as necessary. With the machine running, add the oils in a thin trickle until the mixture is thick and glossy like mayonnaise. Taste and re-season if necessary. Turn into a small bowl, cover with clingfilm (plastic wrap) and chill until required. Serve with soups and grilled birds.

Caviare Cream

SERVES 4–6

150 ml/¼ pt/⅔ cup crème fraîche
5 ml/1 tsp finely grated lemon rind
15 ml/1 tbsp chopped dill (dill weed)
50 g/2 oz/1 small jar of Danish lumpfish roe, chilled
Freshly ground black pepper

Put the crème fraîche in a small bowl with the lemon rind and dill. Chill. Just before serving, fold in the lumpfish roe and season with pepper. Serve with all types of plain grilled (broiled) or fried (sautéed) poultry or game.

Bread Sauce

SERVES 4

1 onion, peeled but left whole
1 clove
75 g/3 oz/1½ cups soft white breadcrumbs
1.5 ml/¼ tsp grated nutmeg
Salt and white pepper
Milk

Stud the onion with the clove. Place in a small ovenproof dish with the breadcrumbs. Add the nutmeg and some salt and pepper. Just-cover the breadcrumbs with milk. Cover and place in the oven with any roast poultry or game and cook for about 40 minutes. Remove the onion and beat with a fork to make a thick sauce. Serve hot.

Cranberry Sauce

SERVES 6

100 g/4 oz/½ cup granulated sugar
Finely grated rind and juice of 1 orange
225 g/8 oz cranberries

Put the sugar in a saucepan. Measure the orange juice and make up to 150 ml/¼ pt/⅔ cup with water, if necessary. Add to the sugar and heat gently, stirring, until the sugar dissolves. Add the cranberries and bring to the boil, reduce the heat and simmer gently for about 5 minutes until the cranberries pop. Skim the surface if necessary, then stir in the orange rind. Cool.

Cumberland Sauce

SERVES 4–6

1 orange
1 lemon
5 ml/1 tsp grated onion
60 ml/4 tbsp redcurrant jelly (clear conserve)
120 ml/4 fl oz/½ cup port
5 ml/1 tsp Dijon mustard
A pinch of ground ginger
Salt and freshly ground black pepper

Thinly pare the rind from the orange and lemon and cut into very thin strips. Boil in water for 3 minutes. Drain, rinse with cold water and drain again. Squeeze the juice from the orange and lemon. Put the onion, redcurrant jelly and port in a saucepan and heat until the jelly melts. Add the juices, rinds, mustard and ginger and season to taste. Simmer for 4 minutes, then pour into a sauceboat and serve hot or cold.

Apple Sauce

SERVES 4–6

450 g/1 lb cooking (tart) apples, peeled, cored and sliced
15 ml/1 tbsp caster (superfine) sugar
30 ml/2 tbsp water
25 g/1 oz/2 tbsp butter or margarine

Put the apples in a saucepan with the sugar and water. Cover and cook gently until the fruit is pulpy, stirring, occasionally. Beat in the butter or margarine, turn into a sauceboat and serve warm.

Gooseberry Sauce

SERVES 4–6

Prepare as for Apple Sauce, but substitute gooseberries, topped and tailed, for the apples and add a pinch of grated nutmeg to the mixture.

Basic Quick White Sauce

SERVES 4

20 g/¾ oz/3 tbsp plain (all-purpose) flour
300 ml/½ pt/1¼ cups milk
20 g/¾ oz/1½ tbsp butter or margarine
Salt and white pepper

Put the flour in a saucepan and gradually blend in the milk. Add the butter or margarine. Bring to the boil and cook for 2 minutes, stirring all the time, until thickened and smooth. Season to taste and use as required.

Quick Béchamel Sauce

SERVES 4

Prepare as for Basic Quick White Sauce, but add a bay leaf and half an onion to the mixture before cooking. Remove before use.

Velouté Sauce

SERVES 4

Prepare as for Basic Quick White Sauce, but use chicken stock instead of milk and add 15 ml/1 tbsp single (light) cream before serving.

Mushroom Sauce

SERVES 4

Prepare either the Basic Quick White Sauce or the Quick Béchamel Sauce. In a separate pan, gently fry (sauté) 50 g/2 oz sliced or chopped button mushrooms for 2 minutes until softened. Stir into the cooked sauce and spike with a little lemon juice.

Mustard Sauce

SERVES 4

Prepare either the Basic Quick White Sauce or the Quick Béchamel Sauce. Add 15 ml/1 tbsp made English mustard, 15 ml/1 tbsp light brown sugar and 30 ml/2 tbsp malt vinegar to the sauce. Heat through before serving.

Parsley Sauce

SERVES 4

Prepare either the Basic Quick White Sauce or the Quick Béchamel Sauce. Stir in 30 ml/2 tbsp chopped parsley.

Cheese Sauce

SERVES 4

Prepare either the Basic Quick White Sauce or the Quick Béchamel Sauce. Stir in 2.5 ml/½ tsp made English mustard and 50 g/2 oz/½ cup grated Cheddar cheese and heat until melted.

Green Sauce

SERVES 4

Prepare either the Basic Quick White Sauce or the Quick Béchamel Sauce. Add 225 g/8 oz chopped cooked spinach and a good pinch of nutmeg and heat through before serving.

Caper Sauce

SERVES 4

Prepare either the Basic Quick White Sauce or the Quick Béchamel Sauce. Stir in 30 ml/2 tbsp chopped capers and 15 ml/1 tbsp vinegar from the jar. Heat through before serving.

Aurora Sauce

SERVES 4

Prepare as for Velouté Sauce, but stir in 15 ml/1 tbsp tomato purée (paste) and whisk in 25 g/1 oz/2 tbsp butter or margarine, in small pieces, until thickened and smooth.

Supreme Sauce

SERVES 4

Prepare as for Velouté Sauce, but omit the cream and whisk in 1 egg yolk and 15 g/½ oz/1 tbsp butter or margarine. Heat until thickened but do not boil.

Polish Sauce

SERVES 4

Prepare as for Velouté Sauce, but stir in 1 finely chopped onion, softened in 15 g/½ oz/1 tbsp butter or margarine, 15 ml/1 tbsp paprika and 5 ml/1 tsp white wine vinegar. Sprinkle the cooked sauce with a few caraway seeds before serving.

Chantilly Sauce

SERVES 4

Prepare as for Velouté Sauce, but fold in 150 ml/¼ pt/⅔ cup whipped cream until creamy and fluffy and serve straight away.

Onion Sauce

SERVES 4

Stew 2 chopped onions in 60 ml/4 tbsp of water in a covered pan until tender. Stir into Basic White Sauce.

Tomato Sauce

SERVES 4

1 onion, chopped
15 ml/1 tbsp olive oil
400 g/14 oz/1 large can of chopped tomatoes
15 ml/1 tbsp tomato purée (paste)
5 ml/1 tsp caster (superfine) sugar
Salt and freshly ground black pepper

Soften the onion in the oil for 2–3 minutes, stirring. Add the remaining ingredients and bring to the boil. Simmer for about 5 minutes until pulpy. Use as required.

Provençal Sauce

SERVES 4

Prepare as for Tomato Sauce, but add 1 chopped green (bell) pepper, 1 or 2 crushed garlic cloves and 12 halved stuffed olives to the sauce before simmering.

Goulash Sauce

SERVES 4

Prepare as for Tomato Sauce, but add 15 ml/1 tbsp paprika and a crushed garlic clove to the softened onion and cook for 1 minute before finishing the sauce. Serve the sauce topped with a spoonful of crème fraîche and a sprinkling of caraway seeds.

Curry Sauce

SERVES 4–6

295 g/10½ oz/1 medium can of condensed celery or mushroom soup
90 ml/6 tbsp water
30 ml/2 tbsp tomato purée (paste)
5 ml/1 tsp garlic purée
5 ml/1 tsp dried onion granules
15 ml/1 tbsp curry paste
5 ml/1 tsp garam masala
5 ml/1 tsp turmeric
30 ml/2 tbsp mango chutney
50 g/2 oz piece of creamed coconut
Salt and freshly ground black pepper

Put all the ingredients in a saucepan. Heat gently, stirring, until the coconut has melted and the mixture is bubbling. Thin with a little more water if necessary. Season to taste and serve with grilled (broiled) chicken, hard-boiled (hard-cooked) eggs or add any cooked poultry or game to the sauce, heat through until piping hot and serve with rice.

Pesto for Poultry

SERVES 4

14 large basil leaves
2 garlic cloves, chopped
½ chicken stock cube
30 ml/2 tbsp pine nuts
30 ml/2 tbsp Parmesan cheese, grated
45 ml/3 tbsp olive oil
Freshly ground black pepper

Put the basil leaves in a blender or food processor with the garlic and stock cube. Run the machine until they form a paste. Add the pine nuts and cheese and blend again until smooth, stopping and scraping down the sides as necessary. With the machine running, add the oil a drop at a time, until a glistening paste is formed. Season with pepper and use as required. Store for up to 3 weeks in a sealed container in the fridge.

Red Almond Pesto

SERVES 4

Prepare as for Pesto for Poultry, but use 2 sun-dried tomatoes instead of the basil and chopped almonds instead of the pine nuts. Substitute 15 ml/1 tbsp of the sun-dried tomato oil for 15 ml/1 tbsp of the olive oil.

SAVOURY BUTTERS

Use any of these to brighten up plain grilled (broiled) poultry or game. They look like you've taken an enormous amount of time and trouble. In fact they are so easy, it's a doddle! They will turn any simple meal into a gourmet experience.

Parsley Butter

SERVES 4

50 g/2 oz/¼ cup butter, softened
15 ml/1 tbsp chopped parsley
10 ml/2 tsp lemon juice
Freshly ground black pepper

Cream the butter until soft. Beat in the parsley and lemon juice and add a good grinding of pepper. Roll into a sausage shape on a piece of greaseproof (waxed) paper. Wrap and chill. Cut into slices for serving.

Lemon Butter

SERVES 4

Prepare as for Parsley Butter, but omit the parsley and add the finely grated rind of ½ lemon.

Curry Butter

SERVES 4

Prepare as for Parsley Butter, but add 5 ml/1 tsp curry powder and 1.5 ml/¼ tsp turmeric to the mixture.

Devilled Butter

SERVES 4

Prepare as for Parsley Butter, but use only 5 ml/1 tsp lemon juice and add 2.5 ml/½ tsp made English mustard, 5 ml/1 tsp tomato purée (paste), 5 ml/1 tsp Worcestershire sauce and 1.5 ml/¼ tsp chilli powder to the mixture.

Chive Butter

SERVES [illegible]

Prepare as for Pa[illegible] substitute snipped [illegible] parsley.

Garlic Butter

SERVES 4

Prepare as for Parsley Butter, but add a large crushed garlic clove to the mixture.

Green Herb Butter

SERVES 4

Prepare as for Parsley Butter, but use only 5 ml/1 tsp parsley and add 5 ml/1 tsp each of chopped tarragon and thyme. Add, too, a large sprig of watercress, finely chopped, to the mixture and 1.5 ml/¼ tsp onion powder.

Tomato Butter

SERVES 4

Prepare as for Parsley Butter, but omit the lemon juice and add 5 ml/1 tsp tomato purée (paste), 1 sun-dried tomato in oil, finely chopped, 5 ml/1 tsp of the tomato oil, 2.5 ml/½ tsp icing (confectioners') sugar and 2.5 ml/½ tsp Worcestershire sauce.

Mustard Butter

SERVES 4

Prepare as for Parsley Butter, but use only 5 ml/1 tsp lemon juice and substitute snipped chives for the parsley. Add 10 ml/2 tsp Dijon mustard and a pinch of icing (confectioners') sugar.

RUBS AND MARINADES

All of these can be used to flavour any poultry or game before grilling (broiling) or roasting. They can be stored in an airtight container in the fridge for up to a week.

White Wine Marinade

MAKES 450 ML/¾ PT/2 CUPS

1 onion, chopped
A sprig of parsley
A sprig of thyme
1 small bay leaf
300 ml/½ pt/1¼ cups dry white wine
30 ml/2 tbsp white wine vinegar or lemon juice
15 ml/1 tbsp clear honey
20 ml/2 tbsp olive oil
5 ml/1 tsp juniper berries, crushed (optional)
1.5 ml/¼ tsp salt
Freshly ground black pepper

Whisk together all the ingredients and use to marinate any poultry or game for at least 30 minutes, preferably longer.

Red Wine Marinade

MAKES 450 ML/¾ PT/2 CUPS

1 onion, chopped
1 garlic clove, crushed
A sprig of parsley
A sprig of rosemary
300 ml/½ pt/1¼ cups red wine
30 ml/2 tbsp red wine vinegar
15 ml/1 tbsp light brown sugar
30 ml/2 tbsp olive oil
5 ml/1 tsp cumin seeds, crushed (optional)
1.5 ml/¼ tsp salt
Freshly ground black pepper

Whisk together all the ingredients and use to marinate any poultry or game for at least 30 minutes, preferably longer.

Chinese-style Marinade

MAKES 450 ML/¾ PT/2 CUPS

Finely grated rind and juice of 1 lime
45 ml/3 tbsp rice wine or white wine vinegar
30 ml/2 tbsp soy sauce
15 ml/1 tbsp dry sherry
15 ml/1 tbsp sesame oil
60 ml/4 tbsp sunflower oil
15 ml/1 tbsp clear honey
2.5 ml/½ tsp Chinese five spice powder
15 ml/1 tbsp chopped coriander (cilantro)

Whisk together all the ingredients and use to marinate any poultry for at least 30 minutes, preferably longer. I don't recommend this marinade for game.

Taiwanese Marinade

MAKES 450 ML/¾ PT/2 CUPS

Finely grated rind and juice of 2 limes
45 ml/3 tbsp Thai fish sauce
75 ml/5 tbsp sesame oil
75 ml/5 tbsp sunflower oil
2 large garlic clove, crushed
45 ml/3 tbsp roasted salted peanuts, finely chopped
1 stalk of lemon grass, crushed
1 green chilli, seeded and chopped
30 ml/2 tbsp chopped coriander (cilantro)

Whisk together all the ingredients and use to marinate any poultry for at least 30 minutes, preferably longer. I don't recommend this marinade for game.

Curried Yoghurt Marinade

MAKES 450 ML/¾ PT/2 CUPS

300 ml/½ pt/1¼ cups plain yoghurt
30 ml/2 tbsp chopped coriander (cilantro)
30 ml/2 tbsp mild curry paste
30 ml/2 tbsp red wine vinegar
45 ml/3 tbsp sunflower oil
15 ml/1 tbsp light brown sugar

Whisk together all the ingredients until thoroughly blended and use to marinate any poultry or game for at least 1 hour.

Sesame Citrus Marinade

MAKES 450 ML/¾ PT/2 CUPS

Finely grated rind and juice of 1 lemon
Finely grated rind of ½ orange
Juice of 1 orange
150 ml/¼ pt/⅔ cup sunflower oil
30 ml/2 tbsp sesame oil
2 garlic cloves, crushed
5 ml/1 tsp ground cumin
5 ml/1 tsp dried mixed herbs
45 ml/3 tbsp chopped parsley
30 ml/2 tbsp sesame seeds, toasted and lightly crushed
A pinch of salt
A pinch of freshly ground black pepper

Whisk together all the ingredients and use to marinate any poultry or game for at least 1 hour.

Garlic and Parsley Marinade

MAKES 450 ML/¾ PT/2 CUPS

300 ml/½ pt/1¼ cups dry white wine
120 ml/4 fl oz/½ cup olive oil
1 large bay leaf, split in half
2 large garlic cloves, crushed
5 ml/1 tsp caster (superfine) sugar
Salt and freshly ground black pepper
30 ml/2 tbsp chopped parsley

Whisk together all the ingredients and use to marinate any poultry or game for at least 30 minutes, preferably longer.

Italian-style M

MAKES 450 ML/¾

Finely grated rind and
60 ml/4 tbsp balsamic
30 ml/2 tbsp red wine vinegar
200 ml/7 fl oz/scant 1 cup olive oil
2 garlic cloves, crushed
2 canned anchovies, mashed
10 ml/2 tsp capers, chopped
45 ml/3 tbsp chopped basil
Freshly ground black pepper

Whisk together all the ingredients and use to marinate any poultry or game for at least 2 hours.

Tropical Marinade

MAKES 450 ML/¾ PT/2 CUPS

120 ml/4 fl oz/½ cup mixed unsweetened tropical fruit juices from a carton
2 garlic cloves, crushed
30 ml/2 tbsp white rum
60 ml/4 tbsp sunflower oil
30 ml/2 tbsp light brown sugar
Finely grated rind and juice of 1 lime
5 ml/1 tsp Tabasco sauce
5 ml/1 tsp ground cumin
5 ml/1 tsp dried oregano
15 ml/1 tbsp chopped coriander (cilantro)
Salt and freshly ground black pepper

Whisk together all the ingredients, adding salt and pepper to taste. Use to marinate any poultry or game for at least 2 hours.

Cranberry Marinade

MAKES 450 ML/¾ PT/2 CUPS

350 g/12 oz jar of cranberry sauce
60 ml/4 tbsp red wine vinegar
45 ml/3 tbsp pure orange juice
1 onion, chopped
1 garlic clove, crushed
60 ml/4 tbsp sunflower oil
5 ml/1 tsp dried thyme
Salt and freshly ground black pepper

Whisk together all the ingredients, adding salt and pepper to taste. Use to marinate turkey, duck or game for at least 2 hours.

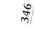

Peking-style Marinade

MAKES 300 ML/½ PT/1¼ CUPS

15 ml/1 tbsp hoisin sauce
90 ml/6 tbsp plum jam
30 ml/2 tbsp soy sauce
2 garlic cloves, crushed
10 ml/2 tsp grated fresh root ginger
5 ml/1 tsp sesame oil
45 ml/3 tbsp sunflower oil
5 ml/1 tsp lemon juice
30 ml/2 tbsp dry sherry

Whisk together all the ingredients or process in a blender or food processor untl smooth. Use to marinade any poultry or game for at least 3 hours.

Chilli Rub

ENOUGH FOR POULTRY OR GAME TO SERVE 4–6

1 garlic clove, crushed
1 small onion, grated
5 ml/1 tsp chilli powder
1.5 ml/¼ tsp salt
1.5 ml/½ tsp coarsely ground black pepper
Sunflower oil, for brushing

Mix together the rub ingredients and use to rub all over the poultry or game. Leave to stand for at least 2 hours before cooking. Brush with oil before grilling (broiling) or roasting.

Rosemary and Garlic Rub

ENOUGH FOR POULTRY OR GAME TO SERVE 4–6

2 garlic cloves, crushed
60 ml/4 tbsp finely chopped rosemary
5 ml/1 tsp dry mustard powder
5 ml/1 tsp dried oregano
A pinch of cayenne
Salt and freshly ground black pepper
Olive oil, for brushing

Mix together the rub ingredients or grind in a blender or pound in a pestle and mortar. Rub all over the poultry or game and leave to stand for at least 3 hours. Brush with oil before grilling (broiling) or roasting.

Cajun Rub

ENOUGH FOR POULTRY OR GAME TO SERVE 4–6

2 garlic cloves, crushed
1 small onion, grated
45 ml/3 tbsp paprika
15 ml/1 tbsp cayenne
10 ml/2 tsp dried thyme
10 ml/2 tsp dried oregano
15 ml/1 tbsp light brown sugar
Salt and freshly ground black pepper
Sunflower oil, for brushing

Mix or pound the rub ingredients together until well blended. Rub all over the poultry and game and leave to stand for at least 3 hours. Brush with oil before grilling (broiling) or roasting.

Totally Dry Onion Rub

ENOUGH FOR POULTRY OR GAME TO SERVE 4–6

10 ml/2 tsp dried onion granules
5 ml/1 tsp garlic salt
5 ml/1 tsp celery salt
15 ml/1 tbsp coarsely ground black pepper
10 ml/2 tsp dried basil
30 ml/2 tbsp paprika or pimenton
Sunflower oil, for brushing

Mix together all the rub ingredients and rub all over any poultry or game. Leave to stand for at least 2 hours. Brush with oil before grilling (broiling) or roasting.

Those Little Extras

It's often the traditional accompaniments apart from sauces that make many poultry and game dishes so special. There's bacon-wrapped chipolatas with the Christmas roast turkey, game chips with roast game birds and so on. You'll find everything you need here to complement every poultry and game recipe you can think of.

Game Chips

Serve these with any roasted game birds

Peel as many potatoes as you like (I usually allow one average-sized one per person). Cut into very thin slices with either a knife or a mandolin cutter. Soak in cold water for at least 10 minutes. Drain and dry well. Heat oil for deep-frying until a cube of day-old bread browns in 30 seconds. Deep-fry the game chips for about 3 minutes until crisp and golden brown. Do not overload the pan; it is better to cook two smaller batches than one big one. Keep the cooked chips warm in the oven while cooking the remainder. Drain on kitchen paper (paper towels) and sprinkle with salt before serving.

Cheat Game Chips

Buy a bag of good-quality pan-fried salted crisps (chips) and heat in the oven after removing the roast bird for 2–3 minutes before serving.

Royal Roast Potatoes

If your oven is slightly hotter (for cooking game birds, for instance), simply cook the potatoes for slightly less time. But watch to make sure they don't over-brown. Use the cooking liquid as stock for another recipe.

SERVES 4

4 good-sized potatoes
1 chicken stock cube
15–30 ml/1–2 tbsp sunflower or olive oil

Peel the potatoes and cut each into 3 or 4 even-sized pieces. Parboil in water to which the stock cube has been added for 3–4 minutes. Drain and, holding the lid tightly on the pan, shake the pan vigorously to rough up the edges. Meanwhile, heat the oil in a roasting tin (pan) towards the top of a preheated oven at 190°C/375°F/gas mark 5. When sizzling, tip in the potatoes and turn over in the hot oil. Roast for about 1 hour or until golden brown, turning once.

Sesame Seed Royal Roast Potatoes

SERVES 4

Prepare as for Royal Roast Potatoes, but sprinkle the potatoes with 15 ml/1 tbsp sesame seeds after tossing in the hot oil.

Poppy Seed and Mustard Royal Roast Potatoes

SERVES 4

Prepare as for Royal Roast Potatoes, but sprinkle the potatoes with 10 ml/2 tsp poppy seeds and 10 ml/2 tsp white mustard seeds after tossing in the hot oil.

Caraway Royal Roast Potatoes

SERVES 4

Prepare as for Royal Roast Potatoes, but sprinkle the potatoes with 15 ml/1 tbsp caraway seeds after tossing in the hot oil.

Speciality Creamed Potatoes

Use the cooking liquid as stock for another recipe.

SERVES 4

1 kg/2¼ lb potatoes, peeled and cut into chunks
1 chicken stock cube
25 g/1 oz/2 tbsp butter or margarine
A little milk
Freshly ground black pepper

Boil the potatoes in plenty of water to which the stock cube has been added until tender. Drain and return to the pan over a moderate heat. Shake the pan for 1 minute to dry out the potatoes. Mash the potatoes well, then beat in the butter or margarine and a little milk until soft and fluffy. Season to taste.

Cheese Potatoes

SERVES 4

Prepare as for Speciality Creamed Potatoes, but add 75 g/3 oz/¾ cup Cheddar cheese, grated, with the butter or margarine and continue as before.

Perfect Potato Wedges

SERVES 4

4 large unpeeled potatoes
30 ml/2 tbsp sunflower or olive oil
5 ml/1 tsp barbecue seasoning
1 chicken stock cube

Scrub the potatoes, prick them all over and either boil in water for about 20 minutes or cook in the microwave according to the manufacturer's instructions until almost tender. Drain, if necessary. When cool enough to handle, cut the potatoes into halves, then each half into wedges. Lay in a roasting tin (pan) and drizzle with the oil. Sprinkle with the barbecue seasoning and crumble the stock cube over. Cook at the top of a preheated oven at 220°C/425°F/gas mark 7 for about 20–25 minutes until crisp and golden, turning once.

Garlic Potato Wedges

SERVES 4

Prepare as for Perfect Potato Wedges, but add 5 ml/1 tsp garlic powder to the barbecue seasoning.

Super Sauté Potatoes

SERVES 4

4 average-sized potatoes
1 chicken stock cube
25 g/1 oz/2 tbsp butter or margarine
30 ml/2 tbsp sunflower oil

Cut the potatoes into dice. Boil in water to which the stock cube has been added for about 3 minutes until almost tender. Drain and dry on kitchen paper (paper towels). Heat the butter or margarine and oil in a large frying pan (skillet). Add the potatoes and fry (sauté), turning gently occasionally, until golden brown and cooked through. Drain on kitchen paper before serving.

Super Sauté Potatoes with Garlic

SERVES 4

Prepare as for Super Sauté Potatoes, but add 2 halved garlic cloves to the butter or margarine and oil. Discard before serving.

Hot Potato Salad

SERVES 6–8

1 kg/2¼ lb potatoes, scrubbed, halved, if large
1 chicken stock cube
50 g/2 oz/1 small can of anchovies, drained
250 ml/8 fl oz/1 cup crème fraîche
5 ml/1 tsp lemon juice
A pinch of caster (superfine) sugar
Freshly ground black pepper
Paprika, for dusting

Cook the potatoes in plenty of boiling water to which the stock cube has been added until just tender. Drain. Peel off the skins, when cool enough to handle. Cut into chunks and return to the pan. Reserve 4 anchovies for decoration and finely chop the remainder. Mix with the crème fraîche, lemon juice, sugar and a little pepper. Add to the potatoes and toss lightly over a gentle heat. Turn into a warm serving dish. Halve the reserved anchovies lengthways and arrange attractively on top. Dust with paprika and serve hot.

Puréed Potatoes

SERVES 4

700 g/1½ lb potatoes, peeled and cut into neat pieces
1 chicken stock cube
A large knob of butter or margarine

Cook the potatoes in plenty of boiling water to which the stock cube has been added until really tender. Drain (reserve the stock for another recipe). Tip the potatoes into a blender or food processor and add the butter or margarine. Run the machine until the mixture is smooth. Serve straight away.

Jerusalem Artichoke Purée

SERVES 4

700 g/1½ lb Jerusalem artichokes
15 ml/1 tbsp lemon juice
1 chicken stock cube
Freshly ground black pepper
A pinch of grated nutmeg
25 g/1 oz/2 tbsp butter or margarine

Scrub, peel or scrape the artichokes. Cut into neat pieces and place immediately in a saucepan of water to which the lemon juice and stock cube have been added. Bring to the boil, reduce the heat, cover and simmer for about 15 minutes or until really tender. Drain thoroughly and return to the pan. Stir over a gentle heat for about 2 minutes to dry. Tip into a blender or food processor. Add a little pepper, the nutmeg and butter or margarine. Run the machine until smooth. Taste and re-season if necessary. Serve with game.

Brussels Sprouts with Chestnuts

SERVES 6–8

450 g/1 lb Brussels sprouts
1 chicken stock cube
A large knob of butter or margarine
320 g/12 oz/1 medium can of chestnuts

Trim the sprouts. Cook in boiling water to which the stock cube has been added for 4–5 minutes or until just tender but still with some bite. Drain (reserve the stock for another recipe). Melt the butter or margarine in the saucepan and add the chestnuts. Toss for 2–3 minutes until piping hot. Add the sprouts and toss again until well mixed. Turn into a warm serving dish.

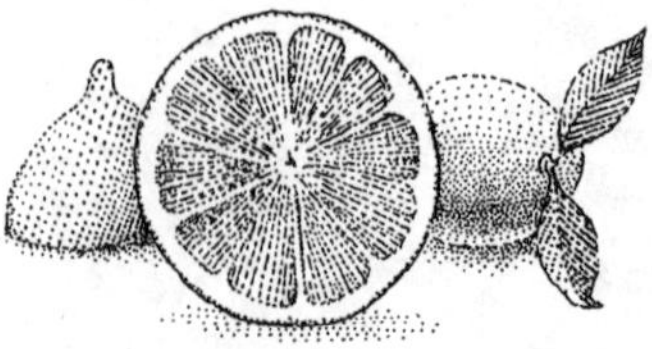

Plain Boiled Rice

SERVES 4

175 g/6 oz/¾ cup long-grain (preferably basmati) rice
1 chicken stock cube

Wash the rice well until the water is no longer cloudy. Drain thoroughly. Bring a large pan of water to the boil and add the stock cube. Add the rice and stir to separate the grains. Bring back to the boil and boil rapidly, uncovered, for 10 minutes. Test by lifting out a few grains and pinching them between the finger and thumb or biting between the front teeth. The grains should be almost soft but still with a little resistance – not crunchy – in the middle. Drain in a colander and rinse with boiling water. Replace over the saucepan with just a little water in it (to prevent the pan burning) over a gentle heat for a few minutes to dry out. Fluff up with a fork and serve.

Brown Rice

SERVES 4

Prepare as for Plain Boiled Rice, but use brown rice and cook for 30–35 minutes.

Buttered Rice

SERVES 4

Prepare as for Plain Boiled Rice, but toss the cooked rice in 25 g/1 oz/2 tbsp butter and sprinkle with 30 ml/2 tbsp chopped parsley before serving.

Thai Fragrant Rice

SERVES 4

Prepare as for Plain Boiled Rice, but use Thai fragrant rice. The rice will be slightly stickier than when using basmati or another long-grain rice.

Egg Fried Rice

SERVES 4

1 quantity of Plain Boiled Rice
30 ml/2 tbsp sunflower oil
50 g/2 oz frozen peas
1 egg, beaten
A pinch of Chinese five spice powder
A little soy sauce

Cook the Plain Boiled Rice. Heat the oil in a frying pan (skillet). Add the rice and peas and toss for 2 minutes. Push the rice to one side and tilt the pan. Pour in the egg. Cook the egg, stirring, then gradually draw in the rice until it is filled with tiny strands of egg. Add the five spice powder and a sprinkling of soy sauce. Toss and serve.

Special Egg Fried Rice

SERVES 4

Prepare as for Egg Fried Rice, but add 50 g/2 oz/½ cup finely chopped cooked chicken with the peas and 50 g/2 oz cooked, peeled prawns (shrimp), thawed if frozen. Then continue as before.

Quick Pilau Rice

SERVES 4

Prepare as for Plain Boiled Rice, but add 5 ml/1 tsp turmeric to the water, 4–6 split cardamom pods and a small piece of cinnamon stick. Cook a finely chopped onion in 15 ml/1 tbsp sunflower oil until golden brown and soft and fork through the rice. Remove the whole spices, if preferred, before serving.

Oven Pilaf

This is ideal to cook under birds being roasted or casseroled.

SERVES 4–6

100 g/4 oz dried fruit salad, soaked overnight in cold water
1 onion, finely chopped
25 g/1 oz/2 tbsp butter or margarine
225 g/8 oz/1 cup long-grain rice, well washed and drained
600 ml/1 pt/2½ cups chicken stock
Salt and freshly ground black pepper

Put the fruit and its soaking water in a saucepan, bring to the boil and simmer for 10 minutes or until tender. Leave to cool. Drain, and then roughly chop the fruit, discarding any stones (pits). Fry (sauté) the onion in the butter or margarine for 2 minutes in a flameproof casserole (Dutch oven). Stir in the rice until glistening. Pour in the stock and add a little seasoning. Bring to the boil, cover and transfer to a low shelf in a preheated oven at 200°C/400°F/gas mark 6. Cook for 12 minutes. Add the chopped fruit and fork through. Cover with foil and the lid and return to the oven as low down as possible for a further 10 minutes until the rice is cooked and has absorbed all the liquid. Fluff up and serve.

Wild Rice Mix

SERVES 4

175 g/6 oz/¾ cup wild rice mix
1 chicken stock cube
Freshly ground black pepper

Rinse the rice mix in several changes of cold water. Drain thoroughly. Bring a saucepan of water to the boil and add the chicken stock cube. Stir until dissolved. Add the rice mix and stir well again. Bring back to the boil and boil for 20 minutes or according to the packet directions until the rice is tender but still has some bite. Drain in a colander. Place the colander over the saucepan with just a little water in it (to prevent the pan burning). Simmer for 2–3 minutes to dry out, stirring the rice occasionally. Fluff up and serve.

Buttered Crumbs

SERVES 4

25 g/1 oz/2 tbsp butter or margarine
100 g/4 oz/2 cups white breadcrumbs

Melt the butter or margarine in a frying pan (skillet). Add the crumbs and toss over a moderate heat until golden and crisp and evenly coated in the fat. Serve hot with any roasted game bird.

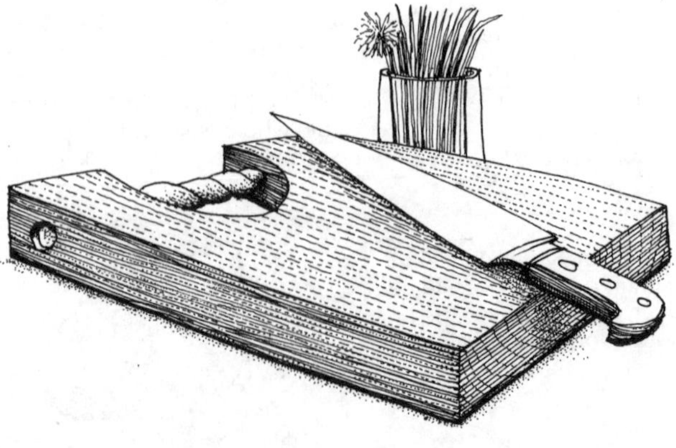

SIMPLE STUFFINGS

Unless otherwise stated, the quantity of stuffing in these recipes is enough to stuff the neck end of an average chicken or duck. For a turkey, double the quantity.

Sage and Onion Stuffing

If using to stuff a turkey, double the quantities but use 1 whole egg instead of 2 egg yolks.

SERVES 4

50 g/2 oz/1 cup white breadcrumbs
1 small onion, finely chopped
8 fresh sage leaves, finely chopped
Salt and freshly ground black pepper
15 ml/1 tbsp melted butter or margarine
1 egg yolk
15 ml/1 tbsp milk

Mix the breadcrumbs with the onion, sage and some salt and pepper. Stir in the melted butter or margarine, egg yolk and milk. Use as required.

Parsley and Thyme Stuffing

If using to stuff a turkey, double the quantities but use 1 whole egg to bind instead of doubling the egg yolks.

SERVES 4

50 g/2 oz/1 cup white breadcrumbs
30 ml/2 tbsp chopped parsley
15 ml/1 tbsp chopped thyme
Salt and freshly ground black pepper
1 egg yolk
15 ml/1 tbsp boiling water

Mix together all the ingredients and use as required.

Herby Bacon Stuffing

SERVES 4

50 g/2 oz/1 cup wholemeal breadcrumbs
1 small onion, finely chopped
2 streaky bacon rashers (slices), finely diced
2.5 ml/½ tsp dried mixed herbs
Salt and freshly ground black pepper
1 small egg, beaten

Mix together all the ingredients and use as required.

Nutty Rice Stuffing

SERVES 4

100 g/4 oz/1 cup cooked long-grain rice
30 ml/2 tbsp raisins
25 g/1 oz/¼ cup walnuts, chopped
15 ml/1 tbsp snipped chives
15 g/½ oz/1 tbsp butter or margarine, softened
Salt and freshly ground black pepper

Mash the rice, raisins, walnuts and chives into the butter or margarine and season to taste with salt and pepper. Use as required.

Liver and Garlic Stuffing

If using to stuff a turkey, use the one liver and double the quantity of the remaining ingredients.

SERVES 4

Liver from the bird, trimmed and chopped
15 g/½ oz/1 tbsp butter or margarine
1 garlic clove, crushed
50 g/2 oz/1 cup fresh breadcrumbs
15 ml/1 tbsp chopped parsley
Finely grated rind and juice of ½ small lemon
Salt and freshly ground black pepper

Fry (sauté) the liver in the butter or margarine for 2 minutes. Stir in the remaining ingredients. Use as required.

Caraway Sausage Stuffing

SERVES 4

50 g/2 oz button mushrooms, sliced
15 g/½ oz/1 tbsp butter or margarine
100 g/4 oz pork sausagemeat
5 ml/1 tsp caraway seeds
Freshly ground black pepper

Fry (sauté) the mushrooms in the butter or margarine for 3 minutes. Remove from the heat and stir in the sausagemeat, caraway seeds and a little pepper. Use as required.

Prune and Pecan Stuffing

If using to stuff a turkey, double the ingredients but use 1 whole egg to bind rather than doubling the egg yolks.

SERVES 4

50 g/2 oz/⅓ cup ready-to-eat dried prunes, chopped
25 g/1 oz/¼ cup pecan nuts, roughly chopped
50 g/2 oz/1 cup fresh breadcrumbs
15 ml/1 tbsp chopped parsley
Salt and freshly ground black pepper
1 egg yolk

Mix together the dry ingredients thoroughly in a bowl, then mix with the egg yolk to bind. Use as required.

Forcemeat Balls

SERVES 4

50 g/2 oz/1 cup white breadcrumbs
25 g/1 oz/2 tbsp shredded (chopped) vegetable suet
30 ml/2 tbsp chopped parsley
5 ml/1 tsp dried mixed herbs
Salt and freshly ground black pepper
1 egg, beaten
Sunflower oil, for greasing

Mix together the dry ingredients and stir in enough of the egg to bind the mixture together without being too wet. Shape into small balls and place in a lightly oiled shallow baking dish. Roast for about 30–40 minutes with any bird until golden.

Bacon-wrapped Chipolatas

Allow 1 or 2 chipolata sausages, and 1 or 2 rindless streaky bacon rashers (slices) for each person. Cut the sausages in half. Stretch the bacon rashers with the back of a knife, then cut in half. Wrap half a slice of bacon round each sausage half. Place in a suitably sized roasting tin (pan) with the bacon ends underneath. Cook towards the top of the oven while roasting your bird for about 30 minutes until richly browned, turning once. Drain on kitchen paper (paper towels) before serving.

Devils on Horseback

Allow 2 or 3 ready-to-eat prunes and 1 rindless streaky bacon rasher (slice) for each person. Discard any stones (pits) in the prunes. Stretch the bacon rashers with the back of a knife, then cut each rasher into two or three pieces. Wrap a piece of bacon round each prune. Place in a small roasting tin (pan) with the bacon ends underneath. Cook towards the top of the oven when roasting your bird for about 20 minutes until the bacon is crisp and brown. Serve with any bird.

Angels on Horseback

Prepare as for Devils on Horseback, but substitute a small button mushroom for each prune. Serve with any bird.

Corn Fritters

SERVES 6

100 g/4 oz/1 cup plain (all-purpose) flour
1 small onion, grated
1 egg
150 ml/¼ pt/⅔ cup milk
350 g/12 oz/1 medium can of sweetcorn (corn), drained
Salt and freshly ground black pepper
45 ml/3 tbsp sunflower oil

Sift the flour into a bowl. Add the onion. Make a well in the centre and add the egg. Gradually beat in the milk to form a thick batter. Stir in the corn and some salt and pepper. Heat the oil in a frying pan (skillet), add spoonfuls of the corn mixture and fry (sauté) for about 2 minutes on each side until golden brown. Drain on kitchen paper (paper towels) and keep warm while cooking the remainder. Serve with any grilled (broiled) poultry.

Fried Bananas

SERVES 4

4 small bananas
40 g/1½ oz/3 tbsp butter or margarine

Peel and halve the bananas lengthways. Melt the butter or margarine in a frying pan (skillet) and fry (sauté) the banana halves for about 2 minutes on each side until golden but still holding their shape. Drain on kitchen paper (paper towels) and serve hot with fried (sautéed) or grilled (broiled) chicken or turkey dishes.

Popadoms

The best way to cook popadoms is in the microwave with no added oil. Place one at a time on a plate. Microwave for about 20–30 seconds until beginning to puff up. Turn over and microwave until puffy all over. Repeat with as many as you like.

Onion Bhajis

SERVES 4

75 g/3 oz/¾ cup gram or plain (all-purpose) flour
2.5 ml/½ tsp salt
A good pinch of turmeric
1 green chilli, seeded and chopped
15 ml/1 tbsp chopped coriander (cilantro)
2 onions, chopped
Sunflower oil, for deep-frying

Mix the flour, salt and turmeric in a bowl. Stir in the chilli and coriander. Mix with enough water to form a thick batter. Leave to stand for 30 minutes. Stir in the onions. Heat the oil in a deep frying pan (skillet) or wok until a cube of day-old bread browns in 30 seconds. Drop spoonfuls of the batter into the pan and cook until golden brown. Drain on kitchen paper (paper towels) and keep warm while cooking the remainder. Serve hot with any curries.

Mushroom Bhajis

Prepare as for Onion Bhajis but omit the onions. When the batter has been standing, stir in 5 ml/1 tsp bicarbonate of soda (baking soda) and add 100 g/4 oz button mushrooms. Drop individual coated mushrooms in the hot oil and deep-fry as before.

Potato Bhajis

SERVES 4

Prepare as for Onion Bhajis, but omit the onion. Dip 1 large potato, thinly sliced and dried on kitchen paper (paper towels), into the batter and deep-fry as before.

Potato Pakoras

SERVES 4

1 large potato, cut into 5 mm/¼ in thick slices
100 g/4 oz/1 cup gram or plain (all-purpose) flour
A good pinch of chilli powder
A good pinch of ground cumin
A good pinch of turmeric
5 ml/1 tsp salt
Oil, for deep-frying

Dry the potato slices on kitchen paper (paper towels). Mix together the flour, spices and salt in a bowl. Add enough water to form a batter the texture of extra-thick cream. Heat the oil until a cube of day-old bread browns in 30 seconds. Dip the slices of potato in the batter, then fry (sauté) in the oil for 3–4 minutes until golden brown. Drain on kitchen paper and serve hot.

Crisp Onion Rings

SERVES 4

2 large onions, thinly sliced and separated into rings
50 g/2 oz/½ cup plain (all-purpose) flour
Salt and freshly ground black pepper
Oil, for deep-frying

Toss the onions in the flour, seasoned with salt and pepper, until well coated. Heat the oil in a large frying pan (skillet) or wok until a cube of day-old bread browns in 30 seconds. Add about a quarter of the onion rings and deep-fry for about 4 minutes until crisp and golden. Drain on kitchen paper (paper towels) and keep warm. Reheat the oil and continue frying until all the onion rings are cooked. Serve hot with fried (sautéed) and grilled (broiled) poultry dishes.

Crispy Noodle Cake

SERVES 4

225 g/8 oz Chinese egg noodles
45 ml/3 tbsp sunflower oil

Cook the noodles according to the packet directions. Drain and dry thoroughly on kitchen paper (paper towels). Heat 30 ml/2 tbsp of the oil in a frying pan (skillet). Add the noodles and spread out in the pan to an even layer. Fry (sauté) until golden brown underneath. Lift out of the pan. Add the remaining oil, turn over the noodle cake and return to the pan. Continue to fry until crisp and golden. Serve whole with any of the Chinese-style dishes spooned over or cut into wedges and serve as an accompaniment.

Crispy Noodles

Other pasta shapes can also be deep-fried. They make a good garnish for oriental dishes and soups too.

SERVES 4

225 g/8 oz cooked ribbon noodles, cut into short lengths
Oil, for deep-frying
Coarse sea salt

Make sure the pasta is completely dry and that the strands are separate. Heat the oil to 190°C/375°F or until a cube of day-old bread browns in 30 seconds. Deep-fry the noodles in small batches in a wire basket until crisp and golden brown. Drain on kitchen paper (paper towels), then toss in coarse sea salt.

Garlic Bread

SERVES 4

50 g/2 oz/¼ cup butter or margarine, softened
1 or 2 garlic cloves, crushed
30 ml/2 tbsp chopped parsley
1 small baguette

Mash the butter or margarine with the garlic and parsley. Cut the baguette into 12 slices, almost through to the bottom crust. Spread the butter between the slices, spreading any remainder over the top. Wrap in foil. Bake in a preheated oven at about 200°C/400°F/gas mark 6 for 15 minutes or until the crust feels crisp when squeezed with an oven-gloved hand.

Hot Herb Bread

SERVES 4

Prepare as for Garlic Bread, but omit the garlic and mix 5 ml/1 tsp dried mixed herbs and the finely grated rind of ½ lemon into the butter or margarine with the parsley.

Index

accompaniments 347–357
all-weather barbecue-spiced drummers 133
almond chicken 92
almond cream of chicken soup 45
almost instant chicken soufflé 71
amazing chicken and broccoli bake 152
American-style hot chicken salad 307
anchovy and pâté eggs with vermicelli 253
Andalusian rice 271
angels on horseback 354
apples
  apple harvest salad 305
  apple sauce 339
  curried chicken and apple warmer 55
Arabic chicken bloomer 194
arancini Siciliani 261
around the world warm salad 326
arroz con pollo 268
arroz poblano 277
artichokes
  Jerusalem artichoke purée 350
  lasagne with chicken and artichokes 246
aru murgh 295
asparagus
  asparagus, strawberry and quail's egg salad 40
  chicken and asparagus bake 245
  chicken and asparagus quiche 187
  chicken and asparagus soufflé omelette 71
  gamekeeper's asparagus 40
  rosti with chicken and asparagus rolls 72
aubergines
  Cypriot stuffed aubergine 33
  grilled aubergine slices with chicken livers and peanut sauce 32
aurora sauce 341
Austrian Schinkenfleckerl 243
avocados
  avocado à l'Indienne 24
  avocado and chicken soup 55
  avocado rasher grills 81
  baked avocados with chicken 26
  chicken and avocado cocktail 21
  chicken and avocado coolers 75
  chicken, olive and avocado mousse 24
  creamy chicken and avocado vol-au-vents 192
  turkey and avocado platter with mushroom dressing 324
baby chicken fillets with cognac 91
bacon
  angels on horseback 354
  bacon, chicken and tomato pancakes 96
  bacon-wrapped chipolatas 354
  chicken and bacon terrine with pistachio nuts 30
  devils on horseback 354
  herby bacon stuffing 353
bacteria 7–10
baguettes
  chicken, egg and tomato baguette 69
  chicken mayo and lettuce baguette 69
  chicken stir-fry sticks 68
  fragrant chicken and pesto baguette 69
  pimiento chicken sticks 69
  see also bread; pitta bread; sandwiches
baked avocados with chicken 26
baked barbecued chicken drumsticks 156
baked beans
  bean and sausage toppers 83

turkey bean chowder 60
baked chicken with apricots and walnuts 150
baked chicken with orange and pine nuts 157
baked chicken with prunes and almonds 150
baked Chinese chicken 161
baked main meal turkey, ham and vegetable soup 58
baked pasta Bolognese 248
balti chicken 290
bananas
chicken, banana and bacon savoury 65
fried bananas 355
Bangkok supper 264
barbecue sauce 336
barbecued buffalo wings 133
barbecued spatchcock baby chicken 134
barbecued turkey steaks 115
basic quick rice sauce 340
basil and lemon barbecued chicken 136
beans
bean and sausage toppers 83
butter beanie 66
pheasant and five bean salad 330
turkey bean chowder 60
beetroot layer 320
bhajis
mushroom bhajis 355
onion bhajis 355
potato bhajis 355
bigarde sauce 335
birds
boning 15–16
carving 17–18
jointing 15
roasting 144–145
trussing 16
types 12–14
see also poultry
biryani salad 317
blackcurrant duck 119
blanquette of chicken 206
blue cheese and chicken fluff 152
blueberries
warm chicken livers with blueberries 31
boned stuffed pigeons 181
boning 15–16
Boxing Day pie 195
braised chicken in black bean sauce 211
braised pigeons with red cabbage 233
braised quail in hock with seasoned rice 285
braised squab with white cabbage and caraway 233
braised turkey with bacon and vegetables 221
braised turkey with redcurrant and mushrooms 224
brandied turkey liver and walnut pâté 37
bread
Arabic chicken bloomer 194
bread sauce 339
buttered crumbs 352
garlic bread 357
hot herb bread 357
see also baguettes; pitta bread; sandwiches
Bridgetown chicken with yam muffins 218
brinjals 338
Brittany chicken 209
broccoli
chicken and broccoli quiche 186
brown onion salsa 336
brown rice 351
brown rice and chicken slow-pot 216
brown turkey pottage 59
Brussels sprouts with chestnuts 350
bubble and squeak special 90
burgers
chicken and cheese burgers 129
chicken burgers with fresh herbs 98
Chinese chicken burgers 153
turkey and cranberry burgers 137
see also rissoles
burritos
chicken burritos with avocado, tomato and pineapple salsa 106
butter beans
butter beanie 66
butter roast chicken and potatoes 145
buttered barbecued chicken 136
buttered crumbs 352
buttered flavoured barbecued chicken 136
buttered rice 351
butters
chive butter 343
curry butter 343
devilled butter 343
garlic butter 343
green herb butter 343
lemon butter 343
mustard butter 343
parsley butter 343
tomato butter 343
see also gravies; marinades; rubs; sauces
cabbage
bubble and squeak special 90
cabbage leaves
Polish stuffed cabbage leaves 36
Cajun chicken wings 26
Cajun rub 346
Californian dreams 80
Californian fruit and rice for poultry or game 305
Californian-style honey roast turkey 168
cannelloni Bolognese 247

Cantonese-style chicken 102
Cantonese-style duck 118
caper sauce 341
capercaillie 13
caraway royal roast potatoes 348
caraway sausage stuffing 354
cardamom chicken 295
Caribbean chicken with coconut soup 44
Caribbean pasta salad 310
carrots
  chicken and carrot tzimmes 165
carving 17–18
cashew nuts
  chicken and cashew nut pittas 74
casseroles 202–238
  blanquette of chicken 206
  braised chicken in black bean sauce 211
  braised pigeons with red cabbage 233
  braised squab with white cabbage and caraway 233
  braised turkey with bacon and vegetables 221
  braised turkey with redcurrant and mushrooms 224
  Bridgetown chicken with yam muffins 218
  Brittany chicken 209
  brown rice and chicken slow-pot 216
  casserole of pheasant with chestnuts and oranges 228
  casserole of pigeons with baby onions and mushroom stuffing balls 234
  casseroled duck with turnips and carrots 227
  casseroled pheasant with Italian sauce 230
  cassoulet 220
  chicken, aubergine and pine nut casserole 208
  chicken Avéronique 205
  chicken crumble casserole 208
  chicken fricassée 206
  chicken goulash 216
  chicken gumbo 217
  chicken harcouet 220
  chicken paprika 210
  chicken pimento 211
  chicken Véronique 205
  chicken with water chestnuts 212
  citrus chicken 215
  coq au vin 207
  coq au vin blanc 207
  cottage rice casserole 258
  country partridge casserole 236
  creamed turkey Grand Marnier 213
  creamy pigeons with redcurrant 234
  Cumberland casseroled quail 237
  curried chicken and celery casserole 219
  curried chicken and mushroom casserole 219
  dry Martini chicken 212
  Fijian chicken 213
  forestry pheasant 229
  French-style duck casserole 225
  grouse in lager 231
  guinea fowl in white Bordeaux 237
  herb-stuffed chicken rolls 209
  hot peanut chicken 214
  Jamaican chicken 213
  lemon chicken 203
  marinated grouse of the ancient Romans 232
  Mediterranean chicken casserole 208
  Moroccan-style duck 225
  New Orleans chicken gumbo 217
  nutty chicken with water chestnuts 212
  old English country duck 226
  partridge in milk 135
  partridge with olives 236
  pheasant with artichokes and chestnuts 231
  pheasant with celeriac and carrot 228
  pheasant with celery and walnuts 228
  pheasant with cider and pears 229
  pheasant with white wine and apples 229
  pink grapefruit and chive chicken 203
  Polonaise chicken 210
  pot roast chicken with orange and pecans 204
  pot roast chicken with tomatoes and cashew nuts 204
  quail ragoût with mushroom selection 239
  quick French chicken casserole 207
  quick Italian chicken casserole 207
  salmi de canard 227
  salmi of grouse 233
  salmi of partridge 236
  salmi of pheasant 230
  salted casseroled duck 226
  sherried chicken casserole 215
  Somerset turkey pot roast with dumplings 222
  spatchcocked pigeons in red wine 235
  spiced chicken casserole 218
  spiced salmi of snipe 238
  tangy turkey wings with ginger 221
  Taunton grouse 231
  tender turkey steaks in smooth cider sauce 222
  three-herb turkey casserole 224
  Tropical chicken 213
  turkey and spring vegetable casserole with bay 223
  turkey cassoulet 221
  turkey herb crumble 224
  turkey pot roast with wine and two cheese 222

Tyrolean turkey 223
Victorian grouse fricassée 232
white chicken and bacon casserole 203
winter chicken and lentil pot 219
winter chicken pot 219
zesty chicken and vegetable casserole 214
cassoulet 220
cauliflower
chicken and cauliflower cheese 151
caviare cream 339
celery
chicken and celery bake 245
Ceylonese rice 259
Chantilly sauce 341
cheat chicken Maryland 124
cheat game chips 348
cheese
blue cheese and chicken fluff 152
cheese and chicken fluff 152
cheese and chicken gnocchi 244
cheese and pickle sausage rolls 81
cheese fondue with chicken bites 68
cheese, pheasant and rice croquettes 284
cheese potatoes 349
cheese sauce 341
cheesy chicken and chive plait 192
cheesy chicken Kiev 92
cheesy chicken pancakes 94
cheesy turkey jackets 84
chicken and cauliflower cheese 151
chicken, broccoli and tomato cheese 151
cottage cheese, chicken and prawn cups 27
hot Leerdammer and turkey bites 35
potted duck with Stilton and redcurrants 38
potted pheasant with two cheeses 41
smoked turkey and cheese balls 34
chestnuts
Brussels sprouts with chestnuts 350
chick peas
peasant pottage 47
chicken
all-weather barbecue-spiced drummers 133
almond chicken 92
almond cream of chicken soup 45
almost instant chicken soufflé 71
amazing chicken and broccoli bake 152
American-style hot chicken salad 307
Andalusian rice 271
apple harvest salad 305
Arabic chicken bloomer 194
arancini Siciliani 261
arroz con pollo 268
aru murgh 295
Austrian Schinkenfleckerl 243
avocado à l'Indienne 24
avocado and chicken soup 55
baby chicken fillets with cognac 91
bacon, chicken and tomato pancakes 96
baked avocados with chicken 26
baked barbecued chicken drumsticks 156
baked chicken with apricots and walnuts 150
baked chicken with orange and pine nuts 157
baked chicken with prunes and almonds 150
baked Chinese chicken 161
baked pasta Bolognese 248
balti chicken 290
Bangkok supper 264
barbecued buffalo wings 133
barbecued spatchcock baby chicken 134
basil and lemon barbecued chicken 136
biryani salad 317
blanquette of chicken 206
blue cheese and chicken fluff 152
braised chicken in black bean sauce 211
Bridgetown chicken with yam muffins 218
Brittany chicken 209
brown rice and chicken slow-pot 216
bubble and squeak special 90
butter beanie 66
butter roast chicken and potatoes 145
buttered barbecued chicken 136
buttered flavoured barbecued chicken 136
Cajun chicken wings 26
cannelloni Bolognese 247
Cantonese-style chicken 102
cardamom chicken 295
Caribbean chicken with coconut soup 44
Caribbean pasta salad 310
cassoulet 220
Ceylonese rice 259
cheat chicken dhansak 291
cheat chicken Maryland 124
cheese and chicken fluff 152
cheese and chicken gnocchi 244
cheese fondue with chicken bites 68
cheesy chicken and chive plait 192
cheesy chicken Kiev 92
cheesy chicken pancakes 94
chicken and asparagus bake 245
chicken and asparagus quiche 187
chicken and asparagus soufflé omelette 71
chicken and aubergine moussaka 154
chicken and avocado cocktail 21
chicken and avocado coolers 75
chicken and bacon stuffed jackets 76
chicken and bacon terrine with pistachio nuts 30
chicken and broccoli quiche 186
chicken and carrot tzimmes 165
chicken and cashew nut pittas 74

chicken and cauliflower cheese 151
chicken and celery bake 245
chicken and cheese burgers 129
chicken and chive stuffed jackets 77
chicken and cider quills 247
chicken and clam risotto 263
chicken and corn chowder 49
chicken and courgette moussaka 155
chicken and cress butter sandwiches 74
chicken and egg fried rice with bacon 259
chicken and egg pie 185
chicken and ham quiche 186
chicken and ham rolls with pineapple sauce 93
chicken and leek pie 189
chicken and leek roulade with mushroom sauce 157
chicken and lentil curry 296
chicken and mushroom cocktail 21
chicken and mushroom flan 193
chicken and mushroom gougère 160
chicken and mushroom muncher 74
chicken and mushroom pizza special 67
chicken and mushroom quiche 186
chicken and mushroom soufflé omelette 71
chicken and mushroom toad 155
chicken and mushrooms with oyster sauce 101
chicken and mussel risotto 270
chicken and parsley quiche 186
chicken and peanut perfection 75
chicken and potato chowder 49
chicken and potato moussaka 154
chicken and potato quiche 187
chicken and prawn bouillabaisse 48
chicken and prawn cocktail 21
chicken and prawn quiche 186
chicken and prawn risotto 263
chicken and prawn wontons with sweet and sour sauce 21
chicken and red wine pasta 246
chicken and rice soup 49
chicken and Ricotta ravioli 241
chicken and roast vegetable fajitas 161
chicken and saffron soup 47
chicken and spiced almond salad 315
chicken and spinach lasagne 249
chicken and spring vegetable jalousie 188
chicken and sweetcorn bake 246
chicken and sweetcorn jackets 76
chicken and sweetcorn quiche 186
chicken and sweetcorn soufflé omelette 71
chicken and sweetcorn toad 155
chicken and tarragon meatballs with spicy spaghetti 245
chicken and tarragon peppered tagliatelle 242
chicken and tarragon risotto 265
chicken and tomato quiche 187
chicken and tuna niçoise 311
chicken and vegetable cassata 309
chicken and vegetable fritters 110
chicken and vegetable moussaka 154
chicken and vegetable pasties 187
chicken and vegetable popovers 155
chicken, aubergine and pine nut casserole 208
chicken Averone 105
chicken Avéronique 205
chicken, bacon and corn kebabs 128
chicken baked custard 20
chicken, banana and bacon savoury 65
chicken bhuna masala 292
chicken biryani 298
chicken, blue cheese and pear salad 315
chicken breasts masala 301
chicken, broccoli and tomato cheese 151
chicken burgers with fresh herbs 98
chicken burritos with avocado, tomato and pineapple salsa 106
chicken chaudfroid 311
chicken chéron 104
chicken, chive and pineapple risotto 265
chicken Cointreau 129
chicken cordon bleu 91
chicken, corn and mushroom pilaf 267
chicken, corn and peanut chowder 52
chicken crumble casserole 208
chicken dhansak 291
chicken dopiaza 293
chicken, egg and tomato baguette 69
chicken fajitas 109
chicken Florentine 188
chicken fricassée 206
chicken goulash 216
chicken gumbo 217
chicken, ham and olive cocktail 21
chicken, ham and pineapple cocktail 20
chicken, ham and pineapple stuffed jackets 77
chicken, ham and tomato grill 127
chicken harcouet 220
chicken, hazelnut and vegetable rice 262
chicken in filo pastry with asparagus sauce 189
chicken Jalfrezi 300
chicken jambalaya 269
chicken Kashmir 294
chicken korma 290
chicken lasagne Bolognese 248
chicken, leek and walnut vermicelli 251
chicken Maryland 146
chicken massage 296

chicken mayo and lettuce baguette 69
chicken moghlai 292
chicken, mushroom and noodle soup 46
chicken, mushroom and pasta chowder 52
chicken, mushroom and tomato kebabs 128
chicken, olive and avocado mousse 24
chicken pal 300
chicken palak 289
chicken paprika 210
chicken parcels with cranberry 187
chicken pesto 108
chicken pesto parcels 156
chicken pimento 211
chicken ravioli 240
chicken, red pepper and chilli sandwiches 75
chicken saag 296
chicken samosas 29
chicken satay 130
chicken seek kebabs 292
chicken shack pie 159
chicken soufflé omelette 71
chicken soup with lemon dumplings 54
chicken soup with matzo meal dumplings 54
chicken, spinach and pecan pies 184
chicken, spinach and Ricotta ravioli 241
chicken stir-fry scramble 103
chicken stir-fry sticks 68
chicken strips in cantaloupes 95
chicken stroganoff 95
chicken supreme salad 314
chicken, sweetcorn and pepper quiche 186
chicken teriyaki kebabs 127
chicken tetrazzini 240
chicken tikka 289
chicken tikka biryani 298
chicken tikka masala 299
chicken toad 155
chicken Tuscany 250
chicken Véronique 205
chicken vindaloo 294
chicken with cashew nuts and noodles 103
chicken with Chinese curry butter 125
chicken with curried butter 156
chicken with curry butter 125
chicken with garlic and herb butter 156
chicken with garlic and lemon butter 155
chicken with lime and garlic 160
chicken with mixed peppers and black bean sauce 100
chicken with mustard and rosemary rub 126
chicken with orange butter 156
chicken with water chestnuts 212
chilli barbecued chicken 136
chilli con pollo 204
chilli winter warmer 44
Chinese chicken and mushroom stir-fry 100
Chinese chicken and spring onion soup 47
Chinese chicken and vegetable soup 51
Chinese chicken burgers 153
Chinese chicken fries 24
Chinese chicken, prawn and beansprout salad 310
Chinese chicken rissoles 102
Chinese chicken wings 160
Chinese curried meatballs 295
Chinese fire chicken 106
Chinese hot and sour soup 46
Chinese meatballs with ginger 22
Chinese mushroom, chicken and king prawn stir-fry 100
Chinese mushroom, chicken and pineapple stir-fry 100
Chinese spring rolls 22
Chinese-style chicken with cashew nuts and rice 107
citrus chicken 215
cock-a-leekie soup 49
Continental chicken and vegetable salad 308
cooling chicken potato toppers 77
coq au vin 207
coq au vin blanc 207
Coronation chicken 316
cottage cheese, chicken and prawn cups 27
cottage rice casserole 258
cream of chicken and walnut soup 54
creamed chicken and tarragon soup 50
creamed risotto with chicken and lemon 260
creamy cardamom chicken 88
creamy chicken and almond pasta 252
creamy chicken and avocado vol-au-vents 192
creamy chicken and ham vol-au-vents 192
creamy chicken and mushroom vol-au-vents 191
creamy chicken and prawn vol-au-vents 192
creamy chicken and sweetcorn vol-au-vents 192
creamy chicken, ham and mushroom risotto 256
creamy chicken pie 184
creamy chicken vol-au-vents 191
creamy chicken with mushrooms 98
creamy chicken with peas and hazelnuts 252
creamy tarragon chicken 105

crisp baked chicken 163
crispy chicken and vegetable rolls 66
crispy tacos 205
crunchy-coated chicken 158
crunchy lemon chicken legs 159
curried chicken and apple warmer 55
curried chicken and celery casserole 219
curried chicken and fresh mango sandwiches 76
curried chicken and mushroom casserole 219
curried chicken and pasta salad 314
curried chicken and peach pittas 74
curried chicken and sultana toppers 77
curried chicken pancakes 94
curried chicken pasta salad 310
curried rice, chicken and cheese salad 309
deep-fried chicken parcels 193
devils and angels 89
dry chicken curry 287
dry Martini chicken 212
Dutch roast 158
Eastern rice with egg 259
Eastern saffron soup 45
easy roast stuffed chicken breasts 148
egg vindaloo basmati 299
enchiladas 204
English country chicken salad 309
extra-fragrant Parmesan rice 257
fast chicken and spiced hazelnuts 316
Fijian chicken 213
fragrant chicken and pesto baguette 69
fragrant chicken with spaghetti 247
fragrant fried chicken 91
fragrant stuffed tomatoes 307
French peasant chicken pasta 249
French-style peasant chicken 104
fried chicken Kiev 92
garlic and chicken soup 53
garlic and lemon chicken 163
garlic butter roast chicken and potatoes 145
garlic fried chicken 91
glazed chicken quills 247
gnocchi alla Romana con pollo 242
gold-kissed chicken grill 127
golden sweet and sour chicken breasts 107
gooey chicken and mushroom crescents 76
gooey chicken parcels 147
gorgeous glazed chicken 88
Gorgonzola speciality 258
Greek chicken and mushroom salad 304
Greek-styled marinated chicken kebabs 129
grilled chicken bites 28
grilled chicken Kiev 124
grilled chicken Kiev with lime and coriander 124
grilled chicken with basil and anchovies 131
grilled chicken with Chinese five spice powder 125
grilled chicken with corn stuffing 124
grilled chicken with hot olive sauce 123
grilled chicken with pasta 242
grilled Italian platter 135
grilled spiced chicken with sweet pepper couscous 126
Hawaiian chicken 308
herb-stuffed chicken rolls 209
hindle wakes 312
hot peanut chicken 214
huevos à la Cubana 20
iced chicken and mango mulligatawny 48
Indian chicken 288
Indian chicken and mushroom pilau 266
Indian fried chicken 288
Indonesian chicken, prawn and egg rice 268
Iranian shireen polow 262
Italian chicken lunch 69
Italian lunchtime fettuccine 243
Italian-style savoury rice cake 255
Jamaican chicken 213
Japanese chicken and shiitake mushroom clear soup 46
Japanese chicken dumplings 194
Japanese peanut chicken stir-fry 108
Japanese-style sesame chicken 270
Kentucky baked chicken 165
Kentucky fried chicken sandwich 70
kosher-style chicken soup 53
kosher-style chicken soup with noodles 53
lasagne al forno 246
lasagne with chicken and artichokes 246
leftover chicken biryani 298
lemon chicken 203
lemon chicken soufflé 72
lime and green peppercorn barbecued chicken 136
Louisiana jambalaya 269
MacArthur Park chicken 133
Malaysian chicken rice 264
marbled tea eggs with sesame chicken 23
marinated Chinese chicken salad 306
meatballs in Greek broth 45
Mediterranean chicken casserole 208
Mediterranean jellied chicken 313
Mediterranean potato toppers 77
melting crescents 76
mighty chicken loaf 159
mild chicken curry 289
mild curried banana chicken 297

minted brown rice ring 304
mixed chicken and vegetable fritters with aioli 109
Monday chicken curry 287
mustard and honey chicken with mangetout and baby corn 101
mustard, chicken, carrot and courgette pittas 73
New Orleans chicken gumbo 217
Normandy chicken 90
nutty chicken rarebit 65
nutty chicken with water chestnuts 212
orchard chicken 130
Oriental barbecued chicken 136
Oriental chicken and beansprout salad 319
Oriental chicken and prawn salad 28
Oriental chicken and soy soup 51
Oriental chicken and sweetcorn soup 50
Oriental chicken curry 294
Oriental green bean, chicken and peanut salad 310
oven-crunched sesame chicken 158
packed with plenty salad 314
paella Valencia 255
Parmesan rice with chicken, tomatoes and basil 257
party rice salad 304
pasta soufflé sensation 241
pâté crunch 79
peasant chicken 104
peasant chicken pasta 249
peasant pottage 47
peppered chicken 92
piazzaiola pancakes 97
picnic pies 190
pimiento chicken sticks 69
pink grapefruit and chive chicken 203
piperade with chicken 70
piquant chicken bake 267
piquant spinach and chicken rolls 26
plain barbecued chicken 134
plain grilled chicken in butter 123
plain grilled chicken with garlic 123
poached chicken with summer fruit and vegetable salad 313
Polonaise chicken 210
Pompeii eggs 27
pot roast chicken with orange and pecans 204
pot roast chicken with tomatoes and cashew nuts 204
pot roast chilli chicken with rice 150
pot roast paprika chicken with rice 150
potato pan pizza 67
potted chicken with sherry and herbs 25
Provençal chicken pancakes 96
prune and chicken-stuffed tomatoes 28
Punjabi butter chicken 297
quick chicken and asparagus soufflé 72
quick chicken and bean soufflé 72
quick chicken and corn soufflé 72
quick chicken and pineapple pizza 67
quick chicken tikka pizza 66
quick Chinese chicken pittas 73
quick French chicken casserole 207
quick Greek-style chicken and vegetable soup 55
quick Italian chicken casserole 207
quick rice supper 269
quick Scottish chicken soup 48
rice with eggs and chicken 260
rich and creamy risotto 257
rich chicken and mushroom soup 51
riso pecorino Romano con pollo 257
risotto al forno 255
risotto bianco con pollo 256
risotto bianco di Napoli 256
risotto with chicken, cheese and wine 260
roast lemon chicken and vegetable platter 147
roast part-boned chicken with lemon grass and rice stuffing 149
roasted spiced flower chicken with barley 151
rosemary and garlic barbecued chicken 136
rosemary chicken with wine-caramelled onions 130
rosti with chicken and asparagus rolls 72
salt roast chicken with potatoes, garlic and parsnips 148
savoury chicken and egg pasta 244
savoury chicken toasts 65
savoury egg rice 258
Scarborough Fair chicken 89
sesame chicken and broccoli stir-fry 99
sherried chicken and pasta soup 50
sherried chicken casserole 215
simple chicken and chive omelette 70
simple chicken and ham omelette 71
simple chicken and mushroom omelette 70
simple chicken and prawn omelette 70
simple chicken omelette 70
simple curried chicken mayonnaise 308
simple dolmas 23
simple fried chicken 91
simple pasta bake 248
smoked chicken and ham vol-au-vent 191
smoked chicken, ham and walnut salad 318
smoked chicken with scrambled egg 25
Somerset chicken bake 250
spaghetti Bolognese 248
spaghetti with chicken and mushrooms 252
spaghetti with chicken and sage 251

spaghetti with chicken, Ricotta and broccoli 243
Spanish rice 263
spatchcocked chicken with lime 134
speciality chicken risotto 265
spiced chicken casserole 218
spiced creamy chicken with brandy 88
spiced yoghurt chicken kebabs 128
spicy chicken and pease pudding crisp 185
spicy chicken and potato cakes 68
spicy chicken parcels 149
spicy chicken wings 127
spicy Chinese chicken 99
spicy fried chicken 92
spicy grilled chicken bites 28
spicy yoghurt chicken breasts 134
spinach and chicken roulade 73
spinach, chicken and peanut loaf 160
spinach pancakes with soft cheese and chicken 95
spring greens with chicken, bacon, cumin and eggs 110
stir-fry chicken and vegetable salad 306
stir-fry chicken with bamboo shoots 102
stuffed cucumber boats 27
stuffed peaches 27
summer paella 317
sun-kissed tagliatelle 241
sunny chicken salad 312
sweet and sour chicken 98
sweet and sour chicken balls 99
sweet and sour chicken delight 251
sweet barbecued chicken fillets 106
sweet spiced chicken with coriander and lemon 123
sweet spiced chicken with mint 123
Swiss chicken salad 305
Syrian chicken dome 266
Szechuan chicken 101
tandoori chicken drummers 287
tandoori-style grilled chicken 135
Thai chicken curry 293
Thai coconut chicken 132
Thai grilled chicken with spiced peaches 132
Thai meat balls 153
Thousand Island chicken and prawn sandwiches 75
traditional Sunday roast chicken 153
Tropical chicken 213
Turkish-style marinated chicken kebabs 129
Tuscan risotto with chicken, spices and raisins 261
Umbrian chicken and pea salad 308
warm brown rice, chicken and nut salad 309
warm chicken, carrot, courgette and wild rice salad 307
washday rice 267
Welsh cream of chicken pie 190
white chicken and bacon casserole 203
white chicken soup 45
winter chicken and lentil pot 219
winter chicken pot 219
wontons in garlic soup 44
woodland chicken soup 53
zesty chicken and vegetable casserole 214

chicken giblets
chicken giblet soup 56

chicken livers
anchovy and pâté eggs with vermicelli 253
chicken liver and hazelnut cannelloni 253
chicken liver and mushroom pâté with celery 32
chicken liver and pea pottage 57
chicken liver and rice-stuffed peppers 271
chicken liver brochettes 136
chicken liver brochettes with persimmons 137
chicken liver gougère 164
chicken liver jackets 79
chicken liver morsels 195
chicken liver nests 111
chicken livers, bacon and spinach 78
chicken soup with chopped liver dumplings 56
chunky chicken loaf 164
grilled aubergine slices with chicken livers and peanut sauce 32
herby chicken liver toasts 79
layered chicken pâté with sweet pepper salad 319
lemony livers with white beans 111
livers in cream and sherry 111
mumbled eggs 78
Oriental chicken livers with spinach and toasted sesame seeds 30
Oriental chicken, spinach and egg noodle soup 43
pâté and horseradish dip 32
pâté fingers 79
pâté nests 31
pheasant, chicken liver and broccoli risotto 285
piquant chicken liver farfalle 254
savoury chicken liver risotto 271
savoury stuffed mushrooms 29
sherried chicken liver lasagne 254
sherried pâté pears 32
speciality chicken liver omelette 78
Tuscan chicken liver soup 56
velvety chicken liver pâté 31

warm chicken livers with blueberries 31
chicken stock
chicken carcass stock 43
Chinese chicken stock 43
Chinese egg flower soup 52
garlic and chicken soup 53
sopa di agio 53
straciatella 52
white chicken stock 43
chilled tomato and cardamom rice with duck 328
chilli barbecued chicken 136
chilli con pollo 204
chilli rub 346
chilli turkey sandwiches 83
chilli winter warmer 44
Chinese chicken and mushroom stir-fry 100
Chinese chicken and spring onion soup 47
Chinese chicken and vegetable soup 51
Chinese chicken burgers 153
Chinese chicken fries 24
Chinese chicken, prawn and beansprout salad 310
Chinese chicken rissoles 102
Chinese chicken stock 43
Chinese chicken wings 160
Chinese chilli dipping sauce 337
Chinese curried meatballs 295
Chinese curry sauce 338
Chinese duck with egg, vegetables and noodles 118
Chinese egg flower soup 52
Chinese fire chicken 106
Chinese fried pigeon 120
Chinese hot and sour soup 46
Chinese meatballs with ginger 22
Chinese mushroom, chicken and king prawn stir-fry 100
Chinese mushroom, chicken and pineapple stir-fry 100
Chinese spring rolls 22
Chinese-style chicken with cashew nuts and rice 107
Chinese-style marinade 344
Chinese tea-smoked roast duck 174
chipolata sausages
bacon-wrapped chipolatas 354
chive butter 343
Christmas turkey lasagne 274
chunky chicken loaf 164
chutney
fresh sweet chutney 338
citrus chicken 215
clams
chicken and clam risotto 263
cock-a-leekie soup 49
Continental chicken and vegetable salad 308
cooking 9
cooling chicken potato toppers 77
coq au vin 207
coq au vin blanc 207
corn *see* sweetcorn
corn fritters 355
corny turkey sausage rolls 80
Coronation chicken 316
cottage cheese, chicken and prawn cups 27
country partridge casserole 236
couscous
grilled spiced chicken with sweet pepper couscous 126
cranberry marinade 345
cranberry sauce 339
cream of chicken and walnut soup 54
cream of turkey and pecan soup 58
creamed baked rice with cheese 276
creamed chicken and tarragon soup 50
creamed risotto with chicken and lemon 260
creamy cardamom chicken 88
creamy cheese and turkey fruity 83
creamy chicken and almond pasta 252
creamy chicken and avocado vol-au-vents 192
creamy chicken and ham vol-au-vents 192
creamy chicken and mushroom vol-au-vents 191
creamy chicken and prawn vol-au-vents 192
creamy chicken and sweetcorn vol-au-vents 192
creamy chicken, ham and mushroom risotto 256
creamy chicken pie 184
creamy chicken vol-au-vents 191
creamy chicken with mushrooms 98
creamy chicken with peas and hazelnuts 252
creamy duck and spinach soup 61
creamy sausage and mushroom rolls 81
creamy tarragon chicken 105
crisp baked chicken 163
crisp onion rings 356
crispy chicken and vegetable rolls 66
crispy noodle cake 356
crispy noodles 356
crispy turkey rolls 81
croissants
gooey chicken and mushroom crescents 76
melting crescents 76
crunchy-coated chicken 158
crunchy lemon chicken legs 159
crunchy meatballs with tomato barbecue sauce 140
crunchy-topped duck and vegetable soup 62
crusty duck with apricots 172

cucumber
  stuffed cucumber boats 27
  turkey, prawn and cucumber boats 34
Cumberland casseroled quail 237
Cumberland sauce 340
curries 286-302
  aru murgh 295
  balti chicken 290
  cardamom chicken 295
  cheat chicken dhansak 291
  chicken and lentil curry 296
  chicken bhuna masala 292
  chicken biryani 298
  chicken breasts masala 301
  chicken dhansak 291
  chicken dopiaza 293
  chicken Jalfrezi 300
  chicken Kashmir 294
  chicken korma 290
  chicken massage 296
  chicken moghlai 292
  chicken pal 300
  chicken palak 289
  chicken saag 296
  chicken seek kebabs 292
  chicken tikka 289
  chicken tikka biryani 298
  chicken tikka masala 299
  chicken vindaloo 294
  Chinese curried meatballs 295
  curried chicken and apple warmer 55
  curried chicken and celery casserole 219
  curried chicken and fresh mango sandwiches 76
  curried chicken and mushroom casserole 219
  curried chicken and pasta salad 314
  curried chicken and peach pittas 74
  curried chicken and sultana toppers 77
  curried chicken pancakes 94
  curried chicken pasta salad 310
  curried jackets 84
  curried rice, chicken and cheese salad 309
  curried turkey and butter bean salad 324
  curried turkey and lentil soup 57
  curried turkey and rice salad 320
  curried yoghurt marinade 345
  curry butter 343
  curry sauce 342
  dry chicken curry 287
  egg vindaloo basmati 299
  game curry 302
  Indian chicken 288
  Indian fried chicken 288
  leftover chicken biryani 298
  mild chicken curry 289
  mild curried banana chicken 297
  Monday chicken curry 287
  Oriental chicken curry 294
  Punjabi butter chicken 297
  tandoori chicken drummers 287
  Thai chicken curry 293
  turkey keema 301
Cypriot stuffed aubergine 33
dark soy dipping sauce 337
deep-fried chicken parcels 193
defrosting 9
devilled butter 343
devilled poussins
devilled turkey-stuffed eggs 35
devils and angels 89
devils on horseback 354
dolcelatte, turkey and watercress mould 277
dolmas
  simple dolmas 23
dry chicken curry 287
dry Martini chicken 212
duck 12–13
  blackcurrant duck 119
  Cantonese-style duck 118
  casseroled duck with turnips and carrots 227
  chilled tomato and cardamom rice with duck 328
  Chinese duck with egg, vegetables and noodles 118
  Chinese tea-smoked roast duck 174
  creamy duck and spinach soup 61
  creamy champagne and duck risotto 282
  crunchy-topped duck and vegetable soup 62
  crusty duck with apricots 172
  duck and apple sandwiches 86
  duck and avocado pancakes 120
  duck and barley broth 61
  duck breasts with dolcelatte dream 280
  duck carcass stock 61
  duck giblet soup 62
  duck, orange and chestnut kebabs 142
  duck, orange and mushroom kebabs 142
  duck shoot rice 281
  duck slivers with grapefruit 117
  duck slivers with orange 117
  duck with ginger 118
  duck with orange rice 281
  duck with orange terrine 38
  duck with port and redcurrant 119
  duck with raspberries 119
  French-style duck casserole 225
  grilled wild duck 142
  honey roast duck 173
  Moroccan-style duck 225
  nutty apricot and duck cooler 327
  old English country duck 226
  Oriental sesame bites 39
  Oriental soy duck with apples 175
  Peking duck 173
  peppered duck 119

plain duck broth 61
potted duck with port and sage 38
potted duck with Stilton and redcurrants 38
risotto with cheese, duck, garlic and parsley 280
roast duck with cherries 172
saffron rice and duck salad 328
salmi de canard 227
salted casseroled duck 226
speciality duck platter 329
spiced duck with lime and potato salad 329
sumptuous duck and apple parcels 174
sweet and spicy duck 141
tangy duck, watercress and orange salad 328
traditional roast duck 171
warming duck soup with peas 62
watercress, duck and egg pasta 279
wild duck with blackberries 182
duck livers
duck liver and apple-stuffed peppers 282
duck liver, pine nut and spinach cannelloni 280
duckling 13
dumplings
chicken soup with chopped liver dumplings 56
chicken soup with lemon dumplings 54
chicken soup with matzo meal dumplings 54
Japanese chicken dumplings 194
Dutch rice ring 331
Dutch roast 158
Eastern rice with egg 259
Eastern saffron soup 45
easy roast stuffed chicken breasts 148
Edwardian rum partridge with grape, lettuce and watercress salad 332
eggs
chicken stir-fry scramble 103
Chinese egg flower soup 52
devilled turkey-stuffed eggs 35
egg and turkey rashers in green sauce 34
egg fried rice 351
egg vindaloo basmati 299
marbled tea eggs with sesame chicken 23
mumbled eggs 78
mushroom, sausage and egg cups 36
Pompeii eggs 27
savoury egg rice 258
savoury jellied egg ramekins 35
smoked chicken with scrambled egg 25
sopa di agio 53
spaghetti all'Uova 244
special egg fried rice 351
straciatella 52
turkey Scotch egg salad 325
see also quail's eggs
enchiladas 204
English country chicken salad 309
Espagnole sauce 335
extra-fragrant Parmesan rice 257
fajitas
chicken and roast vegetable fajitas 161
chicken fajitas 109
fast chicken and spiced hazelnuts 316
fast food turkey chow mein 116
fast macaroni supper 84
fettuccine with turkey and jalopeño pepper cream 273
Fijian chicken 213
food hygiene 7-10
food poisoning 7
forcemeat balls 354
four-cheese melting moments with crunchy turkey 276
fragrant chicken and pesto baguette 69
fragrant chicken parcels 149
fragrant fried chicken 91
fragrant herb poussins with lemon and honey 162
fragrant pheasant hot-pot 176
fragrant stuffed tomatoes 307
freezers 8
French peasant chicken pasta 249
French-roast partridge 178
French-style duck casserole 225
French-style peasant chicken 104
fresh potted pheasant 41
fresh sweet chutney 338
fridges 8
fried bananas 355
fried chicken Kiev 92
fritters
chicken and vegetable fritters 110
corn fritters 355
mixed chicken and vegetable fritters with aioli 109
game
cooking and reheating 9
game broth 63
game broth with mushrooms 63
game broth with onion croûtons 63
game carcass stock 63
game chips 348
game curry 302
game pie 198-199
game soup 63
potted game 40
raised game pie 199
shopping for 7
storage 8
thawing 9
types 13–14
gamekeeper's asparagus 40
garlic

garlic and chicken soup 53
garlic and lemon chicken 163
garlic and parsley marinade 345
garlic bread 357
garlic butter 343
garlic butter roast chicken and potatoes 145
garlic fried chicken 91
garlic potato wedges 349
giant game cushions 283
giblets
chicken giblet soup 56
duck giblet soup 62
giblet gravy 334
pheasant giblet soup 63
turkey giblet soup 60
glazzwill turkey fillets 138
gnocchi
cheese and chicken gnocchi 244
gnocchi alla Romana con pollo 242
gold-kissed chicken grill 127
golden sweet and sour chicken breasts 107
golden turkey and sweetcorn bake 166
gooey chicken and mushroom crescents 76
gooey chicken parcels 147
goose 13
roast goose in cider 175
roast goose with sage, apple and Calvados stuffing 176
gooseberry sauce 340
gorgeous glazed chicken 88
Gorgonzola speciality 258
gougères
chicken and mushroom gougère 160
chicken liver gougère 164
goulash sauce 342
grapefruit
turkey and pink grapefruit pâté 33
grapes
turkey with grape juice and grapes 112
gravies
giblet gravy 334
orange gravy 334
vegetable water gravy 334
see also butters; marinades; rubs; sauces
Greek chicken and mushroom salad 304
Greek-styled marinated chicken kebabs 129
green herb butter 343
green sauce 341
grilled aubergine slices with chicken livers and peanut sauce 32
grilled chicken bites 28
grilled chicken Kiev 124
grilled chicken Kiev with lime and coriander 124
grilled chicken with basil and anchovies 131
grilled chicken with Chinese five spice powder 125
grilled chicken with corn stuffing 124
grilled chicken with hot olive sauce 123
grilled chicken with pasta 242
grilled Italian platter 135
grilled spiced chicken with sweet pepper couscous 126
grilled turkey wrapped in bacon with Oriental sauce 138
grilled turkey wrapped in Parma ham with piazzola sauce 139
grilled wild duck 142
grouse 13
grouse in lager 231
marinated grouse of the ancient Romans 232
old English roast grouse 179
roast grouse with onion buttered crumbs 178
salmi of grouse 233
Taunton grouse 231
Victorian grouse fricassée 232
see also capercaillie; ptarmigan
Guacamole relish 338
guinea fowl 13
guinea fowl in white Bordeaux 237
honey and mustard glazed guinea fowl with roasted roots 179
ham
baked main meal turkey, ham and vegetable soup 58
chicken and ham rolls with pineapple sauce 93
chicken, ham and olive cocktail 21
chicken, ham and pineapple cocktail 20
chicken, ham and tomato grill 127
chicken and ham quiche 186
creamy chicken and avocado vol-au-vents 192
Hawaiian chicken 308
hazelnuts
woodland chicken soup 53
herb-stuffed chicken rolls 209
herby bacon stuffing 353
herby chicken liver toasts 79
Highland pâté 37
Highland pâté with pickled walnuts 37
hindle wakes 312
honey and mustard glazed guinea fowl with roasted roots 179
honey roast duck 173
hot herb bread 357
hot Leerdammer and turkey bites 35
hot peanut chicken 214
hot potato salad 350
huevos à la Cubana 20
hunter's pigeon 180
hunter's spaghetti 282
hunter's squab 180
hygiene 7–10

iced chicken and mango mulligatawny 48
Indian chicken 288
Indian chicken and mushroom pilau 266
Indian fried chicken 288
Indonesian chicken, prawn and egg rice 268
Iranian shireen polow 262
Italian chicken lunch 69
Italian lunchtime fettuccine 243
Italian-style golden fried partridge 121
Italian-style marinade 345
Italian-style savoury rice cake 255
jalopeño hoppin' John 33
Jamaican chicken 213
Japanese chicken and shiitake mushroom clear soup 46
Japanese chicken dumplings 194
Japanese peanut chicken stir-fry 108
Japanese-style sesame chicken 270
jellied turkey mayonnaise 321
Jerusalem artichoke purée 350
jointing 15
kebabs
  chicken, bacon and corn kebabs 128
  chicken, mushroom and tomato kebabs 128
  chicken seek kebabs 292
  chicken teriyaki kebabs 127
  duck, orange and chestnut kebabs 142
  duck, orange and mushroom kebabs 142
  Greek-styled marinated chicken kebabs 129
  spiced yoghurt chicken kebabs 128
  turkey, bacon and pineapple kebabs 141
  Turkish-style marinated chicken kebabs 129
Kentucky baked chicken 165
Kentucky baked turkey 171
Kentucky fried chicken sandwich 70
kitchen cleanliness 10
kosher-style chicken soup 53
kosher-style chicken soup with noodles 53
lasagne
  chicken and spinach lasagne 249
  chicken lasagne Bolognese 248
  Christmas turkey lasagne 274
  lasagne al forno 246
  lasagne with chicken and artichokes 246
  sherried chicken liver lasagne 254
  turkey and basil lasagne 276
layered chicken pâté with sweet pepper salad 319
leeks
  chicken and leek pie 189
  chicken and leek roulade with mushroom sauce 157
  cock-a-leekie soup 49
leftover chicken biryani 298
Leicester macaroni 272
lemon butter 343
lemon chicken 203
lemon chicken soufflé 72
lemony livers with white beans 111
lentils
  curried turkey and lentil soup 57
  winter chicken and lentil pot 219
light dipping sauce 337
light turkey pudding 170
lime and green peppercorn barbecued chicken 136
liver and garlic stuffing 353
liver sausage
  pâté crunch 79
  quick turkey and liver pâté 34
livers in cream and sherry 111
Louisiana jambalaya 269
macaroni
  fast macaroni supper 84
  quick macaroni supper 81
MacArthur Park chicken 133
magnificent turkey centrepiece 322
Malaysian chicken rice 264
mallard 13
mammoth mushrooms 141
mangoes
  iced chicken and mango mulligatawny 48
marbled tea eggs with sesame chicken 23
marinades
  Chinese-style marinade 344
  cranberry marinade 345
  curried yoghurt marinade 345
  garlic and parsley marinade 345
  Italian-style marinade 345
  Peking-style marinade 346
  red wine marinade 344
  sesame citrus marinade 345
  Taiwanese marinade 344
  Tropical marinade 345
  white wine marinade 344
marinated Chinese chicken salad 306
marinated grouse of the ancient Romans 232
matzo meal dumplings
  chicken soup with matzo meal dumplings 54
meatballs in Greek broth 45
Mediterranean chicken casserole 208
Mediterranean jellied chicken 313
Mediterranean potato toppers 77
melons
  chicken strips in cantaloupes 95
  turkey, melon and raisin salad 323
melting crescents 76
microwaves
  defrosting 9
mighty chicken loaf 159
mild chicken curry 289
mild curried banana chicken 297
minted brown rice ring 304

minted yoghurt and cucumber 339
mixed chicken and vegetable fritters with aioli 109
Monday chicken curry 287
Moroccan-style duck 225
mountain special 273
moussakas
chicken and aubergine moussaka 154
chicken and courgette moussaka 155
chicken and potato moussaka 154
chicken and vegetable moussaka 154
mousse
chicken, olive and avocado cups 24
cottage cheese, chicken and prawn cups 27
mumbled eggs 78
mushrooms
chicken and mushroom cocktail 21
chicken and mushroom pizza special 67
chicken and mushroom soufflé omelette 71
chicken and mushroom muncher 74
chicken and mushroom quiche 186
chicken and mushroom toad 155
chicken liver and mushroom pâté with celery 32
chicken, mushroom and noodle soup 46
chicken, mushroom and pasta chowder 52
Chinese hot and sour soup 46
creamy chicken and mushroom vol-au-vents 191
game broth with mushrooms 63
Japanese chicken and shiitake mushroom clear soup 46
mammoth mushrooms 141
mushroom bhajis 355
mushroom sauce 340
mushroom, sausage and egg cups 36
rich chicken and mushroom soup 51
savoury stuffed mushrooms 29
woodland chicken soup 53
mussels
chicken and mussel risotto 270
mustard and honey chicken with mangetout and baby corn 101
mustard butter 343
mustard, chicken, carrot and courgette pittas 73
mustard sauce 341
new age BLTs 81
New Orleans chicken gumbo 217
noodles
chicken, mushroom and noodle soup 46
chicken with cashew nuts and noodles 103
kosher-style chicken soup with noodles 53
Oriental chicken, spinach and egg noodle soup 43
Normandy chicken 90
nutty apricot and duck cooler 327
nutty chicken rarebit 65
nutty rice stuffing 353
nutty turkey Maryland balls 113
old English country duck 226
old English roast grouse 179
old traditional roast partridge 178
omelettes
chicken and asparagus soufflé omelette 71
chicken and mushroom soufflé omelette 71
chicken and sweetcorn soufflé omelette 71
chicken soufflé omelette 71
simple chicken and chive omelette 70
simple chicken and ham omelette 71
simple chicken and mushroom omelette 70
simple chicken and prawn omelette 70
simple chicken omelette 70
speciality chicken liver omelette 78
onions
crisp onion rings 356
onion bhajis 355
onion sauce 341
rosemary chicken with wine-caramelled onions 130
oranges
orange and mango salsa 336
orange and pineapple salsa 336
orange gravy 334
orchard chicken 130
Oriental barbecued chicken 136
Oriental chicken and beansprout salad 319
Oriental chicken and prawn salad 28
Oriental chicken and soy soup 51
Oriental chicken and sweetcorn soup 50
Oriental chicken curry 294
Oriental chicken livers with spinach and toasted sesame seeds 30
Oriental chicken, spinach and egg noodle soup 43
Oriental green bean, chicken and peanut salad 310
Oriental sesame bites 39
Oriental soy duck with apples 175
Oriental turkey with cashew nuts and mushrooms 116
ortolan 14
oven-crunched sesame chicken 158
oven-pilaf 352
packed with plenty salad 314
paella Valencia 255
pancakes
bacon, chicken and tomato pancakes 96

cheesy chicken pancakes 94
curried chicken pancakes 94
duck and avocado pancakes 120
piazzaiola pancakes 97
Provençal chicken pancakes 96
savoury Dutch pancakes 97
spinach pancakes with soft cheese and chicken 95
turkey and corn Scotch pancakes 85
Parmesan rice with chicken, tomatoes and basil 257
parsley and thyme stuffing 353
parsley butter 343
parsley sauce 341
partridge 14
country partridge casserole 236
Edwardian rum partridge with grape, lettuce and watercress salad 332
French-roast partridge 178
Italian-style golden fried partridge 121
old traditional roast partridge 178
partridge and pear salad 330
partridge in milk 135
partridge with bresaola in vine leaves with Waldorf salad 331
partridge with olives 236
salmi of partridge 236
Saxon partridge and mushroom pudding 201
Saxon partridge and oyster pudding 200
pasta
anchovy and pâté eggs with vermicelli 253
around the world warm salad 326
Austrian Schinkenfleckerl 243
baked pasta Bolognese 248
cannelloni Bolognese 247
Caribbean pasta salad 310
chicken and asparagus bake 245
chicken and celery bake 245
chicken and cider quills 247
chicken and red wine pasta 246
chicken and sweetcorn bake 246
chicken and tarragon meatballs with spicy spaghetti 245
chicken and tarragon peppered tagliatelle 242
chicken, leek and walnut vermicelli 251
chicken liver and hazelnut cannelloni 253
chicken, mushroom and pasta chowder 52
chicken tetrazzini 240
chicken Tuscany 250
Chinese chicken, prawn and beansprout salad 310
creamy chicken and almond pasta 252
creamy chicken with peas and hazelnuts 252
crispy noodle cake 356
crispy noodles 356
curried chicken and pasta salad 314
curried chicken pasta salad 310
duck breasts with dolcelatte dream 280
duck liver, pine nut and spinach cannelloni 280
fettuccine with turkey and jalopeño pepper cream 273
four-cheese melting moments with crunchy turkey 276
fragrant chicken with spaghetti 247
French peasant chicken pasta 249
giant game cushions 283
glazed chicken quills 247
grilled chicken with pasta 242
hunter's spaghetti 282
Italian lunchtime fettuccine 243
Leicester macaroni 272
mountain special 273
nutty apricot and duck cooler 327
Oriental green bean, chicken and peanut salad 310
packed with plenty salad 314
pasta soufflé sensation 241
peasant chicken pasta 249
piquant chicken liver farfalle 254
salsa Alfredo for fresh pasta 273
savoury chicken and egg pasta 244
sherried chicken and pasta soup 50
simple pasta bake 248
Somerset chicken bake 250
spaghetti all'Uova 244
spaghetti Bolognese 248
spaghetti with chicken and mushrooms 252
spaghetti with chicken and sage 251
spaghetti with chicken, Ricotta and broccoli 243
spaghetti with Ricotta, pheasant and asparagus 283
spaghetti with turkey and oyster mushrooms 275
spaghetti with turkey carbonara 274
Stilton, turkey and walnut salad 320
sun-kissed tagliatelle 241
sunny chicken salad 312
sweet and sour chicken delight 251
tagliatelle alla panna 275
turkey with grapes, olives and pasta 275
watercress, duck and egg pasta 279
Wraysbury carbonara 274
see also lasagne; ravioli
pastry dishes 183–201
Boxing Day pie 195
cheesy chicken and chive plait 192
chicken and egg pie 185
chicken and leek pie 189
chicken and mushroom flan 193
chicken and mushroom gougère 160

chicken and spring vegetable jalousie 188
chicken and vegetable pasties 187
chicken Florentine 188
chicken in filo pastry with asparagus sauce 189
chicken liver gougère 164
chicken liver morsels 195
chicken parcels with cranberry 187
chicken, spinach and pecan pies 184
creamy chicken pie 184
deep-fried chicken parcels 193
game pie 198-199
pheasant and steak pudding 198
picnic pies 190
pigeon pie 201
quail's egg tartlets 39
raised game pie 199
Saxon partridge and mushroom pudding 201
Saxon partridge and oyster pudding 200
spicy chicken and pease pudding crisp 185
squab pie 201
turkey, bacon and egg pie 197
turkey Christmas parcel 196-197
Welsh cream of chicken pie 190
Yorkshire pigeon pie 200
see also quiches; vol-au-vents
pâtés
brandied turkey liver and walnut pâté 37
chicken liver and mushroom pâté with celery 32
Highland pâté 37
Highland pâté with pickled walnuts 37
layered chicken pâté with sweet pepper salad 319
pâté and horseradish dip 32
pâté fingers 79
pâté nests 31
quick turkey and liver pâté 34
sherried pâté pears 32
turkey and cranberry pâté layer 326
turkey and pink grapefruit pâté 33
velvety chicken liver pâté 31
velvety turkey liver pâté with port 37
peaches
stuffed peaches 27
peanuts
chicken and peanut perfection 75
chicken, corn and peanut chowder 52
peanut sauce 336
pears
sherried pâté pears 32
peas
chicken liver and pea pottage 57
peasant chicken 104
peasant chicken pasta 249
peasant pottage 47
pease pudding
spicy chicken and pease pudding crisp 185
pecan nuts
cream of turkey and pecan soup 58
Peking duck 173
Peking-style marinade 346
Peking-style turkey 112
peppered chicken 92
peppered duck 119
peppers
chicken liver and rice-stuffed peppers 271
duck liver and apple-stuffed peppers 282
jalopeño hoppin' John 33
perfect potato wedges 349
pesto for poultry 342
pheasant 14
casserole of pheasant with chestnuts and oranges 228
casseroled pheasant with Italian sauce 230
cheese, pheasant and rice croquettes 284
Dutch rice ring 331
forestry pheasant 229
fragrant pheasant hot-pot 176
fresh potted pheasant 41
game soup 63
gamekeeper's asparagus 40
giant game cushions 283
hunter's spaghetti 282
pheasant and five bean salad 330
pheasant and steak pudding 198
pheasant, chicken liver and broccoli risotto 285
pheasant giblet soup 63
pheasant mimosa 86
pheasant with artichokes and chestnuts 231
pheasant with celeriac and carrot 228
pheasant with celery and walnuts 228
pheasant with cider and pears 229
pheasant with tomato and cheese cream 120
pheasant with white wine and apples 229
pot roast pheasant with Parma ham 177
potted game 40
potted pheasant with two cheeses 41
risotto with pheasant, cheese and mixed herbs 284
salmi of pheasant 230
spaghetti with Ricotta, pheasant and asparagus 283
sparkling pheasant bortsch 63
sweet and sour pheasant with beans 41
Valencian pheasant 332
Victorian roast pheasant 177
piazzaiola pancakes 97
piazzaiola sauce 335
picnic pies 190

pies *see* pastry dishes
pigeon 14
boned stuffed pigeons 181
braised pigeons with red cabbage 233
casserole of pigeons with baby onions and mushroom stuffing balls 234
Chinese fried pigeon 120
creamy pigeons with redcurrant 234
hunter's pigeon 180
pigeon pie 201
roast pigeons with sherry sauce 180
spatchcocked pigeons in red wine 235
Yorkshire pigeon pie 200
pimiento chicken sticks 69
pink grapefruit and chive chicken 203
piperade with chicken 70
piquant chicken bake 267
piquant chicken liver farfalle 254
piquant spinach and chicken rolls 26
pitta bread
chicken and cashew nut pittas 74
curried chicken and peach pittas 74
mustard, chicken, carrot and courgette pittas 73
quick Chinese chicken pittas 73
see also baguettes; bread; sandwiches
pizzas
chicken and mushroom pizza special 67
potato pan pizza 67
quick chicken and pineapple pizza 67
quick chicken tikka pizza 66
turkey stuffed pizzas 85
plain barbecued chicken 134
plain boiled rice 351
plain duck broth 61
plain grilled chicken in butter 123
plain grilled chicken with garlic 123
poached chicken with summer fruit and vegetable salad 313
Polish sauce 341
Polish stuffed cabbage leaves 36
Polonaise chicken 210
Pompeii eggs 27
popadoms 355
poppy seed and mustard royal roast potatoes 348
pork
cassoulet 220
pot roast chicken with orange and pecans 204
pot roast chicken with tomatoes and cashew nuts 204
pot roast chilli chicken with rice 150
pot roast paprika chicken with rice 150
pot roast pheasant with Parma ham 177
potatoes
bean and sausage toppers 83
caraway royal roast potatoes 348
cheat game chips 348
cheese potatoes 349
cheesy turkey jackets 84
chicken and bacon stuffed jackets 76
chicken and chive stuffed jackets 77
chicken and potato chowder 49
chicken and potato quiche 187
chicken and sweetcorn jackets 76
chicken, ham and pineapple stuffed jackets 77
chicken liver jackets 79
cooling chicken potato toppers 77
curried chicken and sultana toppers 77
curried jackets 84
game chips 348
garlic potato wedges 349
hot potato salad 350
Mediterranean potato toppers 77
perfect potato wedges 349
poppy seed and mustard royal roast potatoes 348
potato bhajis 355
potato pakoras 356
potato pan pizza 67
puréed potatoes 350
ravishing rasher toppers 83
royal roast potatoes 348
sesame seed royal roast potatoes 348
speciality creamed potatoes 348
spicy chicken and potato cakes 68
super sauté potatoes 349
super sauté potatoes with garlic 349
turkey and cranberry toppers 83
turkey and kidney bean jackets 84
turkey and potato pie 170
turkey and stuffing jackets 84
potted chicken with sherry and herbs 25
potted duck with port and sage 38
potted duck with Stilton and redcurrants 38
potted game 40
potted pheasant with two cheeses 41
potted turkey livers 36
poultry
cooking and reheating 9
preparing 15–16
roasting 144–145
shopping for 7
storage 8
thawing 9
types 12–13
see also individual types
poussins
chicken jambalaya 269
devilled poussins 162
fragrant herb poussins with lemon and honey 162
poussins à la Provençal 162
poussins roasted with white wine and rosemary 163
poussins with warm vegetable salad 318

spatchcock poussin with pesto 131
spatchcock poussin with red pesto 131
prawns
chicken and prawn bouillabaisse 48
chicken and prawn cocktail 21
chicken and prawn quiche 186
chicken and prawn risotto 263
chicken and prawn wontons with sweet and sour sauce 21
cottage cheese, chicken and prawn cups 27
creamy chicken and prawn vol-au-vents 192
Oriental chicken and prawn salad 28
turkey, prawn and cucumber boats 34
wontons in garlic soup 44
Provençal chicken pancakes 96
Provençal sauce 342
prunes
devils on horseback 354
prune and chicken-stuffed tomatoes 28
prune and pecan stuffing 354
ptarmigan 14
pumpkin
turkey and pumpkin chermoula 165
Punjabi butter chicken 297
puréed potatoes 350
quail 14
braised quail in hock with seasoned rice 285
Cumberland casseroled quail 237
quail parcels with oyster mushroom sauce 181
quail ragoût with mushroom selection 239
risotto con le quaglie 284
quails' eggs
asparagus, strawberry and quail's egg salad 40
quails' egg tartlets 39
quiches
chicken and asparagus quiche 187
chicken and broccoli quiche 186
chicken and ham quiche 186
chicken and mushroom quiche 186
chicken and parsley quiche 186
chicken and potato quiche 187
chicken and prawn quiche 186
chicken and sweetcorn quiche 186
chicken and tomato quiche 187
chicken, sweetcorn and pepper quiche 186
quick béchamel sauce 340
quick chicken and asparagus soufflé 72
quick chicken and bean soufflé 72
quick chicken and corn soufflé 72
quick chicken and pineapple pizza 67
quick chicken tikka pizza 66
quick Chinese chicken pittas 73
quick French chicken casserole 207
quick Greek-style chicken and vegetable soup 55
quick Italian chicken casserole 207
quick macaroni supper 81
quick pilau rice 351
quick rice supper 269
quick Scottish chicken soup 48
quick turkey and liver pâté 34
quick turkey loaf 169
raised game pie 199
ravioli
chicken and Ricotta ravioli 241
chicken ravioli 240
chicken, spinach and Ricotta ravioli 241
Turkish ravioli 272
ravishing rasher toppers 83
recipe notes 11
red almond pesto 342
red wine marinade 344
redcurrant roast stuffed turkey 166
refrigerators *see* fridges
reheating 9
rice
American-style hot chicken salad 307
Andalusian rice 271
arancini Siciliani 261
arroz con pollo 268
arroz poblano 277
Bangkok supper 264
beetroot layer 320
biryani salad 317
braised quail in hock with seasoned rice 285
brown rice 351
brown rice and chicken slow-pot 216
buttered rice 351
Californian fruit and rice for poultry or game 305
Ceylonese rice 259
cheese, pheasant and rice croquettes 284
chicken and egg fried rice with bacon 259
chicken and rice soup 49
chicken and vegetable cassata 309
chicken, blue cheese and pear salad 315
chicken, corn and mushroom pilaf 267
chicken, hazelnut and vegetable rice 262
chicken jambalaya 269
chicken liver and rice-stuffed peppers 271
chicken supreme salad 314
chilled tomato and cardamom rice with duck 328
Continental chicken and vegetable salad 308
Coronation chicken 316
cottage rice casserole 258
creamed baked rice with cheese 276
curried rice, chicken and cheese salad 309

curried turkey and butter bean salad 324
curried turkey and rice salad 320
dolcelatte, turkey and watercress mould 277
duck liver and apple-stuffed peppers 282
duck shoot rice 281
duck with orange rice 281
Dutch rice ring 331
Eastern rice with egg 259
egg fried rice 351
English country chicken salad 309
extra-fragrant Parmesan rice 257
Gorgonzola speciality 258
Hawaiian chicken 308
Indian chicken and mushroom pilau 266
Indonesian chicken, prawn and egg rice 268
Iranian shireen polow 262
Italian-style savoury rice cake 255
Japanese-style sesame chicken 270
Louisiana jambalaya 269
Malaysian chicken rice 264
minted brown rice ring 304
nutty rice stuffing 353
oven-pilaf 352
Parmesan rice with chicken, tomatoes and basil 257
party rice salad 304
piquant chicken bake 267
plain boiled rice 351
quick pilau rice 351
quick rice supper 269
rice dream 278
rice with eggs and chicken 260
riso pecorino Romano con pollo 257
saffron rice and duck salad 328
savoury cheese timbale 278
savoury egg rice 258
simple curried chicken mayonnaise 308
Spanish rice 263
special egg fried rice 351
summer paella 317
suppli al telefono 277
Syrian chicken dome 266
Thai fragrant rice 351
turkey and tomato rice 278
turkey and tomato rice with sweetcorn and peas 278
Umbrian chicken and pea salad 308
warm brown rice, chicken and nut salad 309
warm chicken, carrot, courgette and wild rice salad 307
washday rice 267
wild rice mix 352
see also paellas; risottos

rich chicken and mushroom soup 51

risottos
chicken and clam risotto 263
chicken and mussel risotto 270
chicken and prawn risotto 263
chicken and tarragon risotto 265
chicken, chive and pineapple risotto 265
creamed risotto with chicken and lemon 260
creamy champagne and duck risotto 282
creamy chicken, ham and mushroom risotto 256
pheasant, chicken liver and broccoli risotto 285
rich and creamy risotto 257
risotto al forno 255
risotto bianco con pollo 256
risotto bianco di Napoli 256
risotto con le quaglie 284
risotto with cheese, duck, garlic and parsley 280
risotto with chicken, cheese and wine 260
risotto with pheasant, cheese and mixed herbs 284
savoury chicken liver risotto 271
speciality chicken risotto 265
turkey liver and pea risotto 279
Tuscan risotto with chicken, spices and raisins 261

rissoles
Chinese chicken rissoles 102
turkey and lentil rissoles 117
see also burgers

roasting 144-145
butter roast chicken and potatoes 145
Californian-style honey roast turkey 168
chicken Maryland 146
easy roast stuffed chicken breasts 148
French-roast partridge 178
garlic butter roast chicken and potatoes 145
gooey chicken parcels 147
honey roast duck 173
old English roast grouse 179
old traditional roast partridge 178
redcurrant roast stuffed turkey 166
roast duck with cherries 172
roast goose in cider 175
roast goose with sage, apple and Calvados stuffing 176
roast grouse with onion buttered crumbs 178
roast lemon chicken and vegetable platter 147
roast paprika turkey 167
roast part-boned chicken with lemon grass and rice stuffing 149
roast pigeons with sherry sauce 180
roast widgeon with chicory and orange salad 182
roast woodcock Rossini 179

roasted spiced flower chicken with barley 151
salt roast chicken with potatoes, garlic and parsnips 148
sixteenth-century roast turkey 169
Thanksgiving turkey 168
traditional roast duck 171
traditional roast turkey 167
traditional Sunday roast chicken 153
Victorian roast pheasant 177
rosemary and garlic barbecued chicken 136
rosemary and garlic rub 346
rosemary chicken with wine-caramelled onions 130
rosti with chicken and asparagus rolls 72
rouille 339
roulades
spinach and chicken roulade 73
royal roast potatoes 348
rubs
Cajun rub 346
chilli rub 346
rosemary and garlic rub 346
totally dry onion rub 346
see also butters; gravies; marinades; sauces
saffron
chicken and saffron soup 47
saffron rice and duck salad 328
sage and onion stuffing 353
salads 303–332
chicken 304–319
duck 327–329
game 330–332
turkey 320–327
salmi de canard 227
salmi of grouse 233
salmi of partridge 236
salmi of pheasant 230
salsa Alfredo for fresh pasta 273
salt roast chicken with potatoes, garlic and parsnips 148
salted casseroled duck 226
samosas
chicken samosas 29
sandwiches
chicken and avocado coolers 75
chicken and cress butter sandwiches 74
chicken and mushroom muncher 74
chicken and peanut perfection 75
chicken, red pepper and chilli sandwiches 75
chilli turkey sandwiches 83
creamy cheese and turkey fruity 83
curried chicken and fresh mango sandwiches 76
duck and apple sandwiches 86
Kentucky fried chicken sandwich 70
new age BLTs 81
pheasant mimosa 86
piquant turkey specials 82
Thousand Island chicken and prawn sandwiches 75
turkey and cranberry toastie 82
turkey mayo sandwiches 82
turkey tartare sandwiches 82
see also bread; baguettes; pitta bread
sauces
apple sauce 339
aurora sauce 341
barbecue sauce 336
basic quick rice sauce 340
bigarde sauce 335
bread sauce 339
brinjals 338
brown onion salsa 336
caper sauce 341
caviare cream 339
Chantilly sauce 341
cheese sauce 341
Chinese chilli dipping sauce 337
Chinese curry sauce 338
cranberry sauce 339
Cumberland sauce 340
curry sauce 342
dark soy dipping sauce 337
Espagnole sauce 335
fresh sweet chutney 338
gooseberry sauce 340
goulash sauce 342
green sauce 341
Guacamole relish 338
light dipping sauce 337
minted yoghurt and cucumber 339
mushroom sauce 340
mustard sauce 341
onion sauce 341
orange and mango salsa 336
orange and pineapple salsa 336
parsley sauce 341
peanut sauce 336
pesto for poultry 342
piazzaiola sauce 335
Polish sauce 341
Provençal sauce 342
quick béchamel sauce 340
red almond pesto 342
rouille 339
supreme sauce 341
sweet and sour dipping sauce 337
tomato dipping sauce 337
tomato sauce 342
velouté sauce 340
see also butters; gravies; marinades; rubs
sausage salad supreme 322
savoury butters *see* butters
savoury cheese timbale 278

savoury chicken and egg pasta 244
savoury chicken liver risotto 271
savoury chicken toasts 65
savoury Dutch pancakes 97
savoury egg rice 258
savoury jellied egg ramekins 35
savoury stuffed mushrooms 29
savoury turkey escalopes 116
savoury turkey toasts 82
Saxon partridge and mushroom pudding 201
Saxon partridge and oyster pudding 200
Scarborough Fair chicken 89
sesame chicken and broccoli stir-fry 99
sesame citrus marinade 345
sesame seed royal roast potatoes 348
sherried chicken and pasta soup 50
sherried chicken casserole 215
sherried chicken liver lasagne 254
sherried pâté pears 32
sherried turkey pottage 59
shopping 7
simple chicken and chive omelette 70
simple chicken and ham omelette 71
simple chicken and mushroom omelette 70
simple chicken and prawn omelette 70
simple chicken omelette 70
simple curried chicken mayonnaise 308
simple dolmas 23
simple fried chicken 91
simple pasta bake 248
simple turkey satay 139
sixteenth-century roast turkey 169
smoked chicken and ham vol au vent 191
smoked chicken, ham and walnut salad 318
smoked chicken with scrambled egg 25
smoked turkey and cheese balls 34
snacks 64–86
  chicken 65–79
  duck 86
  game 86
  turkey 80–85
snipe 14
  snipe parcels with oyster mushroom sauce 181
  spiced salmi of snipe 238
Somerset chicken bake 250
Somerset turkey pot roast with dumplings 222
sopa di agio 53
soufflés
  almost instant chicken soufflé 71
  lemon chicken soufflé 72
  quick chicken and asparagus soufflé 72
  quick chicken and bean soufflé 72
  quick chicken and corn soufflé 72
soups 42–63
  chicken 43–57
  duck 61–62
  game 63
  turkey 57–60
spaghetti Bolognese 248
spaghetti with chicken and mushrooms 252
spaghetti with chicken and sage 251
spaghetti with Ricotta, pheasant and asparagus 283
spaghetti with turkey and oyster mushrooms 275
spaghetti with turkey carbonara 274
Spanish rice 263
sparkling pheasant bortsch 63
spatchcock poussin with pesto 131
spatchcock poussin with red pesto 131
spatchcocked chicken with lime 134
spatchcocked pigeons in red wine 235
speciality chicken liver omelette 78
speciality chicken risotto 265
speciality creamed potatoes 348
speciality duck platter 329
spiced chicken casserole 218
spiced creamy chicken with brandy 88
spiced duck with lime and potato salad 329
spiced salmi of snipe 238
spiced yoghurt chicken kebabs 128
spicy chicken and potato cakes 68
spicy chicken parcels 149
spicy chicken wings 127
spicy Chinese chicken 99
spicy fried chicken 92
spicy grilled chicken bites 28
spicy turkey drummers 170
spicy yoghurt chicken breasts 134
spinach
  chicken and spinach lasagne 249
  chicken Florentine 188
  chicken livers, bacon and spinach 78
  chicken, spinach and pecan pies 184
  creamy duck and spinach soup 61
  Oriental chicken livers with spinach and toasted sesame seeds 30
  Oriental chicken, spinach and egg noodle soup 43
  piquant spinach and chicken rolls 26
  spinach and chicken roulade 73
  spinach, chicken and peanut loaf 160
  spinach pancakes with soft cheese and chicken 95
spring greens with chicken, bacon, cumin and eggs 110
spring onions
  Chinese chicken and spring onion soup 47
  turkey and spring onion wontons with chilli dipping sauce 34

squab
braised squab with white cabbage and caraway 233
hunter's squab 180
squab pie 201
starters 19–41
chicken 20–32
duck 38–39
game 39–41
turkey 33–37
Stilton, turkey and walnut salad 320
stir-fries
chicken and mushrooms with oyster sauce 101
chicken stir-fry scramble 103
chicken stir-fry sticks 68
chicken with cashew nuts and noodles 103
chicken with mixed peppers and black bean sauce 100
Chinese chicken and mushroom stir-fry 100
Chinese mushroom, chicken and king prawn stir-fry 100
Chinese mushroom, chicken and pineapple stir-fry 100
Japanese peanut chicken stir-fry 108
mustard and honey chicken with mangetout and baby corn 101
Oriental turkey with cashew nuts and mushrooms 116
sesame chicken and broccoli stir-fry 99
spicy Chinese chicken 99
stir-fry chicken and vegetable salad 306
stir-fry chicken with bamboo shoots 102
Szechuan chicken 101
turkey and apricot stir-fry 115
turkey and lettuce ribbon stir-fry 114
turkey and pineapple stir-fry with noodles 115
turkey and vegetables in black bean sauce 114
turkey, broccoli and bamboo shoots with yellow bean sauce 115
turkey stir-fry 114
turkey with grape juice and grapes 112
stock
chicken carcass stock 43
Chinese chicken stock 43
duck carcass stock 61
game carcass stock 63
turkey carcass stock 57
white chicken stock 43
see also gravies; soup
storage 8
straciatella 52
stuffed cucumber boats 27
stuffed peaches 27
stuffings
caraway sausage stuffing 354
forcemeat balls 354
herby bacon stuffing 353
liver and garlic stuffing 353
nutty rice stuffing 353
parsley and thyme stuffing 353
prune and pecan stuffing 354
sage and onion stuffing 353
summer paella 317
sumptuous duck and apple parcels 174
sunny chicken salad 312
sunny smoked turkey and nectarine munch 321
super sausage rolls 80
super sauté potatoes 349
super sauté potatoes with garlic 349
suppli al telefono 277
supreme sauce 341
sweet and sour chicken 98
sweet and sour chicken balls 99
sweet and sour chicken delight 251
sweet and sour dipping sauce 337
sweet and sour pheasant with beans 41
sweet and spicy duck 141
sweet barbecued chicken fillets 106
sweet spiced chicken with coriander and lemon 123
sweet spiced chicken with mint 123
sweetcorn
chicken and corn chowder 49
chicken and sweetcorn bake 246
chicken and sweetcorn quiche 186
chicken and sweetcorn soufflé omelette 71
chicken and sweetcorn toad 155
chicken, corn and peanut chowder 52
chicken, sweetcorn and pepper quiche 186
corn fritters 355
creamy chicken and sweetcorn vol-au-vents 192
Oriental chicken and sweetcorn soup 50
Swiss chicken salad 305
Swiss turkey soup 60
Syrian chicken dome 266
Szechuan chicken 101
tacos
crispy tacos 205
tagliatelle alla panna 275
Taiwanese marinade 344
tandoori chicken drummers 287
tandoori-style grilled chicken 135
tangy duck, watercress and orange salad 328
tangy turkey wings with ginger 221
Taunton grouse 231
teal 14

tempting turkey fillets 140
tempting turkey loaf 170
tempting turkey vol-au-vents 196
terrines
  duck with orange terrine 38
Thai chicken curry 293
Thai coconut chicken 132
Thai fragrant rice 351
Thai grilled chicken with spiced peaches 132
Thai meat balls 153
Thanksgiving turkey 168
thawing 9
Thousand Island chicken and prawn sandwiches 75
three-herb turkey casserole 224
tomatoes
  chicken and tomato quiche 187
  fragrant stuffed tomatoes 307
  prune and chicken-stuffed tomatoes 28
  tomato butter 343
  tomato dipping sauce 337
  tomato sauce 342
tortillas
  enchiladas 204
totally dry onion rub 346
traditional roast duck 171
traditional roast turkey 167
traditional Sunday roast chicken 153
Tropical chicken 213
Tropical marinade 345
trussing 16
tuna
  chicken and tuna niçoise 311
turkey 12
  around the world warm salad 326
  arroz poblano 277
  avocado rasher grills 81
  baked main meal turkey, ham and vegetable soup 58
  barbecued turkey steaks 115
  beetroot layer 320
  Boxing Day pie 195
  braised turkey with bacon and vegetables 221
  braised turkey with redcurrant and mushrooms 224
  Californian-style honey roast turkey 168
  cheesy turkey jackets 84
  chilli turkey sandwiches 83
  Christmas turkey lasagne 274
  cream of turkey and pecan soup 58
  creamed baked rice with cheese 276
  creamed turkey Grand Marnier 213
  creamy cheese and turkey fruity 83
  crispy turkey rolls 81
  crunchy meatballs with tomato barbecue sauce 140
  curried jackets 84
  curried turkey and butter bean salad 324
  curried turkey and lentil soup 57
  curried turkey and rice salad 320
  Cypriot stuffed aubergine 33
  devilled turkey-stuffed eggs 35
  dolcelatte, turkey and watercress mould 277
  egg and turkey rashers in green sauce 34
  fast food turkey chow mein 116
  fast macaroni supper 84
  fettuccine with turkey and jalopeño pepper cream 273
  four-cheese melting moments with crunchy turkey 276
  glazzwill turkey fillets 138
  golden turkey and sweetcorn bake 166
  grilled turkey wrapped in bacon with Oriental sauce 138
  grilled turkey wrapped in Parma ham with piazzola sauce 139
  hot Leerdammer and turkey bites 35
  jalopeño hoppin' John 33
  jellied turkey mayonnaise 321
  Kentucky baked turkey 171
  Leicester macaroni 272
  light turkey pudding 170
  magnificent turkey centrepiece 322
  mountain special 273
  mushroom, sausage and egg cups 36
  new age BLTs 81
  nutty turkey Maryland balls 113
  Oriental turkey with cashew nuts and mushrooms 116
  Peking-style turkey 112
  piquant turkey specials 82
  Polish stuffed cabbage leaves 36
  quick macaroni supper 81
  quick turkey and liver pâté 34
  quick turkey loaf 169
  ravishing rasher toppers 83
  redcurrant roast stuffed turkey 166
  rice dream 278
  roast paprika turkey 167
  salsa Alfredo for fresh pasta 273
  savoury cheese timbale 278
  savoury Dutch pancakes 97
  savoury jellied egg ramekins 35
  savoury turkey escalopes 116
  simple turkey satay 139
  sixteenth-century roast turkey 169
  smoked turkey and cheese balls 34
  Somerset turkey pot roast with dumplings 222
  spaghetti with turkey and oyster mushrooms 275
  spaghetti with turkey carbonara 274
  spicy turkey drummers 170
  Stilton, turkey and walnut salad 320
  sunny smoked turkey and nectarine munch 321

suppli al telefono 277
Swiss turkey soup 60
tagliatelle alla panna 275
tangy turkey wings with ginger 221
tempting turkey fillets 140
tempting turkey loaf 170
tempting turkey vol-au-vents 196
tender turkey steaks in smooth cider sauce 222
Thanksgiving turkey 168
three-herb turkey casserole 224
traditional roast turkey 167
turkey and apricot stir-fry 115
turkey and avocado platter with mushroom dressing 324
turkey and basil lasagne 276
turkey and corn Scotch pancakes 85
turkey and cranberry burgers 137
turkey and cranberry pâté layer 326
turkey and cranberry toastie 82
turkey and cranberry toppers 83
turkey and cranberry vol-au-vents 197
turkey and kidney bean jackets 84
turkey and lentil rissoles 117
turkey and lettuce ribbon stir-fry 114
turkey and pineapple stir-fry with noodles 115
turkey and pink grapefruit pâté 33
turkey and potato pie 170
turkey and pumpkin chermoula 165
turkey and spring onion wontons with chilli dipping sauce 34
turkey and spring vegetable casserole with bay 223
turkey and stuffing jackets 84
turkey and stuffing vol-au-vents 197
turkey and tomato rice 278
turkey and tomato rice with sweetcorn and peas 278
turkey and vegetable parcels 166
turkey and vegetables in black bean sauce 114
turkey, bacon and egg pie 197
turkey, bacon and mushroom vol-au-vents 197
turkey, bacon and pineapple kebabs 141
turkey ballantine 325
turkey bean chowder 60
turkey, broccoli and bamboo shoots with yellow bean sauce 115
turkey Caesar salad 323
turkey cassoulet 221
turkey Christmas parcel 196–197
turkey herb crumble 224
turkey keema 301
turkey mayo sandwiches 82
turkey, melon and raisin salad 323
turkey minestrone 59
turkey pockets 139
turkey pot roast with wine and two cheese 222
turkey, prawn and cucumber boats 34
turkey stir-fry 114
turkey stuffed pizzas 85
turkey tartare sandwiches 82
turkey with grape juice and grapes 112
turkey with grapes, olives and pasta 275
Turkish ravioli 272
Tyrolean turkey 223
Wraysbury carbonara 274
zingy turkey steaks 113

turkey giblets
turkey giblet soup 60

turkey livers
brandied turkey liver and walnut pâté 37
Highland pâté 37
Highland pâté with pickled walnuts 37
potted turkey livers 36
turkey and cranberry pâté layer 326
turkey liver and pea risotto 279
velvety turkey liver pâté with port 37
warm turkey liver and Asian pear salad 327

turkey sausages
bean and sausage toppers 83
Californian dreams 80
cheese and pickle sausage rolls 81
corny turkey sausage rolls 80
creamy sausage and mushroom rolls 81
mammoth mushrooms 141
mushroom, sausage and egg cups 36
sausage salad supreme 322
super sausage rolls 80
turkey and cranberry sausage rolls 80
turkey dogs 80
turkey sausage soup 58
turkey Scotch egg salad 325

turkey stock
brown turkey pottage 59
sherried turkey pottage 59
turkey broth 57
turkey carcass stock 57
turkey, onion and rice soup 60

Turkish ravioli 272
Turkish-style marinated chicken kebabs 129
Tuscan chicken liver soup 56
Tuscan risotto with chicken, spices and raisins 261
Tyrolean turkey 223
Umbrian chicken and pea salad 308
Valencian pheasant 332
vegetables
chicken and roast vegetable fajitas 161
chicken and spring vegetable jalousie 188
chicken and vegetable pasties 187
chicken and vegetable popovers 155

Chinese chicken and vegetable soup 51
crunchy-topped duck and vegetable soup 62
poussins with warm vegetable salad 318
turkey and vegetable parcels 166
turkey minestrone 59
vegetable water gravy 334
zesty chicken and vegetable casserole 214
velouté sauce 340
velvety chicken liver pâté 31
velvety turkey liver pâté with port 37
Victorian grouse fricassée 232
Victorian roast pheasant 177
vol-au-vents
creamy chicken and avocado vol-au-vents 192
creamy chicken and ham vol-au-vents 192
creamy chicken and mushroom vol-au-vents 191
creamy chicken and prawn vol-au-vents 192
creamy chicken and sweetcorn vol-au-vents 192
creamy chicken vol-au-vents 191
smoked chicken and ham vol-au-vent 191
tempting turkey vol-au-vents 196
turkey and cranberry vol-au-vents 197
turkey and stuffing vol-au-vents 197
turkey, bacon and mushroom vol-au-vents 197
walnuts
cream of chicken and walnut soup 54
warm brown rice, chicken and nut salad 309
warm chicken, carrot, courgette and wild rice salad 307
warm chicken livers with blueberries 31
warm turkey liver and Asian pear salad 327
warming duck soup with peas 62
washday rice 267
water chestnuts
chicken with water chestnuts 212
nutty chicken with water chestnuts 212
watercress, duck and egg pasta 279
Welsh cream of chicken pie 190
white chicken and bacon casserole 203
white chicken soup 45
white chicken stock 43
white wine marinade 344
widgeon 14
roast widgeon with chicory and orange salad 182
wild duck with blackberries 182
wild rice mix 352
winter chicken and lentil pot 219
winter chicken pot 219
wontons
chicken and prawn wontons with sweet and sour sauce 21
turkey and spring onion wontons with chilli dipping sauce 34
wontons in garlic soup 44
woodcock 14
roast woodcock Rossini 179
woodland chicken soup 53
Wraysbury carbonara 274
Yorkshire pigeon pie 200
zesty chicken and vegetable casserole 214
zingy turkey steaks 113

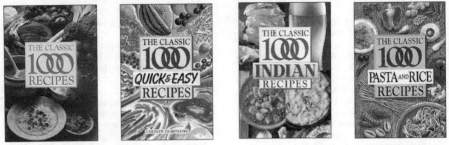